# GOVERNMENT
# AND BUSINESS

# GOVERNMENT
# AND BUSINESS

*John Philip Wernette*

THE MACMILLAN COMPANY, NEW YORK
COLLIER-MACMILLAN LIMITED, LONDON

LIBRARY OF CONGRESS CATALOG CARD NUMBER: 64-12864

THE MACMILLAN COMPANY, NEW YORK

COLLIER-MACMILLAN CANADA, LTD., TORONTO, ONTARIO

PRINTED IN THE UNITED STATES OF AMERICA

# PREFACE

I have pondered using the old term *"political economy"* in the title of this book, for that is what it is about. I have finally rejected the term, however, in the belief that its old-fashioned flavor would be misleading and dissuasive. For under any name the relationships and interplay between government and business is a field of speculation and study and controversy of great and increasing timeliness. Thorough grounding in it is vitally necessary to the competent government official and directly important to the alert business man. But more than that, of far deeper import, wide understanding of the subject among the electors, the citizens, of this representative democracy can be a positive factor in promoting the well-being and good government of the nation, and a bulwark of protection against the dangers from within to which this form of government is vulnerable. To contribute to such an understanding has been my prime purpose in the writing.

The manuscript had the benefit of a superb editing by my friend, Captain E. S. L. Goodwin, U.S. Navy, retired.

J. P. W.

# TABLE OF CONTENTS

# TABLES

# CHARTS AND DIAGRAMS

# 1     INTRODUCTION

The relationships between government and business are important both to individual Americans and to the nation as a whole. Actions of government affect the lives and material well-being of all of us—consumers, taxpayers, workers, businessmen, investors, voters, students, farmers, city people, young, old, employed, unemployed, and retired.

The relationship also runs the other way. We—the same groups, the same people—influence the actions of government, through the processes of our representative democracy. The better the people understand the public problems, the better will be the actions of government.

An examination of the front page of any metropolitan daily newspaper will show news stories on various subjects. Some deal with crime, some with sports. Others describe tense international situations. Many refer to aspects of business–government relations. The following are typical of the latter:

REPORT URGES STABILIZATION POLICY

SUPREME COURT EXAMINES "ROTTEN BOROUGHS"

FOREIGN AID ATTACKED, DEFENDED

JAILINGS EMPHASIZE ANTITRUST LAWS

FEDERAL FARM POLICY CALLED FAILURE

PUBLIC OPPOSES GOVERNMENT OWNERSHIP

CITIES SEEK INCOME TAXES

Study of business–government relationships gives the thoughtful citizen a better understanding of public problems and the ways in which government actions affect him. It also enables him to play better the citizen's role of improving public policies by wise use of vote and voice. The study has special benefits for businessmen, inasmuch as government affects business operations in so many ways. Good business management takes account of government's current actions and tries to anticipate future ones, thereby contributing to continuing business success.

In recent years the importance of public problems has been magnified enormously, and the necessity of solving them rendered more urgent, by the expansion of communism and the appearance of the East–West conflict in all of its forms—ideological, military, diplomatic, economic, political, social, cultural, moral, and even spiritual. As a result of this intensification of the public side of our lives, business and government are brought into ever closer and more complex relationships. The manner in which we handle the problems involved will influence the outcome of this titanic struggle and the conditions of life not only of our own people but of all the peoples of the world into the indefinite future.

## MEANING OF BUSINESS

Like many words in our language, the word *business* has many meanings. One sometimes hears reference to "the conflicting interests of business and labor." Here the word *business* refers to the special interests of business management and of the stockholders or owners of the business. In the statement "The problems of business are different from those of agriculture," the word *business* refers to urban business activities, including manufacturing, wholesaling, retailing, and service industries. There are other meanings of the word, and each is acceptable when used properly.

In this book the word *business* is used in a broad sense to include all of the different kinds of gainful activity; agricultural as well as industrial, professional as well as commercial, individual as well as corporate. It includes all segments of the American economy—business managers, self-employed business and professional men, employees, consumers, investors, farmers, and taxpayers. In short, it includes the American people, all of their economic activities, and all of their business institutions.

## MEANING OF GOVERNMENT

The word *government* also has different meanings. If a citizen says, "I think the government ought to do something about the problem," he is probably referring to the United States Federal Government. Thus used and thus understood, the meaning of the word is clear.

In this book the word *government* is used in a broad sense to include all of the governmental entities and units in the United States. This means not only the Federal Government but all state and local government entities as well. As Table 1.1 shows, in 1962 there were more than ninety thousand such governmental entities.

Note that Table 1.1 does not count the subdivisions of any single gov-

## Table 1.1

## GOVERNMENTAL UNITS IN THE
## UNITED STATES

|  | NUMBER OF UNITS | | | |
|---|---|---|---|---|
| TYPE OF UNIT | 1942 | 1952 | 1957 | 1962 |
| U.S. Government | 1 | 1 | 1 | 1 |
| States | 48 | 50 | 50 | 50 |
| Counties | 3,050 | 3,052 | 3,050 | 3,043 |
| Municipalities | 16,220 | 16,807 | 17,215 | 17,997 |
| Townships | 18,919 | 17,202 | 17,198 | 17,144 |
| School districts | 108,579 | 67,355 | 50,454 | 34,678° |
| Special districts | 8,299 | 12,340 | 14,424 | 18,323 |
| Total | 155,116 | 116,807 | 102,392 | 91,236 |

* There are 2,341 districts that are agencies of other governments, which would make a total of 37,019.
   The tables for 1952 and 1957 have been adjusted to include units in Alaska and Hawaii, which were reported separately prior to their adoption of statehood in 1959. The table for 1942 has not been adjusted to include the two new states.
   SOURCE: U.S. Bureau of the Census, *Census of Governments: 1962* (Washington, D.C.; U.S. Government Printing Office, 1963), V. 1, p. 1.

ernmental entity. For example, it does not count separately the Department of Defense, the Department of State, the Interstate Commerce Commission, the Internal Revenue Service, or any of the dozens of other subdivisions of the Federal Government. The Federal Government is counted just once. The same is true of the states and their many subdivisions. In other words, each of these more than one hundred thousand entities has its own individual life; a kind of corporate existence. The typical one has a governing board and an executive and employees. The typical one takes in money and pays out money, making its contribution to the grand total for all of them, more than $140 billion a year.

This then is what *government* means in this book. The facts substantiate the proposition that we have a tremendous amount of government. Whether we have too much is one of the great issues of our day.

## DECLINE IN THE NUMBER OF
## GOVERNMENTAL ENTITIES

The reader may be surprised to note that the number of governmental units in the United States declined between 1942 and 1962. Might this fact be supposed to indicate a decline in the importance of government in the United States, or perhaps a reduction in the total amount of money collected and spent by governmental entities, or a decrease in the magnitude of the "welfare state"? It indicates nothing of the kind. An inspection of the totals for the figures of governmental entities by types speedily puts us on the track of understanding what actually happened during those years.

The key to the change was a decline in the total number of separate school districts, from 108,579 to 34,678. These figures also, taken by themselves, could easily be misleading, for they might suggest that the number of children in public schools declined, that the amount of money spent on education was reduced, and that, in general, public education became less important in the United States during this period. Actually, the number of children increased enormously, and the amount of money spent on education gained even more. What happened was a *consolidation* of school districts—particularly rural school districts. Small school districts with the traditiona. one-room school houses were merged into larger districts with better schools. At the same time, buses—yellow or red-white-and-blue—began to go around through the countryside, picking up the children and bringing them the greater distances to the consolidated schools.

Table 1.1 shows 17,144 townships. This type of governmental unit does not exist at all in half of the states. Indeed, this fact illustrates another current problem in public policy, namely the question of whether townships are really necessary. This, in turn, is part of a larger question which involves the significance of municipalities and counties and the newly developed metropolitan districts. The great basic question is whether types of governmental entities which were appropriate for America in the bygone horse and buggy age are appropriate for the jet age.

## TYPES OF GOVERNMENT

Throughout history men have lived, and men live today, under different kinds of government. The words that describe these different kinds of government are sometimes used rather loosely with resulting confusion. For the sake of clear thinking, the following tabular presentation suggests a classification by *legal form* on the one hand and by *actual substance* on the other.

### I. *Legal Form*

1.  Kingdom          The chief of state usually inherits his position. His title may be king, emperor, shah, czar, or kaiser.
2.  Republic         The chief of state is usually elected to his position. His title is usually president.

### II. *Actual Substance*

1.  Dictatorship     Rule by one man
2.  Oligarchy        Rule by a few

3. Plutocracy      Rule by the rich
4. Theocracy      Rule by priests or clergy
5. Aristocracy      Rule by the best citizens
6. Democracy      Rule by the people
   a. Pure—by all the people
   b. Representative—by representatives of the people
7. Gerontocracy      Rule by the elderly
8. Agrocracy      Rule by the farmers

It will be noted that the difference in the two legal forms—kingdom and republic—is that in the former the *chief of state* usually or supposedly inherits his position, whereas in the latter he is usually or supposedly elected to it. The chief of state is the ceremonial or protocol head of a nation. For example, in the United Kingdom the chief of state is the King or, if the reigning monarch is a female, the Queen. In the United States the President is chief of state. (Occasionally in some countries men make themselves kings or presidents by illegal means, involving neither inheritance nor election.)

The post of chief of state may be contrasted with that of *chief of government*. The latter is the top man in the actual governing process. In the United Kingdom the chief of government is the Prime Minister; in the United States the President plays two roles: he is chief of government as well as chief of state.

Characteristically, the chief of state has very little power over the actual government of the nation—unless he also happens to be chief of government. In the United Kingdom, for example, it is said, "The King reigns but he does not govern." Since the chief of state is a relatively unimportant person in the governing process, it would be entirely reasonable to ask why this *legal classification* of types of government, on the basis of the manner of selecting the chief of state, is of any importance. The truth is that it is not very important. The legal form of government of a nation is not nearly as important as the actual substance.

## *TYPES OF GOVERNMENT BY ACTUAL SUBSTANCE*

The second part of the tabulation is the significant part. In this connection, it should be noted that *any one of the actual substantive forms of government may exist under either a kingdom or a republic.* The United Kingdom, for example, is (politically) a democracy. On the other hand, the Dominican Republic was, for many years, a dictatorship. A look around the world will enable a thoughtful observer to pick out many other examples of interrelationships of these types.

As has been stated, in the United States the President is both chief of state and chief of government. We have a situation which is considered by many persons to be odd, in that the chief of government does not need to be a member of the majority part in Congress nor, indeed, to be able to command a majority for his proposals. In many other countries the chiefs of government have to be able to command majorities in their parliaments in order to continue to hold their positions. This is sometimes called by political scientists the system of *responsible government.* In our country, both in Washington and in state capitals, the chief executive and the majority in the legislature may belong to opposite parties, with the result that political partisanship is intensified, responsibility is diffused, and in-fighting takes the place of statesmanship.

This classification is largely self-explanatory. A few comments, however, may be helpful.

The word *aristocracy* originally meant, as used by the Greek philosophers "rule by the best citizens." The word comes from the Greek words *aristos,* meaning "the best," and *kratein,* "to rule." It has come, like so many words, to have a secondary meaning and to refer to members of a hereditary nobility or other elite group. In its original political meaning, however, it meant entrusting the government to those best qualified to rule. It is as hard to question the theoretical excellence of this kind of government as it is to determine a reliable way of selecting the best qualified. Should, for example, the right to vote be determined on the basis of education, income, or social standing?

It is a commonplace that a benevolent dictatorship is considered to be an excellent form of government. What is not so clear, however, is how establishment and continuation of the benevolent dictatorship is to be guaranteed. As Lord Acton said, "Power tends to corrupt; absolute power corrupts absolutely." The world's experience with national rule by one-man dictatorships has been sad.

The case for democracy rests on the proposition that, in the long run, a government that reflects the wishes of all the people will make fewer mistakes and will register more positive accomplishments than other forms of government. This proposition is generally accepted in the United States today. At the same time, it is often offered as a prescription for governments in other parts of the world. Indeed, there seems to be a kind of equation prevalent in the minds of many men, which goes like this: "Self-government equals good government." The validity of this equation is seriously open to question, as events around the world have demonstrated in many countries in the past and are demonstrating today.

Even in our own country people sometimes have qualms about democracy. This attitude occasionally takes the form of asserting that the United States is *not a democracy,* but that it is rather a *republic.* Exactly what these observers mean by this distinction is sometimes not at all clear. In many cases, what it boils down to is that they do not like something that the government is doing and believe that the unwise action reflects, in some sense or other, democratic conditions which would not exist in a different form of government.

The words *gerontocracy* and *agrocracy* may be unfamiliar. The former means "government by the elderly." The word is introduced here merely by way of emphasizing the power of the chairmen of the standing committees in the United States Senate and House of Representatives, since these men obtain their positions by seniority and therefore, characteristically, are usually well beyond middle age. A typical age range is from 50 to 80; and the average is in the middle or upper 60s. In some tribes in the world control is deliberately vested in the tribal elders. In the United States Congress this is done to avoid intraparty conflicts. The significance of this will be discussed in Chapter 4.

The coined word *agrocracy*, meaning "government by farmers," is included to point up the disproportionate power exercised by rural areas and farmers in the legislative bodies in the United States. This will be considered in detail later in this chapter. The significance of this problem has become ever greater as the urban parts of the United States have grown in size and relative importance.

## MEANING OF DEMOCRACY

The word *democracy* is used freely and often without recognition of the fact that it is a complex concept. For one thing, there is a difference between *social* democracy and *political* democracy. This is easily seen by looking again at the United Kingdom. It is a political democracy; but it is not a social democracy. In the United Kingdom there is an upper class and a lower class. Members of each know their place and understand what the differences are, and those in the lower class are by no means resentful of their position. Social stratification prevails. The opportunities for the sons and daughters of the members of the lower class are restricted. In the United States there is considerably less social stratification and more social mobility. The opportunities for the children of low-income families are greater than in the United Kingdom.

The concept of political democracy is not a simple one. It means, of course, rule by the people. But *which* people? In a representative democracy the people themselves do not get together to pass laws. An actual essemblage of the voters—*pure* democracy—still prevails in New England town meetings; but the size of the electorate in other cities, to say nothing of the size of the electorate in the states and in the nation, makes this kind of meeting generally impossible. Therefore, the citizens elect representatives who pass the laws and officers who administer them. The people thus "rule" only indirectly. More accurately, they do not rule—they *select their rulers*.

Does democracy mean that *all* the people must be permitted to vote? If children are excluded from the vote, and if convicts and inmates of mental institutions are not permitted to vote, is there a violation of the principle of democracy? A more serious question, perhaps, arises if *women* are not permitted to vote. This is the situation in Switzerland and in a few other countries. Must we therefore conclude that Switzerland is not a democracy? In the United States, in earlier years, there were property qualifications for voting: persons having less than a certain amount of property were not allowed to vote. Was this a denial of democratic principles?

## AGROCRACY

Once the matter of who is allowed to vote is settled, the next question is how many votes each voter shall be allowed to cast. Inasmuch as constitutions and laws rarely, if ever, refer to the specific possibility of some voter's having two or more votes, it may seem that this question is purely academic. In fact, however, it is completely realistic. Because of the differing numbers of people and voters in the representative districts that elect legislators under our system of representative democracy, some voters have far more power in the legislative process than others— amounting in quite literal effect to more votes.

A familiar example is the United States Senate. In that body each state has two senators, regardless of its population. Thus the State of Alaska with a 1960 population of about one quarter of a million is represented by two senators, as is the State of New York with a population of nearly 17 million. In effect, therefore, an Alaskan voter in 1960 had 65 votes, compared to the New Yorker's one vote, in electing members of the United States Senate.

In the case of the Senate, of course, this inequality is a matter of deliberate design, having been written into the Constitution, partly as a matter of political expediency (to induce the smaller states to accept the union), partly under the theory of regional or area representation for the protection of minority subsocieties (for example, to protect the people of sparsely populated agricultural states from undue dominance by those of densely populated industrial ones). The House of Representatives, however, is supposed to be elected on a population basis, but even there the range in the populations of electoral districts is great. The largest district currently has about six times the population of the smallest one, which means that the voters in the latter have six votes to each one in the former.

Many state senates reflect situations similar to that of the Senate of the United States, sometimes combining the regional basis with a partial population-proportional one. In general, the states' lower houses are nominally elected on the basis of population, but in many, perhaps most, cases inequities similar to those in the Federal lower house have gradually appeared and grown, so that now some tremendous variations exist. One reason is that in many states there is no mechanism to *force* redistricting as populations change. In some states the legislatures have disobeyed their constitutions for decades in refusing to redistrict as required by their own basic laws.

More is involved in this matter than violation of the abstract principle of "one man, one vote." The substance of the situation is that, in the United States, the cities and the suburbs have been growing and the rural and farm regions have been standing still or losing population—in either event, declining relative to the urban areas. As this population trend has occurred, urban people have been increasingly underrepresented in legislatures—both national and state—and rural people have been increasingly over represented. In most states a small percentage of the population elects a majority of the state senators, and a slightly larger percentage, but still a minor fraction, elects a majority of the state representatives.

These small minorities, moreover, are characteristically composed of voters in rural regions. The result, it is often contended, of this "agrocracy," or government by farmers, is that state tax burdens are laid more heavily on urban people and less heavily on rural people, whereas state expenditures favor the outlying areas rather than the cities. It is asserted further that many of the pressing problems of our day which have to do with the affairs of cities are neglected or treated inadequately by state legislatures. One of the consequences, it is said, is that the city people, unable to get adequate treatment from their own state legislatures, turn increasingly to Washington for help, and that this helps to explain the growth of the Federal Government.

The extent to which this condition is realized by the citizenry is unknown. Some are acutely aware of it; others seem to have given the matter little thought. It is a frequent subject of discussion in legislative halls and in conventions where revisions of state constitutions are under consideration. In both of these places, however, a common situation is that the representation of those whose duty it is to decide what, if anything, is to be done about rural overrepresentation is heavily weighted in favor of the rural districts and, therefore, in the maintenance of the status quo.

## THE SUPREME COURT AND REAPPORTIONMENT

On Monday, March 26, 1962, the United States Supreme Court in a six-to-two decision (one justice not participating because of illness) handed down a decision on legislative apportionment (*Baker v. Carr**)

* 369 U.S. 186 (1962).

that seems certain to have great significance in the matter of the apportionment of legislative electoral districts. At the very least, the decision is important; at the most, it could turn out to be one of the most important decisions ever rendered by that Court and might come to be seen as a landmark in judicial-political history.

The question of legislative apportionment had been in the courts before that date. The courts, however, had steadily refused to do anything about the alleged unfairness or unconstitutionality of such apportionment. A leading case on the subject was *Colegrove v. Green.** decided in 1946. Two members of the Supreme Court did not participate in that decision, and the decision was four to three. The majority held that legislative apportionment was basically a political question and not one which could be decided by courts.

Therefore, when some Tennessee voters went to court alleging that the representation situation in their state deprived them of Federal constitutional rights, it was not surprising that the three-judge Federal court decided that it lacked jurisdiction in the matter. The Supreme Court permitted an appeal in 1961—an action which, because of the precedent of the Colegrove case, was immediately regarded as having substantial significance. That the Court attached especial importance to this case may be inferred from the fact that the Court heard oral arguments twice, using several hours for this purpose whereas one hour is the usual maximum.

The majority decision in the case says:

> This civil action was brought under 42 [United States Code] sections 1938 and 1988 to redress the alleged deprivation of federal constitutional rights. The complaint, alleging that by means of a 1901 statute of Tennessee apportioning the members of the General Assembly among the State's 95 counties, "these plaintiffs and others similarly situated, are denied the equal protection of the laws accorded them by the Fourteenth Amendment to the Constitution of the United States by virtue of the debasement of their votes," was dismissed by a three-judge court convened under 28 [United States Code] section 2281 in the Middle District of Tennessee. . . .
>
> In light of the District Court's treatment of the case, we hold today only (a) that the court possessed jurisdiction of the subject matter; (b) that a justiciable cause of action is stated upon which appellants would be entitled to appropriate relief; and (c) because appellees raise the issue before this Court, that the appellants have standing to challenge the Tennessee apportionment statutes. Beyond noting that we have no cause at this stage to doubt the District Court will be able to fashion relief if violations of constitutional rights are found, it is improper now to consider what remedy would be most appropriate if appellants prevail at the trial. . . .
>
> The appellees refer to *Colegrove v. Green,* 328 U.S. 549, as authority that the District Court lacked jurisdiction of the subject matter. Appellees

* 328 U.S. 549.

misconceive the holding of that case. The holding was precisely contrary to their reading of it. Seven members of the Court participated in the decision. Unlike many other cases in this field which have assumed without discussion that there was jurisdiction, all three opinions filed in *Colegrove* discussed the question. Two of the opinions expressing the views of four of the Justices, a majority, flatly held that there was jurisdiction of the subject matter. . . .

We hold that the District Court has jurisdiction of the subject matter of the federal constitutional claim asserted in the complaint. . . .

We conclude that the complaint's allegations of a denial of equal protection present a justiciable constitutional cause of action upon which appellants are entitled to a trial and a decision. The right asserted is within the reach of judicial protection under the Fourteenth Amendment.

The judgment of the District Court is reversed and the cause is remanded for further proceedings consistent with this opinion.

The decision instantly drew attention and comment. It became clear at once that the reach of the immediate decision is limited. It does not guarantee court actions to insure approximate arithmetic equality in the numbers of voters in legislative districts. It says only that the Tennessee voters' case was one that was entitled to be tried and decided in a Federal district court. It remained, therefore, to be seen what the outcome of such a trial would be and whether an appeal from that decision might also be taken to the Supreme Court. It further remained to be seen in what circumstances courts thereafter would declare legislative apportionments to be violative of rights guaranteed by the Constitution.

Despite these uncertanties several consequences emerged immediately. One was the initiation of smiliar suits in other states. Another was that public attention was focused on this problem to an unprecedented extent. A third was that a stimulus to changes in the direction of more nearly equal representation was provided. A fourth was that people were set to wondering what the ultimate effects on the operation of government might be if rural overrepresentation should come to be diminished substantially. What would be the effects on the fortunes of the two major political parties? Much of the strength of the Democratic Party lay in central cities. Much of the strength of the Republican Party lay in the suburbs of central cities. Increasing the representation of urban voters would increase the representation of both of these groups. And finally, the prospect of a rearrangement of voting representation suggested the possibility of more active government at state and local levels and a smaller tendency to turn to Washington.

## THE MICHIGAN CASE

On April 23, 1962, the United States Supreme Court handed down a decision in the case of *Scholle v. Secretary of State*,* which, though per-

* 369 U.S. 429.

haps less unexpected than the decision in *Baker v. Carr,* because of the precedent set by that case four weeks earlier, holds the potential of being even more significant.

August Scholle, president of the Michigan AFL-CIO, brought suit in Michigan courts alleging a deprivation of Federal Constitutional rights by virtue of the provision in the Michigan State Constitution that established the districts for members of the State Senate. The suit challenged the apportionment of districts, which varied in population form 61,000 in one Upper Peninsula district to 530,000 in Mr. Scholle's own Detroit suburban district. The Michigan Supreme Court ruled adversely on Mr. Scholle's claim, and the case was then appealed to the United States Supreme Court.

In a brief order the Court directed the Michigan Supreme Court to give the case further consideration in light of *Baker v. Carr.* Justices Clark and Stewart, in a concurring opinion, said, "Today's order simply reflects our belief that the Michigan Supreme Court should be first to consider the merits of the Federal Constitutional claim, free from any doubts as to its justiciability."

The special significance of the Michigan case lies in certain important differences between it and the previous Tennessee case. In the Tennessee case not only was the question of apportionment itself at issue, but also the fact that the Tennessee legislature had for many years disobeyed the requirement of the Tennessee State Constitution that it reapportion itself. This was not the situation in Michigan. There the Senate districts existed as they had been constituted by a 1952 amendment to the State Constitution, which had been approved, in a state-wide referendum, by a vote of more than one million to less than 300,000. In the Michigan case the issue was whether a portion of a state constitution which established senatorial districts that were greatly unequal in population was a violation of rights guaranteed by the United States Constitution. In other words, legislative apportionment by itself, and not supplemented by the factor of disobedience to a state constitution, was the matter at issue.

Before the Michigan decision a state could have contended that, although apportionment was unequal, it conformed to the state constitution. This case thus closed a route by which states could possibly resist reapportionment.

In 1963 Michigan voters adopted a new constitution which provided that Senate districts would be determined 80 per cent by population and 20 per cent by area. The Scholle case apparently then became moot; but the possibility remained of challenging the new constitutional provision after it was seen how great the population inequality of Senate legislative districts would be.

## THE VOTES AND THE VOTERS

Presumably, in a democracy, a large proportion of adults must be allowed to vote. But there is more to it than that—the votes must be *counted honestly*. This is something which we usually take for granted in the United States, although astonishing exceptions occasionally come to light. In some countries, however, control of the counting of the votes is more important than the number of votes itself.

Not only must the votes be counted honestly, but also the outcome of the voting must prevail; it must not be set aside by force or otherwise disregarded.

Moreover, if the representatives are chosen by some kind of geographical districts, the districts must not be rigged in such a way as to favor one political party above another. The ingenious practice of lumping one's opponents into one district, while spreading one's strength by slight majorities into several other districts, is often associated with the name of Elbridge Gerry, a Massachusetts politico. One of the districts that he arranged sprawled about the map in such a meandering way as to prompt an observer to say, "It looks like a salamander." To this came the retort, "It is, in fact, a gerrymander." The word became a part of our language. Today, "to gerrymander" means to arrange an elongated, odd-shaped district for political advantage. These curiously shaped districts are topics of public discussion as they occur in different parts of the United States.

Thus a government based on democracy can easily become infiltrated by practices having characteristics of the other seven substantial forms. We have seen how gerontocracy and agrocracy are embedded in our own version of democracy. The practice of gerrymandering is, in a way, a manifestation of oligarchy. The mounting costs of national political campaigning introduce a potentiality for plutocracy. An unalert electorate can, as history and current events abundantly demonstrate, slip easily under dictatorship. Apparently democracy is a form of government which is unlikely to work well, or even to maintain its nominal character, unless the people have a fairly good level of education and a fairly strong sense of civic responsibility.

## WHICH FORM OF GOVERNMENT IS BEST?

Turning to the question "Which form of government is best?" we take up a problem that wise men have discussed for centuries. It will not be solved in this chapter. In a sense, this entire book discusses the question, since it is a continuing one and not one that can be settled forever even in one country, much less in all others.

In view of the enthusiasm—not to say affection—of the American people for democracy, it may seem strange that the question should be asked at all. Indeed, it might seem almost treasonable to raise it. He who questions whether democracy is the best form of government might be thought equally weak on such subjects as home, motherhood, and the American Way of Life. Not so, however. His question is entirely legitimate, since it is a forerunner to a more important one, namely, How can our democracy be made to function better?

It is, moreover, not a new question. The Founding Fathers had their doubts about democracy, and were perfectly free in expressing them. It is quite possible, indeed, that they would be astonished to discover how well the enlargement of the electorate has actually worked out in our country, since some of them had very little confidence in the common people. These believed—and some people believe today—that if the poor people have the vote they will exploit and expropriate the well-to-do and thereby ruin the nation. This matter will be examined later. For the present, it may be said that neither the evidence of history nor that of public opinion surveys lends much support to this view.

## OBJECTIVES OF OUR SOCIETY

Before we can get far in discussing the question "Which form of government is best?" we need to ask, "What is government supposed to do?" Discussion of this question requires consideration of the goals of our nation. Here are some goals that seem to be generally acceptable: prosperity, economic growth, stability, national strength, justice, freedom, security, opportunity, and other conditions that go to make up the good society, including friendship, culture, and moral and spiritual strength. To the foregoing objectives, most of which have social characteristics, may be added one of no less importance; namely, opportunity for the highest and richest development of each individual person.

If we may suppose that there is a substantial measure of agreement among our people about the desirability of these objectives, the question immediately arises of the proper role of government in their achievement. Inasmuch as the remainder of this book deals with the myriad ramifications of this question, this is not the place to attempt an exhaustive answer.

Certain observations, however, may be made at once. One is that some of these objectives are primarily economic, whereas others are primarily noneconomic. Some of them are of significance in both areas. It may be further noted that it is quite possible for the government either to aid or to injure the attainment of these objectives. There is nothing automatically helpful about governmental action. Indeed, governments, like people, make mistakes. What governments do in a democracy depends in the main on what the people want, and of course especially those people who have political power. The fact intensifies the desirability in such a society of a broad understanding of economics and politics, as well as a civic devotion to the common good.

## ECONOMIC UNDERSTANDING

This broad understanding is not achieved easily. Indeed, because of the complexities of economic analysis, it is doubtful whether any person can obtain a real understanding of a nation's economy without some formal study. It is all too easy to suppose that a citizen who understands a good deal about business must necessarily understand economic analysis as well. This conclusion, however, does not follow. One peculiarity of economic analysis is that it enunciates certain principles which are true of an entire economy, but not true of individuals, families, and firms; and, conversely, it enunciates generalizations that are untrue of an entire economy, whereas they are true of its individual parts.

An example may illustrate the difference. If the depositors in a particular bank become more thrifty and cut down on their consumption expenditures in order to save more and make their bank accounts grow, the deposits in that bank will rise. From this it might be easy to generalize that what is true of one bank is true of all banks and that if the American people generally become more thrifty, the deposits of all banks in the United States will rise. This proposition, however, is not true. When the depositors in the one bank permitted their bank accounts to grow, they were in effect taking deposits away from other banks and were not, by their actions, causing the *total* of bank deposits in the United States to change at all. When all of the American people in the second hypothesis decided to become more thrifty and cut down on their expenditures for consumer goods, this action would not affect the national total of bank deposits at all. It would probably bring on a business depression. In short, increased thriftiness can raise the deposits of one bank, but cannot increase the total of deposits in all banks. Practical experience leads here to a wrong conclusion; a true understanding of the national situation requires the kind of study that is the province of economics.

In view of these considerations, it is pertinent to ask why businessmen sometimes find fault with the pronouncements of economic theorists. One possible reason is that the businessman may disagree with some of the part of economics that he really understands—microeconomics—and therefore he may conclude that the other part—macroeconomics—(which is not his specialty) is also suspect.

Economic theory nowadays is divided into these two principal areas. The subject of macroeconomics deals with the operations of the entire economy. This area of analysis is now rather fully developed as a result of studies that began about 1930.

Microeconomics deals with the actions of individuals, families, and firms. Part of it is called "the theory of the firm," which purports to analyze business operations. Much of it is not based on facts, but on equations and diagrams; and some of it is unrealistic, oversimplified, misleading, or downright wrong. This type of analysis suggests that the firm and its managers have only one activity, namely, deciding on the price and quantity relationship of the one product sold that will maximize the firm's profit.

As a matter of fact, the notion that a business firm is engaged in trying to maximize its profit is a pure assumption. Such evidence as is available makes it altogether doubtful whether firms in fact try to do this. Moreover, this same line of reasoning completely neglects the many management problems in the area of production, personnel, accounting, statistics, finance, marketing, and others which in fact engage the attention of competent business managers.

The net effect of this kind of analysis is to portray the business manager as a kind of Scrooge, who is trying to maximize profits, who doesn't have very much else to do, and who contributes little or nothing to production and economic growth. Perhaps this "theory of the firm" is one reason why business management is underappreciated among our people, including even those (or perhaps especially those) who have taken formal courses in economics. It should be here noted that this book accords the competent business manager a high place in the productive activity of the nation, insists that economic growth is stimulated by the development of competent business managers, and recognizes the contribution that they make.

## CONTRIBUTION OF THE
## SOCIAL SCIENCES

The subject matter of this book can be described by a term that was widely used during the nineteenth century but now has almost completely disappeared from use. The term is *political economy*. Political economy is a mixture of political science and economics. Study of both of these subjects contributes to an understanding of business–government relationships. Other subjects that also contribute to better understanding of this extremely complex subject include history, sociology, social psychology, anthropology, ethics, and constitutional law.

Because of the close connection between subjects taken up in this book and events that are reported daily in our newspapers, the thoughtful reader will experience a sharpening of his interest in news items in these intertwined areas of politics and economics. Rare is the day when our newspapers do not carry one or more stories about subjects in this field. An alert eye in scanning current events will bring home the fact that business and government is a living, developing, growing area of human preoccupation.

## SOCIAL CONTROL

Government influences business in many ways. Government is itself a producer in the sense that it carries on productive activities, such as operating schools. Government also regulates private business—laws tell businesses what they may and what they may not do. Government assists business in many ways—by providing information, statistics, and financial support. Government influences business in direct and indirect ways.

Presumably the purpose of these activities is to aid in the achievement of the objectives of our society. In part this achievement is to be brought about by influencing the behavior of people, by inducing them to do things that they would not otherwise do.

It is important to understand that there are many influences other than government that affect the behavior and attitudes of people. A good society does not need to depend exclusively on government activities, regulations, assistance, and influence in order to secure good behavior from its members. Other influences may be even more powerful.

What are these other influences? They are well known to us all: they include parents, siblings, playmates, friends, school, church, literature, radio, television, clubs, groups, and political and social organizations. It will be seen at once that the foregoing list includes many of the parts of the human being's environment. They are especially those parts that involve other people, or are created or controlled by other people. If these environmental factors are tolerated by society and, a fortiori, if they are encouraged by society, they may be grouped under the heading of "social control."

Some of these forces begin to influence the attitudes and behavior of the human creature in infancy. As the years go by, they shape his thinking and reactions—his very nature. It is not true that "human nature cannot be changed." As a matter of fact, the nature of the mature adult is the end product of what he is born with, plus the many influences that have conditioned him all his life ("nature and nurture," as the phrase goes). If we wish men to be industrious, honest, creative, enterprising, and productive, it is clear that there are many factors that can affect the desired outcome. One, and only one, of these factors is government.

The criminal law is society's *formal* method of trying to prevent stealing (and other undesirable actions). It does so by forbidding stealing and by providing penalties for violation of this prohibition. Opposition to stealing is voiced also by parents, teachers, and religious instructors, among others. On the other hand, a youth's gang may *encourage* theft.

It is quite possible that some of these other forces are in fact more influential than the criminal law. The economic significance of the criminal law will be examined further in the next chapter.

In any event, since one of the necessities of modern society is to try to get men to behave as civilized creatures, it is a mistake to rely or to try to rely exclusively on the actions of government. Instead, the part of wisdom is to understand that there are other methods of influencing the behavior of people and, if a change in people's behavior is desired, to consider the possibility of utilizing mechanisms other than government, perhaps in conjunction with government.

## DIFFICULTIES OF THE STUDY

Serious study of business–government relationships is by no means easy. There are several difficulties. One is the size of the subject. A nation's economy is a very big affair and, although a given problem may deal with only one part of the economy, even that part (agriculture, say) may be very large.

A common error is to suppose that public policy problems are simple. Very few are.

Curiously enough, the enormous volume of available information sometimes turns out to be a disadvantage. In the United States statistics are collected to an extent unknown in any other country. The very mass of the data sometimes obscures the view and hinders understanding.

But the worst handicap to understanding, for some persons, is the combination of political partisanship and political prejudices. These feelings, indeed, seem to be so deeply ingrained in some citizens as to make them almost incapable of thinking clearly about public problems. When strong political partisanship comes in the door, thoughtful consideration is likely to go out the window.

Sometimes these strong feelings take extreme forms. Some persons, on the one hand, seem to believe that government can do no wrong and that increasing governmental activity and intervention is bound to improve our society.

Some, on the other hand, seem to consider that government is basically evil—that it is always wasteful, inefficient, and corrupt. This "again-the-government" attitude comes very close indeed to the original philosophy of *anarchy*. The original meaning of this philosophy was a belief that government generates evil in men and that societies would be better off without governments; it involves open hostility to all governments and, therefore, opposition to political parties. This philosophy has never had very widespread appeal. Indeed, the word *anarchy* has acquired pejorative connotations because most people associate it with lawlessness, chaos, and disorder.

The sense in which the "agin" view and philosophical anarchy are close together may be illustrated by examining a familiar saying which has been attributed to various great men, "That government governs best which governs least." What is presumably not ordinarily noted by those who recite this is that the government which governs least would be one which is virtually nonexistent or but one small step removed from the condition, advocated by philosophical anarchy, of no government at all; they would be astounded and angered if called "anarchists." They are usually registering their objections to something the government is doing, and their real desires are not at all for *less* government, but rather for *more* government—of their especial kind.

## THE  PRODUCTIVITY  OF  GOVERNMENT

The attitude of some persons toward government activity and their corresponding evaluation of the role of government reflect two familiar propositions. The first is the assertion that "government doesn't produce anything." In part this statement seems to reflect the erroneous notion that production means only the creation of tangible goods and does not include the rendering of services. Much of the productive activity of governmental organizations takes the form of rendering services. National defense and education are examples. In general, it is true that the wage and salary payments made by governmental entities pay for the employment of persons who are engaged in productive activity (but those governmental outlays that are called *transfer payments,* such as interest on the national debt and social security payments, do not represent compensation for current productive activity).

The other statement that symbolizes this same attitude is "Government can give the people only that which it has previously taken away from them." It is not always clear what this statement is intended to mean. It surely cannot mean that, in preserving and protecting freedom and liberty, the government has previously taken these valuable conditions away from the people. Perhaps it means that the money that the government pays out is taken from the people in the form of taxation. This proposition—except for those amounts that are obtained by created money of one kind or another—is, of course, true. But it does not prove that the government is merely a parasite or some kind of gigantic Robin Hood. Indeed, the statement in a sense proves too much. The same could be said of any person or any corporation. What a corporation or person pays out to some people is money that has been obtained from other people. In short, the government, like persons and corporations, has receipts and expenditures and is, by this fact, no more parasitic on the economy than any other receiving—expanding entity. Judgment of the wisdom of government actions must depend on other criteria.

## THE POLITICO-ECONOMIC SPECTRUM

The spectrum of politico-economic thinkers is often pictured thus, moving from "Right" to "Left":

Reactionaries
Ultraconservatives
Conservatives
Middle-of-the-roaders
Liberals
Ultraliberals
Socialistic radicals

Two comments are in order. First, the meanings of these words are far from precise. A "liberal" used to be a man who favored greater freedom in political affairs. Nowadays the word may mean one who favors more government activity—one who, in a sense, advocates *less* individual freedom.

Second, the words are often used as *epithets* by unfriendly opponents. Some persons seem to equate governmental activities with socialism and socialism with communism; they then brand proponents of the activities as communists or communist sympathizers.

The net of it is that these labels are often not merely noninformative, but are actually misleading or inflammatory. Cool thoughts, not hot words, help the study of political economy.

Another difficulty that hinders clear thinking about the subject is that many of the topics are controversial, some of them, indeed, fiercely so. Often, controversies stem from political disagreements. Sometimes, however, disagreements reflect differences of opinion about true economic analysis that have nothing to do with political loyalties. Whatever their nature, controversies sometimes generate more heat than light. Occasionally they seem to stand in the way of progress toward appropriate public policies. For example, for many years after 1933 there was a large measure of hostility between Washington and the nation's business community. During this time many businessmen were sharply critical of what Washington, under the label of the New Deal, was doing. Washington, in turn, was heavily critical of many of the things that businessmen were doing. This condition was unfortunate for all concerned. The nation needed then (and still does) all the good advice it could get. Businessmen are well-informed individuals (although some overrate their understanding of national economy as distinguished from private business) and have much to contribute to the formulation and execution of public policies. From 1933 to 1953 the nation did not get as much good advice as it was entitled to expect from the business community.

There were some areas of light in this prevailing murk. An outstanding one was the Committee for Economic Development, or CED, as it is commonly called. Established in 1942, its board of trustees came to include more than two hundred of America's outstanding business leaders. The CED has sponsored studies and research activities and has published books and monographs on public problems. These problems have been approached in a nonpartisan manner and with scientific care, by means of extensive and scholarly researches. One does not have to be in complete agreement with every recommendation ever made by the CED to appreciate that these activities are a model for thoughtful businessmen who wish to make their contributions to the development of sound public policy.

## PUBLIC PROBLEMS

Our nation has always faced problems. In its early days when the country was little and poor and weak, the problems included the British, the Indians, and the structure of government. Today, when the country is big and rich and strong, the problems have changed, although the structure and functioning of government, and particularly the relationships among the different kinds of governmental entities, still involve issues and new problems.

What are today's problems and what will be those of tomorrow? Perhaps the most important is the achievement of a lasting peace and the prevention of a destructive war. This will depend partly on what we do and partly on what other nations do. In the domestic area, our problems are numerous. They include inflation, depression, unemployment, taxation, public spending, union power, business power, farm power, government power, education, housing, economic growth, strikes, competition, monopoly, crime, mental health, atomic energy, natural resources, foreign aid, tariffs, civil rights, freedom. And this multiplicity of domestic problems are all merely aspects of the fundamental domestic problem, which is, how to use material well-being as the firm foundation upon which to build the noble edifice of the good society.

The proper roles of government and of the private sections in dealing with these problems constitute the subject of this book. We shall begin with an analysis of the nature and development of the government in the United States, a realistic consideration of pressures and politics in our government in the American economy. After considering the basic structure and functioning of the American business and governmental systems, we shall go on to discuss specific problems, including some of those mentioned in the preceding paragraph. The aim is to indicate the principal issues and the key facts necessary for understanding them, as well as for appraising existing public policies and discussing possible changes in them.

## QUESTIONS AND PROBLEMS

1. What is the value of understanding the relationships between government and business?
2. Define the terms *business* and *government* as used in this discussion of business and government relationships.
3. Does the decline in the number of governmental agencies in the U.S. mean that we have less government now than formerly?
4. Does your state have townships? Are they desirable?
5. Give present or past examples of the various types of government in specific countries of the world.
6. Rural overrepresentation ("agrocracy") in state legislatures is sometimes defended because it is "enshrined in the Constitution." What do you think of this argument?
7. What is the role of the U.S. Supreme Court in deciding the constitutionality of legislative apportionment?
8. Which type of government is most favorable to economic development?
9. In the new nations of the world, that were formerly colonies, will *self*-government produce *good* government?
10. How do governmental actions and other types of social control complement one another in causing socially desirable behavior?

## SELECTED READINGS

BOULDING, KENNETH E. *Principles of Economic Policy.* Englewood Cliffs, N.J.: Prentice-Hall, Inc., 1958.

CARR, ROBERT K., and others. *American Democracy in Theory and Practice.* New York: Rinehart & Company, 1957.

CLARK, J. M. *Social Control of Business,* 2nd ed. New York: McGraw-Hill Company, 1939.

DIMOCK, MARSHALL. *The New American Political Economy.* New York: Harper and Brothers, 1962.

KNIGHT, FRANK H. *Freedom and Reform.* New York: Harper and Brothers, 1947.
————. *Intelligence and Democratic Action.* Cambridge, Mass.: Harvard University Press, 1960.

LEWIS, ANTHONY. *One Man—One Vote.* New York: Twentieth Century Fund, 1962. A pamphlet.

LIPPMAN, WALTER. *The Good Society,* rev. ed. Boston: Little, Brown & Company, 1943.

McCLELLAND, DAVID C. *The Achieving Society.* Princeton, N.J.: D. Van Nostrand Company, 1961.

PFIFFNER, JOHN M., and ROBERT V. PRESTHUS. *Public Administration,* 4th ed. New York: The Ronald Press, 1960.

President's Commission on National Goals. *Goals for Americans.* Englewood Cliffs, N.J.: Prentice-Hall, Inc., 1960.

RODEE, CARLTON CLYMER, and others. *Introduction to Political Science.* New York: McGraw-Hill Company, 1957.

SMITHIES, ARTHUR, and others. *Economics and Public Policy*. Washington, D.C.:
  The Brookings Institution, 1955.
Social Sciences Staff, University of Chicago. *The People Shall Judge*. Chicago:
  University of Chicago Press, 1949.
WRIGHT, DAVID McCORD. *Democracy and Progress*. New York: The Macmillan
  Company, 1948.

# 2 THE AMERICAN ECONOMY:
## Nature and Development

Consideration of the development of the American economy is appropriate, not for the sake of a mere plowing through masses of historical facts, but rather so that we can acquire a better perspective on where we are today and how and why we got here, plus a better understanding of the factors involved in historical development and some impression of probable future developments if the trends of the past are continued.

The study of the evolution of and changes in our economy has the great advantage of jarring us from our tendency to take for granted things as they are today. It stimulates the realization that conditions have not always been the same and instills an appreciation of the forces and people who have brought about change and improvement. Indeed, the development of the American economy since the beginning of the nation has been so immense, both quantitatively and qualitatively, that a positive effort is required for a visualization of what the economy was like in the early days of the Republic.

One way of doing this is to imagine the Founding Fathers having been able to move either backward or forward in history by means of some kind of *time machine*. If these great men had been able to move back to Imperial Rome in the days of its grandeur, some 16 or 18 centuries before their time, or conversely had been able to move forward in time less than two hundred years to today's America, in which place would they have felt at home? Visiting Imperial Rome, they would have had to admit that the city was much more beautiful than any American city of their day. They would have noted that agricultural and manufacturing methods, on the whole, were similar to theirs, although they would have observed that textile weaving machines were hand-powered, rather than powered by water wheels or steam engines. They would have observed the lack of printing presses, books, magazines, and newspapers. On the other hand, they might have discovered that the plumbing was better than in their day. General George Washington would have found subjects of conversation with a fellow general, Julius Caesar, to have been the problems common to military men of all ages—strategy, tactics, logistics. One of the few things that the American general from the eighteenth century would have had to explain to his Roman counterpart would have been *firearms*.

If, however, we can imagine the Founding Fathers' moving the much shorter time to today's America, it is not unreasonable to suppose that they would be amazed by the changes. They would observe, of course, that the nation is much larger in physical area and many times bigger in population. Perhaps, however, the things that would most astonish them would be the various new products, including automobiles, airplanes, telephones, radios, television sets, electric lights, voting machines, and the many others. They would see the enormous increase in the standard of living of the people possessing and enjoying those products. They would also observe the productive apparatus that creates these goods and would notice technological developments, including power-driven machinery, factories, railroads, and many others.

They would also note, and no doubt be flabbergasted by, the tremendous size of the United States Federal Government. Indeed, it is interesting to speculate which they would find more astonishing, the size of the United States, or the size of its national government. They would naturally wonder how the growth of government had come about; a subject to which we shall turn our attention in the next chapter.

## GROWTH OF AREA AND POPULATION

The extraordinary development of the American economy may also be illustrated by reference to a few statistics. At the time of the first census, August 2, 1790, the area of the United States was 888,811 square miles. Its population was 3,929,214, which means that the simple arithmetic mean of population per square mile was 4.5.

The years and decades passed. In 1860 the area had grown to 3,022,387 square miles, of which 2,969,640 were land. The population had risen in each intervening decade by 32 to 36 per cent, and then stood at 31,443,321. The population per square mile of land area was, therefore, 10.6.

After 1860 the rate of growth of both area and population slowed down. The largest subsequent area additions were Alaska and Hawaii. And from 1930 to 1940 the decade's population rise was only 7.2 per cent.

During that decade something very extraordinary occurred; the national birth rate stopped falling and began to go up! The birth rate had probably been declining in the United States ever since the Republic had been established. One cannot be absolutely certain of this, because the statistics on births prior to 1910 are incomplete. Knowledge of the rate of growth of the total population and of the small contributions by immigration suggest, however, that the birth rate had been very much higher in the early part of the nineteenth century than it was later on. In any event, it seems as though, during a period of more than a century, the birth rate in the United States went down. This led the demographers in the 1930s to do an entirely reasonable thing; that is, to project this decreasing birth rate into the future and on this basis to arrive at the conclusion that the population would rise very slowly, reaching a peak of possibly 160 million around 1960, and thereafter would start to decline.

Contrary to this entirely reasonable expectation, however, the birth rate stopped falling and began to rise about 1935. It should be noted that, notwithstanding a frequently expressed statement, the declining birth rate was not caused by the Great Depression; it had been dropping for a long time before that ghastly experience began. Nor was the rise in the birth rate brought about by an end to the Depression, because the birth rate went up during the latter part of the 1930s, while the depression, although by then somewhat ameliorated, was still more severe than any previously known in the United States.

The increase in the birth rate brought about a faster increase in the total population. The percentage rate of gain jumped to 14.5 per cent in the 1950s and to 18.4 per cent in the 1960s (which becomes 18.5 per cent when newly added Alaska and Hawaii are counted).

In 1960 the area of the United States was 3,615,211 square miles, of which 3,548,974 were land; and on the average, 50.5 persons lived on a square mile.*

If recent trends continue, the population will double in the next half century. Such a rise will probably bring new business–government problems.

## RISING STANDARD OF LIVING

Economic development of other kinds also has occurred. Not only has the population grown, but (somewhat amazingly in view of the law of diminishing returns) output per capita has risen greatly. Although statistics about national income for the year 1800 are not very good, it is probably not far wrong to say that the total national income of the people of the United States in that year was about $1 billion, in dollars more or less equivalent to today's, and therefore the average per capita income was about $200 per year. It should be noted that this was not the income per worker, but the income *per person,* counting men, women, and children.

The significance of the reference to dollars "more or less equal in purchasing power to today's" lies in the fact that the figures have been ad-

* Source of population and area figures: *Statistical Abstract of the United States 1961* (Washington: U.S. Government Printing Office, 1961), p. 5.

justed for changes in the commodity price level. But there is no way of adjusting for the fact that many, perhaps most, of the commodities purchased by Americans today *could not have been bought at any price in 1800.* The necessities, comforts, and luxuries, some of which were mentioned earlier as astounding the Founding Fathers in their imaginary visit to modern America, simply did not exist at that time, and therefore it is impossible to assign any equivalent price to them for the year 1800. In other words, gains indicated for later years are understated rather than overstated by these figures.

Despite this handicap let us go on to examine the increase in total output and the smaller, but substantial, gain in per capita income. A century later—in 1900—total national income was about $60 billions, and the average income figure had risen to $800 per person per year. That was a substantial gain, but it was small compared to what was coming.

Another surge of economic development took place in the twentieth century. In 1950 national income (still in today's dollars) had risen to $300 billions, and the per capita figure to $2,000. The rise continued during the decade of the fifties with the national figure going to $420 billions and the per capita figure to $2,400 in 1960.

The story told by these statistics is as simple as it is impressive. Between 1800 and 1900 the standard of living of the average American quadrupled. In the following 60 years it tripled. At the end of the period of 160 years it was twelve times as high as the beginning.

## INCREASING PRODUCTIVITY

What is the explanation of this enormous increase? One possible explanation might be that people worked harder or worked longer hours as the decades went past. In fact, however, neither change occurred. Actually, the average work week declined during the period of 160 years and probably was about cut in half, from 80 hours a week to 40. Moreover, in terms of physical, backbreaking, sweat-producing toil, the average man did not work as hard in 1960 as had his predecessor in 1800.

No; the explanation is to be found in something completely different, summed up in one phrase: *an increase in productivity.* The nature and causes of this gain will be examined in the discussion of economic growth in Chapter 9.

It is important that we note that this bundle of gains that may be called economic progress—namely, rising productivity, decreasing working hours, and an increasing standard of living—represents a real gain; but its significance should not be instantly equated, without some reservations, to improved welfare or to a better life for people.

Man does not live by bread alone; there *are* noneconomic aspects of the good life. On the other hand, hunger and illness—common among much of mankind—hardly represent good living. Their alleviation presumably contributes to better living. Economic development can be coupled with development in other worthwhile areas. Economic development may or may not contribute to such other development; not only is it not necessarily hostile, it may be favorable. Provisionally, it can be said that improved material well-being provides a *basis* for the better life.

## POVERTY AMIDST RICHES

The gains in the real income of the average American family have been so great that it would be easy to suppose that ours has indeed become an affluent society. Such a conclusion, however, is not borne out by the facts. It is true that in 1960 the 45,370,000 American families had an average annual income of $7,696. That average figure permitted comfortable living. In the same year, however, 3,287,000 families (or 7.3 per cent of the total) had incomes under $2,000 a year. Another 7,161,000 families (or 15.8 per cent of the total) had incomes between $2,000 and $3,999. These two groups contained nearly 10.5 million families, or almost one fourth of the total.*

The problem of poverty has not been solved in our wealthy society—it continues to be an object of concern to private interests and public policy.

## BUSINESS FLUCTUATIONS

The American economy has expanded from the beginning. It has not, however, done so at an absolutely steady pace. There was a spurt in the middle of the nineteenth century and two other periods of rapid advance in the latter part of that century, followed by more vigorous developments in the twentieth.

And there have been occasional contractions in national business activity, followed by renewed expansion. These fluctuations from the steady growth trend are sometimes called "business cycles." A serious slump was experienced in the 1870s and another in the 1890s. A severe but short decline occurred in 1907, another in 1920–1921.

The Great Depression, which began in 1929, however, dwarfed all others. In terms of depth and duration, it was probably five times as bad as the worst previous one, which was the one in the 1870s. By 1933 one fourth of the American work force was unemployed and many of the others were employed only part time. Thousands of banks had suspended payments and the country was economically prostrate. Then came a partial recovery in 1936, followed by another slump. In 1940 the depres-

* Source of family income figures: U.S. Department of Commerce, *Survey of Current Business*, April 1962, p. 12.

sion was eleven years old, and out of a total work force of 55.6 million more than 8.1 million were unemployed, or about 15 per cent.

The Great Depression went so deep and lasted so long that it caused many analysts to believe that something had happened to the long-term growth of the American economy. Two phrases characterize their line of reasoning: "mature economy" and "the stagnation thesis." The gist of both is that economic growth of the American economy had ended.

On the other hand, there were other analysts who believed that this reasoning resulted from confusion between an extraordinarily bad depression and a real cessation of the upward thrust of growth. Eventually this latter view turned out to be correct, as the nation not only emerged from depression during World War II, but after the war continued to enjoy high and rising prosperity, with only minor setbacks.

Prosperity and economic growth have become concerns of government and objectives of policy. They will be analyzed in later chapters.

## QUALITATIVE AND
## STRUCTURAL CHANGE

Immense quantitative growth has characterized American economic history. Qualitative growth and structural change also have been notable. As the standard of living of the American people has risen, so also have their noneconomic achievements. The American family not only consumes more goods than do families elsewhere in the world, but also lives a better life in many respects. To be sure, there are many characteristics of modern America that are unlovely and some that are disagreeable and even dangerous. On the whole, however, the hazards of life are smaller, health is better, infant mortality is lower, and cultural achievements are greater than they were in earlier decades. There is, to be sure, continuing complaint about the moral fiber of our people, about the inability to get a fair day's work from an employee, about the disinclination of people to take care of their own problems. These are not new complaints. Their equivalents can be found in many periods of history. Some of them are undeniably valid, as some of them have been valid in earlier years. Some are exaggerations; some present real problems.

The development of modern America can be realized by reviewing the characteristics of early America. When George Washington was President, the Federal Government spent $4 million in the first year.\* The national government was simple. So were state and local governments. Simple also was the life of the people. Most Americans were farmers. A few lived in villages and small cities and carried on the simple manu-

---

\* It may be hard to realize that nowadays the Federal Government spends that much every *half hour*.

facturing operations and mercantile activities of townsmen of that day. There was little power-driven machinery and no power-driven tools. The chief sources of power were animal and human muscles.

Many families were largely self-sufficient. They raised and prepared their own food—which may have been nourishing but certainly was simple. Families also—perhaps aided by their neighbors—built their own houses and made their own furniture and clothing. Travel was expensive and uncomfortable; few persons other than sailors and politicians ever traveled more than fifty miles from the places of their birth throughout their entire lives.

As the decades passed, the Industrial Revolution spread from England to the United States. Factories were built, and the stock of machinery grew. Cities and towns expanded. Schools multiplied. The urban growth was paralleled by, and indeed was based upon, increasing productivity in the agricultural sector of the economy. Notable inventions—such as the cotton gin, the steel plow, and the combined harvesting and threshing machine—increased agricultural output. Thus it became possible to release manpower from the primary and essential job of producing food and fiber for work in urban surroundings in the expanding manufacturing establishments.

Because of the difficulty of travel and the slowness of communication, many citizens focused their interest in matters governmental on local or state governments. The franchise was extended. Sectional conflicts arose, and in the end, the strong influence of the South upon national government was broken by the Civil War.

## THE CIVIL WAR AS A TURNING POINT

Although it is impossible to break down economic history into sharply defined periods, it is not unreasonable to suggest that the Civil War marked a turning point from a predominantly agricultural America to a nation increasingly characterized by industrialization. After the war railroads were expanded greatly and factories grew and multiplied rapidly. Large agglomerations of wealth and economic power began to appear.

In the three decades following the Civil War the country witnessed the growth of corporate structure, especially in railroads, manufacturing concerns, and combinations of great firms. Historians were later to dwell on this as being the era of the "robber barons," some of them neglecting the fact that the conditions that produced some dubious results also contributed to an immense expansion of industrialization and transportation.

Discontent with some of the conditions of the new industrialization brought about demands for governmental interference. One of the objectives of the Granger Movement was regulation of railroad rates; and the establishment in 1887 of the Interstate Commerce Commission marked the appearance of the first of the great Federal regulatory commissions. State railroad commissions also began to appear.

The enactment of the Sherman Antitrust Act in 1890 made the maintenance of competition and the prevention of abridgements thereof matters of Federal policy; and in the following years the government began to move slowly, and somewhat ineffectually in the beginning, against some of the new giant business combinations.

Federal regulations began to appear in other areas as the years of the twentieth century passed. In addition to the regulatory commissions, the Federal Reserve System was established in 1913. The 1920s saw many new types of government regulation come into being, some sporadically and irregularly. A chronological list of some of the principal ones is presented in Chapter 4.

## THE GREAT DEPRESSION AND THE NEW DEAL

The great change in the role of the Federal Government in the economic life of the country was precipitated, however, by the Great Depression of the 1930s. This experience jolted people into new thinking about the nature of economic activity and the place of the national government in respect to it. Out of that frightful and frightening experience emerged the idea that government has a responsibility for maintaining conditions favorable to high levels of employment and prosperity.

Moreover, this same upsurge of thinking and action resulted in the introduction of some new forms of government regulation which clearly fall into the category of broad reforms, rather than that of *ad hoc* correctives. This group of new laws and new activities, which came to be called the "New Deal," marked a massive change in the role of government in our politico-economic life.

The changes—the new policies and activities—did not command unanimous support. On the contrary, they were highly controversial; indeed, some of the controversy was bitter. A regrettable hostility developed between Washington and the national business community, and this lack of harmony endured, at least in the form of watchful suspicion and distrust, for twenty years.

The election of 1952 returned the Republican Party to power at both ends of Pennsylvania Avenue. This was the opportunity—long awaited, to judge from the utterances of Republicans—to repeal the entire New Deal. What was done? The New Deal was not repealed. On the other hand, the party which had been the "outs" for so many years, now finding itself to be the "ins," reconsidered its attitudes and beliefs about the role of government; and, in the end, not merely left the New Deal substantially unchanged, but actually extended it in some directions.

Controversy did not end, although it became less acrimonious, when the long-time announced foes of the New Deal took over the government.

Controversy about government actions continues, reflecting different opinions about the Great Question in political economy—*What is the proper role of government in a predominantly private enterprise economy?*

A principal objective of this book is to supply materials relevant to the answer or answers to that question. At this point it is appropriate to make only a preliminary examination of the question and to frame a very general answer.

## THE PRIVATE ENTERPRISE SYSTEM

If we were to ask, What is the role of government in a communist or completely socialist society? the answer would be fairly simple. That government's role is to own everything and to run everything. That, of course, is not the kind of society that we have or that we want, although some observers think that we are drifting with dangerous speed in that direction.

Ours is predominantly a private enterprise society. This kind of society is often called "capitalism." In this system the ownership and management of business are chiefly in private hands. There are three principal legal characteristics of the private enterprise system:

[1]   The right to own private property,
[2]   The right to go into business for oneself, and
[3]   The right to earn a profit.

Turning our attention to the nature and functioning of the private enterprise system, we begin by noting that any economic system is confronted with certain problems, common to both collectivist organizations and private enterprise societies. These problems include the following:

[1]   What goods to produce,
[2]   How much of each kind of goods to produce,
[3]   How to produce the goods,
[4]   How to allocate resources to the production of different goods,
[5]   How to produce efficiently, and
[6]   How to distribute the goods among the members of the society.

These problems appear in both primitive and complex societies. Even Robinson Crusoe faced them. After he was joined by his man Friday, he had the labor resource of two persons. His problem involved the essence of *economizing:* the more hours they worked, the fewer they had for rest and leisure. Also, whatever the number of hours they worked, the more they produced of any one good, the less they could produce of others, and therefore they had the problem of achieving a balance in the production of various goods. They had to decide how the goods were to be produced and were naturally interested in increasing the efficiency of their operations, or as we should say in modern language, getting more output per man-hour and doing it without more hard work. And then Crusoe had to decide how much of the total production would go to Friday and how much he would keep for himself.

Similar problems appeared in the frontier societies which used to be characteristic of part of the American economy. There the frontier family comprised the work force, and they had the same series of problems. In both cases—the Crusoe economy and the frontier family—the essential characteristic of the private enterprise system appears clearly. That essential characteristic is the responsibility of individuals to advance their own economic well-being. The output of both of these simple economic units consisted of goods and services which they themselves consumed and which were, in economic language, *their real income*. The relationship between effort and reward was clear and direct: the more effective the effort, the higher the real income; the greater the production, the greater the consumption.

## A COMPLEX SOCIETY

In a complex society like that of modern America, certain important changes appear. One of the principal differences is that, unlike Crusoe and the frontier family, the typical producer consumes very little of his own output. Modern economic society is characterized by division of labor or specialization, in which men work at highly subdivided parts of the production process. The goods thus produced are sold for money, the workers are paid in money, and with their money incomes the workers buy goods produced by other persons.

Even though a modern worker does not literally consume the products of his own efforts, the link between productive effort and real income does not disappear. Presumably, the more a man produces the more money he earns thus increasing both his money income and his real income. He is busily engaged in making goods for other people, not because he loves mankind, but because his diligent effort has the result of improving his own position. Moreover, if, as is likely, he picks an occupation for which his talents are well suited, this also increases his output and, with it, presumably, his income.

The same line of reasoning applies to the use of land. The farmer who has the option of raising corn, tomatoes, or potatoes will take account of the value of the various products and the suitability of the land for their production, and he is likely to select the crop that promises the biggest income. In short, he like the worker, although guided by self-interest, is engaged in directing productive resources so as to make the biggest contribution to the total output of the economy.

Similar reasoning influences the man who is investing capital. He is interested in safety and earnings. In deciding among possible investments of new capital, he looks to these criteria rather than to the well-being of society. Nonetheless, in selecting an investment that promises *him* a good net return, he is thereby putting his capital where it can make a good contribution to the *society's* total output.

## THE INVISIBLE HAND

The manner in which the private enterprise system operates and its superiority to systems that are directed by central authority were described by Adam Smith, in these famous passages:

In almost every other race of animals each individual, when it is grown up to maturity, is entirely independent, and in its natural state has occasion for the assistance of no other living creature. But man has almost constant occasion for the help of his brethren, and it is in vain for him to expect it from their benevolence only. He will be more likely to prevail if he can interest their self-love in his favour, and show them that it is for their own advantage to do for him what he requires of them. Whoever offers to another a bargain of any kind, proposes to do this. Give me that which I want, and you shall have this which you want, is the meaning of every such offer; and it is in this manner that we obtain from one another the far greater part of those good offices which we stand in need of. It is not from the benevolence of the butcher, the brewer, or the baker that we expect our dinner, but from their regard to their own interest. We address ourselves, not to their humanity but to their self-love, and never talk to them of our own necessities but of their advantages.

Every individual is continually exerting himself to find out the most advantageous employment for whatever capital he can command. It is his own advantage, indeed, and not that of the society, which he has in view. But the study of his own advantage naturally, or rather necessarily, leads him to prefer that employment which is most advantageous to the society.

Secondly, every individual who employs his capital in the support of domestic industry, necessarily endeavors so to direct that industry that its produce may be of the greatest possible value.
The produce of industry is what it adds to the subject or materials upon which it is employed. In proportion as the value of this produce is great or small, so will likewise be the profits of the employer. But it is only for the sake of profit that any man employs a capital in the support of industry; and he will always, therefore, endeavour to employ it in the support of that industry of which the produce is likely to be of the greatest value, or to exchange for the greatest quantity either of money or of other goods.

But the annual revenue of every society is always precisely equal to the exchangeable value of the whole annual produce of its industry, or rather is precisely the same thing with that exchangeable value. As every individual, therefore, endeavours as much as he can both to employ his capital in the support of domestic industry, and so to direct that industry that its produce may be of the greatest value; every individual necessarily labours to render the annual revenue of the society as great as he can. He generally, indeed, neither intends to promote the public interest, nor knows how much he is promoting it. By preferring the support of domestic to that of foreign industry, he intends only his own security; and by directing that industry in such a manner as its produce may be of the greatest value, he intends only his own gain, and he is in this, as in many other cases, led by an invisible hand to promote an end which was no part of his intention. Nor is it always the worse for the society that it was no part of it. By pursuing his own interest he frequently promotes that of the society more effectually than when he really intends to promote it. I have never known much good done by those who affected to trade for the public good. It is an affection, indeed, not very common among merchants, and very few words need be employed in dissuading them from it.

What is the species of domestic industry which his capital can employ, and of which the produce is likely to be of the greatest value, every individual, it is evident, can, in his logical situation, judge much better than any statesman or lawgiver can do for him. The statesman who should attempt to direct private people in what manner they ought to employ their capitals would not only load himself with a most unnecessary attention, but assume an authority which could safely be trusted, not only to no single person, but to no council or senate whatever, and which would nowhere be so dangerous as in the hands of a man who had folly and presumption enough to fancy himself fit to exercise it.°

## THE FUNCTIONAL THEORY

This analysis of the private enterprise system may be described as a *functional theory of prices, sales, earnings, and profits.* Productive activity is encouraged by the prospect of increased earnings, efficiency is stimulated by the same incentive, and consumer freedom of choice results in a pattern of production of goods in conformity with what the consumers want. If consumers want less of commodity *A* and more of commodity *B*, the sales (and perhaps also the price) of the former will drop, while those of the latter will rise. The earnings of the producers of *A* will go down and those of the producers of *B* will rise. Thus the carrot and the stick will be in operation to induce transfer of productive resources from the production of *A* into the production of *B*.

In the private enterprise system the millions of independently acting

° Adam Smith, *An Inquiry into the Nature and Causes of the Wealth of Nations.* Page references are to Everyman's Library (London and Toronto: J. M. Dent & Sons, 1910), pp. 13, 398–401.

individuals, motivated primarily by self-interest, are being guided by a gigantic scoring system. Each presumably "sees" only a small part of this impalpable tabulation and is probably not even aware of its existence or its philosophical foundation. The end result, however, is a vast network of unconscious cooperation in which people work and invest to provide the goods and services that other people want. If the rulers of a completely collectivist economy should wish to allow consumers freedom of choice, they would have to pay the private enterprise system what is sometimes counted as the sincerest form of flattery—imitating it by developing and maintaining a gigantic accounting system (this one a palpable one, of paper and ink) to record prices, costs, sales, and earnings, and to signal the need for shifts in allocations of resources as called for by changes in consumers' wants. In both cases *the gigantic scoring system is the fundamental necessity*. In the private enterprise society, no one keeps it—it is *there*; it keeps itself. In the consumer-oriented collectivist society someone would have to keep it—and a Herculean task that would be. *This* is the *essential* difference in the *mechanics of resource allocation* between a free enterprise society and a collectivist one.

It is worth noting here that the existing collectivist governments of the planet are not generally marked by deep concern for their members' desires as consumers and that, to the extent that they give this matter any attention at all, they are somewhat less than successful in meeting these desires.

## THE CRIMINAL LAW

The system of harnessing self-interest to the general good of society is weakened to the extent that people try to get money in unproductive ways, such as stealing, swindling, extorting, and counterfeiting. A simple way of noting the economic consequence of these activities is to imagine a society in which everyone is trying to make a living in one of these ways. What would be the total output of such a society? Zero. What would be the total income of such a society? Zero also. In order to make a private enterprise system work, it is necessary to deter people from trying to make their livings in unproductive ways and thus to insure that they earn them productively.

This is one of the principal purposes of the criminal law. Laws forbid undesired, unproductive activities and provide penalties for violation. Law enforcement officers undertake to apprehend violators, and courts to convict and sentence them. The prospect of fine or prison is supposed to keep men out of these activities. The fact that more than two million major crimes are committed annually in the United States suggests that the apparatus of the criminal law is far from successful. Improvements in law enforcement are a matter of concern to thoughtful citizens, not only for the sake of economic efficiency, but for a variety of noneconomic reasons as well.

In this connection, it is appropriate to make reference to the concept of social control, which was discussed in Chapter 1. The criminal law is not the only mechanism available to influence people away from unproductive activities and toward productive ones. Many of the other elements of social control (such as family, school, and church) also build the attitudes and mold the behaviors of people. Perhaps their strengthening offers an even better possibility of reducing crime than do improvements in the apparatus of the criminal law.

Another self-interest activity that is harmful to the economy is monopolistic exploitation. The monopolistic seller of goods and services can exploit buyers to a greater or lesser extent. The monopolistic purchaser of goods and services can exploit sellers. Not only does the monopolist increase his own profits unfairly, but his actions lead to some misallocation of resources. The prevention or at least limiting of monopoly, therefore, is essential to the proper operation of the free enterprise system.

## THE FUNCTION OF GOVERNMENT

In the operation of the private enterprise system we see people busily enagaged in looking after their own interests and thereby causing the economy to function as it should. Why, then, do they need government? What should government do, and what should it refrain from doing?

The discussion of the criminal law has pointed to one function of government. Unless other forms of social control can completely restrain people from trying to make their livings in unproductive ways, organized society through formal government units steps in to assist in achieving the objective. National, state, and local governments have law enforcement branches. Even adherents to the "laissez-faire" philosophy of government consider that the protection of persons and of property rights, and the prevention of unsocial activities, are proper functions of government. Laissez-faire means "Let people alone; let them do what they want to do." It is a philosophy whose adherents deprecate government interference, especially with business activity. This philosophy also presumably envisages national defense as a proper function of government.

When we consider the many functions now performed by governments, including education, assistance to business, regulation of business, influence upon the economy, and the actual ownership and operation of productive enterprises, we see that government has gone far beyond what are often considered to be its minimum functions. Some of these additional activities are controversial, and an examination of some of them is presented in this book.

## PHILOSOPHY ABOUT GOVERNMENT AND BUSINESS

The basic philosophy of this book about the proper role of government in the economy is this: The government should do those things that are good for the nation and the world, within the framework of a society committed predominantly to the private enterprise system.

As I state this general philosophy, I must observe that even among persons who agree with it, there will be disagreement about its application. There is disagreement about fiscal policy, farm policy, antitrust laws, foreign economic policy, and labor legislation, to mention only a few.

Some persons seem to be inherently in favor of the expansion of government activity. This attitude often accompanies a strong distrust of private business. Other persons condemn any kind of government activity as being socialistic. The historical performance of the private enterprise system in the United States should suggest to the members of the first group, and the contribution of the public schools in the United States should indicate to the second, that both views have their limitations.

They do, to be sure, have the advantage of beautiful simplicity. They do not, however, promise to contribute as much to the formulation of sound public policies as does careful study of specific problems, as well as of the totality of the actions and policies of government.

### QUESTIONS AND PROBLEMS

1. What do you consider to be the most important aspects of the development of the American economy?
2. What are the main factors that have contributed to the growth of the American economy?
3. How does the American economy differ in nature and development from those of other nations?
4. In what ways has government influenced the development of the American economy?
5. Compare and contrast government regulation of business during the early years of the Republic and now.
6. List and explain the main elements of the private enterprise system.
7. What are the proper functions of government in a country which has a predominantly private enterprise system?
8. Explain and evaluate the functional theory of prices, sales, earnings, and profits.
9. How is the criminal law related to this theory?
10. Why might a collectivist economic society maintain a "gigantic scoring system"?
11. What is the future of the American economy? How can the government influence this development? To what extent should the government attempt to influence the economy?

## *SELECTED READINGS*

CLARK, J. M. *Economic Institutions and Social Welfare.* New York: Alfred A. Knopf, Inc., 1957.

GRIFFIN, CLARE E. *Enterprise in a Free Society.* Chicago: Richard D. Irwin, Inc., 1949.

HANSEN, ALVIN H. *The American Economy.* New York: McGraw-Hill Company, 1957.

HARRIS, S. E. (ed.). *American Economic History.* New York: McGraw-Hill Company, 1961.

HART, DONALD J. *Business in a Dynamic Society.* New York: The Macmillan Company, 1963.

HEILBRONER, ROBERT L. *The Making of Economic Society.* Englewood Cliffs, N.J.: Prentice-Hall, Inc., 1962.

JONES, HOWARD MUMFORD. *The Pursuit of Happiness.* Cambridge, Mass.: Harvard University Press, 1953.

KIRKLAND, EDWARD C. *History of American Economic Life.* New York: Appleton-Century-Crofts, Inc., 1951.

MILLER, WILLIAM. *A History of the United States.* New York: Dell Publishing Company, 1958.

SAMUELSON, PAUL A. *Economics.* New York: McGraw-Hill Company, several editions.

SLICHTER, SUMNER H. *Modern Economic Society.* New York: Henry Holt and Company, 1931.

TAYLOR, O. H. *Economics and Liberalism.* Cambridge, Mass.: Harvard University Press, 1955.

U.S. Bureau of the Census. *Historical Statistics of the United States, Colonial Times to 1957.* Washington, D.C.: U.S. Government Printing Office, 1960.

WILLIAMSON, HAROLD F. (ed.). *The Growth of the American Economy.* New York: Prentice-Hall, Inc., 1944.

ZELOMEK, A. W. *A Changing America: At Work and Play.* New York: John Wiley & Sons, Inc., 1959.

# 3       GOVERNMENT:

## Constitution and Court

The Constitution of the United States, the basic document in the relations of our government to business and to individuals, was in part evolutionary from the experience of previous government on this continent. Government began, in a simple way, in the English colonies. An early start was made by the Mayflower Compact, signed by the 41 male adults in that vessel (excepting eight servants and one dying Pilgrim) just before they left the ship, after they had made landfall off Cape Cod. In it they solemnly convenanted and combined into a civil body politic to achieve the ends that they sought by framing "such just and equal laws, ordinances, acts, constitutions, and offices as shall be thought most meet and convenient for the general good of the colony."

Later, other local governments and colonial governments were developed under the authority of the Crown. The colonists, therefore, had had substantial experience with more or less democratic government before the Declaration of Independence.

After the Revolutionary War it became necessary to establish a formal government for the new nation. This was first done under a document usually referred to as the "Articles of Confederation." It provided for a new government of distinctly limited powers. For example, financial support was provided by requiring that the several states contribute money to the central government. There was, however, no provision for compelling recalcitrant states to pay their proper shares, and many refused to do so.

Eventually, the shortcomings of the Articles of Confederation became sufficiently clear to cause the summoning of a convention in Philadelphia in 1787 for the purpose of rewriting the Articles.

Despite the fact that the convention was not authorized to write an entirely new constitution, the delegates decided to do so. They produced a document called "The Constitution of the United States." The new Constitution provided for a somewhat stronger Federal Government than had the Articles. In a key provision it authorized the Congress "to lay and collect taxes."

Despite the fact that the powers granted to the Federal Government under the new Constitution were still limited, many people were dissatisfied with the provisions made for the protection of the people *against* their government. For this reason it was proposed at once that ten more articles (or amendments) designed to strengthen this protection should be enacted. These ten amendments—often referred to as "The Bill of Rights"—were offered to reluctant states along with the new Constitution. Indeed, some made the adoption of these ten amendments a condition requisite to their approval. For practical purposes, therefore, these amendments may be regarded as part of the original Constitution itself.

## ATTITUDES AND CONDITIONS
## OF THE PERIOD

To understand the nature of the government established by the Constitution, it is essential to try to see the United States of America through the eyes of the people who lived in it at that time.

Particularly important was their attitude *toward governments*. State and local governments were close at hand. The people understood them and realized their necessity. The new national government, however, was far away. And people were suspicious of distant centralized government —an attitude that was probably a residue of the feeling toward King George III and the government of England. Presumably they would trust their own national government somewhat more than they trusted the English monarch and his ministers; but in the circumstances it is easy to understand why people mistrusted distant central government.

Technical factors also influenced the attitude toward the powers and functioning of the Federal Government. It is hard for us to realize how slow transportation and communication were at that time and how uncomfortable the former. It required a week to travel by jouncing stagecoach from Boston to New York and another week from New York to Washington. It is no wonder then that, when possible, many preferred travel by sea, even in the small and uncomfortable vessels of the time. The post moved somewhat faster than passengers, but its speed still was limited to that of a rider on horseback. These conditions were reflected quite late into our own time by the original date for the inauguration of the President of the United States, March 4—a date which was not changed until 1933. This date was thus set about four months after the election date partly because it took a long time, first, to discover who had been elected, and second, for those men to get to Washington.

## POWERS OF THE FEDERAL GOVERNMENT

There was much disagreement among the delegates to the Constitutional Convention of 1787, and also among the people whom they represented, about how much power should be given to the new national government. In the end they comprised and gave the Federal Government (as they believed) only modest powers.

Unlike the situation in some other countries where the national government is supreme and provincial governments have only such power as is delegated to them by the national government, the theoretical situation in the United States is that ours is a federal government of "United States." The theory is that the source of power is in the people acting through the states, and that in the Constitution they, via that route, grant certain powers to the Federal Government. Just to make this plain and positive, the Tenth Amendment to the Constitution says, "The powers not delegated to the United States by the Constitution, nor prohibited by it to the States, are reserved to the States respectively, or to the people."

Ostensibly, therefore, the Federal Government is one of *enumerated* powers. The powers not specifically mentioned are sometimes called the *reserved* powers—reserved to the states or the people. Over a period of time some powers have come to be referred to as *concurrent*. These are powers possessed by both the Federal Government and the states. The power to tax is one such important power. Also, through the years, the doctrine of *implied* or *resultant* powers has grown gradually. These are powers that, as their names suggest, are either implied in or result from the existence of the enumerated powers. The manner in which this expansion has come about and its significance will be considered presently.

## SEPARATION OF POWERS

Not only did the Founding Fathers intend to establish a government having only rather limited powers, but also, in order to avoid any kind of tyranny by parts of the government, they undertook to limit the exercise of even those modest powers. They did this by means of arrangements that are sometimes called the *separation of powers* or the system of *checks and balances*. The Founding Fathers provided for a government with three branches—legislative, executive, and judicial. Each of these branches was given certain duties and each was given some veto powers over the actions of the others. The Congress was authorized to lay and collect taxes and to spend money. It therefore has the power of the purse over the other branches of the government. The advice and consent of the Senate must also be sought for important Presidential appointments to Federal offices; the Senate can refuse its consent and occasionally does so.

The powers and responsibilities of the President are not spelled out in great detail in the Constitution except for specific mention that he shall be Commander-in-Chief of the Army and Navy. Many of what have come to be his most important civil duties are not mentioned. He is given the power to veto legislation passed by the Congress, but the legislation may be repassed over his veto by a two-thirds majority. The President appoints—with the advice and consent of the Senate—the judges who comprise the judicial branch of the Federal Government. As matters have turned out, the Supreme Court of the United States has come to have a kind of veto power of its own over legislation passed by the Congress.

Thus, broadly, the intent of the Founding Fathers was to create a modest central government. Let us again utilize the imaginative device of a return to the modern United States by the Founding Fathers as a way of dramatizing the changes that have occurred since their time. Let us picture these wise and patriotic men returning to Washington, D.C., which some of them had known as a muddy village at the confluence of two rivers. As they move along Constitution Avenue, past the huge buildings that house the offices of the Federal Government, they will surely be amazed. As their gaze falls upon one large edifice after another, their astonishment will probably mount, and it might reach a peak after they cross the Potomac and view the Pentagon, which is the largest office building in the world.

At certain times of the day they will note throngs of employees entering or leaving these buildings. They might be astonished to discover how many people work for the Federal Government today in Washington. Their astonishment will probably be heightened if they should learn that this is only about one tenth of the total employees of the Federal Government. If upon inquiry they learn that the Federal Government has 2¼ million civilian employees—exclusive of the armed forces—they will remember that the total population of the United States, when they wrote the Constitution, was only a million larger. From these figures, it would be an easy and obvious inference that the power and activity of the Federal Government had come to be greater—enormously greater—than they had contemplated. They would naturally, therefore, be interested in learning what forces had brought about this enlargement and what kinds of changes in the basic law of the land had implemented it.

## GROWTH OF FEDERAL POWER

It would be altogether natural if the Founding Fathers (continuing their imaginary visit) should conclude that, just as in their day, the people had decided that the nation needed a stronger national government. They might suppose that another Constitutional Convention had been called and the delegates charged with rewriting the Constitution to accommodate the new conditions of a larger industrialized society. It would be easy for the Founding Fathers, after becoming acquainted with today's nation, to note the impact of technological changes on the areas of public problems and to conclude that these changes had created conditions that can be dealt with only by a national government.

On inquiring whether there had been such a Constitutional Convention and learning that there had been none, the time-wanderers would probably reason next that some large and sweeping powers had been given to the Federal Government by important and comprehensive amendments to the Constitution. They would, therefore, be interested in reading the amendments that had been enacted since the original ten that comprise the Bill of Rights.

They would find only 13 of these—and they would read them with growing puzzlement. They would be looking for enumerations of large new additional powers for the Federal Government. But among the 13 amendments they would find only provisions for some rearrangement of governmental processes, articles freeing the slaves and providing for their rights, one that advanced Inauguration Day, and one that was canceled out by a subsequent amendment. In other words, net, there have been only 11 amendments since the Bill of Rights.

Of these they would note only one that gives the Federal Government new power. That one is the Sixteenth Amendment: "The Congress shall have power to lay and collect taxes on incomes, from whatever source derived, without apportionment among the several States, and without regard to any census or enumeration."

In truth, this grant of power might strike them as being not actually an addition, and perhaps redundant, inasmuch as they had authorized the Congress to *lay and collect taxes.* The mystery would be cleared up on its being pointed out to them that Section 9 of Article I of the Constitution provides that "No capitation, or other direct tax shall be laid, unless in proportion to the census or enumeration hereinbefore directed to be taken." Lawyers among the Founding Fathers would realize that the income tax is either a direct or a capitation tax, is not collected in proportion to the census and, therefore, would have been unconstitutional until the Sixteenth Amendment was adopted.

And so the end result of the Founding Fathers' study of the Constitution and its amendments would necessarily be their realization that *the words in the document that give powers to the Federal Government have been changed very little.*

This realization would lead to their next question, How has the Federal Government, which we, in drafting the Constitution, intended to make small and weak, come to be big and powerful *under substantially the same Constitution?*

It is easier for lawyers than for nonlawyers to understand the answer to this question. Its importance, however, suggests that nonlawyers should make the effort—to achieve full appreciation of the processes through which this basic law of the land has come to be called a "living constitution."

## HOW THE FEDERAL GOVERNMENT'S POWERS HAVE GROWN

The process of enlargement of the Federal Government's powers has followed largely from the development of technological, economic, and social changes which have created new conditions and new problems. For one example (having social as well as technological and economic aspects), before the development of railroads, there was no question about the regulation of railroad rates and no problem of distinguishing such regulation on an interstate basis as distinguished from an intrastate one. As such new problems have come along, sooner or later the Federal Government has undertaken to do something about them; the Congress has enacted pertinent legislation.

One of the most important of the enumerated powers which has been used as a basis for such legislation—a foundation upon which to erect the structure of Federal power—is to be found in Article I, Section 8, of the Constitution, which provides that "The Congress shall have power to regulate commerce with foreign nations and among the several states and with the Indian tribes." This is the famous *Commerce Clause*. Much of the enlargement of Federal power has been accomplished under the tent of this clause.

And the constitutionality of such legislation has sometimes been challenged—occasionally the Supreme Court has stopped such new activity by the Federal Government. For the most part, however, the Supreme Court has approved the extension of central governmental activities. The Court has done so through the process of interpreting the meaning of the Constitution, gradually developing the doctrines of implied and resultant powers.

Sometimes the Court has turned around. At one time, for example, the Court held that the business of *insurance* was not "commerce" within the meaning of the Constitution and, therefore, that Federal regulation of the insurance business was unconstitutional. Three quarters of a century later, another Supreme Court reversed this ruling and held that insurance was commerce within the Constitutional meaning and properly subject, therefore, to regulation by the Congress.

We shall see many examples of this gradual expansion of Federal power. At present, let us note that many persons have been alarmed in the past, and many are today, by this continuing development. "Centralization" is its name—a good word or a bad one depending on who uses it.

As "preemption" or "usurpation" it is opposed for a variety of reasons; as "progress" or "realistic meeting of its responsibilities by the Federal Government" it is supported by others.

## THE UNITED STATES SUPREME COURT

We now consider the role and functioning of the Supreme Court because of the key part played by it in the expansion of Federal power and in the control and regulation of business by the states and the Federal Government.

These subjects, somewhat difficult for those not trained in the law, involve an understanding of concepts such as *judicial review, judge-made law, due process of law,* and what critics sometimes call *judicial usurpation of the legislative function.*

One way for nonlawyers to approach an understanding of the critical role of the Court is to consider a not altogether too imaginary situation. Suppose that you are a member of a club or society that has a constitution which stipulates how the club is to be run and what the officers are required to do. Suppose further that you come to be of the opinion that the executive committee of the club, which is given certain power under the constitution and at the same time has certain limitations placed upon it, is disobeying that constitution. What can you do? You can protest to the executive committee. The committee may demur, contending that they have not disobeyed the club's constitution at all, but rather that it is you who are interpreting its meaning incorrectly. Perhaps if you have recourse to the entire club's membership at a meeting you may be able to get the matter straightened out (possibly, by then, too late for your purposes). If, however, you do not have such an opportunity to put the matter before the entire membership, you may find yourself wishing, in effect, that your club's constitution provided for the equivalent of the United States Supreme Court. That is, you may wish that there were some group to which you could turn for an authoritative interpretation of the club's constitution (preferably one agreeing with yours), which would be binding on the executive committee.

This, in essence, is the chief role of the United States Supreme Court. The Court construes the meaning of the words of the United States Constitution. Its decisions, although they are not supported by any police or military force—other than, possibly, United States marshals—are, nevertheless, considered to be binding upon the highest authorities in the land, including the President and the Congress.

## THE NEED FOR INTERPRETATION

The Constitution of the United States is a remarkable document. Its authors worked, and worked with skill, to anticipate difficulties. Many were lawyers and knew the significance of using words carefully and precisely. Nevertheless, the fact remains that few words in the English language other than scientific terms have absolutely precise meanings. It is therefore impossible, even with the best will and the best skill in the world, to write rules which will never encounter any difficulties in interpretation. An exercise demonstrating this fact is presented in an Appendix to this chapter, through an examination of some problems of interpretation of an imaginary city ordinance relating to parking automobiles. The words in the Constitution are bigger and longer, and the ideas more complex, than those in the imaginary ordinance. It is therefore no wonder that disagreements sometimes arise about their meanings and that someone, or somebody, has to be designated arbiter.

Sometimes the question raised is the serious one of whether the Congress of the United States has acted in accordance with the rules of the Constitution in having passed a given law. A law has sometimes been invalidated by the Supreme Court on the grounds that the Congress either lacked power to pass that particular law or had actually disobeyed provisions of the Constitution in passing it.

It has sometimes been suggested that decisions about the constitutionality of laws should be made not by the Supreme Court, but by the Congress itself, it being argued that the former procedure gives too much power to a majority of five men out of the nine who comprise the Court. There is, however, a persuasive argument against allowing the Congress to be the judge of the constitutionality of the laws that it itself passes. If we may again use the example of the executive committee of our imaginary club, we can note that if we left it up to the executive committee to decide whether they were acting in accordance with the constitution of the club, they could do anything they pleased and hold that their action was constitutional. The same proposition applies to the Congress of the United States.

If the constitution of the club is meant to be superior to the executive committee, as the Constitution of the United States is meant to be superior to the Congress, then neither legislative body can rule on the constitutionality of its own acts without, in effect, negating or reversing that superiority. The ruling must be made by some other authority if there is to be any reality in the condition of requiring the body to be subordinate to the document.

## JUDICIAL REVIEW

The Constitution does not specifically provide that the Supreme Court has the power to declare acts of the Congress unconstitutional. This power has developed in an evolutionary way, and from the beginning, the right of the Court to wield it has frequently been questioned. On the whole, however, public opinion and the weight of legal authority appear to support this power of *judicial review*.

What is said about the role of the Supreme Court in judging the con-

stitutionality of laws passed by the United States Congress applies equally
to laws passed by state legislatures. These bodies, too, are subject to the
United States Constitution, and their laws may be reviewed by the
courts, and ultimately by the Supreme Court, if questions about their
constitutionality are raised.

The position of the United States Congress in this respect may be
contrasted with that of the Parliament of the United Kingdom. In the
United Kingdom the Parliament is supreme. It is not subject to any written document. The United Kingdom has, in fact, no written constitution.
There are, to be sure, unwritten traditions and understandings that are
in effect quite as powerful as written rules, but the Parliament is technically free to pass any law that it wishes. If it were to pass a law that
was patently unjust, or violative of the generally accepted notions of the
rights of individuals, the law would stand despite its clear shortcomings
(although, of course, that particular Parliament might be defeated).

In the United States, however, the theory is that the Constitution was
adopted by the people and is the supreme law of the land—to which
even the Congress must be obedient. So must all officers of government.
Judicial review also comprehends scrutiny of the actions of regulatory
agencies and of officers of government—from the President down to the
humblest village official.

## EVOLUTION OF JUDICIAL REVIEW

These important ideas—that the Congress must obey the Constitution,
that legislation violative of the Constitution is void, and that, moreover,
the Courts, and especially the United States Supreme Court, are to pass
judgment on these questions—were set forth in 1803, in the famous case
of *Marbury v. Madison,** when the Supreme Court spoke under the
leadership of the great Chief Justice John Marshall.

The United States Supreme Court had been established in 1791. In the
beginning it was weak and inactive, doing relatively little business. For
a while it had difficulty finding a place to meet. The first two chief
justices resigned—apparently because they saw little future in the position. Then, in 1801, John Marshall became Chief Justice, a post which
he held until his death in 1835. To him goes the credit, more to than
any other one man, for extending the constitutional basis of the power of
the Federal Government. A crucial decision grew out of the unimportant-
looking matter of William Marbury's commission.

Marbury was appointed a Justice of the Peace for the District of
Columbia by President John Adams in the closing hours of the latter's
administration. The written commission which would make his appointment effective had not been delivered to him, however, before the
Adams Administration left office. He therefore brought a legal action to

* 1 Cranch 137 (1803).

compel the new Secretary of State, James Madison, to deliver the commission to him. This action was brought in the Supreme Court because that Court had been authorized by the Judiciary Act of 1789 to hear such cases.

The Court took the position that since the Constitution itself had not conferred upon the Court the power to hear cases of this kind, the Judiciary Act could not enlarge these functions and, therefore, that this section of the Act was unconstitutional and void. In this genuinely dramatic case the Court, in declining to accept the small power granted by the Act, asserted an enormously larger one—the power to void an act passed by the Congress of the United States.

Lest it be supposed that this decision led to a spate of decisions voiding laws passed by the Congress, it should be noted that the Supreme Court's next such decision came a half century later, in the famous Dred Scott case of 1857. The principle of judicial review had been established, however; and it has continued, although it has frequently been the subject of discussion—sometimes acrimonious.

If the foregoing discussion has created the impression that the Court strives to find a constitutional issue in every case brought before it, let it be said at once that this is not true. On the contrary, if a case can be decided on some ground other than the constitutionality of a law, the Court prefers to do it this way.

Moreover, the Court will not give advisory opinions about the constitutionality of proposed bills or enacted laws. It takes cognizance only of actual litigation.

The emphasis here on the United States Supreme Court might create the impression that it is the only court that possesses and exercises the power of judicial review. Not so, however. All courts, including both Federal and state, have power to determine whether an act of Congress, a state constitution, or a state law conforms to the Constitution of the United States.

In addition, state courts have the power of deciding whether state laws conform to state constitutions.

The reason why discussions of judicial review commonly center around the Supreme Court is that the decisions of lower courts are frequently appealed to higher tribunals and, since the Supreme Court is the highest of all, its decisions are the most important.

## EXTENDING THE FEDERAL
## GOVERNMENT'S POWERS

The important case of *McCulloch v. Maryland** was a key case in extending the powers of the Federal Government in two directions.

* 4 Wheat. 316 (1819).

In 1816 the Congress had chartered the Second Bank of the United States, and the State of Maryland had levied a tax on the bank notes of any bank not chartered by the State legislature. McCulloch, an officer of the bank, in Baltimore, refused to pay the tax. Involved in the case were two questions. One was this: Does the Federal Government have the constitutional right to charter a bank? The other was: Is the Maryland law constitutional?

There was no enumerated power of the Federal Government specifically authorizing the establishment of a bank. John Marshall and the Supreme Court might easily have found the act of chartering such a bank to be unconstitutional. Such a decision would have represented what has come to be called the *narrow construction* of the powers of the Federal Government. Instead of doing so, however, Marshall, speaking for the Court, presented a decision that represented the *broad construction*. He pointed out that the Constitution in Article I, Section 8, authorizes the Congress "to make all laws which shall be necessary and proper for carrying into execution the foregoing powers and all other powers vested by this Constitution in the Government of the United States, or in any department or officer thereof." He then went on to interpret the word *necessary* not as meaning "absolutely necessary," but rather as meaning "desirable." He referred to the constitutional authorization for the Federal Government to carry on certain financial activities, such as levying and collecting taxes, and borrowing and coining money. He went on to argue that the right of the Government to charter a bank to assist in carrying on its financial activities must be considered to be authorized by the Constitution as a means of doing so in an appropriate manner. Thus the chartering of the bank was held to be constitutional.

The decision then went on to take up the question of whether the State of Maryland had the power to tax the Bank's notes. There was nothing in the Constitution that specifically forbade such a tax. It was at this point that Marshall adduced his famous proposition, "The power to tax involves the power to destroy." He argued that if states were allowed to tax instruments of the Federal Government, they could limit or even seriously injure the functioning of the national government. The decision then went on to note that in Article VI the Constitution says, "This Constitution, and the laws of the United States shall be made in pursuance thereof; and all treaties made, or which shall be made, under the authority of the United States, shall be the supreme law of the land; and the judges in every state shall be bound thereby, anything in the Constitution or laws of any state to the contrary notwithstanding." On this basis, then—the supremacy of Federal legislation over state legislation—Marshall concluded that Maryland's tax law was inapplicable to the bank notes of the Second Bank of the United States and was, therefore, void under the Constitution.

In review of recent criticism of the Supreme Court, it is interesting to note that, subsequent to this decision, which limited the powers of the states, attacks upon the Supreme Court were so savage that John Marshall felt constrained to write a reply to them—a rare relaxation of the traditional aloofness of the justices of the high court.

## CONTINUED ENLARGEMENT OF FEDERAL POWERS

Another leading case decided by the Supreme Court, presided over by Chief Justice John Marshall, which enlarged the powers of the Federal Government and reduced those of the states, was *Gibbons v. Ogden*.\* This case, sometimes called the "Steamboat Case," involved a monopoly of steamboat transportation on the waters of New York State, which had been granted by the State to Robert Livingstone and Robert Fulton, who had in turn granted a license to Ogden.

John Marshall, speaking for the Court, said that the navigation so regulated was *commerce among the states*, whose regulation was reserved to the Congress, and that, therefore, the New York State law was unconstitutional.

Many subsequent cases have continued the process of enlarging the concept of interstate commerce. The Commerce Clause has been used as the principal justification for the enlargement of the regulation of business by the Federal Government.

Thomas Jefferson once said of John Marshall (who was his first cousin) that Marshall was engaged in writing a constitution. Although the statement is not literally true, it is certainly figuratively true. The process thus begun in the early years of the Supreme Court has continued throughout its history. The Court's continuing interpretation of the meanings of the words of the Constitution has amounted virtually to a rewriting of that document.

For about the first century of its existence, the trend of Supreme Court decisions was in the direction of enlarging the powers of the Federal Government and, in some cases, correspondingly cutting down the powers of the states. During this time very few laws passed by the Congress were declared unconstitutional. Some state laws were, however; and this action sometimes resulted from decisions that enlarged the powers of the Federal Government and reciprocally contracted those of the states.

## DUE PROCESS OF LAW

Beginning in the latter part of the nineteenth century, however, the Supreme Court began to declare unconstitutional certain acts of the

\* 9 Wheat. 1 (1824).

Congress and of state legislatures in decisions which—according to critics —merely reflected the justices' dislike for the laws so voided. The instrument that came to be used frequently by the Court in voiding such pieces of legislation was *due process of law.*

Due process of law is a difficult concept—partly because it has two very different meanings.

One meaning is *procedural due process.* This concept stems from the Magna Charta. In that famous document King John promised not to take criminal action against any freeman except according to "the law of the land." The Magna Charta was written in Latin, and later on this phrase was translated into the English words "due process of law." In the beginning, therefore, due process of law might be described as meaning an end to the "Off with his head!" type of justice which kings often followed and in some countries continued to follow for a long time. What it meant was that persons covered by this guarantee could not be subjected to punishment except in accordance with legal procedures, including fair trial. This meaning of the term prevailed for centuries.

Procedural due process was unquestionably what the Founding Fathers had in mind when they wrote—in the Fifth Amendment to the Constitution (part of the Bill of Rights)—these words: "No person shall . . . be deprived of life, liberty, or property, without due process of law. . . ."

It is by no means improbable that procedural due process was what the framers of the Fourteenth Amendment had in mind, three quarters of a century later. It will be recalled that the Thirteenth, Fourteenth, and Fifteenth amendments were passed shortly after the Civil War. On their face they abolished slavery, provided guarantees of protection for the newly freed citizens, and guaranteed the right of suffrage. The Fourteenth Amendment repeats almost identically the words of the Fifth. It says, ". . . nor shall any State deprive any person of life, liberty, or property without due process of law. . . ."

The alternative to supposing that the framers of the Fourteenth Amendment were thinking of procedural due process is to suppose that they were thinking of the other phrase, *substantive due process.* And in view of the meaning that came to be attached to this second phrase and to the power exercised by the United States Supreme Court in utilizing it, one would have to contemplate the possibility that these people were imagining the Fourteenth Amendment to read thus: "No State shall pass any law which in the judgment of a majority of members of the United States Supreme Court is unjust, discriminatory, arbitrary, unreasonable, or capricious." It may be doubted whether even one state legislature would have voted for this amendment in this form. Yet, as things have turned out, that is what the due process clause of the Fourteenth Amendment has come to mean. How has this remarkable feat been accomplished?

## THE POWER OF SUBSTANTIVE
## DUE PROCESS

This appearance of "substantive due process" in the latter part of the nineteenth century might be regarded as one of the most remarkable inventions of all time. The concept seems to have appeared first in an 1856 case, *Wynehamer v. New York,** in which a New York State court held that "due process of law" meant more than legal procedure, and included, in addition, a consideration of the treatment in inherent rights of the individual to life, liberty, and property.

Many laws—perhaps most—deprive people of liberty, in a broad sense of that word. Deprivation of liberty does, of course, include putting people in jail. But it means more than that. A speed limit, for example, deprives people of the legal liberty to travel above the stated speed. Violation may lead to a fine or to jailing—deprivation of actual physical liberty. And so it is with many laws whose purpose is to deprive people of some liberty which the legislative body considers undesirable for them to have. If the law was passed in accordance with the constitution that governs the legislative body (Federal or state, as the case may be), procedural due process has been complied with.

Substantive due process, however, is different. It involves the concept of a fundamental justice inherently due the individual. Justice Oliver Wendell Holmes, Jr., in effect defined the concept, in the words emphasized (emphasis supplied), in his dissent in the case of *Lochner v. New York*.† In this case, the majority opinion of the Supreme Court declared unconstitutional a law, passed by the State of New York, limiting the hours of employment of men in bakeries. The basis of the decision was the due process clause of the Fourteenth Amendment and the contention that this deprivation of liberty to enter into contracts for longer than certain hours had been accomplished by the State without due process of law—meaning, of course, in this case, substantive due process. In his dissent Justice Holmes provided a test for absence of substantive due process when he said, "I think that the word 'liberty' in the Fourteenth Amendment is perverted when it is held to prevent the natural outcome of a dominant opinion, unless it can be said that a rational and fair man necessarily would admit that the statute proposed would infringe *fundamental principles as they had been understood by the traditions of our people and our law*. It does not need research to show that no such sweeping condemnation can be passed upon the statute before us. A reasonable man might think it a proper measure on the score of health."

It will be seen at once that substantive due process gives a court a

* 13 N.Y. 378 (1856).
† *Lochner v. New York*, 198 U.S. 54 (1905).

versatile weapon with which to strike down legislation which a majority of the members of the court do not like. All that the majority need do is assert basic unjustness, discrimination, arbitrariness, unreasonableness, or capriciousness.

Perhaps it is right that there should be some such concept in the Constitution to guard against genuinely outrageous legislation. On the other hand, it is plain that any court that undertakes to pass upon the fundamental propriety of legislation can, if it wishes utilize this power to veto actions which many persons would consider to be reasonable and which a majority of the legislative body that had passed the law had presumably considered to be reasonable.

The Supreme Court hesitated at first to use the mighty weapon of substantive due process to invalidate laws. An illustration of this self-restraint is the decision in *Munn v. Illinois.*° This case involved the constitutionality of a law which had been passed by the State of Illinois fixing maximum charges for the storage of grain in warehouses. Chief Justice Waite, speaking for the majority of the Court, said of the state's power, "We know that this is a power which may be abused; but that is no argument against its existence. For protection against abuses by legislatures the people must resort to the polls, not the courts."

Later, however, the Supreme Court abandoned that restraint, and during several decades voided many national laws and state laws on the grounds that they violated the constitutional requirement of due process, meaning substantive due process.

Due process was not the only club wielded by the Supreme Court during this assertive period, which lasted until 1937. The Court declared some laws unconstitutional on the ground that they were not proper legislation under the commerce power. Critics declared that these decisions constituted judicial usurpation of the legislative process.

During these decades, inasmuch as many pieces of legislation which the Court voided were what their proponents considered to be progressive socioeconomic legislation (regulating maximum hours, minimum wages, and child labor), these same proponents became sharply critical of the Court. They sometimes referred to it as "the last stronghold of reaction in the United States." People who favored such legislation came to despair of the possibility of getting such new laws into effect because of their belief that if five of what they came to call the "Nine Old Men" disliked the legislation, they would find some constitutional basis for declaring it invalid.

## THE COURT AFTER 1937

Discontent with the actions of the Court came to a head in 1937, after the Court had struck down several New Deal laws as being unconsti-

° 94 U.S. 113 (1876).

tutional. President Roosevelt recommended to the Congress that it exercise its constitutional authority to increase the membership of the Court, with the clearly understood intention of nominating men as justices who were sympathetic to his program, thereby stopping those Court actions which some persons called examples of judicial usurpation of the legislative function. Opponents of the President's proposal called it the "Court-packing scheme." The proposal failed to pass in the Congress.

It would not be unreasonable to supose that after Congress had rejected the President's proposal the Supreme Court might have become even more intransigent. Not so, however. Indeed, some shift in the attitude of the Court had been indicated by decisions made in the spring of 1937, even before the Court-enlargement plan was voted down. Perhaps what took place thereafter was a delayed illustration of Mr. Dooley's famous pronouncement, "The Supreme Court follows the election returns."

Whatever the explanation, a change in the behavior of the Court took place, beginning in 1937, which must be regarded as truly amazing. Since that time the Supreme Court has voided very few laws of either the Congress or the state legislatures, and in those cases where it has it has seemed reluctant to do so. The Court's present policy is sometimes described as one of *judicial restraint*.

Some of the leading cases involving substantive due process—in both its erection and its demolition—are considered in the Chapter 19 discussion of labor legislation.

It is important to note that the Court has never repudiated the doctrine of substantive due process. The doctrine has seldom been used since 1937; but it still exists, and the mighty weapon might be taken out of the closet by a future Court.

## A GOVERNMENT OF LAWS OR OF MEN?

Perhaps the most controversial decision of the Court in recent years was the unanimous decision in 1954 in the case of *Brown v. Board of Education*,\* in which the Court declared a state law requiring racial segregation in public schools to be violative of the Constitution. The issue in this case is not primarily a business or economic problem, although it has some significance along these lines. Not only did the decision strike at the way of life in the South, but it also angered many persons by being yet another reversal of an earlier Court position. In 1896, in the case of *Plessy v. Ferguson*,† the Court had enunciated the famous "separate but equal" doctrine, which held that racial segregation through the provision of two separate sets of public facilities was not unlawful, provided the facilities were "equal."

\* 347 U.S. 483.
† 163 U.S. 537.

After the 1954 decision critics of the Court again raised the question whether ours is in fact a government of laws or a government of men. Critics contended that the case again demonstrated that the Constitution means what the Supreme Court says it means.

Critics also asserted that reversals of Supreme Court opinions make the Constitution meaningless. The Supreme Court has reversed itself 90 times, and it is clear that such changes can be of great significance. The best that can be said for such a reversal is that the previous decision had represented an erroneous interpretation of the meaning of the Constitution, which the later decision corrected. Over against this view, however, may be put this question: If the previous decision had misinterpreted the meaning of the Constitution, why had not the Constitution been amended in the meantime by language deliberately intended to overthrow that decision? Did not the absence of such amendment create the presumption that Congress, the states, and the people agreed with the earlier interpretation? On the other hand, granting such agreement originally, might not the consensus change at some later date, and might it not be possible for a wise, alert, and sensitive Court to detect this shift? And would it not then be its duty to act accordingly?

## JUDGE-MADE LAW

These decisions illustrate another concept that is difficult for non-lawyers—*judge-made law*. Nonlawyers are puzzled by the proposition that judges make laws; the layman's impression is that laws are made by legislative bodies. In fact, however, whenever a law, and even the Constitution of the United States itself, has to be interpreted in court, the decision in effect is an addition to the law, much in the nature of an amendment. As indicated in the last paragraph, the legal amending authority is, of course, in a position to change the "amendment" thus tacked on by a court, if it wishes to do so; and, if it does not, it presumably considers the court's contribution to be proper.

It should be noted that this process of "judicial amendment" is inevitable, inasmuch as the drafters of constitutions and laws cannot anticipate all of the unusual cases and changing conditions that will arise in future years.

In any event, the thoughtful citizen is interested in understanding the important role played by the courts in interpreting—and, by interpreting, *rewriting*—the basic law of the land.

On August 23, 1958, the Conference of Chief Justices of State Courts adopted, by a vote of 36 to 8, a resolution on Federal–State Relationships as Affected by Judicial Decisions. What was said in that report summarizes so precisely an authoritative viewpoint that it is worth quoting in detail.

The outstanding development in Federal–State relations since the adoption of the National Constitution has been the expansion of the power of the National Government and the consequent contraction of the powers of the State governments. To a large extent this is wholly unavoidable and, indeed, is a necessity, primarily because of improved transportation and communication of all kinds and because of mass production.

On the other hand, our Constitution does envision federalism. The very name of our nation indicates that it is to be composed of States. The Supreme Court of a bygone day said in Texas v. White, 7 Wall. 700, 721 (1868): "The Constitution, in all its provisions, looks to an indestructible Union of indestructible States."

Second only to the increasing dominance of the National Government has been the development of the immense power of the Supreme Court in both State and national affairs. It is not merely the final arbiter of the law; it is the maker of policy in many major social and economic fields. It is not subject to the restraints to which a legislative body is subject. There are points at which it is difficult to delineate precisely the line which should circumscribe the judicial function and separate it from that of policy making. . . .

We believe that, in the fields with which we are concerned and as to which we feel entitled to speak, the Supreme Court too often has tended to adopt the role of policy maker without proper judicial restraint. We feel this is particularly the case in both of the great fields we have discussed—namely, the extent and extension of the federal power, and the supervision of State action by the Supreme Court by virtue of the Fourteenth Amendment. In the light of the immense power of the Supreme Court and its practical nonreviewability in most instances, no more important obligation rests upon it, in our view, than that of careful moderation in the exercise of its policy-making role. We are not alone in our view that the Court, in many cases arising under the Fourteenth Amendment, has assumed what seem to us primarily legislative powers.

We do not believe that either the framers of the original Constitution or the possibly somewhat less gifted draftsmen of the Fourteenth Amendment ever contemplated that the Supreme Court would, or should, have the almost unlimited policy-making powers which it now exercises.

It is strange, indeed, to reflect that, under a Constitution which provides for a system of checks and balances and of distribution of power between national and State governments, one branch of one government—the Supreme Court—should attain the immense and, in many respects, dominant power which it now wields. We believe that the great principle of distribution of powers among the various branches of government and between levels of government has vitality today and is the crucial base of our democracy. . . .

We further find that the Court does not accord finality to its own determinations of constitutional questions, or for that matter of others. We concede that a slavish adherence to *stare decisis* could at times have unfortunate consequences; but it seems strange that under a constitutional doctrine which requires all others to recognize the Supreme Court's rulings on constitutional

questions as binding adjudications of the meaning and application of the
Constitution, the Court itself has so frequently overturned its own decisions
thereon, after the lapse of periods varying from 1 year to 75, or even 95
years. . . .

It is our earnest hope, which we respectfully express, that that great Court
exercise to the full its power of judicial self-restraint by adhering firmly to
its tremendous, strictly judicial powers and by eschewing, so far as possible,
the exercise of essentially legislative powers when it is called upon to decide
questions involving the validity of State action, whether it deems such action
wise or unwise. . . .

Symbolic of the rise in the power of the "great Court" is its building.
In contrast to its early days when the Court had no home, today the
United States Supreme Court occupies a $10-million structure especially
designed and constructed for it. It is in the style of a Greek temple and
is located on the plaza facing the Capitol, in Washington. Harsh though
criticism of the Court has been throughout its history and even in recent
years, it seems true that the prestige of the Court is high, even though
the Court's roles as interpreter and enforcer of the Constitution are not
always well understood among the citizenry.

## THE PROPOSED "STATES' RIGHTS" AMENDMENTS

Discontent with Supreme Court decisions and the role of the Federal
Government is reflected in three proposed amendments to the Constitution that are being considered by state legislatures, after passage by
Congress, and have been approved by some. One amendment would end
Federal jurisdiction over reapportionment of state legislatures. Another
would establish a "Court of the Union," consisting of the chief justices of
the 50 states, which, in certain types of cases involving Federal–state
relationships, could overrule decisions of the Supreme Court. A third
would add a method of amending the Constitution, in which the states
could enact amendments without Congressional action.

The question of Federal versus state-and-local governmental rights,
duties, and functions appears in many public policy problems and issues
—as noted at various points in this book. In many instances, however,
the doctrine of "states' rights" seems to be invoked by people who oppose some action taken (or contemplated) by the Federal Government;
but they oppose it not because it is Federal action but rather, in reality,
because they dislike the action itself.

The appeal of these proposed amendments is likely, therefore, to be in
proportion to dislike of current (or contemplated) actions of the Federal
Government.

## APPENDIX

### *AN EXERCISE IN INTERPRETING THE MEANING OF A LAW*

This is an exercise designed to advance an understanding of the nature of the United States Supreme Court's activity in interpreting the Constitution of the United States and in deciding whether laws passed by the Congress or state legislatures are in conformity with that document. It should be noted that although the emphasis in this chapter has been on interpretation of the Constitution, with respect to the *constitutionality* of laws, the Supreme Court and other courts also function in much the same manner in interpreting the meanings of laws.

The recent popularity of television programs with stars playing the roles of lawyers may have increased public understanding of courts and legal processes. The courts in these dramas are usually *trial courts,* and the process is that of determining the facts or the identity of the criminal. However, the work of the Supreme Court, as an *appellate court,* is different. Such a court is concerned not with ascertaining the facts, but with deciding the law. This function is vital, sometimes even dramatic, but its basic nature is not obvious. This exercise is designed to illustrate this basic nature. It may be studied by an individual reader, or it may be used as a group exercise in a classroom.

Involved here is a law rather than a constitution. The law is an imaginary one, and indeed, the entire exercise is not only imaginary but also unrealistic. It is unrealistic in the sense that a person who gets ticketed for a parking violation typically does not go to the bother and expense that are involved in appealing such a conviction to a higher court. He either pays the modest fine or he doesn't; he is unlikely to take expensive legal action.

Why, then, is this admittedly unrealistic series of problems proposed for consideration? The reason is that they permit the use of simple concepts and simple words. In this respect they are unlike some of the concepts and some of the words of the Constitution. The principle involved, however, is exactly the same.

Each of the following cases involves an alleged violation of a parking ordinance. The word *alleged* does not mean that there is any doubt about what the person involved had done. Each of the cases comes to the appellate court on what the lawyers call an *agreed statement of facts.* The question is whether the action violates the ordinance. The issue is the meaning of the ordinance, not the nature or intent of the action.

For the purposes of classroom exercises some or all of the members of the class can be invited to comprise the membership of the appellate court. Two members may be invited to serve as the attorneys, one for the defendant and one for the city; or the instructor may perform both roles or supplement the students' contribution.

Eventually, in each case, the question will be put to the members of the "court," and they will be asked to decide whether the man violated the ordinance. It may be necessary to point out to some of the "judges" that, in difficult cases where it is hard for them to make up their minds, they are not allowed to refrain from voting. Each must vote, unless he has disqualified himself for some personal connection with the case. This happens in real life, but could happen only on an imaginary basis in the classroom.

The imaginary law says: "It shall be unlawful to park a motor vehicle longer than one hour on public streets in the area bounded by Third, Eighth, Jefferson, and Van Buren streets."

1. Adams had parked his car in the prescribed area for about three quarters of an hour. He had then found that the business which had brought him there was taking more time than he had expected. He had, therefore, entered his car, driven it around the corner, and parked it in another location, also within the prohibited area. The car had been in the second location for about three quarters of an hour. Since his actions had been observed by a policeman, the policeman had given him a ticket, believing that the ordinance meant to prohibit parking for more than *a total of one hour in one day* anywhere in the indicated area. Adams had admitted what he had done; indeed, his account had coincided precisely with that of the police officer. He had been found guilty in municipal court and had appealed his case to the appellate court. Adams' attorney argues that the ordinance means to limit parking to *one hour in one location*. The city attorney, on the other hand, contends that the ordinance prohibited parking for a *total* of more than one hour in the affected area in one day.

2. Brown had parked his car near the center of the restricted area for about three quarters of an hour and had then discovered that he needed to be in the neighborhood for a somewhat longer time. He had returned to his automobile and had been happy to discover a vacant parking space directly in front of where his automobile was standing. He had, therefore, moved the car forward a distance of about twenty-five feet and had left it in the second location for another three quarters of an hour. He too had received a ticket and had appealed the case on the same basis that is involved in the case of Adams.

The issue is similar. The difference is the distance the two automobiles had been moved. If the student court has found that Adams had violated the ordinance, the second court will almost certainly find that Brown also has done so. If, however, the court in the Adams case has decided that he had *not* violated the ordinance, the question is still open with respect to Brown. If the court finds that Brown had not violated the ordinance, consideration of the next case is appropriate.

3. Clark also had parked his car for about three quarters of an hour near the middle of the prescribed area. Then, wishing to continue his business, he had returned to the car and had looked about for another parking space. Finding none, he had noted that between his car and the one in front of it was a space of about ten feet, and he had moved his car part way into that space. He too had been found guilty and had appealed the case on the same legal basis. Indeed, if Adams and Brown have been found *not* to have violated the ordinance, his attorney may cite these cases and invoke what the lawyers call the doctrine of *stare decisis,* which means that a court should follow rules or principles laid down in previous decisions.

If the student finds that Clark had not violated the ordinance, then it would be worthwhile to go on to another case involving a man who had moved his car only a few inches. If, however, the court finds that he had violated the law, consideration may be given to a different kind of issue in the next case.

4. Davidson is a businessman who has an office within the prescribed area in the business district. He had come to his office on Sunday to do some work. The street being empty of automobiles, he had left his car in front of his office building for three hours. He had been ticketed and found guilty. In appealing, his lawyer contends that the City Council had certainly never meant to include Sunday within the scope of the prohibition—certainly not in that part of the prescribed area. The city attorney, however, points out that the ordinance does not include the words *except Sunday.* He goes on to state that, on taking office, he had sworn to enforce the laws impartially, and he declares that it is not within his province to enforce the laws on some days and not on others unless the law specifically differentiates among days.

In one or more of these cases the question of the intent of the legislative body may be raised. This factor, "legislative intent," frequently comes up in cases. Sometimes it is easy to determine; sometimes not. In the case of Davidson, for example, if the record can be produced to show that at one time the City Council had debated an amendment providing that Sunday should be an exception, and had defeated the amendment, the matter would be settled. Usually, however, a discussion of these cases is more interesting and fruitful, as well as more realistic, if it is supposed that no such easy solution exists and that the court must construe the meaning of the ordinance without such guides.

5. Evans had been towing his house trailer behind his automobile when he had decided to call on a friend in an outlying part of the city. His wife had decided that she would rather go shopping. He had, there-

fore, maneuvered the trailer into place in the middle of the prescribed area, in front of a department store, and had unhooked the trailer and left it for his wife's convenience; and there it had stayed for two hours until Evans' return. The trailer had been ticketed. In appealing his case Evans' lawyer contends that the ordinance prohibits parking by "a motor vehicle." He insists that the house trailer is not a *motor vehicle* and, therefore, not subject to the prohibition against parking. The city attorney, on the other hand, contends that the trailer had taken up at least as much space as an automobile, that it was covered by the ordinance, and that a violation had occurred.

6. Fox is a farmer who raises excellent sweet corn. On the day in question, he had hitched up his horse and wagon and had taken a load of corn to the very center of the prohibited area. There he had sold corn to passers-by for two hours and had got a ticket. In appealing, his attorney points out that the prohibition in the ordinance applies to "a motor vehicle." He makes the observation that ours is a government of laws and not of men and that the law makes no mention of a horse and wagon, which is clearly not a motor vehicle. The city attorney contends that the horse and wagon had occupied as much space as an automobile and was in fact covered by the ordinance and therefore that Fox had violated the ordinance.

7. The streets referred to in the ordinance enclose an area of several square blocks; they are the streets on the four sides of the area. Green had parked his car for several hours on the *outside side* of one of these streets. In appealing his conviction his attorney points out that when a street serves as a legal dividing line—between precincts or wards, for example—the dividing line usually runs down the *middle* of the street. He argues that this must be taken to be the situation with respect to the present ordinance in the absence of any specific statement to the contrary; and that, therefore, the dividing line between the area in which parking is restricted and the area in which there is no restriction runs down the center of a bounding street. He argues that, since his client's car had been parked on the outside side of the street, it had not been "in the area bounded by Third, Eighth, Jefferson and Van Buren streets." The city attorney contends that the language of the ordinance covers both sides of the street and that Green's action had, therefore, been a violation. In this case it will be noted that the point at issue is the meaning of the words "bounded by."

The question may come up in this case whether there were or were not signs saying "One Hour Parking" on the outside side of the street involved. If so, it may be pointed out that these signs, these pieces of metal, are for the purpose of serving notice on the people and that they themselves in the present situation have no legal force.

Experience indicates that discussion of these cases brings out certain central points. One of them is the fact that the meaning of words is not always clear. The other is that in disputed cases someone has to decide what the words mean. This ultimately is the function of the courts. The cases may also present the situation in which the vote by the student judges is extremely close. Indeed, in some, it may be similar to the five-to-four decisions of the United States Supreme Court. At such a point it might be worthwhile to reconsider the case—to look again at the facts and at the law and to try to understand how people of presumably equal ability can look at the same facts and the same law and come to opposite conclusions regarding the latter's meaning. If this is possible with respect to a simple ordinance relating to simple automobile parking, how much greater its significance with respect to the more complicated matters dealt with in the Constitution and national and state laws!

## QUESTIONS AND PROBLEMS

1. What kind of national government did the Founding Fathers plan? How does our national government today differ from that plan? How were the changes brought about?
2. Explain: enumerated, reserved, concurrent, implied, and resultant powers.
3. Explain: separation of powers, checks and balances.
4. What role does the Supreme Court play in our system of government?
5. What is the basic relationship between the U.S. Supreme Court and the U.S. Constitution?
6. Has the Supreme Court, by its interpretations of the Constitution usurped power from Congress and state legislatures?
7. What does "judicial usurpation of the legislative function" mean? Should it be limited? If so, how?
8. Explain: judicial review. Is it desirable?
9. Some say that the Supreme Court should not be permitted to declare acts of the Congress unconstitutional. What is your opinion?
10. How can one justify the Court's reversing decisions when the question decided and the Constitution remain the same?
11. Is it possible for the Supreme Court to "amend" the Constitution; and if so, what powers does it have at its disposal to carry its "amendments" into law?
12. Explain: procedural due process, substantive due process.
13. Why is substantive due process an important concept?
14. Explain: judge-made law. Is it desirable?

## SELECTED READINGS

BLACK, CHARLES L., JR. *The People and the Court*. New York: The Macmillan Company, 1960.
COMMAGER, HENRY S. *Documents of American History*, 6th ed. New York: Appleton-Century-Crofts, Inc., 1958

CORWIN, E. S. *The Constitution and What It Means Today.* Princeton, N.J.: Princeton University Press, 1954.

———— and J. W. PELTASON. *Understudy The Constitution,* rev. ed. New York: Henry Holt and Company, 1958.

JACKSON, ROBERT H. *The Supreme Court in the American System of Government.* Cambridge, Mass.: Harvard University Press, 1955.

PRITCHETT, C. HERMAN. *The American Constitution.* New York: McGraw-Hill Company, 1959.

SCHWARTZ, BERNARD. *American Constitutional Law.* London, England: Cambridge University Press, 1955.

SWISHER, CARL B. *American Constitutional Development.* Cambridge: Riverside Press, 1954.

# 4

# GOVERNMENT:

## Structure and Growth

In the preceding chapter the constitutional background of government was discussed, together with the vital part played by the United States Supreme Court in interpreting and, in effect, revising the Constitution. We may now turn attention to the structure and growth of government under the "living Constitution."

The operating and initiating branches of the Federal Government are the executive and legislative branches, plus some commissions not specifically provided for in the Constitution. The Supreme Court, as we have seen, has impressive veto powers, but it does not have positive powers to start things and to carry them through to completion. Symbolic and indicative of the difference between the Court and the other branches of the government is a comparison of the amounts of money spent in carrying on their activities. In fiscal year 1960 expenditures for the judicial branch (including the Supreme Court and all other Federal courts) were about $49 million, or $6/100$ of 1 per cent of the total budget expenditures, $76,539 million.

### THE EXECUTIVE BRANCH

Article II of the Constitution and the Twelfth and Twenty-Second amendments relate to the President. Section 1 of Article II vests the executive power in him, sets his term of office, and prescribes the manner in which he is to be elected. This last subject was substantially changed by the Twelfth Amendment. The Twenty-Second Amendment limits his time in office to two terms.

[1] The President is chief of state. This is the ceremonial or symbolic role referred to in Chapter 1. He is the head of the nation and a symbol of national unity somewhat as are the flag and the national anthem.

[2] The President is chief of government. In this capacity he is chief influencer of legislation and chief executive. He stimulates the passage of laws by the Congress. (Some of his methods of stimulation are discussed in the next chapter.) Once the laws are passed, it is his duty to execute them.

[3]   The President is party leader. He is the titular head of his party and its chief director. The fact that the President is chief of state, chief of government, and party leader sometimes produces a troublesome condition for conscientious citizens. In his latter two roles, he is legitimately subject to criticism directed at his actions and the public policies that he advocates. It sometimes seems awkward to direct such criticism at the man who is also the symbolic head of the nation and who, as such, may command, or may be expected to command, respectful or even affectionate regard from all Americans, regardless of party.

[4]   The President is foreign policy chief. Although the Congress has certain roles in connection with the formulation and support of foreign policy, the President is basically responsible for this area of national activity. He delegates much of it, to be sure, to the Secretary of State, but it remains always his ultimate duty and responsibility.

[5]   The President is commander-in-chief of the armed forces. The Constitution provides for this role which, in our nation, is symbolic of the supremacy of the civilian over the military authority.

[6]   The President is the national representative. Excepting only the Vice-President, the President is the only officer of any of the hundred thousand governmental units in the United States (including even the Federal Government) who is elected by the people of the entire nation. United States Senators are elected by states. United States Representatives are elected by Congressional districts—which in a few instances are also states. The constituencies of members of the Congress are parts of the nation, and some of them are very small parts. Congressmen are of necessity (as we shall see in greater detail later on) necessarily concerned with the interests of their local constituencies. This may lead them to support some local interest even when it is not compatible with the national interest.

The constituency of the President, however, is the entire American people. He is not exclusively or substantially concerned with the well-being of any one city, industry, or group. If he is beholden to anyone, it is to the entire electorate. The very nature of the position reinforces what presumably would be the natural inclination of any man of sufficient stature to be elevated to this high office to think and work for the well-being of the entire country.

[7]   The President is a world leader. Because of the position of the United States and because of the power of his post, the President inevitably wears this mantle. Other world leaders there are, of course, in other countries. Our President is only one of several; but his role and his responsibility are great.

In carrying out these various activities the President typically must work with the Congress. Some of his problems in this work will be touched on in the next section.

## THE PRESIDENT AND THE CONGRESS

Article I of the Constitution is the longest article in that document. It deals with the legislative branch of the government. It establishes the House of Representatives and the Senate and provides for their election and their operation. In Section 8 are listed the powers of the Congress, and in Section 9 appear certain restrictions on these powers. Moreover, the first ten amendments—The Bill of Rights—contain further limitations on the legislative branch.

As mentioned in the preceding section, government is carried on by teamwork between the President and the Congress. Sometimes the joint effort is harmonious, sometimes not. Indeed, the President and the Congress occasionally are at outs, even when the President's party has a majority in both houses. In part, this condition results from the fragmentation of interest of Congressmen as against the President's over-all national view. In part, it represents a kind of jealousy on the part of the Congress over the enlargement of the role and power of the Presidency and a resentment over what Congressmen view as the encroachment of executive power upon the legislative process.

This condition reflects what may be referred to as the Congressional Ego. One frequently notes actions by Senators, Representatives, and Congressional committees whose principal purpose seems to be simply assertive—an otherwise pointless flexing of muscles and throwing around of weight. Presidents have tried various ways of appeasing the Congress and attempting to persuade it to enact legislation which they desire. Experience seems to indicate, however, that neither the soft sell nor the tough approach is likely to work. The most effective way seems to be the indirect one (or is it the *direct* one?) of building up among the people such strong support for the President's program that it will make itself felt among Congressmen.

The foregoing comments may seem to be suggesting that Congressmen are human beings rather than statesmen. They are human beings, but some of them are also statesmen; and many of them are men of considerable ability whose concern with the wishes of the electorate is inevitably compelling on them as good practical politicians and properly incumbent on them as good representatives and delegates.

## THE KEY ROLE OF CONGRESSIONAL COMMITTEES

The visitor to the halls of Congress who comes for the first time and without previous preparation is likely to be astonished by what he typically sees when he sits in the visitors' galleries of the Senate and the

House of Representatives. He will see a presiding officer in the chair and a handful of members on the floor. One of these may be talking. Others may be listening, while others read newspapers. From this visual picture, it would be easy for him to form an impression that these men are indolent and perfunctory. This inference would be completely wrong.

The fact is that most of the business of both houses of Congress is done in committees. This is necessary. It is not possible for even an exceptionally able and diligent Congressman to become an expert on all of the many subjects dealt with by these legislative bodies. He does well if he can become knowledgeable on just one. Each house, therefore, has several standing committees whose duty is to consider and screen legislation; to reject it or to prepare bills for consideration by the entire membership. In the committees is the hard work of the Congress done.

In the committees too, in the main, are the decisions made about which bills are going to be passed. No committee, of course, is in a position to force upon its house a bill which is genuinely unacceptable to a majority of the members or to withhold one that the members want. At the same time, a committee is the place where the views of the membership converge and where determination is made of the type of legislation that is likely to be acceptable to the entire membership. It is important, therefore, in understanding the work of the Congress to understand the key role of the committees.

## GERONTOCRACY: THE COMMITTEE CHAIRMEN

It is equally important to understand the power that is in the hands of the typical committee chairman. It is he who selects the committee's legal counsel, if it has one, and who appoints the members of the committee's staff. It is he who arranges hearings on proposed bills—he can have either friendly or unfriendly witnesses predominate. Because of his influence, he may be able to persuade or coerce the votes and attitudes of other committee members, especially younger members. He calls meetings of the committee, and it is not unheard of for a committee chairman to absent himself from Washington and become unavailable even by long distance telephone in order to avoid being requested to call a meeting of his committee. In all these ways, some subtle and some not so subtle, the committee chairman wields a power not generally understood except by those well acquainted with the operations of the Congress.

Committee chairmen obtain their posts by seniority. On each committee the senior member of the majority party automatically becomes chairman. Sometimes the chairmanship goes to a man in his fifties. Most chairmen, however, are in their sixties and many in their seventies.

Occasionally committee chairmen have been past eighty. This means that the great powers of the chairmen reside in a group of men who are well along in years. Most of them typically are past the compulsory retirement age—65—for executives in American business firms. This condition may or may not be desirable, but it is a fact and an important one. It is because of its significance that the term gerontocracy was brought to the reader's attention in Chapter 1.

## THE RULES COMMITTEE

In addition to noting the large powers of all of the Congressional committees, we should make special reference to one committee in the House of Representatives—the Rules Committee.

The name "Rules Committee" may be misleading, even to the well-informed citizen. The name may suggest that this committee has charge of the formulation of the parliamentary rules under which the House of Representatives operates. Not so. It gets its name from the fact that a bill comes onto the floor of the House of Representatives only after getting a "rule" from the Rules Committee. The rule advances the bill and regulates the manner in which it may be handled on the floor of the House. For example, it may indicate the number of minutes or hours that the bill can be debated. It may indicate whether or not amendments may be offered. In short, the rule programs the bill through the House.

The Rules Committee thus functions as a kind of *legislative manager* or *traffic cop* for the House of Representatives. This is an essential function. One needs to reflect only a moment to realize what chaos would prevail in the House of Representatives if bills were taken up on the floor on a first come, first served basis and members were permitted to talk as long as they wanted to on any of them. The volume of business to be done is so great that it is essential that some authority undertake to put first things first and control floor activity so as to make action reasonably expeditious and orderly.

The Rules Committee also serves another important and often unmentioned function. It is a kind of quiet *burying ground*. Bills are frequently introduced which are popular with certain House members' constituents, but which the members themselves regard as undesirable legislation. The situation, therefore, might be that a majority of the House would prefer not to see a bill come to the floor for a vote because they do not favor it, but do not wish to be formally recorded as voting against it. Therefore, the House leadership, in quiet cooperation with the Rules Committee, can bury a proposed bill by simply not giving it a rule, that is, by not permitting it to go to the floor for discussion and vote. In effect, under the right circumstances, this permits House members to indulge in statesmanship without paying the penalty therefor, which popular election often inherently entails. A martyr for his principles is admirable—a man of principle who retains his seat in a legislative body is, in addition, valuable.

The first of these functions (traffic cop) is essential; the second (burying ground) is convenient. Hence, the Rules Committee. The functions of the committee naturally give it great power—sometimes too great. For instance, it can hold up bills that a majority of the *committee* dislike, even though House majority sentiment is favorable.

For example, in 1961 President Kennedy, finding an unyielding group on the Rules Committee that presumably stood in the way of some of his new legislation, backed a proposal in the House to enlarge the membership of the Committee, with the definite intention on the part of the Speaker of the House of appointing to the Committee men friendly to the new administration's program. Only a hard fight on the part of the House leadership carried the day and by only a narrow margin. Moreover, in the end, even after the new appointments, the Committee was still occasionally accused of obstructing the President's program.

It is true, to be sure, that the Committee can be overruled—there are mechanisms by which the House of Representatives can wrest a bill away from a recalcitrant Rules Committee. These mechanisms, however, are so difficult to use that they rarely come into play. As a matter of practice, therefore, the Rules Committee normally is boss.

The Rules Committee, for this reason, has sometimes been referred to as a "fourth branch" of the Federal Government. More commonly, however, this name has been given to the Federal regulatory commissions. To them we now turn attention.

## THE REGULATORY COMMISSIONS: ADMINISTRATIVE LAW

The regulatory commissions represent a type of governmental organization which is not specifically referred to in the Constitution. The first of these was the Interstate Commerce Commission, established in 1887. Since then, these others have been created: Federal Trade Commission, Federal Power Commission, Federal Communications Commission, Securities and Exchange Commission, and Civil Aeronautics Board.

Each of these commissions consists of members appointed by the President, with the advice and consent of the Senate, who hold office for several years. Each is charged with the regulation of certain industries or activities and the administration of certain laws. Each functions under the authority of a statute passed by the Congress.

They were created because attempts to regulate these industries and activities by spelling out the legal regulations in detail, in statutes, had turned out to be an impossible task. Therefore, Congress has passed a law indicating more or less in general terms the authority of each commission. However, the courts, through the continuing process of judicial review, have tended to require that such Congressional delegations of authority have some minimal specificity and detail rather than being mere general directives.

The legislation typically authorizes the commission to enunciate regulations. Once enunciated, these regulations have the force of law. This activity, therefore, is commonly called *administrative lawmaking*. Not only does the commission legislate the details of regulations but also proceeds to enforce them. It executes its own regulations, and in so doing assumes the *executive* role of government. It may also bring and prosecute actions against persons held to have violated its regulations. When it does this, the commission moves into the *judicial* role—one of its employees, an examiner, presides over a hearing which is very much like a court proceeding. The examiner and the commission may decide in the end that there has been a violation, and the commission will then issue an enforcement order. Thus the doctrine of the separation of powers into legislative, executive, and judicial branches of government is violated by the existence of these agencies.

The regulatory commissions have come to be tremendously important —and not only at the Federal level, for their counterparts at the state level have come to function quite similarly. We shall take note of their activities with respect to their various areas of operation in later chapters. For the present we simply observe their position in the structure of our government and acknowledge their importance.

## STATE AND LOCAL GOVERNMENTS

The structure of state governments resembles the Federal setup. There are the three traditional branches—executive, legislative, and judicial— plus commissions and agencies. Their functioning is so similar to that of their Federal counterparts that most of the preceding discussion applies equally to them.

Local governments include counties, townships, municipalities, school districts, and special districts. Most of these governmental units are simpler in structure and function than the Federal and state governments. The typical one has a small unicameral legislative body and an executive officer. A few have courts. Absent, typically, are commissions and other such agencies.

Satisfactory functioning of government in our society involves not only the general problem of the proper role of government, but also the specific question of which governmental entities (Federal, state, or local) are to perform which functions.

Take education. Which level of government should provide, finance, and operate this activity? Should it be divided or shared in some way?

Similar questions may be asked about such other governmental activities as highway construction, urban renewal, conservation of natural resources, public health, welfare, disaster relief, consumer protection, and labor–management regulation.

Many persons contend that government has drifted improperly away from the grass roots to Washington—has become overcentralized. To be sure, some of the opposition to "excessive centralization" is really disguised opposition to any government action at all in some area—the opponents would be no happier to see the action taken by state or local governments than by the Federal Government. But this kind of opposition is unlikely to be persuasive against Federal action, if the action is something that the people genuinely desire. Those who genuinely prefer to see governmental actions taken by state and local governments than by Washington will realize that opposing the latter will fail unless the former succeeds. The way to "get government back home" is to make home government effective, not merely to oppose national government action.

One reason given for the drift to Washington is financial. The assertion is frequently made around the country that state and local activities must be financed by the Federal Government "because state and local taxation has reached its limit." Usually little or no evidence is presented in support of the proposition. One is entitled to ask whether it is in fact true or whether the entire argument is not really a rationalization of the unwillingness of state and local officeholders to advocate higher state and local taxes.

The serious, conscientious student of these matters will find them discussed carefully in the *Report of the Commission on Intergovernmental Relations*, presented in 1955 to the President for transmittal to the Congress. The Commission, established by a 1953 Congressional act, had a distinguished membership. The following substantial excerpts bring out the salient points.

> Early in its study, the Commission was confronted with the fact that many State constitutions restrict the scope, effectiveness, and adaptability of State and local action. These self-imposed constitutional limitations make it difficult for many States to perform all of the services their citizens require, and consequently have frequently been the underlying cause of State and municipal pleas for Federal assistance.
>
> It is significant that the Constitution prepared by the Founding Fathers, with its broad grants of authority and avoidance of legislative detail, has withstood the test of time far better than the constitutions later adopted by the States. . . .
>
> The Commission finds a very real and pressing need for the States to improve their constitutions. . . .

## THE STATE LEGISLATURE

In the early history of our country, State legislatures were the most power-ful and influential instruments of government in the Nation. It was to them that the average citizen looked primarily for initiative and wisdom in the formulation of public policy on domestic issues. They overshadowed the other branches of State government. In power and influence they are no longer as dominant as they were, partly because of the ascendancy of the National Government, partly because of the increased influence of the State executive, but primarily because they have not found effective solutions to problems that become more chronic and more difficult to cope with in a rapidly changing society.

One of these problems is to maintain an equitable system of representation. In a majority of States, city dwellers outnumber the citizens of rural areas. Yet in most States the rural voters are overwhelmingly in control of one legislative house, and overweighted if not dominant in the other.

In a majority of State constitutions, population is the sole or principal basis of representation in both houses. But the basis is in many cases modified, at least for one house, by provision for a certain minimum or maximum number of representatives per county or other district. As cities have grown more rapidly than rural areas, these systems of apportionment have tended to create an increasing imbalance in legislative representation in favor of rural areas. . . .

The constitutions of 43 States call for some reapportionment in at least one house as often as every 10 years. In nearly half of these States, reappor-tionment lags behind schedule. Ten States provide for reapportionment of one or both houses by some agency other than the legislature, either initially or in case the legislature fails to act. In these States, some reapportionment takes place on schedule—a fact worthy of study by States whose legislatures have been reluctant to obey the constitutional mandate to reapportion them-selves.

Revising an outmoded pattern of representation is, to be sure, a difficult act for a legislative body, each of whose members has a vested interest in the *status quo*. Many States would need a constitutional amendment to redistrict, for at least one house, as well as legislation to carry out the Constitutional intent of periodic reapportionment. Since both require action by the legisla-ture, except in States where they may be initiated by petition, a heavy premium is placed upon the farsightedness of legislators and upon the willing-ness of citizens to reconcile their special interests with the general good.

Reapportionment should not be thought of solely in terms of a conflict of interests between urban and rural areas. In the long run, the interests of all in an equitable system of representation that will strengthen State government is far more important than any temporary advantage to an area enjoying over-representation.

The problem of reapportionment is important in the area of study of this Commission because legislative neglect of urban communities has led more and more people to look to Washington for more and more of the services and controls they desire. . . .

Paradoxically enough, the interests of urban areas are often more effectively represented in the National legislature than in their own State legislatures. . . .

For these and other reasons, the Commission has come to the conclusion that the more the role of the States in our system is emphasized, the more important it is that the State legislatures be reasonably representative of all the people. . . .

## THE STATE EXECUTIVE

The American system of separation of powers works best when all branches of government are strong, energetic, and responsible. Men of such diverse points of view as John Adams, Alexander Hamilton, and Thomas Jefferson recognized that the successful operation of a government based on the separation of powers depends on provision for adequate executive authority as well as for a representative legislature and an independent judiciary. Jefferson saw the need for a governor bearing the "whole weight" of executive responsibility. Hamilton insisted that "Energy in the executive is a leading character in the definition of good government." Adams looked upon a strong, independent executive as "the natural friend of the people," the chief defender of their rights and liberties.

Today, few States have an adequate executive branch headed by a governor who can be held generally accountable for executing and administering the laws of the State. State constitutions provide in principle for three equal branches of government, but most of these constitutions and numerous laws based on them include provisions that tend to undermine this principle. . . .

Typically, though not universally, the governor is the nominal chief of a sprawling State administration consisting of scores of separate departments, commissions, and agencies. Department heads, many of them boards of commissions, are often selected or appointed for long or overlapping terms. This enables them to be more or less independent of normal executive controls. Still other agency heads may be separately elected, or may be appointed by the legislature or by someone other than the governor. In most States, the governor's removal power over many of his "subordinates" is so restricted that it is of little value as a tool of administrative control. Few governors have been supplied with modern staff agencies and tools of management adequate to the administrative responsibility presumed to be vested in them. . . .

## STRENGTHENING LOCAL GOVERNMENT

The objective of decentralization cannot be attained by a readjustment of National–State relations alone. It will be fully achieved only when carried through to the lowest levels of government, where every citizen has the opportunity to participate actively and directly. The strengthening of local governments requires that activities that can be handled by these units be allocated to them, together with the financial resources necessary for their support.

The local government map of the United States discloses a maze of approximately 109,000 governmental units, many of them overlapping. This figure includes some 3,000 counties, 17,000 incorporated municipalities, 17,000 towns and townships, 60,000 independent school districts, and 12,000 special districts. It is not uncommon for the same area to be served by a municipality, a school district, a county, and one or more special districts. A considerable number of metropolitan areas ambrace over 100 separate local government units.

More or less hidden in this picture is a paradox that constantly plagues the States and bars an easy solution of the problem of achieving the decentralization of government—too many local governments, not enough local government. . . .

The States have the constitutional responsibility for the future development of local government. This responsibility has two important aspects. One is to create local units of government that are efficient units for providing governmental services. The second is to maintain a system of local government that achieves the traditional American goal of extensive citizen participation in the affairs of government. . . .

While moving toward a more rational pattern of local governments, much can be done with those that exist. There are many States in which even the smallest local units could perform better if given greater discretion to choose their own form of government and to supply themselves with desired local services. The road to greater home rule has already been partially mapped by States that have successfully used constitutional home rule, flexible optional charter systems, and liberal legislative grants of municipal powers. . . .

The most intricate aspect of State–local relations is the problem created by the modern metropolitan area. As indicated earlier, some of these areas contain more than 100 local government units. A standard metropolitan area, as defined by the Census Bureau, is a complex community that includes a central city of 50,000 population or more and an urban fringe. There are 170 such areas. The metropolitan problem is not confined to them, however; it exists also in many other incipient metropolitan areas. . . .

The time is long overdue for an intensive nationwide study of governmental areas with special attention to metropolitan communities. The study should engage the cooperation of National, State, and local governments, as well as universities, private foundations, and civic agencies. Political invention in this field is greatly needed. . . .

## COUNTY GOVERNMENT

The intermediate position of the county between the State and municipal governments in some areas, and its position as the primary area of local government or administration in others, have steadily enlarged its importance in intergovernmental relations. . . .

The States could advance the cause of local self-government by giving all counties the opportunity to obtain modern charters, to use modern methods of administration, and to exercise more home rule powers. The strengthening of rural counties especially would take some of the load off State administration and simplify the task of administering National programs based upon the counties. . . .

By using their power to strengthen their own governments and those of their subdivisions, the States can relieve much of the pressure for, and generate a strong counterpressure against, improper expansion of National action. Thereby they can increase their chances of enjoying an enlarged participation in the total task of governing the Nation. . . ."[*]

One of the possible consequences of the 1962 legislative apportionment case, *Baker v. Carr* (discussed in Chapter 1), could be the strengthening of state and local government, as described and recommended in the Commission's report.

## GROWTH OF GOVERNMENT

Mention has already been made of the fact that in the first year of George Washington's presidency the new Federal Government spent $4 million. State and local governments also were modest. Both kinds of governments have grown as the decades have passed, and their growth has been especially rapid in the twentieth century. The accompanying tables, although composed of cold statistics, dramatically illustrate the enormous expansion of government. Table 4.1 shows the growth in terms of people.

*Table 4.1*

### GOVERNMENTAL EMPLOYMENT AND THE TOTAL LABOR FORCE

#### 1900, 1920, 1940, 1960

(In Thousands)

|                                           | 1900   | 1920   | 1940   | 1960   |
|-------------------------------------------|--------|--------|--------|--------|
| Total labor force                         | 29,164 | 41,371 | 56,180 | 73,126 |
| Federal Government employees              |        |        |        |        |
| Civilians                                 | 312    | 688    | 1,053  | 2,237  |
| Armed forces                              | 126    | 344    | 532    | 2,552  |
| Total, Federal Government                 | 438    | 1,032  | 1,585  | 4,789  |
| State and local governments               | 963    | 1,888  | 3,317  | 6,221  |
| Total regular employees                   | 1,401  | 2,920  | 4,902  | 11,010 |
| Public emergency workers                  | 0      | 0      | 2,892  | 0      |
| Total governmental employees              | 1,401  | 2,920  | 7,794  | 11,010 |
| Percentage of total labor force employed by governments | 4.8%   | 7.1%   | 13.9%  | 15.1%  |
| GOVERNMENTAL REGULAR EMPLOYEES, DEFENSE AND NONDEFENSE | | | | |
| National defense (armed forces plus civilians) | 166    | 581    | 788    | 3,502  |

[*] The Commission on Intergovernmental Relations, *A Report to the President for Transmittal to the Congress* (Washington, D.C.: U.S. Government Printing Office, 1955), pp. 37–56, *passim*.

| Nondefense employees | | | | |
|---|---|---|---|---|
| Federal Government | 272 | 451 | 797 | 1,287 |
| State and local governments | 963 | 1,888 | 3,317 | 6,221 |
| Total governmental regular nondefense employees | 1,235 | 2,339 | 4,114 | 7,508 |

GOVERNMENTAL REGULAR NONDEFENSE EMPLOYEES AS A
PERCENTAGE OF TOTAL LABOR FORCE

| | % | % | % | % |
|---|---|---|---|---|
| Federal Government | 0.9 | 1.1 | 1.4 | 1.8 |
| State and local governments | 3.3 | 4.6 | 5.9 | 8.5 |
| All governments | 4.2 | 5.7 | 7.3 | 10.3 |

SOURCES: Solomon Fabricant, *The Trend of Government Activity in the United States Since 1900* (New York: National Bureau of Economic Research, 1952), pp. 14, 168, 198; *The Economic Report of the President: 1962* (Washington, D.C.: U.S. Government Printing Office, 1962), p. 230; *Statistical Abstract of the United States: 1961* (Washington, D.C.: U.S. Government Printing Office, 1961), p. 210.

The increase in the number of employees at all governmental levels has been substantial. During the same period, the total population and the total work force also have grown greatly. In order to indicate the relative size of government, the table also shows public employment as a percentage of the total labor force.

In order to keep separate the volume of employment in the area of national defense, which, vital though it is, obviously represents something outside the normal civilian functions of government, the table presents the percentage of the total labor force employed by the government excluding national defense employees and also excluding the sizable number who were public emergency employees in 1940. The figures show that even with these exclusions, the proportion of workers employed by governmental entities was nearly 2½ times as large in 1960 as it had been at the turn of the century.

Table 4.2 illustrates the expansion of government in terms of dollar expenditures, which is another significant measure. Here also, in order to segregate the important, but special, type of outlay that is involved in national defense and interest on the national debt (because this too has grown, principally because of defense financing), these figures also have been separated.

Growth of government expenditures has been huge, but the American economy also has grown enormously in the period under consideration. Nevertheless, and even omitting the expenditures basically due to war and national defense, it will be seen that in the fifty-nine-year period covered by the table, the percentage of national income represented by public expenditures has more than doubled.

Both tables tell the same story—expansion of governmental activity at a rate even greater than that of both the growth of population and the even faster growth of the American economy.

*Table 4.2*

## GOVERNMENTAL EXPENDITURES IN RELATION
## TO THE NATIONAL INCOME: 1902, 1961

*(Expenditures for Fiscal Years, National Income for Calendar Years)*

|  | 1902 | 1961 |
|---|---|---|
| National income | $17,200,000,000 | $427,800,000,000 |
| (A) Federal government cash outlays (less grants to state and local governments, to avoid double counting) | $ 476,000,000 | $ 92,200,000,000 |
| Percentage of national income | 2.8 | 21.5 |
| (B) Federal government outlays, excluding national defense and interest on the national debt | $ 270,000,000 | $ 37,200,000,000 |
| Percentage of national income | 1.6 | 8.7 |
| (C) State and local government expenditures | $ 1,088,000,000 | $ 56,200,000,000 |
| Percentage of national income | 6.3 | 13.1 |
| Selected totals |  |  |
| Grand totals (A plus C) | $ 1,564,000,000 | $148,400,000,000 |
| Percentage of national income | 9.1 | 34.6 |
| Nonwar totals (B plus C) | $ 1,358,000,000 | $ 93,400,000,000 |
| Percentage of national income | 7.9 | 21.8 |

SOURCES: Tax Foundation, Inc., *Facts and Figures on Government Finance—1956–57* (New York: The Tax Foundation, 1956), p. 54; *Economic Report of the President: 1963* (Washington, D.C.: U.S. Government Printing Office, 1963), pp. 241, 243, 245.

## MULTIPLYING GOVERNMENTAL
## ACTIVITIES

So much for the totals. Governments employ millions of persons and spend scores of billions of dollars annually. What do the employees do? What functions do these governmental entities perform? How did their expansion come about?

Light can be shed on these matters by looking at some details of government operations. These details provide (as perhaps nothing else could) a realistic understanding of the growth and present scope of officialdom in the United States.

Well-informed citizens are generally aware of the oldline parts of the Federal Government. They know that the legislative branch consists of the Senate and the House, and they may also be aware that directly under the jurisdiction of the Congress are the General Accounting Office, the Government Printing Office, and the Library of Congress.

The Executive Office of the President has been expanded substantially and now includes the Bureau of the Budget, the Council of Economic Advisers, the National Aeronautics and Space Council, the National Security Council, and the Office of Civil and Defense Mobilization.

The judicial branch, in addition to the Supreme Court of the United States, consists of the Circuit Courts of Appeals, the District Courts, the Court of Claims, the Court of Customs and Patent Appeals, the Customs Court, and the territorial courts.

Also rather well-known are the ten departments of the Federal Government whose heads are members of the President's Cabinet, although even the well-informed citizen might have difficulty in swiftly listing them. They and the dates of their, or of their original predecessors', establishment are: State (1789), Treasury (1789), Defense (1789), Justice (1789), Post Office (1789), Interior (1849), Agriculture (1862), Labor (1884), Commerce (1903), and Health, Education, and Welfare (1953) (the Office of Education had been established in 1867).

Perhaps less well-known are what are called the independent offices or independent agencies. A chronology of the establishment of the principal ones follows.

## CHRONOLOGY OF ESTABLISHMENT OF PRINCIPAL FEDERAL INDEPENDENT OFFICES AND AGENCIES

*Previous to 1910*
| | |
|---|---|
| 1846 | Smithsonian Institution |
| 1883 | United States Civil Service Commission |
| 1887 | Interstate Commerce Commission |

*1910–1919*
| | |
|---|---|
| 1913 | Federal Reserve System |
| 1915 | Federal Trade Commission |
| 1916 | United States Tariff Commission |

*1920–1929*
| | |
|---|---|
| 1920 | Federal Power Commission |

*1930–1939*
| | |
|---|---|
| 1930 | Veterans Administration |
| 1932 | Federal Home Loan Bank System |
| 1933 | Farm Credit Administration |
| | Federal Deposit Insurance Corporation |
| | Tennessee Valley Authority |
| 1934 | Export–Import Bank of Washington |
| | Federal Communications Commission |
| | Federal Housing Administration |
| | Federal Savings and Loan Insurance Corporation |
| | National Mediation Board |
| | Securities and Exchange Commission |
| 1935 | National Labor Relations Board |
| | Railroad Retirement Board |

| 1938 | Civil Aeronautics Administration |
| | Civil Aeronautics Authority |
| | (Name changed to Civil Aeronautics Board in 1940) |
| | Federal National Mortgage Association |
| *1940–1949* | |
| 1946 | Atomic Energy Commission |
| 1947 | Federal Mediation and Conciliation Service |
| | Housing and Home Finance Agency |
| | Public Housing Administration |
| 1949 | General Services Administration |
| *1950–1959* | |
| 1950 | National Science Foundation |
| 1953 | Small Business Administration |
| | United States Information Agency |
| 1954 | Urban Renewal Administration |
| 1955 | Federal Home Loan Bank Board |
| 1958 | Federal Aviation Agency |
| | National Aeronautics and Space Administration |

The foregoing list does not include such quasi official agencies as the American Red Cross. Neither does it include such multilateral international organizations as the International Bank for Reconstruction and Development nor bilateral organizations like the Joint Brazil–United States Defense Commission.

Sources of further information about the parts of the Federal Government include the *United States Government Organization Manual*, which is published annually by the Government Printing Office. It lists the offices and describes their organization and operation. The other great source of information is the *Budget of the United States Government*, which also is printed annually by the Government Printing Office. This huge volume—about the size of the telephone book in a large city—with its hundreds of pages of listed expenditures, probably conveys an understanding that can be obtained in no other way of the size, complexity, and cost of the Federal Government.

## GROWTH OF STATE GOVERNMENT

A realistic understanding of the growth of state governments can be gained by study of a historical record which shows the gradual appearance and multiplication of any state's agencies. Such a record is presented for the State of Michigan in the belief that it is typical. The record is based on research embodied in an unpublished report prepared by Mr. Harold C. Young for the author's graduate course in Business and Government in 1961. If the following list seems to be long and detailed, the reader is advised that it actually contains only a small fraction of Mr. Young's complete list, which includes more than three hundred items.

The listing here presented has been restricted to the sixty items judged to be most important.

These agencies are mentioned as of the time of their first establishment. Many of them have subsequently been enlarged, or duplicates have been added, as in the case of insane asylums, or mental hospitals, as they are now called, and some of them have had their names and their functions changed. These additions and changes are not listed, since for the purposes of the outline it is not vitiated by their omission.

## CHRONOLOGY OF ESTABLISHMENT OF PRINCIPAL ACTIVITIES OF THE STATE OF MICHIGAN

*1800–1809*
1805   Probate Courts
       Justices' Courts
*1810–1819*
1817   University of Michigan
*1820–1829*
1824   Circuit Courts
*1830–1839*
1837   State Geological Survey
1838   Bank Commissioner
1839   State Prison
*1840–1849*
1843   Inspectors—Beef, Pork, Flour, and Wheat
1849   State Board of Education
*1850–1859*
1855   Michigan Agricultural College
1859   Asylum for the Insane
*1860–1869*
*1870–1879*
1871   Commissioner of Insurance
1873   State Board of Health
1877   State House of Correction and Reformatory
1879   Industrial Home for Girls
*1880–1889*
1883   Asylum for Insane Criminals
       State Board of Examiners in Dentistry
       Commissioner of Labor
1885   Michigan Mining School
       Reform School
       Board of Pharmacy
       Michigan Soldiers' Home
1887   Game and Fish Warden
1889   State Banking Department

*1890–1899*
    1891    National Guard
    1893    Dairy and Food Commissioner
            Michigan Home for Feebleminded and Epileptic
    1897    State Court of Mediation and Arbitration
    1899    Board of Examination and Licensing Barbers
            Board of Registration in Medicine
            State Veterinary Board

*1900–1909*
    1903    State Board of Law Examiners
    1905    State Board of Accountancy
            State Highway Department

*1910–1919*
    1913    State Hospital for Epileptics
            Michigan Securities Commission
    1915    Board for Registration of Architects
    1919    State Park Commissioner
            State Police

*1920–1929*
    1921    Department of Agriculture
            Department of Conservation
            State Board of Dental Examiners
    1929    Board of Aeronautics
            State Plumbing Board

*1930–1939*
    1931    State Board of Cosmetology
            Motor Vehicle Division
            Unemployment Relief Commission
    1933    Board of Chiropractic Examiners
            Liquor Control Commission
    1936    Employment Security Commission
            Unemployment Compensation Commission
    1939    State Board of Embalmers and Funeral Directors
            Labor Mediation Board
            Milk Marketing Board

*1940–1949*
    1947    Department of Economic Development
*1950–1959*
    1950    Mackinac Bridge Authority
    1953    Office of Civil Defense
            Michigan Turnpike Authority
    1955    Fair Employment Practices Commission

## GROWTH OF MUNICIPAL GOVERNMENTS

A vivid impression of the growth of municipal governments may be obtained by inspection of the historical record of a representative American city—Detroit, Michigan. This list includes eighty-odd activities judged to be the most important ones—of the 396 listed by Upson.* Since the time covered by the Upson tabulation, other activities have been added, but the list as it stands nevertheless shows the expansion of municipal activities which we now tend to take for granted and which helps to explain the level of municipal taxes and expenditures.

## CHRONOLOGY OF THE ESTABLISHMENT OF PRINCIPAL

## ACTIVITIES OF THE CITY OF DETROIT

1824 The territorial legislature provided a new form of city government. Its activities numbered 24, to serve a town of 1,500 persons.

*1830–1839*
 1832 Sidewalk Construction
 1835 Street Paving
 1836 Sewerage
    Water Supply

*1840–1849*
 1842 Elementary School

*1850–1859*
 1850 Street Lighting
 1858 High School

*1860–1869*
 1861 Prison for Male Felons
    Prison for Female Felons
 1865 Organized Police Patrol
    General Library
 1866 Detectives
 1867 Organized Fire Fighting

*1870–1879*
 1871 River Patrol
    Parks
 1873 Police Alarm System
 1879 Food and Meat Inspection

*1880–1889*
 1881 Teachers College
 1883 Emergency Hospital
    Outdoor Relief
    Classes for Incorrigibles
 1885 Inspection of Buildings and Plans
    Contagious Disease Hospital

* Lent D. Upson, *The Growth of a City Government.* Report ,No. 36 of the School of Public Affairs and Social Work of Wayne University (Detroit: Bureau of Governmental Research, 1942).

|       |                                                                 |
|-------|-----------------------------------------------------------------|
| 1887  | Milk Inspection                                                 |
| 1888  | Rubbish and Garbage Collection and Disposal                     |
| 1889  | Water Metering                                                  |

*1890–1899*

|       |                                                                 |
|-------|-----------------------------------------------------------------|
| 1890  | Zoo                                                             |
| 1892  | Free Textbooks                                                 |
| 1893  | Fireboats                                                      |
|       | Art Library                                                    |
|       | Municipal Power Plant                                          |
| 1894  | Bathing Beaches                                                |
| 1895  | Kindergarten                                                   |
|       | Hand Street Cleaning                                          |
| 1897  | Snow Removal                                                  |
| 1898  | Band Concerts                                                 |
| 1899  | Classes for the Deaf                                          |

*1900–1909*

|       |                                                                 |
|-------|-----------------------------------------------------------------|
| 1900  | School Lunches                                                |
| 1904  | Playgrounds                                                   |
| 1905  | High School Evening Classes                                  |
| 1906  | Tuberculosis Hospital                                        |
| 1908  | Public Health Nurses                                         |
| 1909  | Traffic Control                                              |

*1910–1919*

|       |                                                                 |
|-------|-----------------------------------------------------------------|
| 1910  | Children's Clinic                                             |
|       | Classes for Defective Speech, for Cripples, and for Mental Defectives |
| 1911  | High Pressure Water System                                   |
| 1912  | Technical High School                                        |
|       | Classes for the Anemic and for the Blind                     |
|       | Tennis Courts                                                |
| 1914  | Traffic Signs                                                |
| 1915  | Inspection of Swimming Pools                                 |
|       | Ambulance Service                                            |
| 1917  | Auto Patrol                                                  |
|       | Junior College                                               |
|       | Technology Library                                           |
|       | Recreation Camps                                             |
| 1918  | Teachers Summer College                                      |
|       | Children's Museum                                            |
|       | Community Centers                                            |
| 1919  | Executive Preparation for the Budget                         |
|       | Motor Street Sweeping                                        |

*1920–1929*

|       |                                                                 |
|-------|-----------------------------------------------------------------|
| 1920  | Women Police                                                  |
|       | Medical College                                              |
|       | Employment Bureau                                            |
|       | Street Railway Transportation                                |
|       | Regulation of Taxicabs                                       |

| 1922 | Maternity Hospitals |
| | Prison Farm for Men |
| | Golf Courses |
| 1923 | Medical Library |
| | College of Pharmacy |
| | Water Filtration |
| 1924 | Sanding Intersections |
| 1925 | Mosquito Control |
| | General College |
| | Symphony Concerts |
| | Bus Transportation |
| 1926 | Inspection of Hairdressers and Cosmeticians |
| 1927 | Law College |
| 1928 | Cancer Clinic |
| | Boulevard Lighting |
| 1929 | Airplane Landing Field |

*1930–1939*

| 1930 | Use of Radio in Schools |
| | Hangar |
| 1933 | Wayne University |
| 1939 | Sewage Disposal Plant |

## SUMMARY

There's no doubt about it: Today in the United States we have Big Government. During the first 45 years of this century the Federal Government grew faster than state and local governments combined, but since then the growth of the smaller governments has spurted. Throughout the nation's history we note the multiplication of activities of governments at all levels and the expansion of activities once they get started. The total result has been a proliferation of government offices, bureaus, activities, and regulations; an expansion of the total; and a rise in money receipts and expenditures.

Citizens are impressed by this expansion. Some are dismayed by the past trend and appalled by the prospect of its continuation into the future. The problem is both one of detail and one of the totality. Wise formulation of public policy requires attention, not only to the making of sound decisions with respect to individual activities and actions of subordinate parts of government separately, but also to what they all add up to, to what the total in terms of money, personnel, and control amount to in the American economy.

## QUESTIONS AND PROBLEMS

1. Do the various activities of the President involve any conflicts?
2. Is the President's job too big? If your answer is yes, how could its magnitude be reduced?

3. What is the meaning and the significance of "gerontocracy"?
4. Why is the Rules Committee sometimes called the "fourth branch" of the government?
5. What is the meaning and the significance of "administrative lawmaking"?
6. Explain the paradox, ". . . too many local governments, not enough local government. . . ."
7. How do you explain the growth of governmental activities, federal, state, and local?
8. If you consider that we have too much government—federal, state, or local—which activities would you recommend reducing or eliminating?
9. What is the outlook for governmental activities—federal, state, and local? Will any be expanded or contracted? Will new activities be introduced?
10. Are there any ways in which the structure of the government might be changed in order that government might function more effectively?

## SELECTED READINGS

BABCOCK, ROBERT S. *State and Local Government and Politics.* New York: Random House, Inc., 1962.

CORWIN, E. S. *The President, Office and Powers.* New York: New York University Press, 1957.

DAVIS, KENNETH C. *Administrative Law and Government.* St. Paul: West Publishing Company, 1960.

FABRICANT, SOLOMON. *The Trend of Governmental Activity in the United States Since 1900.* New York: National Bureau of Economic Research, 1952.

GALLOWAY, GEORGE B. *History of the House of Representatives.* New York: Thomas Y. Crowell Company, 1961.

————. *The Legislative Process in Congress.* New York: Thomas Y. Crowell Company, 1953.

LANDIS, JAMES M. *Report on Regulatory Agencies to the President-Elect.* Washington, D.C.: United States Government Printing Office, 1960.

U.S. Congress. *Report of the Commission on Inter-Governmental Relations.* Washington, D.C.: United States Government Printing Office, 1955.

*United States Government Organization Manual.* Washington, D.C.: Office of the Federal Register, National Archives and Records Service, General Services Administration. Annually.

# 5 GOVERNMENT:

## General Welfare and Special Interests

The first paragraph of the Constitution of the United States reads:

We the people of the United States, in order to form a more perfect union, establish justice, insure domestic tranquility, provide for the common defense, promote the general welfare, and secure the blessings of liberty to ourselves and our posterity, do ordain and establish this Constitution for the United States of America.

The Constitution does not suggest that one of the objectives of government is to provide special favors for special interests. Not solely for this reason, honorable citizens and thoughtful students of the business–government relationship are inclined to assume that, whatever shortcomings government may have, lack of intention to serve the public interest is not one of them. Such an observer may take note of the fact that critics sometimes accuse government of being inefficient, misguided, or blundering, but he may consider that any such mistakes are the results of human frailty rather than of lack of dedication to the general welfare.

It would be pleasant if this condition could in fact be supposed to prevail. In truth, however, if realism rather than idealism is to dominate our thinking, we must take account of the fact that government sometimes serves special interests. Realistic understanding requires us to look at some of the more unlovely aspects of politics—pressures, pressure groups, lobbying, the personal interests of government officials, even corruption.

It is not intended, in taking up these disagreeable topics, to try to create the impression that government is typically dominated by improper influences. These forces may be small. Nevertheless, they exist, and they are a matter of concern to thoughtful citizens. A clear understanding of both governmental processes and the ways in which government can be improved is facilitated by an understanding of how government can be subverted.

Good government is the aim and interest of decent citizens. Its opposite—*bad* government—can come about in two ways. One is as a consequence of honest mistakes. In the government of human affairs, problems are complex, and it is because they are complex, that the following chapters in this book will take up some of the principal ones and examine them in the light of the question of what proper public policies ought to be.

The other cause of bad government is improper influence. This cause in turn may be divided into two kinds. One is improper influence which is also illegal, involving such things as bribes, graft, and corruption. The other is improper influence which is completely legal, involving pressures and pressure groups and their influence on the actions of public officials.

## LEGAL INFLUENCES TOWARD
## BAD GOVERNMENT

Probably of much larger significance than illegal influence is the impact of special interests on governmental processes when citizens and citizen groups strive to get government to act (or to refrain from acting) for their benefit. Inasmuch as ours is a representative democracy, it is entirely lawful for citizens to attempt to influence government actions, as long as such attempts to influence do not violate specific statutes.

It has been said that politics is economics in action. This statement is an exaggeration. Some political activities and political issues are primarily, perhaps even exclusively, noneconomic in their nature. Although national defense has some extremely important economic entailments, its essential purpose is the preservation of national freedom. Although the subject of civil rights is not without economic significance, it too is a matter which presumably is primarily noneconomic. It is clear, however, that much political activity centers around financial interests. Taxes, expenditures, regulations, and other government actions affect the financial well-being of firms and individuals. The pocketbook nerve is a sensitive one, and therefore, as might be expected, people are alert and even rigorous in attempting to influence the government to take actions financially favorable to them and to refrain from taking unfavorable ones.

Let it be said with haste that in the phrases "improper influence" and "improper pressures and pressure groups" the adjective is a necessary qualification, not a component of a compound. Not all pressures and pressure groups deserve it. The question of impropriety here is a difficult and shaded one—involving intent and understanding. Few would question the propriety of pressure by a number of convinced and sincere individuals, or an organization of them, toward the unilateral abolition of our military strength—however much most of us might disagree with the rightness of a goal which could result in our national humiliation or enslavement. On the other hand, most of us (but by no means all of us) would agree that pressure from, say, a powerful mining interest toward finding a pretext to invade and forcibly annex a weak and undeveloped nation having rich mineral deposits *would* be improper. But how about pressure from the leaders of some specific industry against a proposed broad lowering of tariff barriers against imports? Proper or improper? Assume first that these industrialists are economic illiterates, knowledgeable only in their own field. Possibly "proper"—since they may honestly believe that what is good for their industry must be good for all industries and for the country. Now assume that all of them are trained economists —does our judgment of them change?

It is hoped that the ensuing discussion will be read in the light of this pervading uncertainty. The subject is *legal but improper pressures*— but the only person who can *positively**[*]* identify a specific case in point is the person who applies the improper pressure. And he will not.

But the uncertainty about propriety is even murkier than that. There are decent and indecent *means* of applying pressures. And pressure in a worthy cause, indecently applied, would be justified only by the cynical philosophy that the end justifies the means.

## THE PRESSURE GROUPS

Who are the people who apply the pressures? In the broadest sense the people affected by government and who, therefore, may try to in-influence government actions include all or most of us. Any person who has ever exercised his constitutional right to try to influence a legislative or executive officer or government at any level has used more or less pressure in connection with this effort. Any person belonging to a club, society, or association who has signed a petition or who has voted for a resolution asking for government action has been trying to bring pressure to bear on officers of government.

Pressures may be exercised by individuals, or by groups, or by individuals under the stimulus of groups. Inasmuch as clubs, societies, civic and of the independent offices and agencies, at both Federal and state organizations, religious organizations, professional associations, industry associations, occupational groups, and many others may on occasion attempt to exert political influence, it is clear that the total number of such organizations runs into the thousands and possibly into the tens of thousands.

What are some of the important groups? Business interests are represented at the national level by the National Association of Manufacturers and the Chamber of Commerce of the United States. State chambers of commerce and state manufacturers' associations perform the same function at their level; and local chambers of commerce are active with respect to municipal governments. It would perhaps be accurate to de-

---

[*] The powerful mining interest of the preceding paragraph may have members, and will surely gain supporters, who sincerely believe that taking over the weak and undeveloped nation will, because it introduces "democracy," "progress," and "economic development," be a good thing for all concerned.

scribe the National Association of Manufacturers as ultraconservative in politico-economic matters. The Chamber of Commerce of the United States represents a much larger number of business firms, is less highly centralized in its control and operation, and might be described as somewhat less conservative than the NAM.

In addition to the United States Chamber of Commerce, which represents all kinds of business interests, and the National Association of Manufacturers, which represents a wide variety of manufacturing firms, there are national organizations representing hundreds of specific industries and professions. Examples are the American Medical Association, the Association of American Railroads, the National Education Association, and the American Retail Federation. Many of these national organizations have state counterparts.

Labor's interests are represented at all levels by unions and union representatives. By far the largest labor organization in the country is the AFL-CIO, whose constituent unions have 16 million members.

Three organizations represent the farming interests. The oldest of these is the National Grange. The largest is the American Farm Bureau Federation, which has a membership of more than 1.5 million. The newest and the one considered to be least conservative in its policies is the National Farmers Union. Partly because of the overrepresentation of rural areas in the Congress, it has been said that organized farmers can get anything out of Congress that they want except good growing weather.

Among other powerful and influential groups are the American Legion, the League of Women Voters, and the National Association for the Advancement of Colored People.

## ACTIVITIES OF PRESSURE GROUPS

Since the aim of pressure groups is to influence the actions of government, success will depend on two things: first, getting the "right" men elected to legislative bodies and appointed as administrative officers; and second, influencing their actions when they are on the job in their legislative and executive offices.

Getting the "right" men elected is a process that can begin with the primary election. If the favored man wins the nomination, the interested group then goes on to support him in the election. If he does not win in the primary, the group will have the option of his opponent of another party or of sitting that one out.

There are several ways in which a group can try to help a favored candidate to win an election. One is personal solicitation, sometimes called doorbell ringing. Also, meetings are held, speeches are made, people are telephoned, and other personal efforts are exerted on behalf of the candidate.

Elections cost money—all the way from a few dollars to hundreds of thousands of dollars. Interested parties, therefore, can, subject to the provisions of law, make contributions to political campaign funds.

The actions of appointed officers of the executive branch of government and of the independent offices and agencies, at both Federal and state levels, are often significant to persons, firms, industries, and communities. Here also, from the viewpoint of the interested parties, it is desirable to have men appointed who are friendly to their interests.

Once men have been elected or appointed to office, the next step consists in trying to influence their legislative or administrative activities.

## LOBBYING

One of the principal methods employed is *lobbying*. Neither as a verb nor as a noun does the word *lobby* have a definite meaning. Lobbying has been defined as any attempt by individuals or groups to influence governmental decision. This definition is so broad that it encompasses any correspondence, contact, or conversation—formal or informal—by one or more persons, addressed to any government functionary. The definition is, therefore, too broad to be useful. *Webster's New International Dictionary,* Second Edition, defines the verb thus: "To address or solicit members of a legislative body in the lobby or elsewhere, as before a committee, with intent to influence legislation." The same source defines the noun in this fashion: "The persons, collectively, who frequent the lobbies of a legislative house to transact business with the legislators; specifically, persons not members of a legislative body, who strive to influence its proceedings by personal agency; a particular group of such persons; also, collectively, the practices and methods of such persons."

Despite the lack of definiteness in the meanings of the words, the concepts are fairly well understood by persons familiar with the processes of government. The only point at which precise definition becomes critical is in connection with legal regulation. Both the Federal Government and most of the states have laws regulating lobbyists and lobbying. In such laws, which may require lobbyists to register their names and to report their expenditures, a representative definition of a lobbyist is this one in the Federal act, "Any person who shall engage himself for pay or for any consideration for the purpose of attempting to influence the passage or defeat of any legislation by the Congress of the United States. . . ." The terms *legislative agent* and *legislative counsel* are sometimes applied informally to persons carrying on these activities. Hundreds of lobbyists are employed in Washington and in the state capitals by national and state organizations.

Opinions about lobbying differ tremendously. On the one hand is the statement written into the Constitution of the State of Georgia in 1807 that "lobbying is a crime." On the other hand is the opinion that lobbyists frequently supply busy legislators with facts and information that are useful to them. The fact is that there is both good lobbying and bad lobbying.

The effectiveness of lobbying also is a subject concerning which there is disagreement. Lobbyists who represent organizations are naturally, in their written and oral reports, likely to take credit for the passage of any favorable legislation and for the defeat of unfavorable legislation. Unbiased observers, however, and even some lobbyists, are inclined to rate the power of formal lobbying very much lower than that of some other methods used by pressure groups.

## METHODS USED BY PRESSURE GROUPS

What are some of these other methods? The organization may trigger the sending of letters and telegrams by its members to legislators and other public officials. Despite the fact that careful surveys have shown that Congressional mail is often completely unrepresentative of true public opinion, the impact of dozens or hundreds of letters predominantly favoring or opposing a piece of legislation may not be dismissed lightly as negligible. These organizations have long since learned that, in order to avoid the obvious appearance of lack of spontaneity in such a flood of communications, the members must be urged to express their ideas in their own words. Nevertheless, one suspects that the Congressman who suddenly receives a batch of communications on a particular subject will infer an organized attempt to influence his vote.

The pressure group may also stimulate telephone calls and personal visits to government officers. The effectiveness of these contacts depends on many circumstances, including the power, prestige, and persuasiveness of the caller. An interested group can arrange to have newspaper, radio, and television publicity provided for a legislator if he makes a public statement supporting their viewpoint. If he wishes, they can write the statement for him. They can also write speeches for him to deliver. Entertainment, including cocktail parties and dinners, is a device frequently employed.

Of special significance is the open or veiled promise of support or opposition in the next election. It has been said that the difference between a statesman and a politician is that the politician looks ahead to the next election, while the statesman looks ahead to the next generation. Elected office holders who wish to stay on the job—either because they enjoyed it or because they believe that they are capable public servants—are concerned with getting elected and getting reelected. Pressure groups can help an officeholder, or assist his opponent, with financial contributions or personal efforts.

## THE POSITION OF THE
## GOVERNMENT OFFICIAL

In attempting to assess the influence of pressure groups, we may take account of several different kinds of situations. Let us consider the situation where a government official is being pressured on only one side of an issue, as distinguished from that where he is being pressured on opposite sides. Suppose, for example, that a Congressman is from a predominantly rural district where the farmers raise a crop that has price supports and that he is being pressured to try to get the price support level increased. This situation may be further divided into two cases, the one in which he honestly thinks that the desired action is compatible with the general welfare, as against the one in which he believes that it is not. In the first case he finds himself in the happy situation of being pressed to do something that he believes is genuinely good and so has no problem. He goes along with the pressure and takes the action that he presumably would have taken had there been none at all, with the addition of feeling warm breezes from the home prairie.

If, however, the imaginary representative believes that it is not in the national interest to see the price support increased and, even worse, if he thinks that the price support should be reduced or eliminated, what does he do? In the assumed circumstances, if he wishes to be reelected, he probably goes along with the pressure group.

Indeed, apart from our legislator's political ambitions, a basic philosophical question is raised by situations of this kind. What is an honorable representative supposed to do when, as he sees it, the immediate interests of his constituents are at odds with those of the nation? Is he supposed to work for the interests of his constituents? And who are his constituents? Are they the tight little group of the more influential and articulate voters at home *now*, or the entire population of the home district *now*, or their children's children living in the context of the nation of the future? This is essentially the question of the difference between a politician and a statesman, it is not an easy one, and it is not likely to be settled one way or the other.

Sometimes there may be an out for the representative. If he believes that the bill embodying the action desired by his constituents is pretty certain to lose, he may—to be sure, with a certain amount of hypocrisy— vote for it and figure that he has benefited himself without injuring the nation.

Now let us pass to a case in which the public official is being pressured on *opposite* sides of a controversial issue. If one of the pressure groups is small and weak and the other big and strong, there may be no issue, the situation being essentially the same as in the preceding cases.

If, however, each of the pressure groups is big and strong, the official con-fronts a different problem. He may, to be sure, decide to be a statesman and vote in what he conceives to be the national interest. If, however, he gives attention to the political realities, he may have to try to decide which group has more money and more members. (If one group has more *money* and the other more *members,* he may need the help of a computer.) In the circumstances, he may even exemplify a definition contained in another quip: A statesman is a politician who is kept upright by equal pressures from all sides. His dilemma is real and may properly generate sympathy. Public officials are often fiercely resentful of pressures and pressure groups.

## THE EFFECTIVENESS OF PRESSURES

How effective are the pressures of special interests? Are public policies pretty much determined by what interested parties want, or are they settled in the public interest? A definite answer to this question is im-possible. One reason is that no definite answer would apply equally to all kinds of situations. Circumstances differ at the Federal, state, and local levels, and in legislative, executive, and administrative activities.

For instance, it seems to be easier to stop the passage of an *undesired* bill than to secure the enactment of a *desired* one. The reason is that a bill has to go through many rooms to pass, but one closed door can make it fail. In the Congress, for example, when a bill is introduced, it is referred to the appropriate committee for study. An interest group may be able to influence the committee to kill the bill, and as we have seen, committee action usually settles the matter. If the committee reports a bill out favorably, it is then taken up in the house of Congress to which it is reported.* Here also it may be possible to mobilize opposition suc-cessfully. If it passes in the originating house, it is then sent to the other house, where it goes through the same procedure of first going to a committee for study, where again it may be stopped. If approved by the committee, it again comes to the floor of the second house, where it may be defeated. Finally, if it is passed by both houses, it can be vetoed by the President, as President Truman vetoed the Taft–Hartley Act. It is possible then for the bill to be passed over the President's veto, as also happened with the Taft–Hartley Act.

In short, a bill can be stopped anywhere along the rather long legisla-tive route. An astute pressure group will naturally concentrate its efforts at key points, these include committee chairmen and committee members of standing committees (including—in the House of Representatives—the Rules Committee). The effort involved in getting negative action from one man or a small group of men in this serial screening process may be

---

* In the House of Representatives it usually must get a favorable nod from the Rules Committee before the House can consider it.

much smaller than that of trying to influence a majority of the members of the House or Senate.

The opposite of all this reasoning is involved in considering the problem of how to get a bill passed. The bill must go through all the rooms and through all the doors. Even if there is no strong opposition, sheer inertia may hold up action at one point—and this is all that is necessary to block the proposed legislation. And if there is in fact opposition, and it is substantial, all of this conspires with that opposition and against the bill.

Sometimes the subtleties of the legislative process make parliamentary maneuvers so obscure that the well-informed citizen has difficulty in knowing the side on which his representative has really acted. For example, a common way of killing a bill that has been reported out of a committee is by a vote in the house to *recommit*. This is a motion to send the bill back to the committee, and members voting on the motion understand that the real purpose of the motion is to kill the bill, although ostensibly the purpose may appear to be merely to submit the bill to further study. An affirmative vote on the motion to recommit is, thus, the same thing as a negative vote on the bill itself, and vice versa.

The opinions of the general public about the actual influence and the desirable influence of two of our prominent pressure groups on our lawmaking were surveyed in 1960 by the American Institute of Public Opinion. Two questions asked were: "At the present time, which do you think has the most influence on the laws passed in this country—big business or labor?" and "Which do you think *should* have the most influence?" In a release dated May 13, 1960, the Institute reported the following distribution of responses:

### Which *Does* Have Most Influence?

|  | Business | Labor | No Difference | No Opinion |
|---|---|---|---|---|
|  | % | % | % | % |
| All Adults: | 43 | 34 | 10 | 13 |
| Business and Professional | 38 | 41 | 9 | 12 |
| White Collar | 43 | 37 | 11 | 9 |
| Laborers | 48 | 29 | 10 | 13 |
| Farmers | 42 | 23 | 17 | 18 |

### Which *Should* Have Most Influence?

|  | Business | Labor | No Difference | No Opinion |
|---|---|---|---|---|
|  | % | % | % | % |
| All Adults | 14 | 29 | 46 | 11 |
| Business and Professional | 17 | 16 | 58 | 9 |
| White Collar | 11 | 35 | 42 | 12 |
| Laborers | 12 | 33 | 45 | 10 |
| Farmers | 12 | 36 | 40 | 12 |

The questions in the survey used the term *big business*. It is altogether possible that if the survey had used simply the word *business* the results might have been somewhat different.

## INFLUENCE OF BUSINESS

Business interests are credited with having been extremely influential at all levels of government in the latter part of the nineteenth century and in the very early part of the twentieth century. Prior to 1913, when United States Senators were chosen by state legislatures instead of by vote of the people, certain Senators were often understood to have owed their positions to specific corporations and were referred to as such. The Seventeenth Amendment, providing for the direct election of Senators, changed that condition.

One consequence of the Great Depression seems to have been a decline in the esteem felt by the citizenry for business leaders. The opposition on the part of most of the business community to the measures of the New Deal may have been a factor in causing many Americans to conclude that the business community was opposed to progressive actions by the government. In an unusually frank statement Mr. James K. Vardaman, Jr., then a member of the Board of Governors of the Federal Reserve System, addressing the Eighth District Group of the Georgia Bankers Association on October 19, 1955, said:

> It may be interesting to note here that nearly all major changes in financial customs effected by Congress in the last forty years—especially those from which the economy has derived greatest benefit—have been opposed by bankers. A banker since 1920 and a banker's lawyer before that, I know whereof I speak.
>
> Bankers are not always wrong, even though they usually, and quite naturally, dislike any change in the status quo. When Congress had before it such questions as the establishment of the Federal Reserve System, the Federal Housing Administration, the Federal Deposit Insurance Corporation, the Securities and Exchange Commission, opposition by bankers was widespread, loud, and long.
>
> It is to be hoped that bankers will continue to oppose any change in the status quo that looks suspicious or unsound to them. Opposition and critical analysis usually prove helpful in the drafting of far-reaching legislation and are especially important where effects of the enactment on the people will be lasting. Therefore, I say to you, keep up your guard; continue fighting for what you think is right. Let nothing go by unquestioned. Of one thing you may be certain—if the legislative proposals are good for the country and are really required and demanded, they will eventually be enacted into law whether we oppose or favor.

Discussing both past actions and possible future ones, Henry Ford II enunciated this philosophy in 1961:

I think we must try a whole lot harder than in the past to approach national problems and specific legislative questions in a positive and constructive spirit.

For years, the basic reaction of business and of leading business associations to almost any kind of proposal for governmental action in economic and social matters, tax increases, public works and the rest has been a flat and violent No! I don't suggest that we start saying yes when we ought to say no. But it does seem to me that we are seldom if ever ready with an intelligent alternative solution to a problem.

For every business gripe, there ought to be at least one constructive idea. And if we could begin to even out the ratio of complaints to helpful hints, we would greatly enhance, I'm sure, the effectiveness of business in government.*

Writing in *The New York Times Magazine*, August 30, 1959, Mr. Charles P. Taft was critical of the business-into-politics movement. Mr. Taft said that one thing wrong with the campaign was that it was, in fact, aimed against labor unions. He observed also that the campaign sometimes created the impression that it was basically against all progress. He went on to urge businessmen to study economics instead of relying on private organizations which tend to tell them only what they want to hear.

Study of political economy is important, not merely for businessmen, but also for all thoughtful citizens. He who wishes to influence government policy in the long run must do more than work diligently at the mechanics of politics. In the long run, policies that are good for the nation are likely to be adopted, and he who advocates other policies even with the aid of a powerful political machine is unlikely to achieve lasting success. The serious study of the general welfare and of politico-economic problems is a necessary basis for influencing the formulation of public policies.

## PRESSURE BY GOVERNMENT OFFICIALS

Officials of the legislative and the executive branches of the government as well as those of the independent agencies and regulatory commissions sometimes attempt to sway the actions of officers in the other branches. The White House and other government agencies have Congressional liaison officers. It is the duty of these men to try to influence action by the Congress. If the President's party has a majority in the Congress, the White House gets support from the Speaker of the House and the Majority leaders and whips in both houses.

Many are the appeals that are used. The lures of committee posts, local appointments, and breakfast invitations to the White House may

* Henry Ford II, "Private Business and Public Affairs," *Michigan Business Review*, May 1961, p. 5.

be utilized. Federal judgeships are attractive appointments, and the White House may quietly let it be known that Senators who cooperate with the Administration's program will see their favorites appointed to these posts, whereas those who oppose will receive no such favors.

Defense expenditures have come to be an important factor in these considerations. Contracts and military installations are significant to individual firms and individual communities. In cases where the public interest can be served equally well in two or more locations, the outcome of a contract negotiation, or the site adopted for a new installation, may depend on the political cooperation of individual Congressmen with the White House.

Congressmen are frequently requested by their constituents to intervene for them in their dealings with various executive departments and agencies, and sometimes do so. Because of the fact that Congress passes the laws and holds the purse strings, many administrative agencies in Washington have a special office for handling correspondence and telephone and personal contacts with members of the Congress. Typically, the agency will have a standing rule that letters from Congressmen must get instant replies, but that no reply goes to a Congressman without having been cleared by the head of the Congressional Correspondence Office.

## ILLEGAL INFLUENCES

The preceding discussion has dealt with legal influences, which may or may not be proper. We now turn attention to illegal influences.

Because of the nature of unlawful political activities, they are secret and hidden. Therefore, it is hard to get reliable data on their prevalence. Occasionally they come to the public notice in newspaper stories, legislative investigations, and court cases. It is perhaps not unreasonable to suppose that illegal behavior is like the traditional iceberg, in that only a small fraction of it is exposed to the public view. The scantiness of positive information, however, suggests that there is not very much bad government of the outright illegal kind in our country.

Moreover, its distribution seems to be uneven. There seems to be little unlawful behavior at the level of the Federal Government. The amount of illegal activity in state government seems to differ greatly from state to state, and the same condition seems to prevail among local governments. Some cities have had dubious reputations for municipal morality, whereas others have long been accounted as clean as the proverbial hound's tooth.

The difficulty of drawing the line between legal and illegal actions is considered in the next section.

## CONTRIBUTIONS AND GIFTS

Perhaps one reason for the rarity of illegal influences, such as bribery, is the possibility, seen by interested parties, of achieving the same ends by the entirely lawful method of making contributions to political campaign expenses, and thus assisting the election of legislators who are either favorable to their viewpoint to start with or who may be expected to express their gratitude for the financial assistance by appropriate voting action.

Political contributions are subject to some statutory limitations at all levels of government. Despite the limitations the permitted types and sizes of contributions are substantial. The possibility that such lawful contributions could have ulterior purposes has long been understood.

Public attention has been focused on this problem many times, and one spectacular episode occurred in 1956. At that time a subcommittee of the Senate Privileges and Elections Committee had been concerned to a mild extent with the problem of political contributions, and was contemplating a further inquiry. Activity, however, was languishing—perhaps partly because of active opposition. Then before the Congress came a bill to exempt some five thousand producers of natural gas from direct rate regulation by the Federal Power Commission. The bill passed both houses on a split-party basis—the split being largely between the gas-producing states, whose representatives favored the bill, and the nonproducing or consumer states whose delegations opposed it. In the midst of the legislative process Senator Francis Case of South Dakota revealed that he had been offered a campaign contribution of $2,500, which had come, he said, from the personal funds of the president of a gas-producing company. The Senator judged that this was an attempt to influence his vote and refused. He not only revealed the fact of the proffered contribution, but announced that although he had originally intended to vote for the bill, he was now going to vote against it.

When the bill reached President Eisenhower, he vetoed it, saying that legislation conforming to the basic objectives of the bill was needed, but adding:

> Since the passage of this bill a body of evidence has accumulated indicating that private persons, apparently representing only a very small segment of a great and vital industry, have been seeking to further their own interests by highly questionable activities. These include efforts I deem to be so arrogant and so much in defiance of acceptable standards of propriety as to risk creating doubt among the American people concerning the integrity of governmental processes.

One apparent effect of the veto was to encourage the once-languishing investigation of improper attempts to influence Congress through cam-

paign contributions. The Senate immediately provided money to finance
this investigation.

## COMMITTEE REPORT ON
## CAMPAIGN COSTS

A year later, the subcommittee concerned with the investigation of the
1956 election campaigns produced its report, in the form of a book of
928 pages, which became a best seller in Washington. The book named
names and gave figures. It accounted for contributions of more than $33
million and admitted that the account was incomplete. It suggested that
if total campaign contributions and spending could be ascertained, the
amount might be in excess of $100 million.

A breakdown of these amounts as tabulated by the Committee showed
that members of twelve selected families had contributed more than
a million dollars, the officials of 225 large corporations had contributed
nearly $2 million, officials of 29 of the largest oil companies had put in
$359,647, and labor contributions totaled nearly $2 million. Also mentioned in the report were contributions by officers of airlines, advertising
agencies, and radio and television stations.

According to the reported figures the amounts spent in contests for
seats in the House of Representatives ran up to a top figure (for the two
candidates combined) of slightly more than $43,000. Senatorial races
had involved more money. The most expensive contest had reported
expenditures by two candidates of more than half a million dollars.
At the other end, some Southern Senators who were unopposed had reported zero receipts and zero expenditures.

The financial involvements of campaigns for office—at all levels—and
the important personal efforts and assistance which may not appear in
financial reports at all, but may nevertheless be tremendously effective,
raise a serious question. The question is: To what extent does such election assistance—past or anticipated in the future—influence the thinking
and behavior of public officials? The importance of the question is
matched by the difficulty of answering it.

Personal gifts—at Christmas time and anytime—present a similar
problem. The question is: How big may a gift be without impropriety?

It should be pointed out that this problem is not peculiar to politics; it
is a familiar one in business also. In business the problem arises especially
in connection with gifts to the *purchasing agents* of business firms. Since
the giving of gifts among people, especially at Christmas time, is a commonplace of our culture, it seems to be generally thought that to forbid
completely the acceptance of any gifts would be unreasonable. One line
of demarcation between the proper and the improper gift is its size.

Senator Douglas is frequently quoted: "We have a rule here in the Senate, that if you can eat it up, smoke it up, or drink it up in one day, it is all right."

## PRESIDENT'S COMMISSION ON CAMPAIGN COSTS

In 1961 President Kennedy appointed a commission of nine well-known citizens to recommend ways to improve the financing of campaigns of Presidential and Vice-Presidential candidates.

The Commission reported in April 1962. The report said in part:

> The magnitude of the problem with which we are concerned is obvious. Expenditures on behalf of all candidates for all public offices in the United States probably reached $165,000,000 to $175,000,000 in 1960. While the share of this total spent on behalf of Presidential and Vice Presidential candidates cannot be estimated with precision, the two major parties reported expenditures of almost $20,000,000 in their national campaigns alone: the corresponding totals in 1952 and 1956 were $11,600,000 and $12,900,000 respectively. Both parties ended the campaigns of 1956 and 1960 in debt. In 1960, the Democrats spent $3,800,000 more than they raised and the Republicans spent $700,000 more than they raised.

The Commission noted some overtones of campaign contributions in these words:

> The heavy dependence of political parties in Presidential campaigns upon substantial gifts from and expenditures by a relatively small number of individuals and organizations lends itself to widespread misinterpretation. While the great majority of such contributors to Presidential campaigns is not motivated by expectation of specific preferment, nonetheless, for the vitality and acceptance of the democratic system, we hope to see a significant increase in the number of contributors, both to spread the cost of campaigns and to diffuse more widely through the population the sense and the reality of participation in the politics of democracy.

The Commission made recommendations designed to stimulate an increased number of small contributions. One suggestion was that one half of the total contributions to specified party committees, up to a maximum of $10 a year—a husband and wife filing a joint return could claim up to $20—be an allowable credit against the Federal income tax. An alternative proposal was to permit deduction of contributions to such committees up to a maximum of $1,000 per year from taxable income. The commission pointed to the widespread cynicism concerning the existing legal regulation of campaign finances and proposed changes in the kind of campaign reports required. The Commission also noted that state governments have opportunities, as does the Federal Government, to improve Presidential campaign finances, by permitting similar credits against state income taxes.

The Commission recommended that its tax incentives be adopted only for an experimental period, to include two Presidential campaigns. They also invited consideration of the possibility of developing a greater Federal share in bearing Presidential campaign costs, such as a matching incentive plan, in which stipulated private contributions would be matched by equivalent grants from the United States Treasury.

## CONFLICT OF INTEREST

The ideal of proper government suggests that government officers should not be in positions to influence government actions where such actions might redound to their financial profit. The enforcement of this principle, however, is very uneven. Well-known, for example, have been situations such as that in which the Senate (in 1953) required a prospective Secretary of Defense to rearrange his investments as a condition precedent to his appointment. Similarly, Congressional investigations have examined carefully the financial relationships between officers of regulatory commissions and the industries which they were regulating.

Not subject to the same kind of scrutiny, however, are the special interests of Congressmen themselves. Congressmen may serve on committees and may vote on measures that influence their financial investment. Thus, as only one example, a Congressman may own a farm and, nevertheless, act on programs that influence crop price-supports accruing to his benefit. In addition to these direct links between a Congressman's official actions and his private financial well-being, there is the big group of political actions that have to do with reelection, such as pressures, votes, and financial contributions. These considerations taken together compose a political thicket that constitutes one (but only one) of the hazards along the course in the game of representative democracy.

## THE GREAT GAME OF POLITICS

Politics is a game that is played according to certain rules and sometimes seems as highly stylized as a formal dance, although the general atmosphere is more likely to be one of hurly-burly than of graceful elegance. The party in control of the White House and the Congress or (at the state level) of the governor's mansion and the state house—the "Ins"— are prone to take the credit for every good thing that has happened to the nation or the state since they came into power. In contrast, the "Outs" usually charge the "Ins" with the blame for everything that has gone wrong during that period. If employment is high and business is good, the "Ins" claim the credit. If, however, a slump occurs, the "Outs" will probably blame it on the "Ins," while the latter strive to find some way of disclaiming the responsibility. Charges are made, followed by denials. Claims are asserted, and counterclaims are evoked.

Occasionally the situation becomes confused—especially when the executive branch and the legislative branch are controlled by different parties. In the years 1947 and 1948 Democratic President Truman faced Republican majorities in both houses, and it was they, together with some Democratic assistance, who passed the Taft–Hartley Act over his veto. President Eisenhower had Republican majorities during the first two years of his first administration, but thereafter for the remaining six years, from 1954 through 1960, there were Democratic majorities in the Congress. In this condition, the claiming of credit and the fixing of blame become delicate and difficult operations. Not only do they present problems to the government officers, but they are also confusing to the citizenry. Some of the difficulties of the State of Michigan in the 1950s and early 1960s, for example, have been assessed inaccurately because of the fact that for many years the Governors have been members of one party, while the majorities in the State Legislature have been of the other.

The wise citizen will appraise the actions and the statements of politicians in the light of their loyalties and objectives. Politicians' statements often take the form of special pleading or attempts at persuasion or salesmanship. In these activities they have greater freedom than do commercial firms. The latter are subject to legal regulation. A Federal law forbids unfair and deceptive acts and practices in commerce, thereby making oral and printed statements subject to legal scrutiny. No such external regulation inhibits political activities—other than the laws of libel and slander. In the first instance, of course, there are the inhibitions imposed by politicians' consciences, the self-limitations set by principle and ethics—and nothing herein should be taken as implying that politicians as a breed are less sensitive to this guide than are other men. But where it lacks, or when it breaks down, false and misleading political acts are subject only to the reprisals of the opposing party and to the astuteness of the citizenry.

## QUESTIONS AND PROBLEMS

1. Identify some of the important pressure groups at the federal, state, and local levels.
2. What are some specific governmental actions that are supported or opposed by pressure groups?
3. What are some of the methods employed by pressure groups?
4. Do you agree with the assertion that "a statesman is a politician who is kept upright by equal pressures from all sides"?

5. If you were a governmental official, how much would pressure groups influence your actions?
6. How much actual influence do pressure groups have in the government?
7. Is it necessary or desirable to curb the power of special interest groups?
8. Do the individual Congressmen, in striving to secure the best possible condition for the home state folks, also strive for the best national interests?
9. Does the high cost of running for some offices give monied presssure groups an advantage in aiding the election of men whom they favor? What effects do these conditions have on governmental actions?
10. What is your opinion of the recommendations made by the President's Commission on Campaign Costs?
11. Cite examples of moves in the great game of politics.

## SELECTED READINGS

BLAISDELL, DONALD C. *American Democracy Under Pressure*. New York: The Ronald Press, 1957.

DE GRAZIA, ALFRED. *Public and Republic*. New York: Alfred A. Knopf, Inc., 1951.

EULAU, HEINZ, SAMUEL J. ELDERSVELD, and MORRIS JANOWITZ. *Political Behavior*. Glencoe, Ill.: The Free Press, 1956.

HEARD, ALEXANDER. *The Costs of Democracy*. Chapel Hill: University of North Carolina Press, 1960.

HINDERAKER, IVAN. *Party Politics*. New York: Henry Holt and Company, 1956.

KEY, V. O., JR. *Politics, Parties, and Pressure Groups*. New York: Thomas Y. Crowell Company, 1958.

————. *Public Opinion and American Democracy*. New York: Alfred A. Knopf, Inc., 1961.

LEISERSON, AVERY. *Administrative Regulation*. Chicago: University of Chicago Press, 1942.

"Report of President's Commission on Campaign Costs." Washington, D.C.: United States Government Printing Office, 1962.

SCHRIFTGIESSER, KARL. *The Lobbyists*. Boston: Little, Brown & Company, 1951.

TRUMAN, DAVID B. *The Governmental Process*. New York: Alfred A. Knopf, Inc., 1951.

# 6 GOVERNMENT FINANCE:
## Expenditures and Taxes

Government costs money; *big* government costs big money. Since most of that money comes from taxes, big government means big taxes. The larger the expenditures and the larger the taxes, the more important governmental financial operations become and the more controversial become the subjects of expenditure and taxation.

One of the ways in which government revenues and expenditures affect the economy is through their influence on general business activity. This subject (with special reference to the Federal Government) is discussed in Chapter 10, under the heading "Fiscal Policy." It is useful here to note a distinction between this aspect of government finance and what might be called its ordinary financing or housekeeping aspect. It is the latter that is ordinarily considered under the heading "government finance" or "public finance."

Fiscal policy is concerned largely with changes in the *totals* of Federal taxes and expenditures and the varying consequent surplus or deficit positions, as general business conditions rise and fall. Public finance is not unconcerned with these totals, but concentrates major attention on the individual items. Public finance studies the specific individual taxes at all levels—Federal, state, and local. It also studies the specific items of expenditure for all of the hundred thousand governmental entities in the United States.

Fiscal policy is concerned with the nation's purchasing power, as affected by the absorption of money from the private sectors of the economy by taxation and the injection of money through public expenditures. Public finance considers the proper allocation of public expenditures and the proper levying of taxes to support those expenditures. The difference between the two concepts—fiscal policy and government finance—will be further illustrated as the discussion of these two topics proceeds.

Both lines of analysis are concerned with the aggregate of government receipts and spending in relation to the size of the total economy. Fiscal policy is concerned with the impact of government financial operations on general business levels; public finance, with the important question of the proper relative sizes of the public sector and of the private sector in our economy.

In discussing this last subject some persons contend that we have a situation which is described as *public poverty and private plenty*. In this view, public expenditures should be larger and private expenditures smaller. Such a shift would require an increase in tax rates, and proponents of this viewpoint sometimes seem to be hesitant about indicating just which taxes should be increased and by how much. On the other hand, many persons consider that government and government spending and taxes are too large in relation to the economy and that the government sector should be decreased relative to the private sector.

Since the sum total of taxes is made up of the totals from many taxes at various governmental levels, and since the grand total of expenditures includes public expenditures on many objects, analysis of this public-private sector-size problem requires consideration of the various expenditures. Global totals do not provide a basis for analysis.

Study of public finance is complicated by several of the factors mentioned in Chapter 1. The size and complexity of the operations are so great that they actually make statistical compilations difficult and sometimes hard to understand. Opinions about taxes and spending are frequently influenced by political loyalties and the quivering nerves of the personal pocketbook. Ignorance and misunderstanding sometimes seem to prevail even among well-informed citizens. As a consequence, government financial operations can sometimes look ridiculous. Consider, for example, the hypothetical case of the Benevolent Corporation. This corporation pays one half of the registration fee when an employee takes a useful course in an educational institution. This payment has been held to be part of the employee's *taxable income*. In order further to encourage the employee, the company pays the income tax on that income. The income tax thus paid for the employee also has been held to be taxable income and the employee has to pay income tax on the income tax *payment* made by the corporation in his behalf. This anecdote can be presented in such a manner as to make the rulings on the income tax appear absurd. As a matter of fact, however, careful examination will indicate that the rulings are entirely reasonable. Supplementary payments made by an employer, even though not denominated as salaries or wages, nevertheless benefit the financial positions of employees, and so are properly considered to be taxable income.

## FACTS ABOUT GOVERNMENT FINANCE

Understanding of government finance must necessarily be based on a picture of actual financial data. Table 6.1, therefore, presents the figures for total government revenue, expenditures, and debt for Federal, state, and local government entities in the United States for fiscal years 1902 and 1959. The table shows an increase in the magnitude of these figures over that period, but it should be noted that the national income in 1902 was $17.2 billion, while in 1961 it had risen to $427.8 billion. Government has grown, but so also has the American economy. Nevertheless, even

*Table 6.1*

SUMMARY OF TOTAL GOVERNMENT REVENUE, EXPENDITURES, AND DEBT

Fiscal Years 1902, 1961
(Billions)

| ITEM | 1902 | 1961 |
|---|---|---|
| All Governments[1] | | |
| Revenue | $1.7 | $159.6 |
| General | 1.6 | 134.9 |
| Utility and liquor stores | .1 | 5.0 |
| Insurance trust | — | 19.7 |
| Expenditures (direct) | 1.7 | 164.2 |
| General | 1.6 | 138.8 |
| Utility and liquor stores | .1 | 5.2 |
| Insurance trust | — | 20.2 |
| Debt outstanding | 3.3 | 364.4 |
| | | |
| Federal[2] | | |
| Revenue | .7 | 102.5 |
| General | .7 | 88.3 |
| Insurance trust | — | 14.3 |
| Expenditures | .6 | 104.9 |
| Intergovernmental | [3] | 7.0 |
| Direct | .6 | 97.9 |
| General | .6 | 83.0 |
| Insurance trust | — | 14.9 |
| Debt outstanding | 1.2 | 289.0 |
| State and Local[1] | | |
| Revenue | 1.0 | 64.1 |
| Intergovernmental | [3] | 7.1 |
| Own sources | 1.0 | 57.1 |
| General | 1.0 | 46.7 |
| Utility and liquor stores | .1 | 5.0 |
| Insurance trust | — | 5.4 |
| Expenditures (direct) | 1.1 | 66.4 |
| General | 1.0 | 55.8 |
| Utility and liquor stores | .1 | 5.2 |
| Insurance trust | — | 5.3 |
| Debt outstanding[4] | 2.1 | 75.4 |

[1] To avoid duplication intergovernmental transactions between levels of government are eliminated in the combined totals.
[2] Data are on Census basis.
[3] Less than $50 million.
[4] Debt as of the end of the fiscal year. Data for 1961 are preliminary.
SOURCE: Tax Foundation, Inc., *Facts and Figures on Government Finance*, 12th ed., 1962–63 (Englewood Cliffs, N.J.: Prentice-Hall, Inc., 1963), p. 18.

when allowance is made for the growth of the economy, it remains true that total government expenditures rose from 9 per cent of the national income in 1902 to 32 per cent in 1961.

Table 6.2 shows where the money went in 1961. The largest single expenditure was for national defense and international relations. These took more than one third of total government outlays and more than

*Table 6.2*

## EXPENDITURES OF ALL GOVERNMENTS BY FUNCTION AND LEVEL OF GOVERNMENT

Fiscal Year 1961[1]
(Millions)

| FUNCTION | TOTAL | FEDERAL | STATE | LOCAL |
|---|---|---|---|---|
| Total Expenditures Including Inter-governmental | [2] | $104,863 | $34,693 | $41,978 |
| Intergovernmental Expenditures | [2] | 7,011 | 10,114 | 196 |
| To state governments | [2] | 6,266 | — | 196 |
| To local governments | [2] | 745 | 10,114 | [3] |
| Direct Expenditures | $164,212 | 97,852 | 24,578 | 41,782 |
| General | 138,801 | 82,960 | 19,004 | 36,837 |
| National defense and international relations | 49,387 | 49,387 | — | — |
| Education | 21,022 | 640 | 3,792 | 16,590 |
| Highways | 9,936 | 151 | 6,230 | 3,555 |
| Public welfare | 4,732 | 59 | 2,311 | 2,362 |
| Hospitals | 4,478 | 1,053 | 1,799 | 1,626 |
| Health | 1,132 | 542 | 260 | 330 |
| Police | 2,184 | 193 | 261 | 1,730 |
| Natural resources | 11,409 | 10,082 | 906 | 421 |
| Housing and urban renewal | 1,320 | 377 | 7 | 936 |
| Air transportation | 1,800 | 1,378 | 36 | 386 |
| Water transport and terminals | 1,273 | 980 | 78 | 215 |
| Social insurance administration | 636 | 285 | 351 | — |
| General control | 3,022 | 788 | 725 | 1,509 |
| Interest on general debt | 9,296 | 7,485 | 584 | 1,227 |
| Other[4] | 17,170 | 9,557 | 1,664 | 5,949 |
| Utility and Liquor Stores | 5,221 | — | 873 | 4,348 |
| Insurance Trust | 20,191 | 14,893 | 4,701 | 599 |
| Employee retirement | 2,339 | 956 | 791 | 592 |
| Unemployment compensation | 3,715 | 252 | 3,456 | 7 |
| Old-age, survivors and disability insurance | 11,889 | 11,889 | — | — |
| Railroad retirement | 982 | 982 | — | — |
| Other | 1,267 | 814 | 453 | — |

[1] Preliminary.
[2] Not shown because total would involve duplication.
[3] Transactions among local units of government are excluded.
[4] Includes postal service, corrections, sewers, libraries, sanitation, fire and other and unallocable services.

SOURCE: Tax Foundation, Inc., *Facts and Figures on Government Finance,* 12th ed., 1962–63 (Englewood Cliffs, N.J.: Prentice-Hall, Inc., 1963), p. 19.

one half of the Federal part. The next largest item was education, and it is a sad commentary on the state of the world that the nation felt compelled to spend nearly three times as much for national defense as for education.

Inspection of the remaining figures is rewarding, not only because it helps to explain how the large aggregate has come about, but also because it focuses attention on something of vital importance: If one is concerned that public expenditures and taxes are either too high or too low, one may inspect these specific items of expenditure to find out which ones should be increased or decreased, to permit corresponding increases or decreases in taxes. The reader may find the exercise frustrating as well as enlightening.

Table 6.3 shows that taxes provide most of government revenue, but not all. It also illustrates one of the difficulties of the study of government finance, that of definition. What is a tax? In most cases this question can be answered easily. But what of the amounts paid by employers and employees as part of the Federal Social Security System? Are these taxes or are they insurance payments? This table classifies them as Insurance Trust Revenue rather than as taxes. The question involves the meanings of words, but there is more to it than that. It also involves the proper functioning of government.

*Table 6.3*

## REVENUE OF ALL GOVERNMENTS BY SOURCE AND LEVEL OF GOVERNMENT

*Overlapping in the Sources of Intergovernmental Revenue*

Fiscal Year 1961[1]
(Millions)

| SOURCE | TOTAL | FEDERAL | STATE | LOCAL |
|---|---|---|---|---|
| Total Revenue Including Intergovernmental | [2] | $102,530 | $34,603 | $39,855 |
| Intergovernmental | [2] | — | 6,782 | 10,599 |
| From federal government | [2] | — | 6,412 | 644 |
| From state governments | [2] | — | — | 9,955 |
| From local governments | [2] | — | 370 | [3] |
| Revenue from Own Sources | $159,607 | 102,530 | 27,821 | 29,256 |
| General | 134,907 | 88,251 | 21,911 | 24,745 |
| Taxes | 116,133 | 77,470 | 19,057 | 19,606 |
| Property | 17,806 | — | 631 | 17,175 |
| Individual income | 43,951 | 41,338 | 2,355 | 258 |
| Corporation income | 22,220 | 20,954 | 1,266 | [4] |
| Sales, gross receipts, and customs | 26,094 | 13,631 | 11,031 | 1,432 |
| Customs duties | 982 | 982 | — | — |
| General sales and gross receipts | 5,431 | — | 4,510 | 921 |
| Motor fuel | 5,798 | 2,333 | 3,431 | 34 |
| Alcoholic beverages | 3,837 | 3,124 | 688 | 25 |

*Table 6.3—continued*

| SOURCE | TOTAL | FEDERAL | STATE | LOCAL |
|---|---|---|---|---|
| Tobacco products | 3,063 | 1,986 | 1,001 | 76 |
| Public utilities | 1,791 | 1,092 | 401 | 298 |
| Other selective sales and gross receipts | 4,210 | 3,132 | 1,000 | 78 |
| Motor vehicle and operators Licenses | 1,754 | — | 1,641 | 113 |
| Death and gift | 2,397 | 1,896 | 501 | 5 |
| All other | 2,893 | 633 | 1,632 | 628 |
| Charges and miscellaneous | 18,773 | 10,781 | 2,854 | 5,138 |
| Utility and liquor stores | 5,044 | — | 1,119 | 3,925 |
| Insurance trust | 19,657 | 14,279 | 4,791 | 587 |
| Employee retirement | 3,190 | 866 | 1,745 | 579 |
| Unemployment compensation | 2,669 | 150 | 2,511 | 8 |
| Old-age survivors and disability insurance | 12,131 | 12,131 | — | — |
| Railroad retirement | 571 | 571 | — | — |
| Other | 1,096 | 561 | 535 | — |

[1] Preliminary.
[2] Not shown because total would involve duplication.
[3] Transactions among local units of government are excluded.
[4] Included in individual income tax collections.
[5] Included in "All other."
SOURCE: Tax Foundation, Inc., *Facts and Figures on Government Finance,* 12th ed., 1962–63 (Englewood Cliffs, N.J.: Prentice-Hall, Inc., 1963), p. 22.

Other types of governmental revenue also are illustrated by this table. The revenue from government-owned utilities and liquor stores is a sizable figure. These are not taxes, but are more properly sales revenues, like those of private firms that are in the same lines of business.

Governments also make extensive use of *special charges* and *assessments.* A city which paves a residential street and constructs storm sewers, sanitary sewers, curbs, and sidewalks frequently levies special assessments on the owners of property fronting on the street, often collecting these on the basis of so much per front-foot of the property. These too are not strictly taxes.

## TAXES IN OTHER COUNTRIES

Are our taxes an unduly heavy part of our income? No objective criterion exists, but we can compare their totals with those of some other countries. The basis of comparison in Table 6.4 is the percentage which taxes are of gross national expenditure, or gross national product.

## THE FOUR FEDERAL GOVERNMENT BUDGETS

Study of the financial operations of the Federal Government is complicated by their size and by the fact that there is not one budget but

## Table 6.4

### SHARE OF GNP TAKEN BY NATIONAL, STATE, AND LOCAL TAXES, 1959

|  |  | % |
|---|---|---|
| West Germany |  | 34.0 |
| France |  | 33.3 |
| Austria |  | 33.1 |
| Finland |  | 32.1 |
| Norway |  | 31.8 |
| Luxembourg | (1958) | 30.0 |
| Sweden |  | 29.7 |
| Italy |  | 29.2 |
| Netherlands |  | 29.1 |
| Britain |  | 28.9 |
| United States |  | 26.7 |
| Denmark | (est.) | 24.5 |
| Canada |  | 24.3 |
| Belgium |  | 23.1 |
| Ireland |  | 22.2 |
| Australia |  | 22.0 |
| Greece |  | 20.1 |
| Japan |  | 19.0 |
| Portugal |  | 18.2 |
| Switzerland |  | 14.4 |
| Spain |  | 13.4 |

SOURCE: United Nations, *Yearbook of National Accounts Statistics; United Nations Statistical Yearbook;* U.S. Treasury; as reported in *Business Week,* August 25, 1962, p. 53.

four. A consequence of this condition is that reported figures sometimes differ, and the differences are likely to cause confusion. Table 6.5 shows the totals for the four different budgets. The first three are shown for fiscal year 1960; the fourth, for calendar year 1960 (because the fourth is not available on a fiscal year basis—the difference is not significant).

The Administrative Budget is the old-fashioned, long-standing document which covers the ordinary operations of government. These are the figures which are summarized in Tables 6.2 and 6.3 for fiscal year 1959.

The Consolidated Cash Statement shows the actual cash payments made and cash received by the Treasury. The Administrative Budget contains a few items which do not represent cash payments. An example is the interest on E Bonds, which is included as a bookkeeping item among the expenditures, but which involves no cash payment until the holders of the bonds cash them. If this were the only difference between the two budgets, the Administrative Budget would be larger than the Cash Statement. The big difference between them, however, is something else. The largest single difference is that the Consolidated Cash Statement includes the operations of Federal trust funds, of which the largest is the

*Table 6.5*

## THE FOUR FEDERAL GOVERNMENT BUDGETS

( IN BILLIONS OF DOLLARS )

1. Administrative Budget, Fiscal 1960:
   Budget receipts                                                        $ 77.8
   Budget expenditures                                                    76.5
   
   Budget surplus                                                         +1.2

2. Consolidated Cash Statement, Fiscal 1960:
   Receipts from the public .                                             95.1
   Payments to the public                                                 94.3
   
   Excess of receipts                                                     +0.8
3. National Income Accounts Budget, Fiscal 1960:
   Receipts                                                               94.1
   Expenditures                                                           91.9
   
   Surplus                                                                +2.2

4. Total Federal Government Cash Operations, Calendar 1960:
   Receipts                                                               126.8
   Expenditures                                                           129.7
   
   Deficit ( − )                                                          −2.9

SOURCES: For the first three budgets: The President's Budget Message, January 1962; for the fourth: Joint Economic Committee, *The Federal Budget as an Economic Document* (Washington, D.C.: U.S. Government Printing Office, 1962), pp. 33–79.

Social Security old-age and survivors' insurance operation. These trust fund receipts and payments amount to many billions of dollars.

The budget shown in the third form aims to show the direct effect of government receipts and payments on people's incomes. It excludes government loans and repayments of government loans and otherwise is similar to the Cash Consolidated Statement. Further differences arise from the allocation of the timing of money payments. In the National Income Accounts Budget, for example, taxes are shown on an accrual basis, that is, at the times when they become due, rather than when they are actually paid.

The fourth budget, Total Federal Government Cash Operations, is substantially larger than any of the other three. The principal differences are that this budget includes the total receipts and the total outlays of Federal Government enterprises, whereas the other budgets include only the *differences* between these two figures. For example, in 1960 the United States Post Office took in $8.3 billion and paid out $9.1 billion (including the sale and redemption of money orders); these figures appear in the fourth budget, but only the difference between them—the appropriation necessary to finance the deficit—appears in the others. The other big difference involves the issue of new currency and its retirement, which in 1960 totaled nearly $8 billion under each heading, "Receipts and Expenditures." It should be noted that although the retirement of old currency and the issue of new paper money is an important function, it is a routine one. No problems of government financial policy or of fiscal policy are involved.

## THE CAPITAL BUDGET

The use of yet another type of budget, called the "capital budget," is sometimes recommended. The capital budget (which is used by some other countries) distinguishes between and separates those outlays of the government that are considered to be operating expenses and those that are considered to be capital investments. This procedure may or may not be accompanied by the setting up of depreciation accounts wherein provision is made for the gradual writing off of capital investments as their values expire in use.

A budget of this type focuses attention on the balance between *ordinary* revenue receipts and *operating* expenditures rather than on the balance between *total* receipts and outlays. Expenditures for capital assets—post office buildings, highways, and other durable investments—are thus removed from the necessity of being balanced against current revenues.

Those who have urged that the United States Government adopt this budgetary procedure argue either that it is more businesslike than the present one or that it would make budget balancing easier.

In evaluating this proposal it is vital to observe that the main difference between capital budgeting and ordinary budgeting is in the *labels* that are put on receipts and expenditures; the substance of the financial operations is not affected. Capital budgeting does not in and of itself either increase or decrease any outlays or receipts. It may, however, through the psychological influence of its labels, induce either more or less governmental expenditure—probably the former.

Aside from this possibility there seems to be little to be said about capital budgeting. It is true that the procedure is one that is followed by business concerns, firms which naturally pay attention to their earnings month by month, quarter by quarter, and year by year. The United States Government, however, is not concerned with earnings in any material sense and is, therefore, not obliged to treat capital outlays differently from current operating expenditures. The impact of Federal finance on the national economy and the key decisions about expenditures and taxes would (except for the psychological effect noted above) be unchanged by a capital budget's arrangement of receipts and expenditures.

## THE SPENDING POWER

The Constitution, in Article I, Section 8, provides that "The Congress shall have power to lay and collect taxes, duties, imposts, and excises to pay the debts and provide for the common defense and general welfare of the United States; but all duties, imposts, and excises shall be uniform throughout the United States. . . ." This clause provides the constitutional basis for the Federal Government to spend money.

From the beginning there has been some dispute about the significance of the phrase "provide for the general welfare." Some have contended that it is a grant of additional authority to the Congress, whereas others have argued that it is a restriction on the use of the taxing and spending powers of the Congress. Early in the nineteenth century James Madison and others asserted that the phrase prohibited the spending of tax-raised money for purposes not directly under the control of Congress. Others, including Alexander Hamilton, reasoned that the phrase meant that once the government had collected the tax money it could spend it for any purpose benefiting the general welfare as distinguished from private welfare, without regard to the existence of direct Congressional control of the object of expenditure.

This controversy was intensified by the gradual development of the Federal Government's policy of making *grants* to the states. This policy was criticized on the grounds that it amounted to giving the states bribes to get them to do things that the Federal Government could not itself do under the Constitution. In these cases and in other cases the general trend of the decisions of the United States Supreme Court has been to sustain the broader view of the spending power, as illustrated, for example, in its decision upholding the Federal Social Security Act of 1935.*

## THE EXPENDITURE PROCESS

So large are the expenditures of the Federal Government and so inadequate is the process by which the budget of expenditures is arranged and decided on that some count it a miracle that the business is done at all, while others insist that Federal expenditures have gotten entirely out of hand.

The Constitution states, in Article 1, Section 9, ". . . no money shall be drawn from the Treasury but in consequence of appropriations made by law. . . ." The legal authorization must, of course, come from the Congress. Congress, however, does not take the lead in planning the appropriating process. The President does this. But the Congress does not necessarily go along with the President's plans. The President proposes; the Congress disposes.

---

* In *Helvering v. Davis* 301 U.S. 619 (1937).

Federal expenditures, like other large-scale expenditures, must be planned a long time in advance. The fiscal year of the Federal Government runs from July 1 of one year to June 30 of the following year and is numbered by the year in which it ends.

The planning for the expenditures of a fiscal year begins more than a year in advance of the starting date. In March or April, each year, the Bureau of the Budget begins to make some preliminary estimates of future expenditures. These estimates may originate as requests from the individual agencies, or the Bureau may initiate their preparation. The Bureau reviews the estimates and, after consultation with the agencies, prepares consolidated estimates for their expenditures.

Work continues in the months that follow, and in the following January the President submits to the Congress the figures which in his judgment represent the expenditure needs of the entire Government, for which appropriations should be made for the twelve-month period beginning on the following July 1. This "message" is bound in a large volume entitled *The Budget of the United States Government.*

After the budget is submitted to the Congress it is referred to the House Appropriations Committee, where it is separated into its several parts; these are referred to the appropriate subcommittees of the Appropriations Committee. These parts thereafter become the bases for the various appropriations bills which the Congress considers.

It is significant that the budget of expenditures is never considered as a single document by the Congress, in one piece of legislation. Each subcommittee of the Appropriations Committee holds hearings, prepares an appropriation bill, and reports it to the full Committee; then the bill moves through the normal legislative channels. Each bill is acted upon independently, and all are usually passed by the end of June or early July.

## THE APPROPRIATING PROCESS

The first step in the expenditure of money by the Federal Government is that of *legislative authorization.* This involves the passage of a law by the Congress expressing a basic public policy, for example, on foreign aid or agricultural price supports. Such legislative authorization bills originate in committees other than the Appropriations Committee. In the instances cited they would originate in the Foreign Affairs Committee and the Agriculture Committee, respectively.

The next step is the provision of new *obligational authority,* an authorization by the Congress to an executive agency to commit the government to a specific expenditure or a number of them. The most common form of this authority is the ordinary appropriation. It permits the executive branch to incur obligations and provides the funds to discharge them.

The next step is that of actual *obligation*. The governmental agency given the appropriation obligates the funds—for example, by placing orders for goods.

The final step is *expenditure*—the actual disbursement of funds through government checks as the government pays its bills and its employees.

## THE TAXING POWER

The Constitution empowers the Congress to lay and collect taxes. The taxing power is a *concurrent* power; state and local governments also may exercise it, although the Federal power is supreme in the event of conflict. In this chapter we are concerned with taxes as a method of raising revenue rather than with taxes as a business stabilization device or as regulatory measures. Attention is given in the next chapter and in Chapter 10 to these other aspects of taxation.

By far the largest source of Federal tax revenue is the income tax— the personal income tax and the corporation income tax. This was not always the situation. Prior to the adoption of the Sixteenth Amendment, in 1913, the principal source of revenue of the Federal Government was customs duties.

The financial gods must have been on the side of the United States in World War I because the income tax amendment and the Federal Reserve Act both had been enacted in 1913, shortly before our entry into the struggle. The former provided the basis for raising billions of dollars in taxation and the latter the basis for billions of dollars of the most orthodox manner of creating money. Between these two sources the government had no difficulty in financing World War I. It is hard to imagine, however, how the struggle could have been financed without both of these sources of money.

The Sixteenth Amendment came about in consequence of that passage in the Constitution (Article I, Section 9) which says: "No capitation, or other direct, tax shall be laid, unless in proportion to the census or enumeration hereinbefore directed to be taken." A capitation tax is a head or poll tax. The writers of the Constitution, however, in keeping with the sound philosophy of providing a reasonably short document, had not defined the term *direct tax*. Until 1895 the courts had interpreted this term to mean taxes levied upon the owners of property. In that year, however, the Supreme Court decided that the income tax, which had been enacted in 1894, was a direct tax. The decision went on to note that since this tax was not apportioned according to population, it was unconstitutional.*

And so, in due course, in 1913 the need for a Federal income tax resulted in the adoption of the Sixteenth Amendment. It says simply, "The Congress shall have power to lay and collect taxes on incomes, from what-

* *Pollock v. Farmers' Loan and Trust Company* 158 U.S. 601 (1895).

ever source derived, without apportionment among the several states, and without regard to any census or enumeration."

When the proposed amendment was being debated in the Congress, opponents pointed out that if the amendment were adopted there would be nothing to prevent a future Congress from taking not merely 1 per cent of a man's income, but 5 per cent, or 10 per cent, or even 25 per cent. Others rose to their feet to protest that the danger was only an imaginary one; they asserted that no Congress could possibly do such a thing or survive if it did.

Times change. Today the tax on corporation incomes is 52 per cent. Taxes on personal incomes rise with rising incomes at increasing rates; the highest bracket on the amount of taxable income in excess of $1,-000,000 a year is 91 per cent.

One of the current issues of public policy is whether these tax rates are so high that they are having an adverse effect on economic growth in the United States. This question is taken up in the next chapter.

A significant feature of the financial operations of the Federal Government is that, in the Congress, revenues and expenditures are dealt with by different committees. In the House of Representatives (where, by the Constitution, such bills must originate) revenue measures are considered by the Ways and Means Committee; but expenditures are taken up by the Appropriation Committee. In the Senate, the corresponding committees are the Finance Committee and the Appropriations Committee. The committees considering the two sides of the budget—the income and the outgo—act independently of each other. There is no formal machinery for providing coordination. This condition, in addition to the piecemeal consideration of appropriations in separate bills, represents part of the loose-jointed system whose continued operation amazes some persons, baffles others, and appalls many.

## THE BUREAU OF THE BUDGET

That the creaking Federal financial machinery functions as well as it does is due largely to the existence of the Bureau of the Budget. Because of its importance, in both a financial and a management sense, acquaintance with its operation is essential to the student of government.

A useful—indeed, an almost startling—way of grasping the significance and importance of the Bureau of the Budget is to examine financial procedures prior to its creation in 1921. Before then the President played only a small part in the development of the Federal budget and in the expenditures of the funds provided by Congressional appropriations. Estimates of the expenditures were submitted individually to Congress, via the Secretary of the Treasury, by the various departments, bureaus, and agencies. There was no requirement for Presidential review or clearance or for coordination into a consolidated operating program.

Congress reviewed these estimates in several unrelated and uncoordinated committees, and appropriations were enacted on the basis of reports from these. The departments and agencies then spent their appropriations with little or no regard for the operations of other agencies of the government or for any central executive control. Under this arrangement the President was little more than a nominal business manager of the executive branch. What leadership he provided was often achieved only through force of personality.

Serious consideration of better executive coordination of Federal spending dates back to 1910, with the creation of President Taft's Commission on Economy and Efficiency. The recommendations of this Commission, however, brought no results. Very shortly, however, two developments increased the pressure for a better Federal budgetary system. These were World War I, with its greatly increased expenditures, and the establishment of the income tax.

Budgetary order was finally secured by the passage of the Budget and Accounting Act of 1921. This act created the Bureau of the Budget and provided for the development of a single coordinated Federal budget and the appointment of a designated budget officer for each agency. Congress originally was divided on the organizational placement of the new agency. Some favored independent status under the President; some, a subordinate agency under the Secretary of the Treasury. As a compromise, the Bureau was placed *in* the Treasury Department, but subordinate to the President. It remained under this odd arrangement for 18 years.

The Reorganization Act of 1939 transferred the Bureau to the Executive Office of the President, where its prestige and authority have continued to grow. The Bureau's early authority was extensive, including the powers to assemble, correlate, revise, reduce, and increase the estimates of the several departments and establishments. Gradually, the Bureau's functions were extended to include budget formulation and processing, fiscal planning and policy making, and eventually, administrative organization and management.

Ultimately, the Bureau came to exercise control through advice on pending legislation, the implementation of policy as determined by the administration, and staff surveillance of the operations of the Executive Branch of the government. Since the Executive Branch comprises most of the Federal Government, the Bureau has advisory influence over most Federal activities.

This listing of functions emphasizes the fact that the Bureau has come to be a vital part of the mechanism of the Executive Branch and a right hand to the President in the administration of the affairs of the government.

The Bureau is headed by a director and other senior officers. It has five operating offices. They are named Budget Review, Legislative Reference,

Management and Organization, Statistical Standards, and Accounting. In addition, it has five divisions, each of which is concerned with a broad segment of the Government's operations. The divisions' names are Commerce and Finance, International, Labor and Welfare, Military, and Resources and Civil Works, and each is associated with an appropriate grouping of the departments and agencies of the Executive branch. Each division works directly with, and specializes in the affairs of, its group of departments and agencies; and the offices serve in a functional staff capacity to assist the divisions, but with direct access, for some purposes, to the executive entities and with some independent responsibilities across the board.

Each division, within its program area, examines agency requests for funds, continuously follows the execution of the budget, and reviews and develops recommendations on proposed legislation. It also works with the agencies with which it is concerned to assist them in improving their management and organization, and it undertakes special projects for them, including those related to budgetary and fiscal analysis and organizational planning.

The Bureau has about five hundred employees and its annual budget is about $5 million.

## THE GENERAL ACCOUNTING OFFICE

Whereas the Bureau of the Budget is the administrative right hand of the President, the General Accounting Office is the watchdog of the Congress. This despite the fact that the GAO is under the direction of the Comptroller General of the United States, who is appointed by the President (true, with the advice and consent of the Senate) for a term of 15 years.

The purpose of the General Accounting Office is to perform an independent audit of government financial transactions, thus providing a basis for the settlement of accounts, as well as for determining how well the agencies are managing their financial affairs. It scrutinizes expenditures for their legality, and it has the power to disallow expenditures. It audits receipts, disbursements, and the use of public funds. It performs investigations relating to these matters, and it reports to the Congress the results of its activities and its findings and presents recommendations on measures to improve governmental financial operations.

The Comptroller General may, upon request of the President, make recommendations to him; and he is required to make reports to the Congress regularly and upon special order. He analyzes the expenditures of each agency of the Executive Branch of the Government, including government corporations, in order to enable the Congress to determine whether public funds have been economically and efficiently utilized.

It should be noted that the inspection is for expenditures with respect to the laws *as enacted*; it is not the function of the General Accounting Office to decide whether Federal funds should be spent for fighting wars, or for schools, or for sheer frippery, but merely to determine whether they have been used appropriately as stipulated by law.

## DEPARTMENT OF THE TREASURY

The Department of the Treasury handles the government's money. Most of the money is collected by the Internal Revenue Service. It is with this Service that citizens deal in making income tax payments.

The money thus collected is turned over to the Office of the Treasurer of the United States.* This office is essentially the banking facility for the government. It receives money, pays it out, accounts for it, maintains bank accounts in many banks, furnishes checking account facilities to the agencies of the Government, is responsible for the payment of principal and interest on public debt obligations, and makes daily reports of the position of the Treasury, in addition to less frequent reports. Like natural persons and corporations, the Treasurer needs a working balance which is kept in numerous bank accounts. This cash balance currently is about $5 billion—a large sum, but one presumably not excessive in view of the magnitude of the inflow and outflow of cash in the Federal Government accounts.

## STATE AND LOCAL GOVERNMENT FINANCES

Before World War I (as shown in Tables 6.1 and 6.2) the combined total of the financial operations of state and local governments was about twice that of the Federal Government. Today this total—although there are more than a hundred thousand of these governments—is only about half that of the Federal Government.

However, inasmuch as defense expenditures and interest on the national debt have become so large, it is possible that a more meaningful comparison is to be had by looking at the Federal expenditures other than those in these two categories, that is, at what might be called the civilian operations of the Federal Government. This total is somewhat smaller than the combined total for the state and local governments, and in recent years the latter has been growing more rapidly than has the Federal Government's figure.

State and local governments spend more for education than for any other single function. Highways are second, followed by public welfare

---

* Traditionally, the appointment as Treasurer goes to a woman. Her signature (probably unnoticed by most Americans) appears on our paper currency.

and health and hospitals. Other expenditures are spread over the many other functions, chronological listings of which are presented in Chapter 4.

Table 6.2 contains the figures. Variation in the per capita amounts of state and local government revenues among the states are very large. In 1957 they ranged from a low of $100.94 in Alabama to a high of $237.87 in California. The national average was $169.14.

Inasmuch as average incomes differ among the states, it is appropriate also to compare these tax bills with the average incomes of the people of the several states. Inspection of state and local "tax bites" shows that some of the poorer states tax their people rather heavily in proportion to their incomes and also shows a very large range. In North Dakota, in 1957, state and local taxes took $116.33 out of every $1,000.00 of personal income. The average for all states was $99.40. At the other extreme, Delaware governmental units taxed their people only $48.96 per $1,000.00 of personal income.*

The earmarking of taxes has come to be a major public policy problem in many states. In some states provisions of the state constitutions stipulate that certain taxes may go only for certain types of expenditures or to certain agencies of state or local governments. In other states the proportion of state government receipts thus earmarked is more than one half. The remainder—sometimes called the "general fund"—is subject to appropriation by the state legislatures. The legislatures, however, cannot touch any of the funds that are earmarked for specific destinations.

The growing burden of state and local expenditures and, correlatively, of taxation, and changes in the conditions which had originally given rise to the earmarking of tax revenues, have brought about a condition in which these constitutional provisions are being criticized in many states. Naturally, the status quo is defended by the beneficiaries of the existing constitutional arrangements. Since the earmarking is provided for in constitutions, it cannot be altered by acts of the legislatures, and constitutional amendment is difficult.

The outlook is for a continuing increase in the public demand for state and local government services. This will intensify the financial problems of these governmental units. One result will be more discussion of earmarked monies and of the authority of municipalities to levy taxes of new kinds. If these accommodations are not made, and made properly, the tendency to look to the Federal Government, referred to in Chapter 4, will be further stimulated. The problem of state and local expenditures and taxes, therefore, is closely associated with the large problem of the proper relationships between the Federal Government on the one hand and the other governments on the other and its allied problems of centralization versus decentralization of government in the United States.

* U.S. Bureau of the Census, *State and Local Government Finances in 1957* (Washington, D.C.: Bureau of the Census, 1958), p. 17.

## QUESTIONS AND PROBLEMS

1. What is the difference between fiscal policy and public finance?
2. What are your views on the "public poverty, private plenty" proposition?
3. If you believe that governments are spending too much money, where would you recommend economizing?
4. How does the U.S. "tax bite" compare with those of other nations?
5. What are the similarities and the differences among the four Federal Government budgets? Is it desirable to have four? That is, why not have *one*?
6. Do you believe that any changes should be made in the Congressional appropriations process?
7. What are the functions of the Bureau of the Budget?
8. What are the duties of the Comptroller General and the General Accounting Office?
9. What are the financial activities of the Department of the Treasury?

## SELECTED READINGS

BLOUGH, ROY. *Federal Taxing Process.* Englewood Cliffs, N.J.: Prentice-Hall, Inc., 1952.

BUCHANAN, JAMES M. *Public Finances.* Homewood, Ill.: Richard D. Irwin, Inc., 1960.

GROVES, HAROLD M. *Financing Government,* 5th ed. New York: Holt, Rinehart, & Winston, Inc., 1958.

KIMMEL, LEWIS H. *Federal Budget and Fiscal Policy, 1789–1958.* Washington, D.C.: The Brookings Institution, 1959.

SCHILLING, WARNER R., and others. *Strategy, Politics, and Defense Budgets.* New York: Columbia University Press, 1962.

SHULTZ, WILLIAM J., and C. LOWELL HARRISS. *American Public Finance,* 7th ed. Englewood Cliffs, N.J.: Prentice-Hall, Inc., 1959.

SMITH, D. T. *Federal Tax Reform.* New York: McGraw-Hill Company, 1961.

STRAYER, PAUL J. *Fiscal Policy and Politics.* New York: Harper and Brothers, 1958.

Tax Foundation, Inc. *Facts and Figures on Government Finance,* 11th ed. Englewood Cliffs, N.J.: Prentice-Hall, Inc., 1961.

# 7 GOVERNMENT FINANCE:
## Principles and Problems

A tax is a compulsory payment collected for the support of the government. Its amount is determined by its *rate* and *base*. The rate and base may be X dollars per $1,000 of taxable income, Y dollars per $100 of assessed property valuation, Z cents per dollar of retail sales, or any of many other formulae. Whatever the rate and base, the tax is paid by persons—natural and corporate. Tax money, therefore, comes out of private income or wealth. The well-known saying "Nothing is certain but death and taxes" links what are presumably regarded as two undesirable items. Few seem to agree with the proposition that with taxes one buys civilization and that, therefore, one should not mind paying the price. Many persons seem to believe that the only good tax is one that is paid by someone else. The higher the level of taxes, the more controversial they are, and potentially the more significant their economic effects. An examination of the criteria for good taxes and good groups of taxes provides an objective basis for planning and appraising tax policy. The following are some of the principal criteria that are used for this purpose.

[1] Productivity. A tax should produce substantial sums of money. A tax which does not do so, which produces only pennies, has little to commend it, because it is failing in its primary purpose—to provide money for the operations of government. If one could imagine a tax which is perfect according to all other criteria but produces very little money, it could only be regarded as inferior to a tax that is mildly unsatisfactory according to one or more criteria, but produces adequate amounts of needed revenue.

[2] Economy. Collecting taxes costs money. The costs may run from less than one cent per dollar up to several cents. The costs include not only the money costs (to the government) of the tax-collecting agency, but also the costs and efforts incurred by the taxpayers (for example, in keeping records and in preparing tax returns for corporate and personal income taxes). Obviously, a community accomplishes exactly nothing except pointless effort if it spends one dollar in costs to collect one dollar in tax money. Economy in collection is desirable.

[3] Legal certainty. A tax should be defined in the tax law as precisely as possible, so that both taxpayers and government agents understand exactly the amount of the tax and the circumstances of its collection. A badly drafted tax law which gives rise to uncertainty about these matters leads to litigation, confusion, and dissatisfaction.

[4] Economic (or operational) certainty. This criterion has to do with practical collectibility. Pertinent here is the difference between *avoiding* and *evading* taxes. Avoiding taxes involves legal actions that can be taken by taxpayers to reduce their taxes. For example, if a taxpayer makes a gift to a recognized charitable institution within the provisions of the personal income tax law, he thereby reduces his tax. This is quite proper, and has no bearing on economic certainty. Evasion of taxes, on the other hand, refers to unlawful nonpayment of taxes. The taxpayer who deliberately fails to report income in his income tax return is evading, and the criterion of economic certainty requires that this should be difficult to do both successfully and frequently. It is sometimes alleged that the personal income tax in the United States is such a tax; and one of our important public policy problems is how much reporting and enforcement are required in order to reduce evasion by the dishonest and unscrupulous. (A link with the economy criterion will be noted here.) Evasion of personal income taxes in some foreign countries is reported to be so widespread that well-to-do taxpayers there regularly keep two sets of books and declare only small fractions of their true incomes for tax purposes. It will be seen that where evasion is prevalent, what is being taxed is not incomes but honesty.

[5] Convenience of payment. One of the arguments that has been used in support of the adoption of the system of withholding personal income taxes at the source, by having employers deduct stated amounts from the paychecks of employees, is that this makes the payment of the income tax more convenient for the taxpayer. It avoids the inconvenience of a taxpayer's having to make a large payment in the spring covering the entire amount of his tax. General sales taxes and specific excises such as cigarette taxes are often defended on the same ground, the argument being that the tax is paid gradually as the taxpayer buys the products—a little at a time instead of in one large lump sum once a year.

[6] Justice; and [7] Nonrepressiveness. These criteria are of such complexity that their discussion covers a large part of the remainder of this chapter.

## JUSTICE IN TAXATION

Attempts to explain the criterion of justice frequently associate it with such words as fairness and equitableness. Unfortunately for simple analysis, the importance of justice is equaled by its complexity. The complexity flows in part from the very difficulty of the concept itself.

Philosophers have been wrestling with the question "What is justice?" for a long time. Some have contended that it really has no scientifically valid answer.

A definition that is of special interest in today's troubled world and also especially significant in the study of political economy is that of Professor Thomas Nixon Carver. He wrote, "In the most general terms, therefore, justice may be defined as such an adjustment of the conflicting interests of the citizens of a nation as will interfere least with and contribute most to the strength of the nation."*

Inasmuch as one of the elements of the strength of a nation is its economic strength, this definition ties the concept of justice to that of non-repressiveness in a particularly vivid way.

The first difficulty, then, in appraising the justice of a tax or a tax system is that of defining the thing we are trying to measure.

A second reason for the difficulty in assaying the justice of a tax flows from the fact of tax *shifting*. This concept involves recognition of the difference between the *legal payer* of a tax and the *economic payer*. The law defies the legal prayer. He, however, either individually or through the operation of market forces, may be able to recoup some or all of the tax by shifting the economic payment onto someone else. A tax may be shifted forward onto the buyers of goods and services or backward onto the sellers. A property tax collected from the owner of an apartment house may, in fact, be paid in part or entirely by the tenants.

If the tax is not so shifted, it is said to be *absorbed* by the legal payer, and he is then the economic payer also. If it is shifted, however, the *incidence* of the tax is on someone other than the legal payer.

Not only does shifting of taxes occur, but also (complicating further the analysis of justice) it is difficult or impossible to determine with accuracy how much shifting actually occurs. Scholars write learned papers on this subject—and disagree with one another. Some taxes are held to be shifted more than others. The extent of shifting may differ among commodities and industries or according to times and places. Obviously, if we cannot say who really pays the tax, it is impossible to evaluate the justice of a tax as long as the concept of justice involves the measurement of the amounts paid by specific economic taxpayers.

If the foregoing discussion has created the impression that a tax is either (1) not shifted at all or (2) shifted completely, let a correction be made. Both of the aforementioned possibilities exist, of course. There is, however, another possibility—*partial shifting*, in which a larger or smaller portion of the tax is ultimately paid by the legal payer and the remainder is shifted to someone else who, to only this extent, becomes the economic payer of the tax.

So elusive is the problem of scientific analysis of the shifting and

* T. N. Carver, *Essays in Social Justice* (Cambridge: Harvard University Press, 1925), p. 9.

incidence of taxation that generalizations are risky. Nevertheless, the opinion may be ventured that partial shifting is at least as common as zero shifting or complete shifting; indeed, partial shifting may be the general situation.

A phenomenon that is equally hard to identify is that of *apparent shifting*. Apparent shifting occurs when conditions make it appear that the tax has been shifted to a larger extent than is in fact true. A hypothetical example will illustrate. If an article which is subject to a 20 per cent excise tax shows on the price ticket a price of 80 cents and a tax of 16 cents, for a total of 96 cents, it may appear that the tax is being entirely paid by the purchaser of the article rather than by the seller from whom the tax is actually collected. This, however, is not necessarily true. If there had been no tax at all, it is possible that the actual price of the product would have been 96 cents or any other price between that amount and 80 cents. In other words, although this price tag shows indisputably that someone is paying a 16-cent tax in connection with the sale of the article, it is not conclusive evidence that that someone is the buyer. The fact may be that the tax has not been shifted at all or has been shifted only partially.

## THEORIES OF JUSTICE IN TAXATION

The concept of justice is further complicated by disagreement about theories of its application. One theory suggests that taxes should be collected according to the *benefit* that taxpayers get from the resultant governmental activities. The main difficulty with this rule is that the benefit may be hard to measure. For example, how much benefit does any given family get from the nation's enormous expenditures on national defense? In connection with a few public expenditures such as that for paving a street in a residential area it is often considered that the principal benefit accrues to the people who own property on the street, and recognition of this fact leads to a special nomenclature for collections to finance this; they are called *special assessments* because they are levied on only these beneficiaries.

Education poses a special problem. No doubt the principal beneficiaries of education are the persons who get the education—the children and the young people whose economic and noneconomic well-being throughout their adult lives is increased by it. When they are children, however, they have no money to pay taxes. Should education taxes, then, be collected as a kind of special fee from their parents? Doing so might mean that the children of very poor parents would get little education and that inherited poverty would therefore survive from generation to generation. Public policy in our country favors the idea that education should be free for the specific purpose of benefiting poor families. Thus in this case there is a deliberate rejection of the benefit theory because it is considered to be unsound public policy.

The benefit theory has another weakness, inherent in the simple fact that the services that clearly benefit specific people are the ones that private enterprise quite naturally aims to supply, at a price. One of the special functions of government is to provide services that cannot be sold over the counter, that are hard to measure and hard to collect for, that for one reason or another it would be unreasonable or impossible to charge in full or in equitable proportion to the beneficiaries.

The difficulties of the benefit theory have led many analysts in their quest for justice to favor the *ability to pay* theory. Ability to pay is most commonly measured by *income*. The proposition is that the tax paid should bear an appropriate relation to the income.

There is disagreement about the nature of that appropriate relationship. If the tax rises in exact proportion to the increase in income, so that it is an unchanging percentage of the income, the tax is called *proportional*. If the tax increases more slowly than the income, so that the percentage goes down, it is a *regressive* tax. If the tax increases faster than the income, so that the percentage goes up as the income rises, the tax is labeled *progressive*.

Few analysts favor regressive taxes. The real argument is between proportional and progressive taxes and, given progressive taxes, how high their rates should go. The United States personal income tax takes 91 per cent of a man's taxable personal income in excess of $1 million a year. It also takes 52 per cent of most corporations' income (profits) after a very small exemption.

The ability-to-pay criterion and the argument about proportional versus progressive taxes must also take into account the fact that individuals pay many taxes. Presumably the criterion of justice applies not solely to an individual tax, but to all taxes in the aggregate. An individual's total tax payments must be added up and related to his income in any thoroughgoing evaluation by this criterion. One tax may be progressive; another, regressive. Thus analysis shows that despite the exemption of certain kinds of income from the personal income tax (such as interest on municipal bonds), this tax is, in general, progressive. Conversely, a general sales tax is regressive because, in general, the poorer the family, the larger the proportion of its income that is spent on products subject to the sales tax and, therefore, the larger the fraction these payments are of the family income. If these two taxes and others are just about balanced off so that families in general pay the same constant percentage of their incomes in total taxes, this would satisfy the advocate of proportional taxation. By the same token, of course, it would not satisfy the advocate of progressive taxation.

## TAXES AND ECONOMIC ACTIVITY

Nonrepressiveness as a criterion means that taxation should discourage production and productivity gains as little as possible. Indeed, if possible, it should actually encourage high and rising production and productivity. (To anticipate a subject that is to be discussed in a moment, the total effect of government finance on production depends not only on the tax receipts side, but also on the expenditures side. Many tax-supported activities, such as education, are justified on the grounds that the total operation *stimulates* production and productivity gains.)

The impact of taxes on economic activity is of great importance. Once again we may note that its importance is matched by its complexity and perhaps also by the heat of the disagreement and controversy that attend its discussion. For example, frequent have been the statements in recent years that today's high level of taxation in the United States is slowly but surely strangling the economy. It is asserted that the tax load is destroying the incentive of people to work hard. It is claimed that it is both making it impossible to save and invest and reducing the incentive to provide new capital for American industry. It is stated that it is injuring the spirit of enterprise and reducing the desire to innovate. It is averred that our level of taxation and our types of taxation are responsible for the fact that the rate of economic growth in the United States in recent years has been lower than corresponding rates in some other countries.

In contradiction, it is argued that these statements are not backed up by any substantial evidence and are merely assertions. It is suggested in rebuttal that the American people are, in fact, working hard, that the spirit of enterprise is still active, and that, specifically, many professional men, such as independent lawyers and physicians (who can control their own hours of work), seem to be working too hard, rather than taking long, tax-reducing vacations. Indeed, it is sometimes suggested that the personal income tax *stimulates* economic activity, for if a man wants to make a million, the higher the personal income tax, the harder he has to work in order to have the million left after paying it. It is pointed out that the rate of saving and investing as a percentage of national income and output has remained steady and that, indeed, additional investing, unless accompanied by a reduction of expenditures on consumer goods, might be mainly inflationary in its effect. It is contended that if the rate of economic growth in the United States is slower than it is in other countries, the cause must be something other than taxation, because many of those countries have larger tax bills relative to their economies than we do.

The scientific inquiries that have been made by careful scholars to try to ascertain the truth about the impacts of specific taxes upon economic activity reach two conclusions. One is that determining the truth is difficult if not impossible; the other is that, as far as the analysts can make out, the impact does not seem to be very great.

## HOW MUCH TAXATION CAN A NATION STAND?

Some of the discussion of this matter revolves around Colin Clark's well-known "25-per-cent rule." Clark's proposition is that 25 per cent appears to be about the limit that a nontotalitarian government can take from its people in time of peace without unfortunate consequences on production and in inflation. Since the total of taxation in the United States is now well above that 25 per cent, it is appropriate to ask this key question: How much taxation can a nation stand—as a percentage of its national income? It is the proportion and not the absolute amount that is important, because a nation with a large national income can stand a larger tax bill than one with a small national income.

Examination of this problem can perhaps be facilitated by the use of an analogy (with the full understanding that no analogy ever proves anything): How heavy a load can a man carry as a percentage of his own weight?

Discussion of this problem, which involves concepts familiar to all of us, does not get to far before we find ourselves asking some supplementary questions. The first question might be; How far? If the course over which the man is to carry the weight is a short one, the percentage will be higher than if it is long. And this is true also in tax matters. The longer the tax lasts (or, strictly speaking, the longer the people expect it to last), the smaller will be the tax that can be carried.

In the case of the porter we might next ask, How strong is he? Is he old, feeble, or sick; or is he young, muscular, and vigorous? Similarly the health of a nation's economy, the vigor of its economic system, have a bearing on the tax problem.

Next, the motivation of the man affects how much he can carry. The more intense the motivation, the higher the bearable load. This is true of taxation also. If a nation is at war and its young people are losing their lives on the battlefield, the citizenry can stand a higher level of taxation without cutting their production than they can when the motivation is weaker.

The distribution of the burden may influence the answer for the man. If his load is in a rectangular wooden box, so that no matter how he attempts to put it on his shoulders it squeezes nerves, muscles, and arteries, he will be able to carry less than if the load were distributed uniformly over his back and shoulders in a soft pack. So it is with taxation; the distribution of the tax load is important. Do the taxes impinge on any financial or economic muscles, nerves, or arteries? If so, their repressive effect will be greater and the bearable tax load smaller.

An important psychological factor in determining the size of the load that a man can carry is what he is accustomed to doing. If, over a period of time, he has been carrying gradually heavier and heavier loads, he may eventually get to the point where he confidently shoulders a load whose weight would have appalled or frightened him at the beginning. He is not worried because by now he knows what he can do; past achievement has given him confidence and he goes ahead without debilitating doubt or fear. Taxation follows the same rule. If today's level of income taxation—up to 91 per cent of the top part of a rich man's income and 52 per cent of a corporation's income—had been put into effect immediately after the ratification of the Sixteenth Amendment in 1913, it is possible that the economic machine of the United States would have ground to a stop within a few days. This, however, was not done. Income tax rates started at a very modest level; were raised during World War I; were pushed up substantially during World War II; were reduced very little thereafter; and have stayed at high levels in recent years, for the first time in peacetime. In 1913 a rate of 50 per cent on the top increments of personal income or a rate of 25 per cent on corporation income would probably have been regarded as unbearable. Today a drop to such rates would bring cheers. This does not mean that this tax burden is having no adverse affects, but that the psychological weight of this heavy load is diminished by the fact that we have gradually become accustomed to it.

The content of the load may make a difference to the answer in the case of the porter of our analogy. If, for example, the course is a long one through a desert country, the amount that he will be able to carry across the finish line will be greater if the package includes some drinking water and some nourishing food, even though what is consumed en route is not part of the final, measured pay load. The way in which the tax money is spent affects the answer to the tax problem. If the tax money is spent in wasteful ways, the maximum answer will be reduced. If, on the other hand, it is spent for useful consumer goods (such as school lunches) or in ways that increase the productivity of the people (such as for good education), then the allowable tax burden becomes bigger.

What emerges from this discussion? The answer to the question "How much taxation can a nation stand?" turns out to be this: *It depends.* This is perhaps not a very satisfactory answer, but it at least has the merit of being completely and indisputably correct. In contrast, any answer which purports to say that 25 per cent or any other percentage figure is the maximum that a nation can stand is deceptive in its specificity. It *is* precise—but it is not true and necessarily so.

## THE OUTLOOK FOR FEDERAL TAXES

If governmental budgets are to be approximately in balance, the total of taxes and the total of expenditures go together. What, then, is the outlook for the total of expenditures, and therefore for the total of taxes, in the United States? May we expect that today's heavy burden of taxation will continue indefinitely into the future, or is there a possibility that it can be reduced?

Inspection of Federal expenditures shows that more than half of the budget goes for national defense. Can this immense expenditure be reduced safely? May it actually have to be increased in the future? The international situation holds the answer to these questions.

Another large Federal expenditure is interest on the public debt. This amount is largely governed by conditions in the money market over which the government has little control. Other large expenditures are those for veterans' benefits and for agriculture. In view of the political power of veterans and farm organizations one may question whether substantial reductions in these amounts would be practically feasible. In the rest of the Federal budget there are no doubt some opportunities for cutting costs. Their aggregate, however, must surely be a very small percentage of the total.

The tentative conclusion, therefore, is that Federal expenditures are unlikely to be reduced much and, indeed, because of the growth of the country, are more likely to be increased—at least until the international situation takes a marked turn for the better. By corollary the same is true of Federal tax rates.

## PROPOSED FEDERAL TAX CHANGES

If the total Federal tax bill is not to be reduced, perhaps its composition may be altered. Changes in Federal taxes are proposed in a steady stream. Some of the proposals are worthy of little attention. Others, however, deserve careful consideration.

One such proposal is to reduce the top bracket rate of the personal income tax to a maximum of 50 per cent—so that, in other words, the government does not take more than one half of the top increment of any man's income. The total revenue that would be lost to the Federal Government by this move would be small because, although 91 per cent of the top of a multimillionaire's income may be a handsome sum by itself, there are not many persons in this bracket, and in the aggregate, the yield from them is small compared to the total tax bill.

It has also been suggested that the corporation income tax rate, which is now 30 per cent on the first $25,000 of corporate income and 52 per cent on all income above that, should be reduced.

Another question is whether too much income is exempted or deducted from personal income on which the Federal tax is paid. As will be seen from Table 7.1, the total amount of taxable income in 1959 ($167.9 billion) was less than half the total of the personal incomes of the American people ($383.3 billion). The fact that some income is not subject to the personal income tax is of course to be expected—if there is to be any exemption of small incomes at all. The question which is raised by the facts covered by this table, however, is whether the exclusions are too large. Questions of both justice (involving structure) and repressiveness (involving level) are part of this problem.

Closely related to the personal exemption and deduction problem is the business deduction problem; the question of what are sometimes called "loopholes" in the income tax—legal provisions that reduce taxes. Possibly the most famous of these is the oil depletion allowance. Although there are a hundred other products which also have automatic depletion provisions (including almost everything except *dirt*), oil is the one that gets the principal attention. In computing profits from the operations of oil drilling and extraction it is altogether proper to make some allowance for the fact that the asset is gradually being depleted as the oil is taken out of the ground and to subtract from revenues, in computing net income, a figure representing this exhaustion. The right amount, however, is difficult to estimate. Long ago Congress provided that an oil operator could take off 27.5 per cent of his income as a depletion allowance. This figure is large enough so that it greatly reduces the stated income and, therefore, the taxes payable. Those who believe that this depletion percentage is considerably in excess of the proper amount point out that the excess is really a subsidy to the oil producers. On the face of the matter this appears to be true. In fact, however, the result may be that it encourages investment in petroleum exploration and development and has the end result of making the price of gasoline lower than it otherwise would be. If so, the subsidy is to the buyers of gasoline.

The depletion allowance may or may not be justified. But this is only one detail—there are thousands of business and personal deductions and exemptions. As Table 7.1 shows, more than half of the personal income of the people of the United States is excluded in one way or another from taxable income. The real question, therefore, is the much larger one: What elements of income should be subject to tax, and what elements should go untaxed?

*Table 7.1*

## TAXABLE AND NONTAXABLE INCOMES

[In Billions of Dollars]

|                        | 1959    |
|------------------------|---------|
| Personal income        | $383.3  |
| Deduct:                |         |
| Transfer payments      | 27.0    |

| | 1959 |
|---|---|
| Other labor income | 10.1 |
| Imputed interest | 10.0 |
| Imputed rent | 7.0 |
| Nontaxable military pay | 2.0 |
| Income in kind[1] | 3.5 |
| All other deductions[2] | 7.9 |
| Total deductions | 67.5 |
| Add: | |
| Employee contributions for social insurance | 7.8 |
| Net capital gains | 6.4 |
| All other additions[3] | 5.1 |
| Total additions | 19.3 |
| Personal income adjusted | 335.1 |
| Income not reported on tax returns[4] | 27.9 |
| Adjusted gross income reported on tax returns[5] | 307.2 |
| Adjusted gross income, nontaxable returns | 18.7 |
| Adjusted gross income of taxable returns | 288.5 |
| Deduct: | |
| Standard deduction[6] | 12.1 |
| Itemized deductions[6] | 29.5 |
| Personal exemptions | 79.9 |
| Taxable income of individuals | 167.0 |
| Taxable income of fiduciaries[6] | .9 |
| Total taxable income | 167.9 |
| Tax liability of individuals, statistics of income basis | 38.9 |
| Tax liability of fiduciaries[6] | .3 |
| Adjustment to collections basis[7] | .7 |
| Tax liability, collections basis | 39.9 |
| Effective tax rate (per cent)[8] | 23.3% |

[1] Including food and fuel consumed on farms.
[2] Tax-exempt interest and savings bonds accruals, inventory items, excludable sick pay and dividends, undistributed fiduciary income, dividends and interest reported as capital gains, and so on.
[3] Income from Alaska and Hawaii, miscellaneous reported income, annuities, and pensions.
[4] Includes income of persons not required to file, income disclosed by audit, income of tax evaders, estimating errors in personal income, sampling errors in Statistics of Income, and so on.
[5] Returns with positive adjusted gross income.
[6] Estimated.
[7] Includes tax adjustments, interest, and penalties arising from income of earlier years.
[8] Effective rate on taxable income, after tax credits.
NOTE: Figures are rounded and do not necessarily add to totals.
SOURCE: Joint Economic Committee, *The Federal Revenue System: Facts and Problems* (Washington, D.C.: U.S. Government Printing Office, 1961), p. 10.

## PROPER SOURCES OF
## FEDERAL REVENUE

Another problem is whether our governmental entities rely too much on taxes on income and capital and not enough on taxes on consumption. Table 7.2 compares our National Government tax sources with those of 19 other nations. As the table shows, our Government relies more heavily on taxes on income and capital than any other central government listed—and by a substantial margin. Table 7.3 shows the same distribution for all government entities. It presents a similar picture. A glance at these figures automatically raises the question whether the United States is right and all of the other countries wrong. The same glance, however, by no means settles this question.

### Table 7.2
### DISTRIBUTION OF CENTRAL
### GOVERNMENT TAX LEVIES
### FISCAL YEAR 1960

|  | TAXES ON INCOME[1] % | TAXES ON CAPITAL[2] % | TAXES ON CONSUMPTION[3] % |
|---|---|---|---|
| United States | 83.4 | 1.8 | 14.8 |
| New Zealand[4] | 66.5 | 4.2 | 29.3 |
| Netherlands | 64.6 | 3.4 | 32.1 |
| Canada | 65.0 | 1.6 | 33.4 |
| Japan | 64.9 | 0.6 | 34.5 |
| Germany[5] | 60.2 | 1.6 | 38.2 |
| Australia | 58.1 | 1.3 | 40.6 |
| United Kingdom | 55.3 | 3.7 | 41.0 |
| France | 51.7 | 1.9 | 46.4 |
| Belgium | 51.4 | 1.5 | 47.1 |
| Sweden[4] | 50.6 | 1.5 | 47.8 |
| Italy | 49.7 | 1.7 | 48.6 |
| Switzerland | — | 49.8[6] — | 50.2 |
| Denmark[4] | 40.0 | 5.3 | 54.7 |
| Norway[4] | 37.5 | 2.2 | 60.3 |

[1] Includes personal and corporate income taxes and compulsory contributions by employers and employees for social insurance and similar programs.
[2] Includes property taxes and estate, inheritance, and gift taxes.
[3] Includes all taxes other than taxes on income and capital.
[4] Fiscal year ending 1959.
[5] Also includes tax receipts of Laender.
[6] Breakdown between taxes on income and taxes on capital not available.
NOTE: Details may not add to 100% because of rounding.
SOURCE: First National City Bank of New York, *Monthly Economic Letter*, October 1962, p. 112.

### Table 7.3
### DISTRIBUTION OF TAX LEVIES,
### ALL LEVELS OF GOVERNMENT
### FISCAL YEAR 1960

|  | TAXES ON INCOME % | TAXES ON CAPITAL % | TAXES ON CONSUMPTION % |
|---|---|---|---|
| United States | 63.5 | 14.2 | 22.3 |
| New Zealand[1] | 61.8 | 10.8 | 27.5 |
| Japan | 60.3 | 6.7 | 33.0 |

| | TAXES ON INCOME % | | TAXES ON CAPITAL % | TAXES ON CONSUMPTION % |
|---|---|---|---|---|
| Netherlands | 63.3 | | 3.3 | 33.3 |
| Switzerland | — | 66.1[2] | — | 33.9 |
| Canada | 48.8 | | 17.1 | 34.1 |
| | | | | |
| Germany | 62.0 | | 3.2 | 34.8 |
| Sweden[1] | 63.3 | | 1.1 | 35.6 |
| United Kingdom[1] | 51.7 | | 12.6 | 35.7 |
| | | | | |
| Denmark[1] | 48.6 | | 10.3 | 41.1 |
| Australia | 48.8 | | 9.7 | 41.5 |
| Norway[1] | 53.5 | | 3.0 | 43.5 |
| | | | | |
| Belgium | 52.8 | | 1.5 | 45.7 |
| Italy | 49.3 | | 3.0 | 47.7 |
| France | 45.2 | | 5.1 | 49.7 |

[1] Fiscal year ending 1959.
[2] Breakdown between taxes on income and taxes on capital not available.
NOTE: Details may not add to 100% because of rounding.
SOURCE: *Ibid.*

## OTHER PROBLEMS AND POLICIES

Inasmuch as the rates of the personal income tax are progressive, the government's share of the total national income rises as the average family's money income goes up. This may or may not be a desirable condition, but people should be aware of it.

General improvement in the budgeting and financial processes in the Congress is needed. We have already noted the fragmentation that prevails with respect to the revenue bills on the one hand and the appropriation bills on the other. This is one field requiring action by the Congress.

The Congress also has frequently been urged to give the President the power of *item veto*. At present the President may veto only an entire appropriation bill; and since such a bill usually contains mostly items which he (more or less) approves, he hesitates to veto it and send it back to the Congress for the alteration of only the few items to which he objects.

## FEDERAL GRANTS-IN-AID

The tendency on the part of state and local governments to turn to Washington for help—a part of the process called centralization of government—takes the form in part of Washington's handing money over to the lesser governments. The money, to be sure, has been collected from the people of the several states, but if not unnaturally looks something like a gift when it is returned. The total of these grants has mounted until it is currently more than $6 billion a year. The variety of these grants and their nature are illustrated in Table 7.4.

*Table 7.4*

## FEDERAL GRANTS-IN-AID TO STATE AND LOCAL GOVERNMENTS, 1957

| PROGRAM | YEAR ESTAB- LISHED | FEDERAL DEPARTMENT OR AGENCY ADMINISTERING PROGRAM |
|---|---|---|
| Aid to state soldiers' homes | 1888 | Veterans Administration |
| Agricultural extension work | 1914 | Department of Agriculture |
| Agricultural marketing services | 1946 | " |
| Agricultural research | 1887 | " |
| Airport construction | 1946 | Department of Commerce |
| Assistance to state marine schools | 1911 | " |
| Child welfare services | 1935 | Department of Health, Education, and Welfare |
| Civil defense contributions | 1950 | Federal Civil Defense Administration |
| Crippled children's service | 1935 | Department of Health, Education, and Welfare |
| Defense community facilities and services | 1951 | Housing and Home Finance Agency |
| Distribution of educational materials for the blind | 1879 | ° |
| Donation of surplus agricultural commodities | 1933 | Department of Agriculture |
| Employment service and unemployment compensation administration | 1933 | Department of Labor |
| Fish and wildlife restoration and management | 1937 | Department of the Interior |
| Flood prevention and watershed protection | 1954 | Department of Agriculture |
| Highway construction | 1916 | Department of Commerce |
| Hospital and medical facilities survey and construction | 1946 | Department of Health, Education, and Welfare |
| Library services for rural areas | 1956 | " |
| Major disaster relief | 1947 | Federal Civil Defense Administration |
| Maternal and child health services | 1935 | Department of Health, Education, and Welfare |
| Poliomyelitis vaccination | 1955 | " |
| Public assistance | 1935 | " |
| Public health services | 1935 | " |
| Public housing, low-rent (contributions) | 1937 | Housing and Home Finance Agency |
| Resident instruction in land-grant colleges | 1890 | Department of Health, Education, and Welfare |
| School construction in Federally affected areas | 1950 | Department of Health, Education, and Welfare |
| School operation and maintenance in Federally affected areas | 1950 | " |

| PROGRAM | YEAR ESTAB- LISHED | FEDERAL DEPARTMENT OR AGENCY ADMINISTERING PROGRAM |
|---|---|---|
| School lunch | 1933 | Department of Agriculture |
| Special milk | 1954 | " |
| Slum clearance and urban renewal (capital grants) | 1949 | Housing and Home Finance Agency |
| State and private forestry coopera- tion | 1911 | Department of Agriculture |
| Urban planning | 1954 | Housing and Home Finance Agency |
| Vocational education | 1917 | Department of Health, Education, and Welfare |
| Vocational rehabilitation | 1920 | " |
| Waste treatment facilities | 1956 | " |
| Water pollution control | 1956 | " |

* Operated by American Printing House for the Blind, a private, nonprofit corporation account-able to the Department of Health, Education, and Welfare for its use of Federal funds.
SOURCE: U.S. Congress, House of Representatives, Committee on Government Operations, *Federal-State-Local Relations: Federal Grants-In-Aid*, House Report No. 2533, 85th Congress, 2d Session, 1958, p. 8.

The device whereby the National Government provides aid in the form of money, land, and other valuable considerations is not new. It dates back to the early days of the Republic, if, indeed, it does not actually antedate the Declaration of Independence.

In the Northwest Ordinance of 1787 the Congress of the Confederation dedicated a section of every township in the national domain for the maintenance of public schools. In 1837 the cash surplus in the United States Treasury was apportioned as loans to the states with no expecta-tion of repayment. The Morrill Land Grant Act of 1862 gave the states lands for colleges of "agriculture and the mechanic arts." As the years went by, and grants multiplied, the terms increasingly involved some supervision by the Federal Government, the necessity of matching pay-ments by the recipient governments, and the continuation of the process on a more or less permanent basis. Grants by the Federal Government zoomed during the Great Depression, when they were made to the states for purposes of relief.

The multiplication of grants has resulted from several causes. One is the inequality of income among the people of the different states. An-other is the changed attitude of the people, flowing perhaps from speeded transportation and communication—a tendency to replace the provincial outlook with a national one. The failure of states, previously referred to, to undertake functions deemed by the public to be necessary has caused people to turn to Washington for grants to take care of these functions.

Although these conditions are recognized as furnishing some basis in favor of such grants, critics contend that the process permits the National Government to enter fields of activity reserved by the Constitution to the states, substitutes control by a national bureaucracy for grass roots control by local representatives of the people, coerces states into doing things that they would not undertake or could do better if left to their own initiative, detracts from the incentive for state and local governments to solve their own problems, and is expensive in that (it is claimed) the states never get back as much money from Washington, in the aggregate, as they have sent there. Additional arguments, both pro and con, can be adduced, illustrating both the complexity of public problems and the working of self-interest. The per capita amounts distributed to the various states differ tremendously. It is arguable that some differences are justified, but whether the differences that prevail are in fact the proper ones is another question. In addition, there is the large question whether the inclination to look upon these grants as gifts from Santa Claus diminishes local responsibility and intensifies the maneuvering in Washington by state representatives to secure favorable shares for the folks back home.

The grant-in-aid device, to be candid, offers a way in which, through control of the purse strings, government can be increasingly centralized in the United States. It requires no constitutional amendment and involves the altogether attractive process of apparently receiving money for nothing from Washington. Careful, discriminating, and continuing scrutiny of grants-in-aid is therefore in the public interest.

## STATE AND LOCAL FINANCE AND PLANT LOCATION

The opening of a new manufacturing plant in a community is likely to be viewed by many persons as a favorable event. This feeling springs from the belief that the new industry will, directly or indirectly, enhance the prosperity of the community. First, it is expected to increase the number of workers employed. Second, the increased wage incomes of these workers will benefit local merchants, landlords, and professional men. Third, unless some sort of tax exemption is granted, the new plant will be expected to increase the tax base of the community, permitting qualitative and quantitative increases in governmental services without increase in the tax rates. The actual benefits of a new plant, to be sure, sometimes turn out to be different from the stated ones. Nevertheless, because of the belief that a new plant is good for a community, many communities, states as well as smaller units, actively engage in a kind of race to attract plants to their areas. Among the lures that are extended are favorable tax consideration and the actual financing of the plants.

As this race proceeds, the general question of the impact of taxes on plant location is widely (and, as might be expected, contentiously) discussed. One opinion—or statement—is that tax rates are an important factor in the final selection among different possible communities. Another is that taxes are only a small part of total costs and, therefore, that differences in them are only a minor factor in the choice.

It is hard to get at the truth in this matter. One reason is that opinions are frequently clouded by political loyalties. A plant owner unfriendly to a local or state party administration may move his plant to or locate his new plant in a different place and give as the reason the level of taxes or some other characteristic of government. His statement may reflect party loyalty rather than truth.

A further reason for difficulty is that it is by no means always easy to determine the real reasons for business decisions. The managers themselves are rarely able to give exact weights to the factors involved.

In an attempt to get some information about this subject Professors Bergin and Eagan in 1958 surveyed the managements of more than eight hundred firms which had recently located or expanded in Kentucky, Tennessee, and Mississippi. Over a third of the firms answered the questionnaire, which sought to determine the specific factors that the managements had considered most important in selecting the locations of their new facilities. The factors mentioned, in descending order of frequency and importance, were these:

*Table 7.5*

## REASONS GIVEN BY NEW OR EXPANDED
## FIRMS FOR CHOICE OF PRESENT LOCATIONS*

| RANK | REASONS FOR PLANT LOCATION | TOTAL OF MENTIONS |
|---|---|---|
| 1. | Availability of labor | 143 |
| 2. | Convenience to markets | 116 |
| 3. | Lower labor costs | 102 |
| 4. | Availability of buildings or other property | 99 |
| 5. | Availability of raw materials | 79 |
| 6. | Adequate power | 79 |
| 7. | Local cooperativeness | 76 |
| 8. | Less unionization | 66 |
| 9. | Transportation costs | 56 |
| 10. | Transportation facilities | 44 |
| 11. | Home of management | 41 |
| 12. | Decentralization of operation | 39 |
| 13. | Favorable tax structure | 32 |
| 14. | Center of particular industry | 29 |
| 15. | Financial aid | 25 |
| 16. | Climate | 20 |
| 17. | Plentiful water supply | 8 |
| 18. | Inexpensive plant site | 3 |

* Thomas P. Bergin and William F. Eagan, "How Effective are Industrial Development Programs?" *Michigan Business Review*, January 1960, p. 25.

The fact that taxes were in only 13th place out of 18 factors mentioned does not, however, entirely dispose of the matter, as Bergin and Eagan make clear. Differences in taxes may be significant between two communities which otherwise are approximately equal with respect to other factors. And the significance of taxes differs among different kinds of industries. Moreover, such statistical studies do not show other factors, such as the various *kinds* of taxes involved and the *methods* and *schedules* of their collection.

Furthermore, they do not take account of the other side of the fiscal picture, namely, the uses to which the tax money is put. A community with a low tax rate may have poor schools, and other local services also may be inadequate. In these circumstances the management of a corporation that is considering locating a plant may find the low tax rates counterbalanced by the poor public services available, both for the plant and its employees, and may therefore decide against the low-tax location.

Then, in addition to the actual facts with respect to taxes and public expenditures, there is the subtle and important factor of *reputation* and *climate*. A state or community may acquire a kind of public *image* that does not accurately reflect the true facts; yet the influence of this distorted reputation may easily be greater than that of the facts themselves.

## INDUSTRIAL AID BONDS

One device utilized by some communities to attract industries is the provision of plants which are rented at low figures to business firms and financed by industrial aid bonds. The key to this operation is the fact that the interest on municipal bonds is completely exempt from the Federal corporate and personal income tax, which increases the attractiveness of these bonds to many investors. One of these investors, holding bonds issued by the same business firms, would have to pay personal income taxes on the interest. The result is that many investors are willing to lend money to municipalities at lower rates of interest than they would accept from firms (the difference between the yields on high-grade corporate bonds and municipal bonds in recent years has been running at about one percentage point). Therefore, a municipality wishing to attract a firm can sell a bond issue at a slightly lower rate of interest than could the firm (incidentally, sparing the firm all the expense and red tape incident to the launching of a private bond issue—a not inconsiderable factor) buy a piece of property, build a plant on it, and rent it to the business firm at an attractively low figure, to the benefit of all concerned except the Federal Treasury.

The device of industrial aid bonds thus represents a new weapon in intercommunity competition for plants. It is a significant departure in that the government concerned is borrowing money, not for the purpose of putting the money into local public improvements, but for the purpose of financing a plant for private use. This type of financing represents, therefore, one of the many ways in which the relationships between business and government are continually being extended by innovation.

## STATE AND LOCAL TAX PROBLEMS

As shown in Table 6.3, the largest source of state tax revenues is the group of sales taxes, and the local governments get most of their tax revenues from property taxes.

Mention is made in Chapter 4 of a tendency to let what should be local governmental functions drift toward Washington, with the explanation that state and local tax sources have been milked dry—a proposition not commonly accompanied by any evidence. The foregoing observation by no means implies that these governments should raise sales or property tax rates if they should decide to collect more money. They might well give attention to some other taxes.

At present, 32 states have income taxes, 37 have sales taxes, and only three have neither. Income taxes are increasingly becoming a source of state revenue, and they have been introduced even by some municipalities. The legal authority of municipalities to levy taxes is usually subject to state legislation, and this legislation is frequently extremely restrictive in this respect. One of the current questions, therefore, is whether state governments should relax their restrictions on the types of taxes that municipalities may levy.

In one special sense it is easier for state and local governments to increase taxes than for the Federal Government to do so. The reason is that for tens of millions of taxpayers, Uncle Sam, in effect, pays part of state and local taxes, these taxes being deductible from incomes reported for Federal income tax purposes. If a man pays any personal income tax at all, this means that Uncle Sam pays $20 out of every $100 of his property, sales, and state and local income taxes.* If he has a larger income, the percentage rises along with the percentage in his top bracket. A corporation paying any of these taxes finds that the Federal Government has in effect paid 52 per cent of their amount. To this limited degree the state and local governments are in a preemptive position with regard to taxes, and the Federal Government comes second.

## THE OUTLOOK FOR STATE AND LOCAL TAXATION

State and local taxation and expenditures march together in even closer correspondence than is true of their Federal counterparts. What is the

---

* This statement is rendered somewhat inaccurate by the standard deduction feature of the Federal tax. The inaccuracy, however, is not significant.

outlook for state and local expenditures? In Chapter 4 we review the growth of the activities of state and local governments. Table 6.2 lists the objects and amounts of public expenditures. If historical trends continue into the future, we may expect that the functions performed by state and local governments will continue to proliferate and that the ones now being carried on will be expanded. A larger proportion of young people will attend college; mental hospitals will be expanded; proper treatment of crime and criminals will require increased expenditures; and new city halls and county courthouses will be erected. These increases in the existing functions, plus the addition of new ones, together with the growing population and wealth of our people, seem to foreshadow a continuing expansion in the expenditures of state and local government. And this means, of course, that the total of taxes also will have to rise.

In this area of taxation, like that of the Federal Government, there is the possibility that taxes may be changed, with shifts in the types relied on. Various states have already gone a considerable distance in introducing new types of taxes, including, for example, in the cases of a majority of them, the personal income tax. Municipalities also are moving in this direction, although thus far there has been very little dent made in the proportionate contribution from that old mainstay of local government finance, the general property tax. The argument for some relaxation of the restrictive state laws that inhibit this movement is given earlier.

Our mention of income taxation by states and municipalities makes this an appropriate place for brief reference to the subject of *double taxation*. Opponents of a proposed tax, or even of an existing one, frequently denounce it on the grounds that it constitutes double taxation. A familiar target for this criticism is the Federal taxation of corporation profits and then the further taxation of the same income, or part of it, when it is passed to stockholders as dividends. He who insists that double taxation is in and of itself wrong may be invited to offer reasoning in support of this proposition. He may find this difficult, since there is nothing inherently wrong with double taxation. The rightness or wrongness of taxes is not affected by whether there is one tax or two or three levied on the same base or even against the same persons. It is possible that some of the feeling against double taxation may be a distorted transfer from the idea of double jeopardy in criminal prosecution. True, taxes may strike some people as akin to hanging and jail—but the analogy is extremely thin and completely invalid.

## THE SIZE OF THE PUBLIC SECTOR

Many citizens talk out of both sides of their mouth with respect to the issue of how big the public sector of the economy should be relative to the private sector. A citizen, for example, may denounce government spending and advocate strict economy—calling for, as the phrase goes, cutting expenditures to the bone. At the same time he may defend vigorously an expenditure of significance to him or his firm or his community, such as the dredging of a river or an urban renewal project. This kind of situation was dramatically illustrated by the front page of the *Boston Globe* on May 8, 1957. Stories in the paper reported that local men had costumed themselves as Indians and had thrown simulated bags of tea from a ship in Boston Harbor in protest against Federal expenditures—and other stories in the same paper reported that on the same day the Mayor of Boston had been in Washington seeking Federal aid. The headline read "IKE SCORES HUB AS TAX LESSON" and subheads read "Mayor Wants Federal Aid . . . 'Tea Party' Hits Spending," followed by this additional headline "Not Easy to Do Both, He Remarks."*

When in 1961 the Defense Department named 52 military bases that were going to be closed as unnecessary, protests came from the communities affected, doubtless from many citizens who were strongly opposed to excessive spending.

Any public-spirited citizen can help to reduce public expenditures by taking a Good Citizen's Pledge, sending a copy to his public officials, and thereafter conforming to the pledge. Even within organizations to which he belongs that want special favors, he can contribute by opposing such demands. Here is a draft of such a pledge:

> I should like to see tax rates reduced as soon and as far as sound public policy permits. I realize that tax rates cannot be reduced permanently until expenditures are reduced. An important way of reducing expenditures is to eliminate special benefits. I therefore do not want the government to pay for special benefits for anyone—including me and my group. A factor favorable to getting my vote for a candidate for public office will be a firm stand against special benefits. Such a candidate is a statesman, and commends himself to me.

The reader may judge for himself the prospects of a breakdown of the postal system under a flood of such pledges.

## CONCLUSION

It has been said that all that is necessary for the triumph of evil is for good men to do nothing. While something of an exaggeration, the proposition does contain some truth. If dedicated citizens give little or no attention to the problems of government and, specifically, if they fail to support the efforts of honorable government officers, it may be expected that the representatives of special interests will be the more influential because of a sheer lack of opposition. Nor will it do for the dedicated citizen to wear two hats—one when he is seeking special bene-

* "Hub" is Bostonians' nickname for their city.

fits for himself or his group and another when he is opposing special favors that are not in the public interest. As President Eisenhower pointed out to the people of Boston, it is not easy for the Federal Government to give more money to Boston and simultaneously to spend less. The quality of government will be shaped by the civic quality of the people, and this will be determined by both their understanding of public problems and their devotion to the public good.

## QUESTIONS AND PROBLEMS

1. Evaluate the criteria of good taxes.
2. Explain how a tax is shifted and the significance of shifting to the criterion of justice.
3. Explain and evaluate the benefit theory of taxation.
4. Explain and evaluate the ability to pay theory of taxation.
5. Although Colin Clark contended that a nontotalitarian nation could not carry a tax burden heavier than 25 per cent of national income in peacetime, this figure has been, and is being, exceeded by some of the most developed nations of the world, including the United States. Does this invalidate Clark's contention? What factors must be considered in determining the maximum tax burden a nation can bear?
6. What effects do taxes and expenditures have on the American economy?
7. What changes in Federal taxes do you favor? What changes do you expect will actually be made?
8. What may be said for and against the Federal Government's making financial grants to the states?
9. To what extent are state and local taxes influenced by the desire to attract industry?
10. What changes in state and local taxes do you favor? What changes do you expect will actually be made?

## SELECTED READINGS

ANDERSON, WILLIAM. *Intergovernmental Fiscal Regulations*. Minneapolis, Minn.: University of Minnesota Press, 1956.

COPELAND, MORRIS I. *Trends in Government Financing*. Princeton, N.J.: Princeton University Press, 1961.

DICE, JOHN F. *Government Finance: An Economic Analysis*, 3rd ed. Homewood, Ill.: Richard D. Irwin, Inc., 1963.

GROVES, HAROLD M. *Financing Government*, 5th ed. New York: Holt, Rinehart, & Winston, Inc., 1958.

KENDRICK, MYRON S. *Public Finance*. Boston: Houghton Mifflin Company, 1957.

MUSGRAVE, R. A. *Theory of Public Finance*. New York: McGraw-Hill Company, 1959.

TAYLOR, PHILIP E. *Economics of Public Finance*, 3rd ed. New York: The Macmillan Company, 1961.

Tax Foundation, Inc. *Facts and Figures on Government Finance*, 11th ed. Englewood Cliffs, N.J.: Prentice-Hall, Inc., 1961.

# 8

## DEBT:
### Public and Private

Opinions about debt and its role in economic life vary widely. One view is expressed by the adage "Out of debt, out of danger." Another opinion was that of Alexander Hamilton, who stated, "A national debt, if it is not excessive, will be to us a national blessing." But Shakespeare's Polonius admonishes: "Neither a borrower nor a lender be." If the adage is correct, the American people and their governments are in grave danger, and the danger has been mounting for decades. If, however, Hamilton is right, they have been increasingly blessed, although he might consider that some of the debts have become "excessive." In any event, both people and governments have utterly disregarded Polonius' advice. What are the present facts, their significance, and the outlook for debt in the United States?

The size of the danger or the blessing, and the deviation from the advice of Polonius, is indicated by the following tabulation of net public and private debt on December 31, 1961.

|  | Billions |
|---|---|
| Federal Government and Agency | $ 248.1 |
| State and local governments | 65.0 |
| Corporations | 311.5 |
| Individuals and noncorporate entities | 312.3 |
| Total | $ 936.9 |

SOURCE: U.S. Department of Commerce, *Survey of Current Business*, May 1962, p. 19.

The term *net debt* means the indebtedness of borrowers after elimination of certain types of duplicating governmental and corporate debt. For example, United States Government agencies and trust funds invest their money in Government securities. In 1961 they held $55 billion of such securities.

## HISTORY OF THE FEDERAL DEBT

Like individuals and corporations, the Federal Government is usually either spending more than it is receiving or vice versa. This means that it can either pile up cash and then pay it out, or it can go deeper into debt and then pay off the debts. As a matter of fact, it does both of these things. The fact that through the decades it has paid out much more than it has taken in is demonstrated by the figures above.

Government borrowing on a systematic scale is a relatively modern development. Not until the latter part of the eighteenth-century did it come to be a significant feature of public finance. Prior to that time, governmental borrowing was a difficult and sporadic operation. Sometimes it took the form of a king's borrowing, in effect on his personal note, from a lender who might be a trading operator. Because of political uncertainties, his difficulty in collecting taxes, and the question of whether his successors would honor his debts, the monarch sometimes had trouble borrowing money. As time went on, the continuing evolution of a money and credit economy, coupled with an increase in the general business use of credit, and the development of constitutional monarchies in which the power was really held by parliaments (which gave creditors security in the form of broader representation and taxation) made borrowing a more feasible operation, partly because of the greater willingness of lenders to lend money to governments thus constituted.

As soon as the United States was established in 1776, the Continental Congress faced the problem of financing the Revolution. The total cost of that war, according to Harold U. Faulkner, was slightly more than $100 million. Since the Continental Congress did not have much taxing power, less than $6 million came from taxes, obtained through the states. Paper money provided 40 per cent of the total, and money borrowed by the new national government or the states accounted for 45 per cent.* Later, and primarily at the urging of Alexander Hamilton, the new Government took over the states' debts. In the very early years of the Government, therefore, the national debt stood at $77 million.†

The debt was slightly increased in connection with the purchase of the Louisiana Territory and then was reduced to $45 million in 1811. By 1815, in consequence of the War of 1812, the debt had risen to $127 million. This figure was gradually reduced until in 1835 the debt was entirely paid off, and the Treasury still had a surplus which was returned to the

---

* Harold U. Faulkner, *American Economic History* (New York: Harper and Brothers, 1943), p. 145.

† This figure, and other historical figures on the debt, are taken from the Bureau of the Census publication, *Historical Statistics of the United States* (Washington, D.C.: United States Government Printing Office, 1960), p. 711.

states. That brief period was the only time in the history of our government when there was no Federal debt.

The Mexican War resulted in a modest increase in the debt, and the figure stood at $65 million in 1860. Then came the Civil War, costly in lives and money, much of which was borrowed. In 1866 the national debt had risen to the then enormous figure of $2,800 million.

It was then reduced slowly year by year until, in 1893, it was down to $961 million. The Spanish-American War and the building of the Panama Canal contributed to its growth, but it still stood at a comparatively modest figure, $1.2 billion, in 1916.

A large part of the costs of World War I was met by borrowing, with the result that the debt in 1919 exceeded $25 billion. It was reduced to $16 billion by 1930.

Deficit financing associated with the Great Depression brought the debt up to $40 billion in 1939.

Then came the defense program and World War II. At its end, in 1945, the debt had zoomed to $279 billion.

Some reduction of the debt had been accomplished before the Korean police action plus sizable peacetime deficits pushed the figure past $300 billion in 1962.

This brief review of the growth of the national debt indicates that it originated principally in consequence of the financial needs of the Government in wars and to a smaller extent because of deficit financing during the Great Depression.

## COMPOSITION AND OWNERSHIP
### OF THE DEBT

The debt is represented by different kinds of pieces of paper. Some are called bonds; others are called notes, certificates of indebtedness, and bills. Some are marketable; they can be sold freely by the holders. Others, such as the savings bonds, are nonmarketable; they can be redeemed, but cannot be sold to other persons. The lengths of life of these various types of debt also vary. Some last for only a few weeks; others for many years. These differences are important, but their importance is chiefly of concern to the United States Treasury, in connection with problems of debt management. Their significance for analysis of the general problem of the nature and role of the national debt is smaller.

These pieces of paper—which represent debt of the Federal Government—are assets to the people who own them. A wide variety of persons and organizations own parts of the Federal debt. The table shows their distribution.

*Table 8.1*

## OWNERSHIP OF U.S. GOVERNMENT
## SECURITIES, DECEMBER 31, 1961

|  | (Billions) |
|---|---|
| Commercial banks | $ 67.2 |
| Mutual savings banks | 6.1 |
| Insurance companies | 11.4 |
| Other corporations | 19.4 |
| State and local governments | 18.3 |
| Individuals | 65.6 |
| Miscellaneous investors | 25.0 |
| Total held by the general public | $213.1 |
| Federal Reserve Banks | 28.9 |
| U.S. Government agencies and trust funds | 54.5 |
| Total | $296.5 |

SOURCE: *Federal Reserve Bulletin*, August 1962, p. 1026. Figures do not add precisely because of rounding.

## STATE AND LOCAL DEBT

State and local government debt totaled $13 billion in 1929. It went up a little during the Great Depression and then declined during World War II. In 1946 the figure was only slightly higher than it had been 17 years before.

After World War II, however, state and local governments embarked upon substantial programs of construction and financed them in part by borrowing money. In the late 1950s the total debt of this type rose about $5 billion a year and stood at $60 billion in 1960, with the prospect that it might rise in the future at about the same rate.

In this discussion of the public debt attention will be focused on the national debt because it is so much larger than the total of state and local government debt. Most of what is said about the national debt applies, with appropriate changes, to state and local debt as well.

## THE SIGNIFICANCE OF THE
## NATIONAL DEBT

The *similarities* between the national debt and private debt are obvious. Not so obvious, and quite possibly of greater importance, are the *dissimilarities*.

Opinions about the national debt range over a broad spectrum. The general public seem to be only vaguely aware of its amount, and their estimates of its magnitude tend to run much too low. On the average, they are indifferent to the debt.

Among informed persons, at one extreme are those who contend that since we basically owe the debt to ourselves, it really doesn't matter at all. At the opposite extreme are those who see the debt as a monstrous menace to the American economy. Some of these persons visualize the debt as a millstone around our necks, pulling us down into deflation and depression; others visualize it as a helium-filled balloon, pulling us up into inflation; and still others manage the intellectual feat of seeing it as possessing both of these potentialities at once.

It is true that except for a small (and for the purposes of this analysis unimportant) part of the debt held by foreigners, we do owe the debt to ourselves. The table presented above, which lists the holders of these pieces of paper, shows that they are either individual persons or corporations owned by or using the money of individual persons. The American people, in one form or another, own the debt which is owed by their own national government.

It is true also that if a consolidated balance sheet of the United States of America or of The American People were constructed according to approved accounting principles, the national debt (except for the small part held by foreigners) would again not appear at all. But this does not mean that the debt is of no importance. It would not be the only item that would not appear on such a consolidated balance sheet. Others that would not be listed are stocks, bonds, mortgages, and bank deposits. To conclude that none of these things is important or that their several amounts have no significance is obviously unwarranted.

A national debt is not necessarily either inflationary or deflationary. It may be either, or it may be neutral. This is true both when the total amount of the debt is unchanging and when it is either increasing or decreasing. The monetary impact of the debt depends on how existing debt instruments are refunded when they come due and on how new debt is financed and old debt paid off. This subject is examined further in the discussion of countercyclical policies in Chapter 10.

It is argued that borrowing promotes extravagance. One reason why the Congress puts a legislative ceiling on the national debt is presumably to prevent such extravagance. Because the same Congress passes both the tax laws and the appropriations laws whose imbalance may create a deficit, the debt ceiling represents Congress holding a pistol to its own head and commanding itself to economize.

Wholly apart from the existence of a debt ceiling, it is arguable that the ability to borrow money may loosen somewhat the fiscal restraint on expenditures.

Whether the Government is merely refinancing the $80 billion of debt instruments that come due in a typical year or is increasing or decreasing its debt, these operations are a part of the total capital investment market in the American economy. The Government may add to or subtract from the total demand for borrowed money. It is, therefore, a factor in the capital markets, and its actions affect the amount of money available to private business.

## CAN THE DEBT LAST FOREVER?

Another opinion is that the Government cannot go on indefinitely spending more than it takes in because this will eventually lead to bankruptcy just as it would for a person who does the same thing. In the first place, this outcome is not inevitable for a person or a corporation. A person, whether natural or corporate, can go on increasing his borrowing indefinitely as long as he invests the money wisely enough to get a return adequate to pay interest and to cover maturing principal or justify refunding it. Many a well-managed corporation finds that the total of its debts gradually grows through the years, as its business grows, and quite properly does not feel obliged to reverse this.

. Analysis of the bankruptcy argument involves consideration of some differences between private debt and the debt of the Federal Government. Bankruptcy, in the simple financial sense of inability to meet one's dollar obligations, is in the last analysis impossible for a national government, which can always resort to printing paper money if necessary. This, to be sure, might grow into another kind of bankruptcy ("moral bankruptcy"?), but it is not the simple money bankruptcy that can overtake an individual, to whom (unless he possesses *very* special skills indeed) the recourse of creating money is not available. Moreover, the Federal Government does not depend on success in business operations to pay interest and principal. It depends on its taxing power. The limit to debt expansion, therefore, is set by the *taxability* of the whole economy—its level and health.

This analysis refutes the argument that it is financially wrong and morally indefensible for the government to accept the principle of owing money forever and financially fatal to increase the debt indefinitely.

The debt could be reduced by using tax revenues for this purpose. In the beginning this would mean higher taxes than otherwise would be required; gradually tapering off as the debt and the interest on it are reduced.

The decision to do this would hinge on the significance of this course of action for the economy, rather than on analogies to private financial operations.

One of the economic factors involved is the effect of such an action on the nation's money supply. The money supply is obtained chiefly through commercial bank credit. If the process of reduction of the national debt should come to involve paying off debt held by commercial banks, the effect would be to contract the nation's money supply. (It is quite possible, of course, that expansion of commercial bank credit to private borrowers could be accomplished at the same time at a rate sufficient to offset the contraction of credit extended to the Federal Government.) This role of the Federal debt in sustaining the national money supply is vital to our economy. The question is examined further in the next chapter.

## THE BURDEN OF THE DEBT

The respect in which the national debt is clearly a burden is the taxation that is required to pay the interest on the debt. The annual interest bill is $9 billion. Although this amount is only one tenth of the total Federal budget, it represents a by no means negligible amount of taxes.

In connection with this payment it is argued that the interest is no burden because the amount of money that is collected as taxes is paid back over to the people as interest. This argument proves too much. The same might be said of any taxes—and a simple verbal effort would thus purport to reduce the burden of taxation to zero. Although the taxes to cover the interest bill, and the interest payments themselves, are equal in their totals, *they are not the same for any particular person,* since the amount of tax that he pays is not determined solely by the amount of interest that he receives. A man's personal income tax, for example, is determined by his total income, not merely by whatever income he receives as a holder of Federal Government debt instruments. If he works harder and earns more money, or if he invests in industry and receives dividends, he has to pay more taxes. This is the sense in which the taxes are a burden.

Measuring their burdensomeness—their repressive effect—(as we note in Chapter 7) is difficult if not impossible. Whatever that effect is, the taxes that raise the money to pay interest on the debt are no different from any similar quantity of similar taxes levied by the same government to finance other governmental expenditures.

## TIMING OF THE BURDEN

The debt has been characterized as a burden on the generations yet to come—a "mortgage on the future." The incidence of interest payments and debt retirement on the future taxpayers is claimed to be the grossly unfair result of current and past decisions to create and maintain debt. The opponents of the national debt contend that a particular generation is willing to incur debt in a somewhat reckless fashion if it is secure in the knowledge that generations to follow will bear the burden.

The fallacy in this argument is its implication that the current genera-

tion is enjoying an increased purchasing power at the expense of a reduced purchasing power of the future generations. This contention
fails to recognize the fact that purchasing power can be transferred
neither backward nor forward. When the government borrows, savers
give up purchasing power in lieu of taxpayers' doing so, in the *same
generation*—in effect, purchasing power is transferred from savers to taxpayers. When the government pays the interest on debts of past generations or retires such debt, the transfer is reversed—taxpayers give up purchasing power and bondholders receive equal purchasing power, once
again within the same generation.

Also, the transfer-of-burden argument fails to contemplate that such
a burden, if it in fact exists, may be accompanied by economic benefits
and potential for the future generations which might not have accrued
had not the debt been incurred. It is rather difficult to contend that
World War II was waged and won only for the sake of the wartime
generation and that no benefits will be derived by future generations as
a result of the victory.

Another argument is that the Federal Government should adopt a
more businesslike attitude toward the creation and retirement of national
debt. The advocates of this attitude reason that public debt is similar
to private debt in that it should be backed up and secured by balancing
assets. This would entail repayment of war debts not backed by specific
hardware and no further incurrence of debt unless similarly backed
by tangibles.

This argument of course overweighs what similarity may exist between
public and private debt while failing to give due consideration to the
differences. (It also, be it noted, underweighs the importance of intan-
gibles in private business.) Certainly creation of debt which does not
result in an increase in national production equaling the debt is unfortunate (although, as in wartime, it may be necessary), and in this respect
both types of debt are similar. Public debt differs from private debt,
however, in that its effect on production is less direct. While private debt
is usually related to the specific assets which back it up, its true justification lies in the measure of its contribution to increased earning power
via the assets in which the money is invested. Similarly, the justification
for the incurrence of public debt lies in its contribution toward the raising
of national income, the creation of physical capital, and the development
and preservation of human capital.

## PROSPECTIVE FURTHER GROWTH
## OF THE DEBT

If the national debt is not correspondingly enlarged, the gradual growth
of the gross national product and the national income will have the effect

that the relative burden, both of the principal of the debt and presumably also of the annual interest payment, will gradually be reduced in the sense that they will become a slowly diminishing percentage of annual output and income.

But is it reasonable to expect that the national debt will fail to grow as rapidly as the national economy? An examination of the historical figures indicates that for several decades the total of debt and the size of the American economy have grown together, maintaining, except for the early years of the Great Depression (when the economy actually contracted), a fairly steady ratio to each other. The debt has consistently been between 1.75 and 2.0 times as great as the gross national product.

### Chart 8.1

## DEBT AND THE GROSS NATIONAL PRODUCT

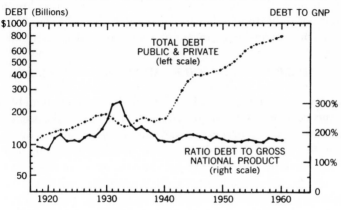

### Chart 8.2

## DEBT: PUBLIC AND PRIVATE

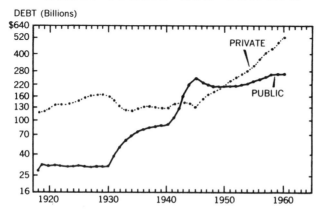

SOURCE: The National City Bank of Cleveland, *Bulletin*, March 17, 1961.

Putting the matter the other way around, we can say that the GNP has regularly been a little more than half as large as the current total of debt. The accompanying charts illustrate both the absolute amounts of the debt and the ratio of the debt to the GNP.

The fact of this parallel growth naturally brings to the fore the question whether it has been a mere accident or whether there is some real functional connection between the size of the debt and the size of the economy. This is a vital question. If the parallel growth has been a mere accident, the economy can presumably grow in the future without further expansion of debt. If, however, there is a real functional relationship, if our economic system depends on and is closely linked to debt, then future economic growth will require expansion of debt. This conclusion does not necessarily mean that the debt will have to expand proportionately to the increase in business, although the past record suggests strongly that this may well be the case. The conclusion, moreover, does not indicate whether the increase in the debt should be public or private, but merely that an increase in the total is required.

## DEBT AND THE MONEY SUPPLY

There are two functional links between the amount of debt and the size of the economy. One is the connection between the debt of commercial banks and the nation's money supply. The outlook for economic growth in the United States suggests that the nation's production will be doubled in the next two decades and doubled again in the equal following period. This growth can presumably be realized only if an equivalent expansion of spending occurs, and this in turn will probably require an approximately equivalent growth in the money supply.

Some of the needed new money will probably come from newly mined gold. A larger part, however, would be expected to come from expansion of commercial bank credit. *Bank credit* is composed of *other persons' debts,* such as mortgages, bonds, and promissory notes. Commercial bank credit can be expanded, and with it the money supply, without expansion of the total debt if the banks buy debt instruments from nonbank holders. For example, this happens whenever commercial banks buy U.S. Government bonds from life insurance companies.

This shifting of existing bonds from nonbank holders into commercial banks could take place in significant volume, of course, only if the life insurance companies and other nonbank investors were willing to sell their securities to the banks. Suppose, however, that they are unwilling to do so, that they want to keep their investments and perhaps even to increase them. Then growth of the money supply could not be accomplished this way, but would have to be done by an actual expansion of debt. This additional debt, to repeat, could be either public or private. Either kind, so long as it is acceptable to the commercial banks, would provide a satisfactory vehicle for expansion of commercial bank credit.

## DEBT AND ASSETS

The second functional link between the magnitudes of debt and of the economy is the connection between debt and wealth, or assets. The historical growth of the American economy has witnessed both a rise in national output and income and an increase in the national wealth—land, buildings, machinery, equipment, and inventories, plus all other kinds of tangible goods. Indeed, these gains are both cause and effect of one another. The total net debt also has gone up.

Table 8.2 shows these figures for two representative years, and also shows the steadiness of the ratio between debt and assets, as the economy grew.

### Table 8.2

### NET DEBT AND WEALTH, 1929, 1955

|  | 1929 | 1955 |
|---|---|---|
| National assets (billions) | $427 | $1,329 |
| Net debt (billions) | $191 | $ 672 |
| Percentage: net debt of assets | 45% | 51% |

SOURCES: National Assets: Raymond W. Goldsmith, in Joint Economic Committee, *Hearings on Employment, Growth and Price Levels,* April 7, 1959 (Washington, D.C.: Government Printing Office, 1959) p. 260; Net Debt: *Economic Report of the President* (Washington, D.C.: Government Printing Office, 1960) p. 210.

One reason why debt and assets increase together is that many assets are financed by borrowing money. Most new homes, for instance, are financed by mortgage money. This condition means that as our country becomes richer and its assets rise, its debts also will rise. The six-percentage point increase in *relative* debt is a reflection of the fact that financing by borrowing was more prevalent in 1955 than in 1929.

This relationship suggests that the total of debt is likely to rise in the future as it has in the past. If the growth of debt is not excessive relative to the assets, it is a part of economic growth and is not something to be viewed with alarm.

## CONCLUSION

Several circumstances make the analysis of debt difficult. One is that the similarities between public debt and private debt are likely to lead to inaccurate conclusions about the significance of the former. The second is that the dissimilarities are not easily seen and require careful study. The third is that the word *debt* has ominous and almost emotional overtones for some persons. And finally, the subject is a highly technical one, and in particular the relationships between debt and the size of the American economy are complex. These difficulties tend to discourage careful study of the subject, and perhaps no one is to be blamed for shirking the chore; but, by the same token, no one who fulminates about the national debt is entitled to a hearing until he has at least tried.

## QUESTIONS AND PROBLEMS

1. How can refunding the national debt have an inflationary or a deflationary effect on the economy?
2. In what sense is the national debt said to be a burden? A benefit?
3. What are the various arguments on the questions as to the effect of a large government debt? Can these same arguments be related to private debt?
4. Does Federal debt promote administrative inefficiencies and extravagance in expenditure?
5. Evaluate these statements: "The government can't go on forever spending more than it takes in. Some time there will be a day of reckoning."
6. Can the Federal Government go on increasing its debt indefinitely?
7. Evaluate these statements: "A Federal tax schedule reduction would increase the deficit and thereby the funded debt. Contrariwise, a cut in expenditures (although not for defense and outer space exploration) to make possible a reduction of the debt at $10 billion a year for 30 years would about extinguish the Federal debt and place the nation upon a sound financial basis."
8. If national debt remains constant and the economy grows, would private debt have to rise at a faster rate than the growth of the economy?

## SELECTED READINGS

ABBOTT, CHARLES CORTEZ. Federal Debt: Structure and Impact. New York: Twentieth Century Fund, 1953.

Commission on Money and Credit. Money and Credit: Their Influence on Jobs, Prices, and Growth. Englewood Cliffs, N.J.: Prentice-Hall, Inc., 1961.

COOKE, HELEN J. Role of Debt in the National Economy. Washington, D.C.: Public Affairs Press, 1961.

COPELAND, MORRIS I. Trends in Government Financing. Princeton, N.J.: Princeton University Press, 1961.

DONALDSON, GORDON. Corporate Debt Capacity. Cambridge, Mass.: Harvard University Press, 1961.

HART, ALBERT G., and P. B. KENEN. Money, Debt and Economic Activity, 3rd ed. Englewood Cliffs, N.J.: Prentice-Hall, Inc., 1961.

ROBINSON, MARSHALL A. National Debt Ceiling: An Experiment in Fiscal Policy. Washington, D.C.: The Brookings Institution, 1959.

WERNETTE, J. P. Growth and Prosperity Without Inflation, Chapter 8. New York: The Ronald Press, 1961.

# 9     ECONOMIC GROWTH

Discussion of *economic growth* has increased so much in recent years that it would not be unreasonable for a well-read citizen to arrive at three conclusions about the subject, namely,

[1]  That the concept of economic growth is new,

[2]  That the condition is new, and

[3]  That concern with the subject is new.

Despite the reasonableness of these conclusions the fact is that none is true.

One reason why the concept of economic growth may seem to be new may be that the topic has been long neglected by economic analysts. This was not always true. Adam Smith's great book of 1776, *An Inquiry into the Nature and Causes of the Wealth of Nations,* might be characterized as a book about economic growth. In it Smith undertook to study the conditions that determine the level of prosperity in nations and to analyze the circumstances that made some nations rich while others were poor, that permitted some to rise in the economic scale while others stood still. Since there had been relatively little technological industrial progress at his time, he naturally did not visualize the potential of this mighty factor. Instead, he stressed the division of labor and specialization as the key contributors. His explanation of what we today call increased productivity is contained in the first sentence of his first chapter: "The greatest improvement in the productive powers of labour, and the greater part of the skill, dexterity, and judgment with which it is anywhere directed, or applied, seem to have been the effects of the division of labour." He then proceeds to illustrate by his famous example of the division of labor in making pins, a comparatively simple operation in which each of several workers specializes in doing just one part of the operation. Smith then says:

> Those ten persons, therefore, could make among them upwards of forty-eight thousand pins in a day. Each person, might be considered as making four thousand eight hundred pins in a day. But if they had all wrought separately

and independently, and without any of them having been educated to this peculiar business, they certainly could not each of them have made twenty, perhaps not one pin in a day; that is, certainly, not the two hundred and for-tieth, perhaps not the four thousand eight hundredth part of what they are at present capable of performing, in consequence of a proper division and com-bination of their different operations.

Most of the well-known economists who followed Smith did not analyze economic growth. Some of them merely neglected the subject. Others ruled it out of their analysis by assuming that they were writing about the kind of changeless economic system which was called the *stationary* state. Instead of discussing how the proverbial pie could be enlarged, they concentrated on analyzing how the prices of the ingredi-ents that went into the pie were determined and how the slices of the unchanging pie were cut and distributed in the form of rent, interest, wages, and profits to the landowners, capitalists, laborers, and en-trepreneurs.

Attention to economic growth, among both the professionals and the public awaited developments of recent years. One development that stimulated interest in the subject was the economic growth of the U.S.S.R. and its significance for military and ideological rivalry.

Today questions that are being asked include these: What is the nature of economic growth? What causes it? Is it desirable? What factors retard it? Are our growth policies adequate?

## NATURE OF ECONOMIC GROWTH

One meaning of economic growth is an increase in the *national total* of goods and services produced and consumed in the United States—as measured by the real gross national product or by the real national income.

Another meaning is a gain in *per capita* figures—a rise in average per capita output and average per capita income.

A third possibility is a combination of both of these—a gain in both the national figure and the per capita figure.

The relationships among these concepts are illustrated in Table 9.1. In it are pictured some hypothetical ways in which economic expansion occurs in a country. (In each case the work force is assumed to change as does the population.) The size of the population, the per capita figures, and the national totals is equated to 1.0 at the start.

In Case A the population is assumed to rise 50 per cent while per capita output and income are unchanged, and so the national total rises 50 per cent. In Case B the population remains unchanged and the per capita figure rises 50 per cent, as does the national figure. In Case C the population goes up 40 per cent and the per capita figure up 30 per cent, so that the national total rises 82 per cent.

*Table 9.1*

## CONCEPTS OF ECONOMIC GROWTH
## IN A NATION

| POPULATION | | PER CAPITA | | NATIONAL TOTAL (Output: GNP) |
|---|---|---|---|---|
| | | (Per Capita Output) (Per Capita Income) | | (Real National Income) |
| Start | 1.0 | × | 1.0 | = | 1.0 |

Three hypothetical cases of economic growth:

| | New Population and Work Force | | New Per Capita | | New National Total |
|---|---|---|---|---|---|
| Case A | 1.5 | × | 1.0 | = | 1.5 |
| | (up 50%) | | (unchanged) | | (up 50%) |
| Case B. | 1.0 | × | 1.5 | = | 1.5 |
| | (unchanged) | | (up 50%) | | (up 50%) |
| Case C | 1.4 | × | 1.3 | = | 1.82 |
| | (up 40%) | | (up 30%) | | (up 82%) |

It will be noted that the population increase is the greatest in Case A, the per capita rise in Case B, and the national total economic increase in Case C.

Which of these hypothetical cases represents the most significant or the most desirable kind of economic growth? In discussing this question we must assume that the circumstances in which the growth occurs are equally desirable, that is, that there is no regimentation, abridgment of freedom, or other undesirable accompaniment.

In Case A the people are living no better, but there are more of them. Whether this means that the country has become crowded is unknown. In Case B there are no more people, but their standard of living has risen 50 per cent. In Case C both the population and the standard of living have risen, but neither as much as in the two preceeding cases. The national total, however, has risen substantially more.

It is impossible to say which one of the three cases offers the greatest increase in potential *military power*—a matter of importance if these nations are in a troubled world. Aside from this consideration, however, Case B, with the largest gain in standard of living, promises the most in the way of better living.

## GROWTH: PAST AND FUTURE

In the United States economic growth has resembled Case C in the past and seems likely to continue to do so in the foreseeable future. Chart 9.1 illustrates how the population of the United States has grown in the past decades (the work force has grown in about the same proportion). The chart also presents a projection of future population in growth in the United States on the assumption that the population will increase 15 per cent per decade during the remainder of the twentieth century.

*Chart 9.1*

## POPULATION GROWTH
### ACTUAL, *1790–1960*
### PROJECTED, *1970–2000*

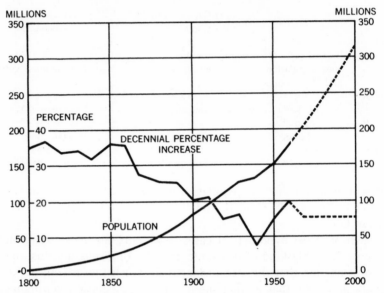

SOURCE OF ACTUAL FIGURES: U.S. Bureau of the Census; projections assume a decennial gain of 15 per cent.

Chart 9.2 shows the increase in total and per worker output since 1910. Inasmuch as the population and the work force have been increasing, total output has increased faster than per worker output, in the manner illustrated in a simplified form in Case C (Table 9.1).

The expansion of the American economy, as the chart shows, does not proceed at a steady rate. Indeed, from time to time contraction occurs. Contraction is then followed by a temporary spurt in which the rate of expansion temporarily exceeds the long-term trend. These deviations from the long-term trend rate are sometimes called "business cycles." Attention is given to this subject in the next chapter.

Here let us note that these fluctuations represent changes in the degree to which productive capacity is being utilized. They are of great significance, but clear thinking is aided by separating their analysis from that of the actual growth of productive capacity itself, which is basic to economic growth.

If past trends continue into the future, average per capita output will increase about 25 per cent per decade, despite a slight shortening of the average work week. Total national output by the same projection will increase by approximately 50 per cent per decade. These trends

*Chart 9.2*

# OUTPUT, EMPLOYMENT, AND PRODUCTIVITY

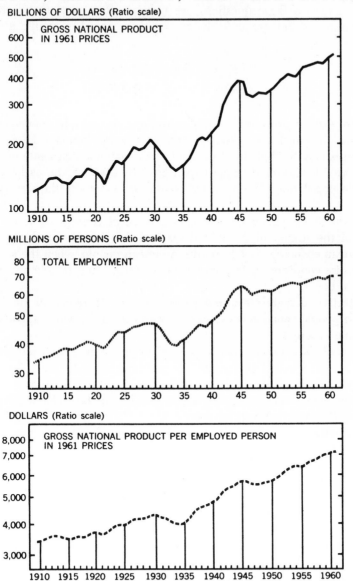

SOURCE: Annual Report of the Council of Economic Advisers in *Economic Report of the President: 1962* (Washington, D.C.: U.S. Government Printing Office, 1962), p. 112.

mean that the real gross national product will be doubled in less than 20 years, and the standard of living of the average American family doubled in about 30 years.

Are these projections reasonable? Do they portray a desirable condition? Should efforts be made to accelerate the prospective growth? To get answers to these questions, we turn attention next from arithmetic examples and definitions to the factors that control economic growth.

## THE CONDITIONS OF ECONOMIC GROWTH

The level of prosperity of our nation and our people depends on two factors: (1) productive capacity and (2) effective demand. Each of these concepts may be thought of in terms of the national aggregate or may be converted to the relevant per capita basis by dividing the national figure by the population. The line of reasoning is essentially the same in each case.

Productive capacity is essentially a *physical* concept. It refers to the size of the stream of goods and services that can be produced by the American economy, that is, by the American people, when the somewhat imprecise condition of full employment prevails and people are working normal hours.

Effective demand is a *monetary* concept. It refers to the rate at which people spend money. For most purposes the word *spending* is a suitable synonym.

Each of these two factors is essential to prosperity. Each sets an *upper* limit to the level of prosperity. If spending tends to grow faster than reproductive capacity, actual prosperity cannot go as high as the spending tendency would rush it, and the result will be inflation—a general rise of the commodity price level.

If, contrariwise, spending does not increase while productive capacity is increasing, or, a fortiori, if spending *declines*, actual production (and employment) also will decline.

In other words, the actual level of prosperity is not set by the higher of the two controlling factors, nor by the average of the two, but by the *lower* of the two. This, of course, is simply another way of saying that neither by itself is adequate; both are essential.

We turn now to the conditions that bring about rising productive capacity and later in the next chapter to an analysis of the problem of achieving a stable, expanding demand.

## FACTORS AFFECTING PRODUCTIVE CAPACITY

Total national productive capacity is influenced by the size of the population and the work force and also by per capita output potential.

*Per capita* output and income are functions of *productivity* and are influenced by population change only insofar as population change itself is a factor affecting productivity.

What does productivity mean? *Productivity* and *economic efficiency* mean the same thing. They refer to the ratio between the *output* of goods and services and the *input* of productive resources. When that ratio rises, productivity and economic efficiency have increased. A rise in productivity or economic efficiency is the essence of *economic progress*.

Productivity is often measured by *output per man-hour*. Output per man-hour depends on workers' skill and industriousness, on the amount of capital equipment used by workers, on the technical sophistication of that equipment and the methods and procedures of its employment, and on the quality of the management that guides and directs the effort.

The importance of productivity lies in the fact that it determines our standard of living. One of the great laws of economics is that the people of any country consume the goods and services that they themselves produce (imported goods being always merely an exchange for some of these). If per capita production or output in a nation is high, per capita income will be high, for they are the same thing viewed, respectively, from the production end and the consumption end of the economic process. If, however, per capita production is low, the people will be poor. If per capita production rises, the standard of living will rise; that is what has happened in our country and in quite a number of others in the past two hundred years.

## ATTITUDES TOWARD PRODUCTIVITY

Since per capita productivity determines real incomes—standard of living—one might expect that, in this and every other nation, people would be striving energetically to increase their productivity, and political and civic leaders would be vigorously developing and promoting programs for increasing the general productivity, which would mean more goods made, which means more goods available for use, which means greater material well-being.

In fact, however, concern with productivity is not universal. Some people, to be sure, do strive to increase their outputs. Some self-employed persons—farmers, businessmen, and professional men—see the connection between greater output and higher personal income. Many employees are motivated by a desire to do a better job, for more pay or more personal satisfaction or both. Some managers push employees to increase output, in order to reduce costs.

Other men, however, are indifferent, ignorant, or restricted by work rules; or they anticipate no gain to themselves from greater productivity. Indeed, they may visualize increased productivity as flooding the market or as displacing workers. If so, they are not merely neutral toward increased productivity but actively opposed to it. These attitudes restrain gains in productivity.

A program directed at promoting an understanding of the importance of raising productivity and improving attitudes toward it would be a desirable national objective.

## FACTORS AFFECTING
## PRODUCTIVITY GAINS

What are the factors that have led to increased productivity and, thereby, to a higher standard of living, shorter hours, and less hard toil?

One of the commonest explanations of the wealth and income of the United States is its possession of great natural resources—land, minerals, water, timber, and climate. These have indeed been valuable. On the other hand, their contribution to the economic well-being of our country or of any nation is easily exaggerated. Thus, great though the natural resources of the United States are, there are four other countries whose natural resources are at least as abundant as ours—Canada, Brazil, China, and Russia. Of these only Canada is a rich country; its standard of living is at a level about three fourths as high as ours. In Russia the standard of living is one third or one fourth of ours. In Brazil it is only one tenth, and in China it is still lower. In addition to these countries, there are some others in which the natural resources *in relation to their populations* offer as favorable conditions as does our own. Such countries include the Union of South Africa, the Republic of Colombia, and Romania. In these countries, however, the typical family income is low.

The explanation of these differences is to be found in a simple but often neglected fact, namely, that most natural resources have to be *developed* in order to be useful. Land, for instance, often has to be cleared and drained before it can be used to produce crops. Minerals must be located, extracted, and refined. Timber must be felled, sawed, and often transported long distances to the points of use. Falling water must be harnessed by water wheels or turbines and perhaps even created by the building of dams.

And who develops the natural resources? The people of the country. The people of Brazil, China, the U.S.S.R., South Africa, Colombia, and Romania have not developed their rich resources as have the Canadian and American people. In short, it is the *human* resources that really count in the economic development of nations rather than the natural resources.* The significance of the activities of the human resources is

---

* This topic is considered in greater detail in Chapter 23.

further emphasized by the fact of the high income level of countries like Denmark, Norway, and Switzerland—nations which nature has not endowed richly with resources, but whose able people have nevertheless created wealth.

The productivity of people depends in part on personal factors. Among them are education, industriousness, the state of labor—management relations, the incentives to activity, and the spirit of enterprise.

## THE ROLE OF BUSINESS MANAGEMENT

A specialized kind of productive activity is that provided by *business managers*. Economic activity does not run itself. Efficiency is not self-generating. Innovations are not introduced automatically. They depend on skillful management.

The contribution that has been made by enterprising business managers to economic development in the United States is often neglected. The businessman has not fared well in either fiction or history. In fiction the businessman is often portrayed as a selfish and dishonest rogue. In history books third-rate generals and politicians may get extensive mention, whereas first-rate business enterprisers may not even be listed.

Our country is fortunate in having a large number of competent business managers per thousand of the population—men who understand the productive management of personnel, machines, plants, inventories, methods, products, and financial resources—in factories, stores, service establishments, and on farms, throughout the land.

The number of competent business managers per thousand of the population is influenced by many factors. Among them are the social standing of businessmen, opportunities for training, and incentives to engage in useful business activity. These factors are more favorable in our country than in other lands.

## THE ROLE OF CAPITAL EQUIPMENT

One of the most obviously visible things in explaining the historical growth of productivity in the United States is the increase in the quantity and quality of tools, equipment, and power-driven machinery. An example that fascinates sidewalk superintendents is the skillful manipulation of the huge power shovel, with which the operator can move many time more dirt per hour than can a worker with a spade. Even when we take into account the man-hours that have gone into making the power shovel, and those that go into providing it with fuel and maintaining it, the amount of dirt moved per man-hour is still much greater than that moved by men using spades.

The expansion of the quality and quantity of capital goods requires a convergence of a number of human efforts, attributes, and conditions, including saving, investing, invention, enterprise, knowledge, and rewards that provide incentives for these.

## TECHNOLOGICAL PROGRESS

Technological development increases productivity by creating more efficient methods of producing goods, more and better equipment, and better working conditions. For farms, technology develops better seeds, breeds, feeds, fertilizers, and insecticides. In urban establishments—factories, stores, banks, and offices—some mechanical and electrical innovations are called "automation." Improved technology raises output per man-hour and provides the basis for higher real wages, even though the workers themselves do not develop the innovations and do not invest capital in them.

Technological progress has been rapid in recent years. Associated with it is a new abbreviation, "R&D," standing for research and development. Public and private outlays on these activities now total some $12 billion a year.

As noted above, the introduction of technological changes is influenced by attitudes toward such changes. Apathy and hostility delay them. Favorable attitudes speed them. Symbolic of the subtle factors that influence economic progress is Charles Kingsley's term *divine discontent*. He wrote, in *Health and Education*, "To be discontented with the divine discontent, and to be ashamed with the noble shame, is the very germ of the first upgrowth of all virtue." For purposes of economic analysis, *divine discontent* stands for three attitudes: (1) a dissatisfaction with things as they are; (2) a belief that things can be made better; and (3) a determination to make them better. If this spirit pervades a nation, there is likely to be economic development. If it is absent, if the spirit of the people is one of *apathetic resignation*, or worse, if the people display active hostility to change, economic progress is unlikely or impossible.

## TAXES AND COMPETITION

Excessive taxes, penalizing activity, can reduce productivity by discouraging saving, investment, invention, innovation, risk taking, and diligence.

As we have already noted, our load of taxation is heavy—not the heaviest in the world, but mighty heavy. How is taxation affecting productivity? As we note in Chapter 6, the evidence suggests that its adverse affect is slight. Nevertheless, some careful tax revision downward is desirable, but it would be a mistake to expect too much stimulus from it.

Proper business competition in business affairs stimulates improvements that increase productivity and decrease costs. Competition seems to be more vigorous in the United States than in some other industrialized countries.

The competitive condition is not due solely to these laws, however. It reflects the competitive spirit of American life in general and of American businessmen in particular.

## THE ROLE OF EDUCATION

The present writer has long been of the opinion that education—*good* education—has been a vital factor in this development. If the several factors discussed above are the *proximate* causes of productivity gains, education may well be described as the cause behind the causes. Despite confidence in this proposition the nagging feeling persists that it might reflect the bias of a professional educator. It has been, therefore, a pleasure to note the importance assigned to education by Edward F. Denison in his careful and comprehensive study of economic growth.*

Looking around the world, we note the correlation between education and economic progress. The causal relationship runs both ways: The poor nations cannot afford education, and therefore remain poor; the richer a nation becomes, the more education it can afford and the greater the contribution to further economic growth that is provided.

## IS A GROWTH POLICY NEEDED?

The United States has experienced great economic growth—both total and per capita. Our average standard of living is the highest in the world. If trends of the past continue, we may expect continued expansion in line with the estimates given earlier in this chapter. Is this, however, enough? Can growth be deliberately fostered; if so, pursuant to such stimulation, should some new policies be adopted or old ones changed?

We may begin by asking whether economic growth is desirable. To ask this might seem as pointless as to inquire about the desirability of progress or of health or of virtue. Nevertheless, the question is not a foolish one.

Growth is not without costs. It does not come about automatically. It requires effort and expenditure. Moreover, the industrial changes that are involved often cause serious inconvenience or even disaster to persons, firms, and communities. Technological developments can make products and skills obsolete and can cause financial loss and unemployment.

Economic growth, in the form of rising material standards, means

* Edward F. Denison, *The Sources of Economic Growth in the United States and the Alternatives Before Us* (New York: Committee for Economic Development, 1962).

easier living, less sweaty and backbreaking toil, and more leisure. Wisdom suggests that we remember that easy living can lead to a weakening of the moral fiber of the people. Oliver Goldsmith warned of this danger in "The Deserted Village":

> Ill fares the land, to hast'ning ills a prey,
> Where wealth accumulates, and men decay.

In the context of today's international situation, moreover, there is a connection between economic growth and national viability. Economic growth contributes to military and diplomatic strength—and stands in the eyes of the world as evidence of the excellence of a nation's economic system as compared with the systems of its rivals.

In the light of international comparisons the relatively slow rate of growth of the United States in the decade of the 1950s has given rise to some concern and discussion. The facts are presented in Table 9.2.

### Table 9.2
### GROWTH RATES, 1950–1959
#### (Average Annual Percentages)

|             | REAL GNP | REAL GNP PER CAPITA | REAL GNP PER MAN-HOUR | TOTAL NEW INVESTMENT |
|-------------|----------|---------------------|-----------------------|----------------------|
| Germany     | 7.6      | 6.5                 | 6.0                   | 11.0                 |
| Italy       | 5.6      | 5.0                 | 4.2                   | 8.1                  |
| Netherlands | 4.9      | 3.6                 | 3.6                   | 8.4                  |
| France      | 4.3      | 3.4                 | 3.8                   | 9.0                  |
| Sweden      | 3.5      | 2.9                 | 3.5                   | 5.1                  |
| Canada      | 3.9      | 1.2                 | 2.7                   | 5.6                  |
| U.S.        | 3.0      | 1.2                 | 2.7                   | 2.2                  |

SOURCE: New England Merchants National Bank, *Monthly Business Letter*, October 1961.

## POPULATION POLICY

The United States has no population policy; nor does this matter promise to become an issue in the near future.

The situation in some other countries is quite different. In some of the poor countries of the world overpopulation is a factor contributing to national poverty. In some of these countries it is hard to visualize an improvement in the standard of living without a check in the birth rate.

Because of many factors favorable to productivity, in the United States the population increase has not been accompanied by a declining standard of living; on the contrary, the standard of living has risen.

No grim economic necessity, therefore, has pushed us toward a policy with respect to this delicate subject. Nor is it to be expected that economic necessity will do so in the foreseeable future. It would seem more likely that population would begin to loom as a public policy question only if people should come to yearn for a less crowded Yellowstone and Yosemite or should become disturbed about the aesthetic concomitants of overcrowding.

## POLICY FOR GROWTH OF EFFECTIVE DEMAND

The foregoing discussion is concerned almost entirely with the conditions that affect productivity and productive capacity. Full employment and prosperity in the future will require the total of effective demand (spending) to increase at about the same rate as productive capacity. If the average velocity of circulation of money and its mathematical reciprocal, the average attitude toward holding cash, remain unchanged in future decades, the total amount of money will have to grow about as fast as productive capacity. If, therefore, productive capacity is doubled in less than two decades, the amount of money also will have to be doubled.

This expansion will require that the Federal Reserve Banks provide sufficient additional reserves to permit the member banks to increase their credit and thereby to create new money. Supervision of this rate of increase is a proper function of the government. If the Federal Reserve Banks and the commercial banks between them do not manage to increase the money supply sufficiently, it would be possible to accelerate monetary growth through government fiscal operations and debt management. This problem—of securing a stable expansion of spending and of the money supply at an appropriate rate—is considered further in the next chapter.

## ECONOMIC GROWTH AND THE GOOD SOCIETY

There is, of course, no guarantee that increasing material well-being will make our people better or happier, since it seems to be true that (as the old saying goes) the more we have, the more we want. Nevertheless, increased productivity can raise the standard of living of millions of families whose present condition is far from affluent. And stable, rising material well-being can provide a firm foundation for that *good society* that the thinkers have been talking about for centuries.

## QUESTIONS AND PROBLEMS

1. What are the different concepts of economic growth? How can each be measured? Which concept is the most significant?

2. Why was the subject long neglected? Why was interest aroused later on?
3. What factors determine economic growth?
4. What are the factors which control productivity?
5. What part do business managers play in economic growth?
6. What are the advantages of economic growth and what are its costs?
7. Should the U.S. worry because some other countries are growing at a faster rate?
8. Should there be a national growth policy? If so, in what areas and of what nature?
9. Is economic growth a goal which can be relaxed as a society reaches a state such as the U.S. finds itself in today?
10. Increasing productivity and, at the same time, increasing per capita consumption is one aspect of economic growth. Is there not a limit on what can be consumed?
11. What is the relationship between economic growth and the good life?

## SELECTED READINGS

ADELMAN, IRMA. *Theories of Economic Growth and Development.* Stanford: Stanford University Press, 1961.

DENISON, EDWARD. *The Sources of Economic Growth in the United States and the Alternatives Before Us.* New York: Committee for Economic Development, 1962.

DOMAR, E. D. *Essays in the Theory of Economic Growth.* Fair Lawn, N.J.: Oxford University Press, 1957.

HOSELITZ, BERT F., and others (eds.). *Theories of Economic Growth.* New York: Free Press of Glencoe, Inc., 1961.

KINDELBERGER, C. P. *Economic Development.* New York: McGraw-Hill Company, 1958.

KURIHARA, KENNETH K. *National Income and Economic Growth.* Chicago: Rand McNally & Company, 1961.

ROSTOW, WALT W. *The Process of Economic Growth,* rev. ed. New York: W. W. Norton & Company, 1960.

————. *Stages of Economic Growth.* London: Cambridge University Press, 1960.

SLICHTER, SUMNER H. *Economic Growth in the United States: Its History, Problems, and Prospects.* Baton Rouge, La.: Louisiana State University Press, 1961.

WERNETTE, J. P. *Financing Full Employment.* Cambridge, Mass.: Harvard University Press, 1945.

————. *Growth and Prosperity Without Inflation.* New York: The Ronald Press, 1961.

# 10    ·STABLE PROSPERITY

The previous chapter deals principally with the gradual long-run increases in national output and income which result from gains in productivity and productive capacity. In this chapter we shall examine a goal which is described thus:

[1] Stable prosperity,

[2] Full employment, and

[3] Full utilization of productive capacity.

Unemployment is the principal form which underutilization takes, and the word also stands as a symbol for the concept of partial utilization. The costs of unemployment in terms of reduced national and personal income and family misery are too well understood to need discussion. Economic and social reasons combine to make the reduction of involuntary unemployment to the lowest reasonable level a vital goal of our society.

As Chart 10.1 shows, the civilian labor force grows gradually, and along with it, national productive capacity. Total employment also grows gradually, but less regularly. Employment never quite catches up with the size of the labor force. Indeed, the gap between the two is sizable. In the decade of the 1950s, which was a time of high prosperity, unemployment averaged 5.5 per cent of the work force.

## TYPES OF UNEMPLOYMENT

Unemployment stems from several causes, and these may be grouped according to several different systems of categorization.

[1] *Seasonal* unemployment results from those declines in business activity that occur normally during certain times of the year, such as the decline in employment that occurs after harvest time in certain kinds of agriculture.

[2] *Cyclical* unemployment occurs when the entire economy is in a slump.

[3] The third kind of unemployment has long been called *frictional*.

171

*Chart 10.1*

## LABOR FORCE, EMPLOYMENT, AND UNEMPLOYMENT, 1929–1961

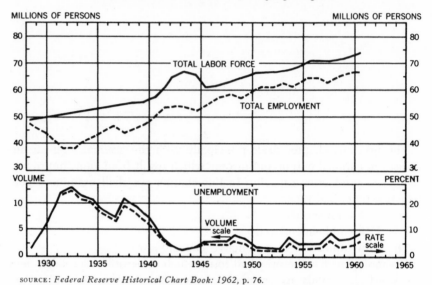

SOURCE: *Federal Reserve Historical Chart Book: 1962*, p. 76.

Nowadays it is often called *structural*. This category includes unemployment resulting from special changes of various kinds.

For example, if the demand for a specific product declines, as the demand for buggies went down some decades ago, workers who have been making the product lose their jobs. Workers sometimes (but not always) lose their jobs in consequence of the introduction of labor saving (that is, output-increasing) machinery, as glass bottle blowers did after the invention of the bottle-blowing machine. When an industry, although prosperous, moves from one location to another, workers in the previous location may become unemployed. In all of these cases the extent of the unemployment is greatly affected by the mobility and flexibility of the workers.

It is sometimes difficult to sort out the specific causes of unemployment and perhaps even more difficult to measure the quantity of unemployment ascribable to each. Nevertheless, the attempt is essential to curative action, because they do not all respond to the same medicine.

Seasonal and cyclical unemployment are discussed briefly below. Frictional unemployment, because it is one of the burning problems of our time, is deferred for fuller treatment later in the chapter.

### SEASONAL UNEMPLOYMENT

Employment offices and their extensive dissemination of information about employment opportunities help to reduce seasonal (and frictional) unemployment by informing workers about employment opportunities. Nevertheless, the correction of seasonal unemployment depends largely upon personal initiative on the part of the workers and employers. A man who is employed, for example, in a marina on one of the Great Lakes in the summertime may be able to find the same kind of employment in Florida in the winter. Or he may be able to find employment in some other industry in his own neighborhood. Employing firms may be able to locate in a region where their production peak coincides with a seasonal slump in the already existing local industries.

One of the public policy questions in connection with the seasonal fluctuations is how much unemployment compensation should be paid to workers who are employed normally during only part of the year. One is inclined to wonder a bit on learning that the New York State unemployment compensation office has opened a branch office in Florida, to facilitate doing business with the recipients of unemployment compensation who go to that southern state during the winter!

Opinions vary about the amount of unemployment ascribable to seasonal and frictional factors. Most estimates suggest a range of 3 to 4 per cent of the work force. This amount of unemployment may be expected even at a time when business in general is excellent—at the top point of the business cycle. In a cyclical sense, a condition in which 96 to 97 per cent are at work is called "full employment."

The excess of unemployment over 3 to 4 per cent is usually considered to be cyclical unemployment.

## THE BUSINESS CYCLE

Chart 10.2 shows both the gradual upward trend in business activity (as measured by industrial production) and the fluctuations around the computed trend line. It is the latter that are commonly referred to as the business cycle.\* The business cycle has many different characteristics stressed by analysts in theoretical explanations. One theory emphasizes the expansion and contraction of *bank credit* as a causal factor. Another points to changes in *psychological conditions* widespread throughout the economy. Fluctuations in *business investment* in plant and inventory occupy an important place in another explanation.

The different theories come together in a general explanation which suggests that in the first instance what varies autonomously is some segment of *demand* (spending). Wherever the initial change in spending starts, it will trigger induced changes—a reaction that may be de-

---

\* The trend line is a mathematical average which runs through the middle of the fluctuating curve. It should not be taken as representing "normal." Nor should its location be presumed to represent a goal for policy; we are entitled to aim for something much better. The desirable goal is a performance line which connects or passes near the *peaks* of the business activity curve.

*Chart 10.2*

INDUSTRIAL PRODUCTION, 1900-1962

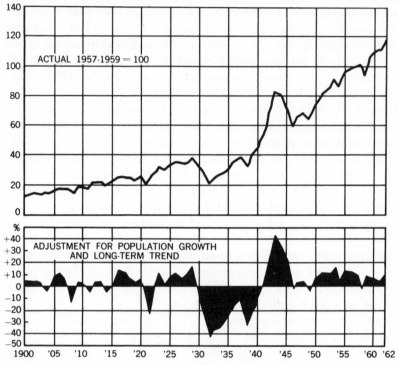

SOURCE: *The Cleveland Trust Company Business Bulletin,* April 25, 1963, p. 4.

scribed as the *multiple effect of changes in spending.*\* Thus the change in spending spreads—a "vicious circle" if downward, a "virtuous circle" if upward, and not too fast or too long. Variations in production and employment accompany these changes in effective demand. The problem of public policy is how to control these cumulative fluctuations.

## SPENDERS AND SPENDING

The three great groups of spenders are consumers, investors, and governmental entities. In addition, there is a smaller but interesting group, foreign buyers. The net excess of exports over imports, added to the

---

\* The term *the multiple effect* is the same one that I used in my book *Money, Business, and Prices* (London: P. S. King & Son, 1933). Students of monetary theory may wonder why I have not changed to using the term *the multiplier*—which is now widely used. The reason is that *the multiplier* is used by many writers as applying solely or especially to changes in investment outlays. I do not mean the term *the multiple effect* to be restricted thus but rather to apply to any change of spending, whether investment outlays, wage payments, consumer expenditure, government outlays, or any other type.

totals of the other three, completes the *gross national product* or *gross national expenditure.*\* Table 10.1 shows how the expenditures for goods and services compare for three significant years, a good year, a poor one, and another fairly good one:

### Table 10.1

## GROSS NATIONAL EXPENDITURE
## IN SELECTED YEARS

|  | 1929 | 1933 (Billions) | 1961 |
|---|---|---|---|
| Personal consumption expenditures | $ 79.0 | $46.4 | $338.1 |
| Investment outlays | 16.2 | 1.4 | 69.3 |
| Government purchases | 8.5 | 8.0 | 107.4 |
| Net exports of goods and services | 0.8 | 0.2 | 4.0 |
| Total | $104.4 | $56.0 | $518.7 |

The total of these spending streams is national effective demand. Their fluctuations bring about business cycles, and therefore may be called *destabilizers*. Why do they occur, and what can be done to reduce or offset them?

## PSYCHOLOGICAL FACTORS

Psychological factors, both in the cause and cure of business cycles, are so important as to deserve special mention. "Money," as Professor Thomas Nixon Carver once observed, "having no organs of locomotion, does not move of itself."† Money is handled by human beings. Their decisions to save or to spend, to hold money or to invest it, involve human psychology and are controlled not only by reason but also by emotion.

It is therefore essential to take account of psychological forces in the planning of a stabilization program. The success of such a program depends to some extent on the confidence that the people have in it.

This factor may be illustrated by observing the difference between the *mechanical links* and the *psychological links* between public actions and the state of business. An increase in government spending, particularly if accompanied by a deficit and especially if the deficit is financed by one kind or another of created money, is stimulating to business in the mechanical sense. It means an increased flow of money in the first instance and an enlargement of the money supply of the nation. If, however, these government actions produce an unfavorable psychological

\* These terms are generally used interchangeably, despite the fact that they stand for different things. Confusion would be avoided if "gross national product" (GNP) were used to refer to the stream of goods and services and "gross national expenditure" (GNE) to refer to spending—to the money paid for the goods and services.

† T. N. Carver, *Principles of National Economy* (Boston: Ginn and Co., 1921), p. 386.

effect among the people, the result may be that private spending is discouraged and in consequence goes down. If such circumstances prevail, what should the Government try to do to get the nation out of depression? This is by no means an imaginary situation. It was the condition that actually prevailed in the 1930s. At that time some persons, worried about the Government's deficit, were heard to say, "We'll never get out of this depression until the budget is balanced." As a matter of fact, we were due not to get out of the depression until the budget was *enormously unbalanced* by the financial needs of World War II.

It appears that since the dismal days of the Great Depression, our people have learned a great deal about the key factors that control the level of business and now have a more sophisticated understanding of the relationship of government finance to aggregate income and spending. Presumably the dilemma has been reduced if not completely extinguished.

## THE GREAT DEPRESSION

The United States had experienced business slumps before 1929. In an earlier period they were sometimes called "hard times." Some were shallow and short; others, deep and long. In the 1930s, however, came a depression which for length and depth was five times as bad as the worst previous one—that of the 1870s. In fact, it was so bad that it caused some analysts to believe that something had happened to the long-time upward growth trend of the American economy. They developed a new line of reasoning characterized by the terms *mature economy* and *the stagnation thesis*, as mentioned earlier. Other analysts, however, thought that they were wrong and were merely confusing the worst of all depressions with an end to secular expansion. Subsequent events have proven this second view correct.

An outstanding characteristic of the Great Depression and one which, all by itself, provides an explanation of the severity of that ghastly slump was the unprecedented contraction of the nation's money supply and its impact on the flow of money. Figuratively speaking, money, as it flows around through the body economic, performs a function similar to that of human blood circulating in the human body. Just as a growing boy requires a larger quantity of blood as the years go by and his body grows, so does an expanding economy require an expanding money supply. The rate of expansion does not need to be absolutely steady; in fact, a countercyclically varying growth rate is desirable in that it contributes to cyclical stability. As Chart 10.3 shows, the money supply in the United States declined about 25 per cent in the four years after 1929, when the requirements of a growing economy would have suggested an *increase* of 15 to 20 per cent. It is no wonder, therefore, that this monetary bloodletting precipitated economic illness in our "growing boy" economy: the wonder is that the bleeding wasn't fatal.

This frightful contraction of the money supply occurred in consequence of a contraction of bank credit, the failure of thousands of banks, and the passivity of the Federal Reserve System in not coming to the rescue of the banks. It is also arguable that, not later than the middle of 1931, the United States Government should have guaranteed all the bank deposits in the United States in an effort to check the monetary contraction.

In any event, the lessons of this bad time—that an expanding economy needs an expanding money supply, that even an unchanging money supply can become harmful in a short time, and that a shrinking money supply is disastrous—now seem to have been learned.

*Chart 10.3*

### THE MONEY SUPPLY IN FOUR DEPRESSIONS

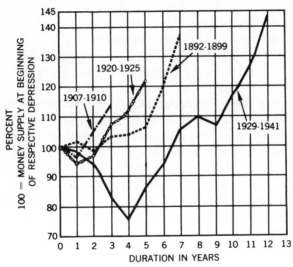

SOURCE: J. P. Wernette, *The Future of American Prosperity* (New York: The Macmillan Company, 1955).

### CONSUMER SPENDING

Destabilizers are discussed in a preceding section. They are the streams of spending that rise or fall and bring about general business fluctuations in the same direction.

Some of the types of spending that have shown large fluctuations are consumer expenditures on durable goods, construction outlays, and business investment in plant, equipment, and inventories.

A proper question at the beginning of a discussion of a stabilization program, therefore, is to ask whether consumers and businesses can reduce the instability of their spending and thus contribute to greater stability.

What can *consumers* do to neutralize business slumps? Theoretically they can, individually, help stability by not going on buying splurges (and running up excessive debts) in time of prosperity and by not slashing their expenditures when business and employment decline. Their *aggregate* behavior, however, is what counts, and this may not be governed by such rationality. One view has it that it is useless to look to consumers in the mass for stabilizing behavior, that consumer spending simply depends mechanically on consumer income and is not affected by consumers' anticipations and beliefs. A contrary view holds that consumer spending is influenced by attitudes as well as by changes in incomes. Studies by the University of Michigan Survey Research Center indicate that the latter view is correct. This suggests that consumer education might hold some promise of inducing steadier spending habits. In any case, the present fact is that consumer spending on nondurable goods (food and other necessities) does tend to hold a steady level, but their spending on durables generally follows the cyclical ups and downs and hence is, by and large, a destabilizing influence.

## BUSINESS AND BANKING

*Business* firms can reduce instability by avoiding cycle-intensifying fluctuations in inventories and outlays for plant and equipment, that is, by refraining from increasing them unduly in good times and contracting them excessively in bad times. Such action would at least reduce the size of these destabilizers and might even change these spending streams into steadiers. Inasmuch as fluctuations in these components of gross national expenditure have been major factors in post-World War II cyclical fluctuations, their stabilization would be correspondingly helpful.

Wider adoption of private supplemental *unemployment benefit plans* would further reduce the instability of workers' incomes and, in addition, would presumably stimulate management to improve production planning with a view to stabilizing output and employment.

*Bankers* can contribute to stability by avoiding both excessive expansion of bank credit when business is good and undue contraction during slumps, actions which intensify the cyclical fluctuations.

The actions that consumers, businessmen, and bankers can take to contribute to stability add up to this principle: In good times, exercise restraint; in a slump, avoid contraction. This principle, however, may be contrary to prudent individual interests. Exercising restraint in good times may mean foregoing profits while one's competitors make big gains. Avoiding contraction in a slump may mean tying up working capital in inventory and losing money and may even lead to bankruptcy. In other words, prudent individual interest may necessarily be a destabilizing factor, and it may be unreasonable to expect much spontaneous improvement in the steadiness of private spending.

The Federal Government, however, unlike consumers, businessmen, and bankers, can take the viewpoint of the economy as a whole and can influence total spending, by means of *steadiers* and *stabilizers*.

## STEADIERS AND STABILIZERS

A "steadier" is a money stream or an influence on a money stream that does not fluctuate cyclically. Many Government *outlays* are in this category. Expenditures on national defense, interest payments, agricultural supports, veterans' benefits, and social security payments are examples.

The more steadiers there are in an economy, the less its instability and the easier the task of achieving stability. But steadiers do not completely solve the problem, because they do not *offset* the effects of the destabilizers.

Offsetting can be accomplished by *stabilizers*—money streams that move in a *countercyclical* direction. Unemployment insurance and supplemental unemployment benefits are examples of stabilizers.

## UNEMPLOYMENT INSURANCE
## AS A STABILIZER

The unemployment insurance system uses money reserves. Payments are made *into* these reserves by employers and *out* of them to the involuntarily unemployed.

When business declines and workers are laid off, they and their families reduce their spending, thus generating the vicious circle of unemployment causing more unemployment. If, however, the laid-off employees receive unemployment compensation payments, their income declines but does not drop to zero, and therefore their spending can continue at a higher level than it would but for the payments.

This benefit is limited, however, by the fact that the unemployment compensation payment amounts to only a fraction of a worker's regular wage. Furthermore, the payments do not continue forever; they last only for a stated number of weeks. If the worker is then still unemployed, he has exhausted his benefits. Moreover, there are several million employees who are not in the groups covered by unemployment insurance.

Because of these limitations, when a thousand average workers are laid off, the total of their unemployment compensation payments amounts while they are unemployed to only some 20 to 25 per cent of their total previous wages. It will be apparent, therefore, that unemployment compensation is only a modest antidote to the cumulative spread of unemployment.

A reasonable question follows: Could this important stabilizer be strengthened? It could be strengthened in three ways: (1) by raising the amounts of the payments, (2) by lengthening the duration of the payments, and (3) by extending the system to cover millions of workers who are not now included.

These changes would present problems. People disagree, for example, about what percentage of take-home pay should be provided by unemployment insurance in order to avoid making unemployment attractive. There are practical difficulties in the way of extending the system to groups of workers not now covered. There are problems of financing the higher level of contributions that would be required to maintain higher benefit amounts and longer durations of payments.

The public (Federal–state) unemployment insurance system has been supplemented by private unemployment benefit plans now operative in automobile firms and other industries. A typical plan provides that the employer make payments into a fund at a stated amount for each employed worker and the fund make payments to workers who are laid off. These payments are in addition to public payments and provide more income for these unemployed persons. Such a supplemental unemployment benefit plan also gives management an additional stimulus to provide steady employment.

## THE ROLE OF THE GOVERNMENT

The proper role of the government in contributing to stability is a controversial subject. Men disagree about it—sometimes for scientific economic reasons and sometimes because of political loyalties. Good citizenship is promoted by careful study of governmental actions and their consequences.

The basic economic policy of the Federal Government is stated in the Employment Act of 1946:

> The Congress hereby declares that it is the continuing policy and responsibility of the Federal Government to use all practicable means consistent with its needs and obligations and other essential considerations of national policy, with the assistance and cooperation of industry, labor, and state and local governments, to coordinate and utilize all its plans, functions, and resources for the purpose of creating and maintaining, in a manner calculated to foster and promote free competitive enterprise and the general welfare, conditions under which there will be afforded useful employment opportunities, including self-employment, for those able, willing, and seeking to work, and to promote maximum employment, production, and purchasing power.

In addition, the Act requires the President to submit an annual economic report and creates the President's Council of Economic Advisers.

In a sense, the Act is a declaration of policy. It does not establish any agencies for carrying out the policies.

If this Act constituted the whole of the Federal program, it could hardly be considered to be very important; but it does not. Even prior to its enactment, the Federal Government had several mechanisms and agencies that influence stability.

Three of the many governmental instruments are especially important and are analyzed here: (1) fiscal policy; (2) credit policy (often called *monetary* policy), administered by the Federal Reserve System; and (3) debt management, administered by the Treasury.

## FISCAL POLICY

The fiscal operations of the Federal Government affect the disposable income of people and corporations in two ways:

[1] Most of the cash out-payments of the government become income to the people who receive the money. For example, if the government buys more missiles, more workers get jobs and incomes. Conversely, if the government buys fewer airplanes, some people lose their incomes.

[2] The government's tax receipts, conversely, come out of people's incomes. The worker whose employer withholds some income tax money has his take-home pay (his *disposable* income) reduced by the tax.

Since the government's fiscal operations affect the people's disposable income in these ways, these operations can be used as a *stabilizer*, reducing disposable income in good years and raising it in slumps. If in a good year the government runs a surplus, with receipts exceeding outlays, the disposable income of the people is restrained. If the government then uses the surplus funds to pay off some government debt held by commercial banks, the restrictive effect is tightened by the consequent contraction of the nation's money supply.

If in a business slump the government runs a deficit with outlays exceeding receipts, disposable income is raised. If the government finances the deficit by borrowing from commercial banks, the stimulating effect is further increased by the consequent expansion of the nation's money supply.

## GOVERNMENT EXPENDITURES

It may seem that the easiest way in which the government could stabilize total spending would be by spending less when the private sectors spend more and, conversely, by spending more when the private sectors spend less. In fact, however, there are some difficulties connected with this countercyclical government-spending plan.

First, changing the rate of government expenditures *takes time*. If a business slump starts and the government already has the blueprints and the proverbial "reserve shelf" of public works, it may take months to get decisions made and contracts let, more months to get the jobs underway, and many more months to finish them. The result might actually intensify business cycles, by doing little during the slump and, instead, providing a tardy stimulus just as the economy rises to the next high level. Furthermore, a public works program emphasizes on *one* industry—the construction industry—and offers no *direct* assistance to other industries. Finally, political factors might prevent cutting expenditures once they had been increased. The higher "temporary" expenditures might become permanent.

## FLEXIBLE TAX RECEIPTS

If countercyclical fluctuations in expenditures (a clumsy and perhaps even harmful weapon) represented the only possible Federal financial stabilizer, not much stabilization could be provided by Federal finance. But it is not the only significant characteristic of the Federal budget. It is also possible to have tax receipts rise and fall with fluctuations in business conditions, and the more they do so, the more they stabilize disposable income.

At the present time the Federal Government has (presumably by accident) erected a system of taxation in which the principal taxes—the personal income tax and the corporation income tax—fluctuate significantly with the state of business. Their yield rises and falls without any new legislation. Moreover, because the rates on the personal income tax are progressive and because any decline in personal taxable income comes off the top taxable brackets first, fluctuations in the personal income tax yield are greater than the fluctuations in the personal income on which the tax is collected. This means that the after tax fluctuations in disposable personal income are smaller than the fluctuations in pretax income and are, therefore, more stable.

Inasmuch as profits are a semiresidual part of national income, they tend to fluctuate more than does business activity and, therefore, contribute to stabilizing corporation incomes after tax.

The cyclical rise and fall in Federal tax receipts is automatic; it occurs without Congressional legislative actions, and it requires no administrative decisions. The consequent tendency toward a (repressive) surplus or a (stimulating) deficit also is automatic. This mechanism is a kind of *economic* thermostat that turns on warmth (a deficit) or cold (a surplus) at different times.

It is important, therefore, that the thermostat be set at the right level —neither too high nor too low. If it is set too *high*, deficits will be too large and surpluses too small, and business will be overstimulated. If, however, it is set too *low*, deficits will be too small and surpluses too large, and business will be chilled too soon in a recovery period—when employment and production are still substantially below capacity.

The latter condition appears to have been the situation of recent years. The Federal budget showed a large deficit in 1958, a rapidly declining deficit in 1959 (as business recovered modestly), and a small surplus in 1960 (while the unemployed were still about 7 per cent of the work force). (See Chart 10.4.)

*Chart 10.4*

FEDERAL  CASH  RECEIPTS  FROM  AND
PAYMENTS  TO  THE  PUBLIC

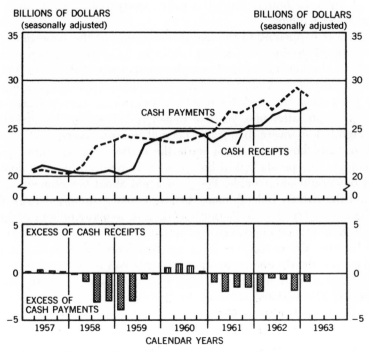

SOURCE: Council of Economic Advisers, *Economic Indicators*, April 1963, p. 36.

This shift from a stimulating fiscal position to a restrictive one, together with a similar shift in Federal Reserve policy, helped to bring on the 1960 slump.

This reasoning leads to the conclusion that the achievement and maintenance of an abundant prosperity in the future would be aided by setting the fiscal thermostat a bit higher. A simple way of doing this would be to enact a modest permanent reduction in the schedule of income tax rates.

CRITICISMS  AND  COMMENTS

Although the idea of compensatory fiscal policy outlined above is now rather widely accepted, and is endorsed by that forward-looking organization of businessmen, the Committee for Economic Development, it does not command universal support.

One criticism is that Government deficit spending was tried for many years during the Great Depression and was not successful. What is the line of reasoning in support of this position? Government expenditures and deficits did rise during the 1930s. The increase started slowly. Indeed, through fiscal year 1930 there was a surplus. Thereafter, however, budget expenditures rose fairly steadily throughout the rest of the decade, going up from $3.3 billion in 1930 to $8.9 billion in 1939. From 1932 through 1939 the budget showed a deficit every year, ranging from $1.2 billion to $4.4 billion.

What was happening to the national economy at the same time? The gross national product was $104.4 billion in 1929, $58.5 billion in 1932, and $91.1 billion in 1939. Unemployment amounted to 12 million, or 24 per cent of the work force, in 1932. In 1939 it averaged 9.5 million, or 17 per cent of the work force, which was still an extraordinarily high figure. In short, after nine years of deficit spending, the depression was only slightly less severe than it had been at its worst point.

These facts, however, do not settle the matter. For one thing, public psychology (the psychological link previously referred to) was doubtful if not downright unfavorable. People worried about Government spending and the deficit. Indeed, many believed that it promised more inflation than recovery. The deliberate spending of so many billions of dollars in peacetime was an unprecedented action.

To be sure, the nation was in an unprecedented depression. As indicated earlier, the decline in the money supply was so severe that by 1933 the nation had only about two thirds as much money as it needed for prosperity. The national economy by that time had slid down into the deepest hole of its history. Getting out required not a modest shove but rather a gigantic push. In the circumstances, the deficit spending, although large by previous standards, was small compared to the actual need.

When World War II came along, the picture changed substantially. Government expenditures soared to $98.4 billion in fiscal year 1945, at which time the deficit was $53.9 billion. Much of the wartime deficit was financed by selling securities to the commercial banks—a process which increased the nation's money supply. Public psychology also changed. It was unorthodox—and, many persons believed, unwise—to spend vast sums on public works and incur substantial deficits in peacetime; but it was entirely orthodox in wartime to spend ten times as much money and to incur a deficit ten times as large.

In short, the financial operations of World War II, at long last, ended the Great Depression. Does this fact mean that financial operations of a similar magnitude would be necessary in order to end future depressions? It does not, unless future depressions should find the nation suffering from the same monetary deficiency that occurred in the early 1930s. Since there is little prospect of such an occurrence in the foreseeable future, it is resonable to conclude that the nation will not again have to cope with such a disastrous depression and that more modest fiscal operations by the Federal Government, together with other policies, will provide adequate assurance that business slumps can be held to tolerable size.

It is also true that there is a wider understanding among the citizenry about these matters than prevailed in the 1930s. Although many are still alarmed by government spending, and some consider that "deficit spending" is a horrid term which represents a dangerous condition, others are able to think in terms of orders of magnitude, functional relationships, and national income analysis and to relate Federal fiscal operations to stabilization policy in the modern manner.

## THE QUESTION OF BUDGET BALANCE

Approval of a balanced budget and concern about the national debt represent the attitudes of some persons. For example, these subjects were analyzed thus in August 1962 in the monthly letter of a great American bank:

> A balanced budget is a hallmark of financial prudence, in family life as well as in government. Borrowing on a major scale by the Federal Government needs to be reserved to great emergencies. At other times we should seek every opportunity to chisel down the magnitude of the debt.

It is perhaps true that a lifetime balanced budget is a hallmark of financial prudence in family life if for no reason other than that no family lasts forever. *People die.* On the other hand, if we turn our attention from people to *corporations,* which are usually administered with the expectation that they will live forever, we find that the situation is different. Here, borrowing is not reserved to meet great emergencies, but is a regular business practice. Corporations do not seek every opportunity to chisel down the magnitude of their debts. On the contrary, growing businesses quite commonly note that their debts rise as the years pass. They not only have no expectation of chiseling down the debt or paying it off; quite the reverse, they expect to see it rise as long as the business is expanding.

## FLEXIBLE TAX RATES

The Federal fiscal system is now a stabilizer of substantial power. Possibly, indeed, it is strong enough (with the thermostat set perhaps a bit higher) to preserve prosperity at a high level. Perhaps, however, it should be strengthened. One way of doing so would be to cause the rates of the income tax to go up in times of prosperity and down in times of depression, thereby cutting off more disposable income in good times and less in low periods.

How could such a plan of flexible tax rates be operated? How would the rates be changed? And by whom?

One possibility is for the Congress to pass a new law each time the rates should be changed. Since the process of enacting a law is usually rather slow, there would always be the danger that the action would be too late.

A second possibility is for the Congress to authorize the President to change tax rates. This arrangement would be similar to the present law with respect to tariff rates, under which the President is authorized to make certain changes in import duties. Such an arrangement would obviate the necessity of passing a new law for each readjustment.

A third possibility is for the Congress to enact a schedule of variable rates, with the amount of variations dependent on some stated rule. One way of providing such automatic changes would be for the amount of each individual exemption under the personal income tax to depend on the current national percentage of unemployment. Thus the law might provide a schedule like that given in Table 10.2. It will be noted that an increase in the value of each exemption is the same thing as a reduction in the effective rate of the tax. The effect, moreover, is concentrated on taxpayers of low incomes in that they gain (by a rise in the exemption) relatively more than do the rich. The rationale of this arrangement is that they are more likely to change their spending as their disposable incomes change than are the well-to-do.

*Table 10.2*

### PROPOSED SCHEDULE OF PERSONAL EXEMPTIONS FROM REPORTED GROSS INCOME

| PERCENTAGE OF LABOR FORCE UNEMPLOYED | EXEMPTION VALUE OF EACH |
|---|---|
| 1.99 or less | $ 300 |
| 2.00—2.99 | 400 |
| 3.00—3.99 | 500 |
| 4.00—4.99 | 600 |
| 5.00—5.99 | 700 |
| 6.00—6.99 | 800 |
| 7.00—7.99 | 900 |
| 8.00—8.99 | 1,000 |
| 9.00—9.99 | 1,100 |

In a discussion of tax policy, there lurks an insidious danger—the danger of relying on common sense. Common sense suggests the time when we should have a tax cut is when the budget shows a sizable surplus; then we can "afford it." Common sense further suggests that if we are running a large deficit, there should be no tax cut; indeed, the thought may be expressed that taxes should be increased in order to reduce the surplus. A surplus is more likely to appear when business is extremely good and a deficit when a business slump is occurring. If one believes in the countercyclical fiscal policy, then one concludes that what common sense tells us is exactly wrong; it is upside down; its recommendations would magnify the business cycle. The countercyclical theory says that the time to raise tax rates is when business is booming and the time to drop tax rates is when business is declining; the former action checks the rise in disposable income, the latter checks its decline, thereby contributing to stability.

Changes in exemptions could be put into effect quickly. Tax deductions of employees, and consequently their take-home pay, would be affected at once. This means that the changes would be likely to have immediate effects on consumer spending.

This third method of providing for tax rate changes—like the second—would obviate the necessity of passing a new law every time the rates were to be varied. It would also offer a degree of certainty, which might be reassuring to businessmen and others—a visible, infallibly responsive weapon of fiscal policy against both boom and bust.

## THE FEDERAL RESERVE SYSTEM

The Federal Reserve System administers credit policy, or monetary policy. The System consists of the 12 Federal Reserve Banks (and 24 branches), located in principal cities all over the country, and the Federal Reserve Board of Governors, located in Washington, plus some six thousand member banks. The Federal Reserve Banks are nominally owned by the member banks; but the entire system is directed as effectively from Washington as though it were owned by the government. The Federal Reserve Banks are *bankers' banks;* they do very little business directly with individuals and business firms, and even a well-informed and financially responsible citizen may never have seen one, much less been inside it.

The Federal Reserve System was created by an act of Congress passed in 1913, and started operations in 1914. That act, as subsequently amended, defines the structure, powers, and duties of the Federal Reserve Banks and of the Board of Governors in Washington; it also provides certain rules that apply to the member banks. The Federal Reserve Act lists these objectives: ". . . to furnish an elastic currency, to afford means of rediscounting commercial paper, to establish a more effective supervision of banking in the United States, and for other purposes."

Since 1913 the last category—other purposes—has risen in importance until now the large "other purpose" of promoting economic growth and stability is near the top.

The Federal Reserve System carries on various activities that influence monetary and credit conditions. It lends money to member banks and sets the interest rate at which such loans are made. It buys and sells government securities—a process called "open-market operations." In addition to these formal activities, it sometimes tries to influence the member banks by exhortation—a process called "moral suasion."

Open market operations are especially important. The reason for this importance lies in a remarkable fact. Just as the member banks by expanding their credit can create money for the corporations and natural persons who are their depositors, so the Federal Reserve Banks, by expanding their credit, can *create cash for the member banks.* In other words, when the Federal Reserve Banks increase their holdings of government securities, they, in effect, manufacture out of thin air additional cash for the country's commercial banks, with whom the public does business. These banks, therefore, have more money to lend. Conversely, when the Federal Reserve Banks reduce their holdings of government securities, they extinguish cash which was formerly in the possession of the commercial banks and restrict the lending powers of these institutions. The member banks, to be sure, do not always expand their credit when their cash reserves are increased by an expansion of Federal Reserve credit, nor do they always contract their credit when the opposite takes place. At the same time, however, this ability of the Federal Reserve Banks to increase and to decrease the cash assets of the nation's commercial banks must be counted as a vital part of any plan for stabilization or expansion of the nation's money supply and, therefore, for economic stability and economic growth.

Twice in the 1950s the Federal Reserve has been criticized by some persons for maintaining excessively repressive policies; others have defended the actions. From 1955 to the end of 1957, the Federal Reserve had the brakes on the American economy, presumably because they were concerned about inflation. They kept the brakes on even after the business decline of 1957 had started, and the critics assert that the repressive action helped to bring on the slump and then to prolong it. Belatedly they shifted from the brake to the accelerator, in 1958. Business improved in 1958 and 1959. In the latter year the Federal Reserve, again becoming disturbed about inflation, put the brakes on again: this action and the appearance of a surplus in the Federal budget are credited with bringing on the business slump of 1960.

Has the Federal Reserve been overly concerned about inflation? If so, they have had plenty of company. Discussion of inflation and an appraisal of its significance are found in the next chapter.

## NATIONAL DEBT MANAGEMENT

The national debt—about $300 billion—consists of obligations of various types—bonds, notes, certificates, and bills, of various face amounts—which come due at various times in a fairly steady stream. In a typical year $80 billion, more than one fourth of the total, are due to mature. The Treasury usually pays off the maturing obligations by selling new securities, a process called *refunding*.

These operations may or may not affect the nation's money supply, depending on who has held the maturing obligations and who buys the refunding issue. If a maturing issue held by nonbank investors is refunded by selling a new issue to commercial banks, the total quantity of money is increased. Conversely, if the maturing securities were owned by commercial banks and the new obligations are purchased by nonbank buyers, the amount of money is decreased as the Treasury draws checks to pay off the banks, thus drawing down its deposits.

Thus the annual refunding of tens of billions of dollars of debt provides opportunities to raise or lower the nation's total money supply, and therefore debt management emerges as an instrument for stabilization—*if* it can be managed so as to transfer the debt to the banks in times of slump and to the nonbank security holders in times of boom.

Shifts from near-term to long-term securities as well as changes in the types of securities also have some effects on the capital markets and the availability of investment funds for private financial operations. These effects can be cycleintensifying if the Federal Reserve does not take care to balance these operations by compensating countercyclical actions.

The flexibility of Treasury operations may be reduced by the existence of statutory limits on the interest rates that it can pay on certain types of securities. If such limits preclude the sale of the affected securities under certain market conditions, the Treasury's hands may be tied.

These considerations lead to the conclusion that the effectiveness of debt management as a stabilization instrument is limited. This modest influence should be used as skillfully as possible and in any event should not be so managed as to intensify cyclical fluctuations.

## CRITERIA FOR ACTION

As noted early in this chapter, the different kinds of unemployment require different types of treatment. A successful stimulus to general spending will reduce and perhaps extinguish cyclical unemployment. At that point the stimulus should be relaxed, since more will not reduce the remaining unemployment, because it is seasonal or frictional.

This reasoning brings us to a key problem: How do we know when cyclical unemployment is down to zero?

This question was pertinent in 1962. Early in that year, business had risen substantially from the low point of 1960, and industrial production and civilian employment were at all-time highs. Nevertheless, more than four million were unemployed, which represented a seasonally adjusted 5.6 per cent of the civilian labor force. The magnitude of this unemployment and its persistence in a period of comparative prosperity caused some persons to wonder whether frictional or structural unemployment had mounted substantially. A contrary view was that aggregate demand or spending simply had not risen enough to provide full employment. After examining this question the Subcommittee on Economic Statistics of the Joint Economic Committee reached these conclusions:

> Relatively high levels of unemployment have persisted in the American economy since late 1957. The unemployment rate has remained over 5 per cent for 4 years. Two alternative approaches—for convenience referred to as the *structural transformation* and the *aggregate demand* theories—have been advanced to explain this adverse development. . . .
>
> A careful canvass of post-1957 developments produced little evidence for the structural transformation hypothesis. Those labor market symptoms which would indicate that higher unemployment has been due to structural causes are almost totally absent. . . .
>
> The evidence adverse to the structural transformation theory confirms the contentions of the aggregate demand theory. Indications of inadequate demand are present in a host of economic time series. Real gross national product increased at a considerably slower rate in 1957–60 than in 1948–57, though the growth of productive capacity did not slow, and in fact probably accelerated. The low level of non-farm job openings and of the help-wanted index in 1959–60 testify to the inadequate availability of jobs. Unemployment rose among workers attached to every occupational and industrial group. The rise in unemployment was particularly sharp among inexperienced workers, the group subject to the fewest wage and mobility constraints. The absence of any unusual concentration of unemployment in 1957–60, studies of interindustry mobility, and the high level of geographic mobility shown by the Census survey—all of these factors indicate that if an adequate number of jobs had been available, workers would have sought them out, regardless of their geographic or industrial concentration.
>
> The above evaluation of the two theories represents the best judgment that can be made on the basis of presently available evidence. . . .[*]

## FRICTIONAL UNEMPLOYMENT

If the view expressed in the foregoing quotation is accepted, it does not mean that frictional or structural unemployment is unimportant but rather that, in 1962, it applied only to limited areas. At that time unem-

[*] Joint Economic Committee, *Higher Unemployment Rates, 1957–60: Structural Transformation or Inadequate Demand?* (Washington, D.C.: U.S. Government Printing Office, 1961), pp. 77, 78, 79.

ployment was very high in West Virginia, Rhode Island, Alaska, Michigan, and Mississippi and was heavily concentrated in certain communities within those states. Unemployment was high also among young people. Dr. James B. Conant startled the nation when, in his 1961 book *Slums and Suburbs*, he pointed to the large proportion of young people between the ages of 17 and 21 who were out of school and out of work and the especially large proportion among Negro young people.

In 1961 an Area Redevelopment Administration was established in the United States Department of Commerce to aid communities plagued by chronic unemployment. In the same year the government undertook to provide funds to retrain workers displaced by automation or other similar causes. Communities and firms also sought to establish programs for retraining unemployed workers. Some of the programs seemed to be successful, while others drew little participation and produced seemingly small benefits.

## A PRIVATE RETRAINING PROGRAM

A private effort to retrain displaced workers attracted substantial attention in 1960. In July, Armour and Company closed a plant in Oklahoma City. In anticipation of this closing the Company had put money into a fund for retraining and had developed a program backed by the union. When the plant closed, 315 workers—mostly unskilled—were left without jobs. The Oklahoma State Employment Service offered free aptitude tests to these people. One hundred seventy took the tests; 58 went ahead with retraining courses in typing, office methods, blueprint reading, upholstering, basic electronics, real estate, auto mechanics, welding, air conditioning, bookkeeping, cosmetology, and tailoring. The fund paid for the courses up to $60 and half of the additional cost up to $150. Later, a survey of the ex-students showed that of the 53 who had completed courses, 40 were employed, but only 17 of these were working in the line for which they had trained. The results of this experiment were widely noted, and did not evoke enthusiasm. Although more than half of those laid off had taken aptitude tests, only about one sixth had taken the retraining courses, and some of these seemed to encounter difficulty in finding employment. One reason cited for the lack of participation in the program was that some of the Armour employees were thought (at ages 45 to 50) to be too old or, having had on the average only a seventh grade education, were lacking in the requisite background for reeducation in the trades for which courses were offered.

## PUBLIC RETRAINING PROGRAMS

The State of West Virginia launched a retraining program in 1960. The State program was supplemented by a pilot operation of the Federal

Government located at Huntington, West Virginia. By 1962 the two programs had turned out about 3,000 graduates. [*]

The significance of these operations was the greater because of the light that they shed on the probable outcome of the half-billion-dollar retraining program launched by the Federal Government in 1962, referred to below.

What were the results? Officials reported widespread interest in the plan among the unemployed. After enrolling, relatively few of the retrainees dropped out. They took courses for small appliance repairmen, stenographers, automatic transmission mechanics, route salesmen, typists, waiters, waitresses, and nurses' aids. The courses were chosen on the basis of a State survey of expected employment openings for the area. About half of the graduates are known to have found jobs, either in the activities for which they were trained or in other positions. At the same time a few jobs were still going begging in West Virginia. These were openings for technicians, physicians, and skilled workers such as machinists. Officials estimated that about 50 per cent of the State's unemployed could not be retrained and could not get jobs because they had insufficient basic education. A sizable proportion, perhaps more than half, had not completed high school.

This last situation focused attention in West Virginia, as it was coming to be focused elsewhere, on the problem of the high school drop-out. The millions of young people who were withdrawing from high schools were handicapping themselves for employment and also, in some cases, were creating serious social and civic problems. In West Virginia the State planned to start a mandatory vocational program for teenage boys who had dropped out of high schools—as a pilot experimental activity.

In 1962 the Federal Government enacted the Manpower Development and Training Act. The objective of the Act was to assist the long-term unemployed, young people, farmers, and others, to acquire the skills needed in a modern and rapidly changing economy. The three-year program was to be operated by the states, under the direction of the Department of Health, Education, and Welfare, and was to be financed by the Federal Government in the amount of $435 million. It was expected that about a million workers would participate in the program, of whom possibly one third would be persons already employed who wished to prepare for better jobs and the other two thirds persons out of work. Men who were unemployed and heads of households, and who had previously had at least three years' work, would be given priority and would receive allowances equal to the unemployment benefits in their states for up to one year. Young people between the ages of 19 and 21 would receive allowances of not more than $20 per week,

[*] This information is based on an article by Peter Braestrup in *The New York Times*, April 14, 1962, p. 11.

and those between 16 and 19, and certain other groups, would receive training without benefit of any allowances.

These programs illustrate the problems involved in trying to cope with this kind of unemployment. Relevant to it are factors that impede mobility, such as sticky wages and sticky prices—and, perhaps, high legal minimum wage rates, which may retard initial entry of young people into the work force if employers feel they are not worth the minimum that must be paid them. Personal factors quite naturally impede the physical movement of laborers from one city to another. Family ties and home ownership sometimes stand in the way of physical movement. Locating new plants in communities of excess labor supply may or may not be successful, depending on many factors, not least of which is whether the unemployed workers can in fact fit the requirements of the new plants.

The entire problem has been made more disturbing by the simultaneous existence of low unemployment and even labor shortages in some European countries. The spectacle of Uncle Sam, the economic giant, floundering in trying to provide reasonably full employment for all Americans is one which is both puzzling and embarrassing to us. The seriousness of the problem suggests that careful thought by private agencies and governmental bodies, followed by appropriate action in both sectors, is essential.

## APPENDIX

### SPENDING, PRODUCTION, AND PRICES

Let $E$ equal gross national expenditure, the $GNE$ (sometimes called the "*money* gross national product")

Let $G$ equal gross national product ($G$ stands for the goods and services that comprise the "*real* gross national product")

Let $P$ equal the average price of these goods and services—the $GNP$ commodity price level

Then $E = PG$

and $\dfrac{E}{G} = P$

Let $M$ equal money

Let $V$ equal average annual GNE velocity of circulation of money

Then $V = \dfrac{E}{M}$

and $E = MV$

Since $MV = PG$

Let $D$ equal the demand for money—the demonstrated desire to hold cash —measured as a fraction of gross national expenditure.*

* Alfred Marshall used the symbol k for what is here labeled D. The symbol k connotes that the value is a constant. Since, however, the demand for money is not a constant, the symbol k is misleading.

Then $D = \dfrac{M}{E}$.

and $E = \dfrac{M}{D}$

Since $E = PG$ (above),

Then $\dfrac{M}{D} = PG$

These equations, which show certain relationships between the basic flows of the American economy, shed light on the monetary conditions that can inhibit achieving satisfactory growth, stability, and full employment.

Achieving these goals requires that the money flow, E (GNE, effective demand, spending) behave in these ways:

[1] Increase in the long run at about the same rate as national productive capacity grows, thereby providing an adequate market for the potentially increasing stream of goods (G) and thus encouraging full employment of the growing work force, with a horizontal commodity price level (P); and

[2] Increase *steadily* rather than in wide swings, thereby avoiding cyclical fluctuations in employment, output, and income.

Achieving this behavior of the national money flow (E) involves bringing about appropriate conditions in the amount of money (M), its velocity of circulation (V), and the desire to hold cash (D).

The last two variables are greatly influenced by psychological attitudes. The first—the amount of money—is also influenced by psychological factors; and is the one of the three that can be influenced directly by fiscal policy and indirectly by Federal Reserve actions.

## QUESTIONS AND PROBLEMS

1. What is stable prosperity, and why is it important?
2. Evaluate this statement: "The economy can be stable without being continuously prosperous; but it can't be continuously prosperous without being stable."
3. Why is it that 97 per cent employment, or thereabouts, is the nearest we can get to full employment?
4. If there cannot be zero unemployment, what is meant by the term *full employment*?
5. What is essential to a stable expanding prosperity? Will any unemployment exist with the most advantageous prosperity level?
6. Evaluate this statement: "We can't spend our way to prosperity."
7. How can the private sectors affect economic stability and prosperity?
8. How can the government contribute to stable prosperity?
9. Evaluate the proposition that the "fiscal thermostat" is set a bit too low and should be raised.

10. Evaluate the proposal for flexible tax rates.
11. What can and should be done—by private or governmental action—to reduce seasonal, frictional, and structural unemployment?

## SELECTED READINGS

Commission on Money and Credit. *Money and Credit: Their Influence on Jobs, Prices, and Growth.* Englewood Cliffs, N.J.: Prentice-Hall, Inc., 1961.

DUESENBERRY, JAMES S. *Business Cycles and Economic Growth.* New York: McGraw-Hill Company, 1958.

GORDON, ROBERT A. *Business Fluctuations,* 2nd ed. New York: Harper and Brothers, 1961.

HANSEN, ALVIN H. *Fiscal Policy and Business Cycles.* New York: W. W. Norton & Company, 1941.

HICKMAN, BERT G. *Growth and Stability of the Postwar Economy.* Washington, D.C.: The Brookings Institution, 1960.

JACOBY, NEIL H. *Can Prosperity Be Sustained?* New York: Henry Holt and Company, 1956.

KEYNES, J. M. *The General Theory of Employment, Interest, and Money.* New York: Harcourt, Brace and Company, 1936.

WERNETTE, J. P. *The Control of Business Cycles.* New York: Farrar and Rinehart, 1946.

————. *The Future of American Prosperity.* New York: The Macmillan Company, 1955.

# 11 THE INFLATION PROBLEM

The attention given to the subject of inflation in recent decades indicates that both the expert and the man in the street consider it one of the nation's most important problems. Few have been the voices that have questioned this proposition, although some ask whether the menace of inflation may not be exaggerated.

What is inflation, and what causes it? Is inflation favorable or unfavorable to prosperity and economic growth? Is it a serious problem?

It now seems to be pretty generally agreed that the word *inflation* means a rise in the commodity price level—the general average of commodity prices. It does not mean that *all* prices go up. Some must, of course, but others may go down as the average goes up. The term does not include average *wage rates*. In a progressive society, in which productivity is increasing, the commodity price level curve may be horizontal, while average wage rates are rising slowly. In the United States inflation is usually measured by the consumer price index (CPI) of the United States Department of Labor.

Historically, inflation in various countries has usually been caused by an exceptionally rapid increase in the nation's money supply. In the United States this has happened most frequently in connection with the needs of financing big wars. At such a time the government budget shows a deficit, which is financed in part by either printing money to pay the bills or borrowing from commercial banks, thereby creating new bank deposits. At the same time, the supply of civilian goods may be restricted, and a condition results described in the familiar phrase "too many dollars chasing too few goods." This is sometimes called *demand-pull inflation* as distinguished from *seller-push inflation*. Chart 11.1 shows the consumer goods price level from 1800 to 1960. Four large, rapid upsurges in prices show plainly: at the times of the War of 1812, the Civil War, World War I, and World War II.

It will be noted that after each of the first three of these wars, the commodity price level declined for a substantial period. The fact that it

*Chart 11.1*

# THE CONSUMER PRICE INDEX, 1800–1960

## (1850–1859 = 100)

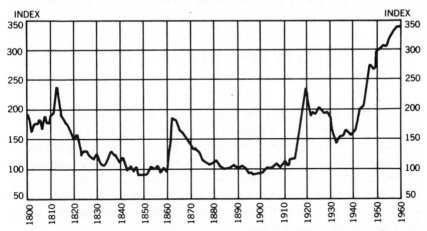

SOURCE: George Rogers Taylor and Ethel Hoover in *Employment, Growth, and Price Levels: Hearings Before the Joint Economic Committee, Congress of the United States: Part 2—Historical and Comparative Rates of Production, Productivity, and Prices* (Washington, D.C.: Government Printing Office, 1959), pp. 397–398.

Figures for 1959 and 1960 calculated by the present writer.

did not decline after World War II surprised some persons. That it actually rose during the Korean War was less surprising. That it went up in 1957–1958 and in 1960–1961, *during business recessions,* alarmed many persons. It was widely—but erroneously—believed that the commodity price level always went down during a general business decline. The persistent upward tendency of the commodity price level during those years therefore caused some persons to wonder whether inflation had become a built-in condition in the American economy.

## THE SIGNIFICANCE OF
## QUALITY CHANGES

Inflation is measured essentially by the extent to which commodities' prices at a certain time exceed the prices of the same commodities at some earlier time. But what does "same commodities" mean? Is this year's better mousetrap the same commodity as last year's less satisfactory one? It is possible that when the consumer price index rises by no more than 1 or 2 per cent in a year, the difference represents merely higher prices for better commodities, and there is no inflation at all.

The experts who put together the consumer price index are not unaware of this problem. They make an effort to allow for quality improvements. It is a difficult job. In automobiles, for examples, they resort to an arbitrary rule: they take account of innovations that are separately priced as "optional equipment" on a new model and omit those that are included in the stated price of the car. This is corrective in the right direction, but not far enough.

## DIFFERENT MAGNITUDES
## OF INFLATION

Not a little of the confusion in the discussion of inflation arises from failure to recognize that inflation comes in many sizes. It may be what is sometimes called creeping inflation or big inflation or hyperinflation. No sharp mathematical dividing lines separate these. They are differences of degree. Differences of degree, of course, if great enough, constitute differences of kind—the difference between the benefit of a gentle rainfall and the harm of a torrential downpour is much greater than the simple difference in their magnitudes.

Hyperinflation occurs when the commodity price level soars rapidly to a hundred or a thousand times its original level. The phenomenon has occurred many times in many countries in past history. It has most commonly been associated with the existence of inadequate tax systems, military defeats, new governments, inept governments, or other conditions that have caused the governments to run the money-printing presses in a helpless or irresponsible manner. Few persons, presumably, expect hyperinflation to occur in the United States, but many seem to be basing their fears of inflation on the disruptive effects of hyperinflation.

Big inflation means a large but not astronomical increase in prices. What is the outlook for a big inflation in the United States—say one in which the commodity price level doubles within a few years? This also is not generally expected unless the nation should become involved in a major war, and in that sad event inflation would be one of our lesser worries.

No; what people are worried about is a creeping inflation, possibly not per se, but because they believe that no inflation can continue at a creep, but must advance to a walk, then a canter, and finally a gallop.

## THE PROBLEM OF CHOICES

Few persons assert that inflation is good in and of itself. Some analysts, however, have suggested that a certain amount of inflation is a necessary price to pay in order to get other desired results. It has been suggested that economic growth is stimulated by high prosperity and full employment and that these conditions cannot be had, along with freedom, without putting up with some inflation.

In this connection, the word *freedom* means several things. For example, it means freedom of labor to organize unions and freedom of these unions and management to engage in collective bargaining without government regulation. It also means freedom of management to set the prices of the products that business firms sell. Implicit in these two freedoms is the fact that in a period of prosperity with high employment, unions are in a position to demand and get much in the way of wage increases because management will grant the increases rather than risk strikes, with the expectation of being able to pass along the increased labor costs to their customers in the form of higher prices.

This reasoning then leads to the conclusion that the nation has to choose among three alternatives: (1) fast growth, full employment, and freedom, but with some inflation; (2) fast growth, full employment, a horizontal commodity price level (no inflation), but with some further abridgement of freedom—that is, with extensive regulation of labor, management, wage rates, and prices; and (3) freedom for labor unions and management and no inflation, but with chronic underemployment and sluggish growth.

Our attitude toward inflation and its relationship to certain desired conditions may be illustrated by an analogy. The analogy is the frightful noise of the jet airplane engine. No one considers that the hideous screech is in and of itself desirable. It is a part, however, of a very powerful engine. If we want to have the powerful engine, we have to put up with the racket. And if we wish to enjoy the benefits of a high-powered economy—it is argued—we have to tolerate a certain amount of inflation.

If it is true that the nation cannot enjoy all the desirable conditions—that they are mutually incompatible—which one of the three combinations is the best, or the least unsatisfactory?

The answer to this question depends on how much of the undesired condition is involved in each one of the alternatives and how harmful that much is. In view of the widespread popularity of freedom, growth, full employment, and prosperity, it must be supposed that the citizenry set a very high value on these conditions and that even a modest impairment of them would be regarded as highly undesirable.

## WHAT HARM IS DONE BY INFLATION?

There is, however, no such agreement among the citizenry or among the experts about the question of the harm done by inflation. The majority view and the one probably subscribed to by most economic analysts is that inflation—even a small inflation—hurts the nation's economy in many ways. It is claimed that inflation has an adverse effect on production by introducing a bias into managerial decision making and discouraging efficiency at the same time that it encourages waste. It is asserted that inflation discourages saving and investing and thereby restricts prosperity and retards economic growth. It is further claimed that inflation cannot possibly continue at a creeping rate, but is bound to be accelerated as people anticipate inflation and buy goods in anticipation of higher prices, and buy in advance of current needs, to avoid paying higher prices later on.

Surprisingly enough, such statements are commonly made without the introduction by their author of evidence in support of their validity. Indeed, their iteration and reiteration sometimes seems to be a sort of chant, in which one man makes a statement, a second man quotes him with approval, and a third says, "Everyone agrees."

Inasmuch as during the past three decades our country has experienced a substantial inflation, one might suppose that the American economy would be in ruins in consequence of its various asserted adverse effects. As a matter of fact, however, every measure of real progress of our economy has repeatedly made new highs during this period.

Some contend that we have been able to achieve economic growth despite the inflation, because inflation has not been an accepted condition; and that if toleration of a small inflation should become public policy, the adverse consequences of a rising commodity price level would then occur. This imaginary proposition cannot be put to the factual test—and deserves close scrutiny.

There is one charge against inflation that is unquestionably true: inflation robs some persons and gives corresponding windfall gains to others. As the economic wheels go around, which have as one consequence of their motion a rise in the commodity price level (the thing called inflation), they also commonly generate increases in the money incomes of most persons. Some persons, however, have fixed money incomes; theirs, therefore, do not rise. Others rise more slowly than the average, while some rise much more rapidly than the average. The laggards, therefore, may witness a decline in the purchasing power of their money incomes; their *real* incomes may actually go down. Their losses, in the aggregate, are equaled by the windfall gains accruing to others whose incomes spurt out far ahead of the average rise in money incomes. This process is patently unjust; but whether it can be considered to be a threat to the soundness of the American economy or to the well-being of the Republic is quite another question.

## IS INFLATION NECESSARY?

It is my considered opinion that the harm done by inflation has been exaggerated and grossly exaggerated in the United States for more than a quarter of a century. In the circumstances, therefore, the reader will not be surprised to learn that if I had to choose among the three alternatives mentioned above, I would have no difficulty in preferring number one—the combination of full employment and freedom, with some inflation.

But is such a choice really necessary? Is it not possible that the choice is not necessary and that, in fact, we can have the happy combination of prosperity and freedom without inflation? The answer to this question is "Yes," provided that the human and social arrangements that are necessary can be brought about. If the happy combination cannot be achieved, it is not on account of any great law of economics which says that this outcome is impossible in our society. It would be on account of the continued unsocial behavior of men. In particular, it would be a consequence of a continuation of annual increases in wage rates, substantially in excess of the average increase of productivity or output per man-hour in the American economy. This kind of outcome of wage bargaining is virtually certain to lead to a little inflation. In view of the importance of this factor, it is significant that in recent years the average percentage *increases* in money wage rates in the United States has been declining slightly. If these increases drop only a little farther, they will be brought into balance with productivity increases, and this source of inflationary pressure, therefore, will end.

If this occurs, it should be observed that this does not mean an end to rising average real *wage* rates in the United States. No, indeed; they will continue to go up, at about the same rate. In an inflationary period the increase in real wage rates is permitted and limited by the same factor that controls it in a noninflationary period, namely the increase in average output per man-hour throughout the American economy. Much of the seeming increase in wages that occurs during an inflationary period is apparent rather than real, because some of the gains in *money* wages are canceled by the increases in the cost of living. If the money wage rate increases are held to a reasonable correspondence with productivity gains, the cost of living can remain horizontal and the increases in the standard of living can be the same as if there were no inflation.

## INFLATION AND PROSPERITY

As long as people in positions of authority are fearful of inflation and consider that it does great harm, a serious complication will continue to exist in any attempt to provide full employment and high prosperity. In a business slump actions by the government to stimulate business, including fiscal measures and various devices of debt management, and actions by the Federal Reserve, are necessarily aimed at increasing the flow of effective demand or spending. But if the nation has already been experiencing inflation, or if it is anticipated that it might do so in consequence of an increase in spending, the people who are responsible for opening the valve of this stimulating force may hesitate to turn it.

Similarly, if the nation is in a period of abundant prosperity and the commodity price level is rising, the regulatory authorities may be tempted to try to damp down effective demand for the purpose of checking the inflation. Presumably, they do not consciously aim at producing unemployment, but the repressive actions are likely to have just that consequence. In short, fear of inflation tends to inhibit expansionist monetary policies and to encourage restrictive ones.

The attitude of William McC. Martin, Jr., Chairman of the Board of Governors of the Federal Reserve System, was tersely expressed by him in an address before the Executives' Club of Chicago on December 12, 1958:

> During the past year, we have had both recession and recovery and now, once again, fear of inflation. Despite the best efforts of the Federal Reserve System to explain its objectives and point of view to the general public, questions are again arising as to the basic purposes of monetary authorities. These queries are legitimate, but the answers have been given repeatedly. The Federal Reserve System is designed to regulate the supply of money in order to foster high levels of employment and stable prices. Stability is not an end in itself but a means by which this higher standard of living can be attained and without which a lower standard of living becomes inevitable.

The Federal Reserve seems to believe that rising prices are worse than rising unemployment, and the beliefs of this central bank, whether right or wrong, are influential, since they are experienced in meaningful actions to control the money supply.

## PREVENTING INFLATION

An anti-inflationary program has three principal features: (1) the restraint of excessive demand, (2) the preventing of seller-push, and (3) the increase of productivity.

Excessive demand may be generated in any of the three great streams of spending—consumer, business, and government. Restraint of private spending is partly a private problem and partly a proper subject of governmental action. Restraint of unnecessary government spending is a problem of government and the citizens. It is the same problem that is discussed in Chapter 7, where the difficulties of reducing government spending are contrasted with the factors tending to cause it to increase.

A Congress that was determined to reduce Federal expenditures could take these steps:

[1] Examine and prune all types of expenditures, even such politically delicate ones as farm subsidies, benefits for veterans, and—that standard "pork barrel"—the rivers and harbors bill.

[2] Restrain the total of government spending by devising a way in which the Congress would pass on that total. At present, as noted in

Chapter 6, the various appropriation bills are passed separately, without regard to what they add up to. The merits of individual appropriations receive extensive consideration; the total receives little or none.

[3] Give the President the power of *item veto* over expenditures, instead of the present system, which permits only his blanket approval or veto of an entire appropriation bill, all items or none. A Gallup poll, on July 16, 1957, reported that American voters favored this proposal by more than two to one. The same report quoted George Humphrey's observation that all but eight states at that time authorized their governors to veto individual appropriation items. Some Congressmen resist this proposal on the ground that it would represent a relinquishment by the Congress of part of its constitutional authority over appropriations, would be an entering wedge for a progressive downgrading of the power of the Legislative Branch—but one is entitled to wonder whether this objection is an expression of a logical fear or the rationalization of an emotional one.

[4] Inspect the expenditures on stockpiling of military commodities. This extra purchasing adds to demand for these products, presumably raises their prices, and has been questioned on the grounds of its necessity.

[5] The government could resist inflation also by reducing tariff rates. This subject is discussed in a later chapter in connection with the subject of international trade. A reduction of tariff rates would presumably lead to some reductions in the prices of the products affected—an anti-inflationary force.

## SELLER-PUSH

Seller-push can come either from the successes of unions in getting excessive wage increases, or from business price policies that lead to unwarranted price increases, or failure to make reasonable price reductions. Some critics, indeed, have gone so far as to claim that the condition called *administered prices* is the real villain of the piece.

This line of reasoning seems to be based on a misunderstanding both of what administered prices actually are and of their role in the American economy. An administered price is simply the amount of money stated on a price tag. Almost all retail, wholesale, and manufactures' prices are administered prices. This is not a new condition. It has prevailed for decades in the American economy. Unless it can be shown, therefore, that some new abuses of this standard price-setting practice have developed, it is hard to see how administered prices can have become a cause of inflation only in recent years.

Increases in wage rates emerge from collective bargaining as a result of the demands of labor unions, presented and defended by their negotiators and officers. Some observers believe that union officers are pushed much as are politicians to get benefits for constituents. According to this view the union officers, although motivated partly by a genuine desire to improve the well-being of the members, also consider that they are in competition with leaders of other unions and are concerned that they may lose their jobs as officers, or their standing with the membership, if they do not make big gains in the wage increase race. To the extent that there is substance in this view, the condition must be counted as likely to produce excessive wage increases as a consequence of tough bargaining by union officers, with concomitant increases in labor costs and prices of products.

Ours is a growth economy, because of both steadily expanding resources and steadily increasing per capita productivity, and our labor is accordingly entitled to steadily rising real wages. It might be expected that both parties to the collective bargaining process would accept this obivous truth as a common starting point. Yet the unions seem often to have to push it alone, as a unilateral contention in bargaining rather than as a bilaterally acknowledged premise. Although some observers see gradual improvement in this respect in recent years, many business managements do a far from skillful job at the bargaining table, succumbing to the easy solution of "Russian bargaining"—simply saying "No"—retreating into the comfortable stasis of absolute obstinacy. But if collective bargaining is to be positive and healthy, and beneficial to the society, *both* participants must bring dynamism and initiative and forbearance to the table. There is necessarily militancy and aggressiveness in the process, but there must be realism and concession too. And the militancy must be bilateral, the realism mutual and concerted, the concession from reason rather than from coercion. That this is not yet true of collective bargaining in this country is perhaps the fault of both parties. In the 1950s more restraint on the part of labor and more vigor on the part of management would have been much in the public interest. It is to be hoped that these movements toward maturity will not be too long delayed.

Increasing productivity is an antidote to inflation because it tends to reduce costs and to increase the size of the stream of goods. The factors that control productivity are discussed in Chapter 9. There it is noted that productivity seems certain to rise in the future without any new special programs on the part of either government or the private sectors. The question whether there should be a "national productivity program" is related to both economic growth and inflation.

## INFLATION AND THE GOLD OUTFLOW

A new aspect of the inflation problem appeared, beginning in the 1950s, as the United States lost substantial quantities of monetary gold. Although throughout this period our *merchandise exports* exceeded our *merchandise imports,* other items such as overseas capital investment by American firms, government military and nonmilitary expenditures, and tourist outlays made our total balance of payments unfavorable on a large scale.

Foreigners, therefore, gained dollar bank accounts. Some of these dollar balances were transferred by their owners to their central banks or governments; and these organizations, being permitted to purchase gold, eventually began to do so and to take gold from the United States. (Sometimes the gold remained in the vaults of the New York Federal Reserve Bank, which guards it.) In part, this represented an entirely proper rearrangement of the world's gold holdings, of which the United States had come to have a disproportionate share.

## COSTS, PRICES, AND EXPORTS

Many analysts blamed the gold outflow on inflation. Although exports rose after 1958, the assertion was frequently heard in those years that we were "pricing ourselves out of the world markets." The reasoning usually was that excessive wage increases had pushed costs up and that these had pushed prices up to our disadvantage in international competition.

Contradicting the foregoing reasoning with data on prices and wage rates here and abroad, Professor Laurence P. Dowd concludes:

> Accordingly, one must look elsewhere for the explanation of the United States' failure to retain its percentage of total world exports. A major explanation appears to lie in the failure of some business organizations to adapt their methods to the dynamic changes in the management of foreign trade as well as to the development of world markets.[*]

The problem of gold outflow is considered further, in Chapter 27. Here we may conclude that neither inflation nor inadequacy of exports is a true explanation of the unfavorable balance of payments. Since these "explanations" are misleading, they are likely to lead to futile proposals for coping with the problem.

## THE STEEL DRAMA

Public attention was focused with unusual force on the steel drama that developed in the spring of 1962. During the early months of that year people were watching the wage negotiations in that great industry for several reasons. One was that memory of the great steel strike of 1959 was still fresh. In that year the basic industry had been shut down for months as a consequence of a labor–management dispute. Moreover, the key position of the product and the industry, and the arguments that

[*] Laurence P. Dowd, "Some Dynamic Developments in the Management of Foreign Trade," *Michigan Business Review,* May 1963, pp. 19 ff.

had swirled about them with respect to the roles played by wage and price increases in the general inflationary movement after 1957, had created the impression that steel was something of a bellwether.

Secretary of Labor Goldberg, formerly a lawyer for the steel workers' union but now representing the Government, urged upon both sides the necessity for a noninflationary settlement and the avoidance of a strike. The negotiations continued for several weeks with occasional interruptions. Finally, on April 6, new formal two-year contracts were signed between the leading steel companies and the United Steel Workers of America. The contracts provided no immediate wage increase, but a gradual increase of fringe benefits estimated to have a value of about ten cents an hour. The contract was immediately hailed as being noninflationary, and concern over the prospect of both inflation and the strike subsided.

Four days later, on April 10, the United States Steel Corporation announced price increases averaging about $6.00 a ton; about 3½ per cent of the existing prices. It is probably no exaggeration to say that the announcement came as a shock to everyone except the members of the Executive Committee of U.S. Steel.

The next day, at his televised news conference, President Kennedy sharply criticized the action, referring to it as irresponsible defiance of the public interest and ruthless disregard of their duty to the nation by what he called a "tiny handful" of steel executives. At the same time, the Department of Justice threatened antitrust investigations, and congressional authorities discussed the possibility of committee inquiries. The Department of Defense announced that steel purchases, both direct and by contractors, would be channeled to firms that did not raise their prices. By this time, however, only two of the eight major companies had failed to raise prices.

Then, almost exactly seventy-two hours after the initial announcement, U.S. Steel rescinded its increase. The president of the company stated that the action was taken "in the light of competitive developments and all other current circumstances." The other steel companies that had announced increases promptly canceled them.

The actions, both of U.S. Steel and of the Federal Government, immediately provoked controversy. Many of the comments reflected partisan viewpoints. Critics of the Administration declared that the Government's actions had been dictatorial, presaging the coming of price control and the socialist state. Contrariwise, other observers suggested that the action by U.S. Steel had represented neither good business nor straightforward behavior. To the U.S. Steel chairman's assertion that there had been no agreement *not* to raise prices, the reply was made that this ingenuous observation seemed to mark him as being one of the few persons in the United States who did not realize that the wage settlement had been effected on an unstated premise that it was noninflationary and would not lead to price increases.

The drama indicated the strength of the Government in certain circumstances. Perhaps one of those circumstances was that public opinion seemed to be strongly on the Government's side. The outcome also hinted that the influence of the Government would be strong in obtaining noninflationary wage settlements and in preventing price increases in other industries.

## ADMINISTRATION GUIDES FOR WAGES AND PRICES

The actions of the Administration in influencing the steel wage negotiations, and the events following the steel price increases, emphasize the importance of the Administration's attitude toward prices and wage rates. In his 1962 Economic Report, transmitted to the Congress a short time before these events, President Kennedy had said:

> But in those sectors where both companies and unions possess substantial market power, the interplay of price and wage decisions could set off a movement toward a higher price level. If this were to occur, the whole Nation would be the victim.
>
> I do not believe that American business or labor will allow this to happen. All of us have learned a great deal from the economic events of the past 15 years. Among both businessmen and workers, there is growing recognition that the road to higher real profits and higher real wages is the road of increased productivity. When better plant and equipment enable the labor force to produce more in the same number of hours, there is more to share among all the contributors to the productive process—and this can happen with no increase in prices. Gains achieved in this manner endure, while gains achieved in one turn of the price-wage spiral vanish on the next.
>
> The Nation must rely on the good sense and public spirit of our business and labor leaders to hold the line on the price level in 1962. If labor leaders in our major industries will accept the productivity benchmark as a guide to wage objectives, and if management in these industries will practice equivalent restraint in their price decisions, the year ahead will be a brilliant chapter in the record of the responsible exercise of freedom.[*]

The line of thinking behind the productivity benchmark and its relationship to wages and prices was spelled out in greater detail in the accompanying Annual Report of the Council of Economic Advisers. Because of its importance and its merits, the statement is presented at some length.

> What are the guideposts which may be used in judging whether a particular price or wage decision may be inflationary? The desired objective is a stable

[*] *Economic Report of the President* (Washington, D.C.: U.S. Government Printing Office, 1962), pp. 16, 17.

price level, within which particular prices rise, fall, or remain stable in response to economic pressures. Hence, price stability within any particular industry is not necessarily a correct guide to price and wage decisions in that industry. It is possible, however, to describe in broad outline a set of guides which, if followed, would preserve over-all price stability while still allowing sufficient flexibility to accommodate objectives of efficiency and equity. These are not arbitrary guides. They describe—briefly and no doubt incompletely— how price and wage rates would behave in a smoothly functioning competitive economy operating near full employment. Nor do they constitute a mechanical formula for determining whether a particular price or wage decision is inflationary. They will serve their purpose if they suggest to the interested public a useful way of approaching the appraisal of such a decision.

If, as a point of departure, we assume no change in the relative shares of labor and nonlabor incomes in a particular industry, then a general guide may be advanced for noninflationary wage behavior, and another for noninflationary price behavior. Both guides, as will be seen, are only first approximations.

The general guide for noninflationary wage behavior is that the rate of increase in wage rates (including fringe benefits) in each industry be equal to the trend rate of over-all productivity increase. General acceptance of this guide would maintain stability of labor cost per unit of output for the economy as a whole—though not of course for individual industries.

The general guide for noninflationary price behavior calls for price reduction if the industry's rate of productivity increase exceeds the over-all rate— for this would mean declining unit labor costs; it calls for an appropriate increase in price if the opposite relationship prevails; and it calls for stable prices if the two rates of productivity increase are equal.

These are advanced as general guideposts. To reconcile them with objectives of equity and efficiency, specific modifications must be made to adapt them to the circumstances of particular industries. If all of these modifications are made, each in the specific circumstances to which it applies, they are consistent with stability of the general price level. Public judgments about the effects on the price level of particular wage and price decisions should take into account the modifications as well as the general guides. The most important modifications are the following:

(1)    Wage rate increases would exceed the general guide rate in an industry which would otherwise be unable to attract sufficient labor; or in which wage rates are exceptionally low compared with the range of wages earned elsewhere by similar labor, because the bargaining position of workers has been weak in particular local labor markets.

(2)    Wage rate increases would fall short of the general guide rate in an industry which would not provide jobs for its entire labor force even in times of generally full employment; or in which wage rates are exceptionally high compared with the range of wages earned elsewhere by similar labor, because the bargaining position of workers has been especially strong.

(3)    Prices would rise more rapidly, or fall more slowly, than indicated by the general guide rate in an industry in which the level of profits was

insufficient to attract the capital required to finance a needed expansion in capacity; or in which costs other than labor costs had risen.

(4) Prices would rise more slowly, or fall more rapidly, than indicated by the general guide in an industry in which the relation of productive capacity to full employment demand shows the desirability of an outflow of capital from the industry; or in which costs other than labor costs have fallen; or in which excessive market power has resulted in rates of profit substantially higher than those earned elsewhere on investments of comparable risk.

It is a measure of the difficulty of the problem that even these complex guideposts leave out of account several important considerations. Although output per man-hour rises mainly in response to improvements in the quantity and quality of capital goods with which employees are equipped, employees are often able to improve their performance by means within their own control. It is obviously in the public interest that incentives be preserved which would reward employees for such efforts.*

Advice on the inflation problem the nation does not lack. The suggestions about how to prevent inflation seem to exceed in quality the observations respecting the harm done by a small rise in the commodity price level. The outcome appears likely to be determined by the conflict of forces, tempered by restraint.

## QUESTIONS AND PROBLEMS

1. What is the significance of the statement "Inflation comes in many sizes"?
2. Why is it argued that fast growth, full employment, and freedom cannot be had without inflation? Do you agree?
3. Evaluate the statements about the harm said to be done by inflation in the light of whatever factual evidence you can discover.
4. Do you think "creeping inflation" can be controlled so that it will not develop into a runaway inflation?
5. If a creeping inflation of not more than 5 per cent per year was expected, would people (consumers and businessmen) buy ahead and stock up on goods, considering the various costs of carrying inventories of goods—storage, insurance, interest, and the risks of obsolescence and deterioration?
6. What is the difference between cost-push and demand-pull as causes of inflation?
7. Why does fear of inflation inhibit expansionist policies and encourage restrictive ones? How important is this matter?
8. Have labor unions become so powerful that the "wage-cost push" insures a little bit of inflation as our economy grows?
9. What degree of responsibility should the Federal Government assume in attempting to halt creeping inflation? Should the Federal Government's authority include the regulation of private business's price increases and labor's demands for higher wages?

* In *Economic Report of the President* (Washington, D. C.: U.S. Government Printing Office, 1962), pp. 188–190.

10. What are some of the reasons for the outflow of gold from the U.S.?
11. Evaluate the statement that the gold outflow, if continued, "could shatter our economy."
12. Evaluate the actions of the various participants in the 1962 "steel drama."
13. Appraise the guideposts to appropriate changes in wage rates and commodity prices suggested by the Council of Economic Advisers.

## SELECTED READINGS

BACH, G. L. *Inflation: A Study in Economics, Ethics, and Politics.* Providence, R.I.: Brown University Press, 1958.

BOWEN, WILLIAM G. *Wage–Price Issue.* Princeton, N.J.: Princeton University Press, 1960.

BURNS, ARTHUR F. *Prosperity Without Inflation.* New York: Fordham University Press, 1958.

Committee for Economic Development. *Defense Against Inflation.* New York: Committee for Economic Development, 1959.

HARRIS, SEYMOUR E. (ed.). *Dollar in Crisis.* New York: Harcourt, Brace and Company, 1962.

SLICHTER, SUMNER H. "On the Side of Inflation," *Harvard Business Review,* September-October 1957.

TRIFFIN, ROBERT. *Gold and the Dollar Crisis,* rev. ed. New Haven: Yale University Press, 1961.

WERNETTE, J. P. *Growth and Prosperity Without Inflation.* New York: The Ronald Press, 1961.

# 12 REGULATION OF PRIVATE FINANCIAL ACTIVITIES

The creation and carrying of such tangible assets as houses, durable consumer goods, factories, stores, hotels, industrial machinery, and inventories of goods—in short, *wealth*—require financing. The total tangible wealth of the United States is probably about $2,000 billion ($2 trillion). All of this tangible wealth in land, buildings, and personal property—on the asset side—is balanced by liability items that represent ownership or debt, and these are documented by paper claims to the wealth. These pieces of paper and the processes involved in their original creation and subsequent purchase and sale (including governmental regulation) are the subject matter of this chapter.

Aside possibly from deeds to property, the largest group of evidences of ownership of all this immense wealth is to be found in stocks and bonds. In 1955 the total market value of stocks and bonds in the United States was $824 billion, and the figure had been rising rapidly. Of that amount, as Table 12.1 shows, government securities totaled $318 billion. These are not subject to the regulations discussed in this chapter (although investment in them by certain types of organizations is regulated).

*Table 12.1*

## MARKET VALUE OF STOCKS AND BONDS — 1955

|  | BILLIONS |
|---|---|
| Corporate securities | |
| Preferred and common stocks | $437 |
| Bonds | 69 |
| Subtotal | $506 |
| Government securities | |
| Federal | 272 |
| State and local | 46 |
| Total | $824 |

SOURCE: U.S. Bureau of the Census, *Historical Statistics of the United States, Colonial Times to 1957* (Washington, D.C.: U.S. Government Printing Office, 1960), p. 150.

A large proportion of the corporate and government securities was owned by natural persons. A sizable segment also was owned by private financial organizations to which people had entrusted their money. The largest of these private organizations, and their total assets, are listed in Table 12.2.

*Table 12.2*

## TOTAL ASSETS OF PRINCIPAL PRIVATE
## FINANCIAL ORGANIZATIONS,
## DECEMBER 31, 1960

|  | BILLIONS |
|---|---|
| Commercial banks | $298.1 |
| Life insurance companies | 119.6 |
| Savings and loan associations | 60.0 |
| Mutual savings banks | 40.6 |
| Investment companies | 18.8 |

Source of first four items: *Federal Reserve Bulletin*, February 1962, pp. 189, 199; source of last item: Arthur Wiesenberger, *Investment Companies*, 1961 (New York: Arthur Wiesenberger & Company, 1961), p. 26.

Commercial banks, life insurance companies, and mutual savings banks hold large quantities of corporate and government bonds and notes. Savings and loan associations put most of their money into mortgages on real property. Investment companies hold both stocks and bonds.

Buying securities—investing money—is not like buying groceries. The special nature of securities and investments and of the organizations that deal in them has led to the development of an immense amount of government regulations.

## BANKING BEFORE 1863

Banking has been a special concern of governmental entities since the very beginning of the Republic. For three quarters of a century, with two exceptions, banks were chartered by states only. In the first years getting such a chapter required the enactment of a special statute by the state legislature, and in many cases obtaining charters became a political activity and the aim of pressure groups.

In 1818 the State of New York created what came to be called "free banking." This law provided that banks could be established if they complied with the state's general banking laws. Many other states subsequently enacted similar legislation.

The Federal Government created the First Bank of the United States in 1791, and it continued for a twenty-year period, until 1811. The Second Bank of the United States, also chartered by the Federal Government, existed from 1816 to 1836. The principal purpose of these two

Federally chartered banks was to assist in the financial operations of the Federal Government. In addition, however, they did a commercial banking business. Also, the Second Bank had a substantial impact on the operations of other banks. It did so by collecting bank notes and presenting them for payment in coin. Since this was a kind of disciplinary action, it was resented. In the end, denounced by President Andrew Jackson as a representative of the money power, the Bank failed to get a renewal of its Federal charter. It obtained a state charter and existed for some years as a state bank.

During this long period, then, most banking activity was carried on by state-chartered institutions. At that time, there was relatively little use of checks and checking accounts, and a common way in which a bank made loans was to lend its own bank notes or promises to pay.

These bank notes comprised the principal currency of the nation. There were great differences in the probity of the bankers, and in the quality of state bank laws and their administration, and the result was that the quality of banks and of bank notes varied enormously. The best of the banks were high-grade institutions, and their bank notes—paper money—were as good as gold. At the other extreme were bank notes on which the promise to pay a certain amount was in large type, followed by small type which stipulated that payment would be made only at the head office and if deemed convenient by the directors at the time. The head office then might be located in the depths of a forest where, as one observer said, the only dwellers were *wildcats*. These institutions accordingly came to be known as "wildcat banks."

In many regions merchants selling goods to the general public found it advisable to subscribe to a publication called the *Bank Note Reporter*. This was a periodical which gave the current quotations on the values of various bank notes, in much the same way that today's papers report the prices of stocks. When a customer tendered state bank notes in payment for goods, the merchant found it necessary to look up the current values of these notes in calculating the face amount to be paid.

## THE NATIONAL BANKING SYSTEM

In retrospect it is hard to see how the nation managed to get along and to grow with such a chaotic and disorderly banking and currency system. Actually, the muddled situation might have gone on for a much longer time if it had not been for the coming of the Civil War.

That struggle, in terms of the standard measures—firepower and manpower, was the biggest war that the world had seen down to that time and was destined to hold that unenviable distinction until much of the world went to war in World War I. Naturally, it was correspondingly expensive. Since the principal source of revenue of the Government at that time was customs duties—a source that is limited and more likely to decline than to rise in wartime—the Government faced a frightful problem in financing the struggle.

The creation of the national banking system in 1863 was spurred in part by a desire to provide a market for government bonds in order to assist the war's financing. The law provided, therefore, Federal charters for banks that met the legal requirements and permitted them to issue bank notes when these were backed by United States Government bonds.

The national banking system was not a success in the beginning. Many bankers preferred to operate with state charters under the rather lax requirements of state laws, and were not eager to come under the more rigorous provisions of the new National Bank Act.

In order, therefore, to accomplish the purposes of strengthening the national bank system and eliminating state bank notes (with their frequent abuses), the Government passed a law levying a tax of 10 per cent a year on state bank notes. The obvious purpose of this law was to extinguish the bank notes, not to raise money. Its constitutionality was challenged, but in 1869 the Supreme Court upheld it.[*]

As a result of these actions, the number of national banks rose from 66 in 1863 to 1,612 in 1870. In the same period the number of state commercial banks declined from 1,466 to 325. In later decades, in consequence of the growing use of checks and checking accounts, it became possible for banks to operate profitably even though they did not issue their own bank notes. Consequently, the number of state banks increased again until, in 1960, there were more than nine thousand state-chartered commercial banks. Each of the states now has a banking act which regulates, in substantial detail, the operations of state banks.

## GROWTH AND SUBSEQUENT HISTORY

The number of banks grew gradually along with the national economy from a few hundred in the early nineteenth century to 30,736 in 1922. At that time there were 1,455 branches, making a total of 32,531 banking offices. During the remainder of the twenties, despite the high level of national prosperity, bank suspensions were numerous, especially in rural regions where many small, undercapitalized, poorly managed institutions had become involved in unwise overextension of credit. As a result of suspensions and consolidations, the number of banks dropped by 1929 to 25,568.

Then, during the early years of the Great Depression, bank failures soared and contributed to the contraction of the national money supply to which reference is made in Chapter 10. All of the banks in the country were closed temporarily in the spring of 1933. Then approved institutions were allowed to reopen, but, at the end of that year the number of

[*] In *Veazie Bank v. Fenno,* 8 Wall. 533 (1869).

banks was down to 14,771, the smallest figure since 1901 and destined to be the smallest until 1943.

After 1933 the number of banks rose slightly and then started to decline—this time not in consequence of suspensions (which were very few), but rather because of mergers and the absorption of small banks as branches of large ones. In the following three decades, when the total number of banks declined slightly, the number of branches quadrupled.

## BANK REGULATION

Some notion of the extent to which national banks are regulated may be had from the fact that the official publication of the Comptroller of the Currency entitled *Federal Laws Affecting National Banks* is a book of 352 pages exclusive of the introduction and the index. Some of the important pertinent subjects that are regulated by these Federal laws are organization, capital, number and qualifications of directors, reserves and reserve requirements, types of magnitudes of loans, investments, borrowing, real-estate ownership, affiliations with other firms, branches, reports, interest rates payable on deposits, fiduciary powers, dividends, trust departments, and many more. The total extent of governmental bank regulation will be appreciated when it is realized that bank legislation in each of the 50 states has similar coverage.

## PROBLEMS AND ISSUES

Two major differences between banking in the United States and banking in most other industrialized countries raise the question whether our systems are correct and theirs wrong. The differences are the number and average size of banks and the amount of government regulation.

In the United States, as we have just seen, regulation by the Federal and state governments is extensive and detailed. In other countries there is little or no regulation of banking. Extensive branch banking is the rule, and there are relatively few unit banks (one-office banks). Banking is carried on by a handful of large banks, each of which has dozens or hundreds of branches located more or less country-wide.

In the United States the number of banks is large, many of them are relatively small, and there is less branch banking. On December 31, 1961, there were 13,946 banks (separate banking corporations); in addition, there were 11,896 branch offices, or a total of 25,842 banking offices.

## BRANCH BANKING

Both the growth and the existence of branch banking in the United States are very uneven among the different states. This is because branch banking is regulated mainly by state laws. The National Bank Act permits national banks to establish branches subject only to the several states' provisions regulating their own state-chartered banks. The state laws vary greatly. Some states do not permit the establishment of any branches whatsoever. Other states allow a bank to establish branches within a limited area, such as the head office city or county, or within a stipulated number of miles of the head office irrespective of city and county lines. Other states permit the establishment of branches anywhere within their borders. The more limited type of branch banking is often called *metropolitan branch banking;* the last type, *state-wide branch banking.*

A bank is not allowed to open branches outside of the state in which the head office is located, except in other countries. There is, therefore, no nationwide branch banking in our country. This is a condition which bankers in other countries, accustomed as they are to nationwide branch banking, find hard to understand. Some strands of explanation are to be found in our long-time mistrust of banking power, the great size of the United States, and the preference in certain circles for state rather than national action in all things.

These and other considerations are examined as we turn attention to this public policy question: Are the existing restrictions on branch banking wise, or should there be some relaxation of these restrictions, or perhaps even should a very considerable enlargement of branch banking be permitted?

Branch banking has existed since the early years of the Republic. The First Bank of the United States had several branches. A pattern of local opposition then developed, compounded of mistrust of a large financial institution whose head office was far away from the branches and dislike on the part of local bankers of the additional competition. The Second Bank of the United States had two dozen branches, and both the branches and the entire organization were the objects of complaint and criticism.

Prior to the establishment of the national banking system in 1863 many state-chartered banks established branches. Some of the banks were successful; others were failures. Apparently, however, the branch banking feature was not the cause of either success or failure in any of these cases.

The supremacy of the national banking system in the latter part of the nineteenth century did not lead, however, to the establishment of many branches. In 1900 there were 13,053 banks and only 119 branches, most of which belonged to state banks.* The emergence of branch banking as a large operation and a problem of public policy stemmed from the substantial development that occurred in the State of California after the

---

* The statistics in these paragraphs on the numbers of banks and branches are taken from *Historical Statistics of the United States, Colonial Times to 1957* (Washington, D.C.: U.S. Bureau of the Census, 1960), Chapter 10; and from current issues of the *Federal Reserve Bulletin.*

passage in 1909 of a law that permitted state-wide branch banking. Taking advantage of that act, A. P. Giannini, who had started a small institution in San Francisco called the Bank of Italy, began an energetic program of opening and acquiring branches. Later the bank's name was changed to the Bank of America, and within his lifetime, Giannini saw it become the largest bank in the world, with hundreds of branches all over the State. Other California branch banks developed also, and several became billion-dollar organizations, with the Bank of America's total assets at the end of 1961 well in the lead, at a figure of more than 11 billion dollars.

Branch banking had a substantial development in a few other states also, a limited development in several others, and none at all in the remainder. The issue of the extension of branch banking has been a live one for many years, and is today. The arguments pro and con have often been expressed in terms of the public interest and the well-being of business but have usually followed the discernible interests of proponents and opponents. Since this is a common situation in connection with public problems, an examination of these arguments may provide insight, with respect, not only to branch banking, but also to other current issues where the same mixture of general welfare and private interest exists.

In a discussion of these matters clarity is aided by noting the difference between *branch banking* and *group banking*. In *branch banking* one legal corporation has banking offices in addition to and located away from the head office. In a case of *group banking* several banks are owned by a holding company and are frequently grouped around a large metropolitan bank. In group banking the banks involved are legally independent corporations with separate charters and boards of directors, but with substantial central management control.

Group banking has been related to branch banking in some instances, but in the main it has developed largely where, and for the reason that, banks were legally prohibited from establishing branches. Inasmuch as branch banking represents the highest degree of centralization of ownership and operating control, also because it is the most prevalent of these forms, and finally because the issues involved with appropriate changes apply (in most cases to a smaller degree) to group banking, attention in this discussion is focused on branch banking.

## PROS AND CONS OF BRANCH BANKING

Some of the pros and cons of branch banking are associated primarily with a factor of *size*, since the more branches a bank has, the larger it usually is. A unit bank may be small—perhaps only a million-dollar institution. But banks with branches may count their assets in the tens or hundreds of millions of dollars or perhaps even the billions.

Other considerations, however, are independent of size and hinge on the fact of the existence of offices in different localities, separate from the head office. Some factors involve a mixture of both the size factor and the dispersal factor.

Many are the arguments adduced on both sides. The following are some of the principal ones in favor of branch banking.

[1] Because it can make loans in several localities and to a variety of industries, a branch banking organization provides a wide distribution of risks.

[2] The larger capital permits a branch banking organization to make its maximum legal loan in any of its branches, whereas a unit bank the size of the branch would have a correspondingly lower maximum loan limit.

[3] Its greater size permits a branch banking organization to avail itself of mechanization and automation and to operate well-staffed central services. (Examples: A group of expert analysts continuously making investment studies of securities; a research activity in the Trust Department studying investments for trust accounts.)

[4] The larger bank is more likely than the small one to know of and to use the latest banking methods, including credit policies and procedures.

[5] Branch banking facilitates the shifting of funds to the places that can make the most productive use of them.

[6] If the peak loads in the various localities in which there are branches occur at different times, the bank may be able to maintain a mobile squadron of tellers and other employees who can move around from branch to branch accordingly, as needed.

Opposed to branch banking are the following arguments:

[1] This system drains capital from small communities and moves it to head office cities or other metropolitan centers.

[2] Branch banking has the characteristics of absentee management, in that the bank is not interested in local problems; branch managers are frequently changed and are often unaware of local conditions.

[3] This kind of banking is impersonal, relying on balance sheets and income statements instead of character as the basis for making loans.

[4] Branch banking tends toward monopoly.

[5] It means a concentration of immense financial power, which is dangerous to our society in many ways.

[6] Where branch banking is permitted, its spread tends to result in the elimination of unit banks. (This is merely the banking version of the greedy-big-business versus worthy-small-business fight.)

Appraisal of the validity of the foregoing arguments is not easy, partly because (as in so many other areas of politico-economic controversy) they often take the form of mere assertions which are not backed up by any evidence. Nevertheless, the present consensus of objective students of the problem leans in the main to acceptance of the arguments favoring branch banking and rejection of those opposed as having less substance.

Perhaps the most interesting argument against branch banking is the last one listed—that it would lead to the elimination of unit banks. This is simply another way of saying that branch banking represents effective competition and in many respects does the job better than do small unit banks. Indeed, it might be regarded as paradoxical that this argument appears under the heading of the stated *disadvantages* of branch banking; it might seem that it should be listed among the *advantages,* since it suggests that, in the competitive struggle, branch banks do better than unit banks.

The monopoly question presents an issue of interest to any analyst who is able to think in terms of *local* monopolies as distinguished from *national* monopolies. To anticipate a line of reasoning that is presented in the later discussion of antitrust policy, it may be observed that many a small-town unit banker has a more effective "monopoly" position than do the industrial giants commonly mentioned in this invidious connection. The local banker who owns the only bank in a town may or may not exploit the advantages of his position; but the fact is that it may be harder for his fellow townsmen to do their banking in a bank elsewhere than to obtain any other kinds of goods or services away from home. Branch banking organizations always encounter competition in their head office cities and usually in other major cities as well. With them competition is a way of life.

The branch banking question is something like the chain store question. Legal restrictions are sometimes laid upon business operations of this latter type. Not infrequently such restrictions appear to be in the interest of *preserving competitors* rather than *improving competition.*

With regard to any honorable way of doing business, the public policy question is this: Why not permit *any* kind of business organization and operation unless it can be clearly shown to be improper and let the various forms engage in competition for patronage. Competition normally means that some will be more successful than others and that some will fail. The fact of failure is not to be applauded, to be sure; but it is a normal part of the competitive picture. Restrictions on ways of organizing and doing business need to be scrutinized carefully to determine whether they are, in fact, in the public interest or whether, instead, they represent attempts to protect competitors against the harsh effects of competition. The advantages of competition sometimes accrue to competitors, but sometimes they do not. In any event, the advantages of competition are usually stated in terms of the gains to customers and suppliers, that is to say, to society at large, rather than to the participants in the game.

## METROPOLITAN BRANCH BANKING

Ten states still prohibit branch banking in any form. They do not allow the opening of branches even within the head office city. One of these states is Illinois. A consequence is that Chicago is the only city in the first ten that has no bank branch offices. Another consequence is that Chicago is less well served with banking facilities than any other large city and, indeed, the nation at large. The United States has on the average one bank office for every 8,000 inhabitants. Chicago has one for each 50,000. If a new bank office is desired in Chicago, in an expanding outlying business district or in a new shopping center, it can be opened only if there is established a new bank—a new banking corporation with its own capital, directors, and officers. This process is not as easy as opening a branch, and this condition explains why Chicago has such a paucity of banking offices. Another consequence of the condition in Chicago is that a larger proportion of wage earners there cash their checks in commercial establishments, or in special check-cashing offices which charge fees for the service.

The situation in Illinois and Chicago is commonly explained on the grounds that the State Legislature is controlled by downstate (that is, rural) interests and that the influence of hundreds of unit banks is felt in Springfield, the capital. The unit banks oppose the enactment of a law permitting the establishment of branches in the head office city, not because this would permit the big Chicago banks to open branches all over the State (which they could not do under such terms), but rather because they regard such a law as an entering wedge which might lead to the later establishment of state-wide banking.

Inspection of the opposing forces in the branch banking controversy is instructive.

Consider first the proponents of branch banking.

[1]  Most of them are large banks; some are giants. They attract the normal opposition to bigness.

[2]  Most of them are located in large cities whose residents are under-represented in the state legislatures.

And now look at the opponents of branch banking, who are opposed to lifting the restrictions on this form of operation.

[1]  Most of them are country bankers in small banks. They represent small business, or the "little fellow," a public favorite.

[2]  They live in small towns and rural regions of the states, whose inhabitants are overrepresented in the state legislatures.

In the circumstances, it is easy to see why the expansion of branch banking has been slow.

As indicated above, the National Bank Act, in effect, subordinates the national banks to state laws as far as opening branches is concerned.

National banks may establish branches only in states where, and to the extent that, state banks are allowed to do so.

One of the current issues is whether this restriction should be lifted from national banks. The proposal is that national banks should be allowed to open branches in any state, *regardless of the state law with respect to state banks.* Sooner or later this proposal will come before the Congress for consideration. It will go through the usual routine of hearings before the appropriate committees and will possibly be eventually embodied in a bill for consideration by the members of the houses of Congress. This would transfer the branch banking controversy from the several state legislatures to the national Congress. There the issues and the forces would be similar, but the drama would be played out before the eyes of the entire nation.

## GROUP BANKING

Action to relax the restrictions on branch banking may get a stimulus as a result of the expansion of group banking, which, it will be recalled, is the arrangement in which the stock of several banks which are separate corporations is owned by a holding company. The holding company through its stock control is in a position to control the election of the directors of the banks, to direct the appointment of their officers, and to regulate their operating policies and procedures. The holding company may prepare an operating manual of rules and regulations and will supervise bank operations. Although the legal structure is loose compared with that of branch banking, group banking, in operation, is similar and therefore shares the advantages and disadvantages—both real and imaginary—of branch banking.

It may be perhaps described as curious that although many states either completely prohibit or severely restrict branch banking, relatively few—only about a dozen—prohibit bank holding companies and group banking. They have grown substantially, and several of them cross state lines. The largest, Western Bancorporation, owns two dozen banks in a dozen states. Expansion of bank holding companies is subject to legal regulation under the antitrust acts and the Federal Reserve Act. A holding company may not acquire banks without permission from the governmental authorities. Concern on the part of these authorities about the expansion of this type of organization has resulted in hesitation to approve acquisitions in recent years. This form of multiple office banking, however, continues to represent an alternative to branch banking, and the status and expansion of each type affect those of the other.

## THE AMOUNT OF REGULATION

As indicated earlier, another difference between banking in this country and in other industrialized countries is the large amount of government regulation in our case. Our banking laws constitute, in effect, a very extensive manual of operations. Large banks sometimes prepare such manuals of their own, and in countries where there are no government regulations the bank manual in effect takes the place of a bank act. With the growth of banking units in the United States, the question naturally arises whether our regulation of banking is too extensive and too detailed. It can be argued that our bank laws are, in large part, aimed at protecting banking and bank depositors against the kind of disastrous depression that the country experienced in the 1930s. Since it is, for reasons discussed elsewhere in these pages, extremely unlikely that the United States will in the foreseeable future experience a depression even remotely resembling that on, it can be further argued that much of our banking legislation is unnecessarily restrictive.

## SECURITY ISSUES AND TRADING

The American people have an enormous stake in stocks and bonds. Exclusive of Federal and state securities, they own hundreds of billions of dollars worth of these pieces of paper. In recent years, new corporate issues of stocks and bonds have been running between $9 billion and $13 billion annually. Securities that are already outstanding are bought and sold through the stock exchanges. The largest of these marts (but not the only one) is the New York Stock Exchange. In 1957 total sales of corporate bonds in this one center topped $1 billion in value. In the same year in the same place 560 million shares of corporate stocks changed hands—with an estimated market value of $10 billion.

The beginnings of governmental regulation of securities issues and dealings date back seven centuries in England and to the earliest days of our Republic. Initially, buyers were protected only by the common-law precedents against fraud. This protection was rendered somewhat ineffective by the legal requirement that he who considered himself to have been defrauded had to prove a degree of knowledge on the part of the seller that made him legally responsible.

The inadequacy of this protection led to a gradual enactment of additional legal regulations. In 1909 the first Federal law which dealt with securities was enacted. The Postal Fraud Law made it a Federal offense to use the mails for the fraudulént sale of goods and services, which included securities, and for the dissemination of misleading statements regarding securities. The law made no provision for the relief of investors who had lost their money in unsound or fraudulent securities. This policing action by postal authorities was not effective.

The states also acted to protect investors. Rhode Island, in 1910, amended its corporation law to require certain issuers to file statements. This, however, was a mere notification statute rather than a licensing act.

Credit for the first general licensing act goes to Kansas for its statute of 1911. By 1933, when the Federal Government entered the field, every state except Nevada had some form of "blue sky law."*

State regulation, however, did not prove effective for several reasons: the generous exemptions of some states, the lack of adequate protective laws in all states, poor administration of the laws, public indifference to the laws, the ease with which promoters were able, by refunding part of the purchase price, to induce victims to drop prosecution, and the possibility of evading state authorities by operating strictly on an interstate basis or in another state.

As has happened in other fields of regulation, the growing need for Federal regulation, occasioned by the inadequacy of state regulation, developed slowly. The triggering force which led national legislation was the great stock market crash which began in 1929. In a few years the Dow-Jones Average of Thirty Industrial Stocks fell from $381 to $41; even bond prices declined disastrously. These conditions, coupled with the drastic decline of business and increase of unemployment, naturally created dissatisfaction and, equally naturally, generated a desire to put the blame for these disasters on someone.

In 1932 the United States Senate Committee on Banking and Currency started its investigation into stock exchange and investment banking practices. These hearings revealed a number of undesirable practices in the securities market. Among them were the formation and operation of pools, manipulation of markets for the benefit of special groups, handling of reorganizations in a manner to permit increased control of a reorganized company, the giving of preferential treatment to certain people in the distribution of securities, and the use by commercial banks of their investment affiliates for the disposal of poor loans. From this committee came recommendations for several laws. One of these was the Securities Act of 1933. This Act was administered for a year by the Federal Trade Commission. In 1934 the Securities Exchange Act provided for the establishment of the Securities and Exchange Commission, which then took over the administration of the 1933 Act and others.

## ORGANIZATION AND OPERATION OF THE SEC

The Securities and Exchange Commission is composed of five members, not more than three of whom may be members of the same political party. The members are appointed by the President, with the advice

* This phrase is said to have come from an angry denunciation of fraudulent stock promoters by a state legislator, who said, "If they could, these rascals would sell shares in the bright blue sky itself."

and consent of the Senate, for five-year terms, one term ending each year. The Chairman is designated by the President.

The Commission is assisted by a staff of lawyers, accountants, engineers, security analysts, and examiners and by administrative and clerical employees. The 1961 budget provided for just over a thousand employees and a budget of $8,900,000.

The Securities Act of 1933 provides that securities offered for public sale in interstate commerce or through the mails must be registered by the filing of a registration statement by the issuer. This statement must contain financial and other information which will permit an informed analysis of the securities and an appraisal of their value. Supplementing the registration, a prospectus containing pertinent facts set forth in the registration statement must be delivered to prospective buyers.

The registration statement is examined by the Commission staff. The statement may be refused clearance if it is found to contain material misstatements or omissions, thus barring the sale of the securities until it is amended. Sometimes the Commission's action results in the permanent abandonment of a proposed issue. The law also prohibits false representation and other fraudulent activities.

Some securities are exempted from this law, including United States Government obligations, state and municipal bonds, certain issues smaller than $300,000, and selected other types of new securities.

It is important to take account of what the Act does *not* do. It does not guarantee that the securities issued will be of good quality. It is entirely possible that an issue of securities in connection with a wild fly-by-night scheme could be cleared for marketing, provided the registration statement and the prospectus set forth all the facts in connection with the business without deception or omission. Nevertheless, the requirement of full disclosure tends inevitably to inhibit such issues.

Besides setting up the Securities and Exchange Commission, the Securities Exchange Act of 1934 contains regulations affecting trading in securities after issue. It extends the "disclosure doctrine" of investor protection to securities listed on national (registered) securities exchanges. An issuer must file a registration statement both with the exchanges on which the securities are listed and with the Commission, as well as subsequent annual and other periodic reports keeping current the data originally filed. The disclosures thus provided for are similar to those contained in the Securities Act registrations.

The Act also regulates proxy solicitations; curbs the use of "inside" information; authorizes the Board of Governors of the Federal Reserve System to prescribe limitations upon the amount of credit which may be extended to those acquiring securities; provides a system for regulating securities trading practice in both the exchange and the over-the-counter markets; seeks to curb misrepresentation, deceit, market manipulation, and other fraudulent acts and practices; and provides for the registration of national securities exchanges, and brokers and dealers who conduct over-the-counter securities business in interstate commerce.

## OTHER LAWS RELATING TO SECURITIES

The Public Utility Holding Company Act of 1935 regulates interstate public utility holding company systems which are engaged in the electric utility business or in the retail distribution of natural or manufactured gas. The law provides for the regulation of the issue and sale of securities by holding companies and their subsidiaries and for the regulation of service charges levied by parent holding companies on subsidiary operating companies, and it sets up requirements for the physical integration and corporate simplification of holding company systems.

The Trust Indenture Act of 1939 applies to bonds, debentures, notes, and similar debt securities offered for public sale and issued pursuant to trust indentures under which more than $1 million of securities may be outstanding at one time. It requires that the indenture trustee be free of conflicting interests which might interfere with the faithful exercise of its duties in behalf of the purchasers of the securities and that the trustee be a corporation with a specified minimum capitalization. It imposes high standards of responsibility and conduct on the trustee and gives the Commission the power to regulate the trustee.

The Investment Company Act of 1940 makes the activities of companies engaged primarily in the business of investing, reinvesting, and trading in securities and whose own securities are held by the investing public, subject to statutory limitations and Commission regulation in accordance with prescribed standards deemed necessary to protect the interests of investors and the public.

The Investment Advisers Act of 1940 requires persons who engage for compensation in the business of advising others with respect to their securities transactions (with certain exceptions) to register and conform their activities to statutory standards.

## THE SEC TODAY

The establishment of the Securities and Exchange Commission and the enactment of the laws which it administers were subjects of intense controversy at the time. While it was admitted that there were serious abuses in connection with the issue of and trading in securities, it was contended that the new governmental surveillance represented an improper intrusion into the field of private enterprise, and would injure the investment banking and securities trading business. Thanks partly to the reasonable administration of the SEC, in addition to the essential soundness of the

Act, criticism of this nature has gradually subsided. Today the consensus among the more informed experts is that the structure of securities regulation is basically sound, and has contributed to the expansion of the number of stockholders in the United States to a total of more than 13 million.

Although there has been great improvement in the propriety of operations in the securities business, occasional improper conditions have been discovered and still come to light from time to time. One such condition is the so-called "boiler room." This is a trade name for a room containing a battery of telephones over which salesmen try to sell securities, using high pressure methods.

Another group of problems centers around the stock specialists on stock exchanges and the over-the-counter broker-dealers. These men act both as principals and as agents. They buy and sell stocks for their own accounts and may thus become involved in conflict of interest situations in either purchasing or selling.

Inasmuch as the law requires full disclosure of relevant information, a company that wishes to make sure that it has omitted nothing from a registration statement tends to perform on the safe side by putting in all available information. The result is that the registration statement frequently becomes a sizable volume, containing so much information that extraction of the genuinely significant data is a substantial research job. Therefore, it has been suggested that the law should be revised to define more usefully and precisely the information to be included, thereby leading presumably to a reduction in the size and an increase in the usefulness of these documents.

Another question is whether the minimum dollar limit for exemption from the registration procedure should be raised, thereby confining the Commission's surveillance to the more important issues. Another proposal is that examination should be made of private placements, which in certain circumstances are exempted completely from the regulations.

These and other questions are being dealt with by the SEC in what may be described as a friendly and cooperative attitude toward the securities industry.


## SAVINGS AND LOAN ASSOCIATIONS AND MUTUAL SAVINGS BANKS

Mutual savings banks hold state charters. They are banks in the true sense of the word, their peculiarity being that, after making provisions for reserves, they distribute their earnings to their depositors. A current public issue in connection with them is the matter of taxation. Since they have this in common with the savings and loan associations, the two institutions are considered together.

Savings and loan associations sometimes look like banks and are sometimes referred to as banks. Properly speaking, however, they are not banks. He who puts money into them is not a depositor; he is a shareholder. What he is paid is not interest on a deposit but rather a dividend on his investment. If the savings and loan association is a member of the Federal Savings and Loan Insurance Corporation, his account is insured up to $10,000; but the terms of the insurance and the payment in case of financial difficulty are not quite the same as those provided for banks through the Federal Deposit Insurance Corporation. Some savings and loan associations are chartered by the Federal Government and others by states, and both are subject to government regulation. Some of the associations are mutual associations; others are stock companies.

Both the mutual savings banks and the savings and loan associations—whether mutual or stock—are subject to a special exemption in calculating their income which is subject to the Federal corporation income tax. In addition to other lawful expenses and deductions, such an institution may deduct amounts transferred to a reserve for bad debts as long as the total of that reserve, plus surplus and undivided profits, does not grow to exceed 12 per cent of its deposit or shareholder's account liabilities. In practice this means that many of these organizations, of both types, pay no Federal income tax at all.

Testifying in 1962 before the Senate Finance Committee on the proposed revenue act, Mr. Joseph C. Welman, past president of the American Bankers Association said:

> In 1960, the 4,700 savings and loan associations which are members of the Federal Home Loan Bank System reported a net income after the payment of dividends of $564 million, but paid Federal income tax of only $4 million, or seven-tenths of one per cent of net income. Insured mutual savings banks had net income of $169 million in 1960, but paid Federal income tax of only $447 thousand, or about one-quarter of one per cent of net income. This contrasts sharply with the commercial banks, which in 1960 paid $1.3 billion in Federal income taxes on a net income of $3.8 billion.

The American Bankers Association believes that these organizations, like other businesses, should be permitted adequate bad-debt reserves to which reasonable additions can be made, tax-free; but the bankers contend that the high allowance in the case of these institutions, coupled with their rapid growth, which results in continuous increase of the deductions, means that they will continue to pay little or nothing in Federal income taxes—a condition which is held to be unfair, particularly in that it gives them a competitive advantage over banks.

## LIFE INSURANCE

Congress did not exercise its constitutional power over interstate commerce to any great extent until many years after the adoption of the

Federal Constitution. Gradually its power grew, but in some cases it was restricted. In the noted case of *Paul v. Virginia,* a case that determined the course that regulation of the insurance business was to follow for three quarters of a century, the United States Supreme Court held that the issue of a policy of insurance was not a transaction of commerce and, therefore, not subject to Federal regulation.* This view was repeated in subsequent decisions.

Then, in 1944 the Supreme Court by a 4-to-3 decision held for the first time that an insurance company conducting a substantial part of its business across state lines was a participant in commerce among the several states and so was subject to regulation by the Congress under the Commerce Clause of the Constitution.†

The decision caused controversy. Many state officials and insurance executives feared that the Constitutional foundation of state regulation had been undermined. In order to deal with this rather ambiguous situation, there was passed in 1945 a law usually called the McCarran Act, which essentially provides that no act of Congress is to be construed as invalidating state acts regulating the insurance business unless it specifically refers to that business. In other words, the Act leaves regulation to the states unless the Congress undertakes to enact legislation specifically directed at this business.

The Congress has not acted, and the regulation of the insurance business remains in the hands of the states. Unlike state regulation of some other businesses, this regulation seems to have been reasonably successful. At present, although there is occasional discussion of the possibility of enactment of a Federal regulatory law, it appears that, unless new developments increase the necessity of such legislation, the present regulatory arrangements will be continued.

## QUESTIONS AND PROBLEMS

1. Why has governmental regulation of financial organizations and activities become so extensive? Is it too extensive? Not extensive enough?
2. What lessons can be drawn from the historical evolution of banking and Federal and state regulation?
3. What characteristics of the banking system in the U.S. distinguish it from those of other industrialized nations?
4. Evaluate the arguments for and against branch banking.
5. Explain the various attitudes toward branch banking found in the different states.
6. Would it be good public policy to permit more branch banking? What is your forecast of probable future branch banking legislation?

* *Paul v. Virginia,* 8 Wall. 168 (1869).
† *United States v. Southeastern Underwriters Association,* 322 U.S. 533 (1944).

7. What lessons can be drawn from the historical evolution of state and Federal regulation of the securities business?
8. Has the SEC been a help or hindrance to security marketing, in the broad sense? Explain.
9. Is there any case to be made for the Federal Government's stepping in to regulate insurance companies? Could a case be made against it? What do you forecast?
10. Are there any financial organizations or activities that you believe should be regulated more than they are at present?

## SELECTED READINGS

ALHADEFF, DAVID A. *Monopoly and Competition in Banking*. Berkeley, Calif.: University of California Press, 1954.

ATKINS, WILLARD EARL, GEORGE W. EDWARDS, and HAROLD G. MOULTON. *The Regulation of the Security Markets*. Washington, D.C.: The Brookings Institution, 1946.

CHAPMAN, JOHN M., and RAY B. WESTERFIELD. *Branch Banking, Its Historical and Theoretical Position in America and Abroad*. New York: Harper and Brothers, 1942.

KIMBALL, SPENCER. *Insurance and Public Policy*. Madison, Wisc.: University of Wisconsin Press, 1960.

LOSS, LOUIS. *Securities Regulation*, 2nd ed. Boston: Little, Brown & Company, 1961.

U.S. Securities and Exchange Commission. *Annual Report*. Washington, D.C.: U.S. Government Printing Office. Annually.

————. *A 25 Year Summary of the Activities of the Securities and Exchange Commission, 1934–1959*. Washington, D.C.: U.S. Government Printing Office, 1961.

WERNETTE, J. P. "The English Banking System," *Harvard Business Review*, Spring 1935.

# 13 SOCIAL WELFARE

The term *social welfare* includes the following Federal, state, and local governmental programs: the Federal Old-Age, Survivors, and Disability Insurance Program (OASDI), unemployment compensation, workmen's compensation, public assistance, health and medical programs, veterans' programs, and other welfare services. Table 13.1 presents the expenditures on these programs for two fiscal years selected to show a decade's increase. The 1949–1950 total was 5.2 per cent of the gross national expenditure ($264.0 billion); the 1959–1960 total was 6.8 per cent of that year's gross national expenditure ($494.6 billion).

*Table 13.1*

## GOVERNMENTAL SOCIAL WELFARE EXPENDITURES SELECTED FISCAL YEARS

(In Millions)

| PROGRAM | 1949–1950 | 1959–1960 |
|---|---|---|
| Social insurance | $ 4,911.2 | $ 19,325.8 |
| Old-age, survivors, and disability insurance | 784.1 | 11,032.3 |
| Railroad retirement | 304.4 | 925.4 |
| Public employee retirement | 743.4 | 2,569.9 |
| Unemployment insurance and employment service | 2,230.1 | 2,824.0 |
| Railroad unemployment insurance | 119.6 | 215.2 |
| Railroad temporary disability insurance | 31.1 | 68.6 |
| State temporary disability insurance | 72.3 | 344.1 |
| Workmen's compensation | 626.2 | 1,346.2 |
| Public assistance (including administrative expenses) | 2,496.2 | 4,100.6 |
| Old-age assistance | 1,510.9 | 2,014.7 |
| Aid to dependent children | 559.9 | 1,130.5 |
| Aid to the blind | 54.7 | 100.2 |
| Aid to the permanently and totally disabled | — | 302.9 |
| General assistance | 363.3 | 490.6 |
| Other public aid | 6.0 | 59.4 |
| Health and medical programs | 2,344.3 | 4,232.1 |

| PROGRAM | 1949–1950 | 1959–1960 |
|---|---|---|
| Hospital and medical care | 1,506.0 | 2,812.5 |
| Maternal and child health services | 29.8 | 139.4 |
| Medical research | 51.3 | 375.0 |
| Other public health activities | 328.4 | 406.1 |
| Medical facilities construction | 428.8 | 499.1 |
| Other welfare services | 401.6 | 1,161.1 |
| Vocational rehabilitation | 30.0 | 100.6 |
| Institutional and other care | 107.9 | 450.2 |
| School lunch | 158.7 | 399.3 |
| Child welfare | 104.9 | 211.0 |
| Veterans' programs (except education) | 3,691.7 | 4,686.5 |
| Pensions and compensations | 2,092.8 | 3,425.8 |
| Health and medical services | 745.8 | 942.1 |
| Welfare and other | 853.1 | 318.6 |
| Total | $ 13,845.0 | $ 33,506.1 |

The figures include the outlays of Federal, state, and local governments.

SOURCE: U.S. Department of Health, Education and Welfare, *Social Security Bulletin, Annual Statistical Supplement,* 1960 (Washington, D.C.: U.S. Government Printing Office, 1961), p. 5.

The OASDI and unemployment compensation programs were among the many features of the New Deal. Like many parts of that program—perhaps most—these programs were controversial. They were denounced as socialistic, visionary, and impractical, as being certain to undermine self-reliance and discourage the individual's provision for his own future, and as an improper intrusion of government into purely personal matters.

As the years have gone by, some of this criticism has declined; but critics who see in "the welfare state" a menace to our way of life continue to question some of these programs. Extension of the programs and enlargement of benefits have occasioned controversy. At the present time the proposal for providing for medical care for the aged within the social security program is a burning issue.

## EARLY DEVELOPMENT OF
## SOCIAL SECURITY

The United States was about forty years behind most of the other leading industrial countries in adopting a policy of social security on a national basis; it is still behind many of them in the scope and extent of protections offered.

The beginnings of social insurance, in this as in other countries, came in the form of laws to protect workers against the results of accidents in industry. Virtually all the European countries and the British dominions adopted such measures between 1884 and 1905. The first effective state laws in the United States were not enacted until 1911, when action was taken in California, New Jersey, Nevada, Washington, and Wisconsin.

Governmental old-age insurance began in the Germany of Bismarck in 1889, and was followed in France and the United Kingdom. By the outbreak of World War I ten European nations and several British dominions had established old-age economic protection plans, and one more, Italy, joined the group after the war.

Unemployment insurance began as a local matter in several countries of continental Europe late in the nineteenth century when scattered city and local governments took steps to subsidize trade union funds for supporting the unemployed. The first comprehensive national compulsory unemployment insurance scheme was established in the United Kingdom in 1911, and similar programs were adopted in most of the other larger European countries during the next two decades.

In the United States pensions for superannuated or permanently disabled employees had been established in a few large enterprises as far back as the 1870s. By 1930 there were several hundred such private plans in operation. Of several million workers covered, 40 per cent were employed by railroads, 18 per cent by public utilities, and the remainder by large manufacturing establishments.

Prior to adoption of the Social Security Act, aged and indigent persons who could not be supported by their families, and who were not able to sustain themselves by doing odd jobs or begging, commonly became inmates of almshouses or poor farms. Montana was the pioneer state, in 1923, in extending pensions to the aged; Wisconsin was second, in 1925. During the next decade such state laws became general, although state benefit payments and residence requirements varied greatly.

Unemployment insurance was unknown in any of the states prior to the Great Depression of the 1930s. Wisconsin, in 1932, was the first state to adopt such insurance, and eight others followed in 1935.

Building a social security system on state legislation alone offered many difficulties. Each state hesitated to burden employers with payroll taxes lest factories be moved to other states where no such levies were imposed. Some Federal program to coordinate action on a national basis seemed to be required. President Franklin D. Roosevelt endorsed a Federal social security program in a message to Congress on January 17, 1935, and the Social Security Act passed both houses by substantial majorities and received the President's signature on August 14, 1935.

## THE FEDERAL SOCIAL SECURITY ACT OF 1935

The new law dealt with old-age pensions, unemployment insurance, public assistance to the needy, aged, and blind and to dependent children, and the extension of additional aid for maternal and child welfare services and public health facilities.

The only one of these programs administered exclusively by the Federal Government was that providing for old-age insurance. All employers and employees except those in certain exempted categories were required to pay a payroll tax. These revenues were to be used to build up reserves in the Federal Treasury out of which retired workers were to receive pensions for life, depending upon their average wages and the lengths of time they had been contributing under the plan.

Provision for unemployment insurance was left to the states, but in order to encourage the establishment of such plans, a Federal unemployment tax was levied upon all employers—except those in exempted categories. The employers, however, were to be allowed a credit up to 90 per cent for any contributions made to state unemployment funds. From the 10 per cent which was retained in such cases the Federal government made grants to the states to assist them with administrative expenses. The inducement proved adequate to secure the enactment of unemployment insurance laws in all the states by 1937.

In other sections the Social Security Act provided for Federal grants-in-aid for states which would match the Federal contribution and administer programs of public assistance to old people in need of relief who were not covered by the insurance plan. Similar Federal grants were available to states which adopted plans for aiding dependent children and the blind. Federal aid on a somewhat different basis was extended for certain health and welfare activities and for vocational rehabilitation.

The Social Security Act of 1935 was strongly opposed by numerous parties. It was denounced as an infiltration by socialism and as the antithesis of sound economic policy. But the man who had no job and no income supported the Act—and there were a great many men in that position in 1935. As far as the general public was concerned, the desirability of social security was heightened by the economic misery so prevalent throughout the land. And when the Act was approved by the Supreme Court in 1937 the future of social security was assured.

## WHAT DO PEOPLE WANT SECURITY AGAINST?

Financial security depends—for most people—on the continuing adequacy of their money incomes. Almost all of today's goods and services are produced not by the user but by someone else and are, therefore, necessarily exchanged through the medium of money. When the money income is more than sufficient to cover the daily necessities of life, the balance can be saved for a "rainy day" or it can be spent on the "finer things of life." But when the money income is less than sufficient to cover the daily necessities the situation is reversed—savings must be spent, homes and other possessions may be mortgaged or sold, and the finer things of life are enjoyed only as dreams or memories. If the family income drops substantially, or necessary expenses soar, the result can be disaster—financial disaster.

If a man loses his job, his income may drop to nothing. In other cases a man's earning power and hence his income may be sharply reduced if he is forced to shift to jobs requiring less skill or ability. If a breadwinner dies or is disabled his family's income is cut—perhaps to zero.

In these modern days of industrialization and specialization the individual worker does not have a great deal of job security. His employment may be terminated for a variety of causes over which he has no control— causes unforeseen and oftentimes beyond understanding. For some workers a semblance of security is provided by intricate seniority rules. But seniority becomes a fiction when it is opposed by the combined forces of shifting market demands and altered business conditions.

Financial disaster may result also from a sudden rise in expenses. It is by no means uncommon for a family to be forced into debt when illness or injury leads to heavy hospital and doctors bills. These costs, or the death or disablement of a family breadwinner, may increase the expenses of related families as they assume support of the bereaved dependents.

These expenses, it must be noted, represent not luxuries but rather real financial burdens which cannot in good conscience be evaded. Responsible people will face up to them, but their effect is always substantial and often tragic. It is to avoid this tragedy—to obtain protection against the financial disaster of a drop in income or a rise in expenses— that our people have resorted to social security.

## OLD AGE AND DEATH

The death of the family breadwinner may result in both types of financial disaster—a drop in income and a rise in expenses. The former is obviously due to the cessation of the deceased's earning power, and it is a permanent or continuing disaster. The latter is occasioned by the expenses incurred in providing a "decent" burial and in the settling of the breadwinner's estate (if any).

With constant improvements in medical science and technology, the probability of the breadwinner's untimely death has been considerably lessened. The problem, however, still exists to a very considerable extent. And, unfortunately, unexpected death often leaves a family with insufficient insurance or savings to ease the financial difficulties.

Social security provides relief from both the immediate, short-term rise in expenses and the loss of income. A lump sum payment of up to $255 is paid to the widow or widower or to the person who has paid the burial expenses. Monthly survivor's benefits are paid to the widow if she is over 65 or if she is caring for one or more children under 18 years of age, to dependent parents if they are over 65, to orphaned children who are under 18, and even to a divorced wife if she is caring for the deceased's children. The specific amount of the monthly benefits is determined by the number and ages of the deceased's dependents and the deceased's average earnings (that were subjct to social security tax) prior to his death. At present, these survivors' benefits range from $44.30 for a widow alone up to a maximum of $254 per month for a widow with two or more children.

Death is, of course, the most final form of job severance; but old age might well be ranked second. Declining mortality rates tend to alleviate the problem of untimely death, but they also tend to aggravate the problem of old age. In 1960 people 65 years of age or over numbered 16,-560,000, or 9 per cent of the total population. The number is rising steadily and even the percentage is rising, slowly.

Unfortunately, many of these older folk are no longer able to earn livings, yet their accumulated savings and insurance, if any, will not support them. Social security legislation attempts to meet this problem by providing monthly retirement benefits to men and women who retire at age 65; or at 62, with smaller benefits. Additional benefits are paid if the wife of a retired worker is over 62. The total benefits payable to a man and wife, at present, range up to a maximum of $190.50 per month.

## DISABILITY—ACCIDENT OR ILLNESS

Grievous financial disaster is caused by disability. The man disabled during his working life loses both his income and his health; he runs up doctors and hospital bills and, to make matters worse, he frequently has a family to support. It is little wonder, then, that the first social insurance program set up in the United States provided for the payment of *workmen's compensation* in the event of occupational disability. This Federal program, enacted in 1908, covered Government employees. Similar programs were subsequently instituted by all the states.

Since workmen's compensation antedated social security legislation by many years, the Social Security Act of 1935 did not provide for disability benefits. However, in 1956 the Act was amended to permit payment of retirement benefits to workers aged 50–64 if they were totally disabled for work, and in 1960 the minimum age requirement was dropped, and it was provided that the period when a worker is temporarily disabled is not counted against him in subsequent determinations of his average earnings for retirement benefit purposes.

Inasmuch as workmen's compensation is primarily a matter of state legislation, there is little uniformity as to the benefits. Some laws cover only work that is considered dangerous, and some cover only those firms that employ more than a specified minimum number of employees. The kinds of injuries for which the employee can be compensated also vary.

Most of the early laws covered only injuries due to accidents, but the majority now include also some or all diseases attributable to workers' occupations. The amount of benefits payable is usually contingent on the worker's wages at the time of the injury or illness. And in most states limits are placed on the number of weeks for which benefits will be paid, or the total amount that will be paid in a given case.

Workmen's compensation laws are designed to furnish a worker prompt medical care and cash benefits when he is injured in connection with his job. If the injury results in death, benefits are paid to his dependents. It should be noted, however, that except in a very few states financial protection is offered only for work-connected disabilities. The majority of the permanent and temporary disabilities that exist at any one time are not work-connected, and hence represent burdens that are not alleviated by workmen's compensation.

## THE COVERAGE OF SOCIAL SECURITY

The original Social Security Act established retirement benefits only for employees working in industry and commerce, or about 60 per cent of the work force. And disability benefits were not provided for at all. But with the passage of numerous amendments in later years, disability benefits were added and retirement benefits were extended to both employees and the self-employed in occupations of nearly all types.

In 1960 sixty million persons were covered by public retirement programs, including OASDI.* The bulk of those excluded were self-employed persons and farm and domestic employees who had not yet met the minimum requirements for earnings or length of time worked. Many of these persons would meet the requirements and hence come under the program before expiration of their working lives. Temporarily employed housewives and students and self-employed doctors of medicine also were excluded, as were numerous employees of the Federal, state, and local governments who were protected by civil service or other retirement programs.

For most workers coverage under OASDI is compulsory, but for a few groups the program is offered on an elective basis. This option is generally limited to those situations where 'compulsory coverage might lead to problems concerning the constitutional barriers on taxation of state and local governments, the tax-exempt status of nonprofit organizations, and the separation of church and state.

In the mid-thirties, 10 per cent of the aged received income from social insurance programs or public assistance. By the end of 1960, 10.3 million, or 60 per cent, were collecting $11 billion as benefits annually under social

* These and other similar statistics in this chapter are taken from U.S. Department of Health, Education, and Welfare, *Social Security Bulletin: Annual Statistical Supplement, 1960* (Washington, D.C.: U.S. Government Printing Office, 1961), *passim*.

security legislation. Another 6 per cent were eligible for retirement checks and would begin receiving them whenever they decided to retire. And a sizable share of the remainder either received or were eligible to receive benefits under veterans' programs or as retired civil service or railroad workers. Thus about 80 per cent of the aged were protected by social security or similar social insurance programs.

In 1934 about 10 per cent of the disabled population (those persons aged 14 to 64 whose activities were impaired for at least six months due to injury or illness) received cash payments from public programs. Twenty-five years later the comparable figure exceeded 40 per cent, and the major part of the gain was attributable to the social security program.

## FINANCING OASDI

When the Social Security Act was first passed, both the employee and the employer each paid a tax of 1 per cent on the employee's earnings of $3,000 or less to finance old age and survivors insurance. Unemployment insurance was financed by a 3-per-cent payroll tax levied on employers only, and public assistance benefits were paid out of general tax revenues. The tax provisions for these latter two programs have not been altered, but the taxes for OASDI have increased substantially, as indicated in Table 13.2. The original Social Security Act provided for a

### Table 13.2
### OLD-AGE, SURVIVORS, AND DISABILITY INSURANCE TAX RATES
#### (Per Cent of Taxable Earnings)

| YEAR | Effective Rates | | | |
|---|---|---|---|---|
| | EMPLOYEES | EMPLOYERS | SELF-EMPLOYED | ON TAXABLE EARNINGS OF |
| 1937–1949 | 1 | 1 | — | $3,000 |
| 1950 | 1½ | 1½ | — | 3,000 |
| 1951–1953 | 1½ | 1½ | 2¼ | 3,600 |
| 1954 | 2 | 2 | 3 | 3,600 |
| 1955–1956 | 2 | 2 | 3 | 4,200 |
| 1957–1958 | 2¼ | 2¼ | 3⅜ | 4,200 |
| 1959 | 2½ | 2½ | 3¾ | 4,800 |
| 1960–1961 | 3 | 3 | 4½ | 4,800 |
| 1962 | 3⅛ | 3⅛ | 4.7 | 4,800 |
| | Scheduled Rates | | | |
| 1963–1965 | 3⅝ | 3⅝ | 5.4 | 4,800 |
| 1966–1967 | 4⅛ | 4⅛ | 6.2 | 4,800 |
| 1968 and thereafter | 4⅝ | 4⅝ | 6.9 | 4,800 |

SOURCES: 1937–1961: Victor Christgau, "Old Age, Survivors, and Disability Insurance After Twenty-five Years, *Social Security Bulletin*, August 1960, p. 27; 1962 on: Wilbur J. Cohen and William L. Mitchell, "Social Security Amendments of 1961," *Social Security Bulletin*, September 1961, p. 7.

small increase in tax rates; but expanded coverage and benefits have necessitated several upward revisions.

From the beginning, the Old-Age and Survivors Program has been a mixture of insurance and current payment. The difference may be seen in the fact that if at the beginning payments to a person over 65 had been made solely to the extent that his previous inpayments had purchased the equivalent of an annuity, the total outpayments of the system would have been tiny. They would have grown gradually, but it would have been years or decades before payments to elderly people under the system came to represent worthwhile amounts. The desire was to get the system underway and to have the payments be immediately meaningful to retired persons. The result was that those who were originally covered under the system got a real bargain. After making inpayments for only a short time they became entitled to the retirement benefits for the rest of their lives. In other words, most of the money paid in was paid out at once as benefits; very little was available to be invested in the trust fund. It was essentially a "pay-as-you-go" operation.

## OASDI TRUST FUNDS

Even in the beginning, however, the system was not entirely on a pay-as-you-go basis. And most of the time since then the inpayments have exceeded the outpayments. In other words, the system has gradually been working toward the point where the retirement benefits are more nearly related to the amounts that the retirees have actually paid in, but it is not there yet. The money accumulated from the excess of inpayments has been turned over to a special trust fund in the United States Treasury. It is invested in United States Government bonds and in 1960 amounted to $22.6 billion. The revenue from these investments was a half billion— a small amount compared to the receipts from social security taxes. The tax rates also have been increased from time to time. Increases in the payments have been provided for principally to offset the decline in the purchasing power of the dollar which has come along with the inflationary rise in the cost of living.

Despite the increase in the tax rates, and partly because of increases in the benefits, the program is still a long way from being on a true actuarial basis. The people who are currently paying in are going to get retirement benefits much greater than they could purchase through annuity contracts with life insurance companies for the same premiums. The excess is coming out of current taxation. This is going to continue to be the situation for a long time to come. Each retired generation is getting part of its old-age retirement payments from taxpayers who are still at work and who are paying into the system. These taxpayers, in turn, when retired, will be benefited similarly by the taxpayers of that later day.

Since the trust funds are invested in United States Government securities, it has been argued that the fund is an illusion. The income on the Government securities comes from taxes, and it has been suggested that, instead of investing the OASDI funds in government securities, they might be used to *retire* Government securities. If this were done, it would then become necessary (sooner or later) either to levy a special tax to balance the social security budget or to increase the tax rates that provide its direct income, thus replacing the income that would have come from the Government securities. It may be questioned whether the end result would be greatly different from the present arrangement. Under either arrangement the OASDI out-payments are financed by the taxpayers.

## UNEMPLOYMENT COMPENSATION

A frequent cause of financial and personal pain or disaster is unemployment.* During the depression years of the thirties, unemployment was extensive and long-lasting. The postwar record has, of course, been much better, yet an unemployment rate of from 3 to 5 per cent has generally prevailed even in periods of general business prosperity.

To the extent that unemployment is seasonal or cyclical, financial protection is offorded by the unemployment insurance provisions of the social security legislation. The immediate purpose of unemployment insurance is to provide the jobless worker with some financial support. A secondary but very important effect is to reduce the decline of purchasing power and cushion the shock of unemployment to the community and to the national economy.

Unemployment insurance is similar to workmen's compensation, in that both programs are administered by the various states. Even though the unemployment insurance program is supervised to some extent by the Federal Government, the states determine the amount and duration of benefits payable to the unemployed, which workers will be covered, and how they can qualify for payments. In general, the weekly payment to an unemployed worker is less than half what he earned before he lost his job.

Most states require a one-week waiting period before benefits are paid, and the maximum duration of benefits ranges from six weeks up to about nine months. During periods of economic recession, many workers use up their unemployment insurance before they are able to find new jobs. This predicament, however, can be alleviated by temporary extension of the maximum duration of compensation. Thus in 1958 a Federal act temporarily extended the compensation period up to 50 per cent longer than the states' original provisions.

* The discussion of this subject is brief here because it is taken up more comprehensively in Chapter 10.

The coverage of unemployment insurance is less extensive than that of old age, survivors, and disability insurance. In the first place, the self-employed are ineligible for unemployment insurance. The Federal Government also makes no contribution toward insurance for agricultural workers, domestic employees, state and local government employees, and a few other groups. Several of the states have extended unemployment protection to some of these occupations, but by and large the Federally excluded individuals are on their own when unemployment strikes.

In all about 45 million workers were covered by the Federal–state unemployment insurance program at the beginning of 1960. (An additional 900,000 were protected by the Federal railroad unemployment insurance program.) Some 13 million employees were not covered by unemployment insurance. Of these over eight million were government employees or domestic servants, and for the first of these groups unemployment probably does not represent a very significant hazard.

Recent years have seen much structural or technological unemployment—a problem that has persisted in both good years and bad. This unfortunate situation has even led to semipermanent pockets of unemployment, as in the coal fields of West Virginia.

In 1958 more than 2,600,000 persons exhausted their benefit rights under unemployment insurance; they constituted nearly a third of those who had received any benefits at all.* Many of these workers were suffering from technological or structural unemployment. The benefits of unemployment insurance serve to counter the financial disasters caused by seasonal or cyclical unemployment, but they are inadequate protection if a worker does not get recalled to his job when business picks up.

The solution to this problem will be found not in social security legislation but rather in policies that promote economic growth and the retraining of unemployed workers—subjects discussed in earlier chapters.

## PUBLIC ASSISTANCE

The public assistance programs under social welfare legislation have served to extend a greater degree of financial security to needy persons who are not eligible for benefits under social insurance or who receive benefits insufficient to meet their minimum needs. These programs have thus played an important part in bridging the gap between the emergency relief programs of the early 1930s and the social insurance provisions of the Social Security Act.

However, as the coverage and benefits of OASDI have expanded, the public assistance programs have declined in relative importance. Fewer than six million people were receiving Federally aided public

* U.S. Senate, *Report of the Special Committee on Unemployment Problems*, 86th Congress, 2nd Session, Report No. 1206, Washington, D.C., March 30, 1960.

assistance in mid-1960, whereas well over 14 million were benefiting from OASDI payments. The number of aged persons dependent on public assistance declined 14 per cent from 1950 to 1959.

Public assistance will continue to be required for those needy persons who are protected inadequately or not at all by social insurance. Unfortunately, some of these are now barred from Federally aided public assistance. Included in this category are the needy unemployed and the underemployed and their dependents, hospital patients suffering from tuberculosis and mental diseases, needy children in public and private institutions and in foster homes, and those individuals who meet some but not all of a state's eligibility requirements.

Total expenditures for public assistance in 1960 amounted to $4 billion. That this program was not free from criticism was dramatically illustrated by the controversy aroused by the actions of city manager Joseph M. Mitchell of Newburgh, New York, in 1960. In May he started a campaign to banish what he called chiselers, loafers, and social parasites from the relief roles. Charging that shiftless migrants were flooding the relief roles and that, in effect, the city was subsidizing immorality, he formulated several rules aimed at getting people off relief. One of the rules cut off assistance to unwed mothers who bore any more illegitimate children. Another required all able-bodied men on relief to work on municipal projects.

His rules evoked vigorous reaction all over the country. Some applauded the program as being long overdue. Others denounced it as heartless and simplistic.

One important consequence of the Newburgh tempest was to stimulate interest in the conditions that put people on relief and keep them there —particularly for long periods of time. Some analysts contended that the worst shortcomings of welfare systems is that most case workers are too overburdened; that they have not enough time to give individual attention to the problems of dependent children, immorality, neglect, divorce, unemployment, and inadequate education; that more careful analysis and better counseling would enable rehabilitation of persons on relief and in the long run reduce the relief load.

In 1962 a step in the direction of helping people on relief to help themselves was taken in Chicago. In that city 16,000 men and 34,000 mothers who were collecting aid-to-dependent-children payments (out of 285,000 persons on relief) were expected to start attending classes conducted in the late afternoons or evenings in elementary and high schools. They were to receive aptitude and education tests to assist them in deciding what courses to take. The subjects were scheduled to include training in household skills and, for the illiterate, reading and writing. More advanced courses would be available for those expected to benefit from them. The similarity of this program to the retraining programs discussed in Chapter 10 is evident.

## PROSPECTS FOR FUTURE CHANGES

If past experience is any guide, we may expect further extensions in both the scope and magnitude of social security legislation. Indeed, some political observers have suggested that biennial amendment of the Act to increase benefits or coverage or both has become the first rule of survival for Congressmen who seek reelection. In any case, the rule has been faithfully observed ever since 1950.

Protection against financial disaster will surely be extended to more and more of those who are now denied some or all of the benefits of social security legislation. Another decade or two may see us at the point where nearly all persons are holders of social insurance, and all needy persons are afforded public assistance regardless of the reasons for their need and no matter where they may live.

Other developments may further expand the scope of coverage. As an example, only four states—Rhode Island, California, New Jersey, and New York—pay temporary disability benefits to compensate wage earners partially for loss of wages caused by nonoccupational injury or illness. As far as financial disaster is concerned, the distinction between work-connected and non-work-connected disabilities is meaningless; they strike equally hard. But since the individual states have been reluctant to furnish protection against the latter type of disability, such protection may come to be offered under Federal social security legislation.

Even more significant changes are likely with regard to the adequacy of financial protection. In the past, social security benefits have represented a floor upon which other protection could be built. And such additional protection has been forthcoming. The years since 1945 have seen a rapid growth in private employee-benefit retirement plans, life insurance, and supplementary unemployment benefit programs. Nevertheless, the fact remains that for many people social insurance is the sole source of income. And, especially for these people, social security benefits have not kept pace with actual needs and the growth of our economy. Public assistance payments have aided some but not all. Undoubtedly, the ranges of benefits enumerated in earlier pages of this chapter will be increased substantially in the years to come.

Bigger and better benefits are not costless. If they come, tax rates will have to be increased even more than they are now scheduled to be.

## MEDICAL CARE FOR THE AGED

At the beginning of the sixties medical care for the aged was a hotly debated issue. The number of aged is, of course, rapidly increasing. For many of these people, longer life has meant smaller income, loneliness, and the necessity of turning to charity. They simply have not sufficient income or savings to pay for their medicine, doctors bills, and hospital expenses. The issue has come to be not whether aid to the aged is required but rather how to furnish it.

In 1960 the public assistance provisions of the Social Security Act were amended to provide Federal grants to help the States pay for medical care for persons aged 65 and over who are unable to pay for such care themselves. Medical care would be provided both to aged persons of low income who do not receive old-age assistance and also as a part of the old-age assistance program. Thirty-eight states are participating in this plan. It is as yet impossible to estimate with any degree of accuracy how many people will benefit from this medical aid. This action, however, has by no means settled the matter. A sizable segment of public opinion has held that public assistance smacks too much of charity —and that the proper solution is a program of compulsory health insurance analogous to that of OASDI. The supporters of public assistance reject such a program on the grounds that it would lead to higher social security taxes, socialized medicine, a lower quality of health care, and a variety of other evils.

## OBSESSION WITH SECURITY?

Some critics assert that our people have become obsessed with the idea of security, and that this obsession extends even to young people who are said to be more concerned with the retirement provisions of their employment than of the opportunity for hard work and promotion. In the absence of any accurate measuring device for the extent of this alleged obsession, perhaps it can be said that concern for security has long been a proper preoccupation for the heads of families and that it might be hard to visualize this as being overdone. In any event, the social security system has relieved millions of Americans from the prospect of having no incomes at all if they lose their jobs and has delivered even more millions from the haunting fear of penniless old age. Widows, orphans, and disabled persons can count on systematic support instead of the uncertain and perhaps grudging charity of relatives and organizations. Social security has not discouraged thrift. Studies conducted by the University of Michigan's Survey Research Center have shown that people covered by social security spend on life insurance as much as or more than those who have not this coverage. Despite criticism the prospect for the future is that social security will not be contracted, and is quite likely to be extended.

## QUESTIONS AND PROBLEMS

1. What does the term *social welfare* mean?
2. Why was the United States slower than some European countries in developing governmental social welfare programs?

3. Why was the Social Security Act of 1935 so controversial? Why is the program still controversial?
4. What types of security do most people look for? How does government aid their quest? How can private actions help?
5. What benefits do the governmental social welfare programs provide? Are they adequate?
6. Evaluate the financing of the OASDI program.
7. How adequate is the present unemployment compensation program?
8. How can public assistance programs be improved?
9. What is a sound program of governmental assistance in financing medical care for the aged?
10. Is there too much social welfare today? Does its expansion undermine the free enterprise system?
11. How would you reconcile expanding social welfare activities of the government and the American attitude toward socialism?
12. Will the progress of social welfare in the U.S. eventually lead to "the welfare state"?
13. Are the individual's independence and initiative being endangered by the government's policy of enlarging its function as a welfare agent?
14. Is it the duty of society to watch out for the individual?
15. Will the expenditure of more funds for social welfare merely cause people to become more dependent and expectant of this aid and hence do little to try to solve their own problems?
16. What should be government's role in the security and welfare of the people?

## SELECTED READINGS

BURNS, E. M. *Social Security and Public Policy*. New York: McGraw-Hill Company, 1956.

DeGRAZIA, ALFRED, and TED GURR. *American Welfare*. New York: New York University Press, 1961.

HABER, WILLIAM, and WILBUR J. COHEN (eds.). *Social Security: Programs, Problems, and Policies*. Homewood, Ill.: Richard D. Irwin, Inc., 1960.

LARSON, ARTHUR. *Know Your Social Security*, rev. ed. New York: Harper and Brothers, 1959.

MORGAN, JAMES N., and others. *Income and Welfare in the United States*. New York: McGraw-Hill Company, 1962.

RAUP, RUTH. *Intergovernmental Relations in Social Welfare*. Minneapolis, Minn.: University of Minnesota Press, 1952.

Rockefeller Brothers Fund. *Prospect for America*. New York: Doubleday & Company, 1961.

TURNBULL, JOHN G., ARTHUR WILLIAMS, JR., and EARL F. CHEIT. *Economic and Social Security*. New York: The Ronald Press, 1957.

———— and others. *Economic and Social Security*, 2nd ed. New York: The Ronald Press, 1962.

WILENSKY, HAROLD L., and CHARLES N. LEBEAUX. *Industrial Society and Social Welfare*. New York: Russell Sage Foundation, 1958.

WITTE, EDWIN E. *Social Security Perspectives*, ed. by Robert J. Lampman. Madison, Wisc.: University of Wisconsin Press, 1962.

# 14 THE PREVENTION OF MONOPOLY:
## The Antitrust Acts

In this chapter we examine the origins and development of antitrust law. We note the difficulties involved in attempting to legislate on this subject and the problems presented to the courts in the interpretation and application of the statutes. We examine the conditions that existed at the time legislation was enacted and the changes that have occurred since. We note the complexity of these problems, the difficulty of defining offenses, and the consequent confusion about the state of the law. We attempt to see why it has come about that, in some respects, the law is vague and uncertain.

In consequence of all these developments, one school of thought is that the antitrust laws need to be completely overhauled and clarified and then enforced vigorously. In the following chapter we examine these interrelated contentions in the light of factual conditions.

The Sherman Antitrust Act was passed in 1890. Since that time, 80 other laws or parts of laws have dealt with these interrelated problems. The United States Government publication *Antitrust Laws with Amendments 1890–1956* is a book of 107 pages.

No other nation has a body of antitrust law even faintly comparable to ours. Some countries have no legislation at all on the subject. Others have acts providing for *investigation* of monopolistic situations. In many countries, indeed, not only is public policy not opposed to monopoly and combination, it actively favors them. In these countries industrial combinations—often called "cartels"—are encouraged by governments, and in some instances private firms are required to join such organizations. This remarkable international contrast prompts the question, Are we right and the other nations wrong, or is it the other way around?

What is our policy? How did it develop? Is it sound? Should it be changed?

Attention in this discussion is focused on the Sherman Act, not because the other laws are unimportant, but rather because they represent, in the main, extensions and amplifications of the key provisions of the Sherman Act, namely, the outlawing of combinations and conspiracies in restraint of trade and the prohibition of monopolizing and combinations to monopolize in trade and commerce. An examination of some of the key cases brought under this Act illustrates the complexities of the legal-business-economic problems that are involved.

Prior to the enactment of the Sherman Act combinations in restraint of trade were governed by the common law—the body of rules and decisions emerging from court cases. Some of such agreements were not only lawful but were actually enforceable in the courts. Others, however, such an agreements among competitors to fix prices, divide markets, restrict output, pool earnings, and employ a common sales agency to effectuate price control, were void and unenforceable. No action could be taken, however, against the parties to such contracts.

The Sherman Act, however, changed this condition by making such combinations and conspiracies unlawful, actionable offenses. The Act grew out of certain business developments in the latter part of the nineteenth century.

## THE HISTORICAL SETTING

The rapid development of a national railway system, augmented by the improved communication facilities afforded by the invention of the telegraph and the telephone, minimized the difficulties of time and distance, previously barriers to effective large-scale business operations. Railroad mileage more than tripled in the two decades following the Civil War—from 36,801 miles in 1866 to 136,338 in 1886.

Great agricultural laborsaving advances, such as sowing, reaping, and threshing machines, freed men for industry; and, with the rapid growth of population, cities in the North and East began developing into centers of finance and commerce. Sources of nonanimal energy, such as coal, gas, and oil were harnessed to use. Electricity was made available for lighting, and in the 1880s, became a practical source of power. Hydraulic lifts, cranes, and elevators; transoceanic telegraph cables; electroplating and electrotype; the rotary press; product standardization and the use of interchangeable parts; and a myriad of other discoveries and technological advances fostered the growth of bigger businesses.

The growth and expansion of industrialization was paralleled by a growing demand for capital—created by the rising investment requirements of specialization. The corporate device facilitated raising capital, and was widely adopted by new and existing firms for this and other reasons. The high initial and fixed costs of industrialization also necessitated larger and larger volumes of sales, and many firms found that they could not longer survive on local product demand. The expanding railroads provided the means whereby firms could enlarge their markets and, in addition, stood out in their own right as industrial giants of the day. As market areas grew, individual enterprisers found their town monopoly positions being challenged by outside competitors, and widely separated businesses became intense rivals.

Individual growth of firms, employment of the techniques of specialization and mass production which necessitated large volumes of sales, and frequent births of new businesses created an intense search for customers that often led to cutthroat competition and business failure. In order to reduce the severity of this intense rivalry, many firms were induced to make agreements and join into combinations of all types. Firms that failed to join these agreements and combinations, and those that were purposely excluded, were often forced into submission or extinction by ruthless and underhanded pressures.

## PUBLIC OPINION AROUSED

Combinations, pools, and practices of the "natural monopolies"—especially the railroads—were the focus of early discontent. In fact, it can almost be said that up until about 1880 discontent with the railroad and land monopolies constituted the core of the antimonopoly movement. The fabulous growth and expansion of the railroads after the Civil War was instrumental, as is pointed out above, in fostering the whole industrial era, but the railroad boom was also stigmatized by many social and economic evils. Not only did the railroads' secret negotiations evoke hostility, but also there were levied against them many charges of high-handedness, discrimination, and exploitation in their dealings with other industries and groups. Individuals, groups, states, and territories purchased railroad securities, and even went into debt to do so, only to find that the securities had been "watered" and were worthless, or worth far less than their promoted value.*

Around 1880 the antagonism began to spread to other combinations. Especially vehement were the attacks made by the early writers against Standard Oil.

In 1879 Standard Oil of Ohio reorganized into a very old legal form of business—the *trust*. The trust is a respectable and still used form of business whereby one person or group of persons (the trustee or trustees) is given the power to handle property for the benefit of another or others (the beneficiary or beneficiaries). As one can readily comprehend, this immense power requires the highest degree of fiduciary responsibility. The Standard Oil Trust, and the other "trusts" which followed in its wake, were not intended to perform this fiduciary function; their goals were power and control. In these "trusts" a few select men were given immense and irrevocable power of attorney to vote the stock as they saw fit, and while the stockholders, who usually received trust certificates,

* Railroad regulation is discussed in Chapter 18.

*could* freely dispose of their shares, *they could not recall* the right to vote.

Standard Oil's practices ranged from intimidation, political bribery, and secret deals to the employment of legal devices and outright purchase. From certain railroads, Standard received rebates of 40 to 50 per cent on shipments of crude oil. These rebate arrangements even went so far as to provide for rebates to Standard for oil *shipped by its competitors!* So effective were Standard's methods that by 1879—only nine years after the formation of the company—it controlled 95 per cent of the country's refining capacity.

The movement against combinations was especially strong in the agrarian South and West, where farmers organized into groups called "granges" and "alliances." This organized discontent was instrumental in fostering the formation of state and national third-party reform platforms and the eventual adaption, in many states, of grain elevator and railroad legislation. However, these state laws soon proved to be ineffective, and the agitation continued. Other groups joined in the movement, and the strong discontent with railroad practices resulted, in 1887, in specific Federal legislation for common carriers—the Interstate Commerce Act.

But the movement did not stop there. By now discontent had spread against all "trusts" and against the restraints of competition practiced by them.

## STATE ANTITRUST LAWS

Again, as had been the case with railroad abuses, the states took the first steps to bolster the common law and provide more effective weapons against monopoly and restraint of trade. Before the passage of Federal antitrust legislation in 1890, twenty-odd states had legal provisions against restraints of trade and monopoly.

Even after the passage of Federal antitrust legislation, states continued to provide their own antitrust laws so that by the turn of the century nearly two thirds of them had done so. Since then, several other states have enacted general antitrust laws, and many special antitrust laws have been legislated to deal with specific practices, industries, and trades.

The state antitrust laws strengthened the attack on monopolies somewhat, by providing harsher penalties and better methods of application. Both criminal penalties and remedies in equity were usually provided, and violations were commonly punishable by imprisonment or fines. If a violation involved a corporation, its officers were frequently covered by separate penal sections. Enforcement of the law was generally charged to the state attorney general, thus relieving injured private parties of the expense of litigation; and, where the outcome of the suit was favorable to an injured party, that party could collect double or even triple damages in some states.

But the state antitrust laws also suffered from deficiencies that limited their effectiveness. Like common-law rules, they were restricted to within state boundaries, which limited their scope of attack on combinations engaging in operations that covered several states or the whole nation. Huge combinations, therefore, could not be touched by state laws. Then too, except in a few states, enforcement was, and still is, sporadic and inadequately financed.

## THE SHERMAN ANTITRUST ACT

The same social and economic forces that impelled the states to act against industrial combinations were felt in Federal legislative halls as well. Public sentiment had become strong enough by 1888 to make antitrust a political issue, and the four principal presidential parties each carried an antitrust plank in its platform.

In that same year Senator Sherman presented his first antitrust bill to Congress, and two years later, on July 2, 1890, President Benjamin Harrison signed into law "An Act to protect trade and commerce against restraints and monopolies"—better known as the Sherman Antitrust Act.

The final bill that became the Sherman Antitrust Act was passed by the Senate with only one dissenting vote and by the House of Representatives without any. Thus it would seem at first glance that the Federal Government was unified in an attack on monopoly and restraint of trade. But the two years preceding its passage, following the introduction of the first Sherman bill in 1888, had witnessed many amendments, debates, proposals, and rejections in antitrust legislation, and the bill that finally became law was far less satisfactory to Congress than the voting suggests.

Since it became law in 1890, the Sherman Act has remained virtually unchanged, except for a few amendments, and has been the backbone of America's attempts at maintaining competition. By 1956, however, it had been supplemented by 80 other Federal laws or parts of laws.

## PROVISIONS OF THE SHERMAN ANTITRUST ACT

The Sherman Act contains only eight, relatively short, sections. The first three sections define the offenses, specify the penalties, and define the limits of its coverage as governed by the Commerce Clause of the Constitution. The other five sections relate to procedural and jurisdictional matters and specify the remedies that are available to injured third parties.

SECTION 1.   Every contract, combination in the form of trust or otherwise, or conspiracy, in restraint of trade or commerce among the several States, or with foreign nations, is hereby declared to be illegal. Every person who shall make any such contract or engage in any such combination or conspiracy, shall be deemed guilty of a misdemeanor, and, on conviction thereof, shall be punished by fine not exceeding five thousand dollars, or by imprisonment not exceeding one year, or by both said punishments, in the discretion of the court.

SECTION 2.   Every person who shall monopolize, or attempt to monopolize, or combine or conspire with any other person or persons, to monopolize any part of the trade or commerce among the several States, or with foreign nations, shall be deemed guilty of a misdemeanor, and, on conviction thereof, shall be punished by fine not exceeding five thousand dollars, or by imprisonment not exceeding one year, or by both said punishments, in the discretion of the court.

Section 3 is substantially the same as Section 1 except that it adds provisions making the Act applicable to trade or commerce.

. . . in any Territory of the United States or of the District of Columbia, or in restraint of trade or commerce between any such Territory and another, or between any such Territory or Territories and any State or States or the District of Columbia, or with foreign nations, or between the District of Columbia and any State or States or foreign nations. . . .

The Act is fundamentally a criminal act, as clearly stated in the provisions that a violator ". . . shall be deemed guilty of a misdemeanor. . . ." However, equity suits also are provided for.


## DIFFICULTY OF DEFINING THE OFFENSE: THE LEGAL DILEMMA

The offenses to be prosecuted under the Sherman Act are stated in its first three sections: It makes illegal "every contract, combination in the form of trust or otherwise, or conspiracy in restraint of trade. . .;" acts by persons who ". . . shall monopolize or attempt to monopolize . . . any part of trade or commerce. . . ." Yet when one attempts to apply the Act, one meets head on the problems of definition: What is the scope of the word *every?* What does *or otherwise* include? Where does competition leave off and "restraint of trade" begin? What does *monopolize* mean? What constitutes a combination when there are no formal agreements? Thus, while the Act may clearly state the offenses in terms of general principles, nowhere does it specify any standard to be used in applying these principles.

Later pieces of antitrust legislation have attempted to define offenses in more specific terms, and, while they have made certain points clearer, they have not been completely free from ambiguity, either. Thus the businessman is often left to operate in areas of unexplored legality. Previous cases can offer him indications of what is legal and illegal under the law, but, because of shifting circumstances and the fact that every case is decided upon unique situations, he becomes certain about the legality of some of his actions only when he himself is brought to the test of the law.

## "COMMERCE" AND "MANUFACTURE"

Some insight into the problems involved in interpreting the meaning and scope of this pioneering statute can be gained by examining a few selected leading cases.

It wasn't until the Knight case* of 1894—more than four years after the passage of the Sherman Act—that the Supreme Court was called upon to interpret its scope and applicability. The decision handed down in that litigation hinged on a distinction between *interstate commerce* and *manufacture*, the result of which sent Federal antitrust enforcement off to a poor start by giving the United States a defeat in its very first case.

Briefly, the facts are that the American Sugar Refining Company of New Jersey, which was already producing about 65 per cent of the nation's sugar, had purchased four Pennsylvania refineries, including the E. C. Knight Company. This action had united control of about 98 per cent of the nation's sugar refining capacity into one firm, often called the "Sugar Trust."

Chief Justice Fuller, who delivered the majority opinion of the court, developed and elaborated on a distinction between interstate commerce and manufacture, concluding that the American Sugar Refining Company held a monopoly of the latter, did not directly affect interstate commerce, and was therefore outside the scope of the Sherman Act. Much of this reasoning appears to be based on the proposition that the rights of the individual states would be circumscribed if monopoly of manufacture were included within the scope of the Act.

This line of reasoning was vigorously opposed by Justice Harlan, who contended that the fundamental inquiry of the case—to decide what was an unlawful restraint of trade—was overlooked. Furthermore, he was of the opinion that the case *did* involve interstate commerce. "Whatever a state may do to protect its completely interior traffic or trade against unlawful restraints, the general government is empowered to do for the protection of the people of all the states—for this purpose, one people—against unlawful restraints imposed upon interstate traffic or trade in articles that are to enter into commerce among the several states."†

* *U.S. v. E. C. Knight Company*, 156 U.S. 1 (1895).
† *Ibid.*, p. 265.

## "*EVERY CONTRACT, COMBINATION*"

The Trans-Missouri Freight Association case* of 1897 provides another interesting interpretation of the Sherman Act. Justice Peckham, who presented the majority opinion of the court in this case, interpreted the Act in a most literal fashion. "*Every* contract or combination in restraint of trade" meant just that to him, and he refused to adhere to standards not written into the Act.

> By the simple use of the term "contract in restraint of trade," *all* contracts of that nature, whether valid or otherwise, would be included, and *not alone that kind of contract which was invalid and unenforceable as being in unreasonable restraint of trade* . . . and no exception or limitation can be added without placing in the act that which has been omitted by Congress.†

In reflecting on the potential consequences of his inflexible stand, Justice Peckham stated further:

> It may be that the policy . . . will, if carried out, result in disaster. . . . Whether that will be the result or not we do not know and cannot predict. These considerations are, however, not for us. . . . Congress is the body to amend it, and not this court . . . the conclusion which we have drawn . . . is that the anti-trust act . . . renders illegal *all* agreements which are restraints of trade or commerce. . . .‡

Peckham's literal interpretation of the Sherman Act, and his refusal to engage in judicial legislation, provoked a vigorous dissent by Justice White, with three other Justices concurring, as he expounded the *rule of reason:*

> I think a brief consideration of the history and development of the law on the subject will not only establish the inaccuracy of this proposition, but also demonstrate that the words "restraint of trade" embrace only contracts which unreasonably restrain trade, and therefore, that reasonable contracts, although they, in some measure, "restrain trade," are not within the meaning of the words.**

A similar case came before the Supreme Court the following year. The Court again split into the same factions, with Justice White leading the dissenters. In fact, White's interpretation of the common law as it was embodied in the Act led him to dissent in several cases over the years until, 14 years later, in the famous Standard Oil case,†† he, then as Chief Justice, was able to secure concurrence in his view by the majority of the Court. (See *The Rule of Reason as an Accepted Standard* below.)

---

* *U.S. v. Trans-Missouri Freight Association,* 166 U.S. 290 (1897).
† *Ibid.,* p. 554. Italics added.
‡ *Ibid.,* pp. 558–559. Italics added.
** *Ibid.,* p. 561.
†† *Standard Oil Company of New Jersey v. U.S.,* 221 U.S. 1 (1911).

The Trans-Missouri Freight Association case is significant for still another reason. Because of the Interstate Commerce Act, which had been enacted in 1887, there was some doubt whether common carriers fell under the jurisdiction of the Sherman Act also. This case decided that ". . . both statutes may stand, as neither is inconsistent with the other,"* and set precedent by bringing the railroads and other common carriers within the scope of the Act.

In the Addyston case† of 1898, presided over by Circuit Judge William Howard Taft (later President of the United States and and Chief Justice of the Supreme Court), we find still another important early interpretation of the Sherman Act as it was felt to be a codification of the common law. Although this was not a Supreme Court case (as yet), the examination and presentation of the common law by Judge Taft were often later referred to by the Supreme Court, and his statement has been widely acclaimed as an outstanding contribution to the understanding of the law.

In this case Judge Taft also rejected the rule of reason. However, unlike Justice Peckham, who refused to apply this common law standard to *any* restraints of trade under the Sherman Act, Judge Taft rejected it in this case only because the restraint was nonancillary—that is, was not subordinate or auxiliary to a larger lawful transaction. This view—that the standard of reasonableness applies only to ancillary restraints of trade—seems to have had the support of the majority of American courts.

It is perhaps worthy of note that this case went on to the Supreme Court,‡ where Justice Peckham relinquished (in effect) his strict stand on literal compliance by concurring in Judge Taft's presentation of the case.

## THE HOLDING COMPANY

In 1888 New Jersey amended its corporation laws to permit firms to hold stock of other firms. This action pointed the way to another organizational device—the holding company—whereby restraints could be placed on competition. By pyramiding small holdings of voting stock, persons holding a relatively small capital investment could control a vast organization.

It was not until the Northern Securities case** of 1904, however, that the Supreme Court faced the holding company form of combination in an antitrust suit. The Northern Securities Company had been formed as a holding company to acquire the controlling interest in two competing

---

* *U.S. v. Trans-Missouri Freight Association*, cited above, p. 549.
† *U.S. v. Addyston Pipe & Steel Company*, 85 Fed. Rep. 271 (1898).
‡ *Addyston Pipe & Steel Company v. U.S.*, 175 U.S. 211 (1899).
** *Northern Securities Company v. U.S.*, 193 U.S. 197 (1904).

railroads. That control, in turn, gave it control over all the leading railroad lines in the northeastern part of the country.

Expressing the conviction that ". . . no device . . . and no combination, by whomsoever formed, is beyond the reach of the supreme law of the land, if such device or combination, by its operation, directly restrains commerce among the states or with foreign nations in violation of the act of Congress,"* the Court in a five-to-four decision, agreed with the lower court, which had found the holding company in violation of the Sherman Act because it had resulted in the pooling of the two companies' earnings and the destruction of every motive for competition between them. Taking a somewhat unusual approach, Justice Holmes, as a dissenter, expressed the opinion (concurred in by three other Justices) that the Act did not apply to ". . . an arrangement by which competition is ended through a community of interest . . ."† but rather only to restraints imposed upon those not parties to the agreement.

In the following year, 1905, the Supreme Court ruled that combinations whose products were eventually sold in other states were subject to the power of the Act, "although the combination alleged embraces restraint and monopoly of trade within a single state. . . ."‡

## THE RULE OF REASON AS AN ACCEPTED STANDARD

In 1906 the United States began proceedings against the Standard Oil Company of New Jersey that were to last for five years and were to end in its required dissolution. This litigation is remembered, however, not only for its length and its outcome, but also for the establishment of the *rule of reason* as the standard to be applied in determining the legality or illegality of restraints under the Sherman Act.**

In this case Chief Justice White, speaking now for the majority of the Supreme Court, stated that the broad general language used in the statute ". . . necessarily called for the exercise of judgment . . .;" otherwise ". . . every conceivable contract or combination . . ." would be ruled an illegal restraint of trade.

> Thus not specifying, but indubitably contemplating and requiring a standard, it follows that it was intended that the standard of reason which had been applied at the common law . . . was intended to be the measure used for the purpose of determining whether, in a given case, a particular act had or had not brought about the wrong against which the statute provided.††

* *Ibid.*, p. 461.
† *Ibid.*, p. 470.
‡ *Swift & Company v. U.S.*, 196 U.S. 375 (1905).
** *Standard Oil Company of New Jersey v. U.S.*, cited above.
†† *Ibid.*, p. 516.

## "*MONOPOLIZING*"

The Sherman Act does not prohibit "monopoly." In Section 1 it forbids "restraint of trade"; in Section 2 it establishes these offenses: (1) to "monopolize"; (2) to "attempt to monopolize"; and (3) to "combine or conspire . . . to monopolize."

The law, however, does not define these offenses, and this duty, therefore, has devolved upon the courts. In the *Standard Oil of New Jersey* case, the Supreme Court linked them to "restraint of trade."

Apparently recognizing—almost intuitively, it would seem—the ubiquity of "monopoly" (as analyzed in the following chapter), the courts have associated "'monopolizing'" with restraint of trade or other unlawful acts. This is of special significance in a situation that involves a single firm, as distinguished from a group.

A firm that achieves a monopoly situation as a result of victory over competitors by legal means presumably has not violated the law. Achieving such a position by acts that constitute restraint of trade or that violate other antitrust laws, however, is another matter; it can be "monopolizing."

In short, the law does not aim at penalizing proper business enterprise that brings about a monopoly situation in consequence of normal economic forces. It forbids calculated attempts to impede or prevent the rise of competitors. The clarity and definiteness of these criteria, however, are questionable.

## THE QUESTION OF SIZE

How does *size* affect legality? There seems to be no clear-cut answer to this question. The Supreme Court pointed out in the Steel case, and again in the International Harvester case,* that mere large size alone, in the absence of unlawful conduct, is not an offense under the Act. This does not mean, however, that the Court has not considered size as a contributory indication of monopoly.†

## WHAT IS THE RELEVANT MARKET?

Closely associated with the question of size is the question of the organization's position in the industry. That is, what effect does the extent of market control have on its legality? Again no clear-cut answers have been given, and a close look at the problem reveals that it is

---

* *U.S. v. United States Steel Corporation*, 251 U.S. 417 (1920); *U.S. v. International Harvester Company*, 274 U.S. 693 (1927).

† *U.S. v. New York Great Atlantic & Pacific Tea Company*, 67 Fed. Supp. 626 (1946).

questionable whether any will soon be forthcoming. For instance, how does one define the limits of a market? Does a "product" that character-izes a market consist of only those things sold which are made out of the same raw material? Or does it consist of those that are produced by similar processes? Or those that serve as substitutes for one another in the eyes of the purchasers? Geographically, what are the boundaries of a market? Local? State? National? International?

Thus, by one definition, a seller's market control can be considered large; by another, it may be considered small. The court has had to face this problem of definition several times. In some cases it has responded by specifying the market within narrow limits, while in other cases it has defined the market scope very broadly. For instance, in the Aluminum Company case* the Circuit Court defined the market as consisting of that for "virgin" domestic aluminum ingot, thus excluding secondary sources, import sources, and substitute materials. On the other hand, in the Cellophane case† it regarded the market as including that for all flexible wrapping materials. Partly as a result of these definitions, it found the Aluminum Company guilty of monopolizing—although certain calcu-lated acts by Alcoa also influenced the decision.

Unfortunately, a definition of the market does not end the problem. Even after it has been defined for the seller in question, the courts must still decide what proportion of market control is illegal. This introduces another problem, since in the first place, it is often difficult to determine the extent of that control and, in the second, the courts have not been able to agree on what proportion separates legality from illegality. In the Aluminum case the court stated quite emphatically that 90 per cent was sufficient to constitute a monopoly, whereas it would be doubtful whether 60 or 64 per cent would be enough, ". . . and certainly 33 per cent is not."‡

## THE SHERMAN ACT AND "LOOSE" COMBINATIONS

In contrast to the uncertainty and contradictions that prevail in the law with respect to single firms and integrated combinations are the relatively clear-cut lines of demarcation between lawful and unlawful practices that the courts have set down for many areas involving "loose" combinations.

Before the passage of the Sherman Act common-law rules dealing with conspiracy and restraint of trade, as practiced by "loose" combinations,

---

*U.S. v. Aluminum Company of America, 148 F. 2d 416 (1945).

† U.S. v. E. I. du Pont de Nemours and Company, 351 U.S. 377 (1956).

‡ U.S. v. Aluminum Company of America, cited above.

had already been well formulated. Therefore, the extension of these common-law rules into the Sherman Act, via court interpretations, has resulted in fairly strict and uniform standards for the measuring of anticompetitiveness in combinations of this type.

The practice of direct price fixing, whether by buyers or by sellers, has been consistently declared unlawful by the Supreme Court. It does not matter that the price setters' intentions are good or that prices charged are reasonable.

> . . . An agreement on the part of the members of a combination controlling a substantial part of an industry, upon the prices which the members are to charge for their commodities, is in itself an undue and unreasonable restraint of trade and commerce.\*

Nor does it matter that prices set are only minimum or maximum prices or that competition has actually been promoted rather than lessened.

> Thus for over forty years this Court has consistently and without deviation adhered to the principle that price-fixing agreements are unlawful per se under the Sherman Act and that no showing of so-called competitive abuses or evils which those agreements were designed to eliminate or alleviate may be interposed as a defense.†

One exception to this firm stand was made in the Appalachian Coals case where the Supreme Court stated that, although the price agreements would raise prices ". . . to a higher level than would otherwise obtain," it concurred in the trial court's finding that ". . . the defendants 'will not have monopoly control of any market, nor the power to fix monopoly prices.' "‡

This reversal of policy by the Supreme Court is generally rationalized on the ground that the case was litigated against a sick industry, at the bottom of the Great Depression. In fact, the Court stated:

> Putting an end to injurious practices, and the consequent improvement of the competitive position of a group of producers, is not a less worthy aim and may *be entirely consonant with the public interest,* where the group must still meet effective competition in a fair market and neither seeks nor is able to effect a domination of prices.\*\*

As a general rule, however, the Supreme Court has followed the contention that:

> The aim and result of every price-fixing agreement, if effective, is the elimination of one form of competition. The power to fix prices, whether reasonably

\* *U.S. v. Trenton Potteries Company,* 273 U.S. 392 (1927).
† *U.S. v. Socony-Vacuum Oil Company,* 310 U.S. 150 (1940).
‡ *Appalachian Coals, Inc. v. U.S.,* 288 U.S. 344 (1933).
\*\* *Ibid.* Italics added.

exercised or not, involves power to control the market and to fix arbitrary and unreasonable prices*

## OUTPUT AND PRICES

Similar to price agreements are the views regarding the regulation of production by concerted action of competitors. There are few cases dealing directly with this problem, but general consensus among students of the law is that such action is illegal per se.

Examination of the American Column and Lumber case† provides some of the basis for this reasoning. The case involved a trade association, as do so many of the cases since trade associations have become such a prevalent form of "loose" combination. The members of this particular trade association, composing only 5 per cent of the total number of mills in the industry but producing about 33 per cent of the nation's hardwood lumber, were engaged in an "Open Competition Plan" whereby they exchanged information concerning their sales, prices charged, and other business facts. The court was "convinced . . . that the purpose and effect of the activities . . . were to restrict competition, and thereby restrain interstate commerce in the manufacture and sale of hardwood lumber, *by concerted action in curtailing production* and in increasing prices. . . ."‡

## PRICE UNIFORMITY

The area of price uniformity is not as clear-cut as the area of direct pricing agreements. This is because the government has to show that prices are uniform due to concerted action of competitors. Where this can be easily shown, as for example, in the American Linseed case,** the court has concluded that competition is being suppressed. In the American Linseed case the members of the trade association not only exchanged price lists, but also gave immediate telegraphic notice to the other members—with buyer's name and the price charged—for any deviation from listed price.

However, where the nature of the facts is such that it can only be inferred that concerted action is being taken, price uniformity has been considered as only *one* fact tending to indicate illegality.

## THE CLAYTON ACT AND AMENDMENTS

Partly because of the vagueness of the Sherman Antitrust Act and partly because of the judicial adoption of the rule of reason, public dis-

* *U.S. v. Trenton Potteries Company*, cited above, p. 379.
† *American Column and Lumber Company v. U.S.*, 257 U.S. 377 (1921).
‡ *Ibid.*, p. 121. Italics added.
** *U.S. v. American Linseed Oil Company*, 262 U.S. 371 (1933).

content with the Act arose during the early part of the twentieth century. It was believed that the law should define monopolistic and restraining actions with greater precision; also, because some huge business combinations had risen to power by the use of unfair methods of competition, people wanted legal prohibition of such activities. In the 1912 elections antitrust legislation was a revived issue.

A consequence was the enactment in 1914 of two new pieces of legislation—the Clayton Act and the Federal Trade Commission Act. The Clayton Act prohibited price discrimination, exclusive dealing arrangements, intercorporate stock acquisitions, and interlocking directorates, where their effect ". . . may be to substantially lessen competition or tend to create a monopoly." The Act was amended by the Robinson–Patman Act of 1936, which strengthened the provisions against price discrimination and outlawed the payment of a broker's commission except when paid for services rendered. The Act was amended again in 1950 by the Celler–Kefauver Act, which prohibited the acquisition by any corporation of any part of the assets of another corporation where the effect of such acquisition ". . . may be substantially to lessen competition or to tend to create a monopoly."

The last words of the previous paragraph appeared in the original Clayton Act as well as in the Robinson–Patman Act. In addition, the Robinson–Patman Act included the limitation where the effect of such price discrimination ". . . may be to injure, destroy, or prevent competition with any person who either grants or knowingly receives the benefit of such discrimination with customers of either of them." These are significant phrases. Whereas the Sherman Act forbade combinations and conspiracies in restraint of trade and monopolizing or attempting to monopolize, these later acts suggest the legal objective of maintaining competition even when it is not threatened by monopoly. In other words, the law now is concerned not only with combinations, conspiracies, and monopolizing, but also with preventing a substantial lessening of competition—an elusive concept.

As might be expected, the court cases under these acts (like those under the Sherman Act) involve wrestling with difficult business issues and the awesome task of drawing a line between actions that lessen or injure competition, on the one hand, from those that do not, on the other hand.

## THE FEDERAL TRADE COMMISSION ACT

The Federal Trade Commission Act, passed at the prodding of President Woodrow Wilson as a part of his reform program, outlawed "unfair methods of competition" and established the Federal Trade Commission to enforce the Act. Despite President Wilson's urging, Congress decided that it was not feasible to specify the unfair methods of competition that were prohibited by the statute. The task, therefore, of defining unfair methods of competition fell to the courts. It has been a troublesome task, and the end result has been uncertainty about borderline types of competitive activities.

The Federal Trade Commission was envisaged by President Wilson as a kind of policeman of American business. To some extent it has performed this role. It may be noted that although the Federal Trade Commission Act is usually listed as part of antitrust law, it has significance apart from preventing the emergence of combinations and monopolies or reducing competition by means of unfair practices. It is directed against unfair practices whether or not these are associated with violation of other antitrust acts. The Commission takes action against unfair trade practices whether they are indulged in by large concerns or small ones. Indeed, the commonest Commission move is an order directed to a small and medium-sized concern, requiring it to stop some practice which the Commission has determined to be an unfair method of competition or unfair or deceptive act or practice. This aspect of the work of the Commission—the protection of buyers as well as competitors—is considered further in Chapter 17.

## THE STATE OF THE LAW

Some parts of antitrust law are clear, some are less clear, and some are nebulous.

Quite clear is the illegality of overt agreements among ostensible competitors (in selling or buying) to fix prices, to exclude competitors, to restrict output, and to divide markets.

Less clear is the legal status of the activities of trade associations, of conscious parallel action, and of vertical integration.

Nebulous is the law respecting monopolizing, especially in situations involving but a single firm.

The reader may reasonably wonder why steps have not been taken to clarify these matters and eliminate these uncertainties, whose existence he might blame on poor legal draftsmanship or judicial confusions. That these "explanations" are far from complete (if, indeed, true at all) will be brought out as we examine the economics of competition, in the next chapter.

## QUESTIONS AND PROBLEMS

1. What lessons can be drawn from the historical evolution of the antitrust acts?
2. Contrast and compare—in terms of the general welfare—the American antitrust legislation with the public policies of European countries.

3. What lessons can be drawn from the court cases involving the Sherman Antitrust Act?
4. How have the courts interpreted the term *to monopolize?* What is its significance?
5. What, if anything, should be done to improve antitrust legislation and regulation?
6. "What our laws need is a good, solid definition of what a monopoly is." Do you agree? What would be such a definition?
7. Is there any basis for saying that there is nowhere near the need for antitrust legislation today that there was in the past? Or, alternatively, more need?
8. What would be a measure of competition which would tell when competition had been "lessened"?
9. It is part of our tradition of jurisprudence that a criminal statute should define the crime with sufficient clarity that an ordinary man can understand it. The antitrust laws do not do this completely. Discuss the reasons why these laws have not been made more clear than they are.

## SELECTED READINGS

DIRLAM, JOEL B., and ALFRED E. KAHN. *Fair Competition: The Law and Economics of Antitrust Policy.* Ithaca, N.Y.: Cornell University Press, 1954.

EDWARDS, CORWIN D. *Maintaining Competition: Requisites of a Governmental Policy.* New York: McGraw-Hill Company, 1949.

GRIFFIN, CLARE E. *An Economic Approach to Antitrust Problems.* New York: American Enterprise Association, 1951.

HANDLER, MILTON. *Antitrust in Perspective: The Complementary Roles of Rule and Discretion.* New York: Columbia University Press, 1957.

LOEVINGER, LEE. *The Law of Free Enterprise; How to Recognize and Maintain the American Economic System.* New York: Funk & Wagnalls Company, 1949.

OPPENHEIM, S. CHESTERFIELD. *Recent Cases on Federal Antitrust Laws.* St. Paul, Minn.: West Publishing Company, 1951.

THORELLI, HANS B. *The Federal Antitrust Policy: Origination of An American Tradition.* Baltimore: Johns Hopkins Press, 1954.

U.S. Attorney General's National Committee to Study the Antitrust Laws. *Report.* Washington, D.C.: U.S. Government Printing Office, 1955.

VAN CISE, JERROLD G., and CHARLES WESLEY DUNN. *How to Comply with the Antitrust Laws.* Chicago: Commerce Clearing House, 1954.

# 15 COMPETITION AND MONOPOLY TODAY

In the previous chapter we trace the tortuous development of antitrust law, observe the attempts of the Congress to define offenses, and note the problems that come before the courts in the application of the laws. One conclusion emerges clearly, namely, that much of antitrust law is far from clear. In some situations even experts are not sure about what is or is not lawful action. In a society having our tradition of Anglo-Saxon jurisprudence, this condition is especially unfortunate when criminal prosecutions are brought under any of these laws. In that tradition every criminal statute should define the crime with sufficient clarity so that an ordinary man can understand what is being forbidden. On the face of it, therefore, it would seem imperative that economists, lawyers, and legislators get together and rewrite the antitrust laws so as to make the nature of the forbidden offenses completely clear. Indeed, so obvious may seem to be the desirability of this move that the question may be asked why it has not been done long since. The reason is that the subjects of competition and monopoly are themselves by no means as simple and as plainly differentiated as they are sometimes made to appear.

Along with a proposal to rewrite the antitrust laws often goes a separate one, namely, that when they are rewritten, they should be enforced much more vigorously than they have been. Appraising this suggestion involves analyzing the nature and extent of competition and monopoly in the United States. Is monopoly increasing? How serious is monopoly? Do the American people need greater protection from monopoly?

In order to examine these questions properly, we need to make a brief excursion into economic theory, and in the doing we shall note that much that has been written on the nature and extent of competition has been misleading and oversimplified. Good economic analysis provides the understanding necessary for formulating sound public policy.

## COMPETITION, MONOPOLY, AND "MONOPOLISTIC COMPETITION"

The analysis, description, and explanation of competition have long been important topics of economic analysts. Adam Smith, who did not use either diagrams or equations, but whose book, *The Wealth of Nations,* is rich in facts, had some interesting things to say about competition and the behavior of businessmen. Much later on, partly under the influence of Alfred Marshall—mathematician turned economist—many writers followed his lead in drawing diagrams purporting to describe and explain economic processes. Two different sets of diagrams were developed—one for competition, the other for monopoly. A product often cited as an example of competition was *wheat.* The monopoly case, on the other hand, might deal with some real or imaginary gigantic national industrial organization. As a result of this oversimplified, unrealistic classification of two categories, these theories must, to businessmen and to others who understood the functioning of business processes, have seemed extraordinarily unrelated to the marketplace.

This condition continued for several decades, until an interesting change occurred, thanks largely to the work of Edward Chamberlin, an American economist, who introduced the concept of *monopolistic competition.* In a formal sense this provided a third category which was held to contain many if not most of the ordinary business firms operating as sellers. At about the same time the English economist Joan Robinson wrote a book entitled *Imperfect Competition.* Since then, these two terms have come into widespread use, often interchangeably, a practice against which Professor Chamberlin protests strongly.

The concept of these three categories in their relations to one another is sometimes presented by the aid of a simple diagram. (See Diagram 15.1.) This diagram shows at one end of the line a condition labeled (depending on the assumptions) "Pure Competition" or "Perfect Competition." At the other end of the line appears something called "Pure Monopoly" or "Perfect Monopoly." Between these two extremes are the labels "Monopolistic Competition" and "Imperfect Competition."

*Diagram 15.1*

### A COMMON BUT MISLEADING PICTURE
### OF MARKET CONDITIONS

| PURE COMPETITION | MONOPOLISTIC COMPETITION | PURE MONOPOLY |
|---|---|---|
| OR ———————————————————————————————————— OR | | |
| PERFECT COMPETITION | IMPERFECT COMPETITION | PERFECT MONOPOLY |

The markets of the world are thus regarded as describable by a linear continuum, with "monopoly" and "competition" as the extreme conditions and continuously varying proportions of both in between.

The markets that writers offer as examples of "pure competition" are rather limited in number. They include the markets for certain standardized products produced by many producers and purchased by many buyers, of which *wheat* is perhaps the most often cited example. At the other extreme it is difficult to imagine any cases of "pure monopoly," or "perfect monopoly," considering the extent to which products and sellers are in competition with one another in virtually all lines. Most business activity, therefore, according to this concept, is not carried on under either of these conditions but, rather, is assigned to the middle group.

Thus, most business operations, according to this description, get branded with the pejorative adjectives "monopolistic" and "imperfect," and practically none receive the accolade of "pure" and "perfect"—which is at the least somewhat unflattering to our business community.

But does this reasoning, with its labels and their connotations, present an accurate picture of actual conditions?

## THE UBIQUITY OF MONOPOLY

Let us begin answering this question by taking another look at the basic concepts—monopoly and competition.

*Monopoly* means "single seller." Plainly it does not mean the single seller of everything in the world. It means the single seller of one or more things in a particular area. This may be the single seller of one particular commodity in an entire country or in a region or locality. Or the single seller may offer a group of goods or services. Indeed, the single grocery store in a small town qualifies under this definition as a monopoly. Furthermore, the grocery store in a shopping center also qualifies under a very strict reading of the definition. Finally, even each of two grocery stores located across the street from each other may, because of some unique characteristics—real or imaginary—that are of importance to their patrons, also may be counted in an even stricter sense as being monopolies. In this sense, the owners of brands, selling their branded goods, are monopolists also.

This definition and its strict interpretations have the unusual result of causing it to appear that virtually all business establishments in the United States except farms are monopolies. This reasoning may be summed up in the phrase "the ubiquity of monopoly."

## THE UBIQUITY OF COMPETITION

If this conclusion were presented to the millions of businessmen associated with the concerns so labeled as monopolies, their reaction would probably be one of mingled astonishment, incredulity, and amusement. The grocer in one shopping center would protest against his business being labeled a monopoly and would insist that his is an exceedingly competitive business. He would point out that he is in competition with grocers in other localities and that he is also in competition for the consumer's dollar with a great many purveyors of nongrocery items, such as motion-picture houses, bowling alleys, and clothing stores. Similarly, the proprietors of well-known national brands of goods would object to being described as monopolists; and they would point out that they too are in competition with other brands of these goods, as well as being in competition with completely different types of goods.

This reasoning may be summed up by another phrase, "the ubiquity of competition."

In short, these two lines of reasoning lead to two completely different conclusions—two contradictory ubiquities. One is that almost every business (except farming) is a monopoly, or has some characteristics of a monopoly. The other is that all these businesses have competitors and are competitive, in some cases intensely so. How is this paradox to be resolved?

## WHAT IS COMPETITION?

It may seem that the answer is simple and, indeed, that it already exists. It may seem that Diagram 15.1 is an adequate explanation, in that the middle category, "Monopolistic Competition" or "Imperfect Competition," adequately characterizes these millions of firms and their behavior.

If, however, analysis should indicate that the typical business competitive situation (in manufacturing, wholesaling, or retailing) is not midway between good and evil, is not an inferior imitation of real competition—and a fortiori if it should be seen that "pure competition" is not an ideal condition—the basic judgments would be altered greatly.

How competitive is the state of affairs called "pure competition?" Consider two neighboring wheat farmers, who raise the same kind of wheat and whose farms adjoin one another in the Wheat Belt. Are these farmers in competition with one another? Does each think of the other as being his competitor? Is there really any competition, in a substantial sense, in this condition? To be sure, if these two farmers are offering sheaves of wheat for a prize at the county fair, they may be conscious of a certain kind of competition. Aside, however, from this interesting but peripheral activity, the farmers do not consider themselves to be competitors, and are not in competition in the sense in which merchants and manufacturers are. If Farmer A improves his methods of farming, raises more wheat, and makes more money, this will have no effect, in and of itself, on the earnings of Farmer B. Farmer A's innovations will not push Farmer B to improve his performance in order to forestall loss of sales and income.

This is not the common condition in urban competition, where a frequent situation is that if one competitor improves his condition he does so at the expense of other competitors. This is a condition well understood by men in urban business. They know that they have competitors.

They know that their actions influence the well-being of their own businesses and may influence the fortunes of their competitors. They know also that the things that their competitors do have a way of affecting them. These interactions may be thought of as a kind of teeter-totter arrangement, in which if *A* goes up *B* must go down. Competition is a driving force among these businesses. It is not such a driving force among the wheat farmers.

Yet the wheat farmers, their product, and their market are the prime exemplars of the condition traditionally called "perfect competition"!

## CONNOTATIONS AND VALUE JUDGMENTS

The question whether there is or is not real competition in the state of affairs called "perfect competition" is not just a matter of semantics or of clever usage of words. True, both the term itself and the simple one-road continuum which is often associated with its use carry a strong connotation of excellence. The adjective *perfect* is a "good" word. The noun *competition* is a "good" word. Taken together, they suggest an ideal condition. But the question has more to it than that.

And when one inspects the diagram, and notes that at the other end of the road is "pure monopoly" (perhaps a strange use of the word *pure*), one is impelled to suppose that anything that lies in between these extremes—the one the ideal of goodness and the other the perfection of evil—must itself be at least partially suspect. It lies somewhere along the road to evil, and is therefore suspect if not downright bad and unlawful. This line of thinking, although not commonly so plainly expressed, shines through many analyses of the antitrust laws and descriptions and explanations of business activities.

This thinking, however, is inaccurate and needs to be corrected. The correction may be pictured with the aid of a new diagram (Diagram 15.2). In this one the base appears as a dotted line because there is much question whether any businesses truly lie in between these lower extremes. At the lower right is the condition labeled "Complete Monopoly." It may be doubted whether, in fact, it really exists. At the lower left appears a new label for a familiar concept. The label is a clumsy phrase —"The Atomistic Condition of Buying and Selling." It is meant to describe, objectively and without the emotional pushes of the words *pure, perfect,* and *competition,* the condition of many buyers and many sellers —so many on each side that no individual can produce an appreciable effect on the market by his own actions. Although the phrase is awkward, it does away with connotations of either excellence or evil. It is appropriately colorless.

*Diagram 15.2*

## MARKET CONDITIONS

BUSINESS COMPETITION

THE ATOMISTIC CONDITION    COMPLETE MONOPOLY
OF BUYING AND SELLING

## BUSINESS COMPETITION

In addition, the diagram is constructed as a triangle. At the apex appears something called "Business Competition." It is the type of competition with which we are all familiar, typified by almost all kinds of manufacturing and wholesale and retail markets, whether involving tangible commodities or services.

It is characterized by conditions that may not prevail under either the lower left or the lower right state of affairs—for example, the use of advertising and selling. These activities would not be useful either to the man engaged in atomistic production and selling or to the man who has a complete monopoly, if such there be.

Drawing the diagram as a triangle, instead of as a straight line, has two advantages. One is that it suggests that business competition is not merely a mixture of characteristics of the other two, but rather is something that has characteristics of its own, and therefore stands apart in some respects from the other two. It has the further advantage, and a marked one it is, of carrying no connotation that this kind of business activity lies somewhere between good, on the one hand, and evil, on the other. In short, it assigns business competition to a new category—one more accurately descriptive of its real nature.

This is the competition of the real business world. It is quite unlike the situation of the wheat growers. In business competition competitors are vying for shares of a limited market. They compete in various ways—by improving the efficiency of their production methods and reducing costs and lowering prices, by improving their products and services, and by sales promotion. These activities lead to progress and increased productivity and economic growth. The benefits accrue both to the consumers and to the successful innovators.

Such competition is often uncomfortable to the participants. Indeed, some may even succumb in the competitive struggle. The success of any competitor may injure his rivals. It is by no means impossible, however, that vigorous competition—though challenging and troublesome to the competitors—may lead all or most of them to improve their positions. In any event, whatever the outcome among the competitors, society as a whole is pretty certain to gain. This stimulus to social gain is stronger than in the atomistic condition of buying and selling.

## THE ANTITRUST LAWS AND MONOPOLY

This new construction, unfortunately, does not solve the problem of clarifying the meaning of the antitrust provisions aimed at monopolizing and at certain actions where the effect may be to substantially lessen competition.

As noted above, under a certain strict definition of monopoly, almost every business in the country, except the farming, has some characteristics of monopoly, and therefore might be called upon to show that it is not "monopolizing." This is obviously absurd; yet the mere mention of it brings strongly to the foreground the true dilemma of the antitrust laws, so far as the concept of monopoly is concerned, in that *there is no clear dividing line between monopoly and business competition.* This is a perplexing and uncomfortable fact, but its recognition is essential to an understanding both of the ambiguity of the antitrust laws and of the difficulty of rewriting them so as to make clear the offenses which are prohibited.

This dilemma, however, is not peculiar to this law or this subject. When the Eighteenth Amendment to the United States Constitution was enacted—forbidding the manufacture, sale, and transportation of intoxicating liquor—it became necessary to define intoxicating liquor. The Congress eventually did so. A similar difficulty is involved in connection with the traffic offense called reckless driving. This too is a matter of degree and a matter of judgment. Many other examples could be cited.

Clarification of the meaning of monopoly by a rewriting of the antitrust laws would be desirable, if it is possible. However, the urgency of doing this and revitalizing antitrust (to use an advocate's phrase) may appear somewhat less pressing in the light of the actual extent and trend of competition in the United States. Concerning these important matters there is not a little misunderstanding.

## THE GROWTH OF COMPETITION IN THE UNITED STATES

A belief held by many is that competition has been diminishing substantially in the United States, either in recent decades or perhaps even since the Republic was established. A second belief (perhaps depending on the validity of the first) is the opinion that public policy to preserve competition must be strengthened. Is the first belief correct? What kind of reasoning supports it?

The following statement by a knowledgeable economist seems to be fairly representative of these intertwined views:

> The role of government in the supervision of the national economy cannot fail to be increasingly important. This follows from the nature of fundamental changes that have occurred over the years since the Republic was founded. Time was when the market was a place in which a substantial number of wholly independent sellers and buyers met to determine through bargaining the price at which the buyers could be induced to take all or practically all the goods or services the sellers had to offer. The essential conditions in such a market place were that both buyers and sellers were relatively numerous and acted independently.
>
> These conditions no longer prevail over much of our industrial economy. Consolidation and concentration have been going on for so long that in some markets you can count on the fingers of one hand the number of sellers who are effectively competing. It follows that we cannot wisely depend as fully as we used to on the interaction of the forces of the market place. The old idea of "the less government the better" no longer holds. The government now has important functions to perform in seeing that the public interest is suitably protected.[*]

Is the foregoing statement accurate? Or does it, rather, conjure up a vision of an idyllic earlier condition that in fact never existed? Does it picture faithfully the degree of competition among today's larger business firms, or does it tacitly accept the proposition that competition among few sellers cannot be as effective as competition among many?

These key questions can be answered by comparing market conditions as they used to be in the United States with what they are now. What, in fact, has been happening to competition?

The total number of business firms in the United States has grown enormously. Industries are frequently cited, however, in which the number of firms has gone down. But all of this statistical analysis leaves out of account a key factor in the total competitive situation—access of buyers and sellers to one another.

Competition occurs at all levels of business—manufacturing, wholesaling, and retailing. Let us begin with retailing. Let us go back a few decades, that is to say, specifically to a time before the coming of the automobile and the motor truck, and look at retailing in small towns and villages and the surrounding rural areas, which were the places in which most Americans lived at that time.

A typical small town might contain one each of several different kinds

---

[*] Edmund E. Day, "National Responsibilities of Business Leadership," *Michigan Business Review*, January 1950, p. 5.

of retail establishments. Thus it might have one grocery store, one dry goods store, one hardware store, one barber shop, and one blacksmith's shop. If it was a somewhat larger place, it might also have one drugstore and one bank. These stores served not only the residents of the village, but also the farmers for many miles around. These people had virtually no option in their selection of places to buy goods. The townsfolk—except for the very well-to-do—did not own horses and buggies and could go to no place other than their home town for ordinary shopping. The farmers, of course, had horses and wagons and came to town from time to time to buy goods. If a farmer lived three miles from one town and nine miles from another, only grossly unfair treatment would keep him from going to the closer town, since the roundtrip difference of an additional 12 miles would mean about four hours of travel, which would be uncomfortable in any weather in his wagon and on the roads of the time and might be downright wretched in the heat of summer or the cold of winter or in rain at any time of the year.

Even in larger towns and cities, the situation was not greatly different. The typical family did not have a horse and buggy. For most of their ordinary purchases they were tied about as closely to the nearest retail establishment as were their country and village cousins. In short, retailing in premotor vehicle, prehighway America consisted of tens of thousands of establishments whose customers were virtually bound to them and which, in the technical sense of the term, were more nearly monopolies than almost any that can be found today.

What was true of retailing was true, to a greater or lesser extent, of wholesaling and manufacturing also. Just as transportation of persons was slow and costly, so also was the transportation of goods. The result was that the market area that a wholesale establishment could serve was rather limited. The same was true for many manufacturers. They could not sell their goods very far away from the factory, unless the goods moved by railroad. In the areas of wholesaling and manufacturing, therefore, quasi monopolistic situations abounded.

## THE MOTOR VEHICLE, HIGHWAYS, AND COMPETITION

The coming of tens of millions of automobiles and trucks, and the building of more than two million miles of paved highways plus many additional miles of improved but unpaved highways, has changed the mobility of both buyers and sellers. Today the housewife thinks nothing of getting into the family automobile and traveling several miles to do her shopping.

The net result of this revolution in transportation has been that America has ceased to consist of thousands of tiny isolated cells in which merchants and manufacturers enjoyed the advantage given to them by the proximity of their customers and the difficulty the customers had of going elsewhere. Instead, America consists of thousands of interlaced communities with both buyers and sellers enjoying a mobility that puts them in touch with one another to a greater extent than ever before. The farmer need no longer go to the nearest village to do his shopping. When he can travel 60 miles an hour over a paved road, instead of three miles an hour bumping over an unpaved one, it is a matter of little importance to him or to his wife whether they shop in an establishment that is three miles away, nine miles away, or even farther.

A situation of widespread local monopolistic situations has yielded to widespread competition. It is important to note that the truth of this proposition cannot be seen if one's mental picture of a "monopoly" is a huge, nationwide trust. One must grasp the reality and importance of *local monopoly* before the proposition becomes meaningful.

Improved transportation does more than permit customers to get to more sellers easily. It also permits the sellers to deliver goods to customers farther away. Great retail stores make deliveries dozens of miles from their sites. Pipe lines bring oil and gas from one side of the nation to the other to compete with other energy sources. Refrigerated freight cars and ships bring fruits and vegetables to places where they were not previously available. Exporters ship goods by air freight halfway around the world. Together with improved communication, better transportation brings sellers' representatives and sales information into new markets.

The introduction of rural free delivery of mail and parcel post has contributed to the development of mail order selling—an important new method of competition.

Nor is the transportation revolution the only stimulus that has been given to intensified competition in the United States. Another is the extent to which new products have been developed that come into competition with one another. Many materials now compete for use in construction, for example, which did not so compete a few decades ago. Examples are aluminum, laminated wood, and new types of glass, of steel, and of concrete. The same is true of the new materials that go into such simple things as pots and pans, including aluminum, stainless steel, and pyrex glass. Indeed, new materials have come along to compete with the older ones in many industries—plastics perhaps providing the most numerous examples.

To put the whole matter bluntly, it just isn't true that "Time was when the market was a place in which a substantial number of wholly independent sellers and buyers met. . . ." This idealized condition—which looks so much like the condition nowadays called "pure competition"—never existed, except for some farm products. No; instead, time was when the United States contained thousands of local quasi monopolies. Since that time important changes in transportation and communication have broken down the walls that surrounded local markets and have intensified *spatial* competition. New products, and new uses for old or improved products, have added to competition. The fact is that the United States has more competition today than it ever had before in its history and, moreover, that this competition is increasing steadily.

## THE MECHANICS OF COMPETITION

The preceding pages treat the question of competition from the general standpoint of its existence or nonexistence in the economy, the extent to which *rivalry in buying and selling* (which is what competition means) is actually a force in business life. It is now necessary to consider the *mechanics* of competition—the specific actions which competitors take to boost their own positions and prevail over the similar efforts of their rivals.

Two types of competition are generally recognized in economic theory: *price* competition and *nonprice* competition. The meaning of the latter term is usually clear; it includes advertising and selling efforts and other activities. The meaning of the former term, however, is unclear—a condition made critical by the fact that it looms large in the history of antitrust enforcement.

This being true, it might be expected that the concept of price competition would give us a firm anchorage for our exploration of the meaning and intent of antitrust legislation and our inquiry into whether that meaning and intent can be clarified (which is, it will be recalled, the point reached at the end of the last chapter and the beginning of this one). Unfortunately, this is not the case. Although the term *price competition* is often used, it is rarely defined, and on close scrutiny we find that it is just as slippery a concept as monopoly. One wonders whether many of those who use the term have taken any time to ponder its meaning. Our examination of this meaning and its application to antitrust interpretation and enforcement is best introduced through the example of another leading antitrust case.

## THE RIGID STEEL CONDUIT CASE

The makers of rigid steel conduit, a special type of pipe for raceways for electrical wires, priced their products for delivery in accordance with a multiple basing point system with two bases—Pittsburgh and Chicago. The delivered prices of the sellers, in any city where they were competing for business, were identical, since all sellers quoted the lowest combination of any seller's base plus transportation.

The Federal Trade Commission, contending that this system of pricing was an unfair method of competition, unlawful under the Federal Trade Commission Act, reported its finding and issued a cease and desist order. The first of the two counts in the findings was a contention that these prices represented a conspiracy, and the corresponding part of the cease and desist order directed the firms, therefore, to stop using it. The United States Circuit Court of Appeals for the Seventh Circuit decided that the Commission was justified in drawing the inference that the petitioners had acted in concert in a price-fixing conspiracy.*

The really important part of the case, however, lies in the second count. This attack by the Federal Trade Commission did not rest upon an agreement or combination. It charged that the makers of rigid steel conduit, through their concurrent use of a method of making delivered price quotations with the knowledge that each did likewise, had had the result that price competition among them was restrained unreasonably. The second part of the cease and desist order, therefore, directed the individual firms to stop using this method of quoting prices. In 1949 the United States Supreme Court upheld the decision of the Circuit Court, on appeal, by a vote of four to four, one of the justices not participating in the case, and issued no explanatory decision.†

The decision of the Circuit Court of Appeals was of significance not only to industries which used the multiple basing point system of pricing, but also to other industries which quoted delivered prices under zone or "postage stamp" methods of pricing, which also resulted in the quotation by several sellers of identical prices for delivery in many cities. The decision raised a question whether any such delivered price systems were lawful, and whether, in order to be lawful, a factory would have to quote "F.O.B. mill prices" and arrive at delivered prices simply by adding the actual freight. Such an F.O.B. mill pricing system would shut out some competitors from meeting prices of other sellers who might be located more favorably with respect to the markets which they sought to enter; in other words, it would actually *reduce* competition! The concern over this question was intensified after the Supreme Court upheld the decision.

In the meantime, the Federal Trade Commission received so many inquiries about this subject that the Commission issued a document which ostensibly was a notice to its own staff with respect to Commission policy toward geographic pricing practices. This document was mailed to persons inquiring about the applicability of the decision to other situations. In this document, the Federal Trade Commission (with Commissioner Mason not participating in approval of the statement) said:

* *Triangle Conduit and Cable Co. et al. v. Federal Trade Commission*, 168 F. 2d 157 (1948).

† *Clayton Mark & Company, et al. v. Federal Trade Commission*, 336 U.S. 956 (1949).

The question raised by geographic pricing practice under the Federal Trade Commission Act is one of elimination of price competition.

This viewpoint was supported in what has become an oft-quoted assertion,

> ... the economic effect of identical prices achieved through conscious parallel action is the same as that of similar prices achieved through overt collusion. ...

On its face this last statement may seem substantial and significant; indeed, a real clincher. Its limitations, however, appear when one considers how a similar proposition might be phrased:

[1]   The economic effect of identical prices achieved through *competition* is the same as that of similar prices achieved through overt collusion. (The condition of identical prices is representative of "perfect competition.")

Variations of this theme might include these statements:

[2]   The economic effect of *unequal* prices achieved through conscious parallel action is the same as that of similar prices achieved through overt collusion.

[3]   The economic effect of *unequal* prices achieved through competition is the same as that of similar prices achieved through overt collusion.

Each one of the foregoing four statements is true. None, however, is meaningful. Neither a condition of equality of prices nor one of inequality of prices—in and of itself—tells anything about the presence or absence of competition, much less offering conclusive evidence on the point.

## THE CONCEPT OF PRICE COMPETITION

Comments on price competition often seem to suggest that it is nonexistent if the sellers of similar products in a market are simultaneously quoting the same price. It might seem, therefore, that price competition exists when two or more sellers are quoting *different* prices. The truth of this conclusion, however, is by no means obvious. Indeed, one may search the books and articles that discuss this subject in vain for a clear and plain statement on the subject.

One sometimes gets the impression that, to some analysts, the term *price competition* contemplates a situation involving a kind of *sellers'* auction as distinguished from the more familiar kind of *buyers'* auction. In the familiar type of buyers' auction the article being auctioned off is sold to the highest bidder. A sellers' auction may be thought of then as one in which a buyer expresses his willingness to buy something and invites representatives of sellers to bid. In this situation one could imagine the representatives' bidding successfully lower prices until no further bids are evoked—at which point the buyer would award his business to the lowest bidder.

As a matter of fact, something that resembles this procedure occurs in connection with certain large purchases of goods (particularly by governments) and frequently occurs in connection with the letting of large construction contracts for big buildings and other structures. In letting such construction contracts, public authorities or private firms release blueprints and specifications for a building and invite construction firms to tender bids. These bids are usually in written form and the bidders are not (or are not supposed to be) in active contact with one another. A time limit is placed for the receipt of bids, and announcement is usually made that the contract will be awarded to the lowest responsible bidder.

Now if a sellers' auction—oral or written—is what the term *price competition* means to some analysts, it becomes clear at once that the procedure is infrequent in the sale—purchase process and, indeed, cannot be very frequent—for a perfectly simple reason. The reason is that it is altogether too expensive to be engaged in by sellers except in connection with extremely large orders and contracts. It is quite clear, for example, that the housewife cannot expect representatives of different grocery stores to make bids on her market purchase basket every few days. The process of inviting and receiving sealed bids on very large orders and on construction contracts is not unreasonable—indeed, in the case of the construction contracts it is extremely sensible because buildings and bridges are not products that are carried in stock—but any extension of this process to buying and selling in general is patently out of the question.

## CONTINUOUSLY QUOTED COMMODITIES

At this point it is essential to distinguish between commodities that may be called "continuously quoted commodities" and commodities and contracts which are completed to special order, or "unique commodities." Ordinarily a *building* is something unique. Builders do not have on hand stocks of factory buildings, store buildings, and apartment houses. The typical one is an individual product, built to individual plans and specifications, and because it represents an expensive transaction the price may normally be expected to be a price negotiated between the prospective buyer and the prospective seller, possibly with the buyer inviting bids from several sellers.

When, however, we turn our attention to continuously quoted commodities, we see an entirely different situation. Here there has emerged the standard practice of putting price tags on the products. The housewife can walk up and down the aisles of the grocery store and see quotations on the grocery items on the shelves. Similarly, at wholesale and manufacturing levels, the sellers commonly have price lists, with, perhaps, stated discounts. The era of bargaining at the retail level has almost disappeared in the United States, and the amount of bargaining in connection with prices at wholesale and manufacturing levels has diminished.

When sellers have continuously quoted prices, these prices become known not only to customers, but also to competitors. In the circumstances, it is perhaps altogether reasonable to suppose that such prices in a particular market will tend toward equality. Indeed, any seller who quotes prices higher than the prices of other sellers for similar products might reasonably be asked why he expects to be able to sell his products at all. If, for example, one were to do a bit of comparison shopping in the retail stores of competing firms in a large city and ascertain the prices on several well-known national brands of food products, surely he would not be amazed if he were to discover that in many of these stores the prices quoted were absolutely identical. Nor should he be amazed to find —at the wholesale and manufacturing levels—that sellers were quoting identical prices on standardized products like cement. Such identity of prices, to be sure, could be the result of collusion; but, on the other hand, it could equally clearly be the result of the working of competition.

In short, the quoting of identical prices by sellers on continuously quoted commodities, whether the orders are large or small, oral or in writing, is a condition that one might normally expect to associate quite as plainly with competition as with collusion.

The situation with respect to sealed bids received for a unique item, such as a building, is quite different from the foregoing. Any firm putting out plans and specifications for a building, and receiving identical bids from two or more bidders, might reasonably infer collusion. Since these are not continuously quoted commodities, and since the computations on which the bids are based are enormously complex, and full of judgment factors, the chances of two or more bidders coming up with identical quotations are so remote as to be out of the question. But to carry this inference of collusion over to cases of identity of prices where goods are on the shelf and in stock, and where price quotations are available to customers and become known to competitors, is a leap of logic carried to absurdity.

## SUMMARY

These interrelated analyses lead to certain general conclusions, which now may be stated briefly.

[1] Some theories of "monopolistic competition" and "imperfect competition" are misleading in important respects—especially in their open contention or tacit implication that business competition is inferior to what these theories call "pure competition" or "perfect competition."

[2] The term *price competition* is used frequently by writers who neither define it nor seem to understand its slippery nature. Those who mean by it the charging by sellers of identical prices for similar products draw unjustified conclusions about its significance in some cases.

[3] What is here called "business competition" is not part way between the "good" condition of "pure" or "perfect" competition and the "bad" condition of monopoly, but, rather, is a different kind of condition which is socially better in some ways than "pure" or "perfect" competition.

[4] Contrary to a widely held opinion, competition has not declined in the United States in recent decades; it has increased.

[5] The unfortunate ambiguities of the antitrust laws that forbid monopolizing and attempting to monopolize cannot, because of the difficulty of defining *monopoly*, be easily eliminated.

[6] Inasmuch as competition has increased—and bids fair to continue to increase—the social need for clear and enforceable laws forbidding "monopolies" and protecting competition may be less pressing than is often asserted. Indeed, when account is taken of their inevitable—and objectionable—ambiguity and of the nature and actual extent of competition, one may ask whether these conditions do not outmode the doctrinaire assumption of the antitrust laws that the way to preserve competition is to outlaw "monopolies."

[7] Because of the difficulties of regulating "monopolies" and protecting competition, and the uncertain desirability of such regulation, it is sometimes argued that the goal of preventing monopolistic exploitation could be achieved by preventing "unfair" competition, thereby restricting business growth to firms that serve customers "fairly." Unfair competition is considered further in Chapter 17.

## QUESTIONS AND PROBLEMS

1. Explain and appraise these terms: *pure competition, perfect competition, imperfect competition,* and *monopolistic competition.*
2. What are the moral and legal connotations of the foregoing terms?
3. Define *monopoly* and name one or more specific examples.
4. Explain why it can be argued that there is both a ubiquity of competition and a ubiquity of monopoly.
5. Is monopoly only a "big business" problem?
6. Farming is often referred to as an example of pure competition. But it has also been argued that farmers are not in competition at all. Discuss.
7. Explain the relationship between the transportation revolution and the increase in the amount of actual competition in this country.
8. Why do some authorities see a lessening of competition and others a strengthening of competition in recent decades? How convincing are the bases for these opposing beliefs?
9. "Monopoly is rising and competition is declining, as anyone can plainly see by looking at the giant businesses existing today." Is this true?
10. Define *price competition* and state how you can test for its presence or absence.

*11.* The fact that several different firms are charging the same price for a good may or may not be indicative of collusive action, depending on whether the good is a "unique commodity" or a "continuously quoted commodity." Explain.

## SELECTED READINGS

BURNS, A. R. *The Decline of Competition.* New York: McGraw-Hill Company, 1936.

CHAMBERLIN, EDWARD. *The Theory of Monopolistic Competition.* Cambridge, Mass.: Harvard University Press, various editions.

CLARK, J. M. *Competition as a Dynamic Process.* Washington, D.C.: The Brookings Institution, 1961.

MACHLUP, FRITZ. *The Political Economy of Monopoly.* Baltimore: Johns Hopkins Press, 1952.

MASON, EDWARD S. *Economic Concentration and the Monopoly Problem.* Cambridge, Mass.: Harvard University Press, 1957.

MASSEL, MARK S. *Competition and Monopoly.* Washington, D.C.: The Brookings Institution, 1962.

ROBINSON, JOAN. *The Economics of Imperfect Competition.* London: Macmillan and Company, Ltd., 1934.

SLICHTER, SUMNER H. "The Growth of Competition," *Atlantic Monthly,* November 1953.

STOCKING, GEORGE W. *Workable Competition and Antitrust Policy.* Nashville, Tenn.: Vanderbilt University Press, 1961.

# 16

## BIG BUSINESS AND
## SMALL BUSINESS

Having examined the concepts of monopoly and competition, we now turn our attention to the question of bigness itself. "Big business" is a problem that has perplexed our country for many decades. Its evils—real or imaginary—have been denounced again and again. It is a favorite target of politicians. Yet with every passing year big business has grown bigger and bigger, and it has not lacked defenders.

In this chapter we shall consider big business from the standpoint of size alone. Perhaps the "problem" will become more manageable if we recognize the important distinction between bigness and monopoly. Bigness and monopoly are not identical. A large chain store corporation is big, but it is not necessarily a monopoly. Contrariwise, a village bank may be small, while coming about as close as any business can to being a monopoly.

First we look at the growth and present extent of big business, so that we can determine just what all the talk is about. Then we consider a rather detailed report on what the public thinks about big business. The pros and cons of bigness are followed by an appraisal of public policy. And finally, we devote some thought to the outlook for big business in the future.

### THE ROLE OF THE CORPORATION

When we think of big business, we usually think in terms of corporations—large corporations. It is true that partnerships and single enterprises hold a wide lead in terms of sheer numbers, but the largest business firms of today are corporations. The dominant position of the corporate structure stems, of course, from its advantages, including those of limited liability and the facility for raising large amounts of capital, both of which become increasingly important as a business grows larger and expands its scope of activities. Thus the story of the growth of big business is for all practical purposes the story of the growth of corporations and the development of the corporate form of business organization.

Although business corporations existed in this country even prior to 1800, they were very few in number and they did not engage in what we would now call big business. The formation of corporations was impeded by the necessity for specific state legislation each time a new firm was organized. However, the number of corporations increased rapidly during the first half of the nineteenth century as the various states enacted general incorporation laws. Additional stimulus was provided when the states began to compete with each other in simplifying the incorporation requirements to provide the most attractive business climate.

As the industrial revolution progressed in this country, transportation and communication facilities were rapidly expanded. Mass markets were created and mass production was developed to serve these markets. Both the number and the size of corporations increased rapidly. Thus one of the significant characteristics of the half century between the Civil War and World War I was the rise of big business in America.

Not all corporations are large, however. Many are small. Some start small and become large. Individual business firms grow larger by reinvesting their earnings, by selling securities to the public to finance expansion or by merging or combining with other business firms. The latter method is obviously the fastest means of growing, and for this reason it has played a major role in business expansion, and especially in the growth of really big business.

## WAVES OF MERGERS

Although forerunners of business mergers can be detected in various gentlemen's agreements and pools of the post–Civil War years, the merger movement first fluorished in the 1880s, as the trust came into popularity. By exchanging trust certificates for stock certificates of different companies, the trustees gained control of the companies and then were able to operate the companies as one. One of the first and most effective of these was John D. Rockefeller's Standard Oil Trust.

The Sherman Antitrust Act of 1890 arrested the growth of trusts but not the further development of big business. During the nineties a new modification of the corporate organization appeared—the holding company—which is a corporation to control and coordinate the operation of other corporations through the simple expedient of owning majorities of their voting stock. A wave of business consolidations using this form of organization occurred during the turn of the century. Numerous big corporations were formed, one of the largest being United States Steel.

The latter part of the Nineteenth Century was truly the era of the big businessmen—the industrial giants and the tycoons of finance—men such as Carnegie, Rockefeller, and Morgan—and they fashioned business firms that were very big indeed. By the end of 1903 there were 41 industrial corporations in the $50-million class. Big business had become a part of the American economy.

The trust-busting activities of Roosevelt and Taft, and public disillusionment with big business, curbed its growth somewhat, but with the twenties came another period of consolidation. These consolidations were on the whole less spectacular than those of the earlier period, since they featured piecemeal absorption rather than wholesale combinations of large numbers of units. The former objectices of market control and increased profits through sheer size tended to be superseded by the desire to share in the commercial advantage of certain competitors or to eliminate the wasteful duplication of selling and distribution costs. Big business giants formed during these years include General Mills, General Foods, and the International Paper Company.

A third merger era began during World War II and is still in process. Whereas the emphasis had formerly been on horizontal combinations of business firms, vertical and conglomerate consolidations have become increasingly important. The vertical combinations have been directed toward assurance of sources of supply and toward improvement of marketing positions. The latter factor has contributed also to the conglomerate combinations, wherein, typically, a company merges with or acquires another firm in a completely unrelated field of business.

It must be recognized that not all mergers invoke or result in big business companies, nor do all big business companies owe their present size solely to mergers. Much growth is attributable to the ability of companies to earn or otherwise acquire capital funds necessary for expansion from within. And, of course, there are underlying factors that have permitted and encouraged business expansion as our nation has prospered. Yet the fact remains that mergers are a part of the history of nearly all big corporations and hence of big business itself.

## THE PRESENT EXTENT OF BIG BUSINESS

To determine the extent of big business requires first that one decide just what is and what is not big business. There is, however, no clear dividing line, easily recognized and commonly accepted, between the big and the small. Probably no one thinks of the General Motors Corporation as a small company. And by the same token, very few would regard the neighborhood grocery store as a part of big business. But for many business firms the proper classification is not so readily apparent. In these cases the distinction between big business and small or medium-sized business might well be based on any or all of a number of characteristics, including such as these:

Dollar value of capital assets,
Dollar value of sales,

Number of employees,
Number of stockholders, and
Size of the market area.

After deciding which characteristic is to be considered, one must still determine the dividing line above which all companies will be considered "big." Are all companies with assets of $50 million or more "big business?" Or should we include only those which have passed the $100-million mark? The final decision is necessarily arbitrary, and may be determined as much by the convenience as by the appropriateness of the division.

Obviously, then, an exact evaluation of the extent of big business would be difficult to prepare and harder still to defend. Instead, we shall merely note some of the data which provide at least a clear and positive indication of the extent of big business.

With regard to the number of people employed, we might conclude from Table 16.1 that big business firms are rather few in number. In 1956 only some 3,100 firms employed 1,000 or more persons. This was less than one tenth of 1 per cent of all business firms then in operation. Even if we drop the cut-off point for big business to those firms employing 500 or more people, big business firms numbered only 6,410. Thus there really weren't very many big business firms. But on the other hand, these relatively few companies—.15 per cent of a total of well over four million concerns—employed 43.6 per cent of all non-government wage-earning and salaried employees. Obviously this figure is heavily influenced by companies with considerably more than 500, or 1,000, or even 10,000 employees. Yet the conclusion is inescapable that, if two of every five workers in private industry are employed by big business, big business is extensive and important.

*Table 16.1*

NUMBER OF FIRMS IN OPERATION AND PAID
EMPLOYMENT, BY SIZE OF FIRM, 1956

| EMPLOYEES | NUMBER OF FIRMS | PER CENT OF TOTAL | EMPLOYMENT | PER CENT OF TOTAL |
|---|---|---|---|---|
| 0—19 | 4,164,400 | 95.05 | 9,621,000 | 23.7 |
| 20—49 | 135,100 | 3.08 | 4,104,000 | 10.1 |
| 50—99 | 44,000 | 1.01 | 3,022,000 | 7.4 |
| 100—499 | 31,310 | .71 | 6,171,000 | 15.2 |
| 500—999 | 3,310 | .08 | 2,271,000 | 5.5 |
| 1000—9999 | 2,880 | .06 | 8,237,000 | 20.3 |
| 10000 or more | 220 | .01 | 7,240,000 | 17.8 |
| Total | 4,381,200 | 100.00 | 40,667,000 | 100.0 |

SOURCE: U.S. Department of Commerce. *Survey of Current Business,* September 1959, p. 15.

In terms of capital assets one could again conclude that there really aren't very many big business firms. Corporate income tax returns for 1957 reveal only 2,084 corporations with assets worth $50 million or more—and this is often cited as one of the measures of big business stature. Of course, $50 million is really quite a bit of money. Some people might be inclined to regard this as "*really* big business," and then many more firms would come under the simple heading of "big business." At any rate, these same 1957 tax returns reveal that the top 2,084 firms owned over 60 per cent of the total assets reported by some 800,000 corporations.

The significance of big business with regard to our national economy is indeed substantial, but it is of course much more substantial with regard to certain specific industries. The automobile industry consists mainly of General Motors, Ford, Chrysler, and American Motors. The influence of the United States Steel Corporation is so great that within the steel industry it is commonly referred to simply as "The Corporation." These are well-known but by no means unique examples. Numerous other industries reflect the importance of big business.

## HOW BIG IS BIG BUSINESS?

While recognizing that big business does occupy a major position in our national economy, we may still find ourselves wondering just how big big business is. What does it mean if a company employs 10,000 or 50,000, or 200,000 people? What if a company has assets worth $50 million, or $500 million, or even $1 billion? Table 16.2 gives us at least one frame of reference for such data, by relating big business firms to government

*Table 16.2*

## FIFTY BILLIONAIRE ENTERPRISES, BUSINESS AND GOVERNMENTAL, RANKED ACCORDING TO SIZE

*(Data Are for 1958)*

| Business Organization or Political Unit | Revenues[1] AMOUNT (MIL-LIONS) | RANK | Employees NUMBER | RANK | Assets[2] AMOUNT (MIL-LIONS) | RANK |
|---|---|---|---|---|---|---|
| *Federal Government* | $69,117 | 1 | 2,405,000[3] | 1 | $262,056 | 1 |
| General Motors Corp. | 9,522 | 2 | 521,000 | 3 | 6,891 | 15 |
| Standard Oil Co. (N.J.) | 7,544 | 3 | 154,000 | 8 | 9,479 | 12 |
| Amer. Teleph. & Teleg. Co. | 6,771 | 4 | 592,130 | 2 | 19,494 | 7 |
| Great Atlantic & Pacific Tea Co. | 5,095 | 5 | 145,000 | 9 | 647 | 41 |
| Ford Motor Co. | 4,130 | 6 | 142,076 | 10 | 2,962 | 20 |
| General Electric Co. | 4,121 | 7 | 249,718 | 5 | 2,398 | 24 |
| Sears, Roebuck & Co. | 3,721[4] | 8 | 205,609 | 7 | 2,036[4] | 26 |
| United States Steel Corp. | 3,439 | 9 | 223,490 | 6 | 4,437 | 16 |
| *State of California* | 2,965 | 10 | 114,675 | 13 | 24,308 | 5 |
| Metropolitan Life Assurance Co. | 2,911 | 11 | 57,554 | 34 | 16,282 | 8 |
| Socony Mobile Oil Co. | 2,886 | 12 | 43,700 | 43 | 3,237 | 18 |

## Table 16.2—continued

| Business Organization or Political Unit | Revenues[1] AMOUNT (MILLIONS) | RANK | Employees NUMBER | RANK | Assets[2] AMOUNT (MILLIONS) | RANK |
|---|---|---|---|---|---|---|
| Gulf Oil Corp. | 2,769 | 13 | 56,000 | 37 | 3,430 | 17 |
| Prudential Ins. Co. of America | 2,648 | 14 | 58,277 | 31 | 14,732 | 11 |
| Swift and Co. | 2,645 | 15 | 63,906 | 27 | 585 | 43 |
| *State of New York* | 2,558 | 16 | 117,474 | 12 | 36,686 | 2 |
| *New York City* | 2,542 | 17 | 254,094 | 4 | 22,450 | 6 |
| Texas Company | 2,328 | 18 | 52,515 | 38 | 3,112 | 19 |
| Safeway Stores | 2,225 | 19 | 59,555 | 30 | 408 | 49 |
| Chrysler Corp. | 2,165 | 20 | 95,846 | 16 | 1,338 | 31 |
| Bethlehem Steel Corp. | 2,006 | 21 | 140,474 | 11 | 2,195 | 25 |
| Westinghouse Elect. Corp. | 1,896 | 22 | 114,652 | 14 | 1,412 | 30 |
| Standard Oil Co. (Ind.) | 1,864 | 23 | 46,033 | 40 | 2,769 | 21 |
| Armour & Co. | 1,850 | 24 | 45,700 | 41 | 412 | 48 |
| E. I. du Pont de Nemours | 1,829 | 25 | 83,875 | 20 | 2,649 | 22 |
| The Kroger Co. | 1,776 | 26 | 40,500 | 44 | 331 | 50 |
| Boeing Airplane Co. | 1,712 | 27 | 92,878 | 18 | 605 | 42 |
| *Commonwealth of Pennsylvania* | 1,680 | 28 | 80,790 | 21 | 16,131[5] | 9 |
| Shell Oil Co. | 1,666 | 29 | 38,572 | 45 | 1,648 | 27 |
| Standard Oil Co. (Calif.) | 1,559 | 30 | 38,395 | 46 | 2,457 | 23 |
| General Dynamics Corp. | 1,511 | 31 | 92,900 | 17 | 651 | 40 |
| *State of Ohio* | 1,478 | 32 | 57,883 | 33 | 24,630[6] | 4 |
| National Dairy Products | 1,451 | 33 | 44,194 | 42 | 558 | 44 |
| Equitable Life Assurance Society of the U.S. | 1,436 | 34 | 11,511 | 50 | 9,298 | 14 |
| *State of Michigan* | 1,421 | 35 | 64,794 | 26 | 15,957 | 10 |
| J. C. Penney | 1,410 | 36 | 75,052 | 23 | 416 | 47 |
| Goodyear Tire & Rubber | 1,368 | 37 | 98,264 | 15 | 915 | 34 |
| Union Carbide & Carbon | 1,297 | 38 | 57,020 | 36 | 1,530 | 28 |
| Proctor & Gamble Co. | 1,295 | 39 | 20,700 | 48 | 756 | 35 |
| Douglas Aircraft Co., Inc. | 1,210 | 40 | 71,925 | 24 | 473 | 45 |
| United Aircraft Corp. | 1,202 | 41 | 57,315 | 35 | 470 | 46 |
| Sinclair Oil Co. | 1,190 | 42 | 23,828 | 47 | 1,500 | 29 |
| International Business Machines Corp. | 1,172 | 43 | 86,736 | 19 | 1,261 | 32 |
| Radio Corporation of Amer. | 1,171 | 44 | 78,000 | 22 | 734 | 38, |
| *State of Texas* | 1,148 | 45 | 66,325 | 25 | 9,369 | 13 |
| R. J. Reynolds Tobacco Co. | 1,147 | 46 | 13,135 | 49 | 743 | 36 |
| *State of Illinois* | 1,111 | 47 | 60,801 | 29 | 28,609 | 3 |
| International Harvester | 1,098 | 48 | 63,206 | 28 | 1,026 | 33 |
| Montgomery Ward & Co. | 1,092 | 49 | 58,152 | 32 | 738 | 37 |
| Continental Can Co. | 1,080 | 50 | 51,000 | 39 | 688 | 39 |

[1] Revenues for all types of organizations and political units are stated on the basis of gross revenues with the exception of corporations, which are based on net sales, and the Federal Government, which are based on net receipts after the deduction of refunds and after the transfer of tax receipts to the old-age and survivors insurance trust fund, to the railroad retirement account, to the Federal disability insurance trust fund, and to the highway trust fund.

[2] Assets of states and municipalities represent total assessed valuation; those for the Federal Government represent personality and realty assets for the executive agencies, offices, and establishments of Government, including the Department of Defense.

[3] Represents the total number of civilian employees, including those outside continental United States.

organizations. We see that, of the leading billionaire enterprises, the Federal Government holds the first position by a considerable margin. But in terms of revenues eight industrial organizations rank higher than any of the state governments, and only two states and one city make the top 25. As employers, four states and New York City are included in the top 25. With regard to assets the government units rank much higher. Still, "big business" is surely not an exaggerated description of those business enterprises that employ more people, take in more money, and own more assets than do many of our state governments.

## THE PUBLIC'S ATTITUDE TOWARD BIG BUSINESS

Although business in one form or another is probably discussed almost as often as the weather, there is very little reliable information on what the general public thinks about big business. The best source on this subject is the report of a national public opinion survey conducted by the University of Michigan Survey Research Center in 1950.* This survey explored the ideas and attitudes of the public about the structure and functioning of large business enterprises in the American economy.

As might be expected, most of the interviewees associated the term *big business* with the names of very large manufacturing companies, such as General Electric, with synonyms for *big business* such as *big companies* or *large corporations*, or with specific industries, such as the steel industry and the auto industry. The most frequently identified characteristics of big business were the involvement of great sums of money, the employment of large numbers of people, the manufacture and sale of great quantities of products, and operation over wide geographical areas.

The most frequently cited *advantages* of big business were its ability to produce great quantities of goods, to produce goods at low cost, and to create numerous jobs. Almost half of those interviewed were impressed with the number of people employed by big business. Additional benefits included a higher standard of living and the development of new and better products.

With regard to the *bad effects* of big business, the greatest concern was expressed over excessive *power* of one sort or another—too much power in interbusiness practices and competition; too much power as opposed to the consumer and the worker; too much power over other

* Institute for Social Research, Survey Research Center, *Big Business from the Viewpoint of the Public* (Ann Arbor, Michigan: Institute for Social Research, 1951).

---

⁴ Data are as of January 31, 1959.
⁵ Data reported are for 1956.
⁶ Data reported are for 1957.
   SOURCE: Theodore J. Kreps, *An Evaluation of Anti-Trust Policy: Its Relation to Economic Growth, Full Employment, and Prices* (Washington, D.C.: U.S. Government Printing Office, 1960) Appendix A.

institutions, such as governments, schools, and newspapers. Other reported disadvantages included high prices and high profits, lack of consideration for the rights and the interests of workers, and even corrupting influence, through the manufacture of such "sinful" products as liquor and cigarettes. Nearly a quarter of those interviewed thought of no bad effects attributable to big business, while only 2 per cent could think of no good effects.

Public concern over the power of big business was further demonstrated in evaluations of the desirability and extent of government control. Seventy-one per cent of the respondents favored some degree of government control over big business, while 18 per cent were opposed. Control was considered most desirable with regard to prices, wages, working conditions, and hours of work. In general, government control was considered appropriate in those matters where big business was believed to affect the living standards of consumers or of employees.

The survey also offered considerable insight into public comparisons of big and small business. From the employee's perspective big business was believed to offer higher wages and greater job security, but the management attitude of small business was considered more favorable to workers. Seventy-one per cent of the respondents felt that big business could lower prices and still make a fair profit; only 36 per cent felt that the same was true for small business. Yet 61 per cent indicated that big plants were more efficient producers, while only 18 per cent supported the small plants in this respect. The greater efficiency of large plants was for the most part ascribed to more machinery, more workers, more capital, and mass production or assembly line methods. Interestingly enough, the survey revealed that most people saw little difference in the quality of products offered by big and small business.

On the whole, the survey indicated that the public recognized both good and bad features of big business. And although no questions were specifically directed toward this point, the bad features apparently were not considered necessary for realization of the good features. As far as the over-all evaluation was concerned, 76 per cent of the interviewees felt that the good things about big business outweighed the bad. Only 10 per cent took the opposite position, while 14 per cent either didn't know, or were confused, or simply felt that the good and the bad were about equal.

Thus, in general, it may be concluded that the public is quite favorably disposed toward big business, but is also reasonably sure that big business can improve on its past performance.

## BIG BUSINESS: ARGUMENTS PRO

To what extent are the public's opinions accurate? What are the arguments pro and con?

It has long been held that big business is the most efficient producer of goods and services. Economies are achieved through mass production, the hiring of topflight management personnel, and the division and specialization of labor. Administrative services are centralized and coordinated; controls are introduced and applied to all phases of the organization. Unit costs of production are reduced, and so are prices, to the benefit of all.

Big business is defended also on the basis of technological developments. Only large enterprises can afford the tremendous costs of present-day research—especially the basic research that is so necessary to technological advance. Many of the research projects carried on by industry prove of no benefit whatsoever; they cannot be translated into sales revenues and profits. Even the cost of applied research into new products and new uses for old products would be prohibitive to many small companies that cannot afford to gamble with large sums of money. Yet without research the flow of new products and improved methods of production would cease, and the rise of our standard of living would be arrested.

Attention is directed also to the role of big business in making the inventor's discoveries available to the general public. When a small firm comes out with a new product, several years may pass before capital investment, marketing programs, sales, and earnings can be built up to the point where the product is available to the entirety of its potential market. On the other hand, big business either has or can quickly procure sufficient resources to telescope this growth period and the ultimate consumer benefits from the earlier enjoyment of the product.

The proponents of big business argue that in its absence many of the products we recognize as everyday necessities would not even exist, at least not for the average citizen. Only in large-scale enterprises are sufficient funds available to assemble the vast complexes of productive equipment that permit the inexpensive mass production and distribution of such basic commodities as steel, aluminum, petroleum products, electricity, plastics, and chemicals.

Big business is also held essential to our national defense. The development and production of intricate weapons systems, rockets and missiles, space satellites, and interplanetary vehicles—all require the special skills and capabilities of big business.

Big business is said to encourage rather than discourage competition. A favorite example is the automobile industry, where industrial giants fight for every sales dollar. Big business stimulates new forms of competition and thereby benefits the consumer. Efforts to improve product quality and to provide products designed to meet the specific needs and desires of the individual buyer are illustrative of the consumer's gain from big business competition. Advertising campaigns beyond the scope or imagination of small business have advised consumers of the availability of products they can use—products they would not even be aware of lacking big business' huge advertising budgets.

Nor does big business discourage the existence and growth of small business—in fact, big business needs small business and will always need it. The small firm can specialize and thereby provide the big companies with needed special products and services. Illustrative of this condition is the following statement contained in the 1962 edition of the General Motors Information Handbook:

> Small businesses comprise the majority of the more than 31,000 suppliers helping General Motors' U.S. divisions make their various products. Located in all 50 states and the District of Columbia, they range from small shops to mass production companies. GM's dependence on thousands of small firms across the nation is evidenced by the fact that more than 76 per cent of the suppliers employ fewer than 100 persons and 92 per cent have fewer than 500.
>
> Over 47 cents of each GM sales dollar goes to suppliers, some of which have been doing business with GM since the company was organized. Direct suppliers, in turn, are often dependent upon thousands of other suppliers.
>
> Only suppliers of goods and services valued at $500 or more annually were included in the supplier count.

Many large firms actually encourage the development of new business firms as outlets for their own industrial products. Consider the case of a large chemical company that produces raw plastics. It could hardly manufacture and market the vast variety of goods of which plastic is the basic raw material. So instead the company spends large sums on product research. As it develops new uses for the raw material—plastic—it also seeks new enterprises desirous of producing the new products. In addition to selling the ideas to the prospective producers, the company also maintains a large sales engineering technical force to assist them in the resolution of technical problems. Both big business and small business thus profit as sales of raw plastic and plastic products increase.

The advocates of big business usually conclude their arguments by urging one to look around and observe all the wonderful things that the average American can enjoy—all the products and services that make up what is by far the highest standard of living in the world. They insist that this high level of living is in large part attributable to the accomplishments of big business.

And, they go on to say, big business provides more than just material advantages. It enables the average American to earn a good living through only a few hours of work each day. Time and effort that our fathers devoted to earning the family bread can now be expended on the "good things of life." Spiritual and cultural pursuits, recreation of all kinds, and even just plain leisure—all are now within reach. Far from being overly materialistic, big business actually permits the best possible life—the free combination of material and nonmaterial advantages to the greater satisfaction of all.

## BIG BUSINESS: ARGUMENTS CON

The opponents of big business do not concede its efficiency. On the contrary, they say that the complexities of administration and organization inevitably lead to inefficient operation. As an organization grows larger and larger, the problem of management control becomes increasingly difficult. Policies and decisions lose their force as they filter down to the operating level. Sales and production data are misinterpreted and distorted before they reach the policy makers. Paper work and staffs multiply. The ratio of administrative expense to actual output increases steadily. The end result is the very opposite of efficiency.

They also argue that the recognized efficiencies of mass production are not contingent upon the existence of industrial behemoths. A plant of a particular size will provide the lowest unit manufacturing cost for a particular product, and it doesn't matter whether the plan represents the entire production facilities of a small company or a minor fraction of the facilities operated by a billion-dollar giant. On a slightly larger scale, critics assert, Chevrolet, Frigidaire, Delco-Remy, and A-C Spark Plug would all be just as efficient if they were completely separate companies rather than divisions of the General Motors Corporation.

Big business is accused of stifling invention and innovation, thereby holding back instead of encouraging technological progress. Critics insist that many big corporations face little competition and so have little incentive to improve their products or develop new products. Maintenance of the status quo offers the greatest possible profit.

In addition, it is asserted that the huge research laboratories of big business are by no means essential to the continued flow of new inventions. On the contrary, say these critics, inventions are for the most part accidents, and so the greatest gain will be achieved from a large number of experimenters working on innumerable individual projects. Massive efforts directed toward a few specific goals will prove less rewarding in the long run.

Another common criticism of big business is the power it wields over our political, economic, and social institutions. From the economic standpoint, statistics are cited to show the wealth of these companies, the number of people who work for them, and the number of people who either buy from or sell to them. The obvious conclusion is that these companies directly or indirectly control or at least strongly influence a disproportionate share of the national economy. Nor is this power of significance only in the aggregate. The economic strength of a big business firm is also evident in its ability to control the prices it pays to its suppliers and the prices it charges its consumers.

On the political front big business is accused of excessive power at all levels of government—national, state, and local. Millionaire big businessmen have held positions of high authority in both Democratic and Republican administrations. It is asserted that these men are going to favor big business, that they cannot be completely impartial, no matter how they try. Big business is also said to carry undue weight with legislative bodies, oil companies in Texas being cited as an example. Whether for personal interests or for the protection of their constituents, it is held that legislators too often find themselves unable to resist the blandishments and threats of big business.

The opponents of big business are particularly concerned over its influence in the editorial offices of the nation's press. They observe that critical comment on the growth of giant corporations is almost nonexistent —indeed, big business is eulogized at almost every opportunity. The reason? Every large newspaper gains most of its revenue from the advertising expenditures of big business. And, of course, radio and television stations are completely dependent on advertising revenue. We all learn at an early age the adage "You don't bite the hand that feeds you." The business managers of our mass communications media make sure that their editorial writers never forget it.

A similar danger is seen in the ever-rising contributions of big business to our colleges and universities. At first glance this support of higher education appears entirely commendable. But what happens if and when a college or university president comes to look upon big business as a major source of funds? Can we then expect that college or university to remain immune to the power of big business? Of course not, say the critics: the dollars buy power; control can be retained by scholars and educators only if the dollars are refused.

Many people believe that big business represents a grave threat to democracy itself. In the first place, it tends to destroy one of the cornerstones of the American way of life—the small businessman, the local entrepreneur. As big business grows bigger, the little competitor is swallowed up or forced out of business. In his place we find salaried management, hourly workers, clerks, and agents. The independent businessman is also losing out in the esteem and ambitions of our youth. Fewer and fewer young people look forward to owning businesses of their own. Most of them desire the safety and security of employment in large corporations. The net result is a social loss for democracy. A nation of wage-earning and salaried employees will lack the qualities of independent thought and vigorous action that our society must possess if the challenges of civilization are to be met in a democratic manner.

A further threat is posed by the rapidly growing distinction between owning and operating a business enterprise. The day-to-day management of productive resources by the owners of those resources has surely been a source of strength to the American economy and hence to democracy. Yet the combination of ownership and management can exist only with small enterprises. We are fast becoming a nation of stockholding employees working under the direction of a managerial class—a group of experts held to be better suited to a socialist than to a democratic society.

## PUBLIC POLICY TOWARD
## BIG BUSINESS

Our national government is not officially committed to the active support of big business. This is perhaps obvious in view of the fact that many government personnel spend all or most of their time investigating the nature, extent, and objectives of big business. Yet there is no denying that every large business enterprise is afforded a substantial amount of government assistance.

The Department of Commerce has actively promoted both domestic and foreign trade. By the very nature of things this promotion is bound to benefit big business. And the services offered by such organizations as the Patent Office and the National Bureau of Standards can be considered almost indispensable. Then too, some government activities oriented toward the business world are of direct and practical significance only to the larger companies. For example, very few small business firms employ personnel capable of evaluating or exploiting the masses of business statistics that are continuously collected and assembled by the government.

The "evils" of big business are a favorite target of campaign oratory and even of postelection speeches and articles. Such oratory, however, does not accurately reflect public policy. Executive policy statements and directives and legislation invariably attack such matters as monopoly, unfair competition, and excessive market control rather than bigness per se. Even the laws regulating corporate mergers—certainly a key factor in the formation and expansion of big business—prohibit only those mergers which tend substantially to lessen competition or to create monopolies. Thus for the most part public policy toward big business may be considered technically neutral or even slightly favorable. Why, then, do we hear so much about government attacks on big business?

In the first place, many people tend to equate big business with such prohibited practices as monopoly and unfair competition. We have already noted that these concepts do not retain their textbook simplicity in actual life. They are difficult to tie to specific cases. Occasionally, bigness is seized upon as an easily measurable substitute. This leads to the feeling that public policy is or should be opposed to big business, since monopoly and unfair competition have long been forbidden. When this feeling is shared by Government officials who direct and implement public policy, then public policy will surely be anti-big-business in their spheres of authority, regardless of what official pronouncements may say on the subject.

Secondly, even though officials are fully cognizant of the distinction between big business and monopoly or unfair competition, the latter usually present a serious problem only as they are practiced by large enterprises. The accusations and investigations of practices prohibited by the antitrust laws invariably involve big business, since it is here that the effect of these practices on our economy and our society is most obvious. Local "monopolies"—in the aggregate—may hurt the nation more, but they are not so conspicuous. With antitrust activity thus focused on big business the appearance of hostility toward big business is well-nigh inevitable.

## PUBLIC POLICY TOWARD SMALL BUSINESS

The well-being of small business has been of particular concern to our Federal Government for many years. Public officials praise small business, both houses of Congress maintain committees to study its problems and in 1956 President Eisenhower formed a Cabinet Committee on Small Business. The general objectives have been to strengthen the economic position of small businesses and to foster their sound development.

At present the primary responsibility for furthering these objectives rests with the Small Business Administration, an independent agency established in 1953. Specific activities of this agency include the following:

[1]  Helping small businesses to gain access to adequate capital and credit through financial counseling, loans shared between banks and S.B.A., direct government loans, and assistance to privately owned small business investment companies. From September 1953 through December 1959, 18,271 business loans had been approved, amounting to $856,-304,000 of financial assistance to small businesses.

[2]  Helping small businesses to obtain a fair share of government purchases and sales. The agency provides other government departments with information about the productive capabilities of small businesses and at the same time furnishes small business firms advice on and guidance in selling to the government. Additional aid is offered through the "set-aside" program. Joint determinations are made by the Small Business Administration and other government agencies to "set aside" certain proposed procurements for competitive bidding only by small firms. The total value of government contracts awarded to small businesses in fiscal year 1959 exceeded $4.7 billion—about 18 per cent of all government procurement actions with business firms.

[3]  Helping small businesses to obtain competent management and

technical and production counsel. This program of counseling has been supplemented by the publication of nearly 300 titles in regular series devoted to such subjects as management aids for small manufacturers, technical aids for small manufacturers, small marketers' aids, and small business management. Nearly eight million copies of these publications had been distributed by the end of 1959.

[4] Making disaster loans to persons whose businesses have been damaged by storms, floods, and other disasters and to small concerns which have suffered substantial economic injury because of excessive rainfall or drought conditions in their areas. On December 31, 1959, 7,769 loans of this type had been approved, with a total value of $82.9 million.

As for unfair competition, the Antitrust Division of the Department of Justice and the Federal Trade Commission are always ready to investigate the complaints of small businesses. Normally, of course, these complaints are directed against big firms.

The suggestion is sometimes voiced that government assistance to small business really misses the mark—that it is generally more suited to the needs of what might be termed the medium-sized companies. This point is partially illustrated by Table 16.3, which indicates that some of the loans approved by the Small Business Administration in 1959 must have gone to companies that were not really small. Yet, in terms of numbers, 75 per cent of the loans were for rather moderate sums. Probably most of these went to truly "small" business firms.

When assistance measures prove to be of little value to small business, the failure is probably in large part attributable to administrative difficulties rather than to deficiencies in the type of assistance offered. Just to make small businessmen aware of the services and facilities available

*Table 16.3*

## BUSINESS LOANS APPROVED BY THE SMALL BUSINESS ADMINISTRATION

| SIZE OF LOANS | 1959 | | 1960 | |
| --- | --- | --- | --- | --- |
| | NUMBER OF LOANS | PERCENTAGE OF TOTAL | NUMBER OF LOANS | PERCENTAGE OF TOTAL |
| $5,000 and under | 343 | 8 | 267 | 7 |
| 5,001—10,000 | 717 | 16 | 581 | 14 |
| 10,001—25,000 | 1,571 | 35 | 1,426 | 36 |
| 25,001—50,000 | 778 | 17 | 705 | 18 |
| 50,001—100,000 | 605 | 13 | 590 | 15 |
| 100,001—150,000 | 217 | 5 | 177 | 4 |
| 150,001—250,000 | 199 | 4 | 174 | 4 |
| 250,001 and over | 103 | 2 | 92 | 2 |
| Total | 4,533 | 100 | 4,012 | 100 |

SOURCE: Small Business Administration, *15th Semiannual Report* (Washington, D.C.: Small Business Administration, 1961), p. 42.

for their use is extremely difficult, and this is only the first step in an effective assistance program. Obviously the larger enterprises are more likely to know about and hence to take advantage of Government aids. However, whether or not public policy could be more effective in its application does not change the fact that public policy is strongly oriented toward the preservation and encouragement of small business enterprises.

## THE OUTLOOK

There seems to be little basis for expecting a decline in the extent of big business. The basic forces that have led to the formation of large industrial enterprises are still with us. The United States is a large country with a growing population—it offers large markets for a wide variety of goods and services. As our nation prospers and the level of real income rises, these markets will continue to grow. And many luxury products that are currently produced in small quantities will in the future become commonplace necessities. Present-day production will be expanded manyfold, and the producers will tend to expand also. Almost every businessman endeavors to hold his share of the market and to increase his share if at all possible. Hence, as the market grows, his firm also may grow. Many of today's small business firms will undoubtedly be included in the ranks of the big businesses of tomorrow.

Public policy will continue to wrestle with the evils of monopoly and unfair competition, and public officials in searching out these evils will continue to concentrate on the activities of big business. The problems of definition and interpretation will not be fully resolved for many years to come. Big business will still be plagued by the vagueness and uncertainties incorporated in the antitrust laws.

Yet these hindrances will not be controlling factors. The containment or contraction of big business will not occur unless and until such becomes the public will. And it does not seem likely that the public will soon demand the dissolution or forbid the growth of large enterprises that endeavor to compete efficiently and to achieve profits honestly. Restrictions may be applied from time to time, but the continued existence and growth of big business is almost assured by the continuous expansion of our national and world economies.

## QUESTIONS AND PROBLEMS

1. What lessons can be learned from the historical development of big business and small business?
2. What are the principal characteristics of big business? Of small business?
3. Do your opinions about big business and small business coincide with those

of the general public? If not, wherein, and what do you surmise is the reason
for the difference?

4. Evaluate the arguments for and against big business and small business.
5. In what ways does "big business" depend on "small business" for survival,
and vice versa?
6. What are the advantages a small business has over its larger competitors,
and how have they held their own amidst the larger concerns?
7. Why do antitrust actions seem to focus on big national firms rather than on
small local ones?
8. What kinds of assistance has small business been getting from governmental
entities? Is this assistance justified? Is it enough?
9. What is the future of small businesses? Are they desirable? In what areas?
10. What changes, if any, would you favor in public policy toward big business?

## SELECTED READINGS

Edwards, Corwin D. *Big Business and the Policy of Competition*. Cleveland,
Ohio: Press of Western Reserve University, 1956.
Fellner, William J. *Competition Among the Few: Oligopoly and Similar
Market Structures*. New York: Alfred A. Knopf, Inc., 1949.
Galbraith, J. D. *American Capitalism*. Boston: Houghton Mifflin Company,
1952.
Glover, John D. *The Attack on Big Business*. Boston: Graduate School of Busi-
ness Administration, Harvard University, 1954.
Kaplan, A. D. H. *Big Enterprise in a Competitive System*. Washington, D.C.:
The Brookings Institution, 1953.
————. *Small Business: Its Place and Problems*. New York: McGraw-Hill
Company, 1948.
Lindahl, Martin L., and William A. Carter. *Corporate Concentration and
Public Policy*, 3rd ed. Englewood Cliffs, N.J.: Prentice-Hall, Inc., 1959.
Maurer, Herryman. *Great Enterprise: Growth and Behavior of the Big Cor-
poration*. New York: The Macmillan Company, 1955.
Quinn, Theodore K. *Giant Corporations: Challenge to Freedom*. New York:
Exposition Press, 1956.
Stigler, George J. "The Case Against Big Business," *Fortune*, May 1952, pp.
123–155.
Survey Research Center, University of Michigan. *Big Business from the View-
point of the Public*. Ann Arbor, Mich.: Institute for Social Research, 1951.

# 17 COMPETITION, COMPETITORS, AND CONSUMERS

The competition whose praises are sung (in a chorus not always joined in by the competitors themselves) and whose maintenance (in most businesses) is an objective of public policy is *fair competition. Unfair competition* may be hurtful to competitors, to consumers, or to both. Federal, state, and local laws, and private efforts, are directed at preventing improper business practices.

The law was concerned with unfair competition long before any statutes were passed on the subject. The common law permitted recovery of damages in cases of unfair competition. One of the early types of such unfair action was "passing off." In this activity, A falsely misrepresented his goods to be the product of B. B then could sue for damages. Proving the damages might be difficult and expensive. If A's goods were inferior to B's, the buyer C also might sue A, alleging fraud. He too incurred the costs and difficulties of proving the fraud. Unless the purchase was a large one, it would not be worth while for him to bring suit.

In order, therefore, to provide better protection for honest competitors and for consumers, many laws have been enacted in the United States. We turn attention first to laws prohibiting unfair competition and, further on, to legislation specifically directed at protecting the consumer, with the understanding that some legislation and governmental activities do both at once.

The extent of governmental activities for the protection of consumers, and their discussion in this chapter, could create the impression that the American consumer is a pitiful creature, who is continually being cheated, misled, swindled, deceived, tricked, and manipulated by scoundrelly businessmen. Not so. Whether in consequence of laws, business ethics, private watchdog organizations, or his own personal wisdom, the American consumer is, in general, well treated.

## THE FEDERAL TRADE COMMISSION

The Federal Trade Commission was organized as an independent administrative agency in 1915, pursuant to the Federal Trade Commission Act of 1914. Additional duties were subsequently delegated to the Commission by the Clayton Act, the Export Trade Act, the Wool Products Labeling Act, the Fur Products Labeling Act, the Flammable Fabrics Act, the Textile Fiber Products Identification Act, and the Lanham Trade-Mark Act of 1946. It will be noted that the Commission is not charged with the enforcement of the Sherman Act. That duty, together with the enforcement of most United States statutes, belongs to the Department of Justice, which has an Antitrust Division for the purpose. With that exception, the Commission is the chief Federal agency charged with maintaining competition and keeping it fair.

The original Federal Trade Commission Act prohibited "unfair methods of competition in commerce." Later the words *and unfair or deceptive acts or practices* were added. The addition grew out of a fascinating case. The FTC ordered the Raladam Company to stop certain practices in connection with the marketing of its product "Marmola"—an antiobesity preparation. The product was held to have some dangerous side effects, and the Commission insisted that the company should not market it without informing the public that it could be safely administered only under medical advice. The company appealed to the Supreme Court, and there the FTC received a setback.[*]

The Court admitted that the order was designed to protect the public on a reasonable basis. In refusing to uphold the order, however, the Court held that, under the law, the Commission must present evidence of injury to the business of competitors. The Court held that these things had not been done and that, therefore, the Commission's action was not within the scope of the law.

In consequence of this and similar situations, the FTC urged the Congress to amend the act. This was finally done in the Wheeler–Lea Act of 1938, which amended Section 5 by adding the words *and unfair or deceptive acts or practices in commerce* to the prohibitions of the Act. The Commission then was able to proceed successfully against the Raladam Company, since the amendment relieved it of the necessity of showing injury to competitors.

In recent years, and especially because of the Wheeler–Lea Act, the FTC has received strong support from the courts, with only occasional setbacks.

## FTC FUNCTIONS AND PROCEDURES

The Commission's principal functions are these: to promote free and fair competition by preventing price-fixing agreements, boycotts, combinations in restraint of trade, other unfair methods of competition, and unfair or deceptive practices; to protect the public by preventing false or

[*] *FTC v. Raladam Co.*, 283 U.S. 643 (1931).

deceptive advertisements of foods, drugs, cosmetics, and therapeutic devices; to enforce truthful labeling of textile and fur products; to prevent the interstate marketing of dangerously flammable wearing apparel and fabrics; and to petition for the cancellation of illegally registered trademarks.

The Commission's activity in enforcing the laws proceeds along two lines: (1) enforcement through formal litigation, leading to mandatory orders against violators, and (2) inducement of compliance by voluntary and cooperative action.

The formal litigation procedure is similar to that used in courts. A case is instituted by issue of a formal complaint charging violation of one of the statutes. If the charges are not contested—or if in a contested case the charges are found after hearings to be true—the Commission may issue an order (often called a "cease and desist" order) requiring discontinuance of the unlawful practice. A respondent who wishes to contest a proceeding has an opportunity to be heard before a hearing examiner. The respondent in the hearing has the right to present evidence, to be represented by counsel, to cross-examine witnesses, and to introduce witnesses, and he has other rights fundamental to judicial proceedings.

The examiner files an "initial decision." This decision becomes a Commission's decision thirty days after it is served unless it is meanwhile appealed to the full Commission or to the courts. An appeal goes to a court of appeals which has the power to affirm or to set aside the order. Thereafter, either party may appeal to the Supreme Court for a review by *certiorari* of the action of the court of appeals.

The second enforcement "procedure" is the use of persuasion and inducement to voluntary cooperation. Voluntary compliance procedures are centered in the Commission's Bureau of Consultation, and often take the form of the trade practice conference. This represents a practical application of the principle of self-regulation. It involves enlisting the cooperation of firms in an industry and their consumers in a joint attack on practices which are harmful to the industry or the consuming public. These persons are invited to meet with the Commission representatives. Out of this conference a draft of proposed rules is prepared for study by the participants. They and others are given opportunity to present their suggestions and objections. After consideration of all these matters, the Commission promulgates rules that specify in detail those practices which are deemed to be unfair.

Other Federal agencies are concerned with improper competition and consumer protection, but the FTC is the one with the largest responsibilities, in the most areas. It is a kind of policeman of the American competitive system. In 1960 it had 750 employees and a budget of $7 million, an amount equal to four cents per American per year—hardly excessive in view of the number and importance of its duties.

## PURE FOOD AND DRUG LEGISLATION

Consumer protection is a big and complex subject. It involves legal devices at the Federal, state, and local levels and also many private efforts, such as those of Better Business Bureaus, Chambers of Commerce, and consumer advisory services. On the positive side, many activities include the area of *consumer education,* whose importance may be greater than that of the essentially negative regulations aimed at preventing undesirable activities by sellers of goods.

Governmental entities at all levels have been concerned with consumer protection for many years—at least to a modest extent. Laws involving the establishment of legal standard weights and measures, and the inspection of weighing and measuring devices, date back many years; and the latter is still an important activity. The first Federal act in this field, passed in 1883, dealt with the regulation of tea. Growing concern about improper food ingredients and unsanitary packing practices led to increasing agitation around the turn of the century for the enactment of a Federal pure food and drug law.

The proposed bill was fought vigorously by certain business interests. Strong opposition to the passage of the law came from "patent medicine" makers, as might have been expected—it was estimated that 95 per cent of the patent medicines on the market at that time were frauds. Also, the bill was opposed by the liquor interests, since, under the law, they would be forced to include "artificial color and flavor added" in their labels on cheap spirits. The many other opponents included the National Mincemeat Makers Association. In view of the fascinating possibilities in the composition of mincemeat, it is interesting to speculate about what the Association feared would be the impact of pure food and drug legislation on their business.

Because of the power of the opposition, the movement for a Federal law made very little headway until after the appearance of Upton Sinclair's book *The Jungle.* The action of the book was laid in and around the stockyards and meat packing plants in Chicago. The author's intended theme was the poverty and miserable living conditions of the workers, most of whom lived in the neighborhoods of the packing plants in which they worked. With the novelist's instinct for "grading," Sinclair presented a vivid unlovely picture of careless and filthy conditions in the meat packing industry. Whatever the reaction of the public to the story of wage slavery, readers were greatly impressed by the description of the unsavory methods in meat packing. In later years Upton Sinclair said, "I aimed at the public's heart and I hit its stomach." According to American tradition, one of those who was hit was President Theodore Roosevelt, who threw his not inconsiderable weight behind the enactment of the proposed pure food and drug law.

So it came to pass that in 1906 a law finally won through, and its enforcement was delegated to existing Federal departments. In the beginning the law was weak, and the appropriation for its administration was small. The law has gradually been strengthened and the appropriation has been increased. As late as 1960, however, the Food and Drug Administration had only 1,656 employees and an appropriation of $13,800,000, or less than a dime per American per year, to carry on its immense responsibilities.

## WEAKNESSES OF THE 1906 ACT

The Federal Food and Drugs Act of 1906 was designed mainly to eliminate misbranding and adulteration. While the bill was being written, many allowances were made to get the support of various pressure groups, and the sum total of these concessions resulted in a less than satisfactory law.

The Government soon encountered many difficulties in the administration of the Act, especially in its enforcement, which was hampered by the following three factors:

[1] Lack of clarity concerning the natures of the offenses defined in the Act,

[2] The size and technical characteristics of the industries affected by the Act, and

[3] The limitations on Federal action imposed under the Commerce Clause of the Constitution of the United States.

The natures of the offenses defined in the Act were hard to ascertain because the Act was written so loosely, the terms used being broad and ambiguous. This meant that many violations had to be tried in the courts and that "judge-made laws" prevailed. In fact, actual legal precedents remained scarce while this (original) law was in effect.

There were only eight inspectors to administer the law for the entire food and drug industry, which was larger, decentralized, and spread out over the entire country. It was impossible to police all of the companies with such a small force of inspectors. Rapid technical changes and developments in processing created additional problems because the Government could not keep up with the scientific advances being made. Industry knew more about concealing adulterations than the Government knew about detecting them.

Action and enforcement were greatly limited because injunctions couldn't be issued. The highest fine permitted under the law was $300, and the average fine paid throughout the life of the Act was $66. The low fines and paucity of convictions under the Act resulted from the fact that a case had to be tried in the home district of the offender, and the jury was usually biased in favor of local industry. Prosecution was limited also by lack of funds available for enforcement and general administration. This all added up to a law without teeth.

Labeling was inadequately covered, since it required only that the quantity of goods (by weight) in the container be stated. In the case of a drug the presence and quantity of a narcotic also had to be stated on the label.

Another difficulty in the administration of the Food and Drug Law of 1906 resulted from the lack of standards. There were no standards in the *food* industry, and the only regulation of food under the law was in reference to misnaming and misbranding. *Drugs* were standardized through standards set in the United States Pharmacopoeia and the National Formulary. However, no limits of allowable *variation* from standard formulas were stated.

As the years passed, it became apparent that the 1906 law had many loopholes, and a move for new legislation was begun. Some of the loopholes in the law were the following:

[1] If a product had a "distinctive name" it was not subject to prosecution for misbranding or adulteration, regardless of what its manufacturer claimed in advertisements and other announcements. This meant that virtually all branded products were excluded from the law.

[2] The label of a product had to be both "false and fraudulent" to be subject to prosecution, and this pertained only to the portion of the label stating the ingredients. Patent medicines were controlled very little by the law. As long as the maker stated the proper ingredients on the label, he could make any wild claims of cure that he desired.

[3] Even though the net weight of the contents of a container was required, the law didn't prohibit deceptive containers and slack-filled packages. People who did not bother to read the net weight on a label and judged the quantity by appearance only could be misled.

[4] The law did not regulate cosmetics.

[5] The law had no control over health devices and appliances.

[6] The law lacked control over advertising claims.

In 1929 a private organization, Consumers' Research, Inc., launched its product survey publication "Consumer Bulletin," which awakened many among the American buying public to the fact that new food and drug legislation was needed. At about the same time many organizations and groups, such as the American Medical Association, joined in with their publications in efforts to safeguard the public. This pressure gradually became more organized, and finally resulted in a new act— the Federal Food, Drug, and Cosmetic Act of 1938.

This Act extended the coverage of Federal regulation to mechanical health devices and cosmetics. It extended control to new drugs, providing for adequacy of manufacturing controls and evaluation of drugs before any could be placed on the market. It increased the penalties for violation, giving the enforcement agency the power to seize adulterated or mis-branded foods, drugs, devices, and cosmetics. It created standards of identification, quality, and fill for containers. It supplied extensive additions to the definitions of adulterated products and misbranded products. The law also contained detailed and specific labeling regulations.

## THE FOOD AND DRUG ADMINISTRATION

Today the Food and Drug Administration consists of a Washington headquarters organization and 17 district territories, each with head-quarters manned by chemists and inspectors and equipped with testing laboratories. Within these district territories are 36 inspection stations. The enforcement program is developed on a selective basis in accordance with provisions of law.

Lest it be supposed that the Act relates only to purity and content labeling, attention is drawn to an event that occurred in April 1962. The Food and Drug Administration seized more than five thousand "giant economy size" jars of Maxwell House instant coffee. Investigation had shown that the ten-ounce "giant economy size" jars were being sold for $1.44, or 14.4 cents an ounce, whereas six-ounce jars of the same coffee were being sold for 75 cents, or 12.5 cents an ounce. Thus, the Government pointed out, the "giant economy size" cost 1.9 cents an ounce more than the regular size.

This example also illustrates a condition that was being complained of increasingly at that time by consumer interests and government representatives, namely, the use of odd-sized containers and of extravagant descriptive phrases. Phrases such as "jumbo quart," "king size quart," and "big pound" were claimed to be misleading.

The practice of manufacturers in putting up their products in odd-sized packages such as 6½ ounces instead of 8 ounces, or 15 ounces instead of 16 ounces, was held to be deceptive in that these packages looked like the more familiar half-pound and pound sizes—especially if they were slack-filled—and, moreover, made it arithmetically difficult for the house-wife to arrive at comparisons of prices per ounce.

A specific example of this mathematical confusion is provided by the four sizes of toothpaste tubes put out by one concern. The "medium" size contained 1⅞ ounces and sold for 31 cents; the "large" size, 3¼ ounces for 53 cents; the "economy" tube had 5 ounces for 69 cents; and the "family" container, 6¾ ounces at 83 cents. It happens in this case (in which respect it is unlike the Maxwell House one) that each size was a better buy than the next smaller one—but the consumer who found this out for himself had to be a dogged and dedicated consumer indeed.

In 1961 the Food and Drug Administration made 158 seizures of different kinds of packaged goods. Of these, 129 involved the offense of giving short weight, and 29 were examples of inconspicuous labeling. The Commission has reported that many manufacturers of packaged foods were putting out products slightly short of weight. Some labels were faulty in that required information appeared in the corners of the packages, in fine print. Ingenious were the examples of a transparent bag of licorice candy on which the net weight figures were printed in black ink and a similar package of raspberry candy with the net weight in lavender.

## ADDITIONAL FOOD AND DRUG LEGISLATION

Lest the impression be created that the Food, Drug, and Cosmetic Act is the only Federal legislation that extends protection to consumers along these lines, the following list of other Federal legislation is presented.

[1] Meat Inspection Act—inspection and grading of meat.
[2] Butter Standard Act—identification of standards of butter.
[3] Skim Milk Act—standard for skim milk.
[4] Import Tea Act—standards for tea.
[5] Import Milk Act—standards for milk.
[6] Filled Milk Act—standards for whole milk.
[7] Filled Cheese Act—standards for cheese.
[8] Oleomargarine Law—standards for oleomargarine.
[9] Standard Grade Apple Law—grading of apples.
[10] Export Apple and Pear Law—grading of apples and pears for export.
[11] Federal Narcotic Drug Law—regulation of narcotics.
[12] Human Biological Drug Law—regulation of biological products for human use.
[13] Animal Biological Drug Law—regulation of biological products for animal use.
[14] Shrimp Amendment—control of seafood industry.
[15] Wheeler–Lea Act—regulation of advertising.
[16] Insecticide Act—regulation and standards for insecticides.

## MEAT INSPECTION

The Meat Inspection Division of the United States Department of Agriculture administers the Meat Inspection Act. It carries on inspection of the handling of livestock in and out of public stockyards. It inspects the wholesomeness and sanitation of the preparation of meat and meat-food products. The inspection is aimed in part at determining that animals slaughtered for meat are free from disease.

It is interesting to note that poultry is not subject to Federal inspection, either in the Food and Drug Administration or in the Meat Inspection Division. George P. Larrick, Commissioner of Food and Drugs, stated in a 1957 interview that he believed that there was much diseased poultry on the market.*

## SOME PROBLEMS OF ADVERTISING

It would be misleading to suggest that a substantial portion of the millions of advertisements that are printed or uttered each year in the United States are substantially false. Many of them, to be sure, contain mild exaggerations of the kind that are sometimes called by the courts "puffing." It is not expected that such statements will be taken literally, and therefore their literal untruthfulness is not considered to be objectionable.

Although state and private agencies exercise some control over false or misleading advertising, regulation of this type is undertaken principally at the Federal level. Major responsibility is exercised by the Federal Trade Commission, the Post Office Department, the Federal Communications Commission, the Alcohol and Tobacco Division of the Internal Revenue Service, the Food and Drug Administration, and the Securities and Exchange Commission. In addition, a dozen other Federal agencies exercise some control over advertising. The effectiveness of their controls depends upon their enforcement. In general, Federal enforcement is much more effective than the enforcement of state regulations.

Part of the difficulty involves the question of drawing the line between mere "puffing" and substantially false and misleading advertising. The following examples of television advertisements are presented so that the reader may practice judging which should be condemned as false or misleading:

> A cake mix manufacturer, aware that hot TV studio lights will melt a cake's icing, frosts his display sample with shaving cream instead.
>
> A coffee producer substitutes hot wine for coffee in television commercials because the cameras tend to make coffee look sludgy and syrupy.
>
> A brewer, urging you to buy his beer instead of a competitor's, puts a salt tablet in his own product as shown on TV to give it a bigger head of foam than his rival's which he doesn't doctor.
>
> A cleansing agent maker uses bleach, not his product, on the sponge that miraculously wipes away hard-to-clean spots in the TV housewife's prop kitchen.†

In a conspicuous decision the Federal Trade Commission in January 1962 ruled unanimously against the use of a shaving advertisement that purported to show how Palmolive Rapid Shave would permit a razor to

* *U.S. News and World Report,* May 31, 1957, p. 78.
† *The Wall Street Journal,* November 25, 1959.

shave coarse sandpaper clean in a single stroke. In its ruling the FTC said that the "sandpaper" was actually a prop made of plexiglass covered with sand and that tests had shown that real sandpaper never could be shaved clean, no matter how long the shaving cream was allowed to soak.

One is sometimes amazed by the amount of ingenuity that goes into devising the tricks of the dishonest trade. One such trick is the "bait and switch" racket. The bait is an advertisement offering a low-priced item to draw a customer into a store. If the bait takes and the customer comes into the store, the salesman talks down the advertised item because he has no intention of letting the customer buy it if he can possibly prevent it. The salesman's aim is to switch the customer to a higher-priced item.

Another deceptive action is that of *fictitious pricing*. This involves pricing an item on sale as having been marked down from a far higher price, when actually it is being sold at its regular price, or for very little less.

A different kind of complaint about advertising—one that does not involve its accuracy—relates to the quantity and quality of radio and television commercials. Critics assert that the quantity is excessive and the quality low. They say that there are too many of them and that many are too long, too loud, or in poor taste. This situation does not lend itself readily to regulation. The broadcasters attempt to exercise some control through their national association and local stations. One consequence of this complaint is the suggestion that there should be some governmentally owned television stations and programs which would have no advertising at all. Another consequence is the movement in favor of *paid television* (referred to in Chapter 18).

## PROPOSED DEPARTMENT OF CONSUMERS

For years it has been suggested occasionally that there should be established a Federal Cabinet-level Department of Consumers. Bills to establish such a department have been introduced from time to time. In general, the proposal would be that the department would represent consumers in court and before regulatory agencies and Congressional committees, and it would investigate complaints and take action where necessary. If such a department were established, to it presumably would be transferred certain existing Federal agencies, including the Food and Drug Administration, the Division of Prices and Cost of Living of the Bureau of Labor Statistics, the Bureau of Human Nutrition and Home Economics, and certain units of the National Bureau of Standards engaged principally in testing consumer goods.

Despite frequent and sometimes fervent advocacy of this establishment, the action does not appear likely, at least in the near future. This unlikelihood might be thought rather strange considering the fact that *all* Americans are consumers and that, in this capacity, they are not formally represented in the Cabinet, whereas several smaller groups are so represented. The Departments of Agriculture, Labor, and Commerce represent farmers, workers, and business interests. On the face of the matter, this would seem to be an anomalous condition which should be altered.

An alternative would be to transfer some of the Government's consumer-oriented activities to the Department of Health, Education, and Welfare, where the Food and Drug Administration is located at present.

In July 1962, President Kennedy named a 12-member Consumers Advisory Council "to give broad consideration to the consumers' needs and point of view." It reports to the Council of Economic Advisers, and is assisted by a small staff and by liaison officers designated by 20-odd government departments and agencies.

## BETTER BUSINESS BUREAUS

The Better Business Bureaus are a nongovernmental, private activity, without legal enforcement power, consisting of the national organization, and Bureaus in more than a hundred cities, whose objectives are promotion of fair competition and protection of consumers. This set of organizations had its start a half century ago with a movement for "truth in advertising," out of which came a national committee for promoting better advertising. The name "Better Business Bureaus" has been used since 1916.

Originally the work was done by volunteers, but now it has become professional. This permits, in any one city, hiring a professional person, with no business connection with the members, to conduct the affairs of the Bureau. The local chambers of commerce originally promoted the Bureaus, and now some cities too small for Better Business Bureaus have divisions devoted to the same activities in their chambers of commerce. The money is provided by the local businessmen, according to the sizes of the chambers and the towns. One of the purposes is to protect both themselves and consumers from unethical businessmen.

Any consumer can take a complaint to the BBB and get free help. Files are kept on firms, and they show how many complaints there have been and how many have been settled satisfactorily. Anyone can ask about the reliability of a store before making a purchase. Of course, the business is not always in the wrong.

Besides acting on complaints received, the BBB initiates action itself. It tries to get better standards. It looks for questionable statements in advertisements and goes out shopping to check up. Often, pressure from a BBB will stop some specific bad business conduct. Newspapers and radio cooperate by refusing to accept some advertisements. Bureaus in different towns can warn each other about objectionable activities.

In 1955 Better Business Bureaus received 2,041,726 requests for information or assistance on everyday business problems.* Home improvement and maintenance, front door and telephoned solicitations, home appliances, insurance, automobiles, radio-TV-musical equipments, photography, furniture and floor coverings, apparel, and magazine subscriptions led the list of subjects for which information was requested.

During 1955 the Bureaus called on advertisers 19,093 times to find out about the accuracy of their claims. Only 525 of these cases were not settled by voluntary advertiser cooperation.†

Though most states have laws on false advertising, the legal approach is often unsatisfactory. Prosecution would be too late, in the case of a sale already made, to help a purchaser anyhow, and prosecution of the smaller crimes, such as advertising as a "huge" price reduction mark-down of 1 per cent or 2 per cent or nothing is unlikely to be pushed or even to be started. Pressure from a BBB in a case of this kind can be very effective. Publicity can be a powerful weapon in combatting false advertising. Offending merchants are very swiftly purified by threats of it.

The BBB gives no leeway to its members; they too must toe the line. It does not recommend or endorse any product, firm, or individual, and a member cannot advertise that he belongs. The Better Business Bureaus form an important policing force whose power and influence seem to have grown steadily.

## CONSUMERS' RESEARCH AND
## CONSUMERS UNION

Consumers' Research, Inc., and Consumers Union of the U.S., Inc., are service-to-consumer organizations with a common ancestry.

Consumers' Research, the first of the two organizations, came about as a response to a book entitled *Your Money's Worth,* by Stuart Chase and F. J. Schlink, which described the problems of the consumer in trying to make intelligent purchases through the maze of conflicting claims, skillfully prepared misinformation, flattery, sex appeal, and exaggerations that then characterized, and still characterize, much advertising of consumer goods. CR was organized in 1929 as a nonprofit corporation entirely supported and managed by consumers. It publishes monthly and annual bulletins containing analyses of products of interest to consumer-members.

* "BBB Efforts in '55 Reached All-Time High," *Editor & Publisher,* May 12, 1956, p. 22.
† *Ibid.*

Consumers Union was organized in 1935 by Arthur Kallet, who, up until that time, had been Secretary of Consumers' Research. It also publishes monthly and annual reports.

Consumers' Research and Consumers Union are the only agencies entirely financed by consumers which test and evaluate a large variety of products and then make their findings available to a substantial portion of the public. Both groups have permanent staffs for testing and investigation, and they make use of outside technical consultants and advisers where their own laboratory facilities are not adequate. After they investigate and test a product, they make available to members lists of recommended, intermediate, and not recommended brands and varieties.

Consumers' Research and Consumers Union have both adopted a policy of remaining at a safe distance from the companies whose products they rate. Along with this policy they deny companies the use of their ratings in advertising because they feel that, if they allowed use of these ratings, they would leave themselves open to charges of bias. They have done an excellent job in upholding this policy. They feel the same way about personal selling, although it is of course impossible for them to control the use of their evaluations by salesmen. Neither organization will sell large quantities of its publication to any company it suspects of using them in its selling efforts.

## ATTITUDES TOWARD "FAIR TRADE" LAWS

Laws relating to resale price maintenance, or "fair trade" laws, as they are often called, have been in existence since 1931. Both prior to that time and since, different parties have been differently interested in the prices at which goods are sold. In general, consumers appear to prefer lower prices to higher ones, except when a reduced price creates a suspicion that something is wrong with the goods. Generally, retailers wish to sell for prices that provide satisfactory profit margins. They are not happy if competition pushes prices down and squeezes the profit margins. For years, therefore, retailer organizations have pushed manufacturers to establish minimum resale prices on their products.

The manufacturer of trade marked goods has an interest in the prices charged by retailers. He wants these prices to provide satisfactory margins so that the retailers will be willing to carry his products and perhaps even push their sale.

Hence, some manufacturers have undertaken to stipulate the actual retail prices of their products, or minimum prices below which retailers could not sell them, and they have entered into contracts with retailers to this end. The legality of such contracts was challenged in 1911 in the Doctor Miles case.* The Doctor Miles Medical Company had signed contracts with wholesalers and retailers to maintain certain minimum resale price levels. The Supreme Court held that these contracts violated the Sherman Antitrust Act.

In the Colgate case† the point at issue was the legality of a list of prices, published by the company, which dealers were expected to adhere to in selling its products. The Supreme Court found that the company had not made contracts with any of the dealers, although it had stated publicly that it would not sell to those who did not adhere to the designated prices. The Court held that this arrangement did not violate the Sherman Act and affirmed the right of the manufacturer to refuse to sell to dealers who would not follow his suggested resale prices, as well as his right to announce in advance the circumstances under which he would so refuse to sell. The net effect of these and other decisions was to leave the situation somewhat hazy.

## SPREAD OF "FAIR TRADE" LAWS

The next big step came with the adoption of state "fair trade" laws, beginning in California in 1931. In that year the Great Depression was well underway—and was to get substantially worse. Competition at all levels had intensified and business profits and sales had declined. The decline of incomes made a few pennies in the prices of consumer goods, especially drugs and groceries, significant to many consumers. The competitive position of small retailers was felt to be especially difficult in view of the intensified competition of chain stores, and organizations of small retailers therefore pushed for "fair trade" laws. Out of these conditions came the enactment in California of a law permitting manufacturers to enter into contracts with retailers (in certain circumstances) stipulating the prices (which in practice turned out to be the minimum prices) at which the retailers were permitted to resell the products.

As a digression, it is interesting to speculate upon the role played by the title given by the proponents of this legislation, namely, "Fair Trade Law." If this law had been labeled "Resale Price Maintenance Law" would its chances of passage have been reduced? What advantage had been gained by the proponents in calling it a *fair trade* law? If a state legislator had voted against it, would he have seemed to be in the position of favoring *unfair trade?*

The law as originally passed in California contained a few typographical errors. Nevertheless, so vigorous was the movement for the enactment

---

* *Doctor Miles Medical Company v. John D. Park and Sons Company*, 220 U.S. 373 (1911).

† *U.S. v. Colgate and Company*, 250 U.S. 300 (1919).

of such legislation that many other states speedily enacted similar laws, and in a few instances the similarity was carried to the extent that the California draft was enacted, *errors and all.*

An early amendment to the California law was of great significance, and was subsequently incorporated into other state laws. The original law soon turned out to be partially ineffective, because, although it provided for enforcement between contracting parties, it provided no basis for control over noncontracting parties—an especially serious matter when noncontracting retailers could easily come into possession of the fair-traded goods. Therefore, in 1933, in response to urging, the California law was amended by the addition of what came to be called the *non-signer clause,* which provided that willfully and knowingly advertising, offering for sale, or selling any commodity at less than the price stipulated in any such contract, *whether or not the offending person was a party to such a contract,* was unfair competition.

The United States Supreme Court upheld these state fair-trade statutes in 1936.[*]

Despite the established legality of these laws, their effectiveness was limited, since each state's law applied only to intrastate transactions. Therefore, the Congress was urged to pass legislation legalizing resale price maintenance contracts in interstate commerce. It did so in 1937, in the Miller–Tydings Act.[†] This Act amended the Sherman Act by exempting from its coverage resale price agreements in interstate commerce for commodities that were shipped into states in which such contracts were legal. It went on to declare that the making of such contracts was not unfair competition.

One effect of the Supreme Court case and the Miller–Tydings Act was an increase in the number of resale price maintenance laws, until, by 1941, 45 states had enacted such legislation.

Resale price maintenance operated almost without challenge until 1951. In that year the Supreme Court upheld the contention of Schwegmann Brothers that the Miller–Tydings Act did not sanction the nonsigner clause and, therefore, that provisions of contracts made by Calvert with other retailers were not binding on Schwegmann, who had not signed such a contract.[‡]

In 1952 was passed the McGuire Act, which made lawful the use of the nonsigner clause, within any state in accordance with the legislation of that state, by manufacturers selling in interstate commerce.

Several states have repealed their fair trade laws, and several state supreme courts have voided the nonsigner clauses. At the same time

---

[*] *Old Dearborn Company v. Seagram Distillers Corporation,* 299 U.S. 183 (1936).
[†] The Miller–Tydings Act was attached to an appropriations bill as a "rider." President Roosevelt stated that he regretted having to sign the bill with this provision.
[‡] *Schwegmann Brothers v. Calvert Distillers Corporation,* 341 U.S. 384 (1951).

there has been agitation for the enactment of a more comprehensive Federal fair trade law.

The problem of resale price maintenance legislation is complex, it does not seem to be easy to reach a conclusion about its desirability from the viewpoint of public policy.

## UNFAIR PRACTICES ACTS

The fair trade laws are *permissive;* they do not *require* any manufacturer to take action. Some manufacturers have done so and have been very energetic in trying to enforce their contracts, while others have refused to fair-trade their products. The continuation of hard times and sharp business competition during the latter part of the 1930s led to further efforts to restrict price cutting. One of these was the enactment of state statutes prohibiting (with stated exceptions) sales of products below cost, plus a minimum mark-up, to "cover the costs of doing business." Several states have adopted such legislation, and some state courts have held the statutes to be unconstitutional. Once again, California led the way with its "Unfair Practices Act" of 1935, which became the model for legislation in other states.

If one inquires why any retailer would want to sell goods below cost or below a stipulated minimum mark-up, presumably the answer is that the product is to be used as a loss-leader to attract customers.

Most of the state laws prohibiting sales below cost do not provide for enforcement by any specific state agencies, and in consequence their enforcement has been ragged. Some wholesale and retail trade associations undertake to police these activities. If violations are found, they first attempt persuasion, and if this is unsuccessful they follow up with legal warnings. Since litigation is expensive, the instances where outright violation is so detected are usually corrected without litigation.

It is altogether possible that the diminished interest in both fair trade laws and unfair trade practices acts reflects the higher level of prosperity that has prevailed in the United States in recent years and which, therefore, has made price cutting both less frequent and less significant than it was during the 1930s.

## THE ROBINSON–PATMAN ACT

Price discrimination means selling goods to some buyers at lower prices than to others. In the Clayton Act (1914) price discrimination was prohibited "where the effect of such discrimination may be substantially to lessen competition or tend to create a monopoly in any line of commerce." The Robinson–Patman Act amended this section of the Clayton Act by adding these words *or to injure, destroy, or prevent competition with any person who either grants or knowingly receives the benefit of such discrimination, or with customers of either of them.* Enactment of this legislation grew out of the claim that giant chain store companies were able to demand and get such large price concessions from manufacturers that they were able to undersell independent unit retail stores. Administration of the Act was delegated to the Federal Trade Commission.

The Act permits price differentials based on differences in the costs of manufacturing, selling, and delivering caused by differences in quantities sold to or in the methods employed in selling to different customers. The Federal Trade Commission is authorized to limit the quantity discounts that can be given if it finds that there are so few large buyers that a quantity reduction, even though justified by a difference in selling cost, gives an undesirable advantage to the buyer or tends to create a monopoly.

The Act also provides that a seller can make a legal defense by showing that his lower price to certain buyers was made in good faith to meet an equally low price of a competitor.

As things have worked out, however, both the cost defense and the good faith defense have been hard to establish in court. The firm that plans to sell a product at two prices is well advised to make plans to prepare a legal defense against prosecution under the Robinson–Patman Act.

The Robinson–Patman Act was and is controversial. It places restrictions on competition in the complex interrelated spheres of outlets, costs, distribution channels, and prices. It illustrates the difficulty that is involved in trying to develop a public policy which protects the parties concerned against improper business actions and preserves competition, while at the same time not restraining the entry into the market of new, effective, and fair methods of business competition—which, in short, encourages competition without perpetuating old and ineffective competitive methods.

## QUESTIONS AND PROBLEMS

1. From the viewpoint of society, what are the advantages and the disadvantages of competition? What are they from the viewpoints of the competitors?
2. Give specific examples of unfair competition. To whom are these actions unfair?
3. What lessons can be learned from the historical development of food and drug regulation?
4. Is government at present doing enough for the protection of the consumer? Too much?
5. Why is it that the consumer, the largest group of all, is not better represented in the Federal government?

6. Is there a need for an organized consumer movement, a pressure group, to protect the consumer interest from similar tactics of agriculture, commerce, and labor?
7. What are the arguments pro and con with respect to establishing a Department of the Consumer in the President's Cabinet? Do you think that such action will ever be taken?
8. Evaluate the activities of private organizations, such as the Better Business Bureaus, Consumers' Research, and Consumers Union.
9. What are the arguments for and against "fair trade laws"?
10. What are the arguments for and against "unfair practices acts"?
11. What are the pros and cons of the provisions of the Robinson–Patman Act?
12. What is the outlook for governmental protection of the consumer?

## SELECTED READINGS

BORDEN, NEIL H. *The Economic Effects of Advertising.* Chicago: Richard D. Irwin, Inc., 1944.

Citizens Advisory Committee. *Report to the Secretary of Health, Education, and Welfare on the Food and Drug Administration.* Washington, D.C.: Multilithed, 1962.

Consumers Research Inc. *Consumer Bulletin.* Washington, D.C. Monthly.

Consumers Union of the U.S. Inc. *Consumer Reports.* Mount Vernon, N.Y. Monthly.

DUNN, CHARLES WESLEY. *Food Law Institute Series: The Food and Drug Law in the United States.* Chicago: Commerce Clearing House, 1955.

GORDON, LELAND J. *Economics for Consumers.* New York: The American Book Company, 1953.

KATONA, GEORGE. *The Powerful Consumer.* New York: McGraw-Hill Company, 1960.

KLEINFELD, VINCENT A., and CHARLES WESLEY DUNN. *Federal Food, Drug, and Cosmetic Act: Judicial and Administrative Record.* Chicago: Commerce Clearing House, 1950.

MILLER, JOHN PERRY. *Unfair Competition.* Cambridge, Mass.: Harvard University Press, 1941.

PAPANDREOU, A. G., and J. T. WHEELER. *Competition and Its Regulation.* Englewood Cliffs, N.J.: Prentice-Hall, Inc., 1954.

TROELSTRUP, ARCHIE WILLIAM. *Consumer Problems and Personal Finance,* 2nd ed. New York: McGraw-Hill Company, 1957.

# 18 REGULATION OF PUBLIC SERVICE INDUSTRIES

The general philosophy of the American economic system favors competition as an important condition. Public policy—as expressed by Federal and state legislation—aims to maintain competition and to prevent abridgments thereof. In the great sea of competition, however, are a few islands of legally restricted competition. These are areas of business in which governments grant certain privileges, such as exclusive franchises or the right of eminent domain. There are several other ways in which the government bestows a monopolylike freedom from competition. We discuss in this chapter the rationale of such special arrangements, the classes of business activity so privileged and restricted, and the laws and agencies which are the instruments of regulation.

These businesses are the *public utilities,* or *public service industries.* The term *public utility* includes the electric, gas, water, telephone, and telegraph businesses. *Public service corporations* includes these, plus railroads, air lines, pipelines, and broadcasting companies.

These businesses are sometimes described as "natural monopolies" because one firm can serve an area better than can two or more firms. This condition encourages governmental intervention—regulation or ownership.

The U.S. attitude toward public service industries is different from that of most other nations. Many of these industries conducted as regulated private business here are nationally owned and operated elsewhere. Public ownership of transportation, communication, and the power utilities is the prevalent method of carrying on these businesses in western nations. The postal service and a part of the electric power industry are owned and operated by our Federal Government. All the others have remained private as far as has been consistent with public needs, and regulation rather than ownership has been the policy.

## EVOLUTION OF REGULATION

Legal regulation of public service businesses has evolved slowly, by means of common-law decisions, statutory enactments, and court interpretations of the statutes.

The famous case of *Munn v. Illinois** prompted the following words in the decision of the U.S. Supreme Court: "When one devotes his property to a use in which the public has an interest, he in effect grants to the public an interest in that use, and must submit to be controlled by the public for the common good to the extent of the interest he has thus created." This decision is an early landmark in the modern application of government regulatory power, but actually it was no more than an expression of a pre-existing authority to regulate.

Other consequential decisions of the early modern period were rendered in *Brass v. North Dakota*,† in which the Supreme Court upheld a state law setting a maximum rate for grain storage, and *German Alliance Insurance Co. v. Kansas*,‡ in which it held constitutional a state law fixing ceilings on insurance rates.

These decisions tended to broaden the concept of public service corporations. The limit of possible extension of the concept was clarified in *Wolff Packing Co. v. Kansas*.** This decision unanimously threw out a state law which in effect made public service corporations out of all businesses concerned with the manufacture and transport of food, clothing, and fuel. In delivering the decision of the Court, Chief Justice Taft attempted to indicate the business activities which up to that time had been deemed as public service. He mentioned principally (1) the railroads and other common carriers; (2) certain occupations, such as proprietors of inns, cabs, and grist mills; and (3) "Businesses which, though not public at their inception, may be fairly said to have risen to be such, and have become subject in consequence to some government regulation."

In recent years there has been little contest of the right of states to regulate selected businesses as public utilities. At present, the chief source of litigation has to do with the nature or fairness of the particular regulations imposed, and not the right per se of the state or Federal Government so to regulate. This is partly because the division of enterprises into the public and private categorization has become well established.

## RIGHTS AND DUTIES OF PUBLIC SERVICE CORPORATIONS

Public service corporations have certain obligations imposed upon them by virtue of regulation; however, there are also certain rights that frequently attach to public service status which are beneficial to the corporations and so tend to encourage activity in these fields.

---

* *Munn v. Illinois*, 94 U.S. 113 (1877).
† *Brass v. North Dakota*, 153 U.S. 391 (1894).
‡ *German Alliance Insurance Co. v. Kansas*, 233 U.S. 389 (1914).
** *Wolff Packing Co. v. Kansas*, 262 U.S. 522 (1923).

These rights are not granted solely as compensation for the companies' submission to regulation. Many of them are granted of necessity, for reasons as compelling as those which prompt the regulation and restriction of these companies.

The principal right or protection given is the right of exclusive operation. Operating rights and a charter or franchise are granted to a utility or transportation company giving it, for a term of years, a protected territory. No other, or only a certain specified other, company in the same business may operate in the restricted area. A legal monopoly is created.

While this is the most frequent and probably most consequential special right of public service corporations, there are others. One example is the right of eminent domain, given to railroads, turnpikes, and certain pipelines. The right of eminent domain gives a company power to purchase lands necessary to it for construction of a right-of-way pursuant to its franchise; even to use judicial process to compel sale to it (at fair prices) in the case of reluctant owners.

This right is so important that companies may seek public service status merely to obtain it. For example, in 1962 the construction of a proposed coal-slurry pipeline depended on acquiring the right of eminent domain. The line was to carry a coal-water mixture from the mine to a generating station, serving only the two parties and carrying only the one commodity.

Within the public service field the law recognizes a variety of degrees of public duty, monopoly power, regulatory need, and other rights and obligations; therefore, it is impossible to generalize to any great extent about these matters. Still, there are some concepts in this connection which are of fairly broad application. These are:

[1] A right to fair return, or reasonable profit. This is necessary to protect the property rights of the stockholders of the corporations and to insure the availability of new capital for expansion.

[2] Rate structures determined by governmental authority, and obligatory upon the regulated companies, which may not set rates higher (and often not lower) than those prescribed by law.

The proper method for calculating a "fair rate of return," and the reckoning of valuation used in making this computation, are subjects of considerable scholarly inquiry and legal debate.

[3] The duty to serve all without discrimination. This imposition requires that public service corporations provide equal and appropriate service to all (objectively) qualified potential patrons. A railroad, for example, may not conspire with a large manufacturer to drive a small shipper out of business by refusing his shipments. Furthermore, railroads are obliged to maintain free interchange of freight with connecting roads at junctions and may not refuse to receive cars from or deliver cars to competing connections as shippers may desire.

This duty is quite extensive, and is imposed for the reason that injury to parties might result if a legal monopoly refused to supply their demands for essential services. However, the rule goes further than monopolies and essential services and applies equally to any public service industry which may impose hardships on members of the public through its unwarranted refusal to serve. Thus innkeepers and taxicab operators are generally obliged to serve all potential guests, unless for good cause.

[4] The right to enjoy certain aspects of monopoly position. The degree of monopoly granted varies from one industry and one location to another. Also, the real power to make use of what appears to be a monopoly position is almost always limited by (in addition to law) the ability of those in different fields to satisfy the need which the monopolist seeks to control. For example, barges and trucks can now thwart any railroad combination's attempt to charge extortionate rates.

On the other hand, quite within the purposes of the monopolies created by law, the public service corporations are able to secure important benefits. The assurance of freedom from direct competition has favorable consequencies for them. The electric utilities, for example, can determine much more safely their future load levels and probable revenues; they can invest in extensive capital installations money borrowed on advantageous terms. The lessened risk in protected utilities enhances the opportunity to make use of financial leverage to the advantage of the owners.

The principal method of obtaining such monopoly is through a governmental grant of a charter or franchise; the monopoly is maintained because it is the policy of government not to grant conflicting charters. For instance, no railroad line may be built without government approval, and no airline may serve specified points unless certified so to do. However, the monopoly is sometimes relaxed in the case of transportation, where competing railroads are sometimes allowed to be built, and where several airlines may be certified on the same route. In no case, however, is entry completely free, and permission to compete is granted only upon evidence that it will not be "destructive" and that it is "in the public interest." The meanings of these terms, as of many other phrases arising out of the administration of public policy, are in doubt. The agency and court decisions are conflicting, and the testimony of litigants in these cases does not tend to lessen the confusion about what is "in the public interest."

[5] There is a duty to maintain a certain standard of service. The extent to which this duty goes is not always precisely known; but the duty is generally closely tied to public expectation and the financial and technical state of the industry. For example, railroads are obliged to operate passenger trains close to advertised schedules under ordinary conditions.

The law not infrequently resorts to rather uncertain terminology in dealing with subjects where the merits of the particular case must necessarily be of paramount importance in the adjudication. Typically, this terminology refers to the mythical "reasonable man" or to "ordinary care" or some other such standard which allows judge or jury some latitude not afforded by more strictly worded, more precise, law. This is the situation with respect to the duty of public service corporations to provide up-to-standard service. Despite numerous decisions the most significant rule that appears is that the quality of service need be only what will satisfy the tribunals as "appropriate and satisfactory" under the existing state of technology and with the existing financial resources of the corporation in question.

## THE ACTS AND THE AGENCIES

The foregoing discussion illustrates the diversity and complexity of public service regulation. We proceed now to a discussion of the governmental bodies that regulate the public service corporations. Of the many government agencies instituted to cope with business matters, the following are foremost in the public service regulatory area:

The *Interstate Commerce Commission*, established in 1887, is the first of the Federal public service regulatory commissions and is the largest, having eleven members. The ICC, although preceded by a few state commissions which attempted to provide regulation at the local level, was a new direction in government activity at its inception. The need for government intervention of this sort was widely recognized at the time; abuses by transport companies were rampant, and the public was incensed. The ICC was given the power to regulate interstate commerce generally, with certain exceptions. Railroads, common carrier trucks, shipping on the inland waterways, many pipelines, and various express, freight-forwarding, and sleeping car companies now fall under ICC jurisdiction.

The *Federal Power Commission* is a five-member board established in 1920. It has jurisdiction over the transmission and distribution of natural gas and electricity in interstate commerce.

The *Federal Communications Commission*, with seven members, was created in 1934. It has authority to regulate the telephone, telegraph, radio, and television industries.

The *Securities and Exchange Commission*, set up in 1934 with five members, has general jurisdiction over the issue of and trading in the securities of all corporations engaged in interstate commerce. Its special meaning for the public service corporations lies in its enforcement of the Public Utility Holding Company Act.

The *Civil Aeronautics Board*, with five members and set up in 1938, has authority to regulate commercial aviation, including freight and passenger service.

The *Federal Maritime Board* in its present form dates from 1950; it has three members and, unlike the other agencies, is a branch of an Executive department, the Department of Commerce. The jurisdiction of the FMB covers shipping between the U.S. and foreign nations and in intercoastal trade.

Supplementing the Federal agencies are numerous state agencies of similar design whose function is regulation of intrastate commerce and the supervision of other matters, control over which is constitutionally reserved to the states. Often the state agencies are combined, and have such names as "Michigan Public Service Commission" or "California Public Utilities Commission."

What are the powers of the regulatory agencies? In general, the powers of each of the agencies enumerated above, in the area of its jurisdiction, are: control of exit from and entry into business; setting rates, including the right to establish minimum as well as maximum tariffs; preventing discrimination among customers; controlling mergers and the pyramiding of stock control; and regulating the services provided, including qualitative and quantitative aspects and extensive and intensive features thereof. Furthermore, the agencies have powers of investigation and may institute hearings or request the Federal courts to enjoin violations. A fuller and more specific appreciation of the power to regulate may be gained from the subsequent discussion of the duties of particular public service industries.

## STATUS OF JUDICIAL REVIEW

All actions of regulatory agencies are subject to judicial review. The courts have the power to examine any agency decision upon an appeal alleging that the agency has acted in violation of its statutory authority. Oftentimes such appeals have resulted in complete rehearings of the original issues.

A leading case on the subject of judicial review is the Hope Natural Gas case, decided in 1944 by the U.S. Supreme Court.[*] This was an appeal to the Court of an FPC rate decision. As was usual, the appellant company had complained of the methods used by the FPC in arriving at its decision. However, the Court enunciated a new doctrine—that commission rulings carry a presumption of validity and that he who would upset them carries the burden of showing that they are invalid. This new view of the courts' role in appeals from rulings of administrative boards was a vote of confidence for the agencies which greatly enhanced their prestige. The net effect of the Hope decision was virtually to take the courts out of the rate-setting business. Since this decision the courts have shown more reluctance to review agency rulings, and ordinarily confine their hearings to the justness of the results, and not the technical bases for the appealed orders.

[*] *Federal Power Commission v. Hope Natural Gas Co.*, 320 U.S. 591 (1944).

Since the regulatory agencies have such broad authority, what can be said of the quality of their personnel? The Hoover Commission reported that the Federal commissioners and their staffs were generally good.* Despite rather low pay, both competence and morale were found high. However, many of the agencies were found to have much more work than they can effectively handle, so that time for investigation and analysis of cases was not always sufficient, and there was a constant backlog of pressing issues awaiting decision. The Commission's findings appear to be still descriptive of conditions.

The *state* counterparts of the Federal agencies are somewhat more spotty in quality. While many of the state commissions are excellent, some have been used to supply sinecures for elderly politicians.

## REGULATION OF RAILROADS

Agency power rests upon statutes, since, at common law, responsibility for public services was vested in the courts of law and equity. Except for a few state agencies, regulatory bodies of the sort we are considering date from the Act to Regulate Commerce of 1887. This Act set up the ICC and the rudimentary machinery for the accomplishment of its objectives. Other major provisions of this Act required that rates be just and reasonable, prohibited unreasonable personal and regional discrimination, provided for the publication of rates, and made the carriers liable for any damages resulting from the violation of the Act's provisions.

Experience in the decades that followed led to amendments and entirely new laws. The Elkins Act was passed in 1903. Prior to this Act, the corporate officers and not the companies themselves had borne the liability for violations of the transportation laws. One provision of the Elkins Act changed this to make the corporations fully liable. Other provisions made recipients of rate rebates equally guilty with the givers, made deviations from approved rate schedules misdemeanors, and generally strengthened the legal enforcement techniques available against persons guilty of violating the spirit, if not the letter, of the then existing provisions.

The Hepburn Act of 1906 brought a number of transport-allied industries under the ICC, including the express and sleeping car companies. Pipelines, other than for water and gas, were placed under the ICC. The Hepburn Act expanded the ICC's authority over rates—the Commission was empowered, not only to set aside unfair or discriminatory rates, but actually to prescribe in advance of hearing certain maximum

---

* Commission on the Organization of the Executive Branch of the Government, *Task Force Report on the Regulatory Commissions* (Washington, D.C.: U.S. Government Printing Office, 1949).

limits for rates. This Act also prohibited railroads from transporting articles which they had produced, or in which they had proprietary interests. This provision prevented railroads from competing unfairly with other producers by virtue of providing free transportation for their own outputs. Previously, several railroads had operated coal mines to the detriment of independent mines, which had to pay steep rates. Another important provision of this Act made the Commission's orders, except orders to forfeit money, binding without court action. This eliminated the tedium of waiting for court action, which, because of judicial delays, often amounted to a new hearing; however, the right to judicial review was acknowledged.

Between 1917 and 1920, because of World War I, the U.S. railroads were taken over and operated by the Federal Government. Because they were for this period separated from private control, there was a respite for this time in the development of regulatory authority.

## POWER AND COMMUNICATIONS

In 1920 the Water Power Act, creating the Federal Power Commission, was adopted. The FPC originally was to construct and operate hydroelectric projects on navigable waterways. It was not until the Public Utility Act of 1935 and the Natural Gas Act of 1938 that the transmission of electricity and gas, respectively, came under FPC jurisdiction.

The Federal Communications Commission was formed in 1934 to assume the duties of several predecessor agencies in regulating the fast-growing communications industries. One of its first acts was to investigate the telephone industry, then as now dominated by the American Telephone and Telegraph Company. The principal result of this investigation was a consent decree accepted in 1956 which loosened somewhat the bonds between AT&T, its subsidiary companies, and its manufacturing and research subsidiaries, Western Electric and Bell Telephone Laboratories.

Regulation of radio and television broadcasting has occupied the FCC to a greater extent. Much of this regulation stems from technical factors. These technical problems of the FCC, and the Commission's involvement with program content, are discussed further in a later section of this chapter.

## OTHER REGULATORY ACTS
## AND AGENCIES

The significance of the Securities and Exchange Commission, organized in 1934, to the public service field arises from a 1935 law giving it the power to supervise the financial and corporate structures of public service corporations. This authorizing legislation was Title I of the Public Utility Act, known as the Public Utility Holding Company Act. A great deal of the action taken pursuant to this authority was directed toward the breakup of holding companies and other forms of undesired power-pyramiding. Such a stern and thorough action of regulation was necessary because of prevalent rate abuses and the difficulty of instituting proceedings for these abuses in a case where the corporate structure was an intricate pyramid.

Air transportation is regulated by the Civil Aeronautics Board and the Federal Aviation Agency. The former is concerned with the *economic,* the latter with the *technical,* aspects of the aviation industry—safety rules, traffic control, and testing of aircraft and airmen. Responsibility for accident investigation is with the CAB, which also has full jurisdiction over economic regulation, including routes, rates, and changes in the frequency of service. The powers of the CAB over aviation are somewhat less than those of the ICC over railroads. It has no jurisdiction over financial securities, and the provision enforced by the ICC prohibiting lower rates for a long haul than for a short haul along the same railroad route has no counterpart in the airways.

## THE TRANSPORTATION INDUSTRY

America's transportation network of today is as different from that of a century ago as the modern supermarket is from the general store. Not only have there been revolutionary changes within the modes of transportation, but also modes unknown only a generation ago have zoomed into prominence.

Freight transportation is conducted by common carriers subject to regulation, by unregulated contract carriers, and by shipper-owned facilities. All railroads and major airlines, many trucks, and some barges are operated as common carriers and hence are regulated. However, a substantial amount of intercity freight transport is unregulated, a fact of considerable concern to the regulated carriers. Although much of the unregulated freight carriage is legal, some of it is undoubtedly conducted in evasion of the law. Stricter supervision of unregulated freight carriers seems a likely prospect for the future; the regulated carriers urge it strongly, and appreciation of their shaky profit position may prompt such aid.

Passenger transportation has been a chronic problem for the common carriers. Even in their heyday the railroads were less than satisfied with their passenger business; today many railroads are dropping passenger services—when permitted to do so.

Nor are the air carriers finding passenger business very profitable. The introduction of faster and more expensive aircraft has triggered a long profit slide which, in 1961, carried many lines into the red.

Intercity bus transportation has been a moderate financial success. However, the automobile is firmly entrenched as the chief means of intercity travel in America. Public carriers of passengers face a difficult struggle to survive against the popularity of private auto travel.

The shopper for transportation, whether freight or passenger, has the opportunity of hiring the service from a regulated carrier or of performing the sevice for himself; and many operate their own trucks. Furthermore, no longer does the shipper who decides on public transportation have only one mode to choose from; often he has the option of truck, rail, barge, or air, to say nothing of the possible choice among the various carriers offering the same mode. For example, it has been estimated by the Association of American Railroads that there is real economic competition between railroads and trucks for about 70 per cent of rail traffic. This condition is significant, since much of the regulatory philosophy we have inherited from our grandfathers is predicated on lack of intermodal competition. Regulation and semimonopoly we have seen to be economic bedfellows. But when the monopoly disappears, what is to become of the regulation? Is it any longer desirable?

In 1920 the first of several general transportation acts was passed. This and the subsequent Transportation Acts of 1940 and 1958 have been, generally speaking, broad statements of public policy, attempting through their numerous provisions to strengthen the nation's transportation facilities, not so much by restrictive measures as by protecting particular areas of the industry. These acts chronicle the nation's struggle. to develop a comprehensive and workable transport policy. From that time until the present such an equitable and efficacious policy has been the goal of most study and legislation in the transportation sector, and an elusive one it has proven to be. Admittedly, without these studies and laws the American transportation situation would be chaotic. Nevertheless, we continue to be faced with the specter of a serious transportation crisis. One of the few things that has become clear from the nation's earnest but befuddled search for a comprehensive transportation policy is that *each mode should have relative freedom to capitalize on its inherent advantages.*

Accordingly, in transportation, regulation seems to be taking a step beyond its customary bounds: it now views, not only particular companies and their relations with the public, but also intercompany and interindustry balances. The regulating agency becomes not only an adjudicator of power-abuse complaints, but an interindustrial center of economic planning and coordination. This outcome is not to be regarded as basically antiprivate enterprise. Indeed, this new trend toward coordinating instead of merely confining the transportation companies may be an indication that the agencies recognize the new, competitive look in transportation, and are paving the way for important new freedoms for the carriers.

## PUBLIC UTILITIES

Public utilities are those enterprises supplying telephone, telegraph, water, electricity, and gas services to domestic and commercial consumers. This definition is the same as that made by Dow-Jones and others in classifying stocks, for computation of the familiar averages.

Generally speaking, this area has been less turbulent than that of transportation. Regulation came to it later, and the abuses that prompted it were not (with a few noteworthy exceptions) as flagrant as those that culminated in the 1887 Interstate Commerce Act and the establishment of the ICC. Also, the utilities as a group have demonstrated greater financial stability and ability to return the maximum permitted rate on investment in recent years than have the transportation companies. There are many reasons for this, all bearing in some way on the different competitive natures of the transportation and utility fields and involving the factors of substitutability of service, number of firms in one region, possibility of private competition, rate of growth of physical plant over the years, and types of physical plant required.

It is probably safe to say that utilities are less competitive today than are transportation firms. There is competition in some users among gas, oil, and electricity and among telephones, telegraph, and the mails. However, competition between firms offering substantially the same utility service in the same region does not often occur, because the utilities are regionalized. For example, freight traffic between Buffalo and the New York City area may use the State Barge Canal, the St. Lawrence Seaway, any of four railroads, or public or private truck carriage on the Thruway. And, except for the Seaway, these facilities traverse not-too-different routes. However, an electricity user has commonly only one supplier, and in many places the same supplier is also the local gas distributor.

Regulation in the utility field, therefore, must be designed more particularly to assure adequate service at fair rates. In transportation the paramount concern seems more and more to be one of protecting the companies from one another; in utilities, of protecting the users.

Another aspect of competition in utilities is the increasing role of the Government in the production and transmission of electricity from hydroelectric installations.* The privately owned electric companies have waged a long battle against the growth of Federal power production, but they have not been successful in preventing some very extensive projects. The net result does not appear to have been catastrophic for the private power companies, however, and many persons consider that the public

* This subject is discussed more extensively in Chapter 25.

welfare has been enhanced by these developments. More government electric projects, many in cooperation with private industry, are proposed or are under way. Often these developments have been in such undeveloped areas, or of such great magnitude, that private industry had shown little willingness to proceed with them.

Some of the largest of the utility companies are those providing telephonic and telegraphic communication. The largest of these, the American Telephone & Telegraph Company, is one of the nation's biggest businesses. However, AT&T is a combination of smaller regional companies, so that the appropriateness of treating it as a single entity is uncertain. As mentioned above, an intensive study of AT&T was one of the first undertakings of the FCC after its inception in 1934; AT&T has been the subject of much government scrutiny and study ever since.

Aside from the problem of AT&T's size and predominance in this industry, the telephone and telegraph utilities under the FCC are in a competitive and regulatory situation similar to that of the other utilities.

The development of artificial earth satellites suitable for facilitating electronic communication—including television, radio, and telephone—presented a new public policy issue, namely, the question of who is to own and operate the satellite communications system. A step toward an answer to this question was provided when in 1962 the Congress passed and the President signed an act establishing an unusual corporation. Stock in the corporation is owned by communications industries and by the general public, each of which groups elects six directors. The remaining three directors are named by the President.

## THE BROADCASTING INDUSTRY

The broadcasting industry is perhaps the most untypical of the regulated businesses. The origin of government regulation of broadcasting was not because of its public service nature, but because certain technical aspects of broadcasting made it necessary to regulate entry into the business and the subsequent conduct of the transmissions. Only a limited number of frequency assignments are available. They are prizes—awarded by the Federal Communications Commission; and the intrusion of political and other influences is sometimes alleged.

Until recently the FCC had not been particularly concerned with the content of broadcasts, beyond controlling certain flagrantly undesirable program material. Recently, however, a growing dissatisfaction with the quality of broadcasting has caused the FCC to make fuller use of its powers to protect this phase of the public interest in broadcasting. Voluntary measures and gentle suggestion seem to have failed in maintaining a generally acceptable quality standard in broadcasting, so the FCC is using its present powers, and is seeking additional authority, to make a thorough housecleaning of broadcast programs. License renewal, once almost automatic, is no longer so certain for stations which cannot show good records of programming. Particularly, those stations which have been heavily complained of are being asked searching questions on how they can justify, from the standpoint of the public interest, their continued operation.

## OTHER "ISLANDS OF MONOPOLY"

Public service corporations are not the only recipients of special grants of immunity from competition. Other businesses and individuals are able to obtain protection of certain aspects of their enterprises. This is because the U.S. Constitution allows the granting of exclusive rights to the use of inventions and other creations of individual human ingenuity and talent. This provision of the Constitution has been implemented by the Congress in the provision of a set of statutes which make patents, trademarks, and copyrights available and give the holders property rights which are transferrable and which may not be infringed without liability.

Patents are granted for inventions. To be patentable, an invention must be unique. It must be a real thing, not just an idea or a process. It must be sufficiently novel that the idea for it "would not readily occur to an experienced practitioner in the same field."

A patent secures to the inventor the exclusive right to manufacture, sell, license, and otherwise exploit his idea for a period of 17 years. Since a corporation can invent nothing, patents are not issued to corporations; but they may be assigned to corporations. For this reason most corporations hire research personnel under contracts requiring them to assign any patents that they get, for nominal considerations.

Copyrights are formal recognition of property rights in literary and certain other artistic works. Again, as with patents, exclusive rights to exploit the properties thus recognized are granted. In such a case the right is enforceable for 28 years, and the copyright may subsequently be renewed for another 28 years.

A third form of protectionable intangible property is the trademark. Like patents and copyrights, trademarks enjoyed some recognition as property at common law before there were statutes on the subject. In the U.S. there are several explicit statutes, including the 1946 Lanham Act, outlining trademark law and practices.

The primary purpose of a trademark is to establish brand preference and identity. As a consequence of the successful attainment of this goal, other firms find entry into competition more difficult and costly. A degree of monopoly is thus attained, and in some instances it is substantial. Trademarks that have not expired may fall into the public domain if they become generic names. For example, "Shredded Wheat" and "Aspirin" were once trademarks; but "Scotch" tape and "Technicolor" color film have so far avoided the loss of their private status, despite widespread generic use of these terms by the public.

Some other rights of less important types may be bought, sold, and sued upon as may copyrights, patents, and trademarks. For example, the "goodwill" of a business is a recognized asset which may be transferred to a new owner. Sale of the goodwill of a business generally involves a provision in the contract of sale that the new owner may continue to use the former owner's name and that the former owner will not reestablish himself in such a way as to detract from the transferred enterprise. These restrictive covenants have been held legal where the prohibitions against reentry and competition are reasonable in their terms as to the regions and periods through which they shall have effect, and where the purpose is legitimately to protect the property interests of the new owners in goodwill, and not merely to restrict competition. All agreements unreasonably in restraint of trade are, of course, absolutely void.

A fifth kind of right of this general sort has been recognized. It has been held[*] that one who conceives of an idea and who formulates and sets down that idea and, expecting to make a profit from the idea, tells it to another may recover damages from that other if the latter takes the idea and uses it to his own gain without making recompense therefor. This occurs most often in connection with advertising and promotion ideas where, in a typical case, an unscrupulous client takes and uses an idea volunteered by an agent and then refuses to pay the agent for it. The rule has been extended to other areas too, but the difficulty of proof maks it speculative to rely upon it.

The problems of government regulation of public service industries are big, tough, and complex; and the regulatory machinery is multifarious, ponderous, and affected by politics. Indeed, it is perhaps amazing that the industries have grown and prospered under the heavy—and occasionally clumsy—hand of government control. Outright government ownership—the rule in most countries—is simpler; but our public service industries seem to have developed quite as well as their foreign, government-owned counterparts, despite the handicap of regulation. Continued development, however, will be encouraged by ever better public policies.

## QUESTIONS AND PROBLEMS

1. Our society relies to a considerable extent on competition, but within this framework there are certain "legal monopolies." Why are they created?
2. What industries may be defined as "public service industries"? What factors or conditions are necessary to classify an industry as a public service industry?

[*] *Belt v. Hamilton National Bank,* 108 F. Supp. 689 (1952).

3. Discuss the pros and cons of government's simply owning the public service industries instead of regulating them.

4. To what extent do the rights and duties of public service industries depend on or are affected by governmental regulation?

5. What is the constitutional basis for the existence of the regulatory agencies? Why are they sometimes called "the fourth branch of the government"?

6. In what sense did the decision in the Hope Natural Gas Case virtually take the courts out of the rate-making business?

7. Is there too much regulation of public service industries today? Do some of their present difficulties stem from this very regulation?

8. Industry by industry, what do you see as the outlook for government regulation?

## SELECTED READINGS

BEHLING, BURTON N. *Competition and Monopoly in Public Utility Industries.* Urbana, Ill.: University of Illinois Press, 1938.

BONBRIGHT, JAMES C. *Public Utilities and the National Power Policies.* New York: Columbia University Press, 1940.

CLEMENS, ELI W. *Economics and Public Utilities.* New York: Appleton-Century-Crofts, Inc., 1950.

DEARING, CHARLES L. *National Transportation Policy.* Washington, D.C.: The Brookings Institution, 1949.

FREDERICK, JOHN H. *Improving National Transportation Policy.* Washington, D.C.: American Enterprise Association, 1959.

GLAESER, MARTIN G. *Public Utilities in American Capitalism.* New York: The Macmillan Company, 1957.

LOCKLIN, PHILIP D. *Economics of Transportation,* 4th ed. Homewood, Ill.: Richard D. Irwin, Inc., 1954.

NELSON, JAMES C. *Railroad Transportation and Public Policy.* Washington, D.C.: The Brookings Institution, 1959.

TROXEL, EMERY. *Economics of Public Utilities.* New York: Rinehart & Company, 1947.

————. *Economics of Transport.* New York: Rinehart & Company, 1955.

# 19 PROTECTIVE LABOR LEGISLATION

In dealing with the relation between government and labor, it is useful to realize that the word *labor* has several meanings. One big difference runs through all the definitions: the word may include just the workers described or the workers *and their families.*

In the broadest sense, labor means all who work or are seeking work and, perhaps, those who are retired after a lifetime of work. If to this classification is added their families, the category includes virtually all of the American people.

Next, the word *labor* may be interpreted to mean what is called in statistical compilations the *labor force*—those who are at work or seeking work in commercial jobs. In 1960 they numbered 73 million. This category excludes the tens of millions of housewives—not employed commercially—whose work, no matter how valuable, does not enter into the calculation of the gross national product and who are not counted as part of the work force. Considering how hard many of them work, it is perhaps ironic that they are excluded. For statistical analysis, however, the classification is reasonable.

In 1960 nearly three million persons were in the armed forces, and several million were self-employed as professional men or businessmen, including farmers. Four million were unemployed. Including the unemployed, but subtracting the armed forces and the self-employed, the total of civilian employees was in the neighborhood of 60 million.

One more step would be to define labor as the 18 million members of labor unions.

It is appropriate to use the word in any of its different meanings for special purposes of analysis, provided the special meaning is stated. Whatever meaning is used, however, it is clear that the word involves, at the very least, labor union members, a large segment of the American population, and, if their families are included, more than one fifth of the American people. As mentioned above, the widest definition includes virtually the entire American population.

The significance of these numbers lies partly in the fact that their size blurs the dividing line between labor legislation in the strict sense of the word and legislation for the general public welfare. Legislation which is good for the country is typically good for labor by any of the definitions above. Some governmental policies and legislation that illustrate this proposition include full employment policy, government employment agencies, restriction of immigration, conservation of natural resources, and free public education.

Having acknowledged this definitional difficulty, we go on in this chapter and the next to consider governmental policies and labor legislation in the narrower sense of the word.

## PROTECTIVE LABOR LEGISLATION

The protection of workers has long been a concern of government. Much of the early legislation was developed by states operating under the *police power*—the somewhat misleading name for the power that is inherent in any government, *just because it is a government,* to legislate with respect to the public welfare, health, safety, and morals.*

Many of these laws have regulated working conditions with special reference to health and safety. Some of the subjects commonly dealt with in these laws include mechanical guards for dangerous machines, proper ventilation and lighting, fire prevention, and sanitation in washrooms and workplaces. In earlier years many of these laws were highly controversial. Rarely, however, was their constitutionality challenged. Some of the laws were not well enforced. More recently, however, employers have come increasingly to find that activities aimed at reducing accidents and disease among their employees result in gains that make these expenditures worth while.

## WORKMEN'S COMPENSATION

In the United States, following British and German precedents, a gradual state-by-state development, begun in New York in 1910, has led to all states providing insurance against occupational accidents and diseases. Such insurance is commonly called "workmen's compensation insurance." These laws operate on the theory that the costs of occupational accidents and diseases are a proper part of the cost of producing the goods and that they should be counted along with other costs and paid for by the buyers of these goods. Some of the laws give an employer the

* Inherent, that is, unless the government is one of enumerated powers—as our Federal Government, theoretically at least, is. Our national government ostensibly has no police power, and this lack forces it to look to some Constitutional grant of power as a basis for such legislation. A Constitutional provision often relied on is the Commerce Clause.

option of coming under this general coverage, but they are all phrased in such a way as to make it practically obligatory for him to do so.

Prior to the enactment of these laws, the employee who suffered an accident or contracted an illness while at work could receive compensation only by suing in court. In such a suit several obstacles stood in the way of his recovering any money. One was the fairly limited duty of the employer as the courts interpreted it. Another was the doctrine that the employee assumed the ordinary risk of employment in which he engaged. Others were his own contributory negligence or the negligence of a fellow employee. The expenses of bringing suit, together with these handicaps in recovering, meant that relatively few workers received compensation for industrial accidents and diseases.

Workmen's compensation insurance replaced the hazards of court suits with a more or less automatic system of payments which cover death benefits, disability benefits, and payments for medical care. The insurance premiums are paid by the employer and are based in part upon his accident and disease record. For this reason, and for others, employers find it advantageous to reduce the incidence of accidents and illness. Indeed, in some companies and plants, extensive safety campaigns are waged continually. Many workers, of course, are not covered by these statutes, and some analysts suggest that the amounts of the prescribed payments are inadequate. Revisions in these amounts have been made from time to time, and the subject continues to occupy the attention of administrators and lawmakers.

Some of the other types of protective labor legislation have also been controversial. They have been challenged in the courts on the grounds of constitutionality and on other grounds. We turn attention to three such areas of regulation, considering each with respect to Federal regulation and state regulation. In the process we watch the gradual evolution of public policy as illustrated by legislation and court review. We also take this opportunity to watch the United States Supreme Court at work and to note the gradual changes in opinions expressed in its successive decisions over the years, including some flat reversals.

## CHILD LABOR

Today it is perhaps difficult to realize the extent of child labor in the United States a century and more ago. The nimble fingers of little children were well suited to tying the broken cotton threads on weaving machines, their pay was low, they were docile (for the most part) and, therefore, made excellent employees. Occasionally, to be sure, as they worked long hours, perhaps through the night, in dimly lighted rooms, they might run away from their work. This difficulty, however, could be coped with by chaining them to the machines.

Gradually, opposition to child labor developed. In 1842 Massachusetts passed the first child labor law. It did not prohibit child labor, but merely provided that children under 12 could not work more than ten hours per day in factories.

In the following years other states added child labor laws, until eventually all had some legislation on the subject. It was not until 1910, however, that any state completely prohibited the labor of children in specified establishments.

These laws were attacked on the ground that they were improper interference with the rights of employers and parents. Their *constitutionality*, however, was rarely questioned—this type of regulation came under the police power.

There were great differences in the strictness of state laws and their enforcement. Some states were rigid; in others the regulations amounted to little. From this condition two consequences flowed. One was that employers located in the states with the strict requirements felt themselves to be handicapped in price and cost competition with employers located in states where child labor was regulated but slightly. The other was that humanitarian persons throughout the land became disturbed at the slowness with which the states were adopting effective child labor legislation.

People of both of these groups, therefore, became interested in Federal regulation of child labor, believing that this would be effective as well as uniform. Since the Congress had no specific constitutional authority to regulate labor, it relied on the commerce power when, in 1916, it passed the Owen–Keating Act, which prohibited the interstate shipment of goods produced in plants that had employed children within 30 days prior to shipment.

The Supreme Court, however, declared the Act unconstitutional.* The majority opinion said:

> A bill was filed . . . to enjoin the enforcement of the act of Congress intended to prevent interstate commerce in the products of child labor. . . .
>
> The power essential to the passage of this act, the Government contends, is found in the commerce clause of the Constitution. . . . The thing intended to be accomplished by this statute is the denial of the facilities of interstate commerce to those manufacturers in the states who employ children within the prohibited ages. The act in its effect does not regulate transportation among the states, but aims to standardize the ages at which children may be employed in mining and manufacturing within the states. The goods shipped are of themselves harmless. The act permits them to be freely shipped after thirty days from the time of their removal from the factory. When offered for shipment, and before transportation begins, the labor of their production is over, and the mere fact that they were intended for interstate commerce transporta-

---

* In *Hammer v. Dagenhart*, 247 U.S. 251 (1918).

tion does not make their production subject to federal control under the commerce power. . . . The making of goods and the mining of coal are not commerce, nor does the fact that these things are to be afterwards shipped, or used in interstate commerce, make their production a part thereof . . . the production of articles intended for interstate commerce is a matter of local regulation. . . . This principle has been recognized often in this court. . . . If it were otherwise, all manufacture intended for interstate shipment would be brought under federal control to the practical exclusion of the authority of the State—a result certainly not contemplated by the framers of the Constitution when they vested in Congress the authority to regulate commerce among the states. . . .

That there should be limitations upon the right to employ children in mines and factories in the interest of their own and the public welfare, all will admit. That such employment is generally deemed to require regulation is shown by the fact that the brief of counsel states that every state in the Union has a law upon the subject, limiting the right to thus employ children. . . .

It may be desirable that such laws be uniform, but our federal Government is one of enumerated powers. . . . To sustain this statute . . . would sanction an invasion by the federal power of the control of a matter purely local in its character, and over which no authority has been delegated to Congress in conferring the power to regulate commerce among the states . . . the act in a twofold sense is repugnant to the Constitution. It not only transcends the authority delegated to Congress over commerce, but also exerts a power as to a purely local matter to which the federal authority does not extend. The far-reaching result of upholding the act cannot be more plainly indicated than by pointing out that if Congress can thus regulate matters intrusted to local authority by prohibition of the movement of commodities in interstate commerce, all freedom of commerce will be at an end, and the power of the states over local matters may be eliminated, and thus our system of government be practically destroyed. . . .

## Justice Holmes, dissenting, said in part:

. . . The statute in question is within the power expressly given to Congress if considered only as to its immediate effects, and that if invalid it is so only upon some collateral ground. The statute confines itself to prohibiting the carriage of certain goods in interstate or foreign commerce. Congress is given power to regulate such commerce in unqualified terms. It would not be argued today that the power to regulate does not include the power to prohibit. Regulation means the prohibiting of something, and when interstate commerce is the matter to be regulated I cannot doubt that the regulation may prohibit any part of such commerce that Congress sees fit to forbid. At all events it is established by the Lottery Case and others that have followed it that a law is not beyond the regulative power of Congress merely because it prohibits certain transportation out and out. . . .

The question, then, is narrowed to whether the exercise of its otherwise constitutional power by Congress can be pronounced unconstitutional because of its possible reaction upon the conduct of the States in a matter upon which I have admitted that they are free from direct control. . . . I should have thought that the most conspicuous decisions of this court had made it clear that the power to regulate commerce and other constitutional powers could not be cut down or qualified by the fact that it might interfere with the carrying out of the domestic policy of any State . . . the States may regulate their internal affairs and their domestic commerce as they like. But when they seek to send their products across the state line they are no longer within their rights. If there were no Constitution and no Congress their power to cross the line would depend upon their neighbors. Under the Constitution such commerce belongs not to the States, but to Congress to regulate. It may carry out its views of public policy what ever indirect effect they may have upon the activities of the States. Instead of being encountered by a prohibitive tariff at her boundaries, the State encounters the public policy of the United States which it is for Congress to express. The public policy of the United States is shaped with a view to the benefit of the nation as a whole. . . . The national welfare as understood by Congress may require a different attitude within its sphere from that of some self-seeking State. It seems to me entirely constitutional for Congress to enforce its understanding by all the means at its command.

## A  SECOND  ATTACK

The proponents of Federal child labor legislation were presumably made unhappy by this decision, but they were not downhearted. Mindful of John Marshall's famous dictum "The power to tax is the power to destroy," they turned to the possibility of using a tax as a regulatory instrument. They recalled that Congress had extinguished state bank notes and the sale of oleomargarine colored to resemble butter by this means and that the Supreme Court had upheld these uses of the taxing power. A Federal law was passed imposing a tax of 10 per cent on the net income of any employer who employed children. The constitutionality of the law was challenged. The Court not only voided the law but, as the following excerpt from its decision shows, was not deceived for a moment with respect to the real purpose of the law.*

> . . . The law is attacked on the ground that it is a regulation of the employment of child labor in the states—an exclusively state function under the federal Constitution and within the reservations of the Tenth Amendment. It is defended on the ground that it is a mere excise tax levied by the Congress of the United States under its broad power of taxation conferred by Section 8, Article 1, of the federal Constitution. We must construe the law and interpret the intent and meaning of Congress from the language of the act. The words are to be given their ordinary meaning unless the context shows that they are differently used. Does this law impose a tax with only that incidental restraint and regulation which a tax must inevitably involve? Or does it regulate by the use of the so-called tax as a penalty? If a tax, it is clearly an excise. If it were an excise on a commodity or other thing of value we might not be permitted under previous decisions of this Court to infer

* *Bailey v. Drexel Furniture Company,* 259 U.S. 20 (1922).

solely from its heavy burden that the act intends a prohibition instead of a tax. But this act is more. It provides a heavy exaction for a departure from a detailed and specified course of conduct in business. That course of business is that employers shall employ in mines and quarries, children of an age greater than sixteen years; in mills and factories, children of an age greater than fourteen years; and shall prevent children of less than sixteen years in mills and factories from working more than eight hours a day or six days in the week. If an employer departs from this prescribed course of business, he is to pay to the government one tenth of his entire net income in the business for a full year. The amount is not to be proportioned in any degree to the extent or frequency of the departures, but is to be paid by the employer in full measure whether he employs five hundred children for a year, or employs only one for a day. Moreover, if he does not know the child is within the named age limit, he is not to pay; that is to say, it is only where he knowingly departs from the prescribed course that payment is to be exacted. Scienter is associated with penalties, not with taxes. The employer's factory is to be subject to inspection at any time not only by the taxing officers of the Treasury, the department normally charged with the collection of taxes, but also by the Secretary of Labor and his subordinates, whose normal function is the advancement and protection of the welfare of the workers. In the light of these features of the act, a court must be blind not to see that the so-called tax is imposed to stop the employment of children within the age limits prescribed. Its prohibitory and regulatory effect and purpose are palpable. All others can see and understand this. How can we properly shut our minds to it? . . .

The case before us cannot be distinguished from that of *Hammer v. Dagenhart.* . . .

The analogy of the *Dagenhart* case is clear. The congressional power over interstate commerce is, within its proper scope, just as complete and unlimited as the congressional power to tax; and the legislative motive in its exercise is just as free from judicial suspicion and inquiry. Yet when Congress threatened to stop interstate commerce in ordinary and necessary commodities, unobjectionable as subjects of transportation, and to deny the same to the people of a state, in order to coerce them into compliance with Congress's regulation of state concerns, the Court said this was not in fact regulation of interstate commerce, but rather that of state concerns, and was invalid. So here the so-called tax is a penalty to coerce people of a state to act as Congress wishes them to act in respect of a matter completely the business of the state government under the federal Constitution. . . .

## FEDERAL CONTROL ACHIEVED

Since these two defeats had exhausted the two powers under which Congress could move in the matter of child labor, advocates of Federal legislation were instrumental (in 1924) in getting the Congress to pass a Constitutional amendment giving the Federal Government the power to regulate child labor. This amendment was sent to the states, but oppo-

sition on the part of farm and industrial interests was more effective than
it had been in the Congress, and approval by the states was slow. The
proposed amendment was short of the required three-fourths majority
when Congress included in the Fair Labor Standards Act of 1938 a general minimum age of 16 for employment in industry.

The constitutionality of this Act was challenged, but it was upheld by
the United States Supreme Court.° The Act provided also for maximum
hours and minimum wages, and these were the matters at issue in the
*Darby* case. It was the more surprising, therefore, that the Supreme
Court went out of its way to discuss child labor. The Court usually follows the eminently reasonable practice of not discussing any issues except
those immediately necessary for a decision in an instant case. Not only
did the Court discuss child labor, an issue not present in this case, but
also its opinion contained a statement which is rather rare in being a flat
reversal of a previous one (in *Hammer v. Dagenhart*). The following
excerpts from the decision show how completely the Court had changed
its thinking since 1918.

> The two principal questions raised by the record in this case are, first,
> whether Congress has constitutional power to prohibit the shipment in inter-
> state commerce of lumber manufactured by employees whose wages are less
> than a prescribed minimum or whose weekly hours of labor at that wage are
> greater than a prescribed maximum, and, second, whether it has power to
> prohibit the employment of workmen in the production of goods "for inter-
> state commerce" at other than prescribed wages and hours. . . .
>
> While manufacture is not of itself interstate commerce, the shipment of
> manufactured goods interstate is such commerce and the prohibition of such
> shipment by Congress is indubitably a regulation of the commerce. The power
> to regulate commerce is the power "to prescribe the rule by which commerce
> is governed. . . ." It extends not only to those regulations which aid, foster,
> and protect the commerce, but embraces those which prohibit it. . . . It is
> conceded that the power of Congress to prohibit transportation in interstate
> commerce includes noxious articles . . . stolen articles . . . kidnapped persons
> . . . and articles such as intoxicating liquor or convict-made goods, traffic in
> which is forbidden or restricted by the laws of the state of destination. . . .
>
> But it is said that the present prohibition falls within the scope of none
> of these categories; that while the prohibition is nominally a regulation of
> the commerce its motive or purpose is regulation of wages and hours of
> persons engaged in manufacture, the control of which has been reserved to
> the states and upon which Georgia and some of the states of destination have
> placed no restriction; that the effect of the present statute is not to exclude
> the proscribed articles from interstate commerce in aid of state regulation . . .
> but instead, under the guise of a regulation of interstate commerce, it
> undertakes to regulate wages and hours within the state contrary to the policy
> of the state which has elected to leave them unregulated.
>
> . . . Congress, following its own conception of public policy concerning

° *United States v. Darby Lumber Company*, 312 U.S. 100 (1941).

the restrictions which may appropriately be imposed on interstate commerce, is free to exclude from the commerce articles whose use in the states for which they are destined it may conceive to be injurious to the public health, morals or welfare, even though the state has not sought to regulate their use. . . .

The motive and purpose of the present regulation are plainly to make effective the Congressional conception of public policy that interstate commerce should not be made the instrument of competition in the distribution of goods produced under substandard labor conditions, which competition is injurious to the commerce and to the states from and to which the commerce flows. The motive and purpose of a regulation of interstate commerce are matters for the legislative judgment upon the exercise of which the Constitution places no restriction and over which the courts are given no control. . . . Whatever their motive and purpose, regulations of commerce which do not infringe some constitutional prohibition are within the plenary power conferred on Congress by the Commerce Clause. Subject only to that limitation, presently to be considered, we conclude that the prohibition of the shipment interstate of goods produced under the forbidden substandard labor conditions is within the constitutional authority of Congress.

In the more than a century which has elapsed since the decision of *Gibbons v. Ogden,* these principles of constitutional interpretation have been so long and repeatedly recognized by this Court as applicable to the Commerce Clause, that there would be little occasion for repeating them now were it not for the decision of this Court twenty-two years ago in *Hammer v. Dagenhart,* 247 U.S. 251. In that case it was held by a bare majority of the Court over the powerful and now classic dissent of Mr. Justice Holmes setting forth the fundamental issues involved, that Congress was without power to exclude the products of child labor from interstate commerce. The reasoning and conclusion of the Court's opinion there cannot be reconciled with the conclusion which we have reached, that the power of Congress under the Commerce Clause is plenary to exclude any article from interstate commerce subject only to the specific prohibitions of the Constitution.

*Hammer v. Dagenhart* has not been followed. The distinction on which the decision was rested, that Congressional power to prohibit interstate commerce is limited to articles which in themselves have some harmful or deleterious property—a distinction which was novel when made and unsupported by any provision of the Constitution—has long since been abandoned. . . . The thesis of the opinion that the motive of the prohibition or its effect to control in some measure the use or production within the states of the article thus excluded from the commerce can operate to deprive the regulation of its constitutional authority has long since ceased to have force. . . .

The conclusion is inescapable that *Hammer v. Dagenhart* was a departure from the principles which have prevailed in the interpretation of the Commerce Clause both before and since the decision and that such vitality, as a precedent, as it then had, has long since been exhausted. *It should be and now is overruled.* [Emphasis supplied]

Inasmuch as the *Darby* decision upheld all the provisions of the Fair Labor Standards Act, including those relating to wages and hours, as well as child labor, the decision must be counted as one of great historic importance. Its significance with respect to Federal regulation of hours and wages is cited in connection with the following discussion of each of these subjects.

One consequence of the *Darby* decision was that attempts to secure the passage of the child labor amendment to the United States Constitution ceased. An interesting interpretation of what had happened is, in layman's language, that the United States Supreme Court had, in effect, adopted the amendment. This series of cases and the final decision (*Darby*), taken together, present a convincing, almost dramatic, example of the power of the United States Supreme Court, as it construes the Constitution and laws.

## THE KEY FACTOR IN THE REDUCTION OF CHILD LABOR

These same decades that witnessed a gradual expansion and tightening of child labor laws also saw a similar expansion and tightening of compulsory school attendance laws. Increasingly, children came to be found in schools instead of in factories. In the circumstances, it would be easy to suppose that this significant chance was coming about solely in consequence of the trends in the two types of laws. Undoubtedly, the laws had something to do with the outcome, but they cannot be credited with being the only factor in the change.

It must be remembered that when children worked in factories, they did so not because employers were in a position to compel them to do so, but rather because their parents caused them to go to work. Nor did this necessarily indicate parental cruelty. In many cases the wages of the children—puny though they were—contributed vitally to feeding and clothing families. In such circumstances, the families would have found it hard or impossible to get along if the children had been in school instead of working in industrial plants.

A significant factor, therefore, in the shift of children's activities was the steady rise in real wages and real family incomes which permitted families to live—at a modest level at least—without the wages of their children.

The process was one of interaction. The more education the children received, the more productive they were when they went to work; the more productive they were, the higher their wages, and the greater their ability, in turn, to release their own children from working, in favor of schooling. The increase in productivity—in output per man-hour—was the key to the entire process. Many factors contributed to the rise in productivity. Compulsory school attendance laws helped, but it is hard to see any contribution from child labor laws.

## MAXIMUM HOURS

State regulation of maximum hours for *women* workers began in slow and originally rather ineffective pieces of legislation in the latter part of the nineteenth century. Both their wisdom and their constitutionality were questioned; but the latter issue was settled early in the twentieth century by the Supreme Court's decision in *Muller v. Oregon.*＊ This was the case in which the briefs were prepared by Lewis D. Brandeis (himself, later, a member of the Court) and Josephine Goldmark and were distinguished by their emphasis on the adverse consequences of long hours of work, rather than on legal citations.

There was no general Federal regulation of hours of work until the passage of the Fair Labor Standards Act of 1938. Prior to that time there had been some Federal legislation affecting a few specific industries, and the government had put certain stipulations with respect to wages and hours into contracts under which it bought goods from private firms.

All this was changed, however, by the 1938 legislation with its sweeping provisions on these subjects. The Fair Labor Standards Act provided that if a covered employee worked more than 40 hours in a week, he must be paid overtime rates at one-and-one-half times the regular rate for the excess hours. This law applied to both men and women, and its constitutionality was upheld in the *Darby* case.

Regulation by the states of maximum hours for *men* has been beset by greater court opposition. Once again, consideration of the leading cases illustrates the role played by the United States Supreme Court in the development of public policy. Regulation of hours of work in dangerous employment or activities of special public importance, such as railroads, has long been considered constitutional. Regulation of hours in ordinary employment, however, was for a while a different story.

An early leading case was *Lochner v. New York.*† The State of New York had enacted a law limiting the hours of employment for men in bakeries. This law was challenged in the courts on the ground that it violated the Fourteenth Amendment, which reads in part, "nor shall any state deprive any person of life, liberty, or property without due process of law. . . ." The word *liberty* is properly interpreted to include the liberty of entering into contracts, and, in that sense, the law certainly constituted a partial deprivation of a liberty—as laws invariably do. The question was: Had the deprivation been accomplished with or without due process of law? The due process involved was not *procedural* due process; it was the *substantive* due process discussed in Chapter 3. The Court voided the statute. It was in his dissenting opinion in this case that Justice Holmes included the sentence that is proffered as a definition of substantive due process in the same chapter. His dissent in this case

＊ *Muller v. Oregon*, 208 U.S. 412 (1908).
† *Lochner v. New York*, 198 U.S. 45 (1905).

became one of the classic examples of a view originally rejected by the Court and subsequently embraced by it. Excerpts from the majority decision and from Holmes's dissent follow.

Said the majority opinion:

It is impossible for us to shut our eyes to the fact that many of the laws of this character, while passed under what is claimed to be the police power for the purpose of protecting the public health or welfare, are, in reality, passed from other motives. We are justified in saying so when, from the character of the law and the subject upon which it legislates, it is apparent that the public health or welfare bears but the most remote relation to the law. The purpose of a statute must be determined from the natural and legal effect of the language employed; and whether it is or is not repugnant to the Constitution of the United States must be determined from the natural effect of such statutes when put into operation, and not from their proclaimed purpose. . . .

Justice Holmes, dissenting, said in part:

This case is decided upon an economic theory which a large part of the country does not entertain. If it were a question whether I agreed with that theory I should desire to study it further and long before making up my mind. But I do not conceive that to be my duty, because I strongly believe that my agreement or disagreement has nothing to do with the right of a majority to embody their opinions in law. It is settled by various decisions of this court that state constitutions and state laws may regulate life in many ways which we as legislators might think is injudicious or if you like as tyrannical as this, and which equally with this interfere with the liberty to contract. Sunday laws and usury laws are ancient examples. A more modern one is the prohibition of lotteries. The liberty of the citizen to do as he likes so long as he does not interfere with the liberty of others to do the same, which has been a shibboleth for some well-known writers, is interfered with by school laws, by the Post Office, by every state or municipal institution which takes his money for purposes thought desirable, whether he likes it or not.

The Fourteenth Amendment does not enact Mr. Herbert Spencer's Social Statics . . . a constitution is not intended to embody a particular economic theory, whether of paternalism and the organic relation of the citizen to the State or of laissez faire. It is made for people of fundamentally differing views, and the accident of our finding certain opinions natural and familiar or novel and even shocking ought not to conclude our judgment upon the question whether statutes embodying them conflict with the Constitution of the United States.

General propositions do not decide concrete cases. The decision will depend on a judgment or intuition more subtle than any articulate major premise. But I think that the proposition just stated, if it is accepted, will carry us far toward the end. Every opinion tends to become a law. I think that the word "liberty" in the Fourteenth Amendment is perverted when it is held to prevent the natural outcome of a dominant opinion, unless it can be said that a rational and fair man necessarily would admit that the statute proposed would infringe fundamental principles as they have been understood by the traditions of our people and our law. It does not need research to show that no such sweeping condemnation can be passed upon the statute before us. A reasonable man might think it a proper measure on the score of health. Men whom I certainly could not pronounce unreasonable would uphold it as a first instalment of a general regulation of the hours of work. Whether in the latter aspect it would be open to the charge of inequality I think it unnecessary to discuss.

Eleven years later, however, the Supreme Court approved an Oregon law establishing maximum hours for all persons, including men.° Key excerpts from that decision follow.

"No person shall be employed in any mill, factory or manufacturing establishment in this state more than ten hours in any one day, except watchmen and employees when engaged in making necessary repairs, or in case of emergency, where life or property is in imminent danger; provided, however, employees may work overtime not to exceed three hours in any one day, conditioned that payment be made for such overtime at the rate of time and one-half of the regular wage." (Laws 1913, Chapter 102, p. 169.)

A violation of the act is made a misdemeanor, and in pursuance of this provision the indictment was found. It charges a violation of the act by plaintiff in error, Bunting, by employing and causing to work in a flour mill belonging to the Lake View Flouring Mills, a corporation, one Hammersly for thirteen hours in one day, Hammersly not being within the excepted conditions, and not being paid the rate prescribed for overtime. . . .

The consonance of the Oregon law with the 14th Amendment is the question in the case, and this depends upon whether it is a proper exercise of the police power of the state, as the supreme court of the state decided that it is.

That the police power extends to health regulations is not denied, but it is denied that the law has such purpose or justification. It is contended that it is a wage law, not a health regulation, and takes the property of plaintiff in error without due process. The contention presents two questions: (1) Is the law a wage law, or an hours-of-service law? And (2) if the latter, has it equality of operation? . . .

There is a certain verbal plausibility in the contention that it was intended to permit thirteen hours' work if there be fifteen and one-half hours' pay, but the plausibility disappears upon reflection. The provision for overtime is permissive, in the same sense that any penalty may be said to be permissive. Its purpose is to deter by its burden, and its adequacy for this was a matter of legislative judgment under the particular circumstances. It may not achieve its end, but its insufficiency cannot change its character from penalty to permission. Besides, it is to be borne in mind that the legislature was dealing with a matter in which many elements were to be considered. It might not have been possible, it might not have been wise, to make a rigid prohibition. We can easily realize that the legislature deemed it sufficient for its policy to

° *Bunting v. State of Oregon*, 243 U.S. 426 (1917).

give to the law an adaptation to occasions different from special cases of emergency for which it provided—occasions not of such imperative necessity, and yet which should have some accommodation; abuses prevented by the requirement of higher wages. Or even a broader contention might be made that the legislature considered it a proper policy to meet the conditions long existent by a tentative restraint of conduct rather than by an absolute restraint, and achieve its purpose through the interest of those affected rather than by the positive fiat of the law. . . .

But passing general considerations and coming back to our immediate concern, which is the validity of the particular exertion of power in the Oregon law, our judgment of it is that it does not transcend constitutional limits. . . .

Any lingering doubts about the constitutionality of state regulation of maximum hours for men, together with the question of the right of the Federal government to legislate in this field, were settled in the *Darby* case.

## MINIMUM WAGES

Regulation of minimum wage rates for women began in a small way early in the twentieth century. In 1923, however, the Supreme Court held* that such legislation constituted a deprivation of liberty (to contract) without due process of law. This case involved the rather unusual situation in which the United States Congress, acting in its constitutional capacity as the city council of the District of Columbia, had passed a law establishing minimum wage rates for women in the District, the constitutionality of which was challenged under the Fifth Amendment, which says, "no person shall be . . . deprived of life, liberty, or property without due process of law. . . ." This restriction has always been interpreted as applying to the Congress, just as the identical restriction in the Fourteenth Amendment has been regarded as applying to the states.

The differences in the reasoning of the majority decision and of Justice Holmes's dissent are striking. Excerpts from both statements follow:

The majority opinion states:

> . . . The statute in question . . . is not a law dealing with any business charged with a public interest or with public work, or to meet and tide over a temporary emergency. . . . It is not for the protection of persons under legal disability or for the prevention of fraud. It is simply and exclusively a price-fixing law, confined to adult women . . . who are legally as capable of contracting for themselves as men. It forbids two parties having lawful capacity—under penalties as to the employer—to freely contract with one another in respect of the price for which one shall render service to the other in a purely private employment where both are willing, perhaps anxious, to agree, even though the consequences may be to oblige one to surrender

* In *Adkins v. Children's Hospital*, 261 U.S. 525 (1923).

a desirable engagement and the other to dispense with the services of a desirable employee. . . .

It has been said that legislation of the kind now under review is required in the interest of social justice, for whose ends freedom of contract may lawfully be subjected to restraint. The liberty of the individual to do as he pleases, even in innocent matters, is not absolute. It must frequently yield to the common good, and the line beyond which the power of interference may not be pressed is neither definite nor unalterable but may be made to move, within limits not well defined, with changing need and circumstances. Any attempt to fix a rigid boundary would be unwise as well as futile. But, nevertheless, there are limits to the power, and when these have been passed, it becomes the plain duty of the courts in the proper exercise of their authority to so declare. To sustain the individual freedom of action contemplated by the Constitution is not to strike down the common good but to exalt it; for surely the good of society as a whole cannot be better served than by the preservation against arbitrary restraint of the liberties of its constituent members. . . .

In his dissenting opinion Justice Holmes said:

This statute does not compel anybody to pay anything. It simply forbids employment at rates below those fixed as the minimum requirement of health and right living. It is safe to assume that women will not be employed at even the lowest wages allowed unless they earn them, or unless the employer's business can sustain the burden. In short the law in its character and operation is like hundreds of so-called police laws that have been upheld.

Inasmuch as the basis of the decision in the *Adkins* case had been absence of substantive due process of law, it was easy for the Supreme Court in subsequent cases to invalidate *state* laws providing minimum wage rates for women.

In 1937, however, the Supreme Court reversed itself in *West Coast Hotel Co. v. Parrish.*° This case involved the constitutionality of a 1913 Washington law which had established minimum wage rates for women and children. Elsie Parrish (possibly the most famous chambermaid in history) brought suit under this law to recover the difference between her actual wage and the minimum wage of $14.50 per week of 48 hours as provided for in the law. Her employer contended that the Washington law was invalid under the *Adkins* decision and subsequent decisions that had invalidated other state minimum wage laws. Once again, a substantial excerpt from the Court's decision is presented to show the manner in which the Court reasoned about this type of problem and laid the basis for its flat and uncompromising reversal of an earlier decision.

. . . The principle which must control our decision is not in doubt. The constitutional provision invoked is the due process clause of the Fourteenth

° *West Coast Hotel Co. v. Parrish,* 300 U.S. 379 (1937).

Amendment governing the States, as the due process clause invoked in the *Adkins* case governed Congress. In each case the violation alleged by those attacking minimum wage regulation for women is deprivation of freedom of contract. What is this freedom? The Constitution does not speak of freedom of contract. It speaks of liberty and prohibits the deprivation of liberty without due process of law. In prohibiting that deprivation the Constitution does not recognize an absolute and uncontrollable liberty. . . . But the liberty safeguarded is liberty in a social organization which requires the protection of law against the evils which menace the health, safety, morals and welfare of the people. Liberty under the Constitution is thus necessarily subject to the restraints of due process, and regulation which is reasonable in relation to its subject and is adopted in the interests of the community is due process. . . .

This power under the Constitution to restrict freedom of contract has had many illustrations. That it may be exercised in the public interest with respect to contracts between employer and employee is undeniable. . . .

The minimum wage to be paid under the Washington statute is fixed after full consideration by representatives of employers, employees and the public. It may be assumed that the minimum wage is fixed in consideration of the services that are performed in the particular occupations under normal conditions. Provision is made for special licenses at less wages in the case of women who are incapable of full service. The statement of Mr. Justice Holmes in the *Adkins* case is pertinent: "This statute does not compel anybody to pay anything. It simply forbids employment at rates below those fixed as the minimum requirement of health and right living. It is safe to assume that women will not be employed at even the lowest wages allowed unless they earn them, or unless the employer's business can sustain the burden. In short the law in its character and operation is like hundreds of so-called police laws that have been upheld." 261 U.S., p. 570. And Chief Justice Taft forcibly pointed out the consideration which is basic in a statute of this character: "Legislatures which adopt a requirement of maximum hours or minimum wages may be presumed to believe that when sweating employers are prevented from paying unduly low wages by positive law they will continue their business, abating that part of their profits, which were wrung from the necessities of their employees, and will concede the better terms required by the law; and that while in individual cases hardship may result, the restrictions will enure to the benefit of the general class of employees in whose interest the law is passed and so to that of the community at large." Id., p. 563.

We think that the views thus expressed are sound and that the decision in the *Adkins* case was a departure from the true application of the principles governing the regulation by the State of the relation of employer and employed. . . .

. . . What can be closer to the public interest than the health of women and their protection from unscrupulous and overreaching employers? And if the protection of women is a legitimate end of the exercise of state power, how can it be said that the requirement of the payment of a minimum wage fairly fixed in order to meet the very necessities of existence is not an admissible means to that end? The legislature of the State was clearly entitled to consider the situation of women in employment, the fact that they are in the class receiving the least pay, that their bargaining power is relatively weak, and that they are the ready victims of those who would take advantage of their necessitous circumstances. The legislature was entitled to adopt measures to reduce the evils of the "sweating system," the exploiting of workers at wages so low as to be insufficient to meet the bare cost of living, thus making their very helplessness the occasion of a most injurious competition. The legislature had the right to consider that its minimum wage requirements would be an important aid in carrying out its policy of protection. The adoption of similar requirements by many States evidences a deep-seated conviction both as to the presence of the evil and as to the means adapted to check it. Legislative response to that conviction cannot be regarded as arbitrary or capricious, and that is all we have to decide. Even if the wisdom of the policy be regarded as debatable and its effects uncertain, still the legislature is entitled to its judgment.

There is an additional and compelling consideration which recent economic experience has brought into strong light. The exploitation of a class of workers who are in an unequal position with respect to bargaining power and are thus relatively defenseless against the denial of a living wage is not only detrimental to their health and well being but casts a direct burden for their support upon the community. What these workers lose in wages the taxpayers are called upon to pay. The bare cost of living must be met. We may take judicial notice of the unparalleled demands for relief which arose during the recent period of depression and still continue to an alarming extent despite the degree of economic recovery which has been achieved. . . . The community is not bound to provide what is in effect a subsidy for unconscionable employers. The community may direct its law-making power to correct the abuse which springs from their selfish disregard of the public interest. . . .

Our conclusion is that the case of *Adkins v. Children's Hospital, supra,* should be, and is, overruled. . . .

Thus the constitutionality of state and Federal laws establishing minimum wages for women was finally upheld.

Up to 1938 there had been relatively little legislation establishing minimum wages for men. In that year, among the sweeping provisions of the Fair Labor Standards Act, was a general minimum wage requirement which applied to both men and women. When the constitutionality of this Act was upheld in the *Darby* decision in 1941, this type of regulation at the state level also was presumably endorsed.

It would perhaps be hard to exaggerate the significance of the enactment of the Fair Labor Standards Act and its subsequent endorsement by the United States Supreme Court. In one rather sudden and comprehensive step the Federal Government had moved into types of regulation one of which—child labor—had previously been closed to it by the Supreme Court; a second of which—minimum wages for women—had been declared by the Court unconstitutional for both states and the Federal government; and others in which the Federal government had not even tried to enact any general comprehensive legislation. The net outcome was that areas long untouched by government, or reserved to the states alone, suddenly fell within the purview of public policy at all levels. Protective labor legislation had come a long, long way.

## QUESTIONS AND PROBLEMS

1. In general, what is the case for protective labor legislation? The case against it?
2. Evaluate child labor laws and compulsory school attendance laws.
3. What light do the decisions quoted from in this chapter shed on the nature and the power of the doctrine of substantive due process of law?
4. In what sense may it be said that in its decision in the Darby case the U.S. Supreme Court enacted the Child Labor Amendment to the U.S. Constitution?
5. Can a flat reversal of an earlier decision by the U.S. Supreme Court be understood? Can such a reversal be justified?
6. Do these cases illustrate "judicial usurpation of the legislative function"? Do they help to understand why some people once called the Supreme Court "the last stronghold of reaction"?
7. Has protective labor legislation become outmoded? Is it still needed? Are there areas in which it should be extended?

## SELECTED READINGS

COMMONS, J. R., and J. B. ANDREWS. *Principles of Labor Legislation,* 4th ed. New York: Harper and Brothers, 1936.

DAUGHERTY, CARROLL R. *The Labor Problems of American Society.* Boston: Houghton Mifflin Company, 1952.

DAVIS, PEARCE. *Modern Labor Economics.* New York: The Ronald Press, 1954.

FALCONE, N. S. *Labor Law.* New York: John Wiley & Sons, Inc., 1962.

GREGORY, CHARLES O. *Labor and the Law,* 2nd ed. New York: W. W. Norton & Company, 1961.

McNAUGHTON, WAYNE L. *Industrial Relations and the Government.* New York: McGraw-Hill Company, 1954.

SCHULTZ, GEORGE P., and JOHN R. COLEMAN. *Labor Problems: Cases and Readings,* 2nd ed. New York: McGraw-Hill Company, 1959.

TAYLOR, ALBION G. *Labor Problems and Labor Law,* 2nd ed. New York: Prentice-Hall, Inc., 1950.

# 20 UNIONS AND UNION– MANAGEMENT RELATIONS

The subject of unions and union–management relations has long been an object of national attention and concern. Many factors have caused our governments, and especially the Federal Government, to increase both the frequency and the extent of their involvement in this field. At the same time, this tendency toward ever greater government involvement is itself a matter of concern to many observers, who feel that labor problems could be better solved if employers and employees were left alone and thus forced to work out their differences by themselves.

In this chapter we consider the development of public policy with respect to these subjects. Various aspects of the history of the union movement in America are examined, and the important Federal labor–management legislation of the past quarter century is discussed in some detail. Then we turn our attention to the more pressing current issues of unionism and union–management relations: "right to work" laws, the problem of strikes, and the political strength of organized labor.

## GROWTH OF UNIONS

Today many unions are big and strong. They were not always so. In the nineteenth century they were subject to the rules of the common law, as formulated in court decisions. The prevailing view among the judges at that time was that labor organizations were criminal conspiracies per se, regardless of their actions. Unions did not begin to gain legal status as lawful organizations until the court decision of *Commonwealth v. Hunt* in 1842.° In this case the Massachusetts Supreme Court held that unions were lawful if their objectives were lawful. Thus the union as an organization received official recognition, and the strike was approved as a legal weapon to be used in industrial disputes.

In spite of the Hunt decision the courts still maintained tight control over unions, since they alone decided whether unions were acting legally

° 4 Metcalf 111.

347

attempting to establish the rights of their members or illegally in causing unjustifiable damage to employers. Union leaders found guilty of unlawful activity were subject to both criminal prosecution and civil suits
for damages.

## INJUNCTIONS IN LABOR DISPUTES

The courts often utilized injunctions in labor disputes, to curb activities. (An injunction is a court order requiring a person to do something
or to refrain from doing something in order to prevent injury that cannot
be recompensed for after its occurrence.) Since to violate an injunction
was to commit contempt of court, the injunction proved to be a very
effective weapon. An employer who could find a friendly judge might
stop a strike by obtaining a temporary injunction on the ground that
strike activities were causing irreparable damage to his property. When
an injunction was issued, it usually restrained the union from interfering
with the employer's business and thereby forestalled the union's chief
weapon, the strike. By the time the temporary injunction could be tested
in court, the strike would have failed, and frequently the union leaders
would have been jailed for contempt. Consequently, the courts were able
to exercise so much control over union activity that the injunction became
a prime object of union hatred.

In order to combat this control, the unions resorted to political pressure.
When the Clayton Act of 1914 was passed, it was termed a great victory
for labor, since one of its provisions was supposed to exempt normal
strike activity from the injunction procedure. Nevertheless, the courts
interpreted the new Act as not really changing things at all. Theoretically,
unions had for many years been free to conduct—peacefully and lawfully—
normal strike activities. But the courts had decided and continued to decide what was "lawful" and "legitimate" and to issue injunctions in
strikes.

With the passage of the Norris–La Guardia Act in 1932, the long
period of common-law control administered by the courts came to an
end. Various strike activities were specifically exempted from the applicability of Federal court injunctions, and in no event could an injunction
issued under the antitrust laws be more extensive than would be permitted
under common law. In addition, new procedural regulations halted the
common court practice of arbitrarily issuing an injunction without first
considering the union's reply to the employer's charges.

Thus—at long last—unions achieved a firm legal position both for their
very existence and for use of the strike—the one weapon that was essential to their continued success. Subsequent labor legislation has reflected
a shifting public policy only on the desirability of unionism and the necessity of regulation of union–management relations.

## THE WAGNER ACT

The National Industrial Recovery Act—a 1939 part of the New Deal—guaranteed the right of labor to organize and to engage in collective bargaining. The Act, however, was invalidated by the Supreme Court in 1935.*

When the Congress quickly enacted the National Labor Relations Act of 1935, usually referred to as the Wagner Act, the Federal Government became officially and firmly committed to the positive support and protection of trade unionism and collective bargaining.

The general provisions of the Wagner Act were as follows: Employees were to have the right to band together into trade unions, to bargain collectively through their union leaders, and to cooperate in other activities for their mutual welfare and protection. To protect these rights, employers were prohibited from engaging in certain antiunion practices that were officially designated as "unfair labor practices": (1) interference with, or restraint or coercion of, employees in the exercise of their rights under the Act; (2) domination of, interference with, or financial support of, a labor organization; (3) discrimination to encourage or discourage union membership except where a closed or union shop had been established by agreement with a majority of the workers; (4) discrimination against an employee for filing charges or giving testimony under the Act; and (5) refusal to bargain with the legal representatives of the employees. A National Labor Relations Board (NLRB) was established to decide disputes and conduct employee elections relating to union representation and to receive, investigate, prosecute, and judge charges of unfair labor practices.

Public support of the principal features of the Wagner Act was evidenced by the passage of "little Wagner Acts" in several states. These state laws materially aided the union movement by extending government protection to organizers in intrastate industries, such as retail trade and building construction.

The application of the Wagner Act was delayed by the many suits that attacked its constitutionality. However, the United States Supreme Court upheld the Act in 1937 (in several cases—most of them decided by five-to-four votes), and it served as the basic labor law of the land for another full decade. The vigorous enforcement activities of the National Labor Relations Board generated both praise by friends of unions and criticism by foes. Over 45,000 unfair labor practice cases were handled by the Board between 1935 and 1947.

The Wagner Act strongly favored the union side of the union–management conflict. No restrictions or obligations were imposed on labor. No

---

* In *Schechter v. U.S.*, 295 U.S. 495 (1935).

mention was made of unfair labor practices on the part of unions. Hence employers argued that the Wagner Act was inequitable in its approach to union–management relations. Additional criticism centered on the absence of protection for the individual and minority rights of workers and on the National Labor Relations Board's serving simultaneously as prosecutor, judge, and jury.

## THE TAFT–HARTLEY ACT

Inasmuch as the avowed purpose of the Wagner Act was to encourage trade unionism and collective bargaining, opposition to the Act by business interests was natural, and they urged its repeal or substantial modification. Other pressures also acted on the proverbial pendulum of public opinion.

Union organizing activity in the late thirties gave rise to considerable industrial warfare. The CIO moved into the mass production industries, but only at the expense of bitter strikes and violence. Laws were passed in some of the states to restrict sit-down strikes, mass picketing, boycotts, and a variety of other union activities; but efforts on the national level to modify or repeal the Wagner Act were always defeated by President Roosevelt and the Democratic majority in Congress.

During World War II labor–management difficulties were overshadowed by the war effort. The imposition of wage and price controls severely restricted bargaining between unions and business firms. After the War ended the industrial relations picture changed rapidly. Union leaders pressed for higher wages and called strikes in major industries.

When the Republicans gained control of the Congress in 1947, the forces of organized labor could no longer resist the pressure for a change in national labor legislation. Even the veto of President Truman could not prevent the passage of the Labor–Management Relations Act, usually referred to as the Taft–Hartley Act.

The general objective of the Taft–Hartley Act was not repeal of the basic provisions of the Wagner Act. The principles of collective bargaining and trade unionism were well established, as was the concept of unfair labor practices. However, the drafters of the Taft–Hartley Act regarded the Wagner Act as giving the unions too much power as compared with employers, with individual workers, and with the public. They attempted to rectify this situation by counterbalancing rather than repealing the Wagner Act.

Therefore, the Taft–Hartley Act added a number of new provisions to the existing labor law. First, a number of union activities were singled out and forbidden as unfair labor practices: (1) interfering with the individual employee's right not to participate in collective bargaining; (2) attempting to cause employers to discriminate against nonunionists;

(3) refusing to bargain collectively with an employer; (4) engaging in secondary boycotts or jurisdictional strikes; (5) charging excessive fees as a condition of membership; (6) attempting to cause an employer to pay for services that had not been and would not be performed, i.e., "featherbedding."

The closed shop was outlawed. Workers were guaranteed the right to present grievances directly to management if they so desired, thus circumventing the union representation provided for in customary grievance procedures. The Act also made it easier for employees to oust a no longer popular union. Under the Act if at least 30 per cent of the employees in a bargaining unit signed a petition for decertification, the NLRB would conduct a secret election to determine if the union had indeed lost its majority support. If the union lost the election, it was then decertified and could no longer represent the employees.

Unions were required to file with the NLRB considerable financial and administrative data and to make these data available to their own members. The automatic deduction of union dues from employees' paychecks was regulated, and some restrictions were applied to the administration of union funds. No union could obtain any of the benefits offered by the Wagner and Taft–Hartley Acts if any of its officers were Communists.

Another provision of the Taft–Hartley Act relates to the handling of national emergency disputes. Whenever the President finds that an impending or existing strike imperils the national health or safety, he can appoint a public board of inquiry to investigate the issues. Upon receipt of the board's preliminary report, the President can initiate a request for a Federal injunction delaying or suspending the strike for a maximum of 80 days. During this period the board of inquiry will further investigate the issues and then make a public report of the union and management positions. In addition, the Federal Mediation and Conciliation Service can enter into the negotiations if they have not previously done so. If in spite of these efforts a contract cannot be agreed upon within the 80-day period, the injunction is dissolved and the union is then free to call or resume the strike.

And finally, the National Labor Relations Board was reorganized. The General Counsel of the Board was given complete authority over the investigation and prosecution of complaints. These duties were thus divorced from the judicial function performed by the Board itself:

As might have been expected, the Taft–Hartley Act was bitterly opposed by organized labor, which called it the "slave labor law" and immediately began a campaign for repeal. And, as also might have been expected, businessmen regarded the Act favorably, since it appeared to reduce union power, especially as seen from the other side of the bargaining table.

Apparently contrary to both management and labor expectations, the

Taft–Hartley Act did not cause any drastic changes in labor–management relations. Union membership continued to increase, and the actual operation of well-established and well-run unions was probably affected very little. The Act supposedly contributed to union democracy, but subsequent events proved that it fell far short in this regard. Labor's power was not greatly curtailed.

## THE LANDRUM–GRIFFIN ACT

The Taft–Hartley Act proved rather ineffective in regulating the internal operation and control of unions. Instances of mismanagement of funds, dictatorial control, and other undesirable practices by a small minority of union offices came to light during the following years. In 1957 the Senate appointed a select committee, chaired by Senator McClellan of Arkansas, to investigate improprieties on the part of both labor and management. The McClellan Committee, sometimes referred to as the Senate Rackets Committee, exposed numerous cases of corruption in union leadership and malpractice by union officers and business representatives.

Public reaction to these revelations led to passage of the Labor–Management Reporting and Disclosure Act of 1959, commonly known as the Landrum–Griffin Act. It was directed primarily at unions, and prescribed a comprehensive code on internal union regulations to eradicate corruption and protect union members from the machinations of their own leaders. The collective bargaining process also was brought under tighter control to eliminate collusion between union and management representatives.

The full impact of the Landrum–Griffin Act has not yet been determined. Many of its provisions are unclear. The rights, duties, and responsibilities of the various parties to labor–management agreements cannot be determined simply by reference to the statute. Questions of interpretation can be resolved only through the slow accumulation of administrative and judicial decisions. The Act has probably led to at least some improvement in the conduct of internal union affairs and union–management relations. But there is considerable doubt whether the improvement is sufficient. One conclusion, though, can be stated with full confidence. The Landrum–Griffin Act unquestionably reflects and extends the tendency toward more government intervention in labor–management relations.

## CONCILIATION AND MEDIATION

Government action with regard to strikes is not limited to the "national emergency disputes" previously mentioned in connection with the Taft–

Hartley Act. On the contrary, government officials frequently serve as mediators or conciliators between unions and management in resolving labor contract disputes. On the national level the Federal Mediation and Conciliation Service maintains a staff of mediators located in major industrial cities throughout the country. Most of the larger industrial states and several large cities also have established mediation boards, which operate in much the same manner as the Federal Service.

Whenever the Federal Service judges that a labor—management dispute threatens to cause a substantial interruption of interstate commerce, it furnishes mediation services on its own initiative; or it may enter in response to a request by one or more of the parties involved. Since it employs only a limited number of mediators, the Service normally avoids those disputes where mediation or conciliation is available from other sources, and only as a last resort will it mediate the settlement of grievance disputes arising under existing agreements.

The role of mediator and conciliator is not restricted to members of government services or boards set up for that specific purpose. Various other officials also serve in this capacity at irregular intervals. The steel industry strike of 1959 was mediated by the Secretary of Labor and the Vice-President of the United States. It is by no means unusual for state governors to assist in mediating important issues, and the same is true of many city officials.

Mediators possess no law enforcement authority. They rely on persuasive techniques, personal experience and standing, and a strictly nonpartisan attitude to achieve their goals. They often enter disputes prior to the calling of work stoppages. Labor unions and business firms subject to the Taft–Hartley Act are required to notify both the Federal Mediation and Conciliation Service and appropriate state mediation agencies of the existence of labor disputes at least 30 days prior to calling strikes or enforcing lockouts over the negotiation of new bargaining agreements. Mediation agencies have helped the parties in many labor disputes to adjust their differences.

## UNIONS TODAY

There are four types of union organizations in America. The basic unit is the local union of workers in a particular trade or industry. The first local union was organized in 1792 by a group of Philadelphia shoemakers. Today the average union member's only direct contact with the union movement is his local, which represents him in day-to-day dealings with his employer.

Local unions combine into city-wide and state-wide federations. These federations serve mainly to promote legislation favorable to labor organizations and to oppose unfavorable legislation.

The most important union structure is the national union of workers in a particular trade or industry. It (the national union) is made up of local unions. Among other things, national unions control the bulk of union finances; they conduct all industry-wide bargaining and normally reserve the right to approve or disapprove bargaining agreements negotiated by their member local unions; they provide direction and financial support when strikes must be called; and they have traditionally taken the lead in organizing nonunion employees. The oldest national union still in existence is the International Typographical Union, founded in 1850.

The fourth type of union organization was developed after the Civil War when national unions banded together to form federations. Although other short-lived federations preceded it, the first really successful union of this type was the American Federation of Labor, established in 1886 under the direction of Samuel Gompers. The AFL traditionally emphasized the organization of workers along *trade* or *craft* lines; but the concept of *industrial* unionism gradually gained more and more supporters, particularly in the mass production manufacturing industries. In the 1930s the advocates of industrial unionism broke away from the AFL, and in 1938 established the Congress of Industrial Organizations as a rival federation. After several years of conflict these two groups merged to form the AFL-CIO in 1955.

Although nominally placed at the top of the union scale of activity, the federation of national unions is not one of supreme importance. Its basic weakness is a lack of power. The member national unions have always insisted on retaining independent control of their internal affairs and finances, so that the only real powers possessed by a federation are the powers of expulsion and persuasion. And, unfortunately, expulsion is self-defeating from the federation standpoint, because while the federation cannot exist without the support of the national unions, the reverse is by no means true. This point is illustrated by the continued success of independent national unions, such as the railway brotherhoods (which have never joined a federation), the United Mine Workers, and the Brotherhood of Teamsters.

A major activity of the AFL-CIO is governmental relations. It pushes favorable legislation and opposes unfavorable bills in the Congress and acts similarly respecting actions of administrative offices and agencies that affect the labor movement.

## UNION MEMBERSHIP

In the past, union membership often fluctuated up and down with business cycles. During the early 1800s membership would increase rapidly during periods of general prosperity and then fall off to almost nothing when depressions occurred. It was not until the depression of 1873–1878 that unions finally demonstrated the ability to ride out the storm of economic disturbance.

The growth of union membership since 1930 is shown in Chart 20.1. While gains have generally been registered during boom periods of rising employment, the most substantial increases occurred between 1935 and 1945. Unemployment and the accompanying hardships suffered by wage earners in those depressed years caused workers to turn to unions as a means of preventing such hardships. Other favorable factors were the change in public policy toward unionism, as reflected by the labor legislation of the New Deal, and the success of industrial unionism's organization drives.

*Chart 20.1*

MEMBERSHIP  OF  NATIONAL  AND

INTERNATIONAL  UNIONS,  1930–1960

SOURCE: U.S. Department of Labor, *Monthly Labor Review*, December 1961, p. 1303.

Chart 20.2 shows union membership as a *percentage* of nonagricultural employment. The chart shows an upsurge in the thirties and a plateau since 1947.

## UNION  PROBLEMS

As is true of many an organization, the first problem of trade unions in their early years was *survival*. The previous discussion of the legal position of unions reflects their efforts to avoid prosecution under common law and then to avoid death by injunction. And we note in later pages that the current dispute over "right to work" laws is at least in part a continuation of the unions' fight for survival against legal restrictions.

*Chart 20.2*

## UNION MEMBERSHIP AS A PERCENTAGE OF TOTAL LABOR FORCE AND OF EMPLOYEES IN NONAGRICULTURAL ESTABLISHMENTS, 1930–1960

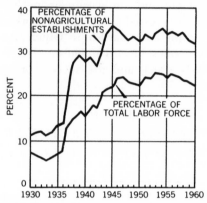

SOURCE: U.S. Department of Labor, *Monthly Labor Review*, December 1961, p. 1304.

Although unionism of large numbers of manual workers is now generally accepted by business management as a fact of life, the struggle to achieve this position was long and often violent. Business leaders resisted the encroachment of unions in many ways, both legal and illegal. Some companies were not above resorting to violence to forestall the efforts of union organizers. "Yellow dog" contracts, which provided that as a condition of employment workers would not join or support labor unions, were quite common until 1932 when, by the Norris–La Guardia Act, they were declared unenforceable in Federal courts. Other means of resistance included the formation of company unions, labor espionage, hiring of strike-breakers, and the immediate discharge of any employee who showed the slightest interest in unionism.

It should not be assumed that all businessmen have now become enthusiastic supporters of trade unions. Many are quite the contrary. But the problem of union security today is far less serious than it was a few decades ago.

Another problem that has plagued union leaders is that of interunion strife. For many years the issue of craft versus industrial unionism split the ranks of organized labor. After World War II some union organizers put much effort into trying to persuade members of other unions to change affiliations. Interunion raiding of membership became increasingly serious, and its prevention was a major factor leading to the union of the CIO and the AFL in 1955.

Unions still engage in both jurisdictional disputes and representational disputes. The former involves the question of who will do the work; e.g., will members of a carpenters' union or members of a metalworkers' union install aluminum casement windows in a housing project? Representational disputes are self-explanatory; they may involve the representation of either organized or unorganized workers. Needless to say, union theory deplores both these types of dispute, since in the aggregate union members cannot achieve gains from each other but from their employers or from the buyers of the goods and services that they produce.

A third problem is that of union democracy. It would seem desirable that the internal affairs of unions should be conducted in a democratic manner because of their fraternal background, because they are in some respects the creation of our democratic society and because membership in unions is not always entirely voluntary. And union democracy should at least include the right of all members to participate in the decision-making process, the right of fair trial or of due process for all members, and the right to equal treatment for all members. Nevertheless, instances of disregard of the basic principles of democratic rule have been revealed from time to time.

On the other hand, the mere fact that a union leader holds his office for a great many years is by no means indicative of a dictator's control. He may well devote a goodly portion of his time to building and maintaining a political machine, but he must also keep in close touch with the members' wishes and opinions, and he must represent the members effectively in collective bargaining negotiations. Otherwise his political machine will not be able to keep him in office.

Most unions are honestly and properly administered, but the unsavory conditions found in a small minority have discredited both good and bad unions. Union officials have insisted that the union movement should be free to conduct its own internal affairs without outside interference. Yet the fact remains that the general public is concerned and even suspicious about the conduct of these internal affairs.

Federal legislation in 1959 (the Landrum—Griffin Act) facilitated the exercise of democratic rights by union members, and the Justice Department has prosecuted numerous union officials on various criminal charges. But, in the final analysis, democratic rule in an organization requires the active, informed, and continuous attention of the members. The attitude that produces this attention cannot be legislated.

## OBJECTIVES

The basic objective of unionism in the United States has always been to improve the lot of its members. This is, of course, a vague, imprecise sort of goal, but its vagueness has greatly contributed to the success of the union movement. Union leaders have often refused to specify ultimate long-term goals. Instead, they have followed the lead of Samuel Gompers, founder of the American Federation of Labor, who supposedly listed the aims of his Federation as simply "More, more, more—now!"

This approach offers the twin advantages of wide appeal and flexibility. Almost any employee can become enthusiastic over union promises of "more." And the chances of attaining "more" are immeasurably improved when the union can adjust its specific objectives and tactics to meet the conditions at hand.

The specific collective bargaining objectives of unions may be grouped into three broad categories: better wages and working conditions, job control and job security, and an equal voice in the drafting and interpretation of working rules and "shop law."

On the political front unions have emphasized social objectives that are more or less unattainable through collective bargaining. These social objectives have included public housing, government medical care programs, unemployment compensation, old-age insurance, good public education, and effective measures to combat unemployment and depressions. And, of course, the protective labor legislation discussed in Chapter 19 has always been high in the unions' political priority lists.

## UNION-MANAGEMENT RELATIONS

Unions deal with management in the formulation of contracts governing working conditions and in dealing with disputes. In these activities the parties use persuasion and force. The methods used and the outcome of the contacts are significant not only to the parties directly involved but also to larger or smaller segments of the general public.

Both employers and unions use weapons in their struggles over labor problems. Union weapons include strikes, picketing, and slowdowns. Management can resort to the lockout* and can hire new workers to replace strikers. Both sides endeavor to win public support, and either the union or management may go to court to obtain an injunction if the opponent is engaging in what appear to be illegal activities.

These weapons stress the application of economic power. Bargaining power, or the ability to secure maximum concessions while minimizing what is given up in return, involves both economic power and negotiating skill. In the forties and fifties union representatives seemed to hold an edge in terms of negotiating skill. Nowadays both union and manage-

---

* Usually management will force the union to call a strike in preference to imposing the lockout, since (a) the lockout places management in a much more difficult position from the standpoint of public relations, and (b) in many states unemployment compensation is paid to workers who are unemployed because of lockouts, but not to workers who are unemployed because of strikes. Obviously the receipt of unemployment compensation strengthens the employees' economic ability to wage a successful strike.

ment negotiators are generally capable and quite evenly matched. As a result, most collective bargaining agreements are hammered out on the basis of relative economic power.

It is possible that labor–management relations are really much better than one might suppose from reading the newspapers. When a union goes out on strike, the event is said to have considerable "news value" and so it is picked up and reported by the news media. If the strike is featured by violence of any kind, or if a very large union or a major industry is involved, the affair may be front-page news. But when a union contract is negotiated without a work stoppage, the "news value" is very slight or even nonexistent.

At the end of 1960 there were approximately 125,000 collective bargaining agreements in force in the United States. Only 3,250 of these agreements had been interrupted by work stoppages during the course of the year. Obviously, then, strikes (or lockouts) are exceptions to the general rule, and should not be considered typical of labor–management relations.

Table 20.1 provides a summary of the number and severity of work stoppages subsequent to World War II. Particularly significant is the downward trend in the percentage of man-days idle due to work stop-

## Table 20.1

### WORK STOPPAGES IN THE UNITED STATES, 1945–1960

| | Work Stoppages | | Workers Involved | | Man-Days Idle | |
|---|---|---|---|---|---|---|
| YEAR | NUMBER | AVERAGE DURATION (CALENDAR DAYS) | NUMBER | PER CENT OF TOTAL EMPLOYED | NUMBER | PER CENT OF ESTIMATED WORKING TIME OF ALL WORKERS |
| 1945 | 4,750 | 9.9 | 3,470,000 | 12.2 | 38,000,000 | .47 |
| 1946 | 4,985 | 24.2 | 4,600,000 | 14.5 | 116,000,000 | 1.43 |
| 1947 | 3,693 | 25.6 | 2,170,000 | 6.5 | 34,600,000 | .41 |
| 1948 | 3,419 | 21.8 | 1,960,000 | 5.5 | 34,100,000 | .37 |
| 1949 | 3,606 | 22.5 | 3,030,000 | 9.0 | 50,500,000 | .59 |
| 1950 | 4,843 | 19.2 | 2,410,000 | 6.9 | 38,800,000 | .44 |
| 1951 | 4,737 | 17.4 | 2,220,000 | 5.5 | 22,900,000 | .23 |
| 1952 | 5,117 | 19.6 | 3,540,000 | 8.8 | 59,100,000 | .57 |
| 1953 | 5,091 | 20.3 | 2,400,000 | 5.6 | 28,300,000 | .26 |
| 1954 | 3,468 | 22.5 | 1,530,000 | 3.7 | 22,600,000 | .21 |
| 1955 | 4,320 | 18.5 | 2,650,000 | 6.2 | 28,200,000 | .26 |
| 1956 | 3,825 | 18.9 | 1,900,000 | 4.3 | 33,100,000 | .29 |
| 1957 | 3,673 | 19.2 | 1,390,000 | 3.1 | 16,500,000 | .14 |
| 1958 | 3,694 | 19.7 | 2,060,000 | 4.8 | 23,900,000 | .22 |
| 1959 | 3,708 | 24.6 | 1,880,000 | 4.3 | 69,000,000 | .61 |
| 1960 | 3,333 | 23.4 | 1,320,000 | 3.0 | 19,100,000 | .17 |

SOURCE: U.S. Department of Labor, Bureau of Labor Statistics, *Monthly Labor Review*, June 1961, p. 615.

pages. This downward trend offers some evidence of a gradual improvement in labor–management relations.

## THE PROBLEM OF STRIKES

Authorities in the field of labor–management relations tend to agree that the power of a union to go out on strike is a prerequisite to free collective bargaining. Effective bargaining requires that the employer and the employees be able to inflict relatively equal economic injury on each other. Otherwise they have little inducement to achieve agreement when differences arise. The union can inflict such harm chiefly by striking—by closing down the plant and keeping it closed. Hence the justification for the right to strike.

This justification, however, has been held generally applicable only to strikes called in order to improve wages, hours, or working conditions. Strikes called for other purposes have often been declared illegal under either common law or statutory law. Included in this category are strikes for the closed shop, jurisdictional strikes to force an employer to assign work to one union rather than other, sympathy strikes to support a strike by another union, and strikes that violate the terms of a labor agreement currently in force.

We have already noted that strikes are not so common in the everyday course of labor–management relations as news reports may suggest. The loss of potential national production due to workers' being out on strike is far less than that due to unemployment. The economic effect of strikes is further mitigated by other considerations. In seasonal industries production always slacks off at certain times of the year. A strike may merely shift the time of the slack season, without actually reducing total production and employment for the year. On the other hand, if the strike comes at the peak time, the season's output may be lost.

Sometimes production that is "lost" due to a strike will subsequently be made up through overtime work. Many workers who are out on strike find temporary employment with other companies, especially if the strike appears likely to last for quite a while. If only one company in an industry or one plant of a company is struck, some of its business may be shifted to unused capacity in other companies or other plants. All of these conditions tend to lower the economic cost of strikes so far as national production is concerned. And, in all but the last, the economic cost to the striker also is reduced.

Yet the fact remains that strikes do occur and do cause economic harm, not only to the parties directly involved but also to the public at large. Sometimes the effect of a strike can be very serious indeed, with losses running into millions of dollars.

Nor is the harm caused by strikes limited to economic damage. On the contrary, a strike probably always causes some unhappiness which cannot be measured but is nonetheless real. Perhaps the best (or worst) example of this is the United Auto Workers' strike at the Kohler Company plumbingware plant in Kohler, Wisconsin. The strike was called in April 1954 and was not finally settled for eight years. This strike engendered violent animosities between strikers and nonstrikers, between the employer and the union, between friends and neighbors, and even between members of the same families. The social scars of conflict in that city may remain long after the economic effects of the strike have run their course.

We have already noted that the Taft–Hartley Act provides for an enforced 80-day "cooling off" period in the event that a strike appears to imperil the national health and safety. This procedure has proved rather unsuccessful in eliminating serious strikes. Two factors account for this. First, the parties involved are seldom in need of "cooling off." Modern day collective bargaining is pretty much conducted by professional negotiators who deal with facts and figures. Histrionics and emotional demonstrations are part of the procedure, but they are often designed to impress the public and the negotiator's own constituents rather than the opposition. Secondly, the findings and recommendations of a board of inquiry will be rejected if the report is seriously objectionable to any one of the parties to the dispute.

Compulsory arbitration has frequently been suggested as a means of eliminating strikes. With this procedure both labor and management are legally required to accept the decision of an arbitrator or board of arbitrators on the proper solution of the issues in question. This would eliminate strikes, if it were enforceable.

It would also imperil collective bargaining. Neither side is apt to concede an issue if the possibility exists that a third party will decide in its favor. Collective bargaining in the vast majority of cases results in peaceful agreement, with some degree of mutual accommodation. Arbitration, since it almost necessarily makes one party a "winner" and the other a "loser," is more likely to leave a residue of bitterness. Nor can arbitration match the flexibility of collective bargaining. Finally, there is doubt as to the constitutionality and the enforceability of compulsory arbitration.

Other means of eliminating strikes have been proposed. Plants can be seized and operated by the government, but this appears practicable only in time of war or similar crisis. Another possibility is the "statutory strike," wherein production would continue but the workers' wages would be sharply reduced and the company would be fined an amount equal to all profits and fixed costs. This supposedly would confine the strike's economic harm to the parties directly involved.

Here, then, is a noteworthy opportunity for social invention: to develop

a technique that will reduce or eliminate strikes, while preserving justice
for all parties concerned—including the general public.

## HOW MUCH GOVERNMENT INTERVENTION?

One of the key current issues is the extent to which the Federal Government and its agencies should interject themselves into collective bargaining settlements. This question received pointed attention in connection with the efforts made by the Administration in 1959 to settle the
long steel strike, and perhaps even more sharply, in 1962, as a result of
Administration influence in the steel wage settlement and the following
episode of announced steel price increases.

A substantial indication of the Administration's attitude, if not of intended specific actions or legislation, was provided in the statements of
the President and of the Council of Economic Advisers referred to in
Chapter 11. After suggesting as a general guide that increases in wage
rates should be related to the trend rate of over-all productivity increase,
the report of the Council of Economic Advisers went on to observe:

> Finally, it must be reiterated that collective bargaining within an industry
> over the division of the proceeds between labor and nonlabor income is not
> necessarily disruptive of over-all price stability. The relative shares can change
> within the bounds of noninflationary price behavior. But when a disagreement
> between management and labor is resolved by passing the bill to the rest of
> the economy, the bill is paid in depreciated currency to the ultimate advan-
> tage of no one.[*]

The more that government becomes involved in settling collective
bargaining disputes, the more the parties to a dispute are likely to
retain fixed positions, expecting this to force a crisis and bring the
government into the picture with the hope of getting a better settlement
than could be obtained across the bargaining table.

### "RIGHT TO WORK" LAWS

One of the most controversial industrial relations issues of recent years
has been the question of state "right to work" laws. The first such law
was passed by Arkansas in 1944. By 1960 similar provisions had been
enacted either by statute or by constitutional amendment in 19 states.[†]

[*] In *Economic Report of the President* (Washington, D.C.: U.S. Government Printing Office, 1962), p. 190.

[†] Alabama, Arizona, Arkansas, Florida, Georgia, Indiana, Iowa, Kansas, Mississippi,
Tennessee, Texas, Utah, and Virginia. Louisiana also passed a right to work law, but
Nebraska, Nevada, North Carolina, North Dakota, South Carolina, South Dakota,
in 1956 revised it to apply only to agricultural workers.

These laws provide that a person cannot be deprived of a job simply because he does not belong to a union. They prohibit the inclusion in collective bargaining agreements of union security devices, such as the closed shop, where employees must be union members before they can be hired; the union shop, where employees must join the union within a stipulated time after they have been hired; and "maintenance of membership," where an employee is required to maintain his membership for a specified time if he voluntarily joins the union.

The applicability to interstate commerce of state right to work laws was permitted by the Taft–Hartley Act. It authorized the union shop, but it allowed state legislation regarding union security to take precedence over the union shop proviso if the state legislation was more restrictive. Thus if a state prohibited any type of union security agreement, the prohibition applied not only to intrastate commerce, which has always been a matter of state jurisdiction, but also to interstate commerce.

Are these laws sound? Arguments of their proponents and opponents are presented in the following paragraphs.

The supporters of right to work laws insist that an individual should have the right to work for whomever he wants, whenever he wants, and under whatever working conditions and financial arrangements he wants. The right to work and freedom of association are claimed as constitutional rights that must not be abridged either by statute or by collective bargaining agreement.

Union leaders counter with these arguments: The right to work is by no means an absolute right. It simply means that an individual may go from one place to another in looking for employment. He may be refused employment for a variety of reasons. The only "rights" that an individual gives up under a union security clause are the right to hold a *particular* job (which is a right that nobody ever has anyway) and the right not to join a union. He is not deprived of the right to work. In fact, union security gives the worker the right to work in the real sense by protecting him from unfair discrimination by the employer. And as far as freedom of association is concerned, the individual is still free to decide whether or not he will associate with the group.

A second major argument advanced for right to work laws is that compulsory unionism tends to give the unions monopoly power. When union officials gain control over all the workers, and at least partial control over the workers' jobs, they are able to press their demands of a union-wide, company-wide, or nationwide basis. Local collective bargaining is ineffective in the face of such power.

The unions advance positive arguments in favor of union security provisions and therefore against the right to work laws. First, compulsory unionism, when supported by a majority of the workers, is held essential to union security. If union membership were not compulsory, union officials would have to spend the major portion of their time defending against employer attacks or attacks from other unions. And the only effective defense would be to attack—by restricting the employer's control over the workers, by battling for the maximum in wages and fringe benefits and better working conditions, by supporting the union members in every grievance against management, and by giving better service to union members than to nonunion employees. In other words, the union would have to be continually built up in the eyes of the workers. The result would be that union officials would have little or no time to exercise the responsible leadership that is most desirable from the standpoint of all concerned. They could not afford to cooperate with management and play a constructive role in the operation of the enterprise.

In answer to this businessmen declare that in our free society an organization such as a union should always be voluntary in nature. If it is well-run and effective, it will attract members and receive their support. Compulsory unionism protects only those unions that do not serve the employees—unions that the employees would prefer to do without.

Unions have opposed right to work laws also on the ground that they permit some workers to receive a "free ride" at the expense of their fellow workers. A union certified as the bargaining agent in a bargaining unit is required to represent all employees in it, regardless of union membership. The cost of representation comes out of the union treasury to which only union members contribute. Thus a nonunion employee receives the advantages of union membership without paying for them. A comparable situation would exist if each citizen of a nation could decide whether or not he would pay any taxes.

Businessmen rebut this argument by noting all the things that a nonmember is denied, such as attendance at union meetings, participation in social activities, and opportunity to benefit from union welfare funds or insurance programs. The nonmember benefits only to the extent that the union is able to win higher wages or other advantages from the employer. And many employees could probably do better in this regard if they could negotiate with the employer for themselves. Then too, many institutions provide benefits to individuals who do not pay for them. Union leaders would be quick to complain if churches, schools, and hospitals charged each and every recipient of their services, so why should unions?

The foregoing paragraphs, then, contain the arguments pro and con. The issue, however, is not entirely rational. The dispute over right to work laws often involves strong emotional differences. Some people tend to decide the issue on the basis of their attitudes toward unionism itself. Those who oppose unionism tend to favor these laws as a step forward in the struggle to contain or reverse the union movement. Those who believe that unions are good for our economy and our society are apt to regard the laws as interfering with peaceful and constructive labor–management relations.

## THE POLITICAL POWER OF ORGANIZED LABOR

Organized labor in the United States has always emphasized the use of economic power to achieve its objectives. In recent years, however, increasing reliance has been placed on the political strength of the union movement. This trend is defended on the ground that (1) business has always indulged in politics and so must labor if it is to hold its own against business interests; (2) some objectives of labor can be achieved only through political activity, e.g., adequate unemployment compensation and other social security benefits; and (3) our democratic society will be strengthened as more and more people take an active interest in political processes.

This tendency to inject union power into the political arena is a matter of great concern to many business leaders and political commentators. They fear that the money and manpower of unions will prove irresistible and that sooner or later the National Government and many of our state and local governments will be under the thumb of organized labor. (Indeed, some observers assert that certain of these governments are already in that position.) In any event, union political power has unquestionably become a matter of public interest.

From the political standpoint, organized labor may best be considered as but one of the many pressure groups that constantly attempt to mold public policy and influence government. There is little factual evidence to support the contention that organized labor is a controlling political power.

It is in the interest of union leaders to foster the belief of labor's political power. Such a belief is bound to facilitate the efforts of their lobbyists in influencing legislative and administrative actions.

There are two reasons for the failure of organized labor to match the claims that are advanced for (or against) it. In the first place, politics costs a great deal of money, and labor unions have been able to provide only a small fraction of the total. Unions were barred by the Taft–Hartley Act from contributing treasury funds to support campaigns for national office, and some states have imposed similar restrictions. (Corporations also are barred from contributing to campaigns for national office.) Hence the bulk of the money that unions spend on political elections comes from voluntary contributions (critics would put the word *voluntary* in quotation marks) by union members to such organizations as the AFL-CIO Committee on Political Education (COPE).

Secondly, the labor vote cannot be *delivered* to the extent that is often implied. Union members are not only union members. They are other personalties also, such as church members, college graduates, home owners, and parents, and their votes are influenced accordingly. An impressive example of the inability of organized labor to control the vote is the reelection of Senator Taft of Ohio after passage of the Taft–Hartley Act. Taft's defeat in 1950 was a major goal of union political activity; nevertheless, the Senator was reelected with a margin of nearly half a million votes.

To hold a position of real influence in American politics requires the ability to deliver votes or money (preferably both). Organized labor can deliver some of both, and hence it does exercise political influence. This influence, however, is one of the many forces that affect elections, appointments, legislation, and administrative actions.

## UNIONS AND THE ANTITRUST LAWS

As we note in Chapter 14, the Sherman Antitrust Act was aimed at huge business combinations. Soon, however, courts began to apply the Act to unions. Unions fought for exemption from the Sherman Act and thought that they had secured it when the Clayton Act was passed in 1914. One of its provisions declares that such organizations are not illegal conspiracies in restraint of trade under the antitrust acts. The joy of the unions gradually disappeared as, in the following decades, the Supreme Court held unions to be subject to these laws.

In a series of decisions, beginning in 1940, however, the Supreme Court turned around and almost eliminated the application of the antitrust acts to unions.

At about the same time, unions were surging in size and power. In the 1950s and 1960s, as we note in Chapter 11, many analysts were holding excessive union wage demands responsible for inflation, via the wage-cost-push route. Critics suggest that the way to curb the power of unions is to remove their exemption from the antitrust laws. The meaning of this proposal is not always clear. Does it mean an end to industry-wide bargaining, to industry-wide unions, or what? Just how would the recommended legal change alter the processes and the outcomes of collective bargaining? Until such questions are answered, the merits of the proposal remain unsettled.

## PRESENT POSITION AND OUTLOOK

Since the beginning of their being reclassified as lawful organizations in 1842, labor unions have come a long way. For decades, to be sure, their progress was slow. Employer antagonism and legal restrictions combined to hold them down. The employers were strong, the unions were weak, and labor's was the role of the proverbial underdog.

Nevertheless, they grew slowly, and a few unions had achieved real strength before the passage of the Wagner Act; but large membership and great general national power did not come to the union movement until after that event.

Today, unions are big, rich, and (economically, if not politically) powerful. In some industries they appear to be more powerful than the corporate employers, large though many of the latter are. Indeed, their power worries many citizens. The majority, however, state that they approve of them. A dozen times since 1936 the Gallup poll has asked, "In general, do you approve or disapprove of labor unions?" The "approve" vote has ranged between 60 and 76 per cent, the remainder dividing between "Disapprove" and "No opinion." The Gallup release dated January 30, 1963, showed these results:

|  | % |
|---|---|
| Approve | 67 |
| Disapprove | 23 |
| No Opinion | 10 |

Here are the results by occupational groups:

|  | Approve % | Disapprove % | No Opinion % |
|---|---|---|---|
| Professional and Business | 61 | 31 | 8 |
| White Collar | 67 | 27 | 6 |
| Farmers | 51 | 30 | 19 |
| Manual Workers | 75 | 16 | 9 |

The meaning of these survey results is perhaps debatable. Nevertheless, they strongly suggest that labor unions have many friends. In the circumstances it is by no means an idle question to ask how Congressional majorities were mustered for the Taft–Hartley Law and the Landrum–Griffin Act—both fought vigorously by unions. Perhaps there is a difference between approving unions in general and approving everything that they do. If so, this difference may be significant in determining future governmental policies, as it seems to have been in the past.

## QUESTIONS AND PROBLEMS

1. Why did the injunction become a prime object of union hatred?
2. Why did it take so long for unions and the right to strike to lose legal fetters?
3. With respect to the principal Federal laws affecting labor–management relations, discuss these subjects: (a) How did the law come to be passed? (b) What are its chief provisions? (c) Evaluate its soundness as public policy.

4. Now that labor and management have reached a state of relative maturity, would it be in the national interest to repeal the Federal laws affecting labor–management relations?
5. Is there a need for stronger legislation to curb the growth and power of labor unions?
6. Why are labor unions exempted from antitrust legislation?
7. Some writers have suggested that the unions be made subject to the antitrust laws. Discuss the arguments for and against this proposal.
8. How useful are governmental conciliation and mediation services?
9. What legislation (if any) might be enacted that would reduce strikes while maintaining justice for all parties concerned, such as labor, management, and the public? Is compulsory arbitration the answer?
10. What are the arguments for and against "right to work" laws?
11. How great is the impact of labor unions in the political arena?
12. What is the outlook for government regulation of labor unions and union–management relations?

## SELECTED READINGS

BAKKE, E. WIGHT, CLARK KERR, and CHARLES W. ANROD (eds.). *Unions, Management, and the Public,* 2nd ed. New York: Harcourt, Brace & World, Inc., 1960.

BUTLER, A. D. *Labor Economics and Institutions.* New York: The Macmillan Company, 1961.

GREGORY, CHARLES O. *Labor and the Law,* rev. ed. New York: W. W. Norton & Company, 1958.

REYNOLDS, LLOYD G. *Labor Economics and Labor Relations.* Englewood Cliffs, N.J.: Prentice-Hall, Inc., 1959.

SHISTER, JOSEPH. *Public Policy and Collective Bargaining.* New York: Harper and Brothers, 1962.

SLICHTER, SUMNER H. *The Challenge of Industrial Relations.* Ithaca, N.Y.: Cornell University Press, 1947.

————. *Union Policies and Industrial Management.* Washington, D.C.: The Brookings Institution, 1941.

U.S. National Labor Relations Board. *Annual Report.* Washington, D.C.: U.S. Government Printing Office. Annually.

WALKER, KENNETH F. *Industrial Relations in Australia.* Cambridge, Mass.: Harvard University Press, 1956.

# 21 THE FARM PROBLEM

Federal farm policy is a tangled situation, compounded of a mixture of economics and politics, that has developed through many decades, with accelerating complication in recent years.

Dramatic evidence of the change in Federal farm policy is provided by a historical incident. In 1887 vetoing an appropriation of $25,000 to buy seed corn for drought-stricken Texas counties, President Grover Cleveland said:

> I can find no warrant for such an appropriation in the Constitution, and I do not believe that the power and duty of the General Government ought to be extended to the relief of individual suffering which is in no manner properly related to the public service or benefit. . . . The lesson should be constantly enforced that though the people support the Government the Government should not support the people. . . . Federal aid in such cases encourages the expectation of paternal care on the part of the Government and weakens the sturdiness of our national character. . . .°

By contrast, in 1961 the Department of Agriculture of the Federal Government spent $6 billion. How did this giant effort evolve? Why was it done? What good has it done? What is the outlook for farm policy?

## EARLY AGRICULTURAL POLICIES

Federal farm policy was not a matter of great public concern during the early history of the United States. The Government engaged in such modest activities as the collection and distribution of seeds and the compilation of agricultural statistics, but for the most part the farmer was left to his own devices.

The first significant development in farm policy occurred in 1862, with the establishment of the U.S. Department of Agriculture. Its purpose was "to acquire and to diffuse among the people of the United States useful

° Quoted by G. O. Dykstra and L. G. Dykstra, *Selected Cases on Government and Business* (Chicago: Callaghan and Company, 1937), pp. 2, 3.

information on subjects connected with agriculture in the most general and comprehensive sense of that word, and to procure, propagate, and distribute among the people new and valuable seeds and plants."

The land-grant colleges also were launched in 1862 as a means of providing technical and general education at the college level in agriculture an dthe "mechanic arts." Each state was assigned an amount of public domain land equal to 30,000 acres for each senator and representative in Congress. This land was to be sold by the states and the proceeds invested in endowment funds for support of the colleges.

Federal support of agricultural research and development was furthered by the Hatch Act of 1887, which provided for state agricultural experiment stations. The Smith–Lever Act of 1914 established a joint Federal–state farm extension program, designed to disseminate to farmers the results of agricultural research and to carry on adult education in rural areas.

Prior to World War I the primary purpose of Federal farm policy was to increase the efficiency of agricultural production and marketing techniques. During the 1920s the economic problems of the farming industry became increasingly apparent. Since the depression days of the thirties the twin objectives of farm income support and farm production control have been emphasized.

Although these have been the major continuing concerns of national farm policy, various measures have been enacted throughout the years to alleviate some of the burdens of our rural population. Programs such as those leading to provision of more adequate credit facilities, development of rural mail delivery and parcel post service, improvement of farm-to-market roads, and rural electrification have contributed greatly to a better life for the American farmer.

## POLICIES IN THE TWENTIES

Although the 1920s are generally remembered as a period of American prosperity, the agricultural industry was less prosperous than the rest of the economy. Production of foodstuffs had increased tremendously during and after World War I, to meet the demands of the export market; and farm income had tripled between 1915 and 1919. However, by 1920, European requirements for food imports had begun to decline, and continued high production led to the inevitable drop in prices. As farm income declined, farm debt that had been incurred during the period of inflated wartime prices became increasingly burdensome; thousands of farms were foreclosed, and many banks in farm communities shut their doors.

The farmers' difficulties led to demands for relief. Attempts were made to develop large-scale, single-commodity cooperative marketing associations, but these voluntary organizations were generally unsuccessful since their objective of higher prices required a degree of control over production and marketing that they were powerless to impose.

A proposal known as the McNary–Haugen plan was widely advocated during the latter part of the decade. Under this plan a Government corporation would have been created to buy up enough of each major export crop to cause the price in the United States to be maintained at a level well above that prevailing in the world market. The products so acquired would have been sold abroad at the lower world market prices, the losses being made up by assessing an "equalization fee" against each unit produced domestically. The plan was supported by the farm groups and by Congress, and failed to become law only because of Presidential vetoes in 1927 and again in 1928.

It is interesting to note that the McNary–Haugen plan had evolved from proposals first advanced by executives of the Moline Plow Company, whose farm implement sales had declined along with farm income.

The belief that most of the farmers' difficulties derived from ineffective marketing methods led to passage of the Agricultural Marketing Act of 1929. This act was intended to place the agricultural industry on a basis of economic equality with other industries. A Federal Farm Board was set up with a $500 million fund from which loans could be made to co-operative and stabilization companies when price-depressing surpluses developed. The loans were to enable farmers to hold products off the market until prices had improved. However, the Act provided no check on production, and when the general economic collapse began shortly after the Act was passed the Farm Board was unable to reverse the mounting surpluses and the falling farm prices.

## THE GREAT DEPRESSION

After 1929, as the Great Depression developed, the position of agriculture relative to the rest of the economy continued to worsen. As a consequence, one of the first measures passed by Congress in the Roosevelt Administration was the Agricultural Adjustment Act of 1933. The objective of this law was to maintain selected farm product prices at levels that would give the raisers of the basic agricultural commodities a purchasing power equal to what they had enjoyed in a base period—August 1909 to July 1914.* As might be expected, these base years had been a relatively prosperous period for farmers as a whole.

The most important feature of the Act provided for the avoidance of surpluses and the support of high prices through *production control*—an element that had been lacking in the Agricultural Marketing Act of 1929. Acreage allotments and marketing quotas were established, and those

* The base period for tobacco was 1919–1929.

farmers who curtailed production were reimbursed by benefit payments which were derived from a processing tax levied on the processors of farm commodities.

The same year, 1933, saw also the creation of the Commodity Credit Corporation (CCC), which initially offered price support loans to growers of cotton and corn. The loan mechanism set a price floor for these commodities in the following manner. Assuming that the Government has set a support price for corn of $1.00 per bushel and that the market price was less than that, a farmer could put up his corn crop, or any part of it, as collateral for a loan in the amount of $1.00 per bushel. If the market price subsequently rose above $1.00, the farmer could sell his grain at the higher price and pay off his loan. If the market price remained under $1.00, the farmer could default on the loan and in effect convert it to a sale. Since the CCC had no recourse when loans were defaulted, they came to be known as nonrecourse loans.

In 1936 the Supreme Court declared, in the Hoosac Mills case,° that the taxation provisions of the Agricultural Adjustment Act were unconstitutional. Thus the granting of benefit payments in return for the curtailment of production was halted.

The Government then shifted its attention to various soil conservation measures as a means of controlling production. Efforts to encourage the growth of "soil-building" grasses and legumes instead of corn, cotton, wheat, and other commodities were generally unsuccessful, however, and crop surpluses continued to mount.

In 1938 a new Agricultural Adjustment Act was passed. This Act incorporated many of the provisions of the earlier Act (but not the tax on commodity processors) and also initiated the Federal Crop Insurance Program. The Commodity Credit Corporation was required to extend loans on wheat, cotton, and corn as necessary to stabilize prices at 52 to 75 per cent of parity. Loans on other commodities and on dairy products were authorized but not required.

## WORLD WAR II AND AFTER

With the advent of World War II, American agriculture again entered a period of abnormally high demand. Commodity surpluses were no longer a problem. To encourage production, acreage allotments were suspended and legislation was enacted providing price supports for the basic crops (cotton, corn, rice, tobacco, wheat, and peanuts) and several other commodities at 90 per cent of parity prices.† The farm industry responded with record yields—and again failed to cut back when the abnormal demand slacked off after the War.

° *U.S. v. Butler,* 297 U.S. 1 (1936).

† Parity prices were those prevailing in a base period high enough to give the farmer a "fair share" of national income.

After 1948 the government reimposed acreage allotments and marketing quotas to stem the excess output, but price supports were held at the 90 per cent level to bolster farm income.

In 1949 Secretary of Agriculture Charles F. Brannan proposed a modified program of farm aid that shifted Federal emphasis from price support to income support. While support loans would still be offered for storable commodities, nonstorable "perishable" commodities such as fruits, vegetables, meats, and dairy products would be permitted to find their free market prices; and direct payments to farmers would raise the farmers' incomes to a level that would be determined by a moving average for the preceding ten years. Thus the consumer would pay a lower market price, but his tax payments would have to provide part of the farmer's income. The plan also included a limitation on the amount of benefits payable for any one farm. The Brannan plan gained considerable support throughout the country, but the difficulty of estimating its probable cost, and the fear that direct government payments to farmers would undermine their independence, ultimately led to the plan's rejection by Congress.

Throughout the 1950s price supports, acreage allotments, and marketing quotas continued to dominate Federal farm policy. However, the requirement for rigid 90-per-cent-of-parity supports was abandoned in 1954 in favor of flexible price supports which at first could be varied between 82.5 and 90 per cent of parity. The minimum was subsequently reduced as low as 65 per cent for some crops. Under the law support levels within these ranges were set by the Secretary of Agriculture.

Commodity surpluses held by the Commodity Credit Corporation mounted rapidly after the Korean War as farm production continued to exceed demand. To equate supply with demand at the desired price levels would have required sharp reductions in acreage allotments and marketing quotas. Recognizing the political impossibility of such reductions, the Administration developed the *soil bank program* to reimburse farmers for voluntarily retiring land from production. Under the acreage reserve provisions (which were dropped after 1958) a farmer could agree to refrain for one year from grazing or cropping a portion of his allotted acreage, and in return he would receive certificates redeemable in cash by the CCC. Under the conservation reserve provisions a farmer could contract with the Government to shift part of his land from crop production to forage, trees, or water storage for a period of three to fifteen years. The Government would pay part of the cost of the conservation measures, such as planting trees or grass cover, and in addition would annually pay the farmer cash benefits for the acres removed from production. By 1960 some 28 million acres had been retired under this program. But, since nearly all of this land was marginal in nature, the effect on total farm output was rather slight.

As the years went by, controls increased, surpluses mounted, costs soared, and opportunities for manipulation multiplied.

## KEY FACTS ABOUT FARMING
## AND FARMERS

The income of farmers has been lower than that of the remainder of our population for many years. Farmers' incomes have gone up, but they have not caught up with nonfarm incomes. In 1960, 4,540,000 farm operator families had an average annual income of $4,518; while the 40,830,-000 nonfarm families' average income was $8,049. The income of 25.6 per cent of those farm families was under $2,000 a year, but only 5.2 per cent of nonfarm families were so poor.*

Although farm poverty was most prevalent in the South, and there among Negro families, it was not confined to that region. Even in relatively prosperous states, such as Iowa, many farm families did not enjoy the conveniences of central heating, indoor toilets, and automatic hot water.

Some farm families were well-to-do; 2.5 per cent had annual incomes of $15,000 or more, compared with 7.9 per cent of nonfarm families in that income category.† The idea that all farmers got rich during the War and drove Buicks or Cadillacs thereafter is wrong. A few farmers did get rich, but many more stayed poor—some desperately so.

## FEWER FARMERS AND
## GREATER OUTPUT

The 25 million people living on farms represented about 18 per cent of our national population of 140 million in 1945. Fifteen years later, national population had climbed to 179 million, but farm population had moved in the other direction—down to 21 million, or 11 per cent of the total. Thus farm population as a percentage of total U.S. population declined by one third from 1945 to 1960. The steady flow of people from rural to urban living has played a large part in the farmer's rising per capita income, by permitting the dollar value of farm output to be shared by fewer and fewer people.

Even though farm population declined by about four million people from 1945 to 1960, farm productivity and total farm output increased. Farm output per man-hour more than doubled during this period, and crop production per acre increased by 25 per cent.

Aggregate farm output in the United States has tended upward since

* Source: U.S. Department of Commerce, *Survey of Current Business*, April 1962, p. 13.
    † *Ibid.*

colonial days. For a long while the increase was primarily associated with the use of additional acres and workers. These trends ended years ago. The peak number of agricultural workers was recorded in the census of 1910, and farm acreage has not changed greatly since 1920. The subsequent rise in production has been brought about chiefly by various technological advances. Fewer than 250,000 tractors were in use on American farms in 1920—by 1960 there were nearly five million. Mechanization represents the most obvious aspect of technological advance, but significant contributions have also been made by chemical and biological developments, such as fertilizers, weed and insect sprays, higher-yielding grains, and improved livestock breeds.

## THE CONDITIONS OF PRODUCTION

A recent history of technological advance and rising productivity is of course not peculiar to the agricultural industry. But this industry is unique in that the producers of most farm products so greatly outnumber their immediate buyers. On occasion, a not overly large number of producers have been able to form an effective marketing organization and thus act as one in market transactions. In this manner the orange growers of Southern California and the dairymen in the milksheds of many of our large cities have been able to coordinate their production and marketing with demand and thereby influence the market prices of their products. But in these and similar instances the suppliers are limited in number and are restricted to specific regions. As far as the mainstays of farm production and farm income are concerned, the individual farmer produces only a drop in the bucket, and neither the doubling nor the halving of his production will affect the market price. This being the case, the farmer will of course try to produce as much as he can.

The incentive for maximum possible output exists so long as the farmer's cash receipts cover his out-of-pocket costs. And inasmuch as these costs are relatively low compared to the fixed costs of land, equipment, and even family labor, commodity prices can drop quite far indeed with no adverse effect on output. Until the cash break-even point is reached, falling prices may even stimulate *increased* production, as each farmer attempts to maintain his income through a greater volume of sales.

This situation prevails even though prices and income drop so low that the farmer who is paying off a mortgage can no longer pay the bank and the tax collector. Foreclosure may result, but the farm does not drop out of production. The financial institution that takes possession will either sell the farm or rent it, and the buyer or the renter will produce as much as possible because the more he can produce the higher his income will be.

## THE DEMAND FOR FOOD AND FIBERS

The total market for agricultural products can be divided into requirements for industrial use and requirements for human consumption. Although in recent years the efforts of agricultural research have emphasized the search for new industrial uses, the results have been less than spectacular. In fact, the proportion of all farm commodities that have been devoted to nonfood uses in the United States has declined during the past 15 years.

As far as the consumer market is concerned, rising incomes have little effect on the amount of food purchased. The human stomach has a limited capacity, so that the average individual does not desire to eat more than a certain quantity of food. Once this quantity is attainable, subsequent income increases are in large part allocated to other areas of the household budget—a new home, a new automobile, appliances, services, travel, and savings. Even when the consumer does spend more money for food, he devotes most of the increase to various packaging or processing improvements, as exemplified in ready-to-bake rolls and cookies, TV dinners, and packaged cake mixes. He also spends more money on expensive foods and less on inexpensive ones. Thus the per capita consumption of meat, poultry, and eggs has gone up, while consumption of potatoes, wheat, and corn products has declined. Rich people eat better, but not more.

The principal cause of increased food consumption (and of increased demand for agricultural commodities) has been population growth. The population of the United States doubled during the first half of this century, and is still growing. This growth insures an expanding market for agriculture, but the rate of expansion is rather slow—much slower than the rate of increase of agricultural productivity.

## THE EFFECT OF PRICE SUPPORTS

With productivity increases outstripping population growth, and with relatively inelastic demand for and supply of agricultural products, one would expect a downward trend in farm prices accompanied by sharp fluctuations due to such factors as changing weather conditions. However, this downward trend has been checked by the Federal Government's price support programs. The Commodity Credit Corporation has consistently held prices above the level that would be necessary to equate demand with supply. And these same price supports have supported the cost of food in every grocery store and supermarket in the country. All consumers have been helping to foot the bill—including all the farmers.

Price supports have helped the rich, efficient farmers to become richer, but they have done little to help the poor, inefficient farmers. Table 21.1

reveals that in 1954 (the latest year for which such data are available) over half of our farms sold less than $2,500 worth of products. When a farmer's gross income is $2,500 and his net income is $1,500, even a sharp rise in price supports for some of his products will not raise his net income very much. A 10-per-cent increase in the support price for his product would mean an additional $250 of revenue. On the other hand, the wealthy and efficient farmer who sells $25,000 worth a year will benefit considerably. His income will go up by $2,500.

### Table 21.1
## FARMS, NUMBER AND OUTPUT, BY ECONOMIC CLASS, 1954

|  | NUMBER OF FARMS | PERCENTAGE OF TOTAL FARMS | PERCENTAGE OUTPUT OF TOTAL DOLLAR |
|---|---|---|---|
| I. Commercial farms having market sales of: |  |  |  |
| $25,000 or over | 134,000 | 2.8 | 31.3 |
| 10,000 to 24,999 | 449,000 | 9.4 | 26.9 |
| 5,000 to 9,999 | 707,000 | 14.8 | 20.5 |
| 2,500 to 4,999 | 812,000 | 17.0 | 12.1 |
| Total, over $2500 | 2,102,000 | 44.0 | 90.8 |
| II. Small full-time commercial farms having market sales of less than $2500 | 1,226,000 | 25.7 | 7.1 |
| III. Part-time, residential, and other farms | 1,455,000 | 30.3 | 2.0 |

SOURCE: U.S. Census of Agriculture, 1954.

Furthermore, many farmers do not raise any of the relatively few products whose prices are supported by the government.* Eggs, fresh vegetables, fruits, nuts, livestock—all these are sold without the benefit of guaranteed loans and minimum prices. Indeed, in 1958 farm market sales were valued at well over $33 billion, yet nearly $20 billion of these sales— 61 per cent—involved products not under the price support program. Thus it is by no means true that farmers are generally dependent on the Government for their incomes. In actual fact, a great many farmers are paying higher taxes and higher prices to raise the incomes of the rest of the farmers.

The general case for Government help to agriculture was put thus by Mr. Herschel D. Newsom, Master of the National Grange, before that organization's ninety-second annual session in November 1958:

Within the present economic structure of America, it should clearly be recognized that farmers are entitled to a reasonably comparable bargaining

* Price supports are currently in effect for corn, cotton, peanuts, rice, wheat, tobacco, butterfat, milk, honey, mohair, tung nuts, wool, barley, grain sorghums, oats, rye, soybeans, cottonseed, flaxseed, and dry edible beans.

power or protective mechanism of some sort, to that enjoyed by nonagricultural labor and nonagricultural industry. Through legislation, government has helped to develop the bargaining power of "labor." Other governmental "institutions" have helped business from the very birth of our Republic to regulate and control the production and the marketing of their products and services. In fact, nonagricultural business and production was insulated from "free competition" long before nonagricultural labor won "fair labor standards" and collective bargaining. Import quotas and controls, duties, excise taxes, and other restraints on competition outside of agriculture are almost as old as the government of the United States itself. . . .

In the same address Mr. Newsom insisted that additional farm income must come from the users of farm products and not from taxpayers. He went on to extol the need for an array of farm programs designed to raise income, reduce Government farm costs, and produce more freedom in farming. He did not, however, indicate exactly what policies, processes, or procedures were to be utilized to bring about these results.

In any appraisal of present Federal farm policy, and proposals for changes, one fact must be recognized at the outset. This is that the Government does assist other industries by regulations of various kinds, and extends to people other than farmers substantial subsidies. The annual expenditure on veterans' benefits, for example, is about equal to that for aids to agriculture. And some people—either the publishers or the readers—are the beneficiaries of a subsidy of several hundred million dollars, representing the difference between low second class mail rates and the actual costs of the postal handling of newspapers and magazines. It is neither fair to farmers nor in accord with sound national policy to assail the regulations and the subsidies applicable to only their branch of the American economy.

## EVALUATION AND OUTLOOK

The farm problem is in reality two problems. The first is that of low income and an unsatisfactory living standard for a large proportion of our farm families. The second problem is that of overproduction, or the excess of supply over demand at desirable price levels.

The Federal Government has actively endeavored to support farm income for three decades, and during most of this time it has also exercised partial control over the production and marketing of farm commodities. Over $15 billion has been spent on stabilization programs, and a comparable sum has been allocated to various other agricultural measures, such as research, conservation, and farm credit. Are the results of all this effort worth the cost?

Per capital farm income has steadily fallen behind that of the nonfarm populace. And the value of farm commodities held by the Commodity Credit Corporation approached the $10 billion mark in 1961. Enough wheat was available in storage to satisfy all our requirements even if no more were produced for a full year.

As noted previously, the incomes of poor farm families have not been and never will be raised to an acceptable level through the use of price supports. These marginal farmers will be able to enjoy a decent income only if:

[1]   They are able to produce a much greater output, through the accumulation and use of additional land and equipment, or

[2]   They are subsidized by the rest of the population, or

[3]   They are able to find other occupations that yield a greater return for their labor and investment.

It is obviously impossible for more than a few to expand their farm operations greatly, and to the extent that they might, the problem of overproduction would be aggravated.

Direct and massive subsidization of the marginal farmer is theoretically possible, but from the practical standpoint this action is not currently foreseeable.

Farmers have been leaving the farms, especially during the past 15 years. The incorporation of farmers into the Social Security program (in 1956) has probably speeded the retirement of farmers reaching 65.

But the key to economic improvement of the low income farmer's status is a generally high level of employment opportunities. The opportunity for other work must be available if farmers are to leave the soil in significant numbers.

A program of special assistance and encouragement would undoubtedly be useful. Educational services in rural areas could be geared to basic subjects and vocational learning, with less emphasis on commercial farming. The relocation of industry to rural locations would make it easier for the marginal farmer to get a job without moving far away from his former home, and in some cases he would not have to move at all. Federal and state employment services could probably do more than they have done to acquaint farmers with employment opportunities. And the outright offer of financial assistance to cover moving costs and immediate cash requirements might stimulate the movement of impoverished families off the land to distant jobs, as suggested by Professor Theodore W. Schultz, in what he has called a "homesteads in reverse" program.

## FOOD FOR PEACE

Our deluge of food does not mean that the United States has succeeded in repealing the law of diminishing returns. What has happened is that, because of remarkable technological developments, the curve of diminishing returns has shifted rapidly to the "Northeast." The result has been that, instead of experiencing the Malthusian misery of pressure of the population on the food supply, we have experienced a Malthus-in-reverse dilemma of the pressure of the food supply on the population.

Thus, while in other parts of the world hunger and starvation are widespread, surpluses of food mount in the United States, and ships, circus tents, and new metal structures are used to store the flood. It would seem to be both simple and humanitarian that we should dispose of our surpluses, if necessary, by *giving them away* (thereby saving the storage costs) to the hungry people of the world.

As a matter of fact, we are doing something of the sort. In 1954 our various gift, grant, and subsidized export programs were brought together when the Congress passed the Agricultural Trade Development and Assistance Act, commonly known as "Public Law 480." The law authorized the sale of commodities below market prices for currencies which were not convertible into dollars and which hence presumably could not be used to purchase foodstuffs through ordinary commercial channels. By June 30, 1961, commodities which had cost the CCC $9.5 billion had been sold for $4.6 billion in soft currencies. The money so acquired was used to make loans and grants to foreign governments, primarily for irrigation, water power developments, rural electrification, and industrial projects.

Selling goods at less than the going market prices is a procedure that has long been condemned as "dumping." This process is injurious to other exporters of the same or competing products. It is, therefore, not unreasonable that such leading agricultural export nations as Canada, Australia, Argentina, and Uruguay have occasionally protested against our Public Law 480 programs, claiming that their traditional export markets were being undercut. Our program may have some less obvious consequences, such as enabling recipient countries to increase their production in exports of other products, such as rice, thereby intensifying competition for rice-exporting nations. And the receipt of fats and oils by Spain may have enabled that country to expand her exports of olive oil in competition with Italy and Greece. Questions may also be asked about the nature of the distribution of these food products within the countries to which they are sent and specifically whether they go to those with the greatest need.

If our key objective is not merely to avert starvation and malnutrition but also to raise the level of real incomes among poor peoples by helping them to help themselves, it follows that subsidized food exports are not a satisfactory substitute for programs contributing to economic growth in low-income countries.

## NEW USES FOR FARM PRODUCTS

Both public and private researchers are devoting time and effort to finding new uses for farm products. The greatest help from this kind of research activity will flow from finding *nonfood uses*. Because of the limited capacity of the human stomach to absorb physical quantities of food, the development of new *food* products enlarges the market for agriculture only in the sense that it may provide more employment and more farm income per thousand calories consumed, in fancier and more expensive forms. Consumption of nonfood goods, however, seems to be capable of more or less indefinite expansion. Scientists, therefore, hunt for ways to use agricultural products to make plastics, paints, varnishes, fungicides, and cosmetics. This research work is carried on in four Federal laboratories, employing more than two thousand persons and spending more than $20 million a year. One of the constituents of wheat and corn is starch. In its standard form, or in a chemically modified form, starch has many uses; and new ones are being sought in the paper, textiles, plastics, and building materials industries. In view of the immense possibilities of modern science it is by no means out of the question that today's surpluses of agricultural products may become the basis for nonfood industries that would require all of today's overabundant output. But that development is not sufficiently certain or imminent to suggest that the problem of surpluses will soon be solved.

## EVALUATION

Some notion of the difficulty of evolving a satisfactory farm program may be had from considering what an "ideal" farm program would include. Presumably such a program would do the following things:

[1] Increase farmers' incomes, particularly the incomes of poor farmers;

[2] Shift productive resources from farming to more socially useful activities;

[3] Reduce Government outlays and the costs to taxpayers;

[4] Get the Government out of the storage and distribution business;

[5] Eliminate acreage and production controls and leave farmers to produce as much as they wish;

[6] Make more friends than enemies in other countries;

[7] Do these things without making food and fiber more expensive; and

[8] Enable legislators and administrators who vote for and favor such a program to get reelected.

What does our present farm program do? It does these things:

[1] Does little for poor farmers;

[2] Retards the shift of resources away from farming;

[3] Tends to become more expensive;

[4] Piles up increasing surpluses;

[5] Requires more production controls;

[6] Complicates some of our international relationships; and

[7] Raises some food and fiber prices.

Considering these odd accomplishments of the program, and the fact that a handful of well-to-do farmers are its principal beneficiaries, whereas the check is picked up by most Americans (including even most farmers), the wonder is that it *does* seem to meet that final requirement of the ideal program.

## QUESTIONS AND PROBLEMS

1. What lessons can be learned from the history of governmental farm policies?
2. Is there really a "farm problem"? If so, precisely what is it? Whose problem is it?
3. What are the key economic characteristics of American agriculture, and what is their significance?
4. What are the chief features of Federal farm policy? What have been its principal consequences?
5. Do we have a "farm" surplus or a "farmer" surplus in this country today?
6. If you could change Federal farm policy, without regard to political considerations and in what you would consider to be the highest national interest, what changes would you make?
7. What is the outlook for Federal farm policy? What changes, if any, do you forecast?
8. If present Federal farm policy is as unsuccessful as asserted and benefits so few, how is it possible for it to be continued?

## SELECTED READINGS

BENEDICT, MURRAY R. *Can We Solve the Farm Problem?* New York: Twentieth Century Fund, 1955.

————. *Farm Surpluses, U.S. Burden or World Asset?* Berkeley, Calif.: University of California, Division of Agricultural Sciences, 1960.

BLACK, JOHN D. "The Agricultural Surplus," *Current History*, September 1956.

————. *Introduction to Economics of Agriculture.* New York: The Macmillan Company, 1953.

BRANDT, KARL. *Farm Price Supports—Rigid or Flexible.* New York: American Enterprise Association, 1954.

Committee For Economic Development. *Economic Policy for American Agriculture.* New York: Committee for Economic Development, 1956.

————. *Toward a Realistic Farm Program.* New York: Committee for Economic Development, 1957.

JESNESS, O. B. (ed.). *Readings on Agricultural Policy.* Homewood, Ill.: Richard D. Irwin, Inc., 1949.

McCUNE, WESLEY. *The Farm Bloc.* New York: Doubleday, Doran & Company, 1943.

SCHULTZ, THEODORE W. *Production and Welfare of Agriculture.* New York: The Macmillan Company, 1950.

# 22 CONSERVATION OF NATURAL RESOURCES

In the half century from 1860 to 1910 the population of the Upper Peninsula of Michigan grew much faster than that of the entire United States. The United States population tripled—from 31 million to nearly 92 million. But the remote Upper Peninsula's population shot up from 21,000 to 326,000—a fifteenfold increase. In the next half century, however, the situation was reversed. The population of the United States nearly doubled, to 179 million in 1960, but the Upper Peninsula's population in 1960 was slightly smaller than it had been in 1910; indeed, it had been virtually horizontal—at the 300,000 level—for the entire 50-year period.

What is the explanation of the large and abrupt change in the U.P.'s growth rate? The answer is: exploitation, followed by exhaustion of natural resources. Prior to 1910 people were developing and exploiting the natural resources of the region. The area had, not *one* rich natural resource, but *three*. They were iron ore, copper ore, and immense forests of towering pines. At its peak of copper production the U.P. was the greatest copper producer in the entire world, and it was a leader in logging and iron ore output. But overexploitation used up the three great natural resources. So tremendous had been these three resources, and so nearly complete their exhaustion, that it is by no means facetious to suggest that the remarkable fact about the U.P. is, not that the population remained stationary for a half century, but rather that there is anyone at all left there. For half a century it had been a chronically depressed area. That the situation is not worse is explained by a substantial development of tourist, resort, and summer home business, plus modest gains from efforts to attract new industries to the region.

Does the experience of this one part of one state have significance for the entire nation? In the discussion of economic growth in Chapter 9 it is suggested that our country's population will double in the second half of the twentieth century and that the real gross national product will be doubled within twenty years and then doubled again in the following two decades. Are these forecasts reliable? And what of the longer future? Is it possible that exhaustion of one or more key natural resources might slow down the growth of the American economy, nay, might even bring about a contracting economy? Although, as is pointed out in the same chapter, comparative abundance of natural resources is a minor factor in explaining the comparative riches of the people of different countries, it is still true that, whatever the productive structure of a nation, unless there is a change in the product-and-service mix or in productive technology, an increase in real national *output* requires approximately the same increase in the *input* of energy and raw materials. Therefore, the American gross national product cannot be quadrupled within forty years unless these inputs also are approximately quadrupled. The relationship of these inputs to total national output and to per capita output and income, therefore, is the reason for a proper interest in the conservation of natural resources—soil, timber, minerals, water, and air.

## PRECONSERVATION PROFLIGACY

Before the colonization of America, European nations had faced problems of conservation of certain types of resources—notably forests, farmland, and wild game—and had developed rudimentary policies for their proper use. The requirements of conservation were somewhat different then. Populations were smaller, and industrialization had not yet started. The laws on conservation were geared to the needs of a static civilization. Many such laws served only the purpose of protecting the vested interests of the nobility. However, the elements of a common-sense attitude toward preserving and protecting the sources of material well-being were in evidence, and law and custom were molded about the need to exercise prudence in consumption.

The discovery and colonization of the New World had a great impact on traditional, conservative attitudes about resources. When America's great untouched storehouse of resources was revealed to her early settlers, the old European ecological balance was upset. At that time both the explosion of population and industrialization were unforeseen; so that thought about need for resources, if any was engaged in, did not recognize the essential changes that were soon to take place in the size and shape of man's demand for natural wealth. As America's abundance began to be revealed toward the end of the seventeenth century, not only did the lack of industrialization and the near-static world population cause demand for natural resources to be stable at a low level, but also the demand was mainly for self-replenishing resources. The stage was properly set for what followed.

Conservation thought did not take root in America along with other philosophies of law and government brought here by our settlers. Perhaps it was the American emphasis on individuality and freedom—responsible for most of the differences between the Old and New Worlds at that time—that established each man's license to do as he chose with what resources he could command. But whatever the moral rationale for the profligacy that became the American way during the settlement of our country, there were sound economic arguments for it as well. The demands of a young, dynamic economy are different from those of a mature system. The great trees that were cut and burned by the thousands of acres to provide clear farmland were, economically speaking, just big *weeds*. Farmland, on the contrary was precious. Laissez-faire policies, and the attendant apparent waste, may, therefore, not have been unwise *at that time*.

## ADMINISTRATION OF THE
## PUBLIC LANDS

Lands not already privately owned at the time the United States gained political jurisdiction over them generally became part of the "public domain," that is, the property of the citizenry at large, subject to the control of the Federal Government. These holdings have included most of the territory of the U.S.; 1.8 billion acres have been in the public domain at one time or another—the total present acreage of the country being 2.3 billion. For years it was national policy to transfer these lands rapidly to private ownership in order to contribute to development of the lands and to national growth. About 1.1 billion acres of the original public domain have been transferred from Federal to private ownership. In 1960 the Federal Government still held 800 million acres.*

Disposition of the public domain lands has been handled in various ways. Following the Northwest Ordinance of 1787 and the Grayson Land Ordinance of 1785, much of the land was surveyed into townships and 640-acre sections. These and similar acts established the transfer policy for years to come. The minimum price was originally set at $1 per acre under the acts; but land sales were regarded as an important revenue source, so the price was raised to $2 per acre until 1820, when it was reduced to $1.25. In addition to sales to individuals, many large grants and sales were made to states and communities.†

As the nation became wealthier, and as the fever of expansion waxed under the promotional activities of railroads and frontier governments, acquiring land was made easier. Acts in 1830 and 1841 gave squatters certain rights in title to the public lands they occupied. In 1862 revenue

* U.S. Bureau of the Census, *Statistical Abstract of the United States: 1961* (Washington, D.C.: U.S. Government Printing Office, 1961), pp. 182, 183.

† Hugh T. Lefler (ed.), *A History of the United States* (New York: Meridian, 1960), pp. 224–228.

considerations disappeared from land disposal laws, and "squatters' rights" were given full Federal blessing with the passage of the Homestead Act. This law (which is still in force with respect to part of the remaining public domain) permitted any settler who made certain improvements and lived on a 160-acre tract for five years to receive a patent of title to the land. In 1912 the five-year tenancy requirement was reduced to three.

Special policies were employed to hasten the disposal of land of certain types. The Timber Culture Act of 1873 and an amending act in 1878 made successive relaxations in the procedure for obtaining valuable forest land not covered by the Homestead Act. The Desert Land Act of 1877 and liberalizing amendments in 1909 and 1916 made potentially valuable desert tracts available at very low cost.

A large portion of the public domain was given to subsidize certain industries, notably the railroads, in order to enhance the value for settlement of the remaining public land. This part of Federal land policy has been criticized sharply. Many have contended that the grants were an unnecessary, overly generous giveaway. On the other hand, although the transcontinental railroads surely would have been built eventually even without land grants, the grants speeded the settlement of the West. Furthermore, the land-grant railroads recompensed the government by carrying its freight at reduced rates for many years.

The need for a change in policy on national resources was first felt with respect to land. As mentioned before, this need for more restriction on developmental consumption came about as the frontier was pushed to the Pacific and our "manifest destiny" became fulfilled.

## EARLY GROWTH OF U.S. CONSERVATION POLICY

The first real evidence of any concern at high levels for our fast-disappearing resources came in the 1870s with the proposal by Carl Schurz, Secretary of the Interior, for a national forest system. Schurz proposed that timberlands remaining in the public domain be set aside for the protection of watersheds and the preservation of saw logs.

Appreciation of the peril in waste of resources developed and spread most rapidly in academic circles at that time. Two reports by the American Association for the Advancement of Science (in 1873 and 1890) spoke critically of our immoderate past practices and urged reform. However, strong vested interests and a somewhat indifferent public prevented any broad measures just then.

General conservation reform was to await the intense campaigns of Gifford Pinchot and Theodore Roosevelt, decades later. But piecemeal progress did continue. In 1871 a Commissioner of Fish and Fisheries was placed in charge of the new U.S. Fish Commission, and in 1885 the broader Bureau of Biological Survey was created, in the Department of Agriculture. In 1888 a forerunner of the present Bureau of Reclamation was established in the Department of the Interior to administer the Government's interests in irrigation, and the first national forest was sequestered in 1891.

In the first quarter of the twentieth century industrialization came of sufficient age so that some could see its proportions and portent for the future. Calculations and projections showed that our economy of plenty was in jeopardy. This quarter century brought such active and influential reformers as Pinchot and Roosevelt into the conservation movement.

Gifford Pinchot was head of the U.S. Forest Service under President Theodore Roosevelt. Pinchot conceived and Roosevelt approved a unified national program for the conservation of vital natural resources. In pursuance of this plan the two conservationists secured a number of fragmentary changes and reforms. The bulk of their proposals met very stiff opposition. An international conference on resources and conservation was planned, but Taft was sworn in as Roosevelt's successor before it could be held. The meeting was canceled on inauguration day. This was a triumph for the antifederalists, who feared that the Government was seizing control of the nation's resources.

Although the real gains of the conservationists in this period were small, conservation had become an issue. It was discussed and studied. The battle lines began to form. Some battles were won easily by the Government: those which required only changes in too-liberal policies or the establishment of supervisory bureaus. The Forest Service (in the Department of Agriculture) was created in 1906 and the Bureau of Mines (in the Department of Interior) in 1910. In 1920 the Mineral Leasing Act placed jurisdiction of certain mineral lands with the Department of the Interior, and hydroelectric projects on navigable waterways were placed under the Federal Power Commission's supervision.

Other battles for conservation were won through education. Not all the nation's primary users of resources were insensitive to pleas for moderation and efficiency. Furthermore, technology prompted some reforms; newer methods had less voracious appetites for raw materials.

## INFLUENCE OF DEPRESSION AND WAR

Two great national convulsions stimulated interest in conservation. The first was the depression of the 1930s. Among the consequences of the upset economy of the time was the creation of a Civilian Conservation Corps (CCC). An activity designed to relieve unemployment and perform needed tasks in the public out-of-doors, the CCC and its work had the desirable side effect of drawing attention to the problems of America's natural resources.

Nor was the CCC the only depression-related public conservation project. The great dust bowl—the drought in the prairies—was an aggravating factor in the depression. The Soil Conservation Service was established in the Department of Agriculture to teach soil conservation methods to farmers. The SCS also did much to stop attempts to cultivate submarginal lands which should have been returned to grass or forest. And the Tennessee Valley Authority (TVA) had conservation as one of its objectives.

Later, World War II and the cold war pounded home the crucial importance of raw materials and other resources to national defense. Production of war materials superimposed a demand for resources on top of the already large civilian consumers' demand. Furthermore, we became aware that foreign sources cannot always be relied upon in a national emergency. Stockpiles or domestic production of critical resources became an integral part of our philosophy of conservation. And because concern is more easily excited over defense needs than over ordinary conservation problems, military necessity began to loom prominent in national conservation policy.

## PRESENT CONSERVATION OBJECTIVES

What is the general national policy on conservation? Is the policy sound? What obstacles lie in the way of an ideal conservation program?

Realistically speaking, conservation is not an ancient, fundamental American institution. It is a condition that has evolved haphazardly through piecemeal legislation and private restraints. It is caught up, at many points of serious conflict, with politics and private interests.

The free market is the primary mechanism of allocation of resources and the chief determinant of their rates of consumption. Public policy, however, is properly concerned with future requirements of resources for economic growth.

Factors other than the need for raw material inputs also influence conservation policy. Foreign policy is one. The U.S. at one time, for diplomatic reasons, imported sugar from Cuba subject to a quota maximum but at a price pegged above that of the market. Such arrangements are still widely used for helping out friendly nations and for gaining tariff concessions for U.S. goods. The conservation aspect arises when the U.S. is also a producer of the commodity imported under such a subsidy.

Another special factor is the use of conservation as a tool for the development of regions. The Tennessee Valley Authority is the outstanding example.

Conservation may be used as an instrument of economic stabilization. The CCC of New Deal days epitomized this factor in the shaping of conservation policy. More usually the stabilization sought comes at a different stage; e.g., a new dam will stabilize the agriculture of the surrounding area by reducing the feast-to-famine cycle of crop production due to uncertain water supply. Or again, a region in general economic decline may undergo a change from marginal farming to grazing or timber as a result of a policy aimed at strengthening the economy of that region.

## ORGANIZATION AND ADMINISTRATION

We practice conservation for such a wide range of reasons, and there are so many categories of resources, that it is not surprising to find many agencies performing administrative tasks in this field. Conservation problems have been tackled at all levels of government, too—from national on down to local—and there are administrative agencies in all of these layers.

At the national level several departments have conservation activities. The Department of Agriculture has the Soil Conservation Service and the U.S. Forest Service. The Department of the Interior has the Bureau of Land Management (managing 475 million acres of Federal lands), the Bureau of Reclamation, the National Park Service, and the Fish and Wildlife Service. The Department of Commerce provides services related to conservation efforts by supplying data on population, weather, foreign trade, and domestic production. It also has an Office of Area Development. The roles of the Departments of State and of Defense follow from their concern with supplies of critical materials and with trade as an instrument of foreign policy.

Several independent agencies are active in conservation: the Atomic Energy Commission, the Tennessee Valley Authority, the Federal Power Commission, and others. Special study commissions have been appointed from time to time to make studies and to report on particular problems.

State governments also have agencies for conservation—some good, some bad, some sufficient, many deficient—patterned according to their several economies and conservation problems.

## THE STATUS OF OUR RESOURCES

Where does the U.S. stand today in reserves of resources? Are we nearly due for serious shortages? Will depletion of domestic raw materials help to price American-made products out of world trade? Or is the picture reasonably bright after all? What are our deficiencies, and where are we strong?

Two prefatory remarks are in order. First, it should be noted that resources may be classified as those that are *renewable*, in that stocks can be replenished or have a natural tendency to replenish themselves when undisturbed, and those that are *nonrenewable*. The former group includes water, farm land, and forests. The latter group includes mineral deposits, which, once exploited, are gone forever. These classes must be viewed somewhat differently. In the case of a nonrenewable resource we need to look at the *magnitude* of the reserve. When a resource is renewable, we should inquire into the *rate of renewal* in the light of future needs.

Second, figures giving reserves of resources in terms of years' supplies can be misleading, being often based on known reserves (often tenuous) and present consumption rates. But new deposits are found at irregular intervals, and suspected reserves are proved up, extending expiration deadlines. Also lower grades of the resource which are not counted in the reserves may become economically workable, sometimes because of tchnological advances rather than shortages.

On the other hand, both population and per capita consumption of materials are increasing; the latter rate being hard to forecast for specific materials into the remoter future.

## MINERALS

The Bureau of Mines compiled in the early 1950s a table of 40 minerals selected as the most essential to industry and national defense. At the time, it was felt that only four could be produced at the current rate for over 1,000 years. Five would last 100 to 1,000 years. The remaining 31 would be exhausted within a century. The outlook for a few sample minerals on the Bureau's list: iron ore, 75 years; natural gas, 55 years; aluminum, 30 years; copper, 25 years; zinc, 20 years; lead, 15 years; petroleum, 14 years. A 1958 study showed that the U.S. was self-sufficient in only magnesium and molybdenum among 32 vital minerals.*

The fossil fuels—coal, oil, and gas—are our major sources of power at present. In addition, they have uses as raw materials for processing and manufacture into such nonenergy products as chemicals, textiles, pharmaceuticals, and lubricants.

As mentioned above, reserves of petroleum were once estimated at 14 years and of gas at 55, but new discoveries have kept advancing the dates for extinction of these resources. Restrictions on domestic production and consequent importing have eased the situation, as have discoveries of methods to squeeze the last possible drops out of old oilfields. Nevertheless, oil and gas are potentially in short supply.

It has been predicted that coal reserves will last for various numbers of years, from several hundred to several thousand. Perhaps the higher estimates are overoptimistic, for the reason that they include coal of lower grades. Coking coal of primary quality is not overabundant. Fur-

* *Science Newsletter,* "U.S. Self-Sufficient in 2 of 32 Vital Minerals," July 5, 1958, p. 5.

thermore, the coal industry has revived somewhat in recent years, and consumption seems to be at a brisker pace.

While many feel that hydroelectricity and atomic energy are our salvation from the consequences of exhaustion of fossil fuels, they would not take care of the nonfuel uses of coal, oil, and gas. Atomic energy cannot replace oil as a lubricant, and falling water does not yield chemical by-products such as come from coal. Many substitutes will have to be found to replace the three fossil fuels in all their diversity of uses.

## MINERALS FROM THE SEA

Sea water is a remarkable substance. It is heavier than pure water, weighing 64 pounds per cubic foot, as compared to 62.4. The additional weight is due to the treasure of mineral wealth dissolved in this vast liquid mine. A single cubic mile of sea water contains 166 million tons of salts. Most of the tonnage is sodium chloride, but also present in quantity are magnesium chloride, magnesium sulphate, calcium sulphate, potassium sulphate, calcium carbonate, and magnesium bromide. Altogether, about 50 elements have been analyzed and found in sea water.

In addition to salts, the sea is full of dissolved organic matter. It has been estimated that the dissolved organic substance in the sea is equal to 20,000 times the world's wheat harvest for one year.

Historically, the removal of minerals from the sea began with the ancient Chinese. Two thousand years ago they tapped sea water trapped underground, brought it to the surface in bamboo pipes, and evaporated it for its salt content. In modern times the noted German chemist, Fritz Haber, became intrigued by the possibility of extracting gold from gold salts dissolved in sea water. Even at the enormous dilution of two parts per billion, there are 11 tons of dissolved gold in a cubic mile of sea. As there are more than 300 million cubic miles of water in the sea, this gold hoard could provide every man with more than Midas ever dreamed of. Haber wanted merely to extract enough of the yellow metal to pay Germany's World War I indebtedness. His floating laboratory, SS *Meteor*, made numerous Atlantic crossings between 1924 and 1928, sampling the water; but no economical method of extraction was discovered. A later experimenter named Blackmore spent $5,000 to obtain five dollars' worth of gold and silver from sea water.

Better success followed when experimenters pursued less valuable but more highly concentrated minerals. Since June 1942, a plant in Freeport, Texas, has produced 36,000 tons per year of the light metal magnesium from sea water. Here at last is a source of metal which does not rely upon exhaustible buried reserves. Bromine is another element recoverable from the sea—99 per cent of the world's production comes from sea salts.

Although only a few elements can be recovered profitably from the sea, at present prices and with present techniques, the future may bring great changes. Better methods of recovery (perhaps brought about by economic necessity) may yield metals other than magnesium, and other elements. Magnesium itself, when properly alloyed, can be put to many uses as a substitute for other materials if necessary.

The sea may yield resources in another way—mines producing solid ores might be developed on the shallow continental shelves. This area already accounts for some important oil production.

## FARM LAND

Millions of acres of farm land have been injured or eliminated by erosion, dust storms, reduction of fertility, highway construction, and residential expansion. At the same time, population has grown and the demands for food and fiber have soared. Nevertheless, we are not experiencing shortages; on the contrary, as we saw earlier, we are burdened with some mountainous surpluses of farm products.

Despite the surpluses, concern is often expressed about the future. Will population growth outrun the contracting farm land supply? Will shortages of agricultural products retard or reverse our economic growth?

These questions are discussed in Chapter 21, and it is appropriate, therefore, merely to restate the conclusion reached there, that the factors making for increased agricultural productivity may be expected to continue to become more favorable in the foreseeable future, at a rate fast enough to accommodate population growth. The foregoing conclusion, however, does not settle the question of the desirability of a national population policy based on aesthetic reasons.

## FORESTS

Our problem of conservation of timber has eased in recent years. A renewable resource, trees can be planted for later consumption, and this is being done. Government has been especially effective in forest conservation because much forest land is Federal or state property. Also, tree farming has recently become an important private enterprise business.

Tree planting and harvesting are about in balance now, with perhaps a slight edge in favor of planting. There is some dispute about the facts, because the numerous one-man operations and the extensiveness of forest lands preclude an accurate census. Other problem areas are a possible future expansion of demand for forest products beyond expectations, and the continuing loss of timber from forest fires, disease, and insects. The present rather satisfactory condition has been brought about by both governmental and private efforts.

Federal Government action has followed two paths: Federal owner-ship of national forests and Federal advice on and regulation of forest conservation, primarily through what is now the United States Forest Service. In the 1800s there were some efforts by state governments, with some local action, to protect their forest resources. But it remained for the combination of Theodore Roosevelt in the White House and Gifford Pinchot as head of the Bureau of Forestry to dramatize the necessity for conservation and to take great strides toward achievement of the con-servation goal.

The establishment of national forests was started on a limited scale in 1892, when President Harrison signed the order which created the Yel-lowstone National Park Timberland Reserve. In 1897 Congress passed an Act for the Administration of Forest Reserves. This Act contained a significant statement which clearly indicated the objective and viewpoint of the Congress. The National Forest Reserves were created, it said, ". . . for the purpose of securing favorable conditions of water flows and to furnish a continuous supply of timber for the use and necessities of citizens of the United States. . . ." Gradually an increasing amount of land was withdrawn from the public domain and established as national for-ests. By 1950 there were 150 national forests, located in 40 states and in Alaska and Puerto Rico, with a combined total area of 180,000,000 acres. Development of these areas to their maximum potential utilization for timber is still proceeding.

The administration of the national forests is under the jurisdiction of the U.S. Forest Service. Besides administering the national forests, the Forest Service also engages in cooperative work with the states and with private owners on forest conservation. In addition, it does research in forestry. Cooperation with the states in forest fire protection was au-thorized by the Weeks Act of 1911 and further expanded by the Clarke–McNary Act of 1924. These Acts authorized the expenditure from Fed-eral funds of amounts not to exceed state and private expenditures for fire protection. This greatly encouraged state action on the forest prob-lem, and as a result many state departments of forestry were established.

Other aspects of cooperative work of the Forest Service with the states include the establishment of forest nurseries for replanting and reforesta-tion purposes. The Forest Service also provides advice on good forestry practices to private firms and individuals. Woodland management proj-ects have been set up in conjunction with the states to educate farm woodland owners in the profitable management and marketing of forest products. Cooperative programs of education have been established with many universities as an extension service of the Department of Agricul-ture. In general, the Forest Service has sought to encourage forest con-servation through advice and education rather than through Federal regulatory laws.

## STATE CONSERVATION ACTIVITIES

The bulk of the regulatory actions to restrict unsound timber cutting and to enforce forest conservation has been left to the states. Regulation and control by the states have followed a variety of patterns, and state legislation has pursued a number of specific objectives. These include forest fire control, forest pest control, and improvement of timber cutting practices. Great achievements have been made in all of these areas. As mentioned above, some of the states' efforts have been in conjunction with the Forest Service and with the aid of Federal funds. In general, state regulation has been accomplished through one or more of the following methods: regulation by statute or by a state agency; regulation through advice to and cooperation with private owners; and regulation through tax concessions. In addition, some states have established state forests pattern after the national forests.

## PRIVATE CONSERVATION ACTIVITIES

It should not be assumed that the governments have been alone in efforts toward forest conservation. Private individuals, organizations, and corporations also have recognized the problem and have contributed to its amelioration. A few examples of such activities are presented in the following paragraphs.

Industrial firms and trade organizations have been ardent and vocal proponents of forest conservation in many instances. For example, American Forests Products Industries, Inc., is a nonprofit industry-sponsored organization which has been formed by the lumber companies to encourage better forest practices and of course to improve public relations. This organization has taken over the "Keep America Green" movement which had originated in the Pacific Northwest and has publicized this slogan until it has become a familiar phrase to school children and motorists in more than 30 states.

Another example is the tree farm movement, originally begun as a formal program on the Clemons Tree Farm, owned and operated by the Weyerhaeuser Timber Company. This movement has spread to more than 7,400 timber owners, managing some 38,000,000 acres of tree farms. The tree farm program is dedicated to maintaining a favorable ratio between the number of trees grown and the number harvested. There are many other examples, similar in nature, of efforts by commercial companies to publicize and practice forest conservation.

Commercial firms have been aided and often spurred on in their efforts toward better forest practices by citizens' societies and professional groups which also have been interested in the subject of conservation. One such society is the Society of American Foresters, organized in 1900, which represents all branches of forestry. Article 2 of the Society's original constitution sets forth the Society's objectives as follows: "to further the cause of forestry in America by fostering a spirit of comradeship among foresters; by creating opportunities for a free interchange of views upon forestry and allied subjects; and by disseminating a knowledge of the purpose and achievements of forestry." The Society has worked for legislation on forest conservation, and has helped to arouse public interest in the subject. In its early years most of its members were governmental employees. Today more than half of its fourteen thousand members work for private firms.

Great progress has been made—by public and private efforts. As our forests once again grow to the point where the supply of timber is adequate for current and anticipated future needs, the need for governmental control and regulation may diminish. In that case voluntary and cooperative programs may well replace the present statutory regulations. However, the interest of government in the general welfare of the people will require some regulation and will justify some governmental ownership of timber lands, not only to assure an adequate supply of timber, but also to provide for such additional purposes as recreational areas for the public, wildlife preservation and watershed management.

## RECREATIONAL LAND

Land for recreational purposes is a less-often-thought-about natural resource. It is directly "consumed" by the general public. Outdoor recreation is an economic good in strong demand and of inestimable value to our highly citified populace. We should plan to have enough to accommodate a rising population and a continuing trend to urbanization.

Good recreational land is becoming scarce and expensive. In order to provide this resource, our governments operate many fine parks, and the national and state forests have been developed for recreation as well as for conservation of timber and wildlife. Eventually, the national and state forests may turn out to be more valuable for recreation than for timber.

Steps are being taken to set aside additional wilderness areas. Such areas would be closed to development other than for recreational purposes, such as camping and fishing. Strong opposition and quarreling over sites has come from local interests which would prefer more intensive development of the proposed reserves. However, the necessity for preserving some wilderness areas seems to be felt strongly enough to assure action.

A step taken in 1962 may turn out to have immense significance, not only for urban America, but also for rural families. The Food and Agriculture Act of 1962 authorizes the Farmers Home Administration to lend money to operators of family-size farms to finance recreational facilities, thereby supplementing their farm incomes by charging fees for their use.

Recreational enterprises for which buildings and equipment may thus be
financed included camp grounds, swimming facilities, tennis courts, golf
courses, riding stables, vacation cottages, picnic grounds, hunting preserves, and ponds and lakes for boating and fishing. Even though these
activities do not promise to solve the farm problem, they may provide
welcome recreational facilities for urban people and income for rural
families.

Also in 1962 was created in the Department of the Interior the Bureau
of Outdoor Recreation. Its principal activities are these:

[1]   Coordination of related Federal outdoor recreation programs;

[2]   Stimulation of and provision for assistance to the states in outdoor
recreation;

[3]   Sponsorship and conduct of outdoor recreation research;

[4]   Encouragement of interstate and regional cooperation in outdoor
recreation;

[5]   Conduct of recreation resources surveys; and

[6]   Formulation of a nationwide outdoor recreation plan on the
basis of state, regional, and Federal plans.

## THE QUANTITY WATER PROBLEM

Water is currently the resource in crisis—in both quantity and quality.
Regional shortages of usable water have already slowed the growth and
delimited the potential of some areas. Pressure at the taps in many cities
drops to a trickle at peak demand periods. Needed suburban developments are sometimes not built because no water is available to them.
Desert lands wait to bloom under irrigation, but the available water is
spoken for.

The water problem is not just one of inadequate quantity relative to
the demand; we have a pollution problem too.

To complicate matters, water has some of the characteristics of a nonrenewable resource. In some locations water is pumped from wells drilled
in semiporous rock beds. When the water is removed, the level of water
in the wells is depressed, and because seepage into the area is impeded
by the rock, recovery is very slow. Also, removal of forests and thick
wild grass cover has stepped up the rate of runoff from land into the
rivers, so that precipitated water returns to the sea without seeping
down to the water table.

The problem can be stated briefly in terms of supply and demand: the
nation's water supply is fixed, but the demand is constantly growing.
Use of water has increased enormously in the United States, and it bids
fair to soar in the future. Here are the figures of the Department of
Health, Education, and Welfare's Water Supply and Pollution Control
Commission.

*Table 22.1*

## PAST AND FUTURE USE OF FRESH WATER

(Billions of Gallons per Day)

|  | 1900 | 1920 | 1940 | 1950 | 1960 | 1970 | 1980 |
|---|---|---|---|---|---|---|---|
| Municipal | 3.0 | 6.0 | 10.1 | 14.1 | 22.0 | 27.0 | 37.2 |
| Industrial | 15.0 | 27.2 | 52.0 | 84.0 | 159.9 | 218.3 | 394.2 |
| Agricultural | 22.2 | 58.4 | 74.1 | 104.6 | 141.0 | 165.9 | 165.7 |
| Total | 40.2 | 91.6 | 136.4 | 202.7 | 322.9 | 411.2 | 597.1 |

SOURCE: U.S. Department of Health, Education, and Welfare, *Clean Water, A National Resource* (Washington, D.C.: Public Health Service, 1960), p. 4.

As shown in Table 22.2, the increase in water consumption closely parallels the rise in the gross national product. The figures suggest that the latter cannot increase in the future without a corresponding increase in usage of water.

*Table 22.2*

## WATER USAGE AND GROSS NATIONAL PRODUCT

|  | DAILY AVERAGE USAGE (Billions of Gallons) | GNP (Billions of 1961 Dollars) | RATIO: WATER USAGE TO GNP |
|---|---|---|---|
| 1930 | 110 | $190 | .58 |
| 1940 | 136 | 237 | .58 |
| 1950 | 203 | 366 | .55 |
| 1960 | 323 | 511 | .63 |
|  |  | Average | .585 |
| 1970 | 411 | Commission's estimate | |
| 1980 | 597 | ” ” | |

SOURCES: Of water usage figures: *Clean Water, A National Resource, loc. cit.;* of GNP figures; *Economic Report of the President: 1962* (Washington, D.C.: U.S. Government Printing Office, 1962), p. 208.

The Commission estimates 1970's daily use at 411 billion gallons, 1980's at 597 billion. These appear to be conservative estimates. If the GNP rises to $780 billion in 1970 (the present writer's estimate), and if the established average ratio between water usage and GNP is maintained (.585), water usage in 1970 will be slightly more than 450 billion gallons. Since the GNP may rise by another 40 to 50 per cent in the 1970s, the Commission's estimate of water usage for 1980 looks low.

Yet, in spite of this growing need for fresh water, the nation's true natural water supply, averaged over the years, is constant. The United States has an average annual rainfall of about 30 inches (4,300 billion gallons a day). Most of this (about 21.5 inches) is dissipated by evaporation, by runoff into the oceans, and by the water uses of natural foliage. A large part of the remaining 8.5 inches goes underground. The fresh water supply actually available for man's use has been steadily increased only through large expenditures involved in building dams and reservoirs to capture and store flood waters, and through the pumping of water from underground sources. However, in some places, particularly in the Southwestern states, the underground water in being drawn up at a much faster rate than it can be replenished by nature. The Water Supply and Pollution Control Commission of the Department of Health, Education, and Welfare estimates that by the employment of other costly techniques, such as reduction of evaporation through the use of chemical films on water surfaces, conversion of salt and brackish waters into fresh water, and the inducing of additional rainfall over land areas through cloud seeding, the dependable fresh water supply can be increased to 515 billion gallons a day by 1980. (See Table 22.3.)

*Table 22.3*

RATE OF USE OF FRESH WATER VERSUS
ESTIMATED DEPENDABLE SUPPLY

(Billions of Gallons per Day)

|                    | 1900 | 1920  | 1940  | 1950  | 1960  | 1970  | 1980  |
|--------------------|------|-------|-------|-------|-------|-------|-------|
| Rate of Use        | 40.2 | 91.6  | 136.4 | 202.7 | 322.9 | 411.2 | 597.1 |
| Dependable Supply  | 95.0 | 125.0 | 245.0 | 270.0 | 315.0 | 395.0 | 515.0 |

SOURCE: *Clean Water, A Natural Resource, op. cit.,* p. 6.

These figures indicate that nationwide demand will exceed supply before long, assuming that every drop is used, and used only once. It would be uneconomical to trap all rainwater for use before it is discharged into the sea, but on the other hand some water is used twice before discharge to sea or atmosphere. Not all water can be reused— most of that which is used in irrigation is lost into the air. We can conclude that the evidence proves that sources other than rainfall over our land area must be trapped to prevent a serious water emergency. Only the date of the emergency can be questioned.

Hence the urgency of developing inexpensive ways of making sea water fresh. The Office of Saline Water was created in the Department of the Interior in 1952 to promote study of this problem. It inaugurated a program of development designed to build water conversion facilities of several types and test them for effectiveness and economy. Thus far, none has managed to get costs down to a practicable level for general use; but scientific and engineering efforts are continuing.

## THE QUALITY WATER PROBLEM

Water pollution is an ugly and sickening subject, but it is also an ugly, sickening, and menacing condition—one that is bad and getting worse.

Crops irrigated by waters containing sewage pollution may transmit disease. Waters carrying industrial pollution, such as chemical wastes, can damage the crops they irrigate. Many natural streams formerly relied on to provide water for livestock have become so polluted that their continued use is unsafe. Fish desirable for food do not thrive in heavily polluted waters. Shad have almost disappeared from some rivers in the East. Large areas of shellfish-producing waters have been closed because of the dangers of pollution. Commercial fishermen find their fish catches smaller and sometimes unmarketable because of bad tastes and odors. Outdoor recreation and the recreation industry suffer from the pollution's damaging effects. Beaches have been closed to swimmers because of health hazards. Boating, camping, and sport fishing are much less desirable, if not dangerous, on polluted waters. Substantial economic loss is suffered by many areas due to water pollution. Some river valleys are nearly closed to further growth for lack of water of sufficiently good quality to nourish industries.

This critical situation is being partially alleviated by the reuse of large quantities of water as it flows in its natural watercourses from city to city and from state to state—a practice which, out of necessity, must be expanded in the future. This reuse of water is dramatically prominent in the hundreds of downstream cities and industries which lie along the banks of great rivers such as the Ohio. Water is taken from this river, used, and dumped back again an average of 3.7 times during its 1,000-mile course from the Alleghanies to its confluence with the Mississippi River at Cairo.*

But water must be of a suitable quality if it is to be reused, and here is where water pollution plays its greatest role as a menace to our society. Water from our streams and rivers currently provides most of our needs. This surface water is drawn off repeatedly from streams to community water systems or industrial intakes, then discharged—polluted—back into the streams. The same polluted watercourse is then used by the next downstream community or industry. There are limits, however, to the extent to which such polluted water can be economically treated at the point of community intake to make it safe for human consumption. In many parts of the country, because of pollution damage, it has already become very difficult for industries and agriculture to obtain usable water. Once pollution impairs the quality of water to the point where it is unfit for these purposes, the water is, in effect, destroyed for one whole natural cycle of evaporation and precipitation.

Pollution may seem to be an exaggerated danger, because modern purification techniques have made our municipal water supplies run clean and clear—and chlorinated. To the majority of us water is so plentiful and inexpensive compared to everything else we have to buy that we find it hard not to take it for granted.

But the truth is, as we have seen in the preceding section, that our

* *Ibid.*, p. 3.

fresh water supply is not inexhaustible, especially in view of the rate at which we are now polluting its sources. Moreover, the cost to treat water in order to make it suitable for use is on the increase. The present national water purification bill amounts to hundreds of millions of dollars yearly, not including the cost of the capital investment in buildings and equipment.* For many industries this cost is prohibitive in certain locations. Polluting our rivers, lakes, and bays, then trying to "purify" these waters to a usable condition, is a costly operation. What is needed is prevention rather than cure. In order to arouse support for and provide for effective administration of any practicable plan of prevention against water pollution, the public must be informed on the basic issues of the problem: What are the pollutants and how do they find their way into our waters? How serious is the situation—now and in the future? What is or is not being done at present in the way of preventive actions? What needs to be done?

The principal sources of pollutants which find their way into our natural waters are sanitary sewage, industrial wastes, and agricultural wastes. Sanitary sewage includes everything that does down the drains of a city and into its sewer system. This includes used water from toilets, bathtubs, and sinks and washings from restaurants, hotels, laundries, hospitals, and other establishments. Industrial wastes include acids, chemicals, oils, greases, and animal and vegetable matter—discharged by our factories, canneries, meat and poultry processing plants, oil fields, and mines. Agricultural wastes consist of the numerous insecticides, herbicides, and pesticides used in spraying and dusting crops and nuisance plants. These modern poisons are often washed into the streams along with silt after heavy rainfalls.

Reducing water pollution is a problem of social control, in which well-enforced laws have a part. It is noteworthy that it is easier to stop a factory from discharging industrial or other pollutants into the waters than to stop a city from emptying untreated sewage into the same waters. If the city refuses to build a sewage treatment plant, the state's enforcement problem is difficult.

Treatment plants remove the solids from the municipal sewage and industrial wastes flowing into them through sewage systems by settling and filtering processes, and then disinfect the effluent by chemical treatment before returning it to the natural watercourse. Wastes, such as radioactive material, which cannot be effectively treated in these plants are disposed of by other means in areas actively concerned with pollution control. One such method is to inject these wastes into deep underground formations where they will not harm fresh waters or mineral resources usable as industrial raw materials.

* United States Department of Health, Education, and Welfare, *Water Pollution in the United States*, (Public Health Service Publication No. 64, 1951), p. 9.

That pollution can be controlled by modern methods has been demonstrated in many areas throughout the country, notably by an interstate effort to clean up the Ohio River. But we aren't doing it on a nationwide scale.

Why has the construction of treatment plants been allowed to lag so far behind the need? The main reason is that the awareness and interest of the public in this problem has not been aroused sufficiently to offset the deterrent of the expense involved in building and operating these plants. Furthermore, when a city or an industry spends money to treat its wastes, the primary benefits are enjoyed by downstream communities and not by the community or corporation which is spending the money.

In a letter to the editor of *Time*, October 24, 1960, Walter M. Culkowski, of Oak Ridge, Tennessee, suggested this solution to the water pollution problem: Require each city, town, and industry to discharge its wastes upstream of its own water intakes. Whatever its other merits, the proposal does illustrate graphically the basic cause-and-effect phenomena of this nasty problem.

## ROLE OF THE FEDERAL GOVERNMENT

The taxpayers need some added impetus, and many municipalities require financial aid, to do their share toward abatement of pollution. Both of these are now being given through governmental programs created by legislation. The Federal Water Pollution Control Act of 1956 greatly broadened and strengthened the earlier legislation by providing grants to improve and strengthen state and interstate programs, more workable Federal enforcement, and more effective research. Yet the pollution problem continued to grow so rapidly that this legislation was seen to be inadequate. Congress responded by enacting the Federal Water Pollution Control Act Amendments of 1961, which provided a statutory basis for a sound Federal-state-local attack geared explicitly to the urgent need. This legislation did five important things: it broadened and strengthened the Federal Government's enforcement powers (the United States Department of Justice was enabled to enter a suit against the City of St. Joseph, Missouri, because that city's citizens had resisted Federal instruction and voted against bonds to finance sewage treatment[*]); it provided the basis for a greatly stepped-up program of construction of works for treatment of waste; it authorized increased Federal support of state and interstate programs for control of pollution; it called for an intensified program of research looking toward more effective methods of such control, with special emphasis on regional variations; and it extended Federal jurisdiction over to all abatement of pollution to all navigable waters.

[*] "Public Health Engineering," *Encyclopedia Britannica Book of the Year, 1961,* p. 581.

## ROLE OF THE STATES

Established policy places principal responsibility and authority for controlling pollution with the states, financial responsibility (with Federal aid) for providing treatment with the cities and industries that create the pollution. Thus the total job of control of water pollution is that of a partnership: cities and industries construct, operate, and maintain works for the abatement of pollution; states are concerned primarily with providing aid to local communities and industries in the design and operation of these works, with carrying on investigations of water pollution, and with admistering the regulatory provisions of the state laws; and the Federal responsibility is primarily a supporting one.

## AIR POLLUTION

*Air* has long been a standard textbook example of a *free good,* as distinguished from an *economic good.* In many parts of the United States today, however, air—*pure* air—is no longer a free good.

Polluted air ("smog") inflicts many costs—losses in crops, deterioration of metals and other materials, plus (greatest of all) losses of health and life.

Nearly anything foreign which may become dispersed in the air may be considered a pollutant, for a human being inhales about thirty pounds of air a day, and the lungs are easily affected by whatever is carried with this air. The air of our cities receives an immense quantity of airborne garbage. The combustion of coal and coke releases (in addition to other gases) sulfur dioxide into the air. This gas, noxious in itself, changes into sulfuric acid in the presence of sunlight and moisture.

Although liquid fuels burn more cleanly, they produce more exotic' poisons: methane, acetylene, aldehydes, alcohols, phenols, and ammoniates.

Programs for the abatement of air pollution have not been extensively installed as yet, but, where tried, such programs are quite effective. Pittsburgh is one city which has effectively combatted industrial smoke.

The elements of a smog-control campaign include systematic detection of specific irritants, tracing them to their source, and securing their elimination there. The technical means are sometimes a problem, but where laws quash the economic objections a workable control method is usually available; elaborate filters, washing systems, electrostatic precipitators, and better control of combustion have helped.

## THE OUTLOOK

The analysis presented here, based on the expectation of a continuation of wise public and private policies plus an almost unlimited confidence in what the scientists, inventors, and engineers will do in the future, suggests that, *in the United States,* shortages of suitable natural resources present some serious problems—problems for which solutions will be found (at a price, to be sure)—and therefore economic growth will not be reversed or even restricted.

If this reasoning is correct, it applies, *mutatis mutandis,* to many other countries. It does not apply, however, to all. In many lands, population pressure on natural resources is critical today and threatens economic growth.

Even in our country there remains the moral question of whether we ought to create problems for future generations. When we skim the cream from resources by taking the purest ores, the biggest trees, and the most fertile soils, we are demanding that our descendants be more efficient than we. They will have more people to support from poorer resources, and they will expect to live at least as well as we. Not only this, but the rising standard of living around the world will make keen the competition for imports of raw materials. The future generations of Americans will have their work cut out for them when they succeed their fortunate ancestors. Tomorrow will test the correctness of American theories on how a nation's natural resources should be managed.

## QUESTIONS AND PROBLEMS

1. Why does our future economic growth depend on our natural resources?
2. "America is making merry today but someday she will be sorry for having depleted her natural resources." Discuss what happens as natural resources are exhausted in an area, a nation, the world.
3. In your opinion, will economic growth in the U.S. be slowed, stopped, or reversed by exhaustion of natural resources?
4. What lessons can be learned from the history of conservation efforts in the United States?
5. Describe and evaluate our governmental policies with respect to the public domain lands.
6. Is it a sound arrangement to have the conservation activities of the Federal Government located in so many different agencies? Would it be better if they were consolidated into a Federal Conservation Agency (or Department)?
7. Why should governmental entities work on conservation? Why not leave it to private enterprise?
8. Why is reduction of water pollution such an intractable problem?
9. Why should the government build more dams to impound more water to irrigate little-used lands when we have farm surpluses?
10. What changes, if any, in governmental conservation programs do you favor? What changes do you forecast?

## SELECTED READINGS

ALLEN, SHIRLEY W. *Conserving Natural Resources*, 2nd ed. New York: McGraw-Hill Company, 1959.

BARNETT, HAROLD J., and CHANDLER MORSE. *Scarcity and Growth: The Economics of Natural Resource Availability*. Baltimore: Johns Hopkins Press, 1962.

DEWHURST, J. FREDERIC, AND ASSOCIATES. *America's Needs and Resources; A New Survey*. New York: Twentieth Century Fund, 1955.

JARRETT, HENRY (ed.). *Science and Resources: Prospects and Implications of Technological Advance*. Washington, D.C.: Resources for the Future, 1959.

KRUTILLA, JOHN V., and OTTO ECKSTEIN. *Multiple Purpose River Development*. Baltimore: Johns Hopkins Press, 1958.

LANDSBERG, HANS H., LEONARD L. FISCHMAN, and JOSEPH L. FISHER. *Resources in American Future: Patterns of Requirements and Availabilities, 1960–2000*. Baltimore: Johns Hopkins Press, 1962.

POTTER, NEAL, and FRANCIS T. CHRISTY. *Trends in Natural Resources Commodities*. Baltimore: Johns Hopkins Press, 1962.

President's Materials Policy Commission. *Resources for Freedom*. Washington, D.C.: Government Printing Office, 1952.

RIDGEWAY, MARIAN E. "The National Water Pollution Control Effort," *Quarterly Review of Economics and Business*, Spring 1963, pp. 51–63.

SPENGLER, JOSEPH J. *Natural Resources and Economic Growth*. Washington, D.C.: Resources for the Future, Inc., 1961.

U.S. Department of Agriculture, Forest Service. *Timber Resources for America's Future*. Washington, D.C.: U.S. Government Printing Office, 1958.

VOGT, WILLIAM. *People! Challenge to Survival*. New York: Sloane, 1960.

# 23 THE DEVELOPMENT OF HUMAN RESOURCES

In the earlier discussion of economic growth we stress the fact that, important though natural resources are in contributing to economic well-being, they are not nearly as important as human resources. Its *people* are a nation's most important potential asset. If their talents are developed, the nation will be progressive and prosperous, whether or not it possesses rich *natural* resources. If, contrariwise, their abilities are not developed, the country will be backward and poor, even if its people live amidst rich natural resources. The essence of the development of human resources is actions and programs that help people to help themselves to lead richer and more productive lives.

Nature provides certain amounts of both natural resources and human resources (if, in deference to ordinary usage, we may be permitted the questionable implication that what is human is anything other than natural). Both have to be developed. In the case of human resources the initial gift is called *heredity*, and the development of it in the aggregate results in *culture*. A low level of this development means a primitive, savage culture; a high level of it is what is called civilization. In the earlier discussion of *social control* we consider some of the *environmental* factors that condition the development of individual human beings. Health, ability, and character—qualities of body, mind, and heart—are developed as a part of the slow process of maturation. Private factors and public agencies influence the outcome. What activities should be carried on by private persons and agencies? What is the proper role of governmental entities? Are there activities that should be carried on through joint public-private action? In view of the primacy of the cultural factor in the determination of human well-being, these problems are perhaps the most urgent confronting our society today. People who are seriously ill, or uneducated, or antisocial, are likely to be low producers, to have small incomes, to be poor. If these people can be helped and thereby enabled to do better, poverty is reduced and economic growth is stimulated.

In families where these handicaps prevail the children are likely to inherit the handicaps—a condition that may be described as "inherited inferiority" results. Body, mind, and spirit are stunted by the home surroundings. The first step in human development, therefore, is the correction of this condition of unfavorable environment of children.

The process, however, does not end there. Adults also may need help— perhaps because they had received inadequate help when they were children, or perhaps because of unfavorably changing conditions that have overtaken them in later years. The nation's concern with its human resources, in short, is not limited to childhood; it continues throughout life.

## THE ROLE OF THE GOVERNMENT

The creation in 1953 of the Federal Department of Health, Education, and Welfare might suggest these inferences:

[1]   That the Federal Government had not been concerned with health, education, and welfare before that date;

[2]   That the Federal Government's concern with these matters finds expression only through that Department; and

[3]   That the Federal Government is alone in this concern, and that state and local governments do not share it.

Not one of these inferences would be accurate. Into the new department went many old Federal activities. One of these was the Public Health Service which had its genesis in an act of July 16, 1798, authorizing marine hospitals for the care of American Merchant Seamen. The Office of Education had been created in 1867. The Social Security Administration dates back to 1935 and the Office of Vocational Rehabilitation to 1943. The Bureau of Federal Credit Unions traces its lineage back to 1934, the Food and Drug Administration and its predecessors to 1907.

A simple listing of the other Cabinet departments of the Federal Government will indicate at once that concern with the general welfare —often on a segmented basis—is a widespread governmental preoccupation—not limited to the Department of Health, Education, and Welfare. One of the independent agencies that is concerned with problems in this area is the Housing and Home Finance Agency. The importance and variety of the activities carried on by this agency may have been among the considerations that prompted President Kennedy, in 1961, to propose the establishment of a new Cabinet Department of Housing and Urban Affairs. The proposal was rejected by the Congress, but the activities if not the title remain important.

State and local governments have been concerned with welfare in both the broad and the narrow sense throughout our history. At the present time, indeed, one of the important issues of public policy is the proper roles of the Federal Government on the one hand and of state and local governments on the other.

## THE DEVELOPMENT OF EDUCATION

Education is a key factor in the development of human resources. This fact seems to have been recognized, dimly at least, throughout the history of mankind. Education—informal or formal—has existed since the beginning of the race; and man's progress from primitive existence to civilized living has been paralleled by and brought about by an increase of education.

In the beginning, education seems to have been carried on informally in families. Later, with the emergence of a class of religious leaders—priests or medicine men—these individuals took over indoctrination in morals and behavior and probably established, however modestly, the first formal schools. It was not until millenia later that education was taken over by the state. And the question whether education should be undertaken and controlled by the family, by the religious authorities, or by the state has long been a social issue.

For many centuries, except for some occupational training, what we should today call really substantial education was limited to the children of the rich. It is only in the last two centuries that free public education, accompanied by compulsory school attendance laws, has blossomed. Today so widespread is public education that it is perhaps hard to realize that social reformers were agitating for nonsectarian public schools, supported by taxes instead of individual tuition, as late as the first half of the nineteenth century.

Free, tax-supported public education began with elementary schools, and legal hurdles had to be overcome before it was decided that taxes could legally be collected for the support of high schools. Provision of free collegiate education proceeded more slowly. In many a state the early pattern was that there would be one state university and one land-grant college (which might or might not be separate institutions), and also one or more normal schools, which in the beginning offered only two-year programs and did not grant degrees. These institutions developed and proliferated. Two-year normal schools became four-year "colleges of education." Presently the qualifier was dropped and they became four-year state colleges, and later, in many cases, "universities." State universities have opened branches; land-grant colleges have become universities; junior colleges have multiplied.

In 1960 total enrollment in schools was 46,259,000—divided thus: kindergarten and elementary, 32,441,000; high school, 10,249,000; and college and professional schools, 3,570,000. About 85 per cent of the pupils in elementary and secondary schools, and about 60 per cent of students at the higher level, were in public institutions.*

## FINANCING EDUCATION

So much has been written and said about the financial problems of schools that it would be easy to conclude that education and educational expenditures have been lagging seriously in the United States. In fact, however, schools and schooling have increased pretty steadily ever since the beginning of the Republic. In 1920 national expenditures on schools and colleges totaled $2 billion, a figure which has risen to nearly $25 billion at present. (It should be noted, though, that the commodity price level is about 50 per cent higher now than it was in 1920.) Of the current amount about 75 per cent comes from public sources—Federal, state, and local governments. About nine tenths of these governmental contributions come from state and local governments, about one tenth from the Federal government.

In short, the fact is that despite the strain on state and local finances, large increases in expenditures for education have been made. The expenditure per student (after correction for changes in the purchasing power of the dollar) has been steady thus far through the twentieth century, and the number of students has increased tremendously.

There will be more students—many more—in future decades; expenditures on education will have to be increased, and increased substantially; the economy also will grow, and past experience suggests that growth of the economy may be counted on to generate much if not all of the additional money that will be needed.

One thing is certain: this is no time in the affairs of the nation to restrict educational activity. Indeed, it is essential that education be expanded and extended; and this will inevitably involve a continuing debate over the proper role of the Federal Government in the process.

## THE FEDERAL GOVERNMENT
## AND EDUCATION

In his 1962 message to Congress on educational needs, President Kennedy said:

No task before our nation is more important than expanding and improving the educational opportunities of all our people. The concept that every American deserves the opportunity to attain the highest level of education of which he is capable is not new to this Administration—it is a traditional

---

* *Statistical Abstract of the United States: 1961* (Washington, D.C.: U.S. Government Printing Office, 1961), pp. 107, 114, 121.

ideal of democracy. But it is time that we moved toward the fulfillment of this ideal with more vigor and less delay.

For education is both the foundation and the unifying force of our democratic way of life. It is the mainspring of our economic and social progress. It is the highest expression of achievement in our society, ennobling and enriching human life. In short, it is at the same time the most profitable investment society can make and the richest reward it can confer.

Today, more than at any other time in our history, we need to develop our intellectual resources to the fullest. But the facts of the matter are that many thousands of our young people are not educated to their maximum capacity —and they are not, therefore, making the maximum contribution of which they are capable to themselves, their families, their communities, and the nation. Their talents lie wasted—their lives are frequently pale and blighted— and their contribution to our economy and culture are lamentably below the levels of their potential skills, knowledge, and creative ability. Educational failures breed delinquency, despair, and dependence. They increase the costs of unemployment and public welfare. They cut our potential national economic output by billions. They deny the benefits of our society to large segments of our people. They undermine our capability as a nation to discharge world obligations. All this we cannot afford—better schools we can afford. . . .

An educational system which is inadequate today will be worse tomorrow, unless we act now to improve it. We must provide facilities for 14,000,000 more elementary, secondary school, and college students by 1970, an increase of 30 per cent. College enrollments alone will nearly double, requiring approximately twice as many facilities to serve nearly 7,000,000 students by 1970. We must find the means of financing a 75 per cent increase in the total cost of education—another $20 billion a year for expansion and improvement —particularly in facilities and instruction which must be of the highest quality if our nation is to achieve its highest goals.

One may agree with the foregoing statements without agreeing with the proposals that followed them in the message. The President went on to state his views that the control and operation of education in America must remain the responsibility of state and local governments and private institutions, that grants of Federal money had not weakened local responsibility, and that their continuation in the future would not do so. He urged Federal assistance in the construction of schools and in increasing the salaries of teachers. He advocated a program including Federally financed scholarships, contributions to medical and dental education and to the development of scientists and engineers, a program of adult education (including but not limited to migrant workers), support of educational television, and aid to the arts. He asserted that Federal money does not mean Federal control.

In its 1959 report "Paying for Better Public Schools" the Committee for Economic Development advocated Federal support for education in the poorer states, plus state assistance to local school districts and re-districting of educational areas under state laws.

The Constitution makes no mention of education. Under the Tenth Amendment the powers not delegated to the Federal Government and not prohibited to the states are reserved to the states or to the people. Some argue that since education is not among the concerns expressly delegated to the United States, it falls within the provisions of the Tenth Amendment.

Others contend that the general welfare clause gives the Government not only the right but actually the duty to promote education. The general welfare clause states:

> The Congress shall have power to lay and collect taxes, duties, imports and excises, to pay the debts and provide for the common defense and general welfare of the United States. . . .

Historically and traditionally in the United States, education has been *principally* a state and local responsibility. There are dangers in departure from this tradition. Nevertheless, through the years the Federal Government has assumed a great number of responsibilities in this field.

Federal support of higher education goes back at least as far as 1802, when each Western state was granted two townships for the support of "seminaries of learning." The Morrill Land Act of 1862, which provided public lands as a subsidy for agricultural and engineering education in every state, reaffirmed this national concern for education. The exemption from Federal income tax of revenue derived from state and local bond issues can be looked upon as a form of Federal subsidy of education.

Despite the antiquity of this financial support Federal aid to education remains a controversial subject. It is defended and opposed by persons equally devoted to the cause of education.

## THE ISSUE OF FEDERAL CONTROL

There are three schools of thought about the effect of Federal aid on the control of education. One contends that Federal aid will not result in Federal control, while the other two claim, one with approval, the other with disapproval, that it will.

The members of the first school hold that, so long as Federal aid consists merely of grants to the states on a per pupil or some other equitable basis, such grants to be spent on education as the states see fit, there is no danger of Federal control. As a matter of fact, however, proponents of Federal aid do not intend it to be completely free of control. They propose some restrictions, which they assert are "needed and reasonable."

Perhaps some degree of Federal control ("needed and reasonable") would be desirable, but there is no guarantee that it would stop at this point. Provisions in a legislative act which prohibit Federal intervention are virtually meaningless, for the act can easily be amended to exclude this restriction. If Federal money comes to represent any meaningful portion of a school's total budget (say, 10 per cent or more), substantial pressure can be placed upon the institution to conform with Federal desires through the mere threat of withdrawal.

A blatant use of Federal power to establish extensive control over education would probably lack enough public support to be successful in the United States in ordinary times; but it is not inconceivable that, if such power had been available during the sway of Senator Joseph McCarthy, a law prohibiting the extension of Federal funds to schools teaching Russian history, the Russian language, or even comparative government could have been passed. Yet these were the very times when there was a desperate need for the American public to understand the Russian people and the communist movement! Can the United States be sure that there will never be another such man or era in its history? Can it even afford to give control over education to one body in view of the chance that there might? Those who view Federal control as desirable argue that even though state and local governments may be financially able to support adequate education, many of them are not doing it now and will not do it in the future, and that for this reason the national government must step in to influence expansion where it is needed.

Aside from the obvious danger that such central control can result in central indoctrination of the public, to the detriment of a free society, there is also the real question whether so-called experts can be counted upon to be always correct. Are not these people influenced by the same self-interest and pressures that affect all human beings? Does not the history of man convince us with an abundance of examples that the mistakes of one "expert" can cause problems that plague many generations —that the safest, perhaps the only safe, course for a *fallible* race is that of plurality, diversity, dispersal of power?

And there is also a positive argument for pluralized control of education. If many different groups control a society, or any aspect of it, the man with slightly different ideas or new ways of doing things can find some place to try them out. And it is this freedom to challenge the old way, to experiment, which has made the United States what it is today. In contrast, under a centralized system, the man who cannot convince the central authorities, the "experts," of the worthiness of his ideas, or at least of the desirability of giving them a trial, has no such opportunity, and sterility and stagnation may result. Some who oppose Federal aid because of the chance that it will result in Federal control do so not because they do not see the value of a uniformly good educational system, or because they are blind to the unevennesses and inequities of the local, plural approach, but because they feel that the dangers to a whole free society inherent in central control are outweighing.

## THE SCHOOL DROP-OUT PROBLEM

Public attention has been focused recently on the problem of youths who drop out of high school, now numbering about a million a year, including a high proportion of Negroes. A large proportion of these youths are unemployed.

With no implication of minimizing the importance of the problem, we may observe that the problem of school drop-outs is not a new one. Indeed, it is reassuring that drop-outs have not been increasing as a percentage of high school youth. On the contrary, the percentage has been declining slowly; that is, the percentage of young people who start high school and complete it has been rising.

Despite that comforting statistic, the fact is that hundreds of thousands of young people have dropped out of school, do not have jobs, are at loose ends on the streets, and many of them are becoming more unemployable with the passage of time. This condition contributes to juvenile delinquency.

Remedial measures must begin with careful studies of the reasons for this condition. Many of the youngsters who drop out of high school come from homes where there are low levels of aspiration, from neighborhoods where schooling is not highly prized. If, in addition, they are somewhat lacking in the aptitudes for schooling, academic failure is likely to generate feelings of discouragement and hostility. The importance of the social mores of the families and the groups from which these young people come can scarcely be exaggerated.

The situation is aggravated by a tendency of the high schools, encouraged by the colleges and universities, to emphasize the college preparatory function of secondary schools. Many of the young people have neither the aptitudes nor the finances to go on to college, and a high school education which is geared to that end may be both uninteresting and impossible for them. Academic resistance to the introduction of courses better suited to the abilities and interests of these young people represents a barrier to desirable change.

Even if courses such as those in shop practice, automobile engineering, and other mechanical work are offered, students may avoid them for various reasons. For example, it is reported that, in some schools, the students who take the courses in automotive mechanics are almost entirely "hoods," so that boys who do not wish to be classified in that category avoid the courses. Other students, including (but not limited to) Negro students, prefer to struggle along with academic subjects rather than shift to occupational ones because the former constitute a kind of status symbol. It appears that these young people would rather fail the academic subjects and withdraw from high school than take subjects for which they are more qualified and which would be more useful to them.

The economic analyst can advise measures calculated to increase employment opportunities for young people. But increasing these opportunities will not remove the causes of dropping out of school. And since the educational requirements for initial employment seems to be going up, it is increasingly hard for the youth who is not a high school graduate to get a job of any kind.

The problem is thus seen to be one that involves a variety of factors. The attack on it will require a combination of approaches involving changes in high school curricula; measures to increase the motivation of students to stay in schools, including influences applied through their home and neighborhood environments (which, by the way, involve problems of wide scope and great urgency, of which this particular one is only one facet); and programs aimed at opening up job opportunities specifically designed for making the most of nonintellectual talents. This is indeed a large order—and the solution is not in sight.

## THE DEVELOPMENT OF CHARACTER

To be a productive citizen, a person needs both competence and character. Competence means ability to do the job—effectiveness in performance. Discussion of the development of human resources, therefore, quite naturally stresses education along the lines of occupational skills, both general and specific.

Competence, however, is not enough. Character also is needed. Without character, the competent promoter may become a swindler, the skillful penman a forger, the expert mechanic a safe-cracker or automobile thief. Many a crook is a man of considerable competence; often of considerable stupidity; never of good character.

Some of the statistics cited in this book may be a source of reasonable pride to Americans; but not those in the following table. The story that they tell is shameful and shocking. The number of serious crimes is huge and has increased rapidly—faster than the population has grown.

Among our people, there is altogether too much dishonesty, crime, vandalism, selfishness, greed, and immorality and too little honesty, decency, unselfishness, and morality. Our modern society needs—perhaps desperately needs—improvement in these respects.

As we note in Chapter 1 in the discussion of social control, the attitudes and behavior of children and adults are conditioned by many environmental forces. The training of character is largely a responsibility of family and church. Relatively little training of character is provided in public educational institutions—at any level. In schools and colleges the emphasis is on the training of the mind.

In view of the national need for better character, it is appropriate

*Table 23.1*

## ESTIMATED SERIOUS CRIMES

### 1947–1962

| | |
|---|---|
| 1947 | 929,530 |
| 1948 | 928,590 |
| 1949 | 951,070 |
| 1950 | 965,060 |
| 1951 | 1,009,290 |
| 1952 | 1,143,310 |
| 1953 | 1,211,860 |
| 1954 | 1,257,380 |
| 1955 | 1,228,990 |
| 1956 | 1,336,330 |
| 1957 | 1,476,020 |
| 1958 | 1,612,430 |
| 1959 | 1,632,200 |
| 1960 | 1,862,680 |
| 1961 | 1,926,090 |
| 1962 | 2,048,370 |

SOURCE: A letter to the present writer from John Edgar Hoover, Director, Federal Bureau of Investigation, September 10, 1963.

"Serious crimes" include murder and non-negligent manslaughter, forcible rape, robbery, aggravated assault, burglary, larceny $50 and over, and auto theft.

to ask whether enough is being done in public educational institutions to inculcate character in our young people. This question has nothing whatever to do with the teaching of religion in the public schools. Religious indoctrination has no place in public educational institutions. Ethics, morality, decency, and unselfishness happen to be subjects of religious teaching in churches, but they are not exclusively religious subjects, and they can be taught without religious connotations, in public schools or anywhere else. Perhaps the time has come when public educational institutions should give more attention to training the heart as well as the head. One of the places in schools where character training is possible and fruitful is in athletics, under the direction of a high-minded coach. Such a coach can instill character in the athletes; and, since athletes are admired by other students, these students are likely to imitate the athletes, thereby multiplying the influence of the coach's teaching.

## PUBLIC HEALTH

Except for those who really *enjoy* poor health, good health—physical and mental—is valuable in and of itself. It is also important in an economic sense. People who are sick cannot work with complete effectiveness any more than can sick draft animals.

Recognition of these facts led early to simple practices among primitive people aimed at promoting public health. In ancient Greece, at a higher level of civilization, emphasis was placed on hygiene. Rome built great aqueducts to bring fresh, pure water to cities and constructed drains and sewers to carry away waste.

In the middle ages the outlook on life changed to the point where many ideas of the ancients were rejected, among them the interest of the Greeks in hygiene and of the Romans in sanitation. One consequence was a sweep of epidemics, which were but little ameliorated by primitive efforts at quarantine.

A substantial push toward the development of activities aimed at public health was given by Sir Edwin Chadwick (1800–1890). As a result of his service on the Poor Law Commission, he reached two conclusions: (1) that sickness was often a factor in causing poverty, and (2) that much of the sickness could be prevented by improving the conditions in which poor people lived. He presented the results of his studies in a notable document, which appeared in 1842, entitled "Report on the Sanitary Condition of the Labouring Population of Great Britain." The impact of this report was substantial in many countries, and led to movements for the provision of pure water supplies, for sewage disposal, and for the elimination of dirt and filth.

Progress in medical and biological sciences, which provided a better understanding of the bases of illness, together with activities of the public health movements, contributed to the reduction of diseases which had been widespread. By the end of the nineteenth century many countries had checked cholera, plague, and typhoid. Later came reduction in the death rates from diphtheria and tuberculosis. Some of the gains were achieved as a result of legal regulations and specific governmental actions. And increasingly it became clear that further progress necessitated educational efforts among the people with respect to their private living.

Public health activities are carried on at all levels of government. Cities, counties, and states have departments of health. The United States Public Health Service in the Department of Health, Education, and Welfare has a billion-dollar annual budget for carrying on its manifold activities. About half of the amount goes for research, and the next largest fraction pays for hospital construction. Other substantial amounts go in grants to the states for their health services.

## MENTAL HEALTH

Although most public health programs have concentrated on physical health, many have been concerned with mental health. Indeed, the medical profession has seemed to be willing to leave the treatment of *mental* illness largely to public programs—in striking contrast to its attitude toward *physical* health. Because of growing need, the public mental health programs have grown enormously. State mental hospitals have multiplied. Recently, private mental health treatment also has burgeoned.

The upsurgence of mental illness prompts the question whether enough is being done of a preventive nature, aimed at reducing the growing threat of mental illness. Is enough being done in the years of childhood, and also for adults, to teach and train people to cope with and endure the mental and emotional stresses of worry, fear, temptation, disappointment, and frustration that occur in everyday living? Some of these conditions originate in the home, and the home is a place where such training could be accomplished. Unfortunately, however, few parents have any technical knowledge along these lines and may not even understand the importance of providing love, firmness, and security for their children. The ability to beget children does not guarantee the existence of the ability to rear them properly. In view of the interrelated high rates of delinquency and of divorce, perhaps all our schools should give courses in Spouse Selection and in Parenthood. Perhaps the courses should be compulsory. The subjects are crucial to our society.

Mental health may easily be thought of as being solely *intellectual*. It is, however, primarily emotional and temperamental. A high level of intelligence coupled with a high level of education and intellectual development do not comprise any guarantee of mental stability. Is it not desirable, therefore, that public schools and colleges should expand their activities in developing mental well-being?

Asking this question does not imply that a large proportion of children or adults are insane. It does no more than acknowledge that normal people have to cope with stress and strain and are afflicted with anxiety and fears. Psychologists and psychiatrists agree that people can be educated to handle these problems and thereby live more serene lives and avoid serious mental illness.

## URBAN RENEWAL

Slums—rural and urban—have existed for decades. These regions of shabby, dilapidated dwellings are sometimes called "blighted areas."

The subject of slum clearance and urban renewal has been a concern of the National Government since World War II. Federal acts have authorized the government to make loans and capital grants to localities to assist them in handling the costs of clearing slum areas for re-development. To be eligible for this money, a project must be initiated by a local public agency and approved by the Federal Government. With appropriate local and state laws, a city can borrow money to buy slum properties and to plan rebuilding. If its program is approved by Washington, the community may obtain Federal grants to pay up to two thirds of the net cost. In fiscal year 1961 the Federal budget included $142 million for urban renewal capital grants.

Justification for the expenditure of public funds to eliminate slums is held to lie in the desirability of reducing the manifestations of poor citizenship, such as crime and juvenile delinquency, which are said to be fostered in such surroundings. This is clearly a desirable objective. On the face of the matter, therefore, urban redevelopment programs would seem to justify instant favorable reaction. Further reflection, however, may lead to the question whether these programs really get at the basic difficulties. Are not the slums a consequence rather than a cause?

If one of the basic causes is poverty, which prevents poor people from being able to afford better homes, does an urban redevelopment program do anything to raise these people's incomes? If it does not do so, is not the end result merely that they have to move and find cheap and ugly housing elsewhere?

To the extent that a basic cause is indifference and lack of pride, the same question may be asked—does an urban renewal program change this attitude? If it does not, will the result not be that families take their unfavorable attitudes with them to new locations?

If crime and juvenile delinquency (or *parental* delinquency, if that is what it really is) flow from psychological conditions rather than from dilapidated houses, changing the housing is no guarantee of changed behavior.

## THE SCOPE OF HUMAN DEVELOPMENT

Much of the content of this chapter seems to be concerned with the lower strata of our society: the ungifted, the maladjusted, the slothful, the vicious, the merely improvident—in short, the dwellers in slums— physical, mental, and spiritual. Any effort to improve society must, of course, start with these and must remain heavily involved with them— ideally, as long as a single human being occupies the category (which sounds like a very long time indeed). But there is more to human development than this and more to the society's collective role in it.

Developing human resources means helping all those who are falling short of attaining their potential—the rich as well as the poor, the moderately diligent as well as the downright lazy, the fairly healthy as well as the sick, the gifted children and the less gifted ones, the educated and the uneducated, the fairly moral citizens and the hoodlums. Human development means improving competence and character, to make *better people,* for the sake of these people themselves, their neighbors, and the society as a whole. Society can approach this in two ways; by letting it work itself out through the painfully slow and uncertain evolutionary operation of its unconscious instruments, or by moving actively to guide and direct the process. Mankind's technology has come to render the purely passive alternative intolerable from several standpoints, not the least of which is that of safety. And since the chief conscious instruments of society are its governments, at all levels, the heavy involvement of these entities in the development of human resources seems to be inevitable and indispensable.

## QUESTIONS AND PROBLEMS

1. Evaluate the comparative importance of natural resources and human resources in achieving both economic and noneconomic progress.
2. Discuss the proper allocation of responsibility for the development of human resources among family, church, school, private organizations, governmental agencies, and others.
3. What shortcomings do you see in American education? How do you think they could be reduced or eliminated?
4. What is the proper way to finance the prospective increases in the nation's education bill?
5. "The Federal Government must contribute to the mounting cost of education, because state and local governments have exhausted the possibilities of their tax sources." Discuss. You may wish to refer to Chapters 6 and 7.
6. What are the issues in the Federal aid to education debate, and how do you evaluate them?
7. How can incentives be created in the present educational system so that all inherent abilities of all persons will be exploited to the best use for economic growth while retaining individual happiness?
8. Would you argue for or against trade schools as a substitute for high school for those desiring them?
9. Discuss the role and problems of the private college in the development of our human resources.
10. Is the public or private sector to bear the major increase in higher education costs?
11. Discuss the problem of keeping young people in school.
12. At what point should governmental entities assume responsibility for an individual's health?
13. Is mental health a legitimate concern of governmental entities? If it is, what programs are reasonable and necessary? Do the problems of mental health pose problems significantly different for those concerned and the government than physical infirmities?
14. List and evaluate the pros and cons of the urban renewal problem.

## SELECTED READINGS

Committee for Economic Development. *Paying for Better Schools*. New York: Committee for Economic Development, 1959.

GINZBERG, ELI, and others. *The Ineffective Soldier: Lessons for Management and the Nation*. New York: Columbia University Press, 1959.

——— and D. W. BRAY. *The Uneducated*. New York: Columbia University Press, 1953.

———. *Human Resources: The Wealth of a Nation*. New York: Simon & Schuster, Inc., 1958.

KOTINSKY, R., and H. L. WITMER (eds.). *Community Programs for Mental Health: Theory, Practice and Evaluation*. Cambridge, Mass.: Harvard University Press, 1955.

LADD, EDWARD T., and WILLIAM E. SAYRES (eds.). *Social Aspects of Education*. Englewood Cliffs, N.J.: Prentice-Hall, Inc., 1962.

MACHLUP, FRITZ. *The Production and Distribution of Knowledge in the United States*. Princeton, N.J.: Princeton University Press, 1962.

MORGAN, JAMES N., and others. *Income and Welfare in the United States*. New York: McGraw-Hill Company, 1962.

MUSTARD, HARRY S. *Government in Public Health*. Cambridge, Mass.: Harvard University Press, 1945.

NEUMEYER, MARTIN H. *Juvenile Delinquency in Modern Society*, 3rd ed. Princeton, N.J.: D. Van Nostrand Company, 1961.

PECK, R. F., and R. J. HAVIGHURST. *Psychology of Character Development*. New York: John Wiley & Son Inc., 1960.

RIDENOUR, NINA. *Mental Health in the United States: A Fifty-Year History* Cambridge, Mass.: Harvard University Press, 1961.

STEEL, RONALD (ed.). *Federal Aid to Education*. New York: H. W. Wilson Company, 1961.

WEISBROD, BURTON. *Economics of Public Health*. Philadelphia: University of Pennsylvania Press, 1961.

WELTER, RUSH. *Popular Education and Democratic Thought in America*. New York: Columbia University Press, 1962.

WOELFEL, NORMAN. *Educational Goals for America*. Washington, D.C.: Public Affairs Press, 1962.

# 24 GOVERNMENT OWNERSHIP OF BUSINESS

In this chapter we depart from the general theme of this book, government *and* business, and turn attention to government *in* business. Federal, state, and local governments own and operate thousands of businesses, ranging from the $4 billion-a-year United States Post Office Department to small municipal enterprises.

This represents partial socialism. Is it proper in a predominantly private enterprise society? How does it happen that governments have become involved in so many businesses? What is the outlook for government ownership of business in the United States?

It is worth noting at the outset that, as suggested above, there is heterogeneity rather than homogeneity in governmentally owned business. Some are huge and important; others are small, although they may be important to the communities served and significant to local businesses with which they are competing.

It is unavoidable that we also have to deal with the question: What is a *business*? For example, is *education* a business? It is carried on by private organizations as well as by governments. Although some of the private organizations are nonprofit corporations, many are businesses run for, and earning, profits.

Is *police protection* a business? It is an activity that has been carried on—at least since Pinkerton's time—by private enterprise, for profit. Where, indeed, would the modern detective story be without the "private eye"? The very term emphasizes the difference between his private status and that of the public authorities.

Even the combat operations of war were in earlier times a private activity. The United States at one time commissioned privateers—private ships authorized to cruise against the commerce or warships of an enemy.

Money—useful although not always legal tender—has frequently been issued by private organizations. Indeed, the bank notes of state banks and of national banks were promises-to-pay of private organizations, although with government backing. Private promises-to-pay without government backing, have occasionally served as currency. In California, shortly after the gold rush, coins were minted by private firms. They were not counterfeits, and they resembled United States coins in size, weight, and fineness.

*Courts* are maintained by many private associations for the adjudication of disputes about contracts, and such courts' awards are binding on the parties.

In each of the foregoing examples, and in others that could be adduced, the issue is whether the activity is essentially a *business* or a natural *function of government*. For our purposes it is unlikely that any useful purpose would be served by prolonging the discussion of the abstract question. It is difficult to draw a sharp dividing line between governmental functions and businesses. It is important to note their resemblance and the difficulty of drawing the dividing line; one conclusion is that the propriety of governmental action cannot be readily determined by reference to such a dividing line. Instead, the key question is a subdivision of the one posed in Chapter 2—Is it sound public policy, in a society committed predominantly to the private enterprise system, for a governmental entity to own and operate a certain specific activity?

Discussion of that question in the following pages proceeds in terms of the total of the activity in question and specific industries. In view of the multiplicity of government businesses, no attempt is made to discuss all of them or even all types. Representative businesses are analyzed, and their discussion utilized as a basis for arriving at general principles applicable universally.

## LEGAL BASIS OF GOVERNMENT BUSINESS

The Constitution explicitly empowers the Federal Government to establish Post Offices and Post Roads; the document is otherwise silent on the general subject of government ownership and operation of business. The Government's power to engage in business activities received early endorsement in the 1819 case of *McCulloch v. Maryland*, which, as noted earlier, approved the chartering by the Federal Government of the Second Bank of the United States.

The constitutionality of government businesses has been challenged occasionally. The Tennessee Valley Authority has been attacked several times. In these cases, the Supreme Court has upheld this activity, basing its approval on the electrical power operations being ancillary to other governmental activities basic to the construction of the dams, locks, and waterways. Of state business, the Supreme Court, in *Puget Sound Power and Light Company v. Seattle*, 291 U.S. 619 (1934), said: "The decisions of this Court leave no doubt that a state may, in the public interest, constitutionally engage in a business commonly carried on by private enterprise, levy a tax to support it . . . and compete with private interests engaged in a like activity." Municipalities share the power of state to operate businesses, and may do so subject to legal regulation by their own state legislatures.

## FORMS OF ORGANIZATION

The two principal organizational forms of government businesses are (1) a department of the government and (2) a separate corporation. The former is by far the commoner type. Examples are the postal service, state liquor businesses, and municipal water plants. Separate corporations are rare at the state and local levels, although there are occasional large ones, such as the Port of New York Authority. The corporate form of organization has been used much more by the National Government. A few corporations were established during World War I; dozens blossomed during the New Deal and World War II until, by the middle forties, there were more than a hundred. Since that time their number has declined.

The principal differences between the two types of organizations are these:

[1] As a corporate body, the corporation is a separate entity for legal purposes and can sue and be sued, enter into contracts, and acquire property in its own name; the department-business is not a corporate body. Corporations conducting business in their own names usually have greater freedoms in making contracts and acquiring and disposing of property than do government departments.

[2] Except for appropriations to provide capital or to cover losses, a governmental corporation is usually independently financed. It obtains its funds from borrowings, from either the Treasury or the public, and from revenues derived from the sale of goods and services. It is authorized to use and reuse its revenues. The department-business is more dependent on its governmental parent.

[3] A governmental corporation is generally exempted from most of the regulatory and prohibitory statutes applicable to expenditure of public funds—statutes which usually control departments.

[4] Usually, the employees of these corporations are not civil servants, and are recruited and compensated under terms and conditions which the corporations themselves determine; the department-business usually operates under civil service laws.

A board of directors is considered by some observers to be one of the essential attributes of a governmental corporation. This view undoubtedly has its basis in the fact that general laws authorizing the creation of business corporations frequently require the establishment of boards of directors elected by the stockholders. The board of a business corporation nominally has the duty to act for the stockholders in formulating basic policies and checking on the results of operations. In government this function is often not performed by a board, but by the chief executive, or by government officers. Governmental corporations have existed and operated effectively without boards of directors. Whether a governmental corporation should be managed by a board of directors or by a single executive depends on the nature of its program, the requirements of public relations, established administrative habits of the government involved, and other factors.

The chief advantages of the corporate form of organization for a *private* business enterprise—limited liability, pooling of investment, transferability of securities, and perpetuity—have little or no significance for a *governmental* enterprise. The principal benefits of the governmental corporation as an organizational device are to be found in its freedom from rigid regulations and controls and its high degree of flexibility in operations and finance.

The special powers granted to these corporations are designed to enable a government, when it undertakes to operate an industrial or commercial enterprise, to render service and discharge its obligations to the public as nearly as possible in the same manner as if it were a private business enterprise. Freedom from restrictive statutes with respect to disbursements, contracts, purchases, and personnel permits a governmental corporation, where desirable, to follow standard commercial practice in carrying on its business. Expansion of facilities to take care of an unanticipated growth in business can be financed, without the delay involved in legislative action, by use of revenues or by borrowing.

In 1945 the United States Congress passed the Government Corporations Control Act, applying to Federal corporations. It made Federal incorporation a requirement, abolished state incorporation for Federal agencies, provided for a limited jurisdiction by the Bureau of the Budget, and established a special unit in the General Accounting Office to audit the accounts of these corporations according to commercial instead of customary governmental methods.

As a consequence of this Act and other factors, the governmental corporation has been so modified during the past twenty years that many of them now resemble regular government departments more than they do corporations.

Neither type of organization—department or corporation—provides any special magic for governmental business. The corporate form provides greater freedom and flexibility, and these given good administration are advantages. Neither legal form, however, guarantees good administration.

Pope's lines—with a small addition, in brackets—are appropriate:

> For forms of government [businesses] let fools contest;
> Whate'er is best administer'd is best.

## EXTENT OF GOVERNMENTAL
## BUSINESSES

To repeat, governmental entities run businesses—thousands of them—ranging from abattoirs to zoos. In the aggregate, however, governmentally owned businesses constitute only a tiny portion of the American economy. In 1960 the national income was $417.1 billion. Of this amount $3,527 million or 0.85 per cent, originated in Federal Governmental enterprises. These enterprises employed 656,000 persons, or 0.97 per cent of total employment. In the same year state and local governmental business enterprises produced a total income of $1,689 billion, or 0.4 per cent of the national total. They employed 340,000 persons, equal to 0.5 per cent of the persons engaged in production.*

The total of these Federal, state, and local governmental businesses produced 1.25 per cent of the national income, with 1.47 per cent of the workers.

## VARIATIONS IN GOVERNMENT
## OWNERSHIP

A conspectus of government ownership is presented in Table 24.1, which shows its relative position in selected industries. In the first column are listed businesses in which the government is dominant, that is, doing more than half the total business. The second column names businesses in which governmental activity can be described as substantial—less than half, but still large. The third column lists some in which government-owned enterprises represent only a small fraction of the activity.

The reader will note that the first column names several economic activities about which the question may be raised whether they are *businesses* or *governmental functions*. These activities are not classified by the U.S. Treasury Department or the U.S. Department of Commerce as "business" activities, and they are not counted as such in the statistics presented in the preceding section and in the following section.

They are, however, important activities *with business aspects*. They should be taken account of, therefore, in any general summary of the total "business" operations of governments in this country.

* Source: U.S. Department of Commerce, *Survey of Current Business*, July 1961, pp. 11, 27.

*Table 24.1*

## POSITION OF GOVERNMENT OWNERSHIP
## IN SELECTED INDUSTRIES

| DOMINANT | SUBSTANTIAL | MINOR |
|---|---|---|
| Highways | Garbage collection | Broadcasting |
| Waterways | Credit extension | Railroads |
| Harbors | Forests | Printing |
| Education | Electric power | Housing |
| Postal service | Agricultural products | |
| Municipal water supply | Life insurance | |
| Sewage disposal systems | Hospitals | |
| Police protection | Medical care | |
| Fire protection | Liquor distribution | |
| Libraries | Research | |
| Museums | Transit systems | |
| Unemployment insurance | Lands | |
| Dams (big) | Ships | |
| Atomic energy | | |
| Retirement insurance | | |
| Airports | | |
| Parks | | |

Table 24.1 shows the tremendous variety in the extent of our governments' dominance in various businesses. It provides also an opportunity to point out a major difference between the United States and many other leading industrialized countries. In many other countries government ownership is dominant in telephones, telegraph, broadcasting, and railroads and in the distribution of matches, salt, and tobacco. So complete, indeed, is government ownership in the railroad industry that, outside of the United States, the only large privately owned railroad system in the world is the Canadian Pacific Railroad.

The greater extent of these governmental businesses in other lands reflects two differences of principle. Distribution of matches, salt, and tobacco are fiscal monopolies in many countries. A government operates these businesses in order to earn a fat profit; they basically represent a type of taxation. On the other hand, government ownership of telephones, telegraph, broadcasting, and railroads represents (as is indicated in Chapter 18), not revenue collection, but an alternative method of dealing with these industries. In the United States our philosophy with respect to them involves private ownership with governmental regulation; in many other countries, the philosophy leads to purely governmental ownership.

## TRENDS IN GOVERNMENT OWNERSHIP
## OF BUSINESSES

Government ownership is small today. What, however, is the trend? Is it expanding or contracting? Table 24.2 and Chart 24.1 shed light on

*Table 24.2*

## NATIONAL INCOME AND GOVERNMENT
## BUSINESSES, 1929–1960

(In Billions of Current Dollars)

| ADMINIS-TRATION | YEAR | NATIONAL INCOME | INCOME ORIGINATING IN FEDERAL GOVERNMENT BUSINESS ENTERPRISES | | INCOME ORIGINATING IN STATE AND LOCAL GOVERNMENT BUSINESS ENTERPRISES | |
|---|---|---|---|---|---|---|
| | | | AMOUNT | PERCENTAGE OF NATIONAL INCOME | AMOUNT | PERCENTAGE OF NATIONAL INCOME |
| Hoover | 1929 | $ 87.8 | $0.581 | 0.66 | $0.177 | 0.20 |
| | 1930 | 75.7 | 0.584 | 0.77 | 0.187 | 0.25 |
| | 1931 | 59.7 | 0.582 | 0.97 | 0.186 | 0.31 |
| | 1932 | 42.5 | 0.544 | 1.28 | 0.161 | 0.38 |
| Roosevelt | 1933 | 40.2 | 0.485 | 1.21 | 0.146 | 0.36 |
| | 1934 | 49.0 | 0.540 | 1.10 | 0.153 | 0.31 |
| | 1935 | 57.1 | 0.614 | 1.08 | 0.164 | 0.29 |
| | 1936 | 64.9 | 0.662 | 1.02 | 0.180 | 0.28 |
| | 1937 | 73.6 | 0.675 | 0.92 | 0.195 | 0.26 |
| | 1938 | 67.6 | 0.698 | 1.03 | 0.200 | 0.30 |
| | 1939 | 72.8 | 0.719 | 0.99 | 0.205 | 0.28 |
| | 1940 | 81.6 | 0.746 | 0.91 | 0.238 | 0.29 |
| | 1941 | 104.7 | 0.808 | 0.77 | 0.277 | 0.26 |
| | 1942 | 137.7 | 0.918 | 0.67 | 0.296 | 0.21 |
| | 1943 | 170.3 | 1.14 | 0.67 | 0.336 | 0.20 |
| | 1944 | 182.6 | 1.19 | 0.65 | 0.340 | 0.19 |
| Truman | 1945 | 181.2 | 1.25 | 0.69 | 0.360 | 0.20 |
| | 1946 | 180.9 | 1.45 | 0.80 | 0.422 | 0.23 |
| | 1047 | 198.2 | 1.44 | 0.73 | 0.516 | 0.26 |
| | 1948 | 223.5 | 1.63 | 0.73 | 0.657 | 0.29 |
| | 1949 | 217.7 | 1.81 | 0.83 | 0.725 | 0.33 |
| | 1950 | 241.9 | 1.90 | 0.79 | 0.779 | 0.32 |
| | 1951 | 279.3 | 2.08 | 0.74 | 0.878 | 0.31 |
| | 1952 | 292.2 | 2.38 | 0.81 | 1.08 | 0.37 |
| Eisenhower | 1953 | 305.6 | 2.37 | 0.78 | 1.15 | 0.38 |
| | 1954 | 301.8 | 2.35 | 0.78 | 1.20 | 0.40 |
| | 1955 | 330.2 | 2.52 | 0.76 | 1.28 | 0.39 |
| | 1956 | 350.8 | 2.67 | 0.76 | 1.32 | 0.38 |
| | 1957 | 366.9 | 2.83 | 0.77 | 1.42 | 0.39 |
| | 1958 | 367.4 | 3.17 | 0.86 | 1.38 | 0.38 |
| | 1959 | 400.5 | 3.27 | 0.82 | 1.47 | 0.37 |
| | 1960 | 415.5 | 3.53 | 0.85 | 1.69 | 0.41 |

SOURCES: 1929–1957, U.S. Department of Commerce, *U.S. Income and Output* (Washington, D.C.: U.S. Government Printing Office, 1958), pp. 130–131; 1958–1960, U.S. Department of Commerce, *Survey of Current Business*, July 1962, p. 6.

this question. They cover the period since 1929—the time for which the United States Department of Commerce has made detailed estimates of national income. In these three decades the American economy grew immensely. In current dollars the national income was nearly five times as large in 1960 as in 1929. The total of Federal Government business enterprises made a contribution to national income that was slightly more than six times as large in the later year, and state and local business enterprises combined grew to nearly ten times their 1929 size. In other words, governmentally owned businesses greatly increased the dollar volume of their operations in this period. (It should be noted that part of the growth, in all three measures, is deceptive in that it reflects the higher dollar values associated with the inflationary increase in the commodity price level which occurred during that time.)

But what of the *relative* position of government businesses in the total economy? Chart 24.1 shows the magnitude of these enterprises as percentages of the national income. The rise in the early 1930s to a peak in 1932 reflects not an upswing of public ownership at that time, but rather the simple arithmetic of the contraction of private businesses as the depression deepened. Similarly, the drop during the war years of the Roosevelt Administration, ending in 1945, results solely from the great expansion of private business in connection with the war effort. Aside from these two major fluctuations, the other slight movements of the ratio seem to have little significance. Economic philosophies of changing administrations seem to have had little to do with the relative expansions and contractions of government businesses in these three decades. The story that Chart 24.1 tells is that, except for the anomalous distortions caused by the Great Depression and World War II, there has been little change in the relative importance of government businesses. In other words, the growth of government businesses has been merely a reflection of the growth of the economy as a whole.

## FEDERAL GOVERNMENT BUSINESSES

Tabulating Federal Government businesses is difficult, for both conceptual and statistical reasons. Is the Commodity Credit Corporation—with two billion dollars in loans and four billion in inventories—a *business*? It does not exist to produce goods and services, but rather to provide financial support for a few crops. The tabulation of the total assets of "Federal business-type activities" in the *Federal Reserve Bulletin* showed a total of $80 billion in 1960.

The largest Federal business, in terms of employees and income, is the Post Office, although it is far from the largest in total assets. Its total assets are listed at about one billion dollars—a figure which substantially understates their current worth.

Chart 24.1

## PERCENTAGE OF CONTRIBUTIONS OF GOVERNMENT AND BUSINESSES TO NATIONAL INCOME, 1929–1960

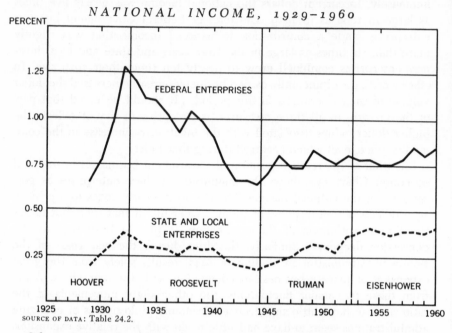

SOURCE OF DATA: Table 24.2.

Other giant Federal business activities and their total assets in billions of dollars include the Rural Electrification Administration ($3.3), Federal National Mortgage Association ($6.0), Export–Import Bank ($3.3), Federal Deposit Insurance Corporation ($2.3), Federal Home Loan Banks ($3.1), Merchant Shipping ($3.2), Tennessee Valley Authority ($2.2), Federal Intermediate Credit Banks ($1.9), and, among the "smaller" organizations, the Panama Canal Company ($0.4).°

The Federal Government is the largest *single* electric power producer in the nation, the largest single insurer, landlord, holder of grazing land, holder of timber land, owner of grain, warehouse operator, ship operator, printer, and truck fleet operator. In most of these businesses, however, large though the Federal Government's activities are, they constitute only minor fractions of the totals of the industries.

The extent to which the Post Office exceeds all other Federal government business enterprises combined may be noted from the fact that in 1960 the Post Office had 563,000 of the 656,000 employees in all Government business enterprises combined. If measurement is based on total assets, however, the Post Office represents only a tiny part of Government investment in business enterprises.

° *Federal Reserve Bulletin,* February 1961, p. 240.

The Post Office has long been a controversial subject, and there have even been occasional proposals that it should be sold to a private organization. Finding a buyer for an organization that runs such a huge deficit would of course be out of the question unless the buyer could be assured that—presumably pursuant to some public utility control arrangement— he would not be restricted in endeavoring to make a fair return on the investment. Controversy rages about the efficiency of operation of the Post Office. Some critics contend that postal systems run by European governments are much more modern and efficient. Programs of modernization, including automated handling of mail, are under way. Most of the employees of the Post Office Department are under civil service; but the top Washington officials and 20,000 postmasters in the larger post offices are not so covered. These positions are regarded by both parties as political plums to be awarded to the party faithful. Moreover, traditionally, the Postmaster General is the chief patronage dispenser of the party in power. In the circumstances, it is perhaps astonishing that the Post Office functions as well as it does.

## THE TENNESSEE VALLEY AUTHORITY

The Tennessee Valley Authority is one of the New Deal's outstanding monuments—and one of the most controversial. Admirers hail it as a great example of regional development. Critics see it as a socialistic, bureaucratic, unconstitutional expansion of central governmental power—both electrical and general.

The TVA had its origin in an installation on the Tennessee River, at Muscle Shoals, Alabama, whose purpose had been to produce power, to make nitrates, and to make explosives for World War I.

In June 1916, the Congress passed the National Defense Act. This Act, in part, empowered the President to make investigations into all phases of the supply of nitrogen in the United States, and to build, maintain, and operate those power and other facilities considered necessary for the production of nitrates for use in the manufacture of explosives and as fertilizer.

At that time the United States was dependent upon foreign sources, especially Chile, for its supply of nitrates, essential to the manufacture of explosives and other war material. With the advent of war in Europe, concern about the availability of a sufficient supply of this essential war material developed in this country. Two processes by which atmospheric nitrogen could be converted to usable form were than known, but these processes required large amounts of *power*. Providing adequate power was one purpose of the National Defense Act.

The potential of Muscle Shoals as a water-power site had been recognized prior to the twentieth century. In 1899 Congress had authorized the construction of a dam there, for a private power project. This authorization had gone unused and had been allowed to lapse. Another proposal to build a dam at Muscle Shoals, in 1906, had failed to win support in Washington.

Late in 1917 President Wilson, under the authority granted him by the National Defense Act, designated Muscle Shoals as the site for the development of nitrate-producing facilities. Authorization was granted for the construction of two nitrate plants, a large dam, and two steam-generating plants, to supply power to the nitrate plants while the dam was under construction; Congress appropriated $20 million for a start.

Actual construction on this project did not begin until 1918, and the four plants were not completed and in operation until after the conclusion of the War. Then the plants were maintained in standby condition, but not operated, while Congress debated what to do with them.

Little progress had been made by the end of the War on the construction of the dam. Work continued until funds ran out in April 1921. Another appropriation was made in 1922 so that the dam could be completed. The Wilson Dam was completed and in operating condition in 1925, at an estimated cost of nearly $47 million.

## MUSCLE SHOALS AFTER THE WAR

At the end of the War the Federal Government tried to dispose of the nitrate-producing plants and the steam-generating facilities to concerns in the fertilizer industry. The fertilizer people were not interested in the Government's proposition because of the high cost of conversion to the production of commercially usable fertilizers.

In 1921 an attempt was made to put a bill through Congress to permit the operation of the plants for the purpose of producing fertilizer.

Other attempts were made to sell the properties, but the private offers were not considered to be acceptable.

In 1928 Congress passed a bill to create a Governmental corporation, for the purpose of producing fertilizer, in the Muscle Shoals plants and to sell any surplus power produced at the Wilson Dam. It was vetoed by President Coolidge. Again, this time in 1931, Congress attempted to dispose of the plants. The bill proposed to lease the nitrate plants to a private concern, but to have the electric power produced and sold by the Government. This bill was vetoed by President Hoover.

## THE IMPACT OF THE DEPRESSION

The Great Depression, along with the New Deal which followed, finally brought about the disposition of the Muscle Shoals power and nitrate-producing facilities.

As part of a program to bring prosperity back to the nation, President

Roosevelt's Administration began many large public works projects designed to provide work for the unemployed and to improve the nation's natural resources.

The Tennessee Valley was hard hit by the depression. The people in this area, poor before the 1930s, saw their standard of living go even lower. The land which these people farmed and on which they lived was wasting away through erosion and a gradual destruction of the soil's mineral content, a result of one-crop farming.

Other problems faced were an average annual flood loss of $1.7 million, high taxes in relation to the incomes of the people, and few good roads, schools, and health services. The people could not have modern conveniences to aid them in their work, because, in the early 1930s, 97 per cent of the farms in the Tennessee Valley had no electricity.

Here was a region which the New Deal was attracted to help. But what form would the aid to the people, and the land, take? This aid came, in 1933, in the form of the Tennessee Valley Authority (TVA), the brainchild of Senator Norris and President Roosevelt.

The Tennessee Valley Authority Act of 1933 covered not only the area of the government-owned property at Muscle Shoals, but the entire Tennessee River Valley. This was an immense extension of the original plans for Muscle Shoals. Muscle Shoals would now be only a small part of the whole development of the Tennessee River.

## A NEW CONCEPT IN GOVERNMENTAL ACTIVITY

The Tennessee Valley Authority Act contained provisions taken largely from the previous bills and included them in an Act of much greater scope. The objectives of the Act (May 18, 1933, 48 Stat. 58), as stated in Section One, were:

> —for the purpose of maintaining and operating the properties now owned by the United States in the vicinity of Muscle Shoals, Alabama, in the interest of the national defense and for agricultural and industrial development, and to improve navigation in the Tennessee River and to control the destructive flood waters in the Tennessee River and Mississippi River Basins, there is hereby created a body corporate by the name of the "Tennessee Valley Authority."

Congress apparently did not fully appreciate nor comprehend the full powers and coverage of the Act. It was felt that this was just another act, creating a corporation to produce power and fertilizer. The TVA wes merely the Muscle Shoals Corporation of previous years, with some additional—ill-defined—powers and functions.

The preamble to the Act enumerated in some detail the reasons for the

Act, as stated by President Roosevelt in his address to Congress on April 10, 1933. In addition to these reasons and purposes the preamble expanded upon the potential of the TVA by ending with a nebulous phrase which allowed the TVA to do almost anything it wished along the Tennessee River and its watershed. The words used to Congress were: "An Act . . . and for other purposes." This left the actions of the Tennessee Valley Authority much to the discretion of the persons whom the President appointed to the Board of Directors.

Senator Norris's ideas for the development of Muscle Shoals were not adhered to in the actual development of the TVA. President Roosevelt's ideas, which *were* followed, changed the idea of a Governmental corporation to be engaged in the manufacture of fertilizers and power into an organization charged with the regional planning and development of an entire river watershed.

Less than three decades later, the TVA, descendant of the nitrate and fertilizer factory, had become a giant, multistate operation in which more than $2 billion had been invested, with annual revenues of more than $250 million dollars and 16,000 employees.

## TVA ORGANIZATION AND ACTIVITIES

TVA is a corporation wholly owned by the Federal Government. In addition to the usual corporate powers, it has the right of eminent domain. The Board of Directors, appointed by the President with the approval of the Senate, is authorized to exercise all powers of the corporation. Under the Board the General Manager is the principal administrative officer. The corporation is financed in part by Congressional appropriations—especially for capital expenditures. Additional funds are obtained from the sale of power and fertilizers, power sales being the principal source of revenue. The Comptroller General of the United States is directed to make an annual commercial audit of the Authority's financial activities. The administration of personnel is based on a merit system authorized by the Act.

The Tennessee River flows 650 miles from its source in the southern Appalachian Mountains; first in a great arc to the south and then west and north, to Paducah, Kentucky, where it empties into the Ohio River. The Tennessee Basin, which includes this river and its tributaries, includes parts of seven states and has an area of approximately 41,000 square miles. The valley has a population of about 3.5 million, about three fourths of which is classified as rural.

TVA facilities consist of 26 major dams with hydroelectric generating stations, ten navigation locks, 12 major fuel-electric generating stations, and a power transmission network of more than 11,000 miles.* The system provides about 12 million acre-feet of flood storage. More than two bil-

* Data in this section from *U.S. Budget, 1963*, Appendix, pp. 851 ff.

lion ton-miles of freight were carried on the river during 1957. In 1958 the system had a power producing capacity of ten million kilowatts, and sold 56 million kilowatt-hours, for $232,217,000. National defense requirements used more than half of the electric power, much of it going to the Atomic Energy Commission's plant at Oak Ridge, Tennessee. Navigation, flood control, and power production are the principal concerns of the TVA, but it has other activities. Research on fertilizers and agricultural activities is aimed to promote conservation and improve use of natural resources. Forestry activities couple use of forest resources with watershed protection. Reservoirs provide recreational facilities for fishing, swimming, boating, and beauty. These artificial lakes have more than ten thousand miles of shore line.

Great changes have occurred in the Tennessee Valley since the establishment of the TVA, and much of the controversy about the TVA rages around the question whether the Valley's gains have been caused by the TVA or by other factors. Incomes and employment have risen, but they have in the rest of the United States also. Partly, no doubt, in consequence of the low rates for electric power made possible through the TVA, the proportion of farms in the valley having power has risen from about 3 per cent to about 95 per cent. Rates are lower, per capita power consumption is higher, and per capita sales of electrical appliances are higher than in similar regions elsewhere in the United States. The TVA contends that the low rates charged by the retail distributors of electricity under its orders explain the high per capita use of electric power.

One of the major areas of controversy relates to the costs and earnings of electric power activities. Inasmuch as the dams are joint-purpose structures, the allocation of costs present a familiar but difficult accounting problem. Private interests contend that the costs of electric power are understated and, moreover, that if the TVA had to pay a corporation income tax, as do the private power companies, it would have very little earnings left. Experts who are connected neither with the TVA nor with private power companies disagree about these matters. That the TVA has accomplished much is clear; less clear, however, are the lessons that it teaches with respect to electric power generation—a subject to which we shall return presently.

Successes of the TVA have led to suggestions that similar regional authorities should be established for the development of other river valleys, such as the Missouri and the Columbia. These proposals stress the multipurpose nature of such a development, including flood control, navigation, power, soil conservation, control of erosion and siltation, recreation facilities, development of resources, and—one not present in the Tennessee Valley—irrigation. Opponents point to the huge cost of these (according to their description) socialistic, bureaucratic, antibusiness organizations.

## STATE AND LOCAL GOVERNMENTAL
## BUSINESSES

Two of the largest areas of state and local governmental activity are educational institutions and highways—their construction, maintenance, and operation. These activities, as mentioned above, belong in that ambiguous category whose nature may be described either as businesses or governmental functions. In fiscal year 1959 state and local governments spent $17.3 billion on education and $9.6 billion on highways, for a total of $26.9 billion out of total expenditures of $58.6 billion, or 46 per cent of total expenditures, on these two activities.* Some charges and fees were collected from users of toll roads and toll bridges and from students in schools and colleges. These fees and charges, however, did not cover the total cost of operation of these activities; gasoline taxes and other taxes financed the larger part of these expenditures.

Aside from education and highways the principal business in which states engage is to be found in those states (fewer than half) in which the state is in the business of distributing liquor—at the wholesale level, the retail level, or both. The total receipts of the state liquor businesses in 1959 amounted to $1,085,000,000; their total expenditures, to $860,000,000.

Local governments engage in a wider variety of substantial business activities as Table 24.3 shows.

The table covers about 2,500 cities, of which 87 per cent own one or more of the listed types of businesses. The concentration of ownership is heaviest in water supply and distribution and sewage treatment plants. It is modest in airports, auditoriums, and electricity generating and distribution. In the other seven businesses municipal ownership is small.

## GOVERNMENTAL BUSINESSES:
## EVALUATION AND OUTLOOK

The pros and cons of government ownership of business—both in general and with respect to specific industries—have been debated for decades in the United States. Argument and appraisal proceed along well-recognized lines. Opponents of government ownership adhere to the philosophical position that in a private enterprise society government should stick to the activity of governing and leave business to private individuals. More specifically they argue that governmental entities which may be able to fall back on the public purse and taxpayers' money

*Source: Tax Foundation, Inc., *Facts and Figure on Government Finance, 1960–1961* (Englewood Cliffs, N.J.: Prentice-Hall, 1961), p. 17.

*Table 24.3*

## OWNERSHIP AND OPERATION OF
## UTILITIES IN CITIES OF 5,000
## POPULATION IN 1955

| TYPE | NUMBER OF CITIES | PERCENTAGE OF CITIES REPORTING |
|---|---|---|
| Water supply and distribution | 1,678 | 67.4 |
| Sewage treatment plant | 1,261 | 50.7 |
| Airport | 525 | 21.1 |
| Auditorium | 413 | 16.6 |
| Electricity generation and distribution | 280 | 11.2 |
| Electricity distribution only | 224 | 9.0 |
| Water distribution only | 159 | 6.4 |
| Gas distribution only | 85 | 3.4 |
| Port facilities | 66 | 2.7 |
| Gas manufacturing and distribution | 41 | 1.6 |
| Bus or trolley | 33 | 1.3 |
| Street railway | 6 | 0.2 |
| Cities having none of the above | 319 | 12.8 |
| Cities not reporting | 70 | 2.8 |

SOURCE: International City Managers Associations, *Municipal Year Book 1956* (Chicago, 1956), p. 64.

can finance losing operations indefinitely and are not subject to the profit-making test of the market place. They argue that it is wrong for governments to compete with their citizens. The question of efficiency is debated, and the comparative skills and diligence of managers and workers in public and private activities are compared. Opponents point to the adverse effect of politics on the governmentally owned businesses, and its reverse, the possible deleterious impact of the governmentally owned businesses on politics. Graft and corruption are alleged to be inherent in governmental businesses. Defenders of government ownership point to instances of devoted service by the staff members of these businesses.

Figures cited earlier in this chapter indicate that the trend of governmental businesses as a fraction of the American economy is approximately horizontal. This condition evidently reflects the state of public opinion. The public attitude toward nationalization of key industries has been surveyed several times by the Gallup Poll. In a release dated October 11, 1953, Dr. Gallup reported the current answers to the question together with a summary of the answers in preceding years. The question asked was this: "Do you think the United States Government should or should not own the following things in this country—Banks? Railroads? Coal mines?" The results of the 1953 poll and previous ones follow:

BANKS

| | Should % | Should Not % | No Opinion % |
|---|---|---|---|
| 1936 | 36 | 56 | 8 |
| 1945 | 27 | 61 | 12 |
| 1947 | 26 | 66 | 8 |
| 1949 | 22 | 63 | 15 |
| 1953 | 14 | 76 | 10 |

RAILROADS

| | | | |
|---|---|---|---|
| 1936 | 30 | 60 | 10 |
| 1945 | 24 | 65 | 11 |
| 1947 | 26 | 67 | 7 |
| 1949 | 22 | 60 | 18 |
| 1953 | 14 | 75 | 11 |

COAL MINES

| | | | |
|---|---|---|---|
| 1936 | 27 | 64 | 9 |
| 1945 | 29 | 59 | 12 |
| 1947 | 33 | 61 | 6 |
| 1949 | 25 | 58 | 17 |
| 1953 | 15 | 73 | 12 |

These polls, to be sure, cover only three industries. Those three, however, were ones in which government ownership had frequently been proposed. It may be supposed that the low public sentiment for nationalizing these industries indicates a lower one—perhaps very much lower—for many other types of business.

The situation with respect to government ownership of businesses seems to be static, with the possible exception of electric power generation and distribution—a subject discussed in the next chapter. Aside from this one industry, governmental entities at all levels seem to go on operating the same business in which they have been engaged for many years. A simple form of inertia seems to govern the situation: the activities and trends of the past continue with few changes.

## QUESTIONS AND PROBLEMS

1. May governmental entities enter any business whatsoever? What is the legal and constitutional basis for governmental businesses? Are there any legal and constitutional limitations on such activities?
2. List and evaluate the advantages and disadvantages of the two principal organizational forms of government businesses.
3. Government ownership of business may be categorized as dominant, substantial, or minor. List several industries in each category.

4. How extensive is government ownership in the United States? Is there a trend? What do you forecast?
5. Give the arguments for and against government ownership of business, and evaluate them.
6. Looking to the future, are there any government businesses that you forecast will be either expanded or contracted substantially?
7. Do you believe that the U.S. Post Office would be operated more efficiently if it were a private business?
8. Evaluate the TVA. Would it be in the national interest to create similar agencies in other river valleys, e.g., a Missouri Valley Authority or a Columbia Valley Authority?

## SELECTED READINGS

ABRAHAM, HENRY J. *Government as Entrepreneur and Social Servant.* Washington, D.C.: Public Affairs Press, 1956.

ALFRED, HELEN (ed.). *Public Ownership in the U.S.A.* New York: Peace Publications, 1961.

CLEGG, HUGH A. *The Future of Nationalization.* Oxford, England: Basil Blackwell & Mott, Ltd., 1953.

Commission on Organization of the Executive Branch of the Government (Second Hoover Commission). *Business Enterprises: A Report to the Congress.* Washington, D.C.: U.S. Government Printing Office, 1955.

DIMOCK, MARSHALL. *Administrative Vitality, The conflict With Bureaucracy.* New York: Harper and Brothers, 1959.

FABRICANT, SOLOMON. *The Trend of Government Activity in the United States Since 1900.* Princeton, N.J.: Princeton University Press, 1952.

FRIEDMANN, WOLFGANG G. (ed.). *The Public Corporation, A Comparative Symposium.* Toronto, Ontario: The Carswell Company, 1954.

GOLDBERG, SIDNEY, and HAROLD SEIDMAN. *The Government Corporation: Elements of a Model Charter.* Chicago: Public Administration Service, 1953.

HANSON, ALBERT H. *Public Enterprise and Economic Development.* New York: Humanities Press, Inc., 1959.

KUHN, TILLO E. *Public Enterprise Economics and Transport Problems.* Berkeley, Calif.: University of California Press, 1962.

MUSOLF, LLOYD D. *Public Ownership and Accountability: The Canadian Experience.* Cambridge, Mass.: Harvard University Press, 1959.

ROBSON, WILLIAM A. *Nationalized Industry and Public Ownership.* Toronto, Canada: University of Toronto Press, 1960.

# 25 ELECTRIC POWER AND ATOMIC ENERGY

As we note in the preceding chapter, some governmental businesses are objects of little or no controversy. There is one, however (and a huge one), that is highly controversial—the various governments' part of the electric power business. Here a batttle rages around the propriety of the Federal Government's engaging in the business of producing and selling electricity. The battle, moreover, has been intensified in recent years by the development of atomic energy as a source of power.

In 1959 Federal power plants—hydroelectric and steam—produced 15 per cent of the electricity used by the general public. Federal Government electricity-generating installations had an allocated investment of $5,232,175,000. The TVA was the largest seller of electricity, and one of its steam plants was the largest steam-electric plant in the nation.

Moreover, national electrical energy requirements are expected to double at least every decade, entailing increasing problems of capital investment and ownership.

## THE GROWTH OF PUBLIC POWER

At the beginning of the twentieth century municipalities were the only governmental entities owning and operating electric power plants. A rather substantial expansion occurred in the first quarter of the century, partly because private electric power companies could not make services available in some cities or because their rates were considered to be too high. Later the expansion of the private electrical utility business and the creation of larger distribution networks had the effect of slowing the development of municipal public power installations. In recent years, however, the capacity of the city-owned installations has been growing rapidly along with that of the rest of the industry. At present they account for between 5 and 7 per cent of the nation's total electric power business.

There are also a few state-owned systems, largest of which is the Nebraska Public Power System. Texas, South Carolina, and Oklahoma have multipurpose dams which were built as public construction projects during the Great Depression, primarily for purposes of flood control and irrigation, with electric power generation as a sideline.

Power marketing policies of the government have changed considerably over the years, chiefly in the extension of Federal activity beyond generation and in the control of the prices at which power is sold. At first the government was reluctant to enter into the business of selling electric power. Before the Tennessee Valley Authority entered the power market in 1933 Federal power was sold at the highest competitive price, since its sale was considered solely as a source of revenue to subsidize other functions. Consequently there was no attempt to undersell private companies.

Federal policy changed in 1933 when the Tennessee Valley Authority announced that it would sell power at the cheapest possible price. It was believed that the rates of the private electrical utilities at that time were too high, and state regulation appeared to be ineffective in holding them down. A feasible approach to this situation appeared to be to subject the private companies to competition from publicly operated plants.

With only 21 per cent of the nation's potential hydroelectric power capacity developed at present, a national question is how large the Federal Government's role will be in the development of the remaining 79 per cent. This, of course, will depend largely on Congress's and the Administration's policy toward hydroelectric development during any particular period. It seems that this matter of water-power development will be a major political issue for some time to come.

## THE PROS AND CONS

When any governmental electric power project is being contemplated, numerous issues arise, many of which apply only the the particular development in question. However, there are certain major arguments, some favoring private development and others favoring development by the government, which are applicable to most electrical projects.

The basic argument used by private power advocates is that public encroachment in the power industry is a violation of the principle of private interprise. Electric power generation is seen as a special case of the general proposition that governments should stick to governing and leave business activities to individuals and firms.

In favor of government ownership is the claim that governmental plants can sell electricity at lower rates than can private enterprise. This is held to be true because of certain cost advantages, such as being able to borrow money at lower rates of interest and being tax-exempt.

Governmental enterprises, such as the Tennessee Valley Authority, can be defended on the ground that they are able to stimulate the economy of an area. It is possible that private enterprise could do this also, but not on such a grand scale. There are definite advantages to being able to develop a large, integrated system, as was done in Tennessee. Perhaps, however, Federal power projects are much more justifiable during times of economic depression than during times of prosperity.

Some people defend the entry of the Federal Government into the power field at least partially on the ground that public rates provide a "yardstick" by which the reasonableness of private rates can be measured. However, conditions of production and distribution differ so widely between Federal and private systems, and from place to place, that making accurate allowances for these differences is extremely difficult, if not impossible.

Since Federal power projects are also multiple-purpose projects, designed to accomplish several major social objectives, many public power advocates will argue that the generation of power should help to defray the costs of these social aspects. They object to the idea of using a public resource for private profit and draw a distinction between navigable waterways, which belong to all of the people, and resources like coal and land, which may be private property. The fact that governments are firmly entrenched in the power business suggests that they will not withdraw from this business in the near future. It is hard to imagine the Federal Government's breaking up the Tennessee Valley Authority or the Bonneville Power Administration and distributing their properties and functions to private interests. These and other governmental activities in the electric power field will probably continue.

What part the Federal Government will play in future hydroelectric developments remains to be seen. The present trend is toward private development of hydroelectric generating capacity, and this appears to be the most desirable course in light of traditional American principles of free enterprise and the predominant aversion toward socialism. One thing is certain: Whatever the prevailing policy, whether it leans toward private or governmental development and ownership in the hydroelectric power field, many people will be dissatisfied.

## RURAL ELECTRIFICATION
## ADMINISTRATION

The Rural Electrification Administration, established partly as an antidepression measure, has become a multi-billion-dollar organization, borrowing money from the U.S. Treasury and lending these funds plus those repaid by borrowers to specified organizations for relending to their customers—consumers of electricity and of telephone service.

The Rural Electrification Administration was created by executive order in May 1935 under authority of the Emergency Relief Appropriation Act of 1935. Statutory provision for the agency was made in the Rural Electrification Act of 1936. This law authorized loans for facilities to bring central station electric service to persons in rural areas who did not have it. REA became a part of the Department of Agriculture in 1939. In 1949 it was authorized to make loans for the purpose of furnishing and improving rural telephone service.

REA is authorized to make loans at 2 per cent and borrows the needed money from the U.S. Treasury at the same rate. The law provides that in making electrification loans preference shall be given to public bodies, cooperatives, and nonprofit or limited dividend associations. In consequence, many REA cooperative associations have been established. Loans are made to these coops, and they, in turn, are authorized under the law to relend the money to their member-customers. Originally, most of these customers were farmers. In 1935, when REA was created, one out of ten American farms had electricity. At the present time about 98 per cent of the nation's farms are electrified.

The financial operations of the REA have become sizable. According to the 1963 Federal Budget the REA had loaned a cumulative total of $3,964,297,000 to more than a thousand organizations; of this amount $1,082,276,000 had been repaid, together with $534,427,000 in interest. Electric energy had been extended to 1,493,000 miles of lines serving 5,011,000 consumers. Total loans under the telephone program amounted to $609,327,000.

In recent years many of the new customers of the REA cooperative associations have been not farmers, but commercial and industrial establishments. REA coops have made loans to many of them, to finance wiring and the purchase of electrical equipment and machinery. This trend has worried defenders of private power distribution and people who are skeptical about the expansion of governmental activities.

## DEVELOPMENT OF ATOMIC ENERGY

An event that may prove to have been a turning point in world history occurred on December 2, 1942, in a laboratory under the stadium of the University of Chicago. On that day—unreported because of wartime secrecy—there was started the first manmade, self-sustaining, nuclear chain reaction; for the first time in history man obtained energy from a source not derived from the fires of the sun.

This development was part of the code-named "Manhattan Project"— the supersecret program to build an atomic bomb. The bomb was built and tested on the New Mexico desert in the early summer of 1945. In August a bomb was dropped on the Japanese city of Hiroshima, and three days later a second bomb was dropped on Nagasaki. The war was over.

After the war scientists and engineers turned attention to the possible peacetime uses of atomic energy. Research quickly developed many promising ones—some of them quite astonishing. One of the obvious uses for nuclear energy was in the production of electric power. At that time approximately 64 per cent of all electric power was being generated from fossil fuels, such as coal, oil, and gas. While there was no immediate need to supplement these fuels, the needs for energy in the future were expected to increase tremendously, and farsighted men could picture the time when we should run out of them. Thus there was a definite need for a new source of energy. The real importance of atomic energy was the assurance that it would give to the United States that this country would have ample fuel to meet its future requirements for electricity, industry's principal form of energy. These large and fast-growing energy requirements were thought to be assured when it was observed that one pound of uranium contains as much energy as 2,600,000 pounds of coal.

With this use in prospect one of the most interesting problems ever to occur in business—government relationships was created. The question became whether private enterprise or the government should develop atomic-power-producing facilities.

## ATOMIC ENERGY COMMISSION

Because of military considerations, the McMahon Act of 1946 made atomic development an absolute monopoly of the government. At the time of its passage people were uncertain about the best way to proceed with the development of atomic power. Therefore, the Act was supported by an overwhelming Congressional majority and by most of the atomic scientists. It transferred the responsibility for atomic development from the military Manhattan Project to a new civilian agency called the Atomic Energy Commission. This Commission was composed of five members appointed by the President for five-year terms. Its major activities included locating raw materials, production, and military and reactor development. The stated purposes of the Atomic Energy Commission in carrying on the above activities were to promote world peace, improve the general welfare, increase the standard of living, and strengthen free competition in private enterprise.

In the early 1950s the Commission undertook a comprehensive program of basic research and experimental development. This program included trial production of atomic electric power, together with many other research programs, such as those in the fields of atomic propulsion of ships and planes, development of weapons, and atomic medicine. The work of the Commission has continued with increasing emphasis on the development of peaceful uses of atomic reactions.

In the meantime, electrical utility companies and other organizations formed groups to study the possibilities of atomic power for the production of electricity. This was done under the industrial study group program of the Atomic Energy Commission. During this period, business became acutely aware of what could happen. As they looked about and saw the tremendous potential in the production of atomic energy, it soon became apparent to them that government had a virtual monopoly on atomic power. Under the spur of this awareness the private groups made substantial progress, but were not permitted by law to proceed beyond the study stage.

While industry, in the early 1950s, was trying to enter the atomic development field after having found itself looking on as an outsider, the Atomic Energy Commission also confronted several problems. Two of these were how to maintain the high secrecy that was necessary in the earlier stages and how to prevent an enterprise in which $14 billion of public funds had been invested by 1956 from becoming an entering wedge for government ownership on a large scale. Many people thought that the second problem might be solved by turning the government's resources over to private industry. Others, however, felt that this also could create many problems. For instance, these people believed that private industries would be "stealing" much of the government's knowledge and equipment, or at least getting a "free ride." Another major problem was that the capital investment required might be greater than any one corporation could afford. A final consideration was that, with atomic energy facilities in the hands of private business, it would be very difficult to control security leaks.

## ATOMIC ENERGY ACT OF 1954

Although reasonably satisfied with the performance of the McMahon Act, Congress, in order to promote the related policies of the Eisenhower Administration, passed the Atomic Energy Act of 1954. This represented a compromise of the positions stated above. The government retained control of atomic energy and did not give its projects to private industry. At the same time industry was given much of the government's information and was now permitted, with the Atomic Energy Commission's approval, to own and operate reactors. The new Act's two general purposes were: (1) to broaden international control and (2) to transfer peacetime development of atomic energy to the private sector of the American economy. This second point caused considerable controversy. It allowed the Atomic Energy Commission to license the private construction, ownership, and operation of reactors and the private possession of nuclear fuels. In addition, it gave private enterprise the right to use the government's patents and to patent new ideas of its own. Under the Act the Atomic Energy Commission was not allowed to enter into the commercial power business, but it could sell power generated in experimental plants.

In adopting the Atomic Energy Act of 1954 the government did not give up its physical assets, but did extend to industry much of its knowledge. The cloak was removed from much of the secrecy which had prevailed earlier, and to the maximum extent possible, the military aspects were separated from the civilian ones. To a large extent information on power reactors no longer remained classified, and frequent exchanges of information were made by some companies with other countries—England, France, and Belgium.

## FUTURE OF ATOMIC ENERGY

The technical feasibility of atomic power is no longer in doubt. We have demonstrated that we can produce electricity safely and efficiently from a variety of types of nuclear reactors. Therefore, the problem of the future, along with the technical one of improvements in the reactors, has become that of determining who should do the necessary developmental construction and operation—private industry or the government. Relevant to it are the factors of national defense, our philosophy of private ownership, and American prestige throughout the world.

Although national defense was one of the major problems in the early history of reactor development, it has become (in this specific context) secondary to the other two problems today. Civilian development of reactors has been divorced from military atomic development. In the past it was necessary to keep most of our atomic information classified. But as Russia and other countries have developed technical knowledge of their own, our country has found it wise to declassify much of the information. It is generally accepted that the progress in declassification to date has substantially reduced and almost eliminated the technical problems in the domestic reactor field.

Consideration of this secrecy requirement would tend to favor public ownership of all atomic information and facilities, including power-producing facilities. In constructing and operating plants the government could use this classified information and still keep it secret. A superficially attractive compromise would be to furnish to private companies only the information needed for actual safe operation and day-by-day maintenance of reactors. Unfortunately the information is not this neatly divisible. With only this minimum of operating information, private companies are not able fully to evaluate the costs of producing power. The prices at which they purchase their nuclear fuels are artificially established by the government and are subject to great changes in the future. There is no free market in atomic fuels, and governmental decisions on price could well make the difference between a private power project's being economic or not.

But private power interests point to the existing progress in declassification: over the years the number of classified items has been greatly reduced. They maintain that there is every reason to believe that, in the future, this reduction will continue, and that it is not unreasonable to expect a free market in the nuclear fuels in the foreseeable future.

If this were not America, the problem would probably be quickly solved in favor of governmental ownership of atomic generation of electric power. This has been the solution in England, France, and Belgium. Whether for these countries this is the better method of developing atomic power remains to be seen. In America, to date, we have taken a different view.

Such questions as the following, in addition to those pertinent to the consideration of national defense, discussed earlier, remain to be answered.

Has our domestic rate of power development been sufficient?

Is there too much danger to surrounding communities in private development?

Can private capital continue to finance an adequate program of expansion?

## PROGRESS OF DEVELOPMENT

When the Atomic Energy Act of 1954 was passed, there was yet no atomic power-producing facility of commercial size in operation or under construction. At that point, industry was given permission to develop atomic reactors. The effect of this Act can be seen by looking at the privately sponsored projects in operation, under construction, under contract, and in the planning and study stages six years later. In 1960 there were three private projects in operation—at Shippingport, Vallecitos, and Santa Susana. In addition, there were 11 more projects under construction or contract, three in the planning stage, and eight in the study stage.

If this Act of 1954 had not been passed and the Atomic Energy Commission had retained the exclusive right to develop power reactors, the results would be conjectural. An advocate of public power would probably cite the extensive research facilities and the apparently unlimited finances of the government. In 1954 the government had a complete monopoly on the available information, and even today it might be in a better position, from the viewpoint of its having ready access to all available data, to do the job. The proponent of private power, on the other hand, would be fortunate in being able to point to tangible evidences of its accomplishments. With private dollars being spent for this development, management—if it expects to continue to stay as management—must show results. From 1954 to date managements have been willing to expand huge sums, with the tangible results listed in the preceding paragraph.

## THE SAFETY CONSIDERATION

A second major consideration is that of safety. Safety in this case means protection from radiation. A reactor cannot explode as does a bomb; an atomic explosion due to the reactor's becoming supercritical for a period of time is physically impossible. If a reactor goes completely berserk, it becomes extremely hot and melts down into a critical mass, which will generate and disperse radioactive fragments locally; this could prove harmful if proper precautions are not taken. Because of this, the government has established a Safeguards Committee to inspect the various installations.

Advocates of public power emphasize the fact that atomic power installations are not completely safe. In support of their contention they can point to the accident that occurred near Calder Hall in England, where radioactive particles contaminated a herd of cows. In this case the government was obliged to buy all the milk from the herds and dispose of it. There was another accident that occurred at Chalk River, Ontario, Canada. Several accidents have occurred in the United States at Arco, Idaho, and one at Argonne. Public power proponents say that, to insure maximum safety, the government should do the actual constructing and operating of atomic installations and should not rely on inspection.

On the other hand, the private power contenders say that the safety issue has been greatly exaggerated. In their opinion every effort is being made to insure safe installations. They do not believe that the government could necessarily provide safer atomic reactors. They point out that mere ownership cannot determine safety—that this is, rather, a function of many other factors, such as design, construction, and mode of operation. From their accidents they are attempting to accumulate experience that can prevent future accidents.

## THE FINANCING PROBLEM

The third basic consideration is whether private industry can continue to finance an adequate atomic power program. By 1954 the government had billions of dollars invested in atomic research and facilities. At that time private investment could not have begun to finance all atomic development. Since then the government has been spending approximately $2 billion a year on atomic development (mostly on military projects); it now owns approximately $7 billion in plants. Most of these plants are for fuel processing and other ancillary operations, and cost up to $.5 billion each. Private industry spent approximately $.5 billion over the same six-year span in developing its reactor facilities.

An opponent of private power can point out how difficult it is for private industry to finance such projects as these. The developments to date have all been experimental. The facilities that have been completed cannot as yet compete with fossil-fueled installations on a basis of costs. Therefore, industry's expenditures are for projects which really must be counted as "research." Funds for work of this type are obviously limited. This, the opponents of private power argue, becomes even more apparent when it is considered that the United States is a country blessed with cheap fuel. We have adequate supplies of inexpensive fossil fuels readily available. Aside from this, fuel cost is only about 16 per cent of the total revenues of an electrical utility. Thus there must be a considerable saving before an atomic power plant will become economically feasible. The technological improvements involved will take time, and so the benefits to be expected from such an investment appear to be somewhat remote. The proponents of public nuclear power feel that this will restrict our development if it is left to private enterprise.

To answer these charges, private companies have formed associations to share the financial burden of developing atomic reactors. In addition, private development is taking place in many associated operations, such as fuel processing and the handling of atomic wastes. By dividing the huge development costs among many companies, the private interests hope to make tolerable the financial burden on any one.

Privately owned business feels that it is obliged to develop atomic power as fast as possible for two reasons: (1) to keep abreast of competition from other sources, such as gas, and (2) to keep government from dominating the power field, Mr. A. C. Montieth, vice-president of Westinghouse, has estimated that atomic electric power will be competitive with fossil fuels in ten years. Hence a reduction in cost of atomic generation would give the electric power industry a competitive advantage over other forms of energy. While their rates are regulated to prevent profits of more than fixed percentages of their assets, very few utilities are actually earning the maximum profits allowed them by the public service commissions. Thus they feel that atomic energy, by reducing their costs, could increase their profits without inducing commensurate rate cuts by the commissions.

The government poses a threat to utilities. At the present time private power generally feels that to date the government has been restricted in the locations where it can reasonably enter into the power business. While it is true that over 60 per cent of the power sold by the government is from fossil fuels, it is still sold largely in areas such as TVA, where the Federal government got into the business for the stated purpose of developing water resources. It is true that, once these installations were established, the government rapidly expanded its activities. For example, today TVA generates about 80 per cent of its electricity by burning coal and only 20 per cent from water power. Private power is concerned that the advocates of public power will use atomic power as an excuse to move into areas where they have not the excuse of needing to develop water resources. Private power, therefore, believes that it must develop atomic power at maximum speed to prevent the government's entering this field and expanding its public power activities to heretofore uninvaded sectors of the country.

## ATOMIC PRESTIGE

An important factor in the international conflict is our prestige around the world. One of the most effective ways of getting prestige is through technological development. In recent years this has centered around rockets and atomic energy. About the only way in which American prestige in nuclear power development can be measured is through comparison of our accomplishments in this field with those of the rest of the world.

It can be contended that, under private ownership, we have not had a sufficient rate of development; although in 1960 the United States had 39 power and prototype reactors compared to 31 for the rest of the world, it can be argued that this difference was not as great as it might have been if the government had been doing the developmental work. But the conclusion is not provable—nor is its reverse.

Private power interests, however, point out that relatively few reactors are being built behind the iron curtain.

Proponents of private power also feel that it is unfair to compare American development with English, French, or Belgian progress. These countries face acute fuel shortages and have been forced by necessity into extensive programs of government ownership and operation. For instance, industrial coal in these countries costs $20 per ton as compared to $4 per ton in the United States.

## PRESENT CONDITION AND OUTLOOK

There would have been no atomic energy industry without governmental development. It is not yet an open competitive field. Under existing laws no one except the government can own uranium. The government has been a foster parent, rearing atomic industry through its adolescence. At this stage, and in the near future, it will be impossible for business to disassociate itself from government in the atomic energy industry.

And so private power is in a most precarious spot. Since 1954 it has accepted the challenge of developing atomic power—and with good results, so far. Business has demonstrated that private development can perform the task of building atomic reactors. This is a good start, but the issue of governmental versus private atomic electric power will be settled by the quality of private industry's continuing performance, for some time into the future.

## THE NEED FOR RESEARCH AND STUDY

As mentioned above, the production of electric power is not the only possible peacetime use of nuclear energy. Many other uses have already been discovered, and are being employed regularly. Research to discover more applications of this great force continues. So great and so significant is this scientific achievement that it may well take rank as one of the most important developments in the history of man, ranking with such earlier ones as the invention of the wheel, the control of fire, the perfection of heat engines, and the development of electrical power.

Historically, great technological developments have sooner or later caused major social changes. It may be expected that this process will be repeated in the case of nuclear energy. Indeed, because of its many possible applications, and also because of the greater rapidity of scientific progress and communication in these days, the consequences are likely to be greater and to follow faster than those of those earlier innovations.

It is clear that this is no time to be walking backward into the future. Just as research on the uses of nuclear energy is proceeding, so should research on the social consequences of these developments be pushed. The general lines along which this research should proceed might include these:

[1] Ascertainment of the principal ways in which atomic energy will affect the American economy;

[2] Visualization of the probable consequences of these influences;

[3] Anticipation of the problems connected with the introduction of atomic energy;

[4] Development of solutions to these problems.

As a part of, or concurrently with, such basic studies, it would be appropriate to consider research into the following subjects:

[1] The possible industrial uses of atomic energy;

[2] Atomic energy as a source of heat, light, and power, and the consequences of such uses in industry and housing;

[3] The probable effects of atomic energy on the size of industrial establishments and on the comparative competitive positions of large and small firms;

[4] The probable effects of atomic energy on agriculture, in creating better agricultural products; on the prices of agricultural products, in promoting better production techniques and increasing output per man-hour; on the incomes of farmers, in possibly creating surplus agricultural population;

[5] The use of atomic energy in providing large supplies of fresh

water, and the resultant effects of this use on the location and productivity of agriculture, on the location of industry, and on the location of population;

[6] The use of atomic energy in improving human health, and the effects of a substantial improvement in health on industrial output, on the demand for different types of consumer goods and services, on life spans, and on retirement programs;

[7] The proper roles (presumably complementary) of government and of private enterprise in the development and application of atomic energy.

The question expressed in this last topic should be raised with respect to the entire suggested program of research on the consequences of the introduction of this new form of energy. Some of the research can undoubtedly be carried on to best advantage by government agencies; other parts of it, by private organizations. Total expenditures on research in the United States have soared in recent years to more than $14 billion annually, and no end to the upward trend seems to be in sight.

A great new force, for good as well as for evil, has entered the life of man. It holds promise both of wholesale destruction and of making great contributions to better living. The very process of making these contributions will create problems, and the purpose of the research mentioned above is to anticipate these situations and to make plans for coping with them.

### QUESTIONS AND PROBLEMS

1. What lessons can be learned from the history of governmentally owned electric power production?
2. Do you favor expansion or contraction of this type of government business in the future? What do you forecast?
3. Do you believe that the Rural Electrification Administration should be continued indefinitely?
4. What special factors have made especially difficult the development of governmental policies respecting peaceful uses of atomic energy?
5. How satisfactory do you consider the present governmental policies respecting peaceful uses of atomic energy? What changes, if any, would you favor? What would you forecast?
6. How important will power obtained from atomic energy be to future American economic growth? Consider, for example, the possible use of solar energy.
7. Do you believe that the Federal Government should sponsor a program of research on the uses and problems of atomic energy? If so, how should the program be structured?

### SELECTED READINGS

American Assembly. *Papers on Atoms for Power.* New York: Columbia University Press, 1957.

AMOROSI, A. *Nuclear Engineering Handbook.* New York: McGraw-Hill Company, 1958.

BONBRIGHT, JAMES C. *Public Utilities and National Power Policies.* New York: Columbia University Press, 1940.

EATON, S. E., and MICHAEL MICHAELIS. *Radiation: A Tool for Industry.* Cambridge, Mass.: Arthur D. Little, 1959.

KRAMISH, ARNOLD, and EUGENE M. ZUCKERT. *Atomic Energy for Your Business: Today's Key to Tomorrow's Profits.* New York: David McKay Company, 1956.

PRITCHETT, CHARLES H. *The Tennessee Valley Authority, A Study in Public Administration.* Chapel Hill, N.C.: University of North Carolina Press, 1943.

SCHURR, SAM H., and BRUCE C. NETSCHERT, with VERA F. ELIASBERG, JOSEPH LERNER, and HANS H. SANDSBERG. *Energy in the American Economy, 1850–1975: Its History and Prospects.* Baltimore: Johns Hopkins Press, 1960.

TEITELBAUM, PERRY D. *Nuclear Energy and the U.S. Fuel Economy, 1955–1980.* Washington, D.C.: National Planning Association, 1958.

THOMAS, MORGAN. *Atomic Energy and Congress.* Ann Arbor, Mich.: University of Michigan Press, 1956.

Twentieth Century Fund. *Electric Power and Government Policy.* New York: Twentieth Century Fund, 1948.

TYBOUT, RICHARD A. *Government Contracting in Atomic Energy.* Ann Arbor, Mich.: University of Michigan Press, 1956.

U.S. Atomic Energy Commission. *Atomic Energy Facts.* Washington, D.C.: U.S. Government Printing Office, 1957.

# 26 THE WORLD CONFLICT

The overwhelming fact of our time is the troubled international situation, characterized by the military, diplomatic, and ideological rivalry between the communist bloc and the West and the holding over of mankind's head the awful possibility of a war of wholesale incineration and world-wide fatal fallout.

At present the Soviet Union is our chief antagonist and the possible source of megatonic destruction. It is possible, however, that in a few years Communist China may take over the number one terror spot. Indeed, the mutual proximity of China and the Soviet Union may turn out to be a divisive factor that might even drive the two huge countries into opposite camps.

Much further ahead, the picture becomes even more ominous. Today only four countries have produced atomic weapons. In future years, however, the membership of this exclusive nuclear club will certainly be enlarged. It is not unreasonable to suppose that within a few decades, nations which today are underdeveloped will (perhaps with aid from the industrialized nations) move from ability to make plows and tractors to competence in manufacturing the implements of war. First would come the simpler weapons of war, and eventually, the atomic bombs and dusts, lethal gases, bacteriological cultures and aerosols, amplified-light-ray projectors, and other awesome weapons which science will probably develop in the future.

Today it seems unlikely that the Russians would deliberately launch a nuclear attack unless they should become convinced that they could destroy a satisfactory portion of our nuclear weapons in an initial strike or that they possessed a satisfactory defense against such weapons. Surely it would be the part of wisdom for the Soviet leaders to concentrate on a program of trying to win the world to communism without becoming involved in a nuclear war, as long as such a war gives promise of being mutually self-destructive.

It is conceivable, however, that in future decades, if it comes to pass that dozens of countries get weapons of total destructive power, ambition or anger or accident might lead to the launching of one country's ballistic missiles. Once launched, they would provoke retaliatory attacks—and, because of the difficulty of determining the direction of origin of the initial rockets, and in the insane confusion of the situation, the counter-attacks might be launched in several directions, triggering a vast, mad chain reaction of indiscriminate destruction.

This is a grim picture. It suggests that unless the techniques of defensive warfare make unexpected strides, the earth could easily end as a depopulated planet whose inhabitants had learned to kill themselves off before they had learned to live in peace with one another. We might well long to dismiss this prospect as a nightmare fantasy, but, technological progress being what it is, we cannot. The chimeras of the race from the cave onward have, one by one, all of them been laid—until this one. This one, finally, is real.

## THE IDEOLOGICAL CONFLICT

The coming of massive war is unpredictable, but the continuation of ideological conflict into the indefinite future seems certain. The struggle between communist civilization and Western civilization for ideological ascendancy and the concomitant struggle for the establishment of the two opposed political, social, and economic systems is already vigorous and may well become intensified.

The struggle involves the claims of the two systems to give the people of any country better lives—economic and otherwise. It sometimes seems to be especially acute in the underdeveloped countries. What countries are these? Table 26.1 presents the data on per capita economic levels for 55 countries. One thing shown by the figures is that no sharp line of demarcation can be drawn between the underdeveloped and the developed countries.

Even should we draw such a line arbitrarily, we should avoid falling into the error of regarding it as demarcating two categories of nations with respect to their susceptibility to the appeals of communist ideology, with "vulnerable" nations below it and "safe" nations above it. For the people of all countries yearn for better lives and a higher standard of living; even the people of the well-developed countries desire improvement. The appeal of communism in well-to-do Western Europe may be smaller than it is in the frightfully poor countries, but the proposition that comparatively rich Western European countries would be even better off under communism is seriously put forth and defended by some persons in those countries.

Because the national income of any nation is only slightly smaller than the net national product, the figures in Table 26.1 may be taken to rep-

## Table 26.1

### ESTIMATES OF PER CAPITA NET NATIONAL PRODUCT OF 55 COUNTRIES EXPRESSED IN U.S. DOLLARS: ANNUAL AVERAGE 1952–1954

At Factor Costs

| RANGE IN U.S. DOLLARS | AFRICA Country | Per Capita | AMERICA Country | Per Capita | ASIA Country | Per Capita | EUROPE Country | Per Capita | OCEANIA Country | Per Capita |
|---|---|---|---|---|---|---|---|---|---|---|
| Over 1,000 | | | United States | 1870 | | | Switzerland | 1,010 | New Zealand | 1,000 |
| | | | Canada | 1310 | | | | | Australia | 950 |
| 750–1000 | | | | | | | Sweden | 950 | | |
| | | | | | | | Luxembourg | 890 | | |
| | | | | | | | Belgium | 800 | | |
| | | | | | | | United Kingdom | 780 | | |
| | | | | | | | Iceland | 780 | | |
| | | | | | | | Denmark | 750 | | |
| 500–749 | | | Venezuela[1] | 540 | | | France | 740 | | |
| | | | | | | | Norway | 740 | | |

| Income class | | | | |
|---|---|---|---|---|
| | | | | Finland 670; Germany 510; Netherlands 500 |
| 250–499 | Union of South Africa 300 | Argentina 460; Puerto Rico 430; Chile 360; Cuba 310; Colombia 250; Panama 250 | Israel 470; Malaya[1] 310; Lebanon 260 | Ireland 410; Austria 370; Italy 310 |
| Under 250 | Egypt 120; Rhodesia and Nyassaland 100; Belgian Congo 70; Kenya 60; Uganda 50 | Brazil 230; Mexico 220; Jamaica[2] 180; Dominican Republic 160; Guatemala 160; Ecuador 150; Honduras 150; Paraguay 140; Peru 120 | Turkey 210; Japan 190; Philippines 150; Ceylon 110; Thailand[1] 80; Korea 70; Pakistan 70; India 60; Burma 50 | Greece 220; Portugal 200 |

[1] 1952 and 1953.

[2] 1952.

SOURCE: Statistical Office of the United Nations, *Per Capita National Product of Fifty-Five Countries: 1952–1954* (New York: United Nations, 1957), p. 7.

resent the average per capita incomes of the peoples of the nations listed. Indeed, at the lower end of the scale, the figures probably do not overstate (slightly) the per capita incomes; they probably understate them substantially. As recognized by the United Nations statisticians, the standard statistical methods of computing national products understate reality in poor countries. This fact is substantiated by Dr. M. K. Bennett's interesting figures on the comparative per capita consumption of goods in various nations. A comparison of his figures (presented in the *American Economic Review*, September 1951) with the Table 26.1 figures, as well as with earlier estimates, suggests that the lowest figures should be multiplied by possibly two or (at the very bottom) three, for accurate comparison with the well-to-do countries.*

Even with such a correction, the fact remains that—as visual evidence indicates perhaps even better than cold statistics—most of the people of the world live in poverty; only a few are well off.

## FACTORS CONTROLLING REAL INCOMES

Why are some nations rich while others are poor? Why have some nations become richer through the years while others have stood still? Light on these subjects may be shed by making (in a slight change of Adam Smith's word *wealth*—but not a change in his meaning) an inquiry into the nature and causes of the *incomes* of nations.

The answers to these questions are basically those that are suggested in the analysis of economic growth in Chapter 9. The key to the level of average per capita income in any country is average per capita productivity. If this is high, the people will be rich; if it is low, they will be poor; and if it is rising, they will be getting richer.

In Chapter 9 we note that the significance of "natural" resources is often exaggerated, that it is the human resources that really count. The productive efficiency of the working population is a key factor. This in turn is influenced by the extent of their education, industriousness, incentives, sobriety, honesty, and health.

The quality and quantity (per capita) of both capital goods and management talent are significant factors. They, in turn, are influenced by investment, education, incentives, knowledge, and the state of technological progress. This last cannot be had if the people are apathetic or actively hostile to change; improvements result only from a favorable attitude toward innovation.

The factors that control productivity are responsible for the levels of real per capita income in all countries. The more favorable the factors, the higher the income; and conversely.

* The earlier comparison and analysis of the basic factors underlying per capita incomes is presented in my book *The Future of American Prosperity* (New York: The Macmillan Company, 1955), Chaps. 4, 5, 15, and 16.

The route to a better standard of living for any country, therefore, lies in improving the controlling conditions. The Marxist–Leninist argues that communism offers a kind of instant improvement. The communist agitator says, "Nationalize the factories and the great agricultural estates; take for the people the excessive shares that have been going to the capitalists and the absentee landowners—and the standard of living of the people can be increased overnight." Before rejecting this proposition as empty propaganda, we should do well to recognize that, in some countries, the shares going to owners are indeed large and that, if these shares could be divided up among the masses of the people, immediately noticeable improvements in living standards would occur. On the other hand, it is easy to exaggerate the extent to which living standards could be thus improved and to overlook the possibility that, under the new management, neither the factories nor the farms would be as efficient as they had been before.

## THE POPULATION QUESTION

A difficult and delicate question is posed in many countries by the growth of populations. A nation which is already overpopulated and is experiencing current rapid growth of population may be effectively blocked from any gain in its standard of living.

The economics of population is simple. The larger the population of a country, the more mouths there are to be fed; but also the more pairs of hands there are to work. Will twice as many hands, however, produce twice as much food? The answer that is right most of the time is "No." This is because of the tendency toward diminishing returns.

The law of diminishing returns states that, at any moment and with given quantities of the other productive factors, an increase in the number of workers will cause total output to increase, but (after a point) the additional output resulting from each additional worker will decrease. In other words, past that point the *marginal product*, that of each added worker, declines.

This principle is often misunderstood because of its being misstated. The rule does *not* say that if, *over a period of years*, the number of workers increases the marginal product will certainly decline. This proposition, to be sure, *might* be true, if the combination of the other productive factors should remain unchanged. But if during these same years the amounts of capital, management, and enterprise also are increased, and technology is improved, the marginal product may *rise* while the number of workers is growing. But the fact remains that, by the end of the period, the marginal product might have been still higher if the number of workers had not increased at all, or had not increased so much.

The tendency to diminishing returns is probably more significant in agriculture than in manufacturing. It is especially important, therefore, in the underdeveloped countries, in which agriculture is the principal form of production.

There are many countries in which standards of living are locked at low levels by current population trends. What are the prospects of reducing the birth rates in these countries? Economic factors, religious beliefs, and cultural mores all bear on this question. Certain methods of birth control cost money, and even modest costs may be prohibitive among poor people. This fact has spurred the search of scientists for what they have come to call "the pill." This word stands for a substance that can be taken orally which will produce temporary infertility, and is so cheap that it is within the means of poor people or could be given away on a wholesale scale by an interested government.

Many persons, however, would be deterred by their religious beliefs from making use of this or any other such means of regulating family size. Moreover, it is unreasonable to suppose that, in any country where a man's prestige is judged by the numbers of his children and grand-children, a program of family limitation could become popular.

The experience of the United States and other Western countries proves that it is possible to have both population growth and a rising standard of living, but this double achievement requires greater effort than would be necessary without the population growth—an improvement in the factors of production sufficient to raise the standard of living by 2 per cent, without population increase, might alternatively permit a population increase of 2 per cent without any gain in the standard of living. To have *both* a 2-per-cent gain in population *and* a 2-per-cent gain in the standard of living would require something on the order of twice as great a gain in the productivity of the factors of production. In short, the overpopulated countries can raise their standards of living much more easily if their populations do not increase; and productivity gains will have to exceed population gains if their populations do in fact increase. Thus the prospect of achieving high real incomes in the over-populated countries without effective birth control is small.

## THE UNDERDEVELOPED COUNTRIES

The well-to-do countries, the industrialized countries, are sufficiently alike in economic conditions, cultural patterns, and institutional arrangements so that what is said about the conditions of economic growth in any one of them applies with only modest changes to the others. The genuinely poor countries, however—the ones commonly called "the under-developed countries"—differ so greatly from the developed countries in many of these respects that their special conditions create some special problems of economic growth.

Most of the underdeveloped nations are countries that were once parts of some colonial network. Their problems are social, political, and economic. Typically in such a country, the people's experience as colonials, followed by their new freedom, has created an emotional national outlook and an antagonism to Western nations. They have an inordinate fear of foreign domination of any type. In these nationalistic emotions they are stimulated further by communist propaganda and hirelings.

The people are generally poor and illiterate, and suffer from malnutrition and disease. Production of everything except human beings is extraordinarily low by comparison with that of the richer nations. The social structures are generally fixed by tradition, with caste or class mobility nonexistent. Most of these nations have little in common in language and cultural traditions, but in anticolonialism and anti-Western emotions they often find strong common ground. They are hampered by traditional concepts—particularly with regard to work and material needs —by lack of motivation in productive enterprise, by a strong affinity with the land, and by a maldistribution of wealth and income.

The political leaders, many of whom are sincere, devoted, and intelligent men, must listen to the mass desires of their constituents. Their wants may include a higher standard of living (usually in a hurry and without sacrifice or effort), land, wider distribution of wealth and income, equality, and recognition of their aspirations.

The political national aims are generally cooperation with both the West and the communists, peace (some Asian cultures exhibit religious pacifism), recognition through the United Nations, equality with other nations, and opposition to colonialism and any sort of domination—political, military, or financial.

Sometimes it seems that their crucial immediate desires are a steelmaking plant, a six-lane highway, a national air line, a huge hydroelectric complex, and an invitation to their president to visit the White House. These five items seem to have become status symbols.

## THE LURE OF INDUSTRIALIZATION

To achieve its goals, an underdeveloped country must take certain primary steps. It must be able to walk before it can run. The creation of a substructure of roads, bridges, docks, water supply, irrigation, housing, and health and educational facilities must precede the agricultural and industrial development. There must be social reforms, agrarian reforms, tax reforms, and population control. Agriculture must be stimulated, productivity increased, light industry begun, enterprise encouraged, and the people motivated to move forward within the frame of their own culture.

The usual urge to industrialize is dangerous. In many cases the problem of producing enough food to keep up with the population takes so much manpower that there is none available for other purposes. Growth must be balanced in many ways. Only as agriculture becomes more efficient can human resources be released to industrial development.

If a per capita income of less than $250 a year might be supposed to mark the underdeveloped countries, they account for over half of the world's population. Though economically primitive, they are being affected and stimulated by the new developments of the twentieth century. They are undergoing transformation, and no one knows what kind of society they will evolve—a condition that presents a serious problem to the United States and its allies. They may turn to communism, or they may develop their own systems, which might be democratic or totalitarian. Because of past colonization by Europeans, they are in general suspicious of the West. It is a concern of the United States to help these countries to develop into nations with which the West can live in peace and security. One way seems to be to help them to accelerate their economic growth. And participation by the United States in the development and trade of these countries could enable her to propagate Western civilization's values of freedom and human dignity, and thus to bridge the political and cultural gulf which now separates the West from the underdeveloped areas.

The importance of building a bridge of understanding lies not only in its own merit, but also in its significance for our survival. We have already helped the other nations of the world extensively—principally in ways that are discussed in Chapter 28. Despite this help they dislike us. If we go on helping these nations, and assist them to achieve industrial and scientific development, it is conceivable that, as the years go by, they will, as mentioned earlier, learn to make fearful weapons. And if during all this time they have continued to dislike us and even to hate us, the end result would be that we would have helped to strengthen potential or actual enemies. It is therefore vital that, at the same time that we help them to help themselves in industrial and scientific development, we should win their friendship.

## IDEOLOGICAL RIVALRY

Throughout much of the world, in poor countries and in rich countries, the ideological rivalry between communism and capitalism, as alternative and mutually antagonistic roads in pursuit of the better life, prevails. The very names—*communism* and *capitalism*—have taken on strong colorations that derive from this struggle. Thus *capitalism* has inseparable connotations of evil in the minds and speech of all convinced socialists, so must so that the pejorative content of the word overflows into our own consciousness, impelling us to seek substitutes. In 1951 *This Week* magazine sponsored a nationwide contest in which 1,500 suggested synonyms for *capitalism* were entered—of which the editors found none satisfactory. Generally, as many pages of this book attest, the terms *free enterprise system* and *private enterprise system* fill the felt need.

The word *communism* has similar overtones in the ears of Americans; although in this case there does not seem to be any carry-over into the consciousness of the opposite camp. We in the United States abhor the word and what it stands for, and many of us take it for granted that this attitude is generally shared by straight-thinking people throughout the world. Confronted with the fact that many people in other lands distrust the private enterprise system and prefer communism or socialism, we find it easy to suppose that these people are ignorant or do not reason clearly. This is a delusion—and a dangerous one. If we are to adjust ourselves to the necessities of the ideological struggle, we had best rid ourselves of it.

Let us suppose that a citizen of one of the nations with low average per capita income (Brazil, India, Egypt, Indonesia) were to say (as many of them, in essence, have said and do say), "Why do you Americans expect my people to prefer private capitalism to socialism or communism? If capitalism means the right of an individual to own private property, to go into business for himself, and to earn profits, my country has been a capitalistic nation for hundreds of years. And in all that time most of our people have been poor, and many have been on the verge of starvation, when not over it. No. We see nothing in capitalism to give us any enthusiasm for it. With us it has been a ghastly failure.

"Many of my fellow countrymen feel that they could not possibly be worse off under communism; and in view of the oppressive nature of our particular brand of industrialism and of the land-tenure system in our country, they suspect that they might be considerably better off. To many of them freedom has meant freedom to starve—and they are ready to give that up with alacrity."

Does this sound like the statement of an ignorant man or of a fuzzy thinker? If so, how might we set him right—which of his facts are in error; where is his logic faulty?

This ideological struggle is not new. Advocates of socialism and communism have been vocal in the world for many years. Much of the argument until recently was of a largely theoretical nature; and much of it continues to be of that nature. The key new factor has been the appearance and experience of the first socialist or communist country, Soviet Russia. Until the appearance of Russian communism collectivism on a national scale was only a blueprint; now it is a reality.

## PROMISE AND PERFORMANCE

The arguments of collectivists run along two main lines. One is criticism of capitalism, and the other is the claimed superiority of socialism

or communism. Capitalism is criticized on the ground that it is basically
a selfish system, that it is immoral and inefficient, that it exploits the common people for the benefit of a handful of the rich; and in the 1930s the
argument was common that it could not even provide full employment
for all of its so-called "wage slaves." The collectivists further contend
that capitalism is wasteful of natural resources and, in its advertising and
selling activities, wasteful of productive resources; that it does not encourage education or the development of the human resources of a
nation.

Collectivism, by contrast, is pictured as an idealistic system in which
"the people" would own and operate the means of producing and distributing goods, in which real incomes would be substantially equal or
adjusted to the needs of the recipients, and in which all, motivated by a
super team spirit, would work together enthusiastically for the common
good.

That is the beautiful blueprint of collectivism. How does the actual
reality in the Soviet Union compare with the blueprint? It does not compare favorably. That the actual reality has been far different from the
blueprint has had as one consequence the fact that—outside the communist countries—the words *socialism* and *communism* are no longer
used interchangeably as they were by Karl Marx and for years after him
by others. Today the word *communism* commonly means the system and
condition in effect in the Soviet Union, Communist China, and the European satellites of the Soviet Union. In those lands the words are not
always used in a uniform meaning.

All over the world many socialists have rejected the cruelties and
inadequacies of the systems in those countries and have become avowed
opponents of communism; the term *socialism* has increasingly come to
mean something different from Sino–Soviet communism. One meaning
is a complete collective ownership of the means of production, but under
a truly democratic government. Another, more limited, meaning involves
only a comprehensive public ownership of heavy industries. By this
standard it could be contended that the United Kingdom is a socialist
country. The difficulty with this definition becomes instantly clear, however, to anyone who is acquainted with the economy of that nation. There
is, to be sure, a sizable amount of government ownership (against which,
by the way, the tide of public opinion seems to have turned) but the
United Kingdom is still predominantly a private enterprise country.

## EARLY YEARS OF SOVIET COMMUNISM

What is the record of Soviet communism, of which the Soviets themselves are so proud?

Immediately after the Bolshevik success and the establishment of the communist system in 1917, predictions were common in other countries that the entire system would soon collapse. In part, these predictions rested on a general belief in the unworkability of collectivism and in part on the patently limited experience of the Russian communist leaders. In later years European socialists were to bewail the fact that the Revolution had come in backward Russia instead of among the orderly, efficient Germans. From the socialistic viewpoint a German socialist state would presumably have been a much greater success than the Russian one. It is true that the men who took over the management of the Russian social, political, and economic system were not experienced managers or executives. For the most part they were conspirators, more likely to be acquainted with the techniques of undercover subversion than with the methods of managing and directing business enterprises, large or small. Indeed, considering their lack of experience and the magnitude of the task that they undertook, there might be said of them what Doctor Samuel Johnson so unchivalrously said when commenting on a proposal that women ministers be ordained in the Church of England: "A woman delivering a sermon is like a dog dancing on its hand legs. The remarkable thing is not that it is not done better but rather that it is done at all."

Nevertheless, despite the inexperience of its managers, and at huge costs, some of which represented deliberate concessions to ideology, the Societ economy gradually expanded. From the beginning to the present, because of confusions in and the unreliability of Soviet statistics, analysts outside Russia have had a difficult time trying to pin down reliable figures on the Russian economy. Opinions naturally differ, therefore, about the true growth of the Russian gross national product and the real standard of living of the Russian people.

## RECENT YEARS

Certain spectacular accomplishments have been plainly visible. One is the Russian accomplishment in World War II. Hurling the first man-made satellite, and subsequent huge ones, into orbit represents another area of accomplishment. A skyscraper university, a palatial subway system, factories, steel mills, and dams are major Russian achievements. And the showing of Russian athletes in the Olympic Games and of Russian chess players in international tournaments has doubtless puzzled those critics who in earlier years asserted that a regimented society is incapable of accomplishing anything, particularly the development of human excellence.

Over against the undeniable gains of the Soviet Union must be put some serious defects. In earlier years millions of Russians perished as a consequence of the policies of the Supreme Soviet. The police state terror may have reached its height (down to the present) at the time when thousands of Russians were killed by order of Joseph Stalin. Within Russia the people are subjected to constant communist party propaganda. For the most part they know only what their rulers want them to know. Newspapers, radio, television, magazines, and books carry only censored information and voice the party line. These media inform the Russian people that they are making more progress than any other people in the world. News stories from the outside world stress the economic misery and hard times in the capitalistic countries. In consequence it seems that most Russians honestly believe that their system is better than capitalism. This situation confounds the opinion held by many outside of the Soviet Union that the Kremlin has never had the support of the masses and that only iron control has prevented the outbreak of a popular revolution.

Communist China and the European satellite communist countries have less in the way of positive gains to boast, and have chalked up many more failures and shortcomings. The Chinese regime has provided the people, not with more rice, but with more cruelty. In the European satellites, since communism took over, the standards of living have stood still in the poor countries and have declined in the formerly well-to-do ones. The contrast between economic and other conditions in East Germany and West Germany finally became so pronounced that in 1961 the communists built a wall to try to check the exodus of East Germans to the West—giving as their ostensible reason their desire to prevent an inflex of spies. The Berlin Wall dramatically illustrates a condition common to all of the communist countries. None of them has to cope with the problem of preventing foreigners from trying to get into the communist peoples' republics. All of them, on the contrary, have the problem of trying to keep their own nationals from escaping to better and freer lands.

## WHAT OF THE FUTURE?

The historical record of actual communism, as distinguished from the blueprint, is mixed. The accomplishments in Russia have been numerous; in other communist countries, few or negative. In all of them propaganda, regimentation, and cruelty have prevailed. One of the avowed objectives of the Soviet Union is to catch up with and surpass the United States. What is the prospect that it will do so? If the apparent present trends of population and productivity are real, and if they continue, it appears that the Russian gross national product may catch up with ours around the end of this century, and the per capita figure may equal ours some time in the twenty-first century.

But are the trends real and will they continue? The experts disagree about the magnitude of the trends and about the periods to be selected for measuring them. The consensus, however, seems to be that in recent years Russia has shown a higher percentage gain in both total and per capita figures than we have.

On the basis of the reliable statistics available, and because of the maturity of our system, projecting the future growth rates of the American economy is an exercise that is not entirely guesswork. But considering the inadequacy of the Russian statistical materials and the comparative newness of their system, trying to do the same thing for the Soviet Union involves much greater uncertainty.

In the light of these facts it might be wise simply to take account of the fact that the comparative economic growth rates of the greatest capitalist country and the largest communist country are factors that will influence the course of the world conflict in every one of its aspects. The future records of history rather than the speculations of today will tell the outcome of the rivalry.

## THE APPEAL OF COMMUNISM

And what has been happening in the rest of the world while the Soviet Union has been chalking up its mixed record and the other communist countries have been doing so badly? Many capitalistic countries have been making tremendous strides in improving the standards of living of their peoples and have been doing it without regimentation or cruelty.

In certain respects the situation in the world today is plain and clear. All of the well-to-do countries are capitalist countries, although not all the capitalist countries are well-to-do. On the other hand, all of the communist countries are relatively poor. Those that are least poor—East Germany and Czechoslovakia—are countries which progressive capitalism had put among the well-to-do before the communists took over and began to reduce their well-being. In short, on the record to date, capitalism at its best has made a very much better showing than has communism at its best. Why then does communism seem to have such a substantial appeal in so many parts of the world?

One explanation often proffered is poverty, as an inducement to what is sometimes called "stomach communism." The influence of this factor is exaggerated. If people are sufficiently hungry, they have little interest in anything and little energy available for starting revolutions. Moreover, the record does not suggest that communism can alleviate hunger nearly as well as can capitalism.

One explanation of the appeal of communism is the sheer magnitude of the untruthful propaganda coming from the Soviet Union. Soviet propagandists misrepresent the living conditions of the Russian people, exaggerting their well-being and denying their troubles.

Ignorance greatly assists the effectiveness of the untruthful propaganda. Many of the earth's inhabitants know little or nothing about the world outside their native villages and farm regions. These folk are poor, illiterate, and uneducated. They have no newspapers, books, or radios. Communist propaganda glowingly misrepresents the life of the Russian people, and these ignorant listeners have no means of discovering the truth or evaluating and refuting the claims.

In many nations much of the best land is owned by handfuls of rich landowners, and the bulk of farm workers labor for them either as employees or as tenant farmers. In this context of economic feudalism communist propaganda easily convinces the toiling farmers that under communism the land would be taken from the exploiting landlords and would become the property of all of the people, who would thereafter receive the rent-share now going to the landlords.

Many countries have governments that are inefficient, corrupt, or reactionary. In some of these the governments are dominated by small groups of wealthy people who run things in their own interests. Republics they may be in legal form, but in actual substance they are oligarchies or plutocracies. In such nations communists can point to wretched governmental performance and can claim that under communism the governmental form would be the "people's republic," operating honestly, efficiently, and in the interests of the common man. The obvious truth of the first part of the statement may convince its dupes that the second part is also true. In such countries revolutions frequently occur and chaos sometimes prevails, quite independently of communistic instigation. But revolutions and chaos serve communist purposes by paving the way for communist sympathizers to take over. So helpful is chaos to communism that communists may attempt to generate it where it does not exist, as a prime technique of their continuing effort.

As we have already noted, the interrelated factors of racism and colonialism generate dislike for and suspicion of the European nations which were the principal colonial powers and which happen also to be among the leading capitalistic countries. It is easy, therefore, to identify colonialism with capitalism and to overlook the fact that in recent years the Soviet Union has been the only expansionistic imperialistic power in the world.

The final explanatory factor is the use of force. Communism has come into power only once without it. In March 1957 a communist government was peaceably elected in the Indian province of Kerala, although it was subsequently able to stay in office only until August 1959. In all other countries in which communism has taken over, the assumption of power has been a usurpation, backed by force.

### A TIME FOR CLEAR THINKING

In assessing the present position and outlook of the two sides in the world conflict, there are four possible errors which we might make. They are:

[1]   To underrate the opposition,
[2]   To overrate the opposition,

[3]  To underrate our side, and

[4]  To overrate our side.

Committing the second or the third of these errors would be awkward. Committing the first or the fourth, however, might be fatal. This is no time in the affairs of our nation and the world to delude ourselves. We would be making a great mistake to refuse to accept facts unfavorable to our side or favorable to the opposition merely because these facts are uncomfortable and disagreeable.

The peoples of other nations and especially of the so-called uncommitted nations are not likely to make this mistake. Indeed, considering their hostility toward the West, they would be more likely to be overly impressed by our opposition and to depreciate our side. Let us therefore, in calm analysis, reconsider the factors that control the economic well-being of countries and the comparative contributions toward improving them that might be made by capitalism on the one hand and by collectivism on the other. This analysis should shed light on probable future trends throughout the world.

## THE PROMISES OF CAPITALISM
## AND OF COLLECTIVISM

Which system would be the more effective in raising the productive efficiency of the working population? Provision of the vital element of education for the people would be a definite matter of public policy under collectivism. Both the avowed aims of collectivist theory and the record of the Soviet Union suggest that this form of organization stresses education heavily. Programs for health and nutrition offer the same choice of alternatives, with a less clear answer. How would the two systems compare in the provision of adequate numbers of those competent managers—in factories, on farms, and elsewhere—that play so vital a part in economic growth? As with all types of training, the collectivist society would be in a position to provide and impose the type of preparation that it desires. And it is arguable that it is easier to train men in the skills used in running a planned economy than to train them to become independent entrepreneurs. This is a key point. In some poor countries of the world thoughtful men say, "Our people lack enterprise; therefore the state must be the enterpriser, and must go into business activities requiring enterprise." The Western viewpoint suggests that it would be better to try to generate the spirit of enterprise among the people, while admitting the difficulty of doing so.

How rapidly could each of the two systems increase the quantity and quality of capital equipment? In capitalist countries industrial equipment is supplied mainly by private investment, while government investment goes into public capital—schools, highways, public works, and the like. Authoritarian collectivist control could increase a nation's domestic rate of investing above the voluntary level by imposing a contraction of current production and consumption of consumer goods. Such action would not be inevitable; collectivism might do the opposite—but the possibility at least exists.

What of the comparative rates of progress in the development of technology? In capitalist countries both public agencies and private organizations contribute to technological development. The experience of the Soviet Union indicates that a collectivist society can concentrate on technological development if it wishes to do so, and the evidence suggests that there is a high rate of technological progress in selected lines there.

Permeating many aspects of economic growth is the factor of *incentives*. What are the incentives to diligent work and productive activity? There are many. In capitalist countries one incentive is the prospect of increasing one's earnings. Would this incentive exist in a collectivist nation? The answer to this question depends on the system adopted for payment of wage and salaries. The Soviet Union has used piece-rate pay systems and other wage arrangements which are admittedly capitalistic. These are held to be a temporary necessity pending the arrival of complete communism. When that condition is achieved, presumably the pay system will be the one long-avowed by communism, "From each according to his ability, to each according to his need." Skeptics insist that such a method of paying wages would remove incentive to effort and would lead to universal soldiering. Collectivists on the other hand contend that in their new society everyone would be trained from childhood to do his best, not because doing so would earn him a larger income than otherwise, but rather because this would be a part of the normal super team spirit of the people of a collectivist state.

In overpopulated nations achievement of improved standards of living depends on the degree of success achieved in birth control. In a capitalist country the government and other sources of social pressure may or may not attempt to influence the psychological and economic factors that influence the birth rate. But the collectivist state, with its rigid control of the mass media of communication and its ability to engage in psychological conditioning, can exert greater influence on the religious and cultural patterns of thought, in addition to being able to help with the economics of the birth control problem, if it wishes to do so.

A collectivist state would have an advantage in dealing with many of these problems if it were able to generate among its people the quasi religious devotion to, belief in, and enthusiasm for its system that seems to prevail among many Russians. Some observers find this dedication puzzling; but there seems to be no doubt that it exists, and that its prevalence facilitates collectivist controls.

## THE CHALLENGE OF COLLECTIVISM

The end result of this analysis is the uncomfortable realization that there are impressive reasons why many of the people of the world prefer collectivism to capitalism. Indeed, considering the wretched record of capitalism throughout most of the world on the one hand, and the glowing promises and basic appeal of collectivism on the other, the question naturally arises why collectivism has not spread much more rapidly through being warmly embraced instead of being forced at gun point. Perhaps among the explanations might be found an instinctive realization by people of the truth of Lord Acton's famous remark (even though they may never have heard of it): "Power tends to corrupt; absolute power corrupts absolutely." When all power is concentrated in the state, can the state—embodied in the ruling group—resist corruption?

In any event, it is the part of wisdom not to allow our own beliefs and attitudes to lull us into the illusion that they represent universal experience and conviction. Collectivism dominates much of the world now and appears likely to make more gains in the future. Those Americans who insist that our goal should be "Victory over Communism" do not make it clear whether they mean military victory or an ideological one. Whichever they mean, they might move us closer to it if they spent less time exhorting the result and more in defining the goal, expounding its desirability, discussing the obstacles to its achievement, and examining the costs.

## THE CHALLENGE OF COMMUNISM

Communism represents a challenge and a menace to us and to the West. Premier Khrushchev has said, "We will bury you." In his characteristically outspoken way he has advertised an intention which we should be ill-advised to ignore. Least of all should we be complacent—overrating our side and underrating his. In the next two chapters we give attention to the policies and programs that we can follow in attempting to meet this challenge. Certain basic actions may, however, be mentioned here. We can contribute to the survival and well-being of our country and our friends by making our nation ever stronger in every good way—military, diplomatic, economic, social, political, cultural, moral, and spiritual. We can work to make friends. We can cooperate in positive programs. And we can attempt to find out whether collectivism must remain a foe or whether it is possible to bring about a condition in which peoples utilizing different kinds of economic systems can live together on this planet in peace and harmony.

Before we reject that thought as being idealistic or impossible, it might behoove us to find out how well we are doing at present. Although there is no "scoreboard"—not even the unofficial one used to count the standings in the Olympic games—we can note such communist successes as the extension of their rule until it has come to control one third of mankind; and we may note also the many technical achievements of the Soviet Union. We may observe on the other hand, the rehabilitation of Western Europe and the containment of major Soviet aggression in recent years. And then we might look at the disconcerting results of a Gallup survey published on October 18, 1961.

Who's Winning The Cold War?

(Percentages of Respondents who Cited Russia or the West)

| Survey made in— | Russia | West |
|---|---|---|
| | % | % |
| Britain | 80 | 20 |
| Vietnam | 77 | 23 |
| Finland | 76 | 24 |
| France | 82 | 18 |
| U.S.A. | 73 | 27 |
| W. Germany | 70 | 30 |
| Ireland | 65 | 35 |
| Uruguay | 63 | 37 |
| Holland | 60 | 40 |
| Switzerland | 50 | 50 |
| Denmark | 40 | 60 |

So much for the situation today. How does the world see the outlook? The results of surveys looking to the future were compiled by the United States Information Office and released in a report dated August 29, 1960. In these surveys the residents of certain foreign countries were asked the following question: "If the U.S. and the U.S.S.R. settle down to competition without war for the next 20 or 25 years, which of the two would end up as the stronger?" The responses should give us pause.

| Country and Date | Number of Cases | U.S. | U.S.S.R. | Both Equal | No Opinion | Net Favorable |
|---|---|---|---|---|---|---|
| | | % | % | % | % | % |
| Philippine students | | | | | | |
| Aug., 1958 | 887 | 50 | 9 | 24 | 17 | 41 |
| Philippines | | | | | | |
| March, 1959 | 1,609 | 42 | 2 | 8 | 48 | 40 |
| Netherlands | | | | | | |
| April, 1958 | 825 | 44 | 13 | 16 | 27 | 31 |
| Uruguay | | | | | | |
| April, 1959 | 1,612 | 36 | 15 | 8 | 41 | 21 |
| Rio de Janeiro | | | | | | |
| May, 1958 | 200 | 39 | 19 | 8 | 34 | 20 |

| Country and Date | Number of Cases | U.S. % | U.S.S.R. % | Both Equal % | No Opinion % | Net Favorable % |
|---|---|---|---|---|---|---|
| Vietnamese students | | | | | | |
| Feb. and March, 1959 | 462 | 27 | 7 | 22 | 44 | 20 |
| Greece | | | | | | |
| Nov., 1958 | 1,207 | 30 | 12 | 8 | 50 | 18 |
| Norway | | | | | | |
| Nov., 1957 | 845 | 38 | 23 | 18 | 21 | 15 |
| Japan | | | | | | |
| Dec., 1958 | 676 | 23 | 27 | 6 | 54 | 6 |
| Mexico City | | | | | | |
| May, 1958 | 200 | 45 | 40 | 3 | 12 | 5 |
| Okinawa | | | | | | |
| Dec., 1958 | 577 | 25 | 21 | 5 | 49 | 4 |
| West Germany | | | | | | |
| Feb., 1960 | 529 | 29 | 29 | 19 | 23 | 0 |
| Italy | | | | | | |
| Feb., 1960 | 591 | 22 | 24 | 32 | 22 | −2 |
| Buenos Aires | | | | | | |
| Feb., 1960 | 560 | 19 | 32 | 23 | 26 | −13 |
| Great Britain | | | | | | |
| Feb., 1960 | 613 | 25 | 44 | 10 | 21 | −19 |
| Turkish students | | | | | | |
| June, 1958 | 230 | 18 | 43 | 30 | 9 | −25 |
| France | | | | | | |
| Feb., 1960 | 608 | 7 | 35 | 25 | 33 | −28 |
| Arab students, Dec. 1, | | | | | | |
| 1957, and Jan. 7, 1958 | 274 | 8 | 40 | 16 | 30 | −38 |

The facts—favorable as well as unfavorable—do not justify compla-cency. Quite the contrary; they make it clear that the world situation is so dangerous today and promises to get so much worse in the future that major national efforts will be required to cope with the multiplying menaces to our (and, we are constrained to believe, the world's) well-being.

## QUESTIONS AND PROBLEMS

1. Do you agree that "the continuation of ideological conflict into the in-definite future seems certain"?
2. Why are some countries rich, others poor? If you were economic adviser to an underdeveloped nation, what would you suggest as methods of raising its low average per capita real income?
3. How real is the population problem?

4. What answer would you make to the visitor from a low-income nation who asks you why his people should be expected to prefer capitalism to socialism or communism in his country, considering what a failure they consider capitalism to be?

5. How do Soviet Russia and other communist countries compare with the theoretical picture of the collectivist system?

6. List, compare, and evaluate the basic advantages and disadvantages of capitalism and collectivism.

7. What is the outlook for the communist countries? What is the outlook for the capitalist countries? What is the relevance of these forecasts to the future ideological conflict?

8. What is your forecast of the ultimate outcome of the ideological conflict?

## SELECTED READINGS

*Annals of the American Academy of Political Science.* Issue entitled "Is International Communism Winning?" July 1961.

BOULDING, KENNETH E. "The Prevention of WW III," *Virginia Quarterly Review,* Winter 1962, p. 1–12.

BAUER, PETER T. *Economic Analysis and Policy in the Underdeveloped Countries.* Durham, N.C.: Duke University Press, 1957.

FRIEDMAN, MILTON. *Capitalism and Freedom.* Chicago: University of Chicago Press, 1962.

JACKSON, BARBARA. *The Rich Nations and the Poor Nations.* New York: W. W. Norton & Company, 1962.

LEIBENSTEIN, H. *Economic Backwardness and Economic Growth.* New York: John Wiley & Sons, 1957.

LOUCKS, WILLIAM N., and J. WELDON HOOT. *Comparative Economic Systems,* 3rd ed. New York: Harper and Brothers, 1948.

MYRDAL, GUNNAR. *Rich Lands and Poor: The Road to World Prosperity.* New York: Harper and Brothers, 1957.

ROSTOW, WALT W. *The Stages of Economic Growth, A Noncommunist Manifesto.* London, England: Cambridge University Press, 1960.

SHANNON, L. W. *Underdeveloped Areas.* New York: Harper and Brothers, 1957.

# 27 POLICIES ON INTERNATIONAL TRADE

Government–business relationships in our country are influenced by these important, interrelated conditions:

[1]  The United States is only one of many countries on planet Earth;

[2]  Our government and our people have economic dealings and other relationships with the governments and peoples of other countries; and

[3]  The world conflict continues, as discussed in the preceding chapter.

The first two conditions are not new; but they have gained new significance in recent years because of the third. Today international trade policy is an important aspect of our foreign policy.

We turn attention, therefore, to basic politico-economic-historical conditions and problems and then proceed to consider them in the context of the world conflict.

## INTERNATIONAL TRADE

As Adam Smith pointed out, one of the conditions of economic progress is increased specialization and division of labor. Such an increase necessitates increased trading—more exchanging of goods and services. The outcome of the entire process is a gain in per capita output and income.

Americans seem to be fully aware of the benefits that have come to them as a result of specialization and trade—*within this country*. Partly because of its, we have greater productivity, more goods and income, more television sets and automobiles—in short, more real wealth—than any other nation in the world. Nevertheless, when imported foreign goods compete with domestic goods, many Americans support the view that it is folly to import goods that we are already producing. They understand the logic of specialization within their country, but they are seemingly incapable of carrying this logic one step further to the realization that world-wide specialization without artificial trade barriers would not only increase the world's wealth, but would enhance their own along with it. Adam Smith went to the heart of the matter in his famous comment on the growing of grapes in Scotland:

> By means of glasses, hotbeds, and hotwalls, very good grapes can be raised in Scotland, and very good wine too can be made of them at about thirty times the expense for which at least equally good wine can be brought from foreign countries. Would it be a reasonable law to prohibit the importation of all foreign wines, merely to encourage the making of claret and burgundy in Scotland?*

Whether the cost of a product made at home is thirty times that of the foreign-made equivalent, as in Adam Smith's example, or only fractionally greater, the principles of free trade remain valid, and the benefits of specialization are contingent only on the element of transportation and other extra costs involved in the international exchange of goods.

## ATTITUDES TOWARD FOREIGN TRADE

In basic economic analysis the rationale of trade between Americans and peoples of other lands is identical with that of trade between Californians and New Yorkers. But when the semantically loaded labels *foreign* and *domestic* enter people's thinking, differences seem to appear.

What are some of the conditions that help foster this biased attitude toward "foreigners" and foreign trade? One of them is the different monetary arrangements of the various nations. Each nation has its own currency, and the various currencies may not be freely exchangeable for one another. National boundaries, and the languages, customs, cultures, and religions that they enclose, may prevent a common basis for communication and understanding and may heighten suspicion and mistrust.

## BARRIERS TO TRADE

Men build ships, highways, railways and airplanes to carry goods from one nation to another and then erect legal barriers to this movement. There are many types of trade barriers. A principal one is tariffs. Others are quotas, embargoes, boycotts, restrictions, and monetary controls and manipulation. Since tariffs are typical and widespread we focus our attention on them.

A tariff is a duty or tax on an imported product. Tariff rates may be assigned in three ways: (1) as a percentage of the value of an item (an ad valorem rate); or (2) as a specific duty rate, such as $1.50 per ton of steel; or (3) by a combination of these two methods.

Quotas are often confused with tariffs. A quota is a stated maximum

---

* Adam Smith, *The Wealth of Nations* (Everyman's Library; New York: E. P. Dutton & Co., 1910), p. 402.

limit on the amount of an item that may be imported in a unit of time, say a year. In the United States, tariffs are generally used except for farm products, for which quotas are used.

Tariffs have several different objectives. The two basic ones are to raise revenues for the government and to protect domestic industries. And the second objective, protection, can have several different motives, as discussed in later pages of this chapter.

How does a tariff "protect" a domestic industry? It raises the price of the competing imported product (perhaps to a prohibitive level) and thereby allows the domestic outut to be sold at a higher price and in a larger quantity than would otherwise be possible. The tariff thus, in effect, gives an indirect subsidy to the domestic producers. The subsidy is paid, not by the government, but by the consumers of the product. An alternative to the protective tariff is direct payment of an actual subsidy by the government to the industry (in which case, presumably, the taxpayers rather than the consumers get the final bill).

## EARLY TARIFF LAWS*

The first law passed by the first Congress, on July 4, 1789, was a tariff law, designed primarily to furnish the government with revenue. (Duties on imports continued to be a main source of governmental revenue until World War I, after which they declined to a position of relative unimportance in this respect.)

Later tariff laws raised the rates, reflecting a desire to afford protection to infant industries and to foster a stable and self-sufficient economy. It is interesting to note the conflict involved in early tariff policies— the more protective the tariff, the fewer goods entered, and hence the smaller the revenue.

The Tariff Act of 1816 is considered by some to have been the first protective tariff. A desire for protection of domestic manufactured goods was developed because of the War of 1812, which had cut off foreign sources. Here was planted the seed of protectionism for infant industries and defense industries. These are examples of some of the rates: new boots $1.50 a pair, hats 30 per cent, leather 30 per cent, rolled or hammered iron 30 per cent, and carriages 30 per cent.

In 1818 increased protection was given to the iron industry. In 1819 there was a reduction in wine rates. In 1824 the rates were increased to protect the iron, glass, linen, hemp, lead, cutlery, and woolen industries. This was our first tariff to apply mixed duties—not only ad valorem rates but also specific duties on the same commodities. During the debate over the Act of 1824 Henry Clay gave his famous speech on the

---

* This summary of tariff history is based on F. W. Taussig, *The Tariff History of the United States* (8th ed.) (New York: G. P. Putnam's Sons, 1931).

American system. His theory was that protection of manufactured goods had the virtues of providing revenue for the government, of reducing our dependency on foreign nations, and of increasing our home market for agricultural goods.

The Act of 1828 is of special interest to the student of politics. It was the first tariff act where political considerations became more important than economic principles. It was an act that was never intended to be. The tariffs of the period had aligned the country into sections. The South was against high protective tariffs, the middle states favored them, and the New England states were somewhere in between. In a special maneuver a bill was framed by "Jackson men" who intentionally put the rates on raw materials so high that the conservative New Englanders would defeat it. The plan was that the middle states would vote for the act while the Southern and New England states would vote against it. The middle state "Jackson men" could then go down on record as the friends of American industry and weaken the prestige of the two protectionist presidential aspirants, Clay and Adams. However, the woolen interests in New England were strong enough to pass the bill, and the United States got its "Tariff of Abominations."

In 1830 and 1832 rates on coffee, tea, cocoa, molasses, salt, and wine were reduced. The tariff of July 14, 1832, had the effect of reducing rates to the lower levels of the Act of 1824. Criticism of protectionism led to the Compromise Tariff of 1833. This act provided for a gradual horizontal cut of all ad valorem rates above 20 per cent by 1842.

During the period of the Compromise Tariff the country went through the panic of 1837, and the government had a large deficit. The Tariff of 1833 was blamed for the panic and the deficit. The Tariff of 1842 raised the rates back to the 1832 level.

The Tariff of 1846 was composed by the executive branch of the government and included a plan by the Secretary of the Treasury. It was generally considered to be a free-trade act, but it retained some protection.

The Tariff Act of 1857 was basically the same as the Act of 1846, but since revenues had become excessive, it reduced the rates and listed more free items.

## TARIFFS DURING AND AFTER
## THE CIVIL WAR

The Tariff Act of March 2, 1861, raised the rates back to the level of 1846. Increases in tariff rates were frequent during the Civil War because of the need to finance the war. The Act of June 30, 1864, fixed average rates of 47 per cent on 1,450 separate articles.

In view of an increase in surplus revenue the Tariff Act of 1872 provided for a 10-per-cent horizontal cut and an increase in the number of free goods. However, there was a panic in 1873 and a large reduction in custom receipts, so the Act was repealed in 1877.

In 1881 the Tariff Commission was organized. It proposed a general reduction of tariffs. This recommendation was not heeded, however; and the Act of 1883, while reducing the rates on some commodities, increased them on others.

In 1884, for the first time since the Civil War, a Democratic president, Cleveland, was elected. True to the Democratic principle of low tariffs as opposed to the Republicans' advocacy of high protective tariffs, Cleveland tried unsuccessfully six times to get legislation for tariff reductions.

During the Harrison Administration, the McKinley Act of 1890 was passed; it increased average rates to approximately 50 per cent. The Act contained a reciprocity provision. In enabled the President to impose certain duties on selected products whenever he found that countries exporting these commodities were imposing duties on American products which he deemed to be unjust or unreasonable.

After a Democratic sweep in 1892 Cleveland tried to revise the tariff policy of the country. The result of his effort was the Wilson–Gorman Act of 1894. It was presumably a step toward free trade; but it followed no uniform principle whatsoever. Cleveland was not happy with the Act and, to register his disapproval, allowed it to become law without his signature.

## HIGH PROTECTION

When McKinley became President, he called a special session of Congress for the problem of raising revenue. Congress gave him the Dingley Tariff of 1897. This Act raised the average rate to approximately 57 per cent. It also restored the reciprocity provision of the Act of 1890 and put wool back under protection.

The Dingley Tariff lasted twelve years. During this period the anti-trust movement surged. There was a widespread belief that high tariffs and trusts went hand-in-hand, and there was a cry for reduced rates. President Taft tried to get a reduction in rates, but the result was the Payne–Aldrich Tariff Act of 1909, with a general rise in rates. This Act stated that the rates were only minimum ones, and that if any country discriminated against the United States these rates, as applicable to that country, could be increased by 25 per cent. The President was given authority to set up a Tariff Board to collect information applying to the rates. Also a Court of Custom Appeals was set up to review the legal aspects of the provision. The Act of 1909 also eliminated the reciprocity provision of the Act of 1897.

Under President Wilson there was a movement for reduction in tariff rates, and the Underwood–Simmons Act of 1913 was the result. The Democrats called this a competitive tariff—claimed that it represented a new policy on tariffs. In general, it reduced the rates to 29 per cent and placed sugar and wool on the free list. It eliminated fixed duties in favor of ad valorem rates and extended the free list. Because of the outbreak of World War I, the consequences of this tariff are not clear.

After the war farmers suffered a severe cut in income as compared to the high levels of the war. The Republicans blamed the slump on the low rates of the Tariff of 1913. When they took over Congress they immediately passed the Emergency Tariff Act of May 27, 1921. It placed specific rates on farm products and higher rates on textile materials, dyes, and chemicals. It was scheduled to remain in force only six months; but it lasted over a year.

The Fordney–McCumber Tariff of September 19, 1922, returned tariffs to a protective level. Agricultural products continued to enjoy high rates, and so did other industries which feared competition. The bill contained a flexibility clause which authorized the President to vary the rates as much as 50 per cent to compensate for differences between American and foreign costs.

## THE CLIMAX OF PROTECTIONISM

The Tariff of 1922 lasted until the Hawley–Smoot Tariff Act of 1930 was passed. According to its framers the latter was to protect American industries from the changing conditions in Europe. However, its extremely high rates seemed more than enough for this purpose.

While in the Senate the bill came under fire in two unusual ways. First came protests from foreign countries which, although phrased in diplomatic language, warned of retaliation. A second protest came in the form of a letter signed by 1,028 American economists asking President Hoover (in vain) to veto the bill. The letter generally made the following comments:

[1]  The higher tariffs would permit inefficient producers to operate, thus causing excessive waste, and would give higher profits to more productive producers, at the expense of the consumers.

[2]  Few people would gain from this tariff since the majority of the businesses in the country did not come under its protection.

[3]  People that depended on exporting and those with capital invested overseas would lose.

[4]  Other countries would undoubtedly retaliate in kind.

[5]  Unemployment would certainly not be aided by restricting trade.

[6]  American industry did not need this protection.

[7]  Bitterness would be generated in foreign nations.

With the passage of the Act came immediate retaliation by other countries, as the economists' letter had predicted. In not altogether rational moves several nations raised their tariffs on American goods.

## THE WALL COMES DOWN

With the defeat of Hoover in 1932 there came a demand for a reduction of tariffs. The answer to this was not a new tariff act but rather the Reciprocal Trade Agreements Act of 1934. This law did not repeal the Act of 1930 but rather amended it. The amendment gave the President the authority to raise or lower the rates within 50 per cent of statutory rates as he saw fit to the benefit of the United States. The amendment also stated that any agreement made with one country would apply to all others. This was an unconditional form of the "most favored nation clause." From that time until 1962 the practice in the Congress was to renew and extend the Reciprocal Trade Agreement Amendment for periods of one to three years and on occasion to allow more reductions of rates.

In 1962 came the Trade Expansion Act, which, representing as it does a substantial move in the direction of tariff reduction, is the most important development in American tariff legislation since the 1934 law. Its enactment stemmed in large part from the development of the European Economic Community and the challenge which this great continental organization poses to other nations. One of the objectives of the Act is assisting the United States to meet this challenge by enabling our representatives to bargain more effectively with other countries and, of course, especially with the countries comprising the EEC.

The Act gives the President authority to decrease by 50 per cent any rate of duty and to change other types of import restrictions. It also gives the President authority to remove tariffs altogether on certain specified categories of products.

Since it appears that the tariff reductions made both within the EEC and by the United States may be hurtful to some producers of goods, the Act further provides that if increased imports arising primarily from tariff concessions under this Act cause serious injury to an industry, two types of adjustment assistance may be invoked. One is authority to readjust tariffs or impose quotas; the other is a provision for direct assistance to firms and workers in industries so injured. Under conditions specified by the Act, certain types of technical, financial, and tax assistance will be extended to such firms, and readjustment allowances lasting as long as 52 weeks may be given to workers who are adversely affected.

Even though the Administration threw its weight behind the enactment of the Trade Adjustment Act, the comparative ease of its passage in the Congress was a source of surprise to many observers who were familiar with the power that industries desiring protection have been able to mobilize against tariff reductions.

As Chart 27.1 shows, our tariff rates were high throughout most of our history; in recent years they have declined to today's modest level, and it seems not unreasonable to conclude that passage of the Trade Expansion Act signals a period of further reduction in these duties and other impediments to international trade.

*Chart 27.1*

## TOTAL DUTIES AS A PERCENTAGE
## OF DUTIABLE IMPORTS

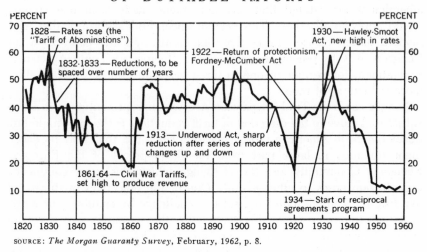

SOURCE: *The Morgan Guaranty Survey*, February, 1962, p. 8.

## THE PROS AND CONS

There is basically only one argument for free trade and against protection. It is the one cited earlier—the gain to most parties from specialization and the division of labor.

Arguments in favor of protection, however, are numerous, and most of them are fallacious. Only one of the invalid contentions is worthy of mention here—the one that might be called the *basic* invalid contention—the argument that tariffs are necessary to prevent the American standard of living from being dragged down by floods of imported goods made cheaply by the "pauper-paid" labor of "less advanced" nations. This argument is false, because, as we note in Chapter 9, per capita income depends on per capita output—on productivity. As long as American productivity remains high relative to that of other countries, the American standard of living will remain high compared with theirs. If and when the productivity of other countries rises to the level of

American productivity, we shall no longer be ahead, but we shall not have dropped to their level—they will have risen to ours, and the world will be better off. And, in this process of exchange of goods among people having different productivities, a protective tariff cannot possibly produce a gain for us in the long run; indeed, to the extent that it reduces the incomes of other nations, and hence their imports from us, it must reduce our own real income a little.

A valid reason for a temporary trade barrier is the need to protect an "infant industry" in order to promote economic development. It is perfectly possible for a country to possess the resources to render it potentially competitive, or even dominant, in a certain industry, but to find it difficult to get the industry started and on its feet because other nations have been first in the field and have preempted the markets. In such a case, resort may be had to a protective tariff, to keep up the domestic price of the imported product until domestic makers of the same product can become solidly established. In theory, such a tariff should be removed when the infant grows up.

Another valid reason for a trade barrier is the "essential defense industry" argument. It may be necessary to protect a domestic industry which would not normally be viable against foreign competition, but which must be maintained in good health and steady operation because it would be genuinely essential for the prosecution of a war in which the foreign sources might, for one reason or another, be cut off. An example is the optical industry, which arose in the United States after World War I as a result of America's experience in that war of being shut off from the German source, which had theretofore enjoyed a virtual world monopoly. Another is the synthetic rubber industry which was created in World War II to replace the Southeast Asian source of natural rubber, blocked off by the Japanese. The use of a direct subsidy as alternative to a protective tariff is particularly applicable in a situation of this sort.

The infant-industry argument, it should be noted, does not validate permanent barriers (although, conceivably, the essential-defense-industry one might). Once a domestic industry has become sufficiently well established that its product is ready or almost ready to compete successfully with the imported equivalent without a barrier, the retention of the barrier means only that the arguments for specialization are being disregarded, and the benefits of specialization are being foregone. Vested interest sometimes argues for temporary continued protection after an industry has reached maturity and self-sufficiency. In such a case "temporary" often really means forever. Yet there may be a valid argument for a truly temporary extension—too hasty elimination of a protective tariff can result in economic catastrophe for some innocent people. Consideration should be given here to a gradual reduction of protection, to give the industry time to adjust in an orderly manner and without undue hardship. At the end of such a transitional period, if it has been properly planned, the industry will either have built up its efficiency to the point where it is genuinely competitive, or it will have proven itself genuinely unable to compete, in which case it will presumably, and properly, cease operation. This procedure is no more harsh than the normal attrition caused by technological improvement. The Reciprocal Trade Agreements program has in effect followed this policy, with a not unreasonable resultant mortality rate.

## PRESSURES AND POLITICS

An anomaly in the tariff issue is the position of *consumers*; they, the largest single group in the United States (being, in fact, the entire population), have been weak in voicing appeals for the lower tariffs and the freer trade which would benefit them. Paradoxically, their individual voices have spoken out more loudly for higher tariffs and protection. Why? Because they are far more conscious of themselves as producers than as consumers—it is as producers that they receive their paychecks; and, if these are large enough, their consumers' concern over prices is a secondary one. In their universal mass as consumers, they make only a confused and muffled clamor; but, in their localized groups as producers, they are articulate and specific.

It is the localized groups of citizens as producers—the farm states, the regions that specialize in woolen textiles, the steel-making countries —that send representatives to Congress. These representatives are likely, for reasons discussed in Chapter 5, to pay less attention to the generalized clamor than they do to the loud and clear voices of their own constituents; and, through the familiar techniques of logrolling, to cooperate in keeping tariffs high. These facts give validity to the saying, "The tariff is a local issue."

In view of this condition it is perhaps surprising that tariffs have been lowered at all. Lower tariffs have resulted mainly because the trade agreements have made it possible to isolate, to turn spotlights on, various individual protectionist interests. And encouragingly, more and more people and segments of the economy are becoming educated to the gains to be had from freer trade. A Gallup poll in January 1962 indicated that 40 per cent of the respondents favored lower tariffs, 31 per cent higher ones, 14 per cent no change, while 15 per cent expressed no opinions.

## IMPACT OF OUR TARIFFS ON
## OTHER NATIONS

The international relations of the United States have occasionally been adversely affected by increases in our tariff rates. A substantial increase in one of our import duties may stop or greatly reduce the import of the commodity affected. If that commodity is one of the principal exports of another, friendly, country, and if in that country exports are a larger proportion of the gross national product than they are in the United States (a common condition), the effect will be that a significant proportion of the foreign nation's income is eliminated. The consequence may be serious injury to its economy. The gain—such as it is—for a segment of the American economy represents, on the other hand, only a tiny portion of our economic activity. That which is merely a ripple on our side of the ocean may be a tidal wave on the other.

In the light of these conditions we should do well, before adjusting any of our tariff rates upward, to take account of the probable impact of the change on other countries. Foreign policy as well as domestic policy may be pertinent.

## THE COMMON MARKET

January 1, 1958, may go down in history as one of the most significant dates of all time—significant for Europe and the world, including the United States. On that date six countries—France, Germany, Italy, Belgium, Holland, and Luxembourg—signed the Treaty of Rome, creating the European Economic Community, which has come to be called "The Common Market." Primarily an economic document, the Treaty nevertheless foreshadows the possibility of eventual political union of the six signers into a United States of Europe.

In the Treaty the signatory nations pledged themselves to accomplish gradually over a period of years the following things:

[1] Removal of tariffs, quotas, and other trade barriers among themselves;

[2] Creation of a uniform tariff schedule applying to imports from the rest of the world into the Common Market;

[3] Abolition of restrictions on the movement of labor, capital, services, and business enterprises within the EEC;

[4] Coordination of monetary and fiscal policies;

[5] Establishment of a common agricultural policy;

[6] Endorsement of the need to improve living and working conditions;

[7] Establishment of a social fund to help to relieve economic injury to workers resulting from tariff reductions; and

[8] Inclusion of other countries in associated arrangements.

The original plan contemplated completion of these objectives in ten to 15 years, but developments have been faster than scheduled. Furthermore, several other countries have applied for membership or are contemplating doing so.

It is clear that the Common Market will improve economic conditions within the participating nations. What is less clear is the nature of the effects of this great development on the rest of the world. Specifically, will the national tariffs be replaced by a Common Market tariff surrounding the new giant entity with its 250 million people? There will unquestionably be increased international trade within the Common Market. Is it likely that one consequence will be diminished international trade between member countries and nonmember countries? Specifically, what will be the effects on the United States? One thing is clear: the establishment of the European Economic Community intensifies the importance of our own international trade policies.

Fortunately for the United States, international trade is a relatively small fraction of our gross national product and our national income; and our economic well-being depends almost entirely upon domestic trade. Nevertheless, it is important that legislation and negotiations be handled in such a way as to minimize any adverse effect of the new organization on our economy.

As additional countries become members of the Common Market, and as other countries are permitted to become associated with it, the relationships between the United States and the EEC will become increasingly important. Involved is not only the modest problem of reducing or preventing adverse economic impact on our country, but the much more important matter of preventing this huge new combination from becoming a divisive force in the Western community.

## THE GOLD AND BALANCE OF PAYMENTS PROBLEM

A continuing unfavorable international balance of payments, together with a large loss of monetary gold, has intensified the importance of our international trade policies and also has introduced a complicating factor into our domestic monetary situation.

For several years after World War II the United States was in the position of being able to export goods easily to most countries, partly because many of the other leading industrial countries were devastated and were temporarily handicapped in production. As a part of our foreign economic policy under the Marshall Plan, and other arrangements, the United States contributed substantially to the industrial rebuilding of other nations—both friends and former foes. One consequence was that these nations in many instances found themselves possessed of new plants and equipment more modern than those in our country. With their traditionally greater reliance on export trade, they went after new business and did so successfully. As a result, our net favorable balance of payments declined and then became negative.

The international balance of payments looks more complicated than it actually is; but it is complicated enough. When we Americans buy goods from other lands, or travel abroad, or make military expenditures or grants, or invest money in other nations, we create in foreign hands supplies of dollars to be exchanged for other currencies. Conversely, when the peoples of other lands do these things vis-à-vis the United States, a supply of foreign currencies appears, offered in exchange for dollars. In recent years the number of dollars offered for exchange has exceeded the quantity of foreign currencies offered; in other words, we have been spending and investing more abroad than foreigners have been spending and investing here. When this condition occurs, foreigners first come into the possession of increased bank accounts in the United States. If these bank balances, which stand to the credit of foreign banks, corporations, and individuals, rise above levels that they consider to be necessary and useful, they can sell their dollar bank accounts to their own central banks. These foreign central banks, under our law, are permitted to buy gold and to withdraw it from our stocks. This is what has been going on in recent years.

This gold movement, together with sales of gold by the Soviet Union and other world gold producers, has produced a substantial improvement in the gold liquidity positions of other countries, and this has strengthened their currencies. From the viewpoint of the world the United States had a disproportionately large share of the world's gold when this process began, and the redistribution is generally advantageous.

Desirable though the gold movement was from the viewpoint of other nations (to which it has been a gold *inflow*), it presents a problem to us. The United States is a world banker. If the gold outflow were to continue very much longer, people might become concerned lest the United States either run out of gold or suspend gold payments. Having this fear, they might hasten to sell their dollar bank balances to central banks, and the central banks might quickly exchange the dollar bank balances for gold, thereby intensifying the outflow. It would be a condition something like that of depositors' rushing to take their money out of a bank because they fear that it might close its doors.

## APPRAISING THE SITUATION

How significant is the unfavorable balance of payments? How important is the gold outflow? There is some difference of opinion about these matters.

In 1962 a noted writer asserted that the gold outflow, if continued, could shatter our economy.

Less dismal, perhaps, but more important are the views of William McChesney Martin, because as Chairman of the Board of Governors of the Federal Reserve System, and Chairman of the Federal Open Market Committee, his influence on Federal Reserve actions is substantial. In a statement before the Joint Economic Committee, February 1, 1963, he said:

> There is the tendency to speak of international versus domestic goals. This seems to me to be only the latest version of a series of problem formulations in terms of unrealistic alternatives. Over the years, we have seen counterposed full employment *or* price stability, social objectives *or* financial objectives, and stagnation *or* inflation. In the last case there was even serious discussion of the number of percentage points of inflation we might trade off for a percentage point increase in our growth rate. The underlying fallacy in this approach is that it assumes that we can concentrate on one major goal without considering collateral, and perhaps deleterious, side effects on other objectives. But we cannot. If we were to neglect international financial equilibrium, or price stability, or financial soundness in our understandable zeal to promote faster domestic growth, full employment, or socially desirable programs, we would be confronted with general failure.°

If the gold loss were to continue, the United States would, sooner or later, have to suspend gold payments—cease selling gold to foreign governments and central banks. What consequences would follow?

We should surely be criticized—at home and abroad—for breaking faith with our creditors, in going back on our promise to redeem our money in gold. Our international banking business would be likely to suffer in the future.

Another consequence might be a decline in the international exchange value of the dollar, taking the form of a rise in the prices of other currencies in United States money. Such a decline in the dollar's foreign exchange value would tend to stimulate our exports and reduce our imports. Most American businesses, however, would be unaffected. The general prosperity of the nation would not be altered. Our prosperity depends basically on what goes on within our borders, not on what goes out across them.

Suspension of gold payments would immediately solve the balance of payments problem, since with a floating foreign exchange rate (unconnected to gold), the rate moves to balance the supply of and demand for dollars.

At the same time, such a suspension would alarm those who consider that our money and our economy are sound only if the dollar is soundly based on gold.

Depreciation of the dollar (if it occurred) would injure our nation's prestige—something serious in today's troubled world.

In short, an end to the gold loss is desirable—some would say essential—to our economic well-being.

° *Federal Reserve Bulletin,* February 1963, p. 124.

## DEALING WITH THE GOLD PROBLEM

The United States could take certain direct, negative measures to check the gold outflow, such as raising tariff duties on imports and cutting our military and economic assistance to other nations. These steps would be highly effective for the purpose, but as cures they might, for obvious reasons, be worse than the disease.

Positive measures would include attempts to encourage and build up our exports. As noted in Chapter 11, this approach might involve restraining increases in wages and prices, but should not be limited to such restraints. Another helpful step would be securing more participation in international development programs by other nations.

A treatment of the difficulty rather than a cure would be to bring about some international arrangement involving a pooling of gold reserves—figuratively a sort of international Fort Knox (although the physical presence of metallic gold in such a pool would probably not be necessary). This international gold pool, with appropriate accompanying arrangements, might relieve some of the strain on the dollar, and might also go some distance toward relieving an international problem—the general world shortage of gold as a proportion of growing economies and expanding world trade. World monetary gold stocks have not been increasing as fast as world business has been growing. At the moment, the possible brake on economic expansion that could be imposed by a failure of gold supplies to keep pace with other forms of economic growth is not crucial for many nations; but it is by no means inconceivable that the gold brake could become a serious matter for other countries as it has already become for the United States.

Since it would be foolish for nations to restrain their economic growth to keep it in step with the expansion of the gold supply, it is appropriate to consider possible steps for economizing gold and, possibly, to go beyond that point and make arrangements for simultaneous proportionate devaluations of leading world currencies in terms of gold (say by one fourth of 1 per cent each month). This process would multiply the number of dollars, francs, or pounds represented by any given weight of metallic gold and would also tend to stimulate gold mining. In any event, the outcome would be an increased quantity (in terms of monetary units) of gold. Among the countries thus simultaneously devaluating their several currencies, there would be no change in exchange rates.

## THE GOLD STANDARD

Discussions of alterations in the gold standard run into a barrier to clear thinking in the form of the quasi religious attitude toward gold. Many persons believe adherence to the gold standard to be a sure guard against inflation. Those who express this opinion are apparently unaware of or indifferent to the fact that between 1896 and 1920, when the United States was on the gold standard, the commodity price level rose considerably more than it has risen since 1933, when the nation abandoned the full gold standard in favor of the modified gold bullion standard.

In a modern nation which has become accustomed to the use of paper currency and bank checks, it is not necessary that the bank deposits and the currency be convertible directly or indirectly into any physical substance. The soundest money is not that which is convertible into gold (or diamonds, or radium, or sea shells), but rather that which serves a nation best. It is hardly arguable that the American economy was encouraged between the end of the Civil War and 1896, when a shortage of monetary metals caused the commodity price level to decline for three decades. With or without gold, the proper national monetary objective is to manage the money system so as to contribute to growth and stable prosperity.

## OUTLOOK FOR INTERNATIONAL TRADE

After more than a century of protectionism, the United States has recently moved away from that viewpoint and toward lower import duties and freer trade. The vigorous political pressures and lobbying activities of bygone years in favor of high tariffs seem to have lost much of their potency. It can honestly be stated that our recent international commerical policy has not been shaped solely with an eye to the well-being of this nation, but rather has taken account also of the well-being of the peoples of other lands. We not only have not followed a "beggar my neighbor" policy; we have, in fact, followed policies designed to aid and strengthen our friends throughout the free world.

## QUESTIONS AND PROBLEMS

1. Explain how specialization, division of labor, and exchange of goods affect economic well-being. Who gains from these conditions? Who loses?
2. Would the United States have developed to its present extent if it had followed a policy of free trade since its inception?
3. How does a protective tariff work—specifically, how does it "protect" an American industry?
4. What lessons can be learned from the history of tariff legislation?
5. State and evaluate the arguments for tariff protection.
6. Under what conditions might trade restrictions, such as tariffs and quotas, be justifiable? What other course of action (e.g., subsidies) might produce more satisfactory results and why?
7. Evaluate the proposition that "the tariff is a local issue," and indicate its significance for democracy as a type of government.

8. How may changes in our tariff rates affect exporting nations and our relations with them?
9. What is the significance of the European Common Market for the U.S. businessman?
10. What effects will the European Common Market have on U.S. policy?
11. Do you agree with the analysis of the gold outflow problem and the suggested program for dealing with it?
12. Evaluate the Trade Expansion Act.

## SELECTED READINGS

BENOIT, EMILE. *Europe at Sixes and Sevens: The Common Market, the Free Trade Association and the U.S.* New York: Columbia University Press, 1961.

Committee for Economic Development. *A New Trade Policy for the United States.* New York: Committee for Economic Development, 1962.

ENKE, STEPHEN, and VIRGIL SALERA. *International Economics*, 3rd ed. Englewood Cliffs, N.J.: Prentice-Hall, Inc., 1957.

GRIFFIN, CLARE E. "A Tariff Policy for Modern Times," *Michigan Business Review*, September 1953, pp. 6 ff.

HABERLER, GOTTFRIED. *A Survey of International Trade Theory*, rev. ed. Princeton, N.J.; Princeton University, 1961.

LLOYD, LEWIS E. *Tariffs, The Case for Protection.* New York: Devin-Adair Company, 1955.

McCRACKEN, PAUL W., and EMILE BENOIT. *The Balance of Payments and Domestic Prosperity.* Ann Arbor, Mich.: University of Michigan, Graduate School of Business Administration, 1963.

ROOSA, ROBERT V. "The Balance of Payments and International Financial Cooperation," *New York Federal Reserve Letter*, March 1962, p. 44–51.

TAUSSIG, F. W. *The Tariff History of the United States*, 8th ed. New York: G. P. Putnam's Sons, 1931.

# 28 POLICIES FOR INTERNATIONAL DEVELOPMENT

In turning attention to description, analysis, and appraisal of our policies on international development, it is wise at the outset to recognize certain unwelcome and uncomfortable but important conditions, stemming from the fact that throughout the world people dislike us.

Well known in ordinary interpersonal relations is the operation of the *sympathy–antipathy principle*. In accordance with this principle an action by a man who is liked will rate approval for it and for him. Conversely, this same action by a man who is disliked will draw criticism. Thus if a man is careful in his charities, those who like him will call him *thrifty*; those who dislike him will call him *tight*. And a man who is openhanded in his giving will be regarded by those who like him as friendly and generous, and by those who dislike him as profligate or condescending.

The same perverse rule applies among nations; indeed, in some respects, its operation is intensified in national attitudes. Since World War II the United States has given or lent more than $80 billion in foreign aid. What kind of reactions has this program—unique in world history in its giant size—provoked throughout the world? A few foreign friends share what must be the predominant American opinion that it represents unparalleled generosity. Many foreigners, however, perhaps believing that our wealth is more fabulous than in fact it is, consider that it has been a stingy performance. In the matter of motivation some foreigners probably agree with the view of many Americans that we have been moved by a combination of humanitarian friendliness and calculating self-interest. Many other foreigners—perhaps most of them—think of our programs as motivated solely by selfish interest, representing an attempt to buy friendship. There is also foreign criticism that we do little for those who are our demonstrated friends and much for those who might otherwise be foes. And there is criticism that much of the money is misdirected—goes into the wrong pockets or maintains cruel and dictatorial regimes.

Our foreign relations are complicated further by what might be called the *outsider resentment principle*. This principle is observed in our ordinary domestic interpersonal relationships. Thus an inhabitant of an American city may angrily denounce his municipal administration for what he regards as stupid and incompetent failure to fill and repair the chuckholes in the city streets after a hard winter. If, however, an out-of-town visitor should mildly observe that the streets do not seem to be in their usual excellent condition, this citizen may become as angry with the visitor as he already is with his own city administration.

This principle becomes greatly intensified where comments by foreigners are involved. A dramatic example occurred in 1961. A young woman member of the American Peace Corps wrote a postcard to a friend in which she reported on the squalor and primitive living conditions in Nigeria, where she was stationed. Her postcard was accidentally dropped, picked up by a local person, and brought to the attention of others. It stirred an angry demonstration in which speakers charged that the Peace Corps was designed to spread American imperialistic propaganda and to spy on other nations. One of them denounced the organization as "a penetration corps." The young woman's communication was merely a postcard to a friend; it was not an article, a book, or a broadcast. The message was not unfriendly; indeed, the writer characterized her activity as a very rewarding experience. Moreover, and the significance of this fact can hardly be exaggerated, the torrent of abusive criticism contained no allegation that any of the statements on the postcard were untrue or even misleading.

What are some of the reasons for the widespread dislike of the United States throughout the world? There are both good ones and bad ones. The actions of individual Americans often give justifiable offense. Occasional actions by our government, such as landings by the Marines, have stirred reasonable resentment.

Possibly, however, the biggest reason for the world-wide antipathy toward our country is that it is big and rich. Fear of the big and rich is felt by persons, by organizations, and by nations. Indeed, the world's experience with big rich nations throughout history lends much support to the view that, sooner or later, they menace smaller, poorer nations.

We, of course, do not feel that this dislike is justified. Many of us are not even aware of it, and tacitly assume, if we think about the matter at all, that the world must surely love the greatest giver of all time. This is a dangerous delusion. The part of wisdom is to accept the hard fact of the world's dislike of our country, to take account of it in our policy formulation and execution, and—where possible and desirable—to do something about it.

## FOREIGN AID PROGRAM

One erroneous belief about foreign aid can be quickly put aside. The magnitude of the program has caused some Americans to believe that we were giving away our national heritage or spending ourselves into bankruptcy. Indeed, it prompted an American machinery manufacturing company in a 1961 magazine advertisement to list individually the amounts given or lent to eighty countries, headlined "No Wonder We Are Broke!"

The reasoning behind that sensational headline is mysterious, considering that the total net national assets then exceeded $2,000 billion, the annual national income was $430 billion, and the standard of living of the American people was at an all-time high. In the 15 years after World War II the national income amounted to more than $4,500 billion, of which the $80 billion of foreign aid amounted to less than 2 per cent. At the present time foreign aid takes about 1 per cent of the national income.

Foreign aid may be a mistake; it may not have been handled well; it may have many shortcomings—but it is absurd to claim that it can impoverish or bankrupt us.

## HISTORY OF FOREIGN AID

Foreign aid in a sense dates back to the lend-lease program, an economic weapon which helped us to win World War II. At the close of that war the United States became concerned with the problems of relief. We therefore participated in the United Nations Relief and Rehabilitation Administration, contributing almost three fourths of the funds disbursed by that organization.

As a result of pressure by the Soviet Union on Greece and Turkey, we began extending military and economic aid to those countries in 1947; later, under similar circumstances, to Iran.

The next stage of American economic aid was involved in the problem of European recovery. Here the idea was to go beyond mere relief and to help European countries to get back on their feet. This program derived its initial impetus from an address by Secretary of State George Marshall at Harvard University in June 1947. In that address he almost casually threw out the suggestion that we develop a large program of economic assistance. The idea caught on. In the form of what came to be called "The Marshall Plan" it involved an outlay of more than $12 billion over a three-year period.

President Truman's inaugural address in 1949 might by now be completely forgotten except by historians were it not for its fourth point. This was a proposal, which attracted immediate support, to set up a long-range plan to raise the levels of all friendly nations, industry, agriculture, health, education, and public administration. In 1950 the Congress passed the first Act for International Development, giving form to what came to be called the "Point Four Program." The start of the Korean War in the same year had the consequence of shifting much of the emphasis to military assistance. This kind of assistance continued for many years, some of it being direct and some of it taking the form of what was called "defense support"—economic aid designed to help the receiving nations to carry out military programs.

Later in the 1950s the United States began programs of exporting surplus agricultural products under the provisions of Public Law 480. In 1957 a loan program involving long-term low-interest loans for economic projects was established, and the Development Loan Fund was organized to administer the credit program.

As time went by, the foreign aid program was administered successively by various organizations—the Economic Cooperation Administration, the Technical Cooperation Administration, the Mutual Security Agency, the Foreign Operations Administration, the International Cooperation Administration, and the Agency for International Development. The military assistance program was carried out by the Department of Defense. Coordination of the military and economic aspects of these programs was eventually assigned to the Department of State under the title of the Mutual Security Program.

## AGENCY FOR INTERNATIONAL DEVELOPMENT

The Foreign Assistance Act of 1961 established a new agency to handle the program, called the Agency for International Development (AID), an arm of the Department of State, headed by an Administrator with the rank of Under Secretary. The Act and the Agency provide a substantial measure of central control for the direction of foreign aid operations in place of the earlier system in which the authority had been diffused among the several agencies. The new Agency was formed by a merger of the International Cooperation Administration and the Development Loan Fund. In addition, certain functions of the Export–Import Bank were transferred to it. The military assistance program, however, remains an operation of the Department of Defense, which is supposed to coordinate these activities with the new Agency.

AID began its activities on November 4, 1961. It started with a staff of 15,000 employees, of whom 13,000 were serving overseas and 2,000 in the United States. It immediately confronted problems of accomplishing the transition in organization and programming from the old system to the new.

The new AID program stresses the following points:

[1]  It recognizes that foreign aid can furnish only one of the factors needed for development, namely, imported resources of capital, personnel, and technology. To these imported resources must be added

indigenous resources if the program is to be successful—a process which has often been neglected in the past.

[2] The program emphasizes the need for action by recipient countries to develop long-range plans with definite goals and methods. This does not mean the adoption of planned economies in the socialist sense. On the contrary, it includes measures designed to stimulate and support private enterprise.

[3] The program expects to undertake advance commitments for loans —subject, of course, to Congressional appropriations—wherever such commitments are essential to encourage governments to engage in development programs.

[4] The program stresses the need for social progress within the countries receiving American aid, such as programs in education, health, agriculture, and tax reform.

[5] The program recognizes that foreign aid should increasingly become a cooperative effort shared by the nations of the free world and the United Nations.

The AID program is coordinated with the credit operations of the International Bank for Reconstruction and Development, generally known as the "World Bank." The other principal international agencies with which AID coordinates the task of overseas development are the International Development Association, an affiliate of the World Bank which provides long-term loans; the InterAmerican Development Bank, which specializes in Latin American long-term financing; the International Finance Corporation, which encourages productive private enterprise in member countries; and the United Nations, which through its Expanded Technical Assistance Program and Special Fund makes resources available for development in many parts of the world. At present foreign aid costs us $4 billion a year, of which $2.5 billion represent direct and indirect military assistance and the remainder, $1.5 billion, go for economic and financial assistance.

## THE ALLIANCE FOR PROGRESS

Growing out of meetings held by United States representatives with those of Latin American countries, the United States announced in March 1961 the establishment of the Alliance for Progress. This program is directed at providing assistance to economic growth in Latin America.

Latin America comprises twenty independent nations, each with its history, its cultural and political traditions, its own problems, and its own pride. Despite this diversity, most of the nations have common problems of social unrest, poverty, disease, illiteracy, political instability, and wide differences among individuals in income and opportunity. In many Latin American countries tiny handfuls of rich families own most of the good farm land and the large urban financial and industrial establishments and also exercise political control of the governments. The basic philosophy of the Alliance for Progress is that assistance will be given to those nations that go ahead with internal programs of social improvement. One expectation is that the characteristically regressive pattern of the taxation in some of these countries will be modified by the introduction of some progressive features, so that the finances necessary to accomplish certain improvements will be obtained by increasing the taxes of the well-to-do, who have heretofore paid relatively little, rather than through the universally unwelcome step of merely raising existing rates. In addition, there must in some cases be marked improvements in the administration and collection of taxes.

A key need is for improvement of education and its extension to the masses of the people. In some of these countries the children of the poor do not have access to education.

Agricultural reform is seen as another key necessity. This will involve making plots of land available for individual ownership by small farmers, and in some areas this action will mean breaking up or at least subtracting from some of the huge land holdings of the rich few.

In his message to Congress, March 14, 1961, on Latin American aid, President Kennedy said of the program: "Its effectiveness depends on the willingness of each recipient nation to improve its own institutions, make necessary modifications in its own social patterns, and mobilize its own domestic resources for a program of development."

Will the recipient nations be willing and able to do these things? Will the oligarchies in certain of these countries be willing to relinquish some of their privileges and assume a share of the burden of providing the basis for social progress and economic growth? How many of the privileged few will be as wise as the member of a prominent Latin American family who said, "Either we give, or they take"? Will the owning and ruling oligarchies refuse to yield an inch until popular revolutions take all their wealth—except that stored in Switzerland?

Since the creation of the Alliance for Progress, there has been little time for the desired political, social, and economic reforms. Resistance to change also has been encountered. Some Latin Americans who had heard of the Alliance for Progress immediately expected too much from it too soon, and were either disappointed or abusive when instant benefits did not appear. On the other hand, many Latin Americans have heard little or nothing about the program. In both the United States and Latin America the program has been criticized by conservative folk as "pushing Latin America toward socialism."

The logic of the entire program of the Alliance for Progress has caused it to be hailed by thoughtful people; but their enthusiasm in some cases has led to an underestimate of the difficulties involved in implementing the program, together with a reciprocal overestimate of the speed with which substantial improvements can be brought about.

Thus the Alliance receives forehanded slaps from its enemies and backhanded ones from its friends. In this it is by no means unique among the important reform efforts of history.

## THE PEACE CORPS

The Peace Corps was established in 1961. It represented a new concept of United States Governmental activity abroad, designed, as stated by the Congress, "to help the peoples of interested countries and areas in meeting their needs for trained manpower, and to help promote a better understanding of the American people on the part of the peoples served and a better understanding of other peoples on the part of the American people." To accomplish these objectives, the Peace Corps built up membership from volunteers who were carefully selected and trained extensively in special programs, some of which were located in American universities.

The work of the Peace Corps is quite distinct from that of the Agency for International Development. It is not a financing organization. It makes available men and women, who, by working and teaching in less developed areas, can help the people of these countries to help themselves. It consists of volunteer personnel rather than career employees. They are not high-level experts or advisers, but rather workers and doers. Many of them are teachers, and it is their expectation to work under simple conditions and make contributions to the development of the host countries.

The Peace Corps has attracted volunteers of both sexes and all ages. They characteristically see in the organization and its efforts a social opportunity to be of service to less fortunate peoples. Within a year after its establishment the Peace Corps had nearly 1,000 volunteers in service or in training for thirteen countries, and that number was expected to increase to 6,700 by the end of fiscal year 1963. In Thailand 45 peace corpsmen have gone to work in the country's schools and as entomologists and laboratory technicians assisting in a nationwide campaign to eliminate malaria. In India 26 (which seems a pitifully small number for so large a job) have started on an agricultural project aimed at increasing food production for that country's expanding population of more than 400 million.

Critics of the Peace Corps have been inclined to make light of its possibilities or even to ridicule the whole idea. Enthusiasts, however, have seen in this organization and its devoted personnel not only an opportunity to help poorer people to get on the road to the better life, but also a chance to modify the "image" of America from one of size and wealth toward one of humanitarian friendship.

## THE DIFFICULTIES IN FOREIGN AID

The difficulties in connection with extending foreign aid were so graphically described in 1950 by C. D. Jackson in an address, "The Battle for Men's Minds," that his vivid statement is presented at length.

We in our lifetime have seen America pour out billions of dollars in foreign missions, in disaster aid, in countless propaganda efforts. More recently we have expended some $7 to $10 billion in ECA aid alone, and hundreds of millions in such attempts as the Voice of America and the State Department's information program. Yet millions of non-Americans in Asia, India, China, in South as well as North Korea, still hesitate to choose our democracy over Russia's Communism.

The explanation of that one, I think, can be given to you by another illustration. Before we left the Chinese mainland so hastily, our government sent millions of dollars' worth of medical supplies, food, and machinery to the aid of that ravaged land. But what to us looked in its over-all bulk like unparalleled generosity (and there has never been a nation so generous as ours) was something else again to Joe Chang.

The gimmick in this is how you look at it. Chinese eyes do not see things the way our eyes see them. For instance, *we saw* penicillin as the salvation of 300,000,000 people. *He saw* an untouchably costly item on the black market. *We saw* shiny new tractors as the simple answer to a backward agricultural people. *He saw* loss of face in the humiliation he suffered because no one bothered to show him how to use it—so there it is, rusting.

*We saw* the huge dynamo as the magic machine to raise his standard of living. *He saw* the dams which ruined his farmland for this year's desperately needed crops. *We saw* unselfish Americans sacrificing income, family life, and civilized comforts to work for their fellow man. *He saw* white snobs who could not even speak his language, herding together in officers' club bars. *We saw* ECA shields and American flags and U.S. initials stencilled on the tons of crates unloaded at his docks. *He saw* incomprehensible and suspicious foreign symbols. *We saw* carefully trained and educated Chinese students and missionaries. *He saw* Chinese who had become Americanized, who had lost the common touch.

## ROLE OF PRIVATE INVESTMENT

There is much to be said for encouragement of American private investment abroad along with a gradual cut in public loans and grants. One now prominent but underdeveloped country of the eighteenth century, the United States, was aided in reaching its present heights not by grants but by private capital, much of it from Europe. A flow of private American capital to underdeveloped countries could help to alleviate their shortages of capital and aid in establishing productive, profitable business enterprises, paying wages at the going rate or better. Most of the workers may be local nationals, and some of the capital for the project may be supplied by local sources, while the American firm supplies the bulk of the capital, management, and technology.

Moreover, private investment does not burden American taxpayers, and may generate fewer international disputes and disagreements than do government loans and grants. Finally, from the point of view of the American investors, there is the opportunity for profit.

However, private investment will flow into foreign fields only if there is a prospect of capital preservation plus a return commensurate with risk. The factors which discourage American investors include imbalance and dislocation in trade and currency relationships, the problem of transfer of profit, harsh and unreasonable internal regulation, economic nationalism, the threat of unstable political situations, and the danger of confiscation of property.

Spokesmen for private investment interests have asked for more government aid to stimulate the flow of capital abroad; in particular, some tax advantages and guarantees against loss. And they ask our Government to impress upon the foreign governments, via the diplomatic route, that they must change some of their policies in order to establish favorable climates for the investment of private capital. They also argue that, as long as we support government-owned industries abroad, we are cutting off opportunities for private capital; and some of them suggest that we are in effect "subsidizing creeping communism" on the ground that "experiments in socialism" tend to lead to communism.

They suggest that the "private enterprise system" is the one we know best, the one that we know will produce the most efficient results, and that it is therefore "the only effective answer" to the problem. Private investment will stimulate the foreign economy; it will provide markets for American goods, sources of raw materials at reasonable prices, and additional investment opportunities for American capital.

At the extreme, Spruille Braden has said, "The plain truth is that the United States is going broke, committing suicide, by uselessly giving away billions of dollars to the rest of the world. . . . I respectfully urge that the foreign aid programs rapidly be reduced to the most modest dimensions, at most, a few million dollars per year . . . and in due course replaced entirely by private investment and enterprise."[*]

Since we are neither going broke nor committing suicide, there doesn't seem to be substantial pressure to cut out all governmental foreign economic aid. In fact, it seems to be recognized by the more thoughtful advocates of private investment abroad that there are some areas where private capital will not venture, where the risks are too great or the prospective return too small. There are also certain scene-setting projects which are essential before any agricultural or extractive or other indus-

[*] Spruille Braden, "Our Disastrous Foreign Aid Policies," *Commercial and Financial Chronicle*, August 8, 1957, p. 22.

trial development is feasible, and these are normally, almost essentially, governmental.

A word of caution. When we provide the capital by direct private investment, and privately own the enterprises in foreign lands, we open our door to propaganda by whispers of these nations about foreign domination by the "Yankee Dollar"—a topic that many of them do not reason too carefully about. The usual impact of this phrase is an emotional reaction, and a powerful one.

As for the government help, there is an investment guaranty program, administered by the Agency for International Development, that will insure approved foreign investments against these risks:

[1]  Inability to convert foreign currency receipts into dollars;

[2]  Loss through expropriation or confiscation; and

[3]  Loss from damage to physical assets caused by war.

## THE SOVIET TRADE AND AID PROGRAMS

While we have been developing trade and aid programs, the U.S.S.R. has not been idle. It has put into effect energetic programs that in some respects surpass ours.

The Russian economic offensive consists of three main elements: (1) a program of economic assistance to the less developed countries outside the communist orbit, (2) increased technical assistance to these countries, both through the sending of their technical personnel to the U.S.S.R. for training and the sending of Russian technicians to them, and (3) a rapid increase in trade, both export and import, between Russia and them.

This program of aid, trade, and technical assistance is being promoted by means of an effective advertising campaign. Soviet participation in world fairs and exhibitions is extensive. Trade missions are sent to the underdeveloped countries. Top Soviet leaders have made numerous well-publicized visits to these countries. Modesty is set aside in order to make maximum propaganda gains from all of these efforts.

Although there is the usual difficulty in collecting and evaluating figures on the magnitude of this Soviet assistance, it appears that the amount extended in intermediate and long-term credits for the purchase of goods and services from the Soviet Union since the outset of their assistance program equals several billion U.S. dollars. A comparison of U.S. assistance to selected underdeveloped countries with that of the Sino-Soviet bloc is shown in Table 28.1.

Russia maximizes the political and psychological impact of its aid programs by concentrating its effort on a few recipients who best lend them-

*Table 28.1*

## U.S. AND SINO-SOVIET BLOC ECONOMIC ASSISTANCE TO CERTAIN NEAR EASTERN AND ASIAN COUNTRIES

*(June 1, 1955 to February 1, 1958)*

(Millions of U.S. Dollars)

| COUNTRY | U.S. AID | SINO-SOVIET AID |
|---|---|---|
| Afghanistan | $    47 | $   136 |
| Burma | 43 | 42 |
| Cambodia | 96 | 22 |
| Ceylon | 11 | 20 |
| Egypt | 16 | 235 |
| India | 419 | 295 |
| Indonesia | 124 | 109 |
| Iran | 140 | — |
| Iraq | 7 | — |
| Israel | 88 | — |
| Jordan | 28 | — |
| Lebanon | 16 | — |
| Nepal | 7 | 13 |
| Pakistan | 272 | — |
| Philippine Islands | 135 | — |
| Saudi Arabia | — | — |
| Syria | — | 194 |
| Thailand | 75 | — |
| Turkey | 222 | 10 |
| Yemen | — | 16 |
| Totals | $1,959* | $1,092 |

* U.S. private investment is included in total, but not by country.
SOURCE: Douglas Dillon, "Economic Activities of the Soviet Bloc in Less Developed Countries," *U.S. Department of State Bulletin*, March 24, 1958, p. 473.

selves to exploitation and the attainment of Russian political objectives. Six countries—Yugoslavia, Afghanistan, India, Indonesia, Egypt, and Syria —have received over 95 per cent of the total Russian aid.

"[Russian] credits for economic development cover a wide range of fields and an obvious effort made to select projects which will have an important psychological impact in the recipient country and can hence be exploited by [Russian] propaganda organs seeking to make political capital. Since most of the less developed countries place a high priority on industrialization, [Russia] has concentrated its efforts in the industrial field." An example of the impact which these large projects can have in host countries is a $132-million steel mill which the Russians have built in India. This mill will boost India's steel capacity by some 60 per cent and will save that nation $80 million yearly in much needed foreign exchange.

* "Soviet Bloc Economic Offensive in the Less Developed Areas," *U.S. Department of State Bulletin*, No. 38, January 27, 1959, p. 145.

All but a very small part of the Russian aid is in the form of loans, as compared with that of the United States, whose program consists to a much greater extent of outright grants and gifts. The Soviet loan rate is between 2 and 2.5 per cent, a rate considerably under the rates charged by our financing institutions. By giving assistance in the form of loans instead of grants, but charging low interest rates, the U.S.S.R. caters successfully at the same time to both the pride and the poverty of the underdeveloped nations.

A key feature in the attractiveness of Soviet assistance programs is that they accept raw materials and agricultural products in repayment of loans.

Although communist bureaucracy is inherently slow and inflexible, when political gain is in sight it can move with great speed and adaptability. Since foreign trade is a state monopoly it can be easily tied to over-all government policy without regard to the ordinary commercial considerations that would be pertinent for us. For example, it can offer to buy surpluses from backward agricultural countries for purely political purposes, even at above-market prices. In thus being able to combine business with politics, it can in selected instances, operate with an advantage over the free world.

"Technical assistance provided by the Soviet Union is closely related to its trade and credit activities and is not a separate program on a grant basis as is that of the United States. Over 2,300 Soviet technicians spent a month or more in nineteen less developed countries during the last half of 1957, while another 2,000 technicians and students from the less developed countries went to the Soviet Union for study and training during that year."* As in the case of economic assistance, technical assistance is highly concentrated in a few countries; 80 per cent of Soviet technical personnel abroad are found in Egypt, Syria, India, Indonesia, and Afghanistan.

Soviet technicians in underdeveloped countries are reported to be competent in their fields of specialty. Their living standards while on assignment are kept close to those prevailing in the countries in which they are serving. This, a result of deliberate Soviet policy, makes a favorable impression on the people of the poor countries, although it has been reported that it has caused dissatisfaction among the Soviet technicians themselves and increased their desire to return to their own land.

Soviet offers of assistance have usually been readily accepted. It would, indeed, be remarkable if this were not so, considering the needs and desires of these desperately poor nations.

The new leaders of these countries are committed to promoting economic development as rapidly as possible, and they will hold their jobs

* "The Sino-Soviet Economic Offensive in the Less Developed Countries," U.S. Department of State Publication 6632, Released May 1958, p. 29.

only as long as they show results in this respect. Certainly then it is not surprising that they are anxious for Soviet assistance, nor that some of them accept help from the Soviets with one hand and from the Western nations with the other.

Many of these countries were formerly parts of colonial empires of Western Europe, and as is brought out in Chapter 26, this historical fact has understandably given rise to continuing hostility toward the West and to a tendency to blame present economic ills on previous political status. Communist propaganda plays heavily on this theme by misrepresenting the American aid programs as merely a new disguise for the old imperialism. Since the U.S.S.R. has risen from a backward economy to an industrialized one only in recent years, its offers of assistance have a special appeal for the people of the underdeveloped countries.

The efforts of the Russian aid programs to date seem to have had a great impact in the recipient countries and to have won friends for the communist world. As President Eisenhower said in his message to Congress, February 19, 1958, "If the purpose of Soviet aid to any country were simply to help it overcome economic difficulties without infringing upon its freedom, such aid could be welcomed as forwarding the free world purpose of economic growth. But there is nothing in the history of international communism to indicate this can be the case. Until such evidence is forthcoming, we and other free nations must assume that Soviet bloc aid is a new, subtle, and long range instrument directed toward the same old purpose of drawing its recipient away from the community of free nations and ultimately into the communist orbit."

## APPRAISAL AND OUTLOOK

Faultfinding with American foreign economic policy is easy—and not merely the irrational antipathetic foreigners or the subversive faultfinding of communist propagandists. There have been blunders and mistakes. On the whole, however, we need not feel ashamed of the major aspects of the program—its magnitude and its motivation, although its accomplishments are somewhat uncertain. Perhaps most important and encouraging of all is the fact that we are not satisfied with it. Complacency would be a dangerous attitude with which to pursue a line of policy having such potentiality for the peace and prosperity of America and the world—or the opposite.

One of the shortcomings of the present program is the lack of appraisal. We seem to be operating in the dark and planning programs and expenditures on the basis of speculation.

We need a scientific evaluation—on a country by country and item by item basis. The accomplishments—economic and diplomatic—of our international development activities cannot be measured with precision;

nay, perhaps not even roughly. Nevertheless, it is very much in the national interest that a continuing effort be made to compute a "cost-effectiveness" measure for each aid activity. If even approximate indicators could be developed, our actions surely would become more effective.

## QUESTIONS AND PROBLEMS

1. Why do people dislike the United States? What is the significance of the fact? Should we try to change this condition?
2. What lessons can be learned from the history of our foreign aid program?
3. What should be the U.S. role in international development?
4. Should international development be confined to the UN, or would this jeopardize the U.S. in its present race to preserve freedom as opposed to Russia's goal of world socialism?
5. Should the U.S. continue to give aid to those countries which are communist-inclined?
6. Should the U.S. give aid to countries receiving aid from Russia, or should we force them to make a choice?
7. In aid to underdeveloped areas, which is more desirable, technical or capital assistance?
8. In light of our present balance of payments deficit, are the billions of dollars going into foreign aid justified?
9. Evaluate: the AID program, the Alliance for Progress, the Peace Corps.
10. Should the government subsidize private business to increase investment in underdeveloped countries? If so, how?
11. Is our free market system capable of competing with the Soviet Union's state trading monopoly in the sphere of economic warfare? If not, is *state trading* desirable for the U.S.?
12. How, in your opinion, could our foreign economic policies be improved?

## SELECTED READINGS

*Annals of the American Academy of Political Science.* Issue entitled "American Foreign Policy Challenged," July 1962.

BLACK, EUGENE R. *The Diplomacy of Economic Development.* Cambridge, Mass.: Harvard University Press, 1961.

Committee for Economic Development. *Cooperation for Progress in Latin America.* New York: Committee for Economic Development, 1961.

ELLIOT, WILLIAM Y. *The Political Economy of American Foreign Policy.* New York: Henry Holt and Company, 1955.

ENKE, STEPHEN. *Economics for Development.* Englewood Cliffs, N.J.: Prentice-Hall, Inc., 1963.

FATOURAS, A. A. *Government Guarantees to Foreign Investors.* New York: Columbia University Press, 1963.

GALBRAITH, J. K. *Economic Development in Perspective.* Cambridge, Mass.: Harvard University Press, 1962.

HOSELITZ, B. F. (ed.). *The Progress of Underdeveloped Areas.* Chicago: University of Chicago Press, 1961.

*International Economic Affairs.* Title of this issue: "The Alliance for Progress," Summer 1962.

KNAPPEN, MARSHALL. *An Introduction to American Foreign Policy.* New York: Harper and Brothers, 1956.

Rockefeller Brothers Fund. *Foreign Economic Policy for the Twentieth Century.* New York: Doubleday & Company, 1958.

STALEY, EUGENE. *The Future of Underdeveloped Countries,* rev. ed. New York: Harper and Brothers, 1961.

WALLICH, HENRY C. *The Cost of Freedom, A New Look at Capitalism.* New York: Harper and Brothers, 1960.

# 29  MILITARY ACTIVITIES

In earlier decades military activities were significant in terms of government–business relationships only in time of war. In major wars, and most of all in World War II, military operations were temporarily of great importance to our nation and its economy, but between wars the military part of the economy was tiny. Since the end of the Korean action, however, we have had a large defense program, although without wartime economic controls.

## *PRIOR TO WORLD WAR I*

Although the United States waged several wars during the eighteenth and nineteenth centuries, most of them did not require the full or even the major effort of the national economy. Since only a few thousand men were engaged in hostilities at any one time, and since their military equipment was neither extensive nor costly, there was no need for mobilization or governmental controls. On the home front "business as usual" was, by and large, the order of the day.

The lone exception was the Civil War. As measured by any criterion, this war was until 1914 truly the most gigantic war in world history. More than half a million soldiers died in it, and its economic costs to both the North and the South were staggering.

The Civil War was the forerunner of the "total" wars of the twentieth century. It involved the exercise of all aspects of national strength—political, economic, and moral, in addition to the military. And it was the North's economic strength which finally proved decisive.

Although neither side was adequately prepared for such a long and bitter conflict, the North's manufacturing industry gradually shifted to production of war goods and eventually provided a sizable flow of military supplies and equipment for the Union armies. The South, on the other hand, was primarily an agricultural area, and from the very beginning experienced great difficulty in properly supplying the Confederate troops. This situation went from bad to worse as the Union armies occupied and devastated the Southern states, and as the Union navy's blockade slowly constricted the importation of military supplies from Europe. Eventually the attrition of its resources, of both men and materiel, reached the point where the South had no alternative but to capitulate.

## WORLD WAR I

Although World War I started in 1914, American wartime mobilization did not commence until shortly before America's official entry into it. The first major step toward mobilization was the appointment in 1916 of the Council of National Defense, composed of the Secretaries of War, Navy, Interior, Agriculture, Commerce, and Labor. Operating only in an advisory capacity, and Council was able to initiate some attention to the economic problems of fighting a war. The Council was assisted by an advisory commission (of which Mr. Bernard M. Baruch was a member), and the Commission in turn appointed committees of industrialists to formulate the actual mobilization plans. But since the entire organization had no real authority, progress was slow.

The United States declared war in April 1917, and shortly thereafter the War Industries Board was established. Numerous other agencies also were organized to expedite the economy's transition to war. Yet, until the early part of 1918, this transition left much to be desired. Material shortages, labor difficulties, inflation, and hoarding hampered the output of military goods.

In March of 1918 the War Industries Board was reorganized under the direction of Mr. Baruch, who assumed the primary responsibility for industrial mobilization. As Board Chairman he directed the administration of various economic controls, such as the assignment of priorities and the allocation of critical materials.

A major improvement was the centralized coordination of the government's procurement. During the first part of the war various governmental departments had competed with one another and with our allies for goods and services. The Board corrected this situation by instituting positive action to balance civilian needs, military requirements, and the productive capacity of American industry.

The Board operated with full powers for only the nine months from March to November of 1918. In that brief period the national economy was not brought under regulation to the degree later found necessary during World War II. Many economic controls were introduced, including price ceilings, rationing, priorities, and measures for conservation, but on the whole the impact of these controls was not very great. Industrial mobilization in World War I was short, slow, and modest.

On the other hand, the economic significance of the war itself was substantial. The Federal Government spent only $305 million for national security in 1916. In 1917 the figure almost doubled, moving up to $602 million. Then the cost of war mounted very rapidly, reaching $7,110 million in 1918 and the high mark of $13,548 million in 1919. These dollar volumes are small compared with more recent national security budgets, but as fractions of corresponding national incomes they are not unimpressive.

## PEACETIME PLANNING

For many Americans World War I was the "war to end war." Although this unfortunate misconception was by no means universal, the fact remains that military preparedness, and the possibility of war, were not of any real concern to the average citizen in the decades of the twenties and thirties. Official policy stressed security through neutrality—and the instruments of war were renounced time and time again. It is not surprising that mobilization planning between the two world wars was modest in scope.

The National Defense Act of 1920 assigned responsibility for industrial mobilization planning to the Assistant Secretary of War. Shortly thereafter the Army Industrial College was established to train military officers in the fundamentals of industrial procurement and mobilization, and the Army and Navy Munitions Board was organized to coordinate the mobilization activities of the two services.

The planners attempted to analyze and improve upon the experiences of World War I. In 1931 they issued an Industrial Mobilization Plan (IMP), which outlined the general features of the regulatory agencies, controls, and procedures that might be employed should the need for wartime mobilization again arise. Even though the IMP was modified several times during the thirties, the planners were always handicapped by inadequate data and sketchy assumptions of the conditions under which mobilization would be required. The identity of the enemy, the possible theaters of war, the sizes of armies, the duration of conflict, and other relevant matters could only be estimated. It is not surprising that actual mobilization during World War II did not follow the course prescribed during the thirties.

## WORLD WAR II

Although war broke out in Europe in 1939, the United States did not really begin to mobilize until after the fall of France, in the spring of 1940. Then, despite domestic preoccupation with the presidential election campaign, several agencies and offices were established and charged with various functions relating to preparation for war.

The pace of mobilization and of planning for industrial mobilization increased steadily in 1941. Some progress was made in planning the curtailment of production of civilian goods, the expansion of supplies of raw materials, the adoption of a system of materials priorities, and the conversion of our manufacturing capacity to the production of war goods. Lend-lease was initiated, and our military forces began to be built up by means of the draft.

With the official declaration of war in December 1941, mobilization became the first objective of both business and government. There soon emerged numerous Federal boards, offices, commissions, committees, and administrations to deal with specific aspects of the war economy. The most important of these was the War Production Board, which was created in January 1942.

The Board was responsible for general direction of war production and procurement. It coordinated the plans and policies of the other Federal departments and agencies that influenced war production, and it controlled the assignment of priorities and the allocation of materials and production facilities. Production was regulated on the basis of programs supplied by the war procurement agencies (Army, Navy, Maritime Commission, and Treasury Procurement Division) and the authorities concerned with civilian requirements.

While the powers of the War Production Board were very considerable, they did not encompass the entire economic mobilization program. Price control, for example, was handled by the Office of Price Administration. At first one man—President Roosevelt—coordinated all of the controlling agencies. Because of the increasing complexities of coordination and control, the President in 1943 established the Office of War Mobilization as a supercoordinating agency at the apex of the pyramid of Federal mobilization activities. A year later, in anticipation of the approaching problems of peace, this agency became the Office of War Mobilization and Reconversion.

The problems of the mobilizers were almost indescribable; many of them were unforeseeable. Every decision seemed to generate the need for several more decisions; every solution seemed to result in more problems. The fact that their efforts met with success is a tribute to their perseverance and to the unity of purpose with which the American people faced the task of winning the war.

Despite the lessons of World War I the planning of the thirties, and the inception of limited mobilization prior to America's entry into the war, our war production did not reach the desired level until late in 1943. But by then we had created a wartime arsenal that dwarfed our own accomplishments in World War I and the contemporary output of the Axis powers.

Industrial production more than doubled from 1939 to 1944, real gross national product rose by 70 per cent, and direct military production climbed to an annual rate of over $89 billion. This war production appears even more astounding when we note that it was not achieved at the expense of the civilian economy. Personal consumption of goods and services (except for certain durables, such as automobiles) actually went up during World War II.

## A PLANNED ECONOMY

For the few years of World War II ours was a planned and regulated economy. Various conditions, including the need for quick and positive shifts in resources, led the nation to modify temporarily the free market's mechanism for allocating men, machinery, and materials. Selective service inducted millions into the armed forces. The pattern of production and consumption of goods, both military and civilian, was determined by the War Production Board, largely through the use of its Controlled Materials Plan. Prices and rents were controlled by the Office of Price Administration. But civilian labor was subject to relatively little regulation; indeed, in 1944 and 1945 the President and the Congress gave consideration to legislation imposing additional regulation on civilians in the form of a National Service Act. This idea, which would have involved controls on both employers and employees, had not come to a head when the war ended.

It is scarcely possible to convey an accurate impression of the size and complexity of the task of managing an entire economy, determining the amounts of various commodities to produce, scheduling the component parts and the raw materials necessary for their production, and allocating capital facilities involved. But even a cursory consideration of the difficulties, the problems, and the opportunities for the mistakes associated with such central control can lead to an appreciation of the marvelous flexibility of the private enterprise system, under which millions of decision makers, acting independently within the framework of the price system, day in and day out, week in and week out, month in and month out, continuously make and alter their economic judgments and plans and prosecute their myriad activities accordingly.

It is therefore remarkable not that so many mistakes were made in World War II, but rather that so few were made. The accomplishment was prodigious. Early in the war President Roosevelt had announced our aim to produce 50,000 planes a year. Many had scoffed at this huge projection. Before the end of the war, however, the production rate had reached 90,000. A similar story had unfolded in connection with almost all kinds of war production. Production had started slowly and haltingly, and this had been the more critical in 1942 when German submarines were sinking, per month, 500,000 tons of shipping, together with their cargoes. Then had come a gradual build-up of facilities and the beginning of a stream of output. From this point on the production curves had soared. Whereas in the early days of the war men in the armored divisions had trained with civilian trucks mounting stovepipes to simulate cannon, by the end of 1943 production of many types of military goods had zoomed to such heights that the procurement schedules of the armed forces had actually to be cut back. By the end of the war the Air Force was the largest in the world, and the United States Navy had more ships than all the navies of the world combined, throughout history, had previously floated on the seas of the earth.

With the lid of insufficient demand taken off the American economy and with Uncle Sam calling on American industry to produce more and yet more, the slack in employment had been taken up, the work force enlarged, and the entire economy galvanized to heights of production which were unprecedented, largely unanticipated, and almost unbelievable.

The lessons of this immense achievement are still fresh in our minds. With the aid of the knowledge and techniques learned in World War II, if we should again go to war we could, within three years from its outbreak, expand the national output enough to be able to put $500 billion worth of resources into the war effort and still leave $250 billion worth for nonwar purposes.

With the coming of the nuclear age, however, it is quite possible that these lessons will never be useful. The figures quoted are contingent on there being no noticeable destruction within our country. The present possibilities of nuclear armaments, however, suggest that this assumption is unrealistic. It now appears that a nuclear war might reduce both sides to ruins within a few hours or a few days. In these circumstances, there would be no time for industrial mobilization; the war would have to be fought with the weapons in being at the start.

Although World War II did not end until 1945, the problems of demobilization were already being considered early in 1944. In many quarters it was believed that the reversion to a peacetime economy would entail mass unemployment and even a resumption of the Great Depression. Actually these predictions proved untrue; indeed, the national problem turned out to be not deflation, but inflation.

Demobilization of our armed forces was so rapid that it might better be termed disintegration. But reconversion of our economy to civilian production proceeded at almost as fast a pace. Demobilized soldiers, sailors, and airmen found jobs when they came home. The production of civilian goods and services skyrocketed. And because of the money that families and business firms had saved during the war, and because of the unsatisfied demands that had accumulated both during the war years and during the prior years of depression, everything that was produced found a ready market.

## THE NUCLEAR AGE

In June of 1950 the United States was once again forced to resist overt military aggression. The problems posed by the Korean War differed considerably, however, from those of the two World Wars.

In the first place, Korea marked the beginning of what has come to be known as limited war. And to the extent that the war was limited, economic mobilization also could be limited.

Moreover, our state of military preparedness at the beginning of the Korean War was much better than it had been in either 1917 or 1941. Our reserves of military equipment and supplies were substantial, and much of the materiel was stored in Japan and hence readily available to our armies in Korea. The military personnel situation also was better— the forces on active duty were immediately augmented by trained National Guard and reserve units, and this enabled us to meet our initial Korean requirements fairly quickly.

Finally, the experiences of mobilization in World War II were well remembered by many industrialists and government administrators. Many of the problems which had been solved once did not prove so perplexing the second time around.

Because of the limited nature of the Korean War (at least as compared with general war) mobilization at first proceeded rather slowly. The element of urgency did not become apparent until the intervention of the Chinese communists, in November 1950. This act significantly altered the military situation and hence the economic situation back home.

President Truman declared a state of emergency in December and set up the Office of Defense Mobilization. The Director of this office was given sweeping powers over all economic mobilization activities. This provided the machinery for shifting the economy rapidly to a wartime basis and for resolving conflicting viewpoints or requirements of mobilization without the President's personal involvement.

Military production was stepped up considerably in 1951. Inasmuch as the economy was already at a high level of employment and production, the added emphasis on military output necessitated the imposition of numerous governmental controls. These controls, however, were by no means so extensive and tight as those of World War II, and most of them were terminated by the spring of 1953.

Although national security expenditures more than tripled from 1950 to 1953, only a small part of the increase was necessitated by the Korean War. It has been estimated that, of some $116 billion expended for national defense during the three-year conflict, the War itself cost only $18 billion.* The remainder was devoted to building up a sustained level of military readiness.

### THE COLD WAR

National security expenditures have constituted the major portion of the Federal budget since 1951. In the past, the end of a war had always been followed by a sharp reduction in military costs, but after the Korean

* Seymour E. Harris (ed.), *American Economic History* (New York: McGraw-Hill, 1961), p. 231.

War these costs dropped by only 20 per cent. The continuing heavy burden of defense has been necessitated by these basic premises of our national military policy:

[1] Our strategic arms and defenses must be adequate to deter any nuclear attack on the United States or our allies.

[2] Our tactical military forces must be capable of successful resistance against nonnuclear attack, i.e., limited war.

[3] The nature of military technology is such that the signifiance of our economy's military *potential* has been considerably reduced; full mobilization of a peacetime economy would be appropriate and possible only in the event of a nonnuclear conflict of both long duration and large magnitude. A conflict of this type is not likely to occur.

In short, we must be ready to fight any type of war, big or small, nuclear or nonnuclear, at home or abroad. This requires a large and costly military establishment. And the never-ending race for supremacy in arms requires fantastic outlays for military research and development. The sum total has for several years amounted to about 10 per cent of our gross national product.

The responsibility for defense mobilization and management of resources and production was assigned in 1958 to the Director of the Office of Civil and Defense Mobilization (which, in 1961, was placed under the Secretary of Defense). This office was established to centralize authority for all nonmilitary defense functions in a single agency. The broad scope of these functions is evident from the following list of assigned activities:

[1] Advise the President concerning the coordination of military, industrial, and civilian mobilization.

[2] Prepare and direct national civil defense plans and programs.

[3] Determine which raw materials are critical and strategic, and the quality and quantities of these materials to be stockpiled.

[4] Assist and advise the President with respect to telecommunications in the executive branch of the government.

[5] Coordinate the administration of Federal disaster relief programs.

The task of civil defense has received much more public attention than that of mobilization. Perhaps this is inevitable in view of the probable destruction inherent in a nuclear war and the declining urgency of full mobilization planning.

## PAYING THE BILL

The costs of war and defense, or of any other governmental activity, may be financed by taxation, by borrowing, or by printing more money. None of these alternatives is particularly popular. Nobody likes to pay high taxes; borrowing controverts the thrifty "pay-as-you-go" principle;

and the printing press solution carries a certain implication of irresponsibility.

But from the standpoint of the nation as a whole, the question of how to pay for military activities is really a question of mechanics. Depending on which method or combination of methods is selected, some people will pay more and some people will pay less, but the total will always be the same. For the cost of today's defense must be paid today—it cannot be postponed.

The cost of a war, or of defense, consists of goods and services that are not consumed, of leisure that is foregone, of equipment and buildings that are not repaired or replaced, and of lives and property that are destroyed. These costs cannot be shifted to a future generation. Efforts to do so result only in a redistribution of national income now and again in the future. Our descendants may have to pay for their own defense, but they will not be burdened by the costs of safety today.

Americans all too often think of military expenditures as being necessary to our continued existence, but a complete waste of money from any other standpoint. Some defense dollars, however, are of direct and significant benefit to the national economy.

For example, in fiscal year 1961 the government spent $47.5 billion for national security costs. Of this, $6.5 billion (13.5 per cent) was for research and development, some of which was carried out at colleges and universities throughout the nation. The lasting value of such research is evident when one considers the sizable segment of present-day civilian industry that has evolved from governmental research conducted during World War II.

Another little publicized activity of the defense establishment is the training and educational function performed for society. Many servicemen receive expensive training as specialists, serve their obligated service, and then depart for the lucrative fields of private industry. The value of this training would be very difficult to assess, but its existence cannot be denied.

## HOW MUCH FOR DEFENSE?

There is little to be gained in predicting the magnitude of future military expenditures. There is too much uncertainty in military technology, in the behavior of the communist nations toward each other and toward the free world, in the attitudes and desires of our allies, and even in our own responses to changing world affairs. Continuation of the status quo might lead to a gradual reduction in defense costs as a percentage of our gross national product. If we endeavor to improve our capacity for protection and retaliation, our defense budget may have to increase at the same rate as does our GNP—or even faster, if the rate of increase in communist military expenditures so dictates. On the other hand, a gradual easing of world tension, the reduction of the ground forces of the communist bloc, or significant progress in control of nuclear weapons might lead to major reductions in expenditures for defense. Of course, if a general nuclear war is to be our lot, there may not be much point in attempting to predict anything.

One common approach to the question of how much should be spent for defense might be labeled the "defense first" approach. Advocates of this line of reasoning argue that there are certain absolute requirements for defense that can be expressed in specific terms of manpower, airplanes, missiles, and other elements of military strength. These requirements must be met regardless of cost if we are to have confidence in our national security.

This approach is especially prevalent among military officials, who are the people most familiar with our defense problems. It is their responsibility to develop plans and assemble forces appropriate to assigned military objectives. Naturally, they tend to be insistent and specific about what is needed to do the job.

At the other extreme we find the "budget first" approach. The budget first group argues that the national security requires a healthy economy and that the health of the economy is jeopardized by heavy governmental spending. These men know that costs are important, that national security does not represent the only claim on our resources, and that military demands are virtually insatiable. They are also aware of inefficiencies within the defense establishment. They believe in forcing efficient use of limited resources by squeezing hard on the military budget.

We may expect that the element of uncertainty will force military expenditures upward toward the recommendations of the "defense first" group. Although uncertainty lessens the validity of the absolute requirements generated by the military, it is even more damaging to the budget-firsters' estimates of the sufficiency of military forces and the relative merits of various weapons systems. The difference lies in the severity of the *penalty for being wrong.*

If we spend *too much* for defense, the penalty will consist of our foregoing some consumption and leisure. But this will likely be less than the cost of even a very limited hot war. Spending *too little* increases the risk of hot war, whether a localized police action or a world-wide holocaust. And cold war losses may occur through default, if we find ourselves unable to meet an unexpected challenge.

The *"best"* defense position is an ultimate that can never be determined with certainty—and perhaps never attained. Even hindsight will not provide the true answer. But if we should experience military disaster in either hot or cold war, we should then be certain of just one thing— that our defense program had not even been a *good* one.

## A COMPARISON WITH RUSSIA

In conclusion, it may be worthwhile to compare the defense expenditures of the United States and of Soviet Russia. The United States spent $47.5 billion for defense in fiscal 1961, or about 9 per cent of her gross national product. This is certainly a lot of money. But is it too much? Or even enough?

On the basis of rather limited statistical data it has been estimated that Russia's defense expenditures, in dollars, are about the same as ours, even though her gross national product is considerably lower. Even more important is the fact that for several years Russia has been allocating to military activities a relatively *constant share* (about 20 per cent) of her *rapidly rising* gross national product. The United States, on the other hand, has stabilized the dollar level of military expenditures; the share of her gross national product devoted to defense has been declining.

If these trends continue, Soviet Russia will soon be spending more for military activities than does the United States. And the question is not whether *they* can afford this luxury but whether *we* can. Keeping up with the Joneses is a silly vanity of suburban neighborhoods—but in the international neighborhood, where survival may be at stake in addition to mere prestige, it is wise not only to keep up with the Joneses but to surpass them.

## DEFENSE AND THE AMERICAN
## ECONOMY

The foregoing sections arrive at the conclusion that, from the standpoint of national security and survival, there can be no question of whether we can "afford" an "adequate" defense. But there is another standpoint from which the matter should be viewed—the economic one; the two questions that arise when this standpoint is adopted are quite contradictory in their implications:

[1] Can we afford economically to continue such huge defense expenditures into the indefinite future?

[2] Can we afford economically *not* to continue huge defense expenditures into the indefinite future? That is, does the prosperity of the American economy depend on a continuation of defense expenditures?

The answer to the first question depends on the effect of the taxes required to finance the defense program in addition to all other taxes on the American economy. The reasoning presented in Chapter 7 suggests that today's level of taxation is having little or no adverse affect on the total of our economic activity. Since the longer the program continues the more we become accustomed both to the program and to the correlative levels of taxation, the conclusion follows that we can carry the program into the indefinite future. And if international conditions should take a turn for the worse, we could certainly manage a very much larger program over a considerable period of time. In World War II, in 1944, we put 44 per cent of our gross national product into the military effort, as contrasted with today's 9 per cent. The problem of how much national defense we can afford turns out to be one of national necessity and national morale. We can afford whatever our people consider to be necessary.

With regard to the second question neither history nor theory substantiates the proposition that American prosperity depends on a continuation of defense expenditures at any particular level, including their present one. Putting to one side the question whether such a development is likely, let us consider the hypothetical case in which our military expenditures are greatly reduced.

Examination of this hypothesis is best begun by looking at a precedent. Historically, this is exactly what happened at the end of World War II. In 1944 military expenditures amounted to $88.6 billion out of a total gross national expenditure of $211.4 billion. In 1946 military expenditures were $20.6 billion. What happened to total national expenditures? There was a barely perceptible decline—to $210.7 billion. In other words, civilian expenditures rose almost as much as military expenditures dropped.

It must be admitted that the prodigious increase in civilian expenditures was aided by two factors which are not present now. These were (1) a considerable accumulated backlog of consumer demand resulting from shortages generated during the Great Depression and World War II; and (2) an immense increase—during World War II—of cash and other liquid financial items among our people, representing great purchasing power.

At the present time, however, there are two favorable factors which were not present then. The first is that the total military expenditures are a comparatively small percentage of the gross national expenditure. The hole to be filled upon a decline of 9 per cent of gross national expenditure is a very much smaller one than the immense hole that yawned at the end of World War II. The second advantage is to be found in the state of the budget. The Federal budget of $95 billion in 1944 was financed only to the extent of $48 billion of taxes, and showed a deficit (financed by borrowing) of $47 billion. There was, therefore, little room for tax reduction at the end of World War II even though government expenditures were slashed. Today, however, the budget is almost in balance. If military expenditures were cut substantially, it would be possible to reduce taxes by about the same amount, releasing that much civilian purchasing power.

A big decline in defense expenditures, even accompanied by a corresponding increase of civilian expenditures, would, to be sure, still pose a serious problem of shifting of resources. Particularly difficult would be the transition in employment from the missile-making plants and the airplane plants to the consumer-goods-making plants, which would be uncomfortable for some regions and for many individual workers. It would not, however, pose the prospect of a prolonged general business slump.

Certainly, few Americans would maintain that an economic depression would be too high a price to pay for the establishment of a permanent peace and a consequent great reduction of armaments. In being able to hope for that priceless event without having to fear paying any such price for it, we are, then, doubly blessed.

## PLUMS AND POLITICS

Even though the prosperity of the national economy is not dependent on defense spending, individual segments are very much affected by this $50-billion stream. The huge volume of defense spending has made military installations and business contracts significant sources of income to many firms and communities. Defense spending as a tree yielding financial plums dwarfs the historical monetary plum tree, the rivers and harbors bill. The economic fortunes of firms and communities rise and fall with defense allocations. Naturally, therefore, a military-industrial-political complex is deeply involved in the destiny and destination of these billions of dollars. Congressmen are pressured and pressure in turn. Governors, business leaders, citizen organizations, and sheer privateers fight to get and to keep the military prizes. Focal points of the pressures are the White House and the Pentagon, and the former is rumored sometimes to use awards as a pressure to Congressmen. It is a malodorous condition now, and might become seriously hurtful if special interests were to gain ascendancy over the national welfare.

Generals and admirals, loyal to the nation and to their several services, sometimes resist decisions made by the Secretary of Defense and get support from Congressmen, business firms, and communities. A determined Secretary may find that his problems involve more than defense against external attack.

## QUESTIONS AND PROBLEMS

1. Compare the effectiveness of industrial mobilization during World War II with that during World War I.
2. Evaluate the administration of the economic side of our national activity in World War II.
3. Are we, right now, as some have claimed, "spending ourselves into national bankruptcy"? How much *can* we afford to spend on national defense?

4. Are we spending enough for defense? Too much? Spending for the wrong things?
5. How necessary is a strong military (in number of troops) in today's nuclear era with a potential "push-button" war?
6. How important to the economy are military expenditures? Does American prosperity depend on the defense program?
7. What would be the effects of a substantial decrease in military expenditures on the economy?

## SELECTED READINGS

BENOIT, EMILE, and KENNETH BOULDING. (eds.). *Disarmament and the Economy*. New York: Harper & Row, 1963.

Committee for Economic Development. *The Problem of National Security: Some Economic and Administrative Aspects*. New York: Committee for Economic Development, 1958.

DIRECTOR, AARON (ed.). *Defense, Controls, and Inflation*. Chicago: University of Chicago Press, 1952.

HAMMOND, PAUL Y. *Organizing for Defense: The American Military Establishment in the Twentieth Century*. Princeton, N.J.: Princeton University Press, 1961.

HARRIS, SEYMOUR E. *Economics of Mobilization and Inflation*. New York: W. W. Norton & Company, 1951.

LINCOLN, GEORGE A., and others. *Economics of National Security*, 2nd ed. Englewood Cliffs, N.J.: Prentice-Hall, Inc., 1953.

PECK, MERTON J., and FREDERIC H. SCHERER. *Weapons Acquisition Process: An Economic Analysis*. Cambridge, Mass.: Harvard University Press, 1962.

SCHILLING, WARNER R., and others. *Strategy, Politics, and Defense Budgets* New York: Columbia University Press, 1962.

WALLACE, DONALD H., and J. M. CLARK, *Economic Controls and Defense*. New York: Twentieth Century Fund, 1953.

# 30

## THE OUTLOOK IN RELATIONSHIPS BETWEEN GOVERNMENT AND BUSINESS

Our nation, our economy, and our government have grown prodigiously since the War of the Revolution. At the war's end the nation's area was .9 million square miles; today it is 3.6 million, or 4 times as large. The population at the first census, in 1790, was 3.9 million; in 1960, 179.3 million—46 times the first figure. The 1790 gross national product (in today's dollars) was of the order of $1 billion; the 1960 figure, $503 billion, was larger in that same proportion. The 1790 receipts of the Federal Government were $4.4 million, expenditures $4.3; in 1962, budget receipts totaled $94 billion, expenditures, $86 billion—20,000 times the figures in George Washington's time! Even in the absence of figures on state and local government finance, it is clear that the financial operations of government have outstripped the other key characteristics of the nation.

The figures presented in Chapter 4 demonstrate the same trend for the twentieth century—governmental financial operations and employment have expanded faster than private finance and employment.

These figures do not measure the extent of governmental *regulation;* but they do provide significant measures of the place of government in our lives. Governments, in 1960, employed 15 per cent of the work force, and governmental financial operations involved 35 per cent of the national income. The employment figures suggest that we were one sixth governmental, five sixths private. The financial figures suggest an even higher degree of government—one third.

As we note in Chapter 24, the *business* activities of Federal, state, and local governments originated only 1.25 per cent of the national income in 1960. The nonbusiness or "purely governmental" activities (if you wish) of these governments, however, generated $47.3 billion of the $417 billion national income, or 11.3 per cent. In total, then, governments were responsible for 12.55 per cent.* By this measure, our economy was one eighth governmental, seven eighths private.

* U.S. Department of Commerce, *Survey of Current Business,* July 1961, p. 11.

The historical record of economic progress hardly suggests that the nation has suffered from excessive government. Indeed, on the face of the matter, the record might be cited as evidence of sound governmental activity—in both quantity and quality. There is, however, a contrary opinion.

## CONCERN ABOUT BIG GOVERNMENT

Government has become so big, so powerful, and so influential that some persons are alarmed by its present size and frightened by the prospect of a continuation of the upward trend. They foresee a future expansion of governmental power and a reciprocal contraction of individual liberty. They visualize the end of the road in a completely collectivized society.

The validity of this view does not depend on the proposition that the American people have accepted socialism as an ultimate goal and are deliberately working toward it by a gradualistic process. If it depended on this proposition, it would have little substance, for, as demonstrated by public opinion surveys, the American people are overwhelmingly opposed to collectivism. No; the expectation of ultimate complete socialism rests only on a possibility of *inadvertent transformation*. According to the theory behind this phrase people who openly and perhaps even loudly proclaim the virtures of the private enterprise system and denounce the shortcomings of collectivism turn to the government for specific kinds of assistance or regulation. Confronted with their inconsistency, they reply that *their* programs are *special* cases which represent *justified* exceptions to the general principle. The theory goes on to suppose that the resultant extensions of governmental activities gradually nibble away at the people's sense of personal initiative and feeling of personal responsibility, so that the private enterprise system eventually becomes weakened and no longer viable. At this point, the theory continues, private weakness is so great that the citizenry, even if they comprehend the gradual process of undermining, are too feeble to reverse the trend. They are unable to join the proponents of this theory in crying, "In one small step after another, we have, during these past decades, undermined the private enterprise system. Let us go back, therefore, and repeal all of the enfeebling legislation and eliminate all of the enervating governmental activities. Let us go back to the private enterprise system with only the necessary minimum of government." Since individualism has been so weakened by creeping collectivism, the theory concludes, the nation finds itself an economic point of no return and therefore—reluctant but helpless—becomes a fully collectivized society.

It would be easy to dismiss this theory of creeping collectivism and the inadvertent acceptance of socialism as a mere figment of ill-informed and frightened imaginations. But the fact remains that government and governmental activities are *essentially* collectivistic and socialistic. The Department of Defense, the Pure Food and Drugs Act, the Federal Reserve System, Social Security, highways, schools, and policemen; all answer this description.

And governmental activities—their number, size, scope, significance, and cost—have increased enormously during the life of our nation. This increase has not occurred in consequence of a general public affection for socialism; indeed, it has occurred despite strong opposition to this philosophy. It has come about through gradual extensions of governmental functions—triggered by officials of government or stimulated by public pressures—at Federal, state, and local levels, in the many areas discussed in this book.

The record shows that governmental activities have rarely been extinguished, although specific operations sometimes decline, as a result of circumstances. Thus the passing of the last of the Civil War veterans ended the payment of pensions to the soldiers of that war; but not to their widows. Few laws are repealed; they are more often amended and extended. Bureaus, offices, agencies, and departments are rarely extinguished or even contracted; they usually proliferate and grow bigger. Regulations are rarely relaxed; they are usually extended and tightened. Taxes and tax rates are not often dropped; new levies are imposed and the rates of old ones are increased. Governmental subsidies are more likely to be increased than decreased. Although there is no general public sentiment for increased government ownership of businesses, those which governments own grow gradually with the growth of the economy.

## THE OUTLOOK

This, then, is the record—our nation has expanded, the American economy has grown, and government has grown faster than the economy. This trend—the relative increase of government—does not seem to have ceased.

Some say that we now have too much government (although they may not agree about where to reduce it).

Others, contrariwise, contend that we do not have enough government— that the public sector should be enlarged for the benefit of the nation.

Certain trends seem inevitable, such as upward trend in the proportion of young people who attend governmentally supported colleges and who, increasingly, continue in graduate study. In general, however, it does not seem that there is much current public pressure for a huge program of assorted new governmental activities which might be described as a "New New Deal," although there are some specific proposals, such as increased medical care for the aged financed via Social Security, which incline in that direction. The great group of extended governmental activities commonly called the New Deal seems to have enlarged Federal Governmental activities to a point satisfactory to most of the citizenry. At present, some of the key issues involve the proper functions of state and local governments.

In view of the subtle and insidious manner in which gradual extensions of governmental power can nibble away our freedom, we should do well to keep in mind the penetrating warning of Justice Brandeis:

> The makers of our Constitution . . . sought to protect Americans in their beliefs, their thoughts, their emotions and their sensations. They conferred, as against the government, *the right to be let alone*—the most comprehensive right and the right most valued by civilized man. Experience should teach us to be most on our guard to protect liberty when the government's purposes are beneficent. Men born to freedom are naturally alert to repel invasion of their liberty by evil-minded rulers. The greatest dangers to liberty lurk in insidious encroachment by men of zeal, well-meaning, but without understanding. (Emphasis supplied)*

At the same time, the Brandeis warning does not amount to a flat opposition to any and all increases in governmental action.

## SOCIAL CONTROL

The future trends in the relationships between government and business will result from the continuing operations of our representative democracy, our private enterprise system, and private, nongovernmental controls. In Chapter 1 and elsewhere we have noted that one of the principal objectives of government is to cause men to refrain from behaving in socially undesirable ways and to influence them to behave in socially desirable ways. We have also emphasized that government is not the only force that influences the attitudes and behavior of people. We have noted the existence of other conditioning factors which are other forms of *social control*. We have observed that government and the other means of social control vary in their effectiveness and also they are not necessarily alternatives, that they may complement one another.

Growth of population, technological changes, and other factors tend to introduce new social problems. Whether our problems—old and new—will be handled in the future by government or by other sources of social control will depend on conscious choices made by the people more or less deliberately and more or less advisedly. In general, the rule appears to be that the more effective the nongovernmental social controls the less need there is for governmental ones; and vice versa. Indeed, it is perhaps not merely "idealistic" to suggest that governmental leaders—and

* Justice Louis D. Brandeis, in his dissenting opinion in *Olmstead v. U.S.*, 277 U.S. 438 (1928).

most of all, the President of the United States—should take to television and other media of mass communication from time to time for the deliberate purpose of exhorting the American people to socially desirable attitudes and behavior. It would be easy to scorn this suggested action as *preaching*—useless and even objectionable. Perhaps it would be. On the other hand, an occasional carefully prepared presentation, completely nonpartisan and backed by the prestige of office, might have real influence on our people. To conclude otherwise is to believe that Americans are little sensitive to noble leadership—a proposition which, if true, suggests a dismal outlook for our nation.

## INFORMATION AND MISINFORMATION

The functioning of a democracy depends in part on how well informed the citizenry are about public problems. Since the daily newspaper is a principal source of information, it is not encouraging to note the criticisms of our papers voiced by newspaper publishers themselves— in a survey made by Edward Bernays.[*] One fourth of the publishers were critical of the press, and listed the following as the deviations from ideals: failure to perform public service, response to economic pressures, slanting the news, political bias, sensationalism, bias and self-interest of the publishers, group pressures, inaccuracy, and incompetence. The Bernays survey showed *The New York Times* as the paper mentioned by the most respondents as among the best ten.

Certain individual columnists and commentators who discuss national problems have large audiences. The present writer, therefore, has sought to determine the quality of their observations, by surveying the opinions of his professorial colleagues in the University of Michigan School of Business Administration and Department of Economics. Four times in recent years questionnaires have been sent to several dozen, and replies —down to a minimum of 12—tabulated and averaged. The question asked and the average grades in the 1963 survey follow.

> How good (profound, reliable, comprehensive, unbiased) are the following reporters, columnists, and commentators as reliable observers of governmental actions and policies, especially with respect to economic and business matters? Please grade A, B, C, D, or E; and describe in a few words what you think best characterizes the man. Please grade only those whom you read or hear relatively regularly.
>
> The average grades:
> A  James Reston
> B  Walter Lippman
>    David Brinkley

[*] Edward L. Bernays, "Press and Public Agreed on Deviation From Ideals," *Editor & Publisher*, May 17, 1952.

       Arthur Krock
       Marquis Childs
       Sylvia Porter
       Joseph Alsop
C   Drew Pearson
D   Henry Hazlitt
       David Lawrence
       Fulton Lewis, Jr.
E   Westbrook Pegler

## THE NATION AND ITS PROBLEMS

The United States has faced problems ever since its birth. In the early years the problems included the British, the Indians, and the structure of government. Now our problems include domestic ones, plus a troubled and dangerous world situation, whose ultimate outcome will be substantially influenced by the state of our future politico-economic development.

In the early years, although the nation was small and poor and weak, men of wisdom and courage—despite occasional dismaying disasters—carried on, coped with the problems, built a great nation, and handed it on to us.

Today, when the nation is big and rich and strong, it is still true that our problems can be dealt with satisfactorily only if we display wisdom and courage. If we deal with our problems satisfactorily we shall achieve further economic progress and we shall utilize the increased material well-being as the firm foundation upon which to build the edifice of the good life and the good society.

## QUESTIONS AND PROBLEMS

1. How valuable, in your opinion, have been the contributions of government to our social and economic progress?
2. Do we have too much government today?
3. Are there any areas in which you *favor* (as distinguished from *forecasting*) additional governmental activity?
4. Into what areas do you *forecast* that governmental activity will expand in the future?
5. What, in your opinion, is the outlook for government–business relations?
6. What can businessmen and other citizens do, properly, to affect this relationship?
7. How big is the governmental fraction of our economic life going to become?
8. Is there a real danger of creeping collectivism?
9. How effective do you think Presidential messages to the people could be?

## SELECTED READINGS

DIMOCK, MARSHALL. *The New American Political Economy*. New York: Harper and Brothers, 1961.

GRIFFIN, CLARE E. *Enterprise in a Free Society*. Chicago: Richard D. Irwin, Inc., 1949.

HANSEN, ALVIN H. *Economic Issues of the 1960s*. New York: McGraw-Hill Company, 1960.

HAZARD, LELAND. "Can We Afford Our National Goals?" *Harvard Business Review*, May-June 1962, pp. 6 ff.

————. "Our National Goals—The Hard Choices," *Harvard Business Review*, May-June 1963, pp. 22 ff.

HOOVER, CALVIN B. *The Economy, Liberty, and the State*. New York: Twentieth Century Fund, 1959.

KEEZER, DEXTER M. *Making Capitalism Work*. New York: McGraw-Hill Company, 1950.

President's Commission on National Goals. *Goals for Americans*. Englewood Cliffs, N.J.: Prentice-Hall, Inc., 1960.

Rockefeller Brothers Fund. *Prospect for America*. New York: Doubleday & Company, 1961.

SLICHTER, SUMNER H. *Economic Growth in the United States: Its History, Problems, and Prospects*. Baton Rouge, La.: Louisiana State University Press, 1961.

WERNETTE, J. P. *The Future of American Prosperity*. New York: The Macmillan Company, 1955.

# GENERAL INDEX

# INDEX OF CASES